Understanding Java

Pearson
Education

We work with leading authors to develop the
strongest educational materials in computer science,
bringing cutting-edge thinking and best learning
practice to a global market.

Under a range of well-known imprints, including
Addison-Wesley, we craft high quality print and
electronic publications which help readers to
understand and apply their content,
whether studying or at work.

To find out more about the complete range of our
publishing please visit us on the World Wide Web at:
www.pearsoneduc.com

Understanding Java

Barry Cornelius
University of Durham

Addison-Wesley

An imprint of **PEARSON EDUCATION**
Harlow, England ● London ● New York ● Reading, Massachusetts ● San Francisco
Toronto ● Don Mills, Ontario ● Sydney ● Tokyo ● Singapore ● Hong Kong ● Seoul
Taipei ● Cape Town ● Madrid ● Mexico City ● Amsterdam ● Munich ● Paris ● Milan

Pearson Education Ltd
Edinburgh Gate
Harlow
Essex CM20 2JE
England

and Associated Companies around the World.

Visit us on the World Wide Web at:
www.pearsoneduc.com

First edition 2001

© Pearson Education Limited 2001

ISBN 0201-71107-9

British Library Cataloguing-in-Publication Data
A catalogue record for this book can be obtained from the British Library

Library of Congress Cataloging-in-Publication Data
Cornelius, Barry, 1948–
    Understanding Java / Barry Cornelius.
      p. cm.
    ISBN 0-201-71107-9
    1. Java (Computer program language)   I. Title.
QA76.73.J38 C665   2001
005.13′3—dc21

                                00-051089

10 9 8 7 6 5 4 3 2 1
05 04 03 02 01
Typeset by 59 in 10/12 pt Times Ten
Printed and bound in Great Britain by Henry Ling Ltd., at the Dorset Press, Dorchester, Dorset

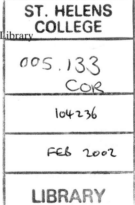

Contents

···

Trademark Notice

Preface

....

The objectives of this book

This book has three principal objectives:

- to introduce the main aspects of programming;
- to explain the constructs available in the Java programming language;
- to create an appropriate foundation for the construction of large programs.

Books on Java abound, and a lot of books will have the above three objectives. What makes this book different is that it aims to give you a thorough introduction to Java, to give you an *understanding* of the way things are, rather than just give you a superficial view of the Java programming language. Hence, the title of the book is *Understanding Java*.

How this book teaches Java

But don't panic! This book starts from scratch: it assumes you have done no programming before. It gradually introduces you to the various aspects of programming, and uses the Java programming language to do this. To begin with, the programs you write will be for simple tasks, but later we move on to produce programs that solve more involved problems.

One of the key aspects of Java is that it is an object-oriented programming language. A language is described as *object-oriented* if it is easy to write programs that model objects in the real world. In this book, you will find out that in Java this is done using *class declarations*. And, although the Java programming language is accompanied by a large number of classes that can be used to model some real-world objects, we will need to know how to provide our own class declarations in order to model the particular objects that we are interested in. So we will spend some time looking at class declarations and how to write good class declarations.

Although being able to provide good representations of real-world objects is a important skill to acquire, there are other aspects of programming we need to know about. For example, we also need to provide our programs with user interfaces that people will want to use. So, in this book, we also look at how we can provide a Java program with user interfaces involving components such as buttons, textfields, dialog boxes and menus.

When programming, we also need to know how to deal with vast quantities of data: how can we best represent this data within a program? In this book, we look at three important ways of representing a collection of items: they are *lists*, *sets* and *maps*.

Although some Java programs are programs that we want to run on our own computer, others will be programs that we will want people to run when they visit our WWW page. So, in this book, we will also look at how we can write *Java applets*, code that is executed on visiting a WWW page.

Besides constructing lots of the code of programs ourselves, another important idea of programming is to use code that already exists. One of the benefits of using Java is that the language is accomplished by a vast quantity of code that is simply waiting there for us to use.

We will use this pre-existing code in almost everything we do. For example, we will rely on it when giving our programs user interfaces. Instead of doing all the hard work ourselves, we will just build on code that someone else has already produced.

We will see that it is easy to use this pre-existing code because it is comprehensively documented in WWW pages. So this book frequently refers you to these WWW pages.

Besides making the construction of new programs easier, there is another reason why the existence of this code is beneficial: it means that we can more quickly and easily build programs that do useful and complicated tasks. The existence of this code gives the Java programmer a head start on those programming in other languages.

Using the book

Most chapters of this book have a final section entitled *Curios, controversies and cover-ups*. These sections contain a collection of esoteric points. They may be ignored on a first reading of a chapter.

Some parts of the book are based on problems that are mathematical in nature. They are indicated by the symbol ◊ appearing in the margin. The reader who does not have a strong mathematics background can ignore these parts of the book.

The *Understanding Java* web site

Every book has to have a web site, and this book is no exception! This book's web site is at:

http://www.booksites.net/cornelius

This web site includes WWW pages containing:

- all the code of the examples that appear in the book;
- the code of other examples including the code of a WWW browser that is written in Java;
- solutions to some of the exercises;
- a list of corrections to the book – hopefully there will be few of these!
- a comments form where you can suggest corrections or submit comments;
- a list of frequently asked questions (with answers!).

Acknowledgements

For the last two years, I have been teaching the Java programming language to first-year students at the University of Durham. Earlier drafts of this book were used to support this course. So, first, I would like to thank the students attending this course for being the guinea-pigs for this material. I would also like to thank the Department of Computer Science for giving me the opportunity to teach this course, and to thank my own department, the Information Technology Service, for permitting me to do this.

Earlier drafts were a bit more rough than the final book, and, in producing subsequent drafts, hardly a page did not get drastically attacked. In particular, I would like to thank Claire Knight for her comments on the first draft; Frank Doherty for useful feedback during the first year the course was taught; those students that have given me feedback during the two years; and the anonymous reviewers of the manuscript.

I would like to thank Craig Gaskell both for his technical review and for his encouragement. A draft of this book is being used as part of Craig's teaching at the Centre for Internet Computing at the Scarborough Campus of the University of Hull.

Finally, I would like to thank two people who gave the draft manuscript a really hard time. First, thanks to James McKinna, a lecturer in Computer Science at the University of Durham. In many places, my ideas have been sorted out by stimulating discussions with James and he is responsible for some of the more interesting curios. Thanks James. I would also like to thank Stefan Nilsson of the Kungl Tekniska Högskolan (the Royal Institute of Technology) in Stockholm. He provided an extremely thorough review of the manuscript, and, as a result of his critical but constructive comments, the book has been enormously improved. Thanks Stefan.

Barry Cornelius
Durham, September 2000

Technical preface

The overall approach of this book

Any person teaching Java will be aware that there are hundreds of books that teach the Java programming language. So why is there a need for another one? To help you decide whether this book is suitable for your course, here are ten points giving an outline of the ways in which this book differs from other books.

1. One of the seriously neglected constructs of the Java programming language is the interface declaration. Although many books teach this after derived classes and abstract classes, I think this is the wrong way to teach interfaces. Instead, interfaces are an appropriate vehicle for describing the operations of a new type: an interface declaration should be produced before developing a class declaration that implements the interface.

   So, in this book, interfaces are taught at the same time as classes, and derived classes are left until a lot later. Besides being an appropriate construct for new types, there are other benefits from teaching interfaces early. In particular, many aspects of Java such as establishing listeners (for GUI components) and working with Java 2's Collections API require an understanding of interfaces.
2. The book advocates that each interface–class should always provide a standard set of methods, i.e. each should have get methods, `toString`, `equals` and `hashCode`. It may also be appropriate for there to be set methods and `compareTo`.
3. Many of the interfaces–classes developed in earlier chapters are re-used in later chapters. For example, Chapter 11 develops an interface–class to produce a new type for representing dates. These are then used (in Chapter 12) in the interface–class for a person (because a person has a date of birth). The latter is later

used (in Chapter 17) when producing an interface–class for a population, and (in Chapter 14) when representing a queue of people.

4. The book uses Java 2's Swing classes in preference to the AWT classes.

5. Instead of teaching all the details of how to manipulate linked lists and trees, the book teaches the reader how to use Java 2's Collection API. For example, with this API it is easy to use an object that has the `List` interface (which is created as an object of the `ArrayList` or the `LinkedList` class). The reader can learn how to use such an object without being concerned at this point with how it is implemented.

6. The book explains the advantages of using the Model-View-Controller technique, i.e. the advantages that are obtained by separating a data structure from the user interface that is used to change it and view its contents.

7. The book introduces the various ideas to do with exceptions gradually, i.e. when they are needed, rather than all at once in one chapter.

8. The book uses Java's classes for keyboard input rather than using the author's own class.

9. The book uses a convention for identifiers. This convention is used to help the reader of some code locate where an identifier is declared.

10. The book refers extensively to the WWW pages that document the Core API; it gives syntax diagrams to illustrate the syntax of the language; it uses UML's class diagrams to show the dependencies between a program's interfaces/classes; it uses tables to list some of the constructors and methods of commonly-used classes; it points out some of the patterns that appear when designing the code of programs; and it ends each chapter with programming tips, debugging hints, *curios* and exercises.

More details about the approach taken by this book

Introducing objects early?

Although Java is a language in which one can pursue object-oriented programming, it is not a pure object-oriented programming language: in Java some values are represented by values of a primitive type. One approach to teaching Java would be to try to ignore the primitive types as they do not fit in comfortably with an *object-first* approach. However, with such an approach, you would have to ignore Java's Core APIs (as these classes make extensive use of primitive types); instead you would have to develop your own classes. And you would have to ignore the `for` and `while` statements as these require values of the type `boolean`.

Although this approach could be adopted, it is not one that I would want to pursue. In my opinion, it is not teaching Java as it really is. One of the key features of Java is its well-stocked library of already written code, i.e. the Core APIs. For this reason, I believe that any course that teaches Java should make extensive use of the Core APIs, and use these from the start of the course. This reinforces the idea that you do not write all the code yourself: there is a wealth of code out there waiting for you to use.

If primitive types have to be taught reasonably early, how do we teach both primitive types and reference types? In this book, this material is taught in the following order:

1. introduce primitive types;

2. demonstrate that operations can be performed on values of a primitive type by using methods (and operators);

3. point out that the primitive types are not sufficient to represent real-world objects;

4. introduce some of the reference types (class types) of Java's Core APIs as a way of representing other real-world objects.

During this process it is important to use the WWW pages that document Java's Core APIs in order to show what is possible with these class types.

Handling control statements and method declarations

One of the key aspects of a class declaration is a method declaration. And there is a lot of complexity in writing both the header and the block of a method declaration. In my view, it is wrong to explain how to write class declarations at the start of a course and hope that the students can take on the idea of method declarations at the same time.

So, in this book, the following order is used to teach the bread-and-butter topics:

- output to the screen
- input from the keyboard
- if statements
- for statements
- method declarations
- other control statements

I'm not ashamed that you will find these taught in this order in many books that are teaching a language other than Java.

Interfaces and classes

The role of interfaces and classes

Both Ada and Modula-2 separate out the interface from the implementation. Ada divides a *package* into a *package specification* and a *package body*; similarly, in Modula-2, you provide a *definition module* and an *implementation module*. Although a similar idea can be achieved in C++, it is not so cleanly done. In Java, an interface declaration can be used to specify the *what* and the class declaration can be used to specify the *how*.

In this book, interface declarations are taught in the same chapter as class declarations, and students are encouraged to develop an interface declaration before developing a class declaration that implements the interface.

When a student gets to writing their own interfaces and classes, they are already familiar with the WWW pages of some of the classes of Java's Core APIs, and so they are aware of what classes often provide. And, by the time they get to this chapter, they are also already familiar with method declarations. As a result, they are more in a position to concentrate on the actual interface/class declaration.

The book stresses that there are two main characteristics to a type:

- a type has a set of values associated with it;

- a type has a set of operations that are permitted on these values.

So, we can use a class declaration to introduce a new type because the fields of the class declaration can represent the values of the type, and the methods of the class declaration can provide the operations. The associated interface declaration is there to expose the operations that are available on the values of the type.

The book also stresses that other code (called the *client* code) should be written in terms of the interface and that the name of the class should only be used when you want to create an object (of the class that implements the interface):

```
Date tTodaysDate = new DateImpl(2000, 9, 1);
```

The book points out that:

- The interface is better at expressing the contract between the client and the supplier of the class.

- The use of an interface helps to delineate in the client the code that is dependent just on the interface from the code that is dependent on the implementation.

- Although there will be some client classes that need to create DateImpl objects, it is possible that the code of some client classes can be written solely in terms of Date rather than DateImpl. Such classes need not be re-compiled and re-tested if DateImpl is changed. The extreme of this is to declare an interface and a class for a factory class which is responsible for creating DateImpl objects. In this way, all the other interfaces and classes can be written in terms of Date and so only the factory class and the program class need to be re-compiled if DateImpl is changed. The details about the use of a factory class are left until the final chapter of the book.

Although this first chapter on interfaces and classes (Chapter 11) emphasizes that one of their primary roles is to represent a new type, the following chapter introduces some of the other ways in which class declarations can be used.

Minimal public interfaces

What is meant by minimal public interface?

This book suggests that each interface–class should always provide a standard set of methods (a *minimal public interface*):

- methods called equals, hashCode, toString, and (if appropriate) a method called compareTo;

- get methods;

● set methods (if appropriate);

● some means for cloning an object.

Some of these (e.g. equals, hashCode, compareTo) are needed if objects of the class are to be stored in a collection. When we produce a class, we may be uncertain as to what the client code will want to do with objects of the class. I do not believe we should change the class later or produce a subclass later. Instead, whenever possible, we should provide these methods at the outset.

The need to provide equals *and* hashCode

I find it incredible that so many books on Java introduce classes as a means of representing real-world objects and yet do not provide each class with the ability to find out whether two objects of the class have the same value.

Suppose a book introduces a class called Point. Then, if the book does mention equals, often you will find it declared with a parameter of type Point. If a client attempts to use objects of this class with objects of the Collections API (or Hashtable or Vector), they are in for a shock. None of the following methods will work with that declaration of equals:

```
Hashtable   contains, containsKey, get, put, remove
   Vector   contains, indexOf
     List   contains, remove, indexOf
      Map   containsKey, containsValue, get, put, remove
      Set   add, contains, remove
```

This book teaches that for the equals method to be useful it needs to have a parameter of type Object. If you declare equals properly, you need also to declare hashCode.

The need to provide compareTo

If the interface and class that you are providing is for a type where there is a natural order for the values of the type, the interface and class should also provide a means for finding out whether one value of the type is less than another value. So in such situations this book teaches that your interface should be a subinterface of the interface Comparable (from the package java.lang), and the class is then obliged to provide a method declaration for compareTo. In fact, there are some parts of the Collections API (e.g. TreeSet and TreeMap) that work better if your class implements this interface.

The need to provide a cloning operation

Few books explain that, when producing an interface–class, it is desirable to provide a cloning operation. Without this, it is difficult to make copies of existing values of a type. This book shows two ways of cloning. The easy way is to provide a constructor:

this is presented in Chapter 11. The better way is to override `Object`'s `clone` method: this is discussed in Chapter 19.

A turning point

The previous sections have described the contents of the first 12 chapters. This is a turning point in the book. Although there are a few important aspects of the Java language that are still to come, most of the important ones have now been introduced. The remaining chapters of the book are mainly concerned with introducing two important APIs: the Swing API and the Collections API.

Although both of these APIs came into being when Java 2 was released, they are both considered by Sun Microsystems to be part of the Core APIs of Java.

One of the main aims of the second half of the book is to become familiar with these two APIs. They are both quite large: the book's aim is to introduce the basic ideas giving the students sufficient knowledge to look at the other parts of the API on their own.

Note the emphasis in this part of the book is on using the code of existing libraries. By taking a ride on the work of others, Java gives even the beginner the possibility of easily building reasonably powerful pieces of code.

The Swing API

The book looks at the Swing API in two takes. In the first take, the students are introduced to the following ideas:

- creating a new window using `JFrame`;
- putting GUI components such as `JButtons` and `JTextFields` into the pane of a window;
- introducing an object to listen for the event of a click of a button;
- grouping components together using a `Box` (in preference to a `JPanel`);
- providing a form to allow multiple values to be input;
- using a `JDialog` to force the user to complete the form.

In order to use the Swing API, a programmer is required to be familiar with the idea of declaring a class that implements an interface. In this book, this has already been done as the first chapter on the Swing API (Chapter 13) appears immediately after the chapters introducing interfaces and classes.

In a later chapter (Chapter 18), the classes `JMenuBox`, `JMenu` and `JMenuItem` are introduced. These three classes are needed to build a menu system. Because `JMenuItems` are another form of button, responding to a click of a menu item can be handled in a similar way to that for buttons (which were discussed in the earlier chapter).

This later chapter also introduces material on how to create popup menus (using `JPopupMenu`) and how to create windows within a parent window (by using `JDesktopPane` and `JInternalFrame`).

The Collections API

The Collections API provides a useful set of interfaces and classes that can be used for building data structures that represent collections of data. The emphasis in this book is on how to make effective use of this API rather than on how to implement the various data structures.

The book describes and explains the differences between the capabilities of the three main interfaces called List, Set and Map (and subinterfaces called SortedSet and SortedMap), and the six classes called ArrayList, LinkedList, HashSet, TreeSet, HashMap and TreeMap. The use of the Iterator interface is also described.

Once again, the book advises writing the code of clients in terms of the interface, only mentioning the name of a class when you want to create a collection object.

Although the book stresses the use of this API for representing collections of data, the more advanced example in the chapter on arrays (Chapter 15) looks at how an array can be used to implement the List interface.

The use of MVC and the Observer pattern

Whilst introducing the Collections API, the book explains and demonstrates the advantages of using the Model-View-Controller pattern to decouple a data structure from any user interface. The simpler form in which the view and the controller are combined (sometimes called Model-UserInterface) is also discussed. By having the class that implements the model derived from java.util.Observable, it is easy to provide multiple views of the model (the class for each view implementing the java.util.Observer interface). These ideas are illustrated by two examples.

Implementation inheritance

Often books on Java teach the following topics in one chapter:

- deriving classes from base classes
- polymorphism (dynamic binding)
- abstract classes
- interfaces

These topics are taught in this order because it seems to be an obvious order: first introduce the advantages of deriving classes from base classes; then explain polymorphism (dynamic binding); then explain that an abstract class is a special form of base class; and finally introduce an interface as a special form of an abstract class. However, a chapter that has these topics introduces a lot of new ideas and explaining them all at once will overload the reader.

Although there is some logic to teaching interfaces in this way, it is better to make a clearer separation between implementation inheritance and interfaces. I think it is important to teach interfaces early, and to leave implementation inheritance until later.

Although the chapter on implementation inheritance appears late in this book, some of the basic ideas are introduced in earlier chapters:

- When `toString`, `equals` and `hashCode` are introduced, the book also introduces the idea that, by default, classes are derived from `Object`; that you can use methods of the class `Object` on any object; and that methods of a superclass can be overriden.
- When discussing the classes of the Swing API, the book mentions the Swing API's use of implementation inheritance and explains the usefulness of organizing classes in a class hierarchy.
- When using `java.util.Observable`, the book produces a class that is derived from a class of the Core APIs and explains why this is being done.

It is only towards the end of this book (in Chapter 19) that students learn how to derive a class from one of their other classes. This chapter also introduces the idea of abstract classes.

Applets

Because the full details of implementation inheritance are taught late, the material on applets also appears late (in Chapter 20). However, a large amount of the ground work needed to understand applets has already been covered.

Exceptions

Some books seem to include exceptions as an afterthought: often the whole topic is taught in the last chapter. As with implementation inheritance, this book gradually introduces the various aspects of exceptions:

- In this book, exceptions first need to be mentioned when discussing the manipulation of `Strings` and when values are read from the keyboard. So the students first meet the exceptions called `StringIndexOutOfBoundsException` and `IOException`. A distinction can be made at this stage between unchecked exceptions and checked exceptions. So, the throws clause for `IOException` on the main method is also explained.
- When method declarations are introduced, the book explains why a throws clause is needed with a method declaration as well as the main method.
- The chapter on control statements introduces the use of a try statement to handle an exception, e.g. to handle `NumberFormatException`.
- The chapter on using files introduces the need for a finally clause.
- The chapter on class declarations shows how a throw statement can be used to generate one of the standard exceptions.

Although in Java it can be tempting to overuse exceptions, in this book it is recommended that they are only used for untoward situations. For this reason, the idea of introducing your own exceptions is mentioned only briefly at the end of the book (in Chapter 21).

Keyboard input

Often, books that teach Java provide their own package of classes. One reason for doing this is that it makes it easy to provide a class that facilitates the reading of a value of some primitive type from the keyboard.

Although this approach has its advantages, it is also inconvenient for students:

- if a student has their own computer, they have to obtain the package and install it;
- if they read more than one book, they have to become familiar with more than one package;
- they can easily fall into the trap of always using a book's package and never shifting to using the classes defined in Java's Core APIs.

In this book, the horrors of Java's keyboard input are introduced early (in Chapter 4):

```
BufferedReader tKeyboard =
        new BufferedReader(new InputStreamReader(System.in));
String tHeightString = tKeyboard.readLine();
double tHeight = Double.parseDouble(tHeightString);
```

Note the use of both instance methods and class methods and the need to use the wrapper classes of the primitive types.

Teaching devices

- A consistent style is used for the layout of the code that is presented in the book.
- A naming convention is used for the identifiers used in the code. This convention uses a lower-case letter as a prefix to indicate where an identifier is declared, i.e. i is used for a private member of a class, p is used for a parameter, and t is used for a temporary (i.e. a local) variable of a block.
- The book uses syntax diagrams to explain the syntax of the language. To make things easier, some simplifications are made to the syntax.
- The book uses UML's class diagrams to provide a visual representation of the dependencies that exist between the interfaces/classes of a program.
- The book presents tables containing a description of some of the constructors and methods of commonly-used classes.
- The book often refers the student to the WWW pages that document the Core APIs.
- Each chapter of the book has a collection of tips (i.e. hints about programming pitfalls and debugging hints).
- Each chapter of the book has a section entitled *curios, controversies and cover-ups*.
- Each chapter of the book has a set of exercises.

Chapter 1

Examining the structure of Java programs

The main aim of this first chapter is to present some details of the structure of Java programs. A program consists of a number of *class declarations*: however, for the time being, we will be concentrating on programs that have just one class declaration which will be called the *program class declaration*.

Although later we will find out that a program class declaration can have many different parts, once again, to keep things simple, initially the program class declaration will only have one *method declaration* which will be called the *main method declaration*.

In this chapter, we are only concerned with examining the structure of Java programs. To help do this, a notation called a **syntax diagram** will be introduced. In this chapter, we will use this notation both to define the overall structure of a Java program, and also to define the names (**identifier**s) that can be used for the entities that occur in programs.

The chapter will also introduce ways which we will be using to make programs more understandable: the use of meaningful identifiers, the judicious use of layout, and the introduction of comments.

Although an example of a program will be given and will be broken up into its various parts, the actual meaning of these parts will be deferred to the next chapter. In this chapter, our concern is with being able to recognize the structure of a program.

1.1 The Java programming language

1.1.1 Introduction

A **program** is simply a set of instructions that can respond to our inputs, carry out actions, and display information to us. Most aspects of modern life involve the running of programs. We might use a PC to browse the World Wide Web (WWW), to send electronic mail messages, to manage our finances, or to produce an essay using some word-processing package. When we perform these activities, we are running different programs on the PC. However, we also indirectly run programs when we perform a large number of other common day-to-day activities. Examples are:

- financial transactions, such as buying a ticket to see a movie;
- household devices, such as washing machines and TVs;
- remote control devices for controlling TVs and VCRs;
- smart cards, pagers, mobile phones and PDAs (handhelds).

Although until now these programs have been written in different programming languages, it is possible that in the future one language will be used for programs in all of these application areas: the Java programming language.

1.1.2 Notations to aid communications

But why do we need to use a programming language to get a computer to do something? Well, human beings often devise languages to aid communications. Some examples are:

- the notation used in music scores ensures that everyone in the group/band/orchestra knows what to play;
- the notation used in knitting patterns tries to ensure that the garment being produced has the right size, shape and style;
- the notation used in recipes tries to ensure that the finished product tastes good and does not harm us!

In a similar way, it is useful to have some notation that enables us to say what we want a computer to do; such a notation is called a **programming language**.

So a **program** is just a set of instructions written in some programming language. Later in this chapter, we will be looking at the program given in Figure 1.1. In many ways, a program is similar to a score, a knitting pattern or a recipe. So, as with scores, patterns and recipes, the text of the program is a useful way of discussing with others what we want to happen.

However, although we sometimes discuss scores, patterns and recipes with other people, the main reason for producing them is so that they can be *executed*: the score of Mahler's Fourth is played by an orchestra; your grandmother uses a knitting pattern to produce some bootees for your newly-born niece; and your spouse uses a recipe

```
// This program displays the sum of 2.7 and 4.2.
// Barry Cornelius, 28 May 2000
public class SimpleSum
{
   public static void main(final String[] pArgs)
   {
      double tFirst, tSecond, tSum;
      tFirst = 2.7;
      tSecond = 4.2;
      tSum = tFirst + tSecond;
      System.out.print("The sum of the two numbers is: ");
      System.out.print(tSum);
      System.out.println();
   }
}
```

Figure 1.1   A program that displays the sum of 2.7 and 4.2.

to produce a dish for impressing your parents when they come to dinner. In each of these situations, the instructions of the score/pattern/recipe are being played out or *executed*.

And that is the main reason for producing a program: we produce a program so that it can be **run** or **executed** by some computer.

1.1.3 Getting the program executed

When we produce a program using the notation of some programming language, the notation that we are using is one that is convenient for us to write and read. Like those used in knitting patterns and recipes, the notation is a textual notation.

However, this textual notation is inappropriate for computers to use. So, each program will actually appear in two forms: the program in textual form (referred to as a **source program**) and the program in a binary form (known as **bytecodes**). It is convenient for humans to write a program in source form, whereas a computer needs the binary form. Luckily, there are other programs known as **compilers** that are able to translate from the source form of a program to its corresponding binary form. This translation process is known as **compilation**. Having compiled a program, we can then get the computer to **interpret** the bytecodes, i.e. to obey the instructions of the binary form of the program.

The two stages to getting a program executed are illustrated by the diagram in Figure 1.2.

1.1.4 The key components of a programming language

In the notations used by music scores, knitting patterns and recipes, there are three key components: sequence, repetition and conditional sections.

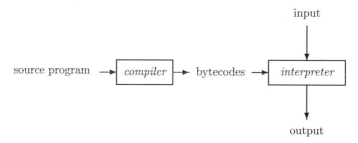

Figure 1.2   The two stages of compiling and executing a program.

Sequence

A music score is a sequence of bars of music: each bar is played after the previous bar. In a knitting pattern, you will get sequences of instructions. For example:

```
K1, P1
```

is a sequence meaning knit one stitch and then purl one stitch. With a sequence, it is important to execute the instructions in turn: you cannot choose the order in which to execute them. And so, often in these notations, the items of a sequence are numbered just to point out that the order is important. For example, in a recipe, the instructions for making a white sauce might start with:

1. *Melt the fat.*
2. *Remove from the heat and add the flour.*
3. *...*

Repetition

There are several ways of indicating in a music score that you want a section of the piece of music to be repeated. One possibility is to use the words Da Capo to mean *repeat from the beginning.* Another is to use a special notation on two of the bar lines in order to signify that the bars in between are to be repeated:

In knitting patterns, you will find instructions such as:

```
(K1, P1) 6 times
```

or:

```
(K1, P1) until the end of the row
```

And in cookery you will find instructions such as:

Continue to beat until it comes to the boil and thickens.

Conditional sections

Having indicated that a section of the piece of music is to be repeated, it may be that on the first two repetitions you want the bars to end in some way whereas on the final occasion you want the music to do something else. In a music score, you can indicate this using the following notation:

Both knitting patterns and recipes deal with many variants of the same basic product, and you will find that some of the instructions only have to be used if you are wanting the particular variant. For example:

> *If the cake is round, fill the centre and spread the remaining icing on top and down the sides.*

And you will also find that some instructions are optional:

> *Season and strain; it may be necessary to skim off excess fat.*

But what about programming?

These three ideas of sequence, repetition and conditional sections are also important when producing programs in some programming language.

We need sequencing in order to say that we want the computer to do this instruction first, and then to do this instruction, and so on. We need repetition in order to indicate that we want some instructions to be executed for each person or for each bank account or.... And we need conditional sections in order to indicate that we only want some instructions executed if the person is over 21, or if the bank account is in credit, or....

1.1.5 Top-down development

One approach for creating a computer program is to break the problem up into subproblems. Then, imagining for the moment that we have instructions to solve each of these subproblems, we could put the instructions together using sequence, repetition and conditional sections in order to produce a program that solves our problem.

If a subproblem is small, it will be easy to produce some instructions to solve it. However, if any of the subproblems is big, it should itself be broken up into *sub-subproblems*, and we can put the solutions to each of these together using sequence, repetition and conditional sections in order to produce a solution to the subproblem. And if a subsubproblem is big.... Eventually, the problems that are involved are so small that they can easily be coded in a programming language.

This method for generating a program is often known as **top-down development** (or **stepwise refinement** or **divide and conquer**). It leads to the production of a program containing the **code** for the **algorithm** needed to solve the problem.

It is not a new idea. Humans always find it easier to solve problems if they are broken down into subproblems – so, in fact, we use this technique all the time.

Although this approach works well for small programs, it suffers from two drawbacks:

1. It does not scale well: it falls over if the problem is too big for us to have a full grasp of the problem. For example, is it easy to use this approach to write down the steps for processing transactions on thousands of bank accounts?

2. Producing a program in this way would not help us to produce another program. We might reuse some of the ideas in the next program, possibly copying some of the lines, but we could not simply just use the code produced previously.

1.1.6 An object-oriented approach

The problem with the top-down development method is that its driving force is to consider what instructions we want to be executed and the order in which we want the computer to execute them. The design of early programming languages concentrated on these aspects. They were targeted at ensuring that we could easily code the algorithm being used to solve the program.

However, with computers being used to tackle bigger and more complicated problems, it was recognized that programming was not just concerned with being able to code algorithms.

We are also dealing with data: we want to store information about people, bank accounts, transactions (on a bank account), and so on. These are the real-world objects that we want to model in our program. And, as with any form of modelling, we are not interested in representing all the aspects of the real-world object: we are only concerned with those that are important to the programs we want to produce.

So, if we produce programs for a bank, we are unlikely to want to represent the beer that a person prefers, or their favourite football team. Instead, we will want to represent their name, their date of birth, their address, their marital status, and so on.

Besides identifying the data of the real-world object that we wish to represent, we will also want to represent some aspects of its behaviour. For the banking program, we will want the program to be able to create a new person (when the bank gets a new customer); we will want it to add some details each time they open a new account; we will want it to be able to change the address of the person if they tell us that they have moved house; or to change their marital status if this changes; and so on.

So, in our programs, we will have objects that in some way model real-world objects. Each object will contain values and will provide some means for modelling the behaviour of the real-world objects.

With any banking program, we will want to manipulate objects representing people, objects that represent the different types of bank accounts, objects that represent transactions, and so on. At some point while a program is executing, it might have received some data that describes a transaction for the bank account of one of the customers of the bank. Although a program might be manipulating many different objects at once, we can classify these objects: some objects represent people, others represent bank accounts, others represent transactions. We will use the term **class** to distinguish between the different kinds of objects.

When constructing a big program, it is hard work to develop the program by the top-down development method that was described earlier. Instead, it is easier to look at each class of objects separately. To say, I need to represent people; what data do I need to store about each person, and what instructions do I need to provide in order to change this data. Then to move on and say I need to represent a bank account – so again what data do I need to store, and what instructions do I need to provide in order to change this data. And the same with transactions.

So we are concentrating on each class of objects separately, looking at each of them in turn. Although when designing each class we have to have some idea of what we want to do with an object of this class, we do not have to be hampered with all the details of the program we are currently producing.

Having used a programming language to describe for each class of object the data and the instructions that are applicable, it is a lot easier to build programs that perform particular tasks. This approach to producing a program is called the **object-oriented approach**.

It is important to note that this approach deals with both of the drawbacks described earlier for the top-down development method. Not only does it help us with the development of a big program, but it also produces classes that can be reused in later programs. If, for example, as part of the task of creating one program, we produce a set of instructions for the class of objects that represent a person, then that work is done: those instructions can instantly be used in the next program.

During the 1980s and the 1990s, there was a shift to using the object-oriented approach. However, this does not mean that the top-down development method is no longer useful. If the operation you want to perform on an object is complicated, the code that you need can be produced using top-down development.

Because the programs of the earlier chapters of this book are *simple* in that they involve few objects, the top-down development method can be used to produce the code. However, in Chapter 11, we will learn how to define our own classes for representing real-world objects. From that point, an object-oriented approach will be adopted.

1.1.7 In what ways is Java different from other programming languages?

Although the object-oriented approach can be achieved with some success even with programming languages that are not object-oriented, it is a lot easier to use a language that has been designed with the object-oriented approach in mind. There are many programming languages, including Ada, BASIC, C, C++, COBOL, FORTRAN, Pascal and Modula-2. Object-oriented programming languages include Simula (from 1967), Smalltalk (from 1976), C++ (which evolved during the period 1980–1992) and Java (from 1995). Although the design of C++ does not force the adoption of the object-oriented approach, the design of Java encourages programs to be built as object-oriented programs.

Java was designed by employees of a computer company called Sun Microsystems during the first half of the 1990s. Although Java is often associated with the WWW, it can be used in most areas of programming: for this reason, it is sometimes described as a general-purpose programming language.

Its design builds on that of a large number of other programming languages, and so in many aspects it is a state-of-the-art programming language. For example, it has facilities for handling exceptions, for establishing more than one thread of control, for building graphical user interfaces, and for handling collections of data (such as lists, sets and maps). Although these buzzwords probably do not mean much to you at this stage, these ideas will be explained later in this book. And whereas, in other programming languages, programmers often run into trouble with manipulating things called *pointers*, most of these problems do not occur in Java because it has garbage collection, array index checking, and no pointer arithmetic. Again, this description includes more jargon that will be dealt with later.

When writing programs, it is useful not only to have a well-designed state-of-the-art language, but also to have a well-stocked library of existing code. If a lot of code already exists, the chances are that someone has already produced some code that is going to be useful to you. Java comes with a large number of **application programming interface**s (APIs): these are libraries of code which have been written by other people and we can access their facilities from our Java programs.

Some of the APIs that have been produced by Sun Microsystems together form what are called the *Core APIs*, and we will make extensive use of these Core APIs in this book. But besides these, there are hundreds of APIs in many other subject areas being announced by Sun Microsystems and by other software developers. Many of these can be freely downloaded from the WWW.

Finally, there is one aspect that makes Java exceptional. It does not have any architecture-dependent constructs: its publicity uses the slogan of *Write Once Run Anywhere*. With most other programming languages, it is a not insignificant task to move a program from one platform (e.g. a computer running UNIX) to another platform (e.g. a Windows 95/98/NT computer, or a UNIX computer from a different supplier): you will usually have to make numerous changes to the program to get it to compile and execute on the new platform. The program will then have to be tested again. However, with Java, a program written and compiled on one platform will run on another platform without any platform-specific code or any recompilation: the bytecodes can be run straightaway. This particular aspect makes the language very attractive to those developers who supply their products on many different platforms.

1.1.8 The different versions of Java

Since its first public release in 1995, the language definition and the Core APIs for Java have been evolving, with versions 1.0, 1.0.1, 1.0.2, 1.1, 1.1.1,..., 1.3 of Java being released during the period 1995–2000. At the release of 1.2 in December 1998, Sun Microsystems chose to announce it under the new name *Java 2*. The language definition and the Core APIs are now referred to as the **Java 2 Platform**. At the time this book was being prepared, the latest version is **Java 2 Platform v 1.3**.

One way of compiling and running Java programs is to use the **Java 2 SDK**. This Software Development Kit is a collection of software including a *compiler* and an *interpreter*. It can be downloaded free of charge from one of Sun's WWW pages. At the time this book was being prepared, the latest stable version of this software is **Java 2 SDK v 1.3.0**. Previous versions of the software were known as the **JDK** (**Java Development Kit**) and many Java programmers still use versions such as **JDK 1.0.2**, **JDK 1.1.8** and **Java 2 SDK v 1.2.2**.

This book assumes that you have access to some software that implements the Java 2 Platform. Details of how to obtain the Java 2 SDK are given in Appendix A.

1.1.9 The definition of Java

Although this book provides an introduction to the major parts of Java, there are some aspects of Java that will not be covered, and there are some places where for the sake of simplicity we will ignore some of the details. The primary book that defines all aspects of the Java language is *The Java Language Specification* by James Gosling, Bill Joy, Guy Steele and Gilad Bracha. A full reference for this book is given at [19] in the References section of this book. We will use the shorthand **JLS** to refer to this book. Note that the JLS is not a tutorial: instead it is a complicated book that is the bible defining the language.

The text of the JLS is also available on the WWW at [20].

1.2 The structure of a Java program

Earlier we looked briefly at the Java program shown in Figure 1.1. You can see that it consists of words and punctuation symbols, and that some letters of some of the words are in upper-case whereas other letters are in lower-case.

You will find that there is relatively little freedom when writing Java programs. When you ask a compiler to compile your source program (in order to produce the bytecodes that can be executed), you will find that the compiler will complain if you depart from the rules. It will produce a list of errors called **compilation error**s. Because we need to get the symbols right, we will spend some time in this chapter looking at the structure of Java programs. After this has been done, in the next chapter we will find out what happens when a program (such as the one in Figure 1.1) gets executed.

While analysing a program splitting it up into its various parts, the lines starting with / / will be ignored:

```
// This program displays the sum of 2.7 and 4.2.
// Barry Cornelius, 28 May 2000
```

Each of these lines forms a *comment*. More details about comments will be given in Section 1.6.1.

A Java program consists of a number of **class declaration**s. However, to begin with, our programs will just contain one class declaration which will be called the **program class declaration**.

Looking at the program in Figure 1.1, the program class declaration consists of all of the lines from:

```
public class SimpleSum
```

down to the last line:

```
}
```

The first few symbols of a program class declaration are called the **header** (of the program class declaration). The header ends just before the first {. Essentially all the header of the program class declaration does is to give a name to the program. In this case, the program has the name SimpleSum.

Between this { and its matching } (which is at the end of the program), there may be many declarations: but to begin with we will only have one declaration called the **main method declaration**.

The main method declaration consists of all of the lines from:

```
public static void main(final String[] pArgs)
{
    double tFirst, tSecond, tSum;
```

down to:

```
    System.out.println();
}
```

Like the program class declaration, the main method declaration also has a header that ends just before a {. Between this { and its matching } (which is just before the other }), there is what is called a **block**. This starts at the { and goes as far as the matching }:

```
{
    double tFirst, tSecond, tSum;
    tFirst = 2.7;
    tSecond = 4.2;
    tSum = tFirst + tSecond;
    System.out.print("The sum of the two numbers is: ");
    System.out.print(tSum);
    System.out.println();
}
```

(1.3) Syntax diagrams

Because of the need to be precise, it is useful to introduce a notation to show the rules for constructing the individual parts of a program. Giving rules like these is known as specifying the **syntax** of the language – the notation we will use to describe the syntax is referred to as a **syntax diagram**.

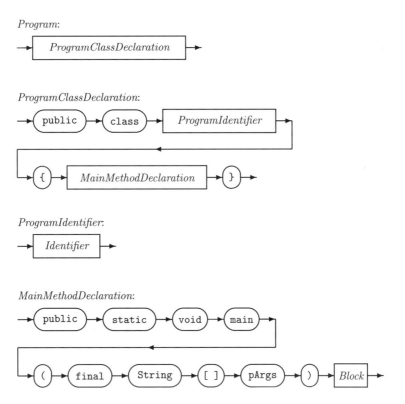

Figure 1.3   The syntax of a program.

Figure 1.3 includes a number of syntax diagrams. All these do is to state more formally some of the information that was presented in the previous section.

The first diagram does not do very much: it just says that a *Program* is a *ProgramClassDeclaration*. The parts of a syntax diagram that appear inside **rectangular boxes** need further explanation, and this is done by other syntax diagrams.

The next diagram tells us what a *ProgramClassDeclaration* looks like. The diagram contains some symbols that are given inside **oval boxes**: a symbol that is given within an oval box is a symbol that actually appears in a program. So, a *ProgramClassDeclaration* starts with the symbol public, followed by the symbol class, followed by a *ProgramIdentifier*, followed by the symbol {, followed by a *MainMethodDeclaration*, followed by the symbol }. The public, class, { and the } will appear in the program, whereas the actual characters that form a *ProgramIdentifier* and a *MainMethodDeclaration* are defined by other syntax diagrams.

Another syntax diagram explains that a *ProgramIdentifier* is an *Identifier*. Again, this does not seem to have got us much further forward! However, the only bits that are left unexplained by the syntax diagrams in Figure 1.3 are the rules for *Block* and *Identifier*. The easiest one to get rid of is *Identifier*, so we will deal with that in the next section; and the details of a *Block* will be given in the next chapter.

1.4 Identifiers

We need to give names to almost all of the **entities** that appear in a program, and this is the purpose of an **identifier**. For example, in a *program class declaration*, the program is given a name – in the case of the program given in Figure 1.1, the name SimpleSum is used. This program also uses something called print and something called println – both of these are associated with something called out that is from a *class* called System. So, you can see that there are lots of identifiers in a program.

Figure 1.4 contains a set of syntax diagrams for *Identifier*. These diagrams illustrate that syntax diagrams can contain bits which are optional and bits which may be

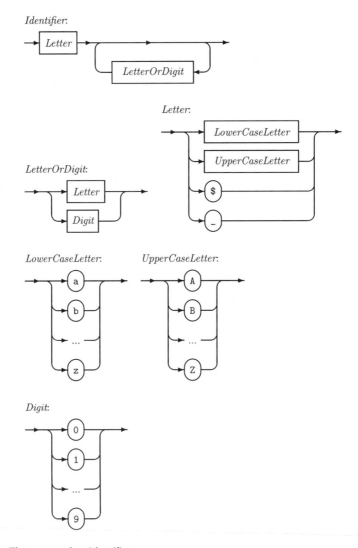

Figure 1.4   The syntax of an identifier.

repeated many times. All you need to know is that any path through a syntax diagram from its starting point to its finishing point can be used to produce an instance of the construct being defined by the syntax diagram.

All the examples of identifiers that we have seen so far (e.g. `SimpleSum`, `print`, `println`, `out` and `System`) have just involved letters. However, the syntax diagrams show that each character of an identifier may be a letter, a digit, a dollar or an underscore character – but the syntax diagram for *Identifier* states that an identifier must start with a letter.

The **case** of any letters in an identifier is significant. This means that `SimpleSum`, `SIMPLESUM`, `simplesum` and `simpleSum` are different identifiers. So, they cannot be used to refer to the same entity – you must choose one and be consistent. Although these four identifiers could be used to refer to four different entities, this would probably cause confusion for a reader of the program, and so it is not recommended.

Certain words cannot be used as identifiers – these are the **keyword**s of Java. If one of these words appears in a program, it has a special meaning. Examples that we have already seen include `public`, `class`, `static` and `void`. Besides the keywords, there are three other words that cannot be used as identifiers: they are the words `false`, `true` and `null`. A complete list of words that cannot be used as identifiers appears in the table in Figure 1.5. Although the word `assert` can currently be used as an identifier, it is possible that `assert` will be a keyword in a later revision of the Java Platform. For this reason, it is also included in the table in Figure 1.5.

abstract	default	if	private	throw
assert	do	implements	protected	throws
boolean	double	import	public	transient
break	else	instanceof	return	true
byte	extends	int	short	try
case	false	interface	static	void
catch	final	long	strictfp	volatile
char	finally	native	super	while
class	float	new	switch	
const	for	null	synchronized	
continue	goto	package	this	

Figure 1.5   A table giving words that cannot be used as identifiers.

The table in Figure 1.6 gives a list of other words that are commonly used for a special purpose. Unlike the keywords, you could use one of these words for an identifier within a program. For example, when choosing what name to give to a

Class	hashCode	length	out	toString
clone	in	main	print	util
equals	io	notify	println	wait
finalize	java	notifyAll	String	
getClass	lang	Object	System	

Figure 1.6   A table giving other words to be avoided when choosing an identifier.

program, you could choose the name `print`:

```
public class print
{
   ...
}
```

Because Java uses the name `print` for something that is commonly used in a Java program, also using the name `print` for the name of a program might be confusing for a reader, and hence it is not considered to be a good idea. Later (e.g. when we look at *method overriding* in Section 11.7), we will see that there are occasions when we will deliberately be reusing some of these identifiers. However, for the time being, avoid using the words in Figure 1.6 for any of the identifiers that you want to introduce.

1.5 Choosing identifiers

This book will encourage you to use identifiers that are meaningful. It is much easier to read or modify a program written by someone else if the identifiers in it are well chosen.

For example, a more meaningful name such as `temperature` will be chosen in preference to `temp`, or even worse, `t`. In particular, it is better to avoid short identifiers, such as `i` or `j`, and identifiers that are vague such as `count` or `loop`. And it is often better to choose a name associated with the problem being solved (such as `accountIsOverdrawn`) rather than one concerned with some aspect of the programming (such as `sumOfValuesIsNegative`).

Occasionally, this advice will not be followed. There are some problems, such as mathematical problems, in which it has been traditional to use single character names such as x and y. It is appropriate to use the same names in a program to solve the problem.

Java programmers have adopted some conventions about the case of letters in an identifier. In particular, where an identifier is composed of several words, each word (except the first) is started with an upper-case letter as in `accountIs-Overdrawn`. This identifier is chosen in preference to `accountisoverdrawn`, `account_is_overdrawn` or `ACCOUNTISOVERDRAWN`. As far as Java is concerned, it does not matter which one of these four is chosen. However, the convention is to use something like `accountIsOverdrawn` because it is easy to read. Another convention is to use an upper-case letter for the first letter of an identifier only when the identifier is the name of a *class*. Examples are `SimpleSum` and `System`. There are other conventions that are often adopted by Java programmers – these will be looked at later.

In this book, most of the identifiers that we choose will start with a single-letter prefix. For example, the identifiers `tFirst`, `tSecond` and `tSum` of the `SimpleSum` program start with the lower-case letter `t`. Later, we will find out that this prefix gives some indication of where the identifier was *declared*. Here the `t` means *temporary*: in Section 8.2 we will use `i` meaning *internal* and in Section 8.5 we will use `p` meaning *parameter*.

Although this convention is unusual, it is the view of this book that this convention will help both when we are constructing programs and when people are trying to understand our programs.

In our programs, we will also be using entities from classes written by other people. For example, we have seen that the `SimpleSum` program uses entities called `print` and `println` (that are associated with `out` which is from a class called `System`). In cases like these, the name of the entity (e.g. `System.out.print`) has already been chosen. So, when using entities from classes written by other people, we will have to use the names that they have chosen.

1.6 Comments and layout

1.6.1 Comments and their uses

We saw earlier that the `SimpleSum` program contains two lines that are **comment**s. The purpose of a comment is to add some description to the program that helps the person reading the program.

There are two ways in which you can put comments into a Java program. First, a comment can be introduced by the `//` symbol: anything that appears on a line after this symbol is taken as a comment. There are two examples of this form of comment in the `SimpleSum` program given in Figure 1.1.

In the second form of comment, a comment starts at a `/*` symbol and ends at a `*/` symbol. Here is an example:

```
/* This program displays the sum of 2.7 and 4.2.
   Barry Cornelius, 28 May 2000 */
```

With this form of comment, the comment may stretch over several lines. Note that it can be disastrous to omit the `*/` at the end of the comment. The compiler will treat the subsequent lines of the program as part of the comment, and will continue to do this until it reaches another `*/` symbol or the end of the file. In some situations, the compiler can detect that you have failed to close a comment, but in others the error will go undetected.

In order to try to avoid this problem, some programmers arrange for the `*/` to be lined up under the `/*` symbol:

```
/* This program displays the sum of 2.7 and 4.2.
   Barry Cornelius, 28 May 2000
 */
```

A comment is equivalent to a space, and can appear in a program whenever a space is permitted. The contents of a comment (no matter what it contains) will be ignored by the compiler.

Comments are included in a program as an aid to the reader to understand the program. In particular, a comment should be used to explain a part of the program that is difficult to understand. In this book such a comment is placed *before* the part that is difficult.

However, there is no point in using a comment just to restate the task being performed by a construct of the language. For example, there is no point in including the following comment:

```
// display the characters "The sum of the two numbers is: " on the screen
System.out.print("The sum of the two numbers is: ");
```

There should always be a comment at the start of a program which gives details of the purpose of the program, the program's author, and the date the program was created. This is illustrated by the comments contained in the SimpleSum program. If, at a later date, a program is altered, further details should be added to these comments. These additional details should include the maintainer's name, the date the program was altered, and the purpose of the alterations.

Finally, it should be noted that a comment only describes the *intention* of the author of the program: what the comment says may in fact be incorrect. Alternatively, it may have been true when the program was created; however, subsequently, a change has been made to the code of the program, but the comment attached to the code was not updated.

1.6.2 The layout of programs

There is no mention of **layout** in the syntax diagrams. This is because spaces which can be used to control the layout of the text of a program can occur almost anywhere, and so their inclusion in syntax diagrams would cause confusion. However, here are some rules about their use:

- A space must not appear within a keyword, within an identifier, or within a **compound symbol** (such as the // and /* symbols that were introduced in the previous section).
- Several spaces are equivalent to one space.
- At least one space must appear between two consecutive symbols when each symbol is a keyword or an identifier (e.g. public class cannot be written as publicclass).
- There is an implicit space between any two consecutive lines of a program. So any line can be split into two, and continued on the next line, at any point where a space is permitted. It follows that the characters of a keyword, an identifier, or a compound symbol cannot be split between two lines.

To a compiler, a program is merely a string of symbols. A compiler would accept the program given in Figure 1.1 even if it had been typed in as shown in Figure 1.7. As far as the compiler is concerned, they are the same program. It is for your own benefit, and for the benefit of other people reading your programs, that you should adopt a sensible layout. Although the actual style of layout varies from one programmer to another, it is important to use a style consistently throughout a program and to choose a style in which the actual structure of a program is reflected by the layout of the program. One particular style is illustrated by the layout chosen for the programs in this book.

```
// This program displays the sum of 2.7 and 4.2. Barry
// Cornelius, 28
// May 2000
public class
SimpleSum { public
static void main(final String
[]pArgs){double          tFirst          ;double
tSecond;double tSum;tFirst = 2.7;tSecond
= 4.2;tSum = tFirst
+
tSecond;System.out.print("The sum of the two numbers is: ");System.
out.print(tSum);System.out.println();}}
```

Figure 1.7 A program that is badly laid out.

Curios, controversies and cover-ups

1.1 There are three editions of both the Java 2 Platform and the Java 2 SDK. They are called the **Micro Edition (J2ME)**, the **Standard Edition (J2SE)**, and the **Enterprise Edition (J2EE)**. In this book, we will be concentrating on the Standard Edition. The Micro Edition is a slimmed-down edition suitable for use when Java is running in embedded systems such as smart cards, pagers, mobile phones, PDAs (handhelds), whereas the Enterprise Edition has more facilities than the Standard Edition, enabling Java to be used with distributed systems.

1.2 Unlike other programming languages, the characters of a Java program are not just restricted to the *ASCII* character set: instead Java's character set is based on the *Unicode* standard. According to the syntax diagrams in Figure 1.4 the only characters allowed in an identifier are 26 upper-case letters, 26 lower-case letters, 10 digits, a dollar character and an underscore character.

However, Figure 1.4 is very much a simplification of what is allowed. A letter/digit of an identifier may be any of the letters/digits of a large number of languages from around the world.

For more details, see the entry in the documentation of the Core APIs for the class `java.lang.Character`. There are details about how to look at this documentation in Curio 3.2.

1.3 When describing the use of a **dollar** character in an identifier, the JLS says that it 'should be used only in mechanically generated Java code or, rarely, to access pre-existing names on legacy systems'. In this book, we will not use the dollar character in identifiers.

1.4 According to the JLS, the **underscore** character is permitted in identifiers 'for historical reasons'. It is not clear as to what this means. It probably refers to the fact that, in some programming languages, programmers use the underscore character to break up the words of a multi-word identifier, as in `account_is_overdrawn`. However, as was pointed out in Section 1.5, this is not usually done in Java: `accountIsOverdrawn` is used instead.

Java programmers tend to use underscore characters in identifiers for two main purposes: these will be considered in Curio 2.9 and Curio 11.3. In this book, we will not use the underscore character in identifiers.

1.5   All Java programs have a main method declaration. In other Java books, you are likely to see it declared with the header:

```
public static void main(String[] args)
```

or:

```
public static void main(String args[])
```

However, in order to be consistent with the style adopted (in this book) for method declarations and array declarations, this book will use the header:

```
public static void main(final String[] pArgs)
```

There are three differences: the use of `final`, the position of the `[]` characters and the use of `pArgs` rather than `args`. These are explained in Section 8.7, Curio 15.1 and Section 8.5.

Exercises

1.1   Make a list of all the keywords that appear in the `SimpleSum` program – see Figure 1.1.

1.2   Make a list of the identifiers that appear in the `SimpleSum` program.

1.3   Produce syntax diagrams that describe the syntax of a date and time.

1.4   Produce syntax diagrams that describe the syntax of a postal address.

Chapter 2

Constructing simple programs

....

One of the main parts of a program's syntax diagram, which was left unexplained in the previous chapter, is the part that refers to *Block*.

In this chapter, we will see that a block consists of a list of the actions that we want the computer to carry out. Each of these actions is coded by means of a *statement*.

The statements will refer to entities called *variables* – these are places where temporary values can be stored. The purpose of a *declaration* is to mention the names of any variables that are used in the block.

It is no use getting a computer to perform a set of actions if you are unable to see what results it has produced. So, this chapter finishes with some discussion of how we can use some *method invocations* to display results on the screen of the computer.

2.1 Blocks

In the previous chapter we pulled the wrappings off a program; we discovered some of the paraphernalia that is needed to produce a program. However, we did not look at the part of a program where we tell the computer to do some work. Looking again at the syntax diagrams for a program given in Figure 1.3, the exciting part is in the section marked *Block*.

A block contains the actions we want the computer to execute. Here is the block of the SimpleSum program:

```
{
    double tFirst, tSecond, tSum;
    tFirst = 2.7;
    tSecond = 4.2;
    tSum = tFirst + tSecond;
    System.out.print("The sum of the two numbers is: ");
    System.out.print(tSum);
    System.out.println();
}
```

The syntax diagram for a **block** is shown in Figure 2.1. It just says that a *Block* is introduced by a { symbol and terminated by a } symbol, and in between these two symbols there are zero or more occurrences of a *Statement*.

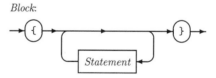

Figure 2.1   The syntax of a block.

When a block is executed, each of the statements of the block is executed one after another in the order that they are given. For the SimpleSum program, the block contains seven statements; each of these will be executed in turn. The first statement is:

```
double tFirst, tSecond, tSum;
```

and the last one is:

```
System.out.println();
```

2.2 The different kinds of statements

The name **statement** is badly chosen because what we are actually referring to is some form of *action* or *command* rather than a *statement*. However, programming languages have been using the term *statement* since the late 1950s, and so we are stuck with it!

In Java, a statement can take many different forms. However, in this chapter we will only be looking at *variable declarations*, *constant declarations*, *assignment statements*, statements formed from an *increment-decrement expression*, and some examples of statements that involve *method invocations*. Other kinds of statements will be introduced later. A simplified version of the syntax diagram for a statement is shown in Figure 2.2.

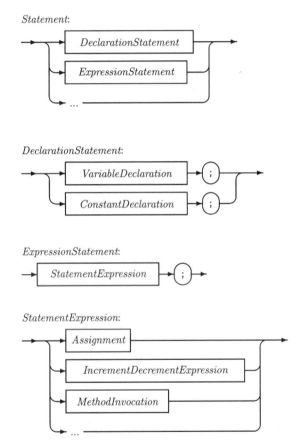

Figure 2.2   The syntax of a statement.

To give you some idea as to what statements look like, here are a few examples taken from the `SimpleSum` program. There is one statement in the program that is a variable declaration:

```
double tFirst, tSecond, tSum;
```

There are three assignment statements – here is one of them:

```
tSum = tFirst + tSecond;
```

And there are three method invocations – here is one:

```
System.out.print(tSum);
```

and here is another:

```
System.out.println();
```

The next few sections of this chapter will explain the meaning of the seven statements of the `SimpleSum` program.

2.3   Variable declarations

A **variable** is a place where an intermediate value can be stored when a program is executing. Most pocket calculators and many telephones have a *memory*, and a variable fulfils a similar purpose.

A **variable declaration** of a program *declares* the names of some variables that are used by the program. For example, in the `SimpleSum` program, the variable declaration:

```
double tFirst, tSecond, tSum;
```

states that the program will use three variables called `tFirst`, `tSecond` and `tSum`. So, there are three places in which three values can be stored when this program is executing:

The syntax of a *VariableDeclaration* is given in Figure 2.3. The part involving an *Initializer* is optional, and so, for the moment, we will ignore it. Looking at the syntax

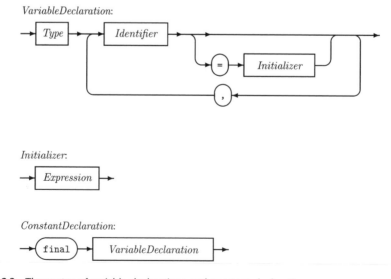

Figure 2.3   The syntax of variable declarations and constant declarations.

diagrams and at:

```
double tFirst, tSecond, tSum;
```

you will see that a variable declaration does not just list the names of the variables that are going to be used: it also specifies the *type* of the variables. Thus, the variable declaration in the `SimpleSum` program states that the variables `tFirst`, `tSecond` and `tSum` are variables of type 'double'.

2.4   What is meant by a type?

Type is an important concept in programming languages like Java. So, we now look more closely at the idea of types. A **type** has two main characteristics:

- a type has a set of values associated with it,
- a type has a set of operations that are permitted on these values.

Consider, for example, values which are integers. In mathematics, there is an infinite set of integers. However, in computing, the number of integers is usually limited to some finite range. Java has four types for representing whole number values, each of these having a different range of values. In this book, we will mainly be using one of these types: it is a type called `int`.

In Java, the type `int` refers to the set of whole numbers from some large negative value to some large positive value together with operations such as addition and subtraction. If a variable is declared to be of type `int`:

```
int tNumberOfStudents;
```

only `int` values can be stored in the variable. So, we will not be able to store a person's name in this variable, or put non-integral numeric values (such as 6.7) into it. Some languages are more relaxed about the typing of values and variables: Java, however, is quite strict – it is said to be a language with **strong typing**.

There are parallels in the real world. If you have a fruit bowl, a milk bottle and a petrol can, you put fruit into the fruit bowl, milk into the milk bottle, and petrol into the petrol can. You normally do not put fruit into a milk bottle, or milk into a petrol can, or . . . !

2.5   Some of the primitive types of Java

In most programming languages there are some types which are predefined. In Java, the predefined types are called the **primitive type**s. To begin with, we will only use two of the primitive types in our programs: they are the type `double` which is used in the `SimpleSum` program and the type `int` mentioned in the previous section.

Some of the characteristics of the types `int` and `double` are given by the table in Figure 2.4. In particular, this table shows the **range** of values for both types. When representing non-integral values (**floating-point** values), the table indicates that not every real number of mathematics is represented exactly by a value of

```
int
```
   Set of values:

      The whole numbers from –2147483648 to 2147483647.

   Examples of operations:

      `+, -, *, /`

   Examples of literals:

      `0, 42, 2147483647`

```
double
```
   Set of values:

      Some of the real numbers (of mathematics) from approximately $-1.8E+308$ to $1.8E+308$. Values are stored with a precision of about 15 significant digits. Values in the range from approximately $-4.9E-324$ to $4.9E-324$ are treated as if they were equal to 0.0.

   Examples of operations:

      `+, -, *, /`

   Examples of literals:

      `0.0, 2.7, 0.5e100, 6.6252e-34, 2.99792458E8, 1.1E-100`

Figure 2.4   Some of the characteristics of the primitive types `int` and `double`.

the type `double`. In fact, there are only a few that are represented exactly: all the other numbers are represented by an approximation with a **precision** of about 15 significant digits. The table also lists some of the operations that are permitted on values of each type – these will be considered again in Section 5.3. Finally, the table shows how a **literal** of the type is written – this illustrates how a program can refer to a value of the type. Note that a literal of the type `double` can have an **exponent part** where the letter E (or the letter e) is used to mean *times ten to the power of*.

Unlike other programming languages, in Java the range of values (for both `int` and `double`) and the precision of the type `double` do not vary from one implementation of Java to another. They are always the same. There are some more details about the precision and the range of the numeric types in Curio 2.2, Curio 2.3 and Curio 2.4.

Besides `int` and `double`, Java has six other primitive types. Like `int`, the types `byte`, `short` and `long` are primitive types for representing whole number values. However, each one of these types has a different range of values. We will rarely use these other integer types in this book. There are more details about them in Curio 2.2. Similarly, the type `float` is similar to the `double` type but with a different range and precision. We will not use `float` much either. There are more details about the type `float` in Curio 2.3.

So far, we have looked at the six primitive types for representing numerical values; the remaining primitive types are called `char` and `boolean`. The type `char` is important as it is used for manipulating characters, but most of the useful things that can be done with characters require the handling of a *string*, a sequence of characters. So, the type char will be left until we deal with the type String in Chapter 3. Finally, the type boolean is also important, as it is used for making decisions in a program: it will be covered in Section 6.13.

2.6 Assignments

Variables were introduced as a means by which we can store intermediate values. One way of giving a variable a value is by executing an **assignment**. The syntax of an assignment is given in Figure 2.5. There are two parts to an assignment, and these parts are separated by an = symbol. This symbol is one of Java's 12 **assignment operator**s and is often read either as *becomes* or as *becomes equal to*.

Assignment:

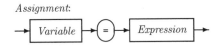

Figure 2.5 The syntax of an assignment.

The part to the left of the = is usually simple as it is often the identifier of a variable. However, the part to the right of the = can be very complex. Syntactically, it is an *expression*, and, in many places where an expression is used, you can view it as the computing equivalent of a mathematical formula. We will find that expressions are not only used in assignments: they are also used in other statements such as *if statement*s and *method invocation*s.

Sometimes the expression is simple – it might be a literal or the name of a variable, but, as mentioned earlier, expressions can be complex. There are two main forms of complicated expressions: we will look at *arithmetic expression*s in Chapter 5, and at *boolean expression*s in Chapter 6.

Having discussed the syntax, we now move on to look at what happens when an assignment is executed. Two things happen in the following order:

1. The value of the expression on the right-hand side of the = symbol is obtained.

2. This value is stored in the variable named on the left-hand side of the = symbol.

An assignment is usually used to form a statement called an **assignment statement**. The syntax diagrams of Figure 2.2 show that this can be done by following an assignment by a semicolon. The following fragment of Java includes two simple assignment statements:

```
double d;
int i;
d = 2.7;
i = 3;
```

These are instructions to introduce two variables called d and i, to place the value 2.7 in the variable d and the value 3 in the variable i.

So the following two assignment statements of the `SimpleSum` program simply store values in the `tFirst` and `tSecond` variables:

```
tFirst = 2.7;
tSecond = 4.2;
```

The other assignment statement of the `SimpleSum` program is slightly more complicated:

```
tSum = tFirst + tSecond;
```

This has the effect of adding together the current values of the variables `tFirst` and `tSecond`, and then storing the result in the variable `tSum`.

Earlier, it was mentioned that Java is a language with *strong typing*. Whether it is legal to assign a value to a variable depends on the type of the expression and the type of the variable. The variable's type is obvious: it is given in the variable's declaration, and, although there are rules for determining the type of an expression, an expression's type will often be obvious.

An assignment is allowed when the expression and the variable have the same type. It is also allowed in other situations: there are rules which deal with these other possibilities. These rules determine whether the type of the expression is **assignment compatible** with the type of the variable. Because we are currently only considering the types `int` and `double`, the only other rule we need to know (at this stage) is that it is possible to assign an `int` value to a `double` variable. Assuming that we have the statements:

```
int tFreezingPoint;
double tSpeedLimit, tStartingTemperature;
tFreezingPoint = 32;
```

here are two examples of assigning an `int` value to a `double` variable:

```
tSpeedLimit = 30;
tStartingTemperature = tFreezingPoint;
```

In the examples we have looked at so far, we have been using an assignment statement to give a variable its first value. This is a task known as **initializing** the variable – we will look at this in more detail in Section 2.8. The other possibility is that the variable (on the left-hand side of an assignment statement) already has a value: in this case, the execution of an assignment statement will cause its current value to be replaced by the new value.

2.7) Operators for assignment, increment and decrement

Sometimes we will want to replace the value that is stored in a variable by some value that is related to its current value. For example, if we want to count the number of students entering a lecture theatre we might want to execute:

```
tNumberOfStudents = tNumberOfStudents + 1;
```

each time a student enters the room. This may look a little odd. However, remember that an assignment calculates the value of the expression on the right-hand side of the = and then assigns this value to the variable on the left-hand side. So the above assignment statement has the effect of increasing the value of tNumberOfStudents by 1.

And the assignment statement:

```
tNumberOfStudents = tNumberOfStudents - 1;
```

could be used whenever a student leaves the lecture theatre.

If instead we are working out the weight of the load of a ferry boat, we might execute the following whenever a vehicle is loaded:

```
tLadenWeight = tLadenWeight + tWeightOfVehicle;
```

However, there are other *assignment operators* that can be used when an assignment is increasing or decreasing a variable. The three assignment statements:

```
tNumberOfStudents = tNumberOfStudents + 1;
tNumberOfStudents = tNumberOfStudents - 1;
tLadenWeight = tLadenWeight + tWeightOfVehicle;
```

can be abbreviated to;

```
tNumberOfStudents += 1;
tNumberOfStudents -= 1;
tLadenWeight += tWeightOfVehicle;
```

We have now met three of Java's 12 assignment operators: they are =, += and -=. There are more details about assignment operators in Curio 2.6.

When a variable is being increased or decreased by 1, an assignment can be abbreviated further by using a **increment-decrement expression**. For example:

```
tNumberOfStudents = tNumberOfStudents + 1;
```

can be abbreviated using an **increment operator**:

```
tNumberOfStudents++;
```

and:

```
tNumberOfStudents = tNumberOfStudents - 1;
```

can be abbreviated using a **decrement operator**:

```
tNumberOfStudents--;
```

The syntax of an increment-decrement expression is given in Figure 2.6. And an increment-decrement expression can be used in a statement because of the syntax diagrams shown in Figure 2.2. So far, we have placed ++ and -- immediately after the name of a variable. However, the syntax diagrams reveal that they may also be used before the name of a variable. There are more details about this in Curio 2.8.

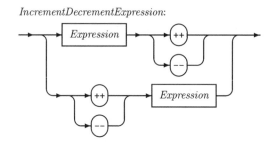

IncrementDecrementExpression:

Figure 2.6   The syntax of an increment-decrement expression.

2.8 Initialization

Up to the point where a variable is initialized, it is said to be **undefined**. A program should not refer to the value of a variable if it has not yet been assigned a value. In fact, if you attempt to do this in a Java program, then, when you submit the program to the Java compiler, it will detect the error: it will produce a *compilation error*.

When a variable is declared, you can include an **initializer** that gives the variable its initial value. For example:

```
double tFirst = 2.7;
```

Often, the initial value of a variable can only be established after the execution of a few statements. In these cases, it is better to leave the declaration until the initial value is known. The initializer will then be an expression that depends on the values of other variables. This is the case with the initializer for the variable tSum in:

```
double tFirst = 2.7;
double tSecond = 4.2;
double tSum = tFirst + tSecond;
```

This approach encourages a style where variables are declared just before they are used and where they can be initialized with an appropriate value: this style is said to cause less errors. It is a style that is adopted by this book.

2.9 Constant declarations

In a program, we frequently use numerical values. For example, we might need to use the fact that there are 2.54 centimetres in an inch, that there are 86 400 seconds in a day, that the freezing point of water is 32 (in degrees Fahrenheit), and so on. Obviously, we can use such *literals* within the statements of a program:

```
tRealTemperature = 32 + tAmountAboveFreezing;
```

However, it is possible to have a variable that is a **constant**: we assign the value of an expression to a variable and indicate that the variable cannot be changed. To do this, we use a variable declaration that has an initializer and we can signify that the variable's value cannot be changed by using the `final` keyword. For example, we could introduce:

```
final int tFreezingPoint = 32;
```

and replace the above assignment statement by:

```
tRealTemperature = tFreezingPoint + tAmountAboveFreezing;
```

The syntax of a constant declaration is included in Figure 2.3. Like variable declarations, constant declarations may appear anywhere in the sequence of statements that form a block.

There are several reasons for introducing constants into a program:

- Values which are difficult to remember (and are therefore difficult to get right) need only be written down once. Examples include the value of the speed of light, the number of seconds in a day, the value of π, etc.
- The resulting program is usually more understandable. Rather than just using the literal `2.99792458E8` in the middle of an expression, it is more helpful to a reader of a program if the expression uses a name like `tSpeedOfLight`, where there has previously been the declaration:

  ```
  final double tSpeedOfLight = 2.99792458E8;
  ```

- It is a lot easier to change all references to a value to some other value. For example, suppose a program needs to contain numerous references to a value representing the additional amount to be paid for some tax (such as VAT or a sales tax). Suppose that this value is currently 17.5 per cent. If the program has used a constant for this value:

  ```
  final double tTaxRate = 17.5;
  ```

  then only the one occurrence of 17.5 within this declaration would need to be changed if the tax rate were changed, e.g. from 17.5 to 18.5.

Some people suggest that all literals that are going to be used in a program should be given a name. However, this is an extreme view. There are some values which are known to everyone, and are never going to be changed to some other value. Examples include the number of days in a week, or the number of months in a year. It is over-zealous to introduce constants for such values.

Remember that a variable declared in a constant declaration, such as `tTaxRate`, cannot have its value changed. So if you include the assignment statement:

```
tTaxRate = 18.5;
```

the program will not compile.

There is one other slightly different use of a constant declaration: besides the constant values described above, a program may have other variables whose values do not change after they have been initialized. Again, this can be indicated by using a `final` keyword when declaring the variables. For example, in the `SimpleSum` program we could use:

```
final double tFirst = 2.7;
final double tSecond = 4.2;
final double tSum = tFirst + tSecond;
```

The use of final at a variable's declaration documents the intention of the programmer to the compiler. If elsewhere in the program the programmer has produced code that assigns to this variable, the compiler will produce a *compilation error*. It also documents the programmer's intention to anyone reading the program: when looking at some statement involving this variable, the reader can be sure that the variable has the value given in its declaration without having to hunt through the code to see whether the variable's value has subsequently been changed.

2.10   Output of values

2.10.1 How are we to see the results of the calculations?

One of the crucial parts of Java that we have not yet considered concerns getting information back from the computer. There is not much point in getting a program to do a series of calculations unless we have some way of finding out the results that it has calculated – we need to get the program to produce **output**.

Consider the SimpleSum program again. Having got the computer to calculate the sum of two numbers, we would then like the computer to output this value. In the context of the SimpleSum program, this means that we want the computer to output the value of the variable tSum.

The task of taking a value from the computer's memory and producing a representation of this value as a sequence of characters on the screen is reasonably difficult – a complicated sequence of statements is needed. Because this sequence is needed so often, someone else has already written this code, and has defined this code within a **method**. Later (in Chapter 8), we will see how to define our own methods; however, for the time being, regard a method as a name for an existing sequence of statements.

So, to summarize: the details of how to transform the double value that is in the variable tSum into characters on the screen need not concern us; this is because Java provides a *method* that performs this task.

2.10.2 The print method

In days gone by, most of the output produced by computers appeared on printers. So it is for historical reasons that the appropriate method for displaying some output is called print. However, we want to send this output not to some printer but to the screen, and we do this by applying the print method to System.out, an *object* that has already been set up to be associated with the screen. So we will be using a statement like:

```
System.out.print(...);
```

We will see later that System.out is a way of referring to a variable called out belonging to the *class* System.

However, in order to use the `print` method, we need to pass it some information: it needs to know the value that we want to be output. In our case, this value is stored in the variable `tSum`. So, here is how `print` is used in the `SimpleSum` program:

```
System.out.print(tSum);
```

This is an instruction to output the value of the variable `tSum`. For example, the characters:

```
6.9
```

might be output.
　The statement:

```
System.out.print(tSum);
```

leads to a **call** of `print`. More formally, a call is known as a **method invocation**, and syntactically it consists of the name of the object to which the method is being applied (e.g. `System.out`), followed by a full stop, followed by the name of the method (e.g. `print`), followed by expression(s) enclosed in a pair of parentheses (e.g. `(tSum)`). This is shown by the syntax diagram in Figure 2.7. And a method invocation can be used in a statement because of the syntax diagrams shown in Figure 2.2.

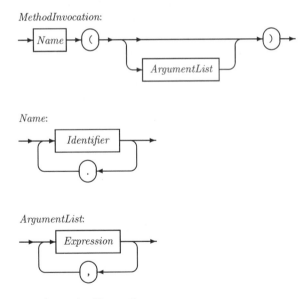

Figure 2.7　The syntax of a method invocation.

2.10.3 The arguments that `print` can take

The expressions (that appear within the parentheses) are referred to as the **arguments** of the call. In the call of print, there is only one argument which is an expression that gives the value that you want to be printed. The important thing about a method is that you can vary the argument(s) from one call to another.

For example, we could modify the `SimpleSum` program to output the values of `tFirst` and `tSecond` as well as `tSum` using:

```
System.out.print(tFirst);
```

and:

```
System.out.print(tSecond);
```

as well as:

```
System.out.print(tSum);
```

We will want to output values of other types besides values of type `double`. For example, we will also want to output values of type `int`. For this, Java provides a method that can output `int`s. Instead of each type having an output method that has a different name (e.g. `printInt`, `printDouble`, ...), all of these output methods are called `print`, e.g.:

```
int tNumberOfStudents = 42;
...
System.out.print(tNumberOfStudents);
```

Defining different methods that have the same name but which take arguments of different types is called **method overloading** – there is more about this topic in Section 8.14.

The output from a program should not just consist of a set of numerical values. It is important that such values are accompanied by text that gives some description of the values being output. In order to do this, there is a version of the `print` method that takes an argument that is the *string* of characters to be output. Here is an example of its use:

```
System.out.print("The sum of the two numbers is: ");
```

The above fragment will have the effect of producing output like:

```
The sum of the two numbers is:
```

An argument like `"The sum of the two numbers is: "` is a *literal* of type `java.lang.String`. The type `String` is a type that we will consider in more detail in the next chapter.

2.10.4 The `println` method

In the `SimpleSum` program, there is one other method invocation that we need to consider:

```
System.out.println();
```

This is the call of a method called `println` (pronounced *print-line*). Here it appears without any arguments, i.e. there is nothing between the parentheses. When `println` is called, the printing position is moved to the start of a new line. For example, the code:

```
System.out.print("The sum of the two numbers is:");
System.out.println();
System.out.print(tSum);
```

has the effect of producing two lines of output such as:

```
The sum of the two numbers is:
6.9
```

There are two shortcuts that you ought to know about. First, like `print`, `println` is heavily overloaded, and so, besides the `println` having no arguments, there is a `println` counterpart for every `print` method. For example, we could use `println` with an argument of type `double` as in:

```
System.out.println(tSum);
```

When `println` has an argument, first the value of the argument is output and then the printing position is moved to the start of a new line. So the above call of `println` is an abbreviation of:

```
System.out.print(tSum);
System.out.println();
```

2.10.5 Use of the string concatenation operator

Here is another shortcut: if you are going to output several values, you do not need separate `print`/`println` calls to output each of the values; instead, you can use the **string concatenation** operator with one call of `print`/`println`. For example, the calls:

```
System.out.print("The sum of the two numbers is: ");
System.out.print(tSum);
System.out.println();
```

can be abbreviated to:

```
System.out.print("The sum of the two numbers is: " + tSum);
System.out.println();
```

or to:

```
System.out.println("The sum of the two numbers is: " + tSum);
```

Each of these will produce a line of output looking like:

```
The sum of the two numbers is: 6.9
```

Because one of the operands of the + is a string, the other operand is converted from a `double` to a `String`. The string concatenation operator is very flexible in that it will convert any operand that is of a permitted type into a `String`.

So we have now seen two uses of the + operator: sometimes it is used for addition, and on other occasions it is used for string concatenation. The meaning of a particular + depends on the types of its operands. For more details, see Tip 2.4.

(2.11) Compiling and executing the `SimpleSum` program

Most of the material necessary to understand the SimpleSum program given in Figure 1.1 has now been introduced. The only aspects left unexplained at this stage are the meanings of `public class`, `public static void`, and `final String[] pArgs`. For the moment, all of our programs will contain these symbols: we will look at what they mean later.

In Section 1.1.3, we saw that there is a two-stage process in getting a program executed. First, we will have to get a compiler to compile the SimpleSum program. This will produce a file containing some bytecodes. When we ask the Java interpreter to interpret the bytecodes of the SimpleSum program, the bytecodes corresponding to each of the following statements will be executed in turn:

```
double tFirst, tSecond, tSum;
tFirst = 2.7;
tSecond = 4.2;
tSum = tFirst + tSecond;
System.out.print("The sum of the two numbers is: ");
System.out.print(tSum);
System.out.println();
```

The first statement is a declaration: it creates the three variables tFirst, tSecond and tSum. The next statement causes the value 2.7 to be stored in the variable tFirst and the following statement causes the value 4.2 to be stored in the variable tSecond. The third assignment statement calculates the sum of the two values stored in the variables tFirst and tSecond and assigns that value to the variable tSum. Finally, the program executes two print calls that cause it to output the line:

```
The sum of the two numbers is: 6.9
```

to the screen. The call of println causes the printing position to be moved to the start of the next line.

Make sure that you understand the meaning of each part of this program before moving on.

At this point, you should try to compile and execute the SimpleSum program. One way of doing this is explained in Appendix B.

(2.12) An improved `SimpleSum` program

After reading the material in this chapter, an improved version of the SimpleSum program can be produced. It is given in Figure 2.8.

```
// This program displays the sum of 2.7 and 4.2.
// Barry Cornelius, 29 May 2000
public class ImprovedSimpleSum
{
   public static void main(final String[] pArgs)
   {
      final double tFirst = 2.7;
      final double tSecond = 4.2;
      final double tSum = tFirst + tSecond;
      System.out.println("The sum of " + tFirst +
                         " and " + tSecond + " is " + tSum);
   }
}
```

Figure 2.8   An improved version of the SimpleSum program.

2.13 Getting programs to do different things each time

Normally, when you run a computer program, you will have some way in which
you can influence what the program does from one run of the program to the next.
However, the Java programs that we have seen so far are very boring: they always
do the same thing.

At the moment, all the variables get their values directly or indirectly from values
given in the program. What we want is some way of specifying some of these values
when the program is running. We will look at this key issue of supplying *input* to a
program in Chapter 4.

2.14 Debugging, testing and maintenance

Even if a program compiles, it does not follow that (when you execute the program)
it will perform the task that you had planned the program to do. This is because the
statements that you have asked to be executed may not be the right ones to perform
the task. If this is the case, the program is said to have a **bug**. Having looked at what
happens when you execute the program, it may be obvious as to what is wrong with
the program. However, on other occasions, you may at first be completely baffled.
This task of removing bugs from a program is called **debugging** – there is more
about debugging in the sections of this book marked *Tips for programming and
debugging*.

Unless a program is exhaustively tested, it may contain bugs that lie undetected
for many years – such bugs are sometimes known as **sleeper**s. So you need to subject a program to a fair amount of **testing** before you can say that its development
is complete. Bugs that are detected after a program has been completed are the
responsibility of the person maintaining the program.

Tips for programming and debugging

2.1   One aim of the various sections of this book marked *Tips for programming and debugging* is to tell you about some of the pitfalls of writing Java programs. The first tip concerns a problem you may get into when calling a method.

When a method is called, you must include a list of arguments (surrounded by parentheses) even if the call does not have any arguments. For example, if you produce a program containing:

```
System.out.println;
```

then, when you compile the program, the compiler will detect the error. It will output a *compilation error* message which may be something like:

```
SimpleSum.java:13: Invalid expression statement.
        System.out.println;
                  ^
1 error
```

Instead, you need to write:

```
System.out.println();
```

2.2   It is important that your main method declaration has the correct header:

```
public static void main(final String[] pArgs)
```

If you forget the `void` symbol, leave out the parentheses, or leave out the `pArgs`, your program will fail to compile. Alternatively, if you misspell `main` or spell `main` using some other case (such as `Main`), or if you forget the `static` symbol or the `[]` symbol, your program will compile but fail when you run the Java interpreter. It will fail with an error message like:

```
Exception in thread "main" java.lang.NoSuchMethodError: main
```

2.3   If a program uses `print`, the output may not actually be sent to the screen until `println` or `flush` (introduced in Section 4.5) is called. Although this is a detail that is usually unimportant, if a program uses calls of `print` the program should always end in a call of `println` (or `flush`) or else the last line of the output may not appear.

2.4   As mentioned in Section 2.10.5, the symbol + is used both for addition and for string concatenation. Suppose we have the following variables:

```
int tYear = 2000;
int tMonth = 7;
int tDay = 11;
```

If you write:

```
System.out.println(tYear + tMonth + tDay);
```

the output will contain the value 2018, the result of the addition of the values 2000, 7 and 11. Suppose that, instead, you use:

```
System.out.println("" + tYear + tMonth + tDay);
```

As will be pointed in Section 3.4.3, the " " is the representation of a string that has no characters: it is called the *empty string*. Because one of the operands of the expression `"" + tYear + tMonth + tDay` is the string literal `""`, this expression uses the string concatenation operator three times – it does not use the addition operator. The above code outputs the line:

```
2000711
```

If you want the three values to be separated by spaces, use:

```
System.out.println(tYear + " " + tMonth + " " + tDay);
```

This will produce:

```
2000 7 11
```

2.5 There is a **debugger**, jdb, that comes with the Java 2 SDK. This can be a useful tool for establishing what is wrong with a program. However, because it is a powerful tool, it is very easy to get confused. In this book, instead of using jdb, we give you some hints to help you with debugging. It is recommended that you have a look at a debugger only when you are confident both with the language Java and with programming.

So, one of the other aims of the sections marked *Tips for programming and debugging* is to give you some idea about how to track down a bug in your program. Often this is done by including additional statements in the program that gets the execution of the program to produce more output. Such statements are called **debugging statements**.

Here are two kinds of debugging statements:

- It may be useful to output different pieces of text at various points if you are uncertain as to whereabouts in the program the execution is going wrong.

- It may be useful to output the values of any temporary variables that are used by the program.

Having detected the cause of a bug, it is tempting to remove the additional statements that helped to locate the bug. However, it may be that subsequent testing shows up another bug, and the existing debugging statements may be useful in detecting the cause of this new bug. So it is often best to leave debugging statements in the program until you have finished testing the program.

The task of removing the debugging statements is quite a tedious one. Needless to say, it sometimes happens that when a programmer is doing this, some statements that are not debugging statements are inadvertently removed. The chances of this happening can be reduced in the following way: whenever you add a debugging statement to a program, put an empty comment in columns 1 to 4 of the line.

For example, here is part of the `SimpleSum` program (Figure 1.1) with some debugging statements added to it:

```
      ...
      tFirst = 2.7;
/**/  System.out.println("*** value of tFirst is: " + tFirst);
      tSecond = 4.2;
/**/  System.out.println("*** value of tSecond is: " + tSecond);
/**/  System.out.println("*** about to do the addition");
      tSum = tFirst + tSecond;
      System.out.print("The sum of the two numbers is: ");
      ...
```

The characters * * * are output at the start of each line of output that is produced by the debugging statements. This helps to distinguish between the output produced for debugging purposes and the normal output of the program. Note that the above code contains an example of each of the two kinds of debugging statements referred to earlier.

Having tagged each debugging statement with a / * * /, the task of removing these statements is a lot easier: there is less chance of removing statements that are not debugging statements. In Section 10.6, we look at a program that actually does the task of removing debugging statements from a Java program.

Curios, controversies and cover-ups

2.1   The syntax of a variable declaration (given in Figure 2.3) allows more than one variable to be declared in the same declaration. It also allows a variable to be initialized at its point of declaration. It is probably best not to combine both of these in the same declaration. Although there is no problem with the declaration:

```
double tFirst = 2.7, tSecond = 4.2;
```

what is the meaning of the declaration:

```
double tFirst, tSecond = 4.2;
```

Is this the same as:

```
double tFirst;
double tSecond = 4.2;
```

or is it the same as:

```
double tFirst = 4.2;
double tSecond = 4.2;
```

Although the Java language defines the answer to be the first of these, it is best not to test the knowledge of the person reading your program!

2.2 Besides the type int, Java also has the primitive types byte, short and long. They are used in much the same way as the type int, the main difference being that they have a different range of values. The ranges of these types are as follows:

type	smallest value of the type	largest value of the type
byte	−128	127
short	−32768	32767
int	−2147483648	2147483647
long	−9223372036854775808	9223372036854775807

2.3 Besides the type double, Java also has one other primitive type for representing the real numbers of mathematics: it is called float. It is used in much the same way as the type double. These types have two main differences. First, double values are stored more accurately: they are stored with a precision of about 15 significant digits, whereas floats are stored with a precision of about 7 significant digits. Secondly, they have a different range of values as shown by this table:

type	smallest value of the type	largest value of the type
float	$-3.40282347E+38$	$3.40282347E+38$
double	$-1.79769313486231570E+308$	$1.79769313486231570E+308$

Values of the types float and double that are small in magnitude are considered to be zero:

type	largest non-zero negative value	smallest non-zero positive value
float	$-1.40239846E-45$	$+1.40239846E-45$
double	$-4.94065645841246544E-324$	$+4.94065645841246544E-324$

A floating-point literal that ends in an F or an f is of type float whereas one that ends in a D or a d is of type double. A floating-point literal that does not end in any of these letters is also of type double. Here are some examples:

type	examples of literals
float	4.2F, 4.2E1F, 4.2f, 4.2E-4f
double	4.2, 4.2E1, 4.2D, 4.2E1D, 4.2d, 4.2E-4d

2.4 From the release of the Java 2 Platform onwards, it has been possible for the intermediate results of floating-point calculations to be done with a different precision, and this may lead to results which are slightly different from one implementation of Java to another. The same results will be produced for all implementations if the strictfp keyword is used. For more details about this, see Section 4.2.3 of the JLS.

2.5 Figure 2.4 gives some examples of literals of the type int. These integer literals are given using decimal notation, a notation based on using powers of 10. It is also possible to use integer literals written in **octal notation** or in **hexadecimal notation**: these are notations that are based on powers of 8 and 16.

Literals given using these notations are written with some special characters: the digit 0 is used at the start of an **octal literal** and the two characters 0x (or 0X) are used at the start of a **hexadecimal literal**. These curious denotations for octal and hexadecimal literals are borrowed from the programming languages C and C++.

So the assignment statement:

```
tValue = 42;
```

can instead be written as:

```
tValue = 052;
tValue = 0x2A;
```

We will not find a need to use these forms of integer literals in this book.

2.6   An assignment may use any of 12 **assignment operators**. They are =, +=, -=, *=, /=, %=, <<=, >>=, >>>=, &=, ^= and | =. Only the first six of these will be used in this book. We looked at =, += and -= in Section 2.7. The *=, /= and %= operators are used in a similar way to += and -=.

2.7   Although in this book an assignment will always be used to form an assignment statement (or to form part of a *for statement*), strictly speaking it is an expression. It can therefore be used anywhere where an expression is required. The value of an assignment is the value of the variable after it has been assigned its new value.

2.8   Although in this book an *increment-decrement expression* will always be used to form a statement (or to form part of a *for statement*), strictly speaking it is an expression. It can therefore be used anywhere where an expression is required. The value of *variablename++* is the value of the variable before it has been incremented. Besides *variablename++*, it is also possible to write *++variablename*. The value of *++variablename* is the value of the variable after it has been incremented. Similar comments apply for the -- operator.

2.9   When choosing the name of a constant, some programmers adopt the convention of using an identifier consisting of upper-case letters. If the identifier is formed from more than one word, the words are separated by an underscore character. Here are some examples:

```
final int FREEZING_POINT = 32;
final double SPEED_OF_LIGHT = 2.99792458E8;
final double TAX_RATE = 17.5;
```

Although this convention is often adopted by Java programmers, it is not adopted in this book.

2.10   It is unclear as to why Java has chosen to use println instead of printLine. Besides being easier to pronounce (!), the latter is consistent with readLine which is what is used for input (see Section 4.2). Interestingly, the choice of print and println is similar to the names write and writeln which are those that are used in the language Pascal.

2.11 Besides sending output to System.out, it is also possible to use print and println to send output to System.err. This is usually only used for error messages or debugging output. Although you may be able to instruct the underlying operating system to route this output to a destination that is different from that used for System.out, by default both go to the window in which the Java interpreter is running.

Exercises

2.1 Type in, compile and execute the SimpleSum program shown in Figure 1.1. If everything has gone well, the program should output:

```
The sum of the two numbers is: 6.9
```

Some details about how to do this using the Java 2 SDK are given in Appendix B.

2.2 Write a program called IntExtremes that:

- declares an int variable called tPositive;
- assigns to the variable the value 2147483647, i.e. the largest value of the type int;
- outputs the value of the variable;
- uses the + operator in an assignment statement to increase the variable's value by 1;
- outputs the value of the variable again;
- declares another int variable called tNegative;
- assigns to the variable the value −2147483648, i.e. the smallest value of the type int;
- outputs the value of the variable;
- uses the − operator in an assignment statement to decrease the variable's value by 1;
- outputs the value of the variable again.

The output from this program demonstrates that the range of the ints is limited. It also shows what silently happens when a program produces a value that is outside the range. There is more discussion about this in Section 5.5.

2.3 Write a program called IntByZero that declares two int variables, gives them the values 42 and 0, and then assigns to a third int variable the result of dividing the value of the first variable by the value of the second. Use the / operator in order to do the division. Finally, get the program to output the value of the third variable. Once again, there is some discussion about what happens in Section 5.5.

2.4 Write a program called DoubleByZero that declares two double variables, gives them the values 42.0 and 0.0, and then assigns to a third double variable the result of dividing the value of the first variable by the value of the second. Use the / operator in order to do the division. Finally, get the program to output the value of the third variable. Again there is some discussion about what happens in Section 5.5.

2.5 Suppose the SimpleSum program (shown in Figure 1.1) is modified to end with the following statements:

```
tSum = tFirst + tSecond;
System.out.print(tFirst);
System.out.print(tSecond);
System.out.print(tSum);
System.out.println();
```

What is the problem with the output that is produced by these statements? How can it be corrected?

Chapter 3

Using objects and classes from Java's Core APIs

Although the primitive types can be used to model some real-world objects, we need some other mechanism if we are to model real-world objects that cannot easily be represented by a value of a primitive type. For this, Java has a construct known as a *class declaration*.

Later (in Chapter 11), we will introduce new types by producing our own class declarations. However, the *Core APIs* already have a lot of class declarations that we can use.

In this chapter, a few of these will be considered. We will look at a class called `Point` that can be used for representing a point in two-dimensional space, and a class called `String` that can be used for representing a sequence of characters. Before looking at the class `String`, we will digress to consider the primitive type `char` which is used for representing values that are single characters.

An instance of a class will be called an *object*. We will find that Java has a special construct for creating an object, and that in a program we use a variable (called a *reference variable*) in order to *refer to* an object, i.e. *point to* an object.

We will find that a class declaration not only defines the values of an object, it also defines what methods are available: each method performs some action on an object.

In this chapter, we will also find out that there are two kinds of *method*s: we will distinguish between *void method*s and *function*s.

3.1 The need for more types

3.1.1 Using a class declaration to introduce a new type

One approach to writing a program is to identify the real-world objects (of the problem) that you need to represent in the program. Each real-world object can be in a number of states (i.e. may possess one of a number of different values) and has a set of operations that can be performed on it.

We saw in the previous chapter that some of these real-world objects can be realized in a program by variables each of which is declared to be of a *primitive type*. For example, if our problem needs to represent the number of students in a lecture theatre, we can use an `int` in a Java program in order to represent this real-world object. Or we might use a variable of type `double` in order to represent the temperature of the air outside.

However, there are many real-world objects that cannot be represented in a Java program by a value that is of a primitive type. For example, we might want to represent a date in history, a point in two-dimensional space, the ISBN of a book, an electronic mail address, the URL of a WWW page, and so on. In most programming languages, you can introduce new types to model these real-world objects. In Java, you can do this by producing a **class declaration** for each of these classes of real-world objects.

For example, you might want to introduce two-dimensional graphic figures such as points, rectangles, circles, squares, and so on. We could start by producing a class declaration to represent any point in two-dimensional space. And then produce another class declaration to represent rectangles, and so on.

Earlier, in Section 2.4, we said that a *type* has two main characteristics:

- a type has a set of values associated with it,
- a type has a set of operations that are permitted on those values.

As we will find out later, when we produce a class declaration, we control what range of values *object*s of our class can take, and we also indicate what operations can be performed on those *object*s. So a class declaration is a means by which we can introduce a new type. This is a subject which will occupy a lot of our time later – we will be producing our own class declarations from Chapter 11 onwards.

3.1.2 Grouping related classes together to form packages and APIs

Java permits related classes to be grouped together in a **package**. For example, if we did produce class declarations for representing points, rectangles, circles and squares, it would be sensible to put the four classes together into a package. Together the classes of a package form a way of programming in a particular area: together they define what is called an **application programming interface** (an **API**).

However, we need not get into the details of writing class declarations straightaway because Java has a large number of classes already defined. There are classes for reading from and writing to files, for producing graphical user interfaces (GUIs), for doing 2D and 3D graphics, for communicating with databases, for reading WWW pages, for accessing objects of Java programs running on other computers, for supporting the writing of applets, and so on. The list of APIs seems endless, and new ones are announced by Sun Microsystems and other software developers almost daily.

3.1.3 The Core APIs

This well-stocked library of already written code is one of the reasons why Java is so successful. And it is important for you to realize that you do not have to write all the code of a program yourself: there is a wealth of code out there waiting for you to use/reuse. However, this book is not going to be looking at all of the APIs: such a book would be enormous!

Some of these APIs are considered to be crucial to Java: they form the **Core APIs**. It is important to be familiar with some of these classes. So, this book will gradually introduce some of the more useful classes of the Core APIs.

3.1.4 The WWW pages that define the Core APIs

When you are writing a Java program, it will be useful for you to be able to look up the details of what is in the classes of the Core APIs. Although you could consult the books mentioned in Curio 3.1, it so happens that the Java 2 SDK is accompanied by many WWW pages that describe these APIs.

If you are using a computer that has a copy of these WWW pages, and your computer has a WWW browser, you should create a bookmark within your WWW browser to the page that is called the **Package Index page**. On Windows 95/98/NT, this will be a page with a URL like:

    file://c:/jdk1.3/docs/api/index.html

On UNIX, the URL will be something like:

    file:/usr/local/java/jdk1.3/docs/api/index.html

It is not possible to give the precise URLs because these will depend on where the Java 2 SDK has been installed. Alternatively, if you have a connection to the Internet, you can always go to Sun's WWW pages at the URL:

    http://java.sun.com/j2se/1.3/docs/api/index.html

There is a mine of information in the WWW pages below the Package Index page. From time to time, this book will refer to the definitions of the classes of the Core APIs that are given in these WWW pages. The book will use the notation $API to refer to any of the above incantations up to (and including) the /docs/api. For example, this book will refer to the Package Index page by the notation $API/index.html. So whenever this book refers to $API, you will need to replace the $API by whichever of the incantations works on your computer.

3.2) The class Point

3.2.1 Introducing a variable of the type java.awt.Point

Suppose that we want to represent a point in two-dimensional space. If you are able to access the WWW pages for the Core APIs, go to the Package Index page, i.e. to $API/index.html. As shown in Figure 3.1, this is a WWW page that has three frames: the top left-hand frame has a list of packages; the bottom left-hand frame has a list of classes; and the right-hand frame has a commented list of packages.

In both the top left-hand frame and the right-hand frame, you will see that it mentions a package called java.awt. This is a package that can be used to produce graphical user interfaces (GUIs).

Move your mouse into the top left-hand frame and click on the **java.awt** link. When you do this, the contents of the bottom left-hand frame should change. If you use the scroll bar of the bottom left-hand frame, you should find that this frame contains separate indexes for *Interfaces*, *Classes*, *Exceptions* and *Errors*. It is important not to let the wealth of information on these WWW pages put you off: just concentrate on the bits of interest. You will soon learn to ignore the other bits: some of these you will learn about later, whereas others may never be of interest.

Now move the scroll bar of the bottom left-hand frame so that the area of the *Classes* index that contains the line referring to the class Point is visible. Click on the Point link. When you do this, the contents of the right-hand frame should change: it should now be displaying a page containing details about the class Point (as shown in Figure 3.2). This frame is displaying the contents of the WWW page $API/java/awt/Point.html.

After some introductory lines, you will see that it says that the class called Point can be used for 'representing a location in (x, y) coordinate space, specified in integer precision'.

Using the scroll bar of the right-hand frame, you will find that this frame next contains *Summary* sections for the *Fields*, *Constructors* and *Methods* of the class Point. These three summary sections are followed by detailed descriptions of the *Fields*, *Constructors* and *Methods*. We will look at the detailed descriptions in later sections of this chapter.

What these WWW pages are doing is documenting the existence of a class called Point that belongs to the java.awt package.

Because each class introduces a new type, we can use java.awt.Point as follows:

```
java.awt.Point tFirstPoint;
```

This is a variable declaration: it declares a variable called tFirstPoint and the variable is of the **class type** called Point that is declared in the package java.awt.

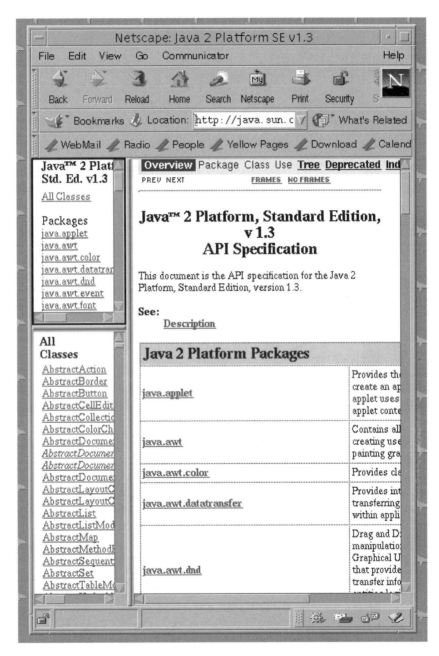

Figure 3.1   The Package Index page of the Core APIs.

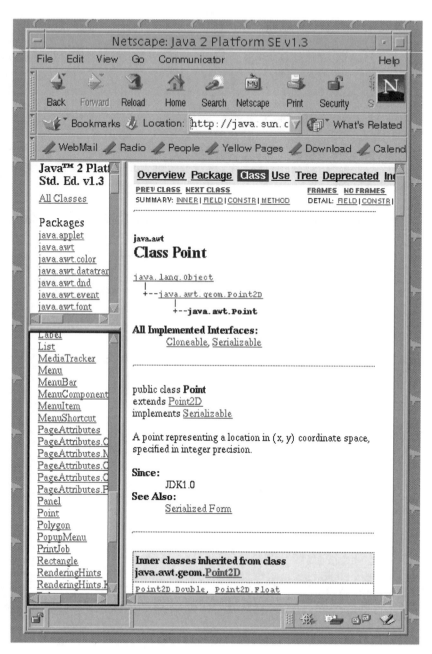

Figure 3.2   The right-hand frame shows the start of `java.awt.Point`'s page.

3.2.2 Using an import declaration

To avoid having to repeat the package name every time a program needs to refer to a class type of a package, the program can use an **import declaration**:

```
import java.awt.Point;
```

Having put this import declaration before the program's class declaration, the tFirstPoint variable can then be declared using the variable declaration:

```
Point tFirstPoint;
```

In Section 1.2 and Section 1.3, it was stated that a program simply consists of a *ProgramClassDeclaration*. This was illustrated by one of the syntax diagrams in Figure 1.3. However, this is a simplification: a *ProgramClassDeclaration* can be preceded by zero or more import declarations, as shown in Figure 3.3. This diagram also contains a syntax diagram for an import declaration.

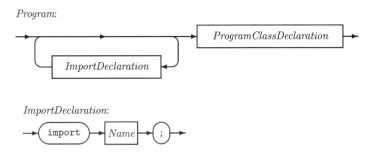

Figure 3.3 The revised syntax of a program and the syntax of an import declaration.

3.2.3 The variable tFirstPoint is only a reference variable

Here is a diagram illustrating the result of the above variable declaration:

Such a declaration does not introduce a variable that contains the details of where in two-dimensional space the point is: instead it is a variable that can *refer to* or *point to* an *object* that contains the details about a point in space.

A variable that just contains a pointer to some *object* is called a **reference variable**. It will be declared to be of one of the three kinds of **reference types**. A classification of the various kinds of Java's types is illustrated in Figure 3.4. The diagram shows that there are three kinds of reference types: they are class types (which we are currently considering), *interface types* (which will be considered in Chapter 11) and *array types* (which will be considered in Chapter 15). So, because Point is the name of a class, tFirstPoint is a reference variable that is of a reference type that is a class type.

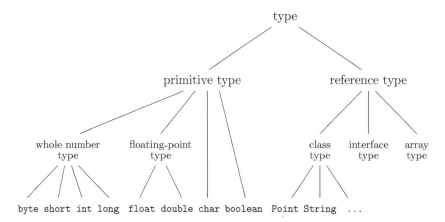

Figure 3.4 The various kinds of types that are available in Java.

3.2.4 Creating an object of the class `Point`

An **object** is simply an **instance** of a class. We can easily get a reference variable to refer to a `Point` object, i.e. a particular instance of the `Point` class. This can be done by using an assignment statement where the right-hand side contains an expression that is a **class instance creation expression**:

```
tFirstPoint = new Point(100, 200);
```

The class instance creation expression `new Point(100, 200)` creates an object of class `Point`. It uses a **constructor** of that class to initialize the object with x and y **field**s of 100 and 200. The syntax of this kind of expression is given in Figure 3.5.

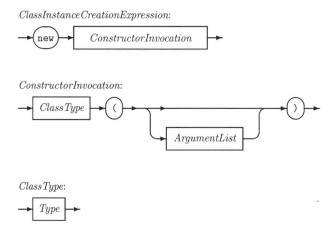

Figure 3.5 The syntax of a class instance creation expression.

We can use this constructor because it has been provided by the designers of the `java.awt` package. If you look at the *Constructor Summary* section of

$API/java/awt/Point.html, you will see that one of these constructors describes itself as `Point(int x, int y)`. If you click on this link, you get to:

> $API/java/awt/Point.html#Point(int, int)

which is at a lower part of the same WWW page. Here you will find a full description of this constructor.

If you do not have access to these WWW pages, look instead at the table given in Figure 3.6. You will find details about constructors in the middle section of this table.

```
public int x;
```
    The x coordinate of the target point.
```
public int y;
```
    The y coordinate of the target point.

. . . .
```
public Point(int pX, int pY);
```
    Initializes the x and y fields of the new **Point** object to the values of **pX** and **pY**.
```
public Point(Point pPoint);
```
    Initializes the new **Point** object to be a copy of the object pointed to by **pPoint**.

. . . .
```
public double getX();
```
    Returns the x coordinate of the target point as a value of type `double`.
```
public double getY();
```
    Returns the y coordinate of the target point as a value of type `double`.
```
public void move(int pX, int pY);
```
    Changes the value of the target point so that it now represents a point with an x coordinate equal to the value of **pX** and a y coordinate equal to the value of **pY**.
```
public String toString();
```
    Returns a textual representation of the target point.
```
public void translate(int pXIncrement, int pYIncrement);
```
    Changes the value of the target point by increasing its x coordinate by the value of **pXIncrement** and its y coordinate by the value of **pYIncrement**.

Figure 3.6 Fields, constructors and methods of the `java.awt.Point` class.

So the statements:

```
Point tFirstPoint;
tFirstPoint = new Point(100, 200);
```

ensure that the variable called `tFirstPoint` refers to a `Point` object. This object represents a point that has an x coordinate of 100 and a y coordinate of 200. You can visualize this as follows:

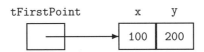

The above declaration of `tFirstPoint` together with the above assignment statement can be shortened to a declaration that has an initializer:

```
Point tFirstPoint = new Point(100, 200);
```

3.2.5 Accessing the fields of a `Point` object

Looking at the *Field Detail* section of `Point`'s WWW page (or at the top section of the table in Figure 3.6), you will find some details about the two fields called x and y. Because these fields are described as being `public`, a program can use the notation `tFirstPoint.x` and `tFirstPoint.y` to access the two fields of the object pointed to by the `tFirstPoint` variable.

For example, the point being represented could be changed by 50 units in the x direction and 75 units in the y direction by the assignment statements:

```
tFirstPoint.x = tFirstPoint.x + 50;
tFirstPoint.y = tFirstPoint.y + 75;
```

Or, instead, by the statements:

```
tFirstPoint.x += 50;
tFirstPoint.y += 75;
```

This produces the situation shown here:

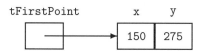

This notation for accessing a field of an object will be called the **dot notation**. As we will see later, it is unusual to be able to access the fields of an object. We are able to do it with objects of the class `Point` solely because the fields are described as being `public`.

3.2.6 Applying methods to a `Point` object

The designers of the `java.awt` package have thought that we may want to change an existing point to a new point in space by specifying increments in the x and y coordinates: they have provided a *method* to do this. The method that they have provided is called `translate`. It is documented at `$API/java/awt/Point.html#translate(int, int)` and it is also listed in Figure 3.6.

On the WWW pages, it is documented as:

```
public void translate(int x, int y)
```

and Figure 3.6 says:

```
public void translate(int pXIncrement, int pYIncrement)
```

This notation is saying that, in a *call* of `translate`, there must be two arguments of type `int`.

So, instead of the above two assignment statements, we could have a statement that calls the translate method:

```
tFirstPoint.translate(50, 75);
```

Note that the dot notation that we used above to refer to the x and y fields of a Point object is also used in the call of a method. You should look at this call in the following way: 'apply the translate method with arguments 50 and 75 to the object that is pointed to by the tFirstPoint variable'.

In this book, the variable to which a method is being applied will be called the **target variable**. And the object that is pointed to by the target variable will be called the **target object**. In this example, the target variable is the tFirstPoint variable and the target object is the object pointed to by tFirstPoint.

3.2.7 Using final with a reference variable

Earlier, we saw that it is possible to use final to document that a variable is a constant, i.e. its value can not be changed. Similarly, if a reference variable is described as being final:

```
final Point tFixedPoint = new Point(100, 200);
```

it is not possible to change its value, i.e. you cannot subsequently do something like:

```
tFixedPoint = new Point(300, 400);
```

You would get a compilation error.

However, it is possible to change the value of the object pointed to by the reference variable. For example, you can do:

```
tFixedPoint.x = tFixedPoint.x + 50;
```

or:

```
tFixedPoint.translate(50, 75);
```

So, although it is possible to signify that a reference variable cannot be changed, it is not possible to signify that the object pointed to by the reference variable cannot be changed.

3.2.8 Point objects are mutable

The examples above show two ways in which a Point object can be changed after it has been created. Here they are again:

```
tFixedPoint.x = tFixedPoint.x + 50;
tFixedPoint.translate(50, 75);
```

Objects that can be changed after they have been created are called **mutable object**s. Some class declarations allow their objects to be changed after they have been created, whereas others do not. The class java.awt.Point is an example of a class that permits objects to be changed after they have been created. In this book, we will refer to a class that permits its objects to be changed as a **mutable class**.

3.2.9 Copying `Point` objects

In programming, we often take a copy of a value that some variable has and then modify the copy. For example, consider the following code to calculate the total weight of a ferry boat. Because we have not yet looked at looping statements, it is written in an informal mix of Java and English.

```
double tLadenWeight, tUnladenWeight, tWeightOfVehicle;
...
tLadenWeight = tUnladenWeight;
for each vehicle:
    1. tWeightOfVehicle = the result of weighing the next vehicle;
    2. tLadenWeight = tLadenWeight + tWeightOfVehicle;
```

In the first assignment statement, we are taking a copy of the value of the `tUnladenWeight` variable and storing this value in the `tLadenWeight` variable. The remaining code then modifies the value of `tLadenWeight`.

Here the real-world objects (the unladen and laden weights of the ferry boat and the weight of the vehicle) are being represented by values of type `double`, a primitive type. However, we have to tackle this in a slightly different way when a real-world object is represented by an object rather than by a value of a primitive type.

Suppose we want to track the movement of some thing that can move through two-dimensional space by a series of horizontal and vertical movements. Assuming that we are using objects of the class `java.awt.Point`, we might try producing code that looks like this:

```
tCurrentPoint = tFirstPoint;
for each move:
    1. find out the values of tXIncrement and tYIncrement;
    2. tCurrentPoint.translate(tXIncrement, tYIncrement);
```

However, the assignment statement:

```
tCurrentPoint = tFirstPoint;
```

does not do what we want it to do: all it does is to make `tCurrentPoint` point to the same object that `tFirstPoint` points to:

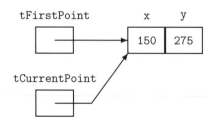

So, the above assignment statement does not produce a copy of an object. Instead, it just copies the value of the reference variable into the other reference variable. As they both now have the same value, they are both now pointing to the same object.

The classes of the Core APIs use two different ways of enabling you to produce a copy of an object:

- a class sometimes provides a method called clone;
- a class sometimes provides a suitable constructor.

Although Point does not provide a clone method, it does provide a suitable constructor. If you look at the list of constructors that Point provides (either by looking at the WWW pages at $API/java/awt/Point.html or by looking at the middle section of Figure 3.6), you will see a constructor that is described as:

```
public Point(Point pPoint);
```

When it is used in a class instance creation expression, this constructor initializes the new Point object to have the same value as that of the object pointed to by pPoint. So if we replace:

```
tCurrentPoint = tFirstPoint;
```

by:

```
tCurrentPoint = new Point(tFirstPoint);
```

we will finish up with the following situation:

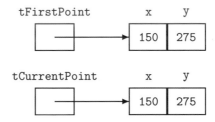

3.2.10 Garbage collection of unwanted Point objects

Assuming that tFirstPoint is a Point variable that points to some object, what happens if we later change its value, as in:

```
tFirstPoint = new Point(100, 200);
...
tFirstPoint = new Point(200, 300);
```

The first assignment statement causes a Point object to be created and tFirstPoint is made to point to it. In the second assignment statement, another Point object is created, and tFirstPoint's value is changed: it is now pointing to the second `Point` object. The result of executing these two assignment statements is shown here:

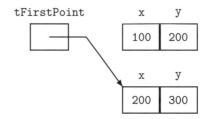

There is now no variable pointing to the first object. It is lost in space! Life's not so cruel: the Java interpreter will notice this, and arrange for a decent burial! Although it may appear that when a Java program is being executed, it simply works through the code of your program, it is not as simple as that: a program's execution actually involves several **threads** of code being executed. In fact, whilst the interpreter is running the thread containing the statements of your program, it is also running a **garbage collector** in another thread. Behind your back, the garbage collector will notice that you no longer want this object: the space occupied by the unwanted object will be reclaimed, and you may get it back on some subsequent use of new. This will happen without you knowing. Although originally the object was an object of the class `java.awt.Point`, at its reincarnation it may be an object of some other class.

Instead of losing the object, we may want to use the `Point` object again later in the execution of the program. In this case, we can keep track of it using another reference variable. Compare the above statements with these:

```
tFirstPoint = new Point(100, 200);
...
tGuardianPoint = tFirstPoint;
tFirstPoint = new Point(200, 300);
```

First, `tFirstPoint` is made to point to a (100,200) object. Then `tGuardianPoint` is also made to point to this object. Finally, `tFirstPoint` is given a new value: it now points to a (200,300) object. This does not change `tGuardianPoint`: it is still pointing to the (100,200) object.

These statements produce the following situation:

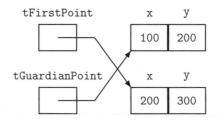

3.2.11 Outputting the value of a Point object

How do we output the value of an object? Well, it so happens that each class has access to a method called toString. If we apply toString to an object of any class, it returns a string of characters that gives a textual representation of the value of the object.

Note: if a class does not itself provide a method called toString, it is still possible to apply toString to an object of the class. The reason why this is the case is explained in Curio 3.5.

At $API/java/awt/Point.html#toString(), you can see that the Point class is a class that does provide a method called toString. In the following example, the toString method is applied to the object pointed to by tFirstPoint:

```
Point tFirstPoint = new Point(100, 200);
String tFirstPointString = tFirstPoint.toString();
```

The call of this method produces a value that is a string, and tFirstPointString is made to point to this string object. This is illustrated by the following diagram:

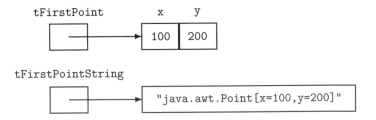

We will look at the type String in more detail in Section 3.4.

The method toString is different from the other methods (print, println and translate) that we have seen: when the toString method is called it executes some code *and returns a result*. This value is then assigned to tFirstPointString. However, when the print, println and translate methods are called, they do some work but no result is returned.

Methods such as toString are often called **function**s and, in this book, the term **void method** will be used to refer to methods such as print, println and translate.

When looking at the WWW pages, it is easy to distinguish between functions and void methods. At $API/java/awt/Point.html#toString(), it describes toString as:

```
public String toString();
```

whereas, at $API/java/awt/Point.html#translate(int, int), it describes translate as:

```
public void translate(int x, int y);
```

For a function, the public keyword is followed by the type of the value that is returned by the function, whereas for a void method the public keyword is followed by the keyword void.

There is another big difference between functions and void methods: they are called in different places. In the above example, the method invocation for the function `toString` appears in the expression on the right-hand side of an assignment statement, whereas the method invocation for a void method is used as a statement. Further differences between a function and a void method will be given later – see Section 8.9.

Earlier the `String` variable `tFirstPointString` was made to point to a string containing a textual representation of a `Point` object. In the previous chapter, we saw that a value that is a string can be passed as an argument to the `print` or `println` method. For example, here is the string `tFirstPointString` being used as an argument of `println`:

```
System.out.println(tFirstPointString);
```

If you do this, you will get some output like:

```
java.awt.Point[x=100,y=200]
```

As you can see, this is not a particularly nice format. Some code that outputs using a nicer format will be produced in Section 8.10.

In Section 2.10.3, we looked at some of the overloadings of the `print` and `println` methods. Both methods have one more overloading that we will find useful. If a value of some reference type is passed as the argument of a call of `print` (or `println`), the object's `toString` method will be applied and the resulting string will be output. This means that the above three statements, i.e.:

```
Point tFirstPoint = new Point(100, 200);
String tFirstPointString = tFirstPoint.toString();
System.out.println(tFirstPointString);
```

can be abbreviated to:

```
Point tFirstPoint = new Point(100, 200);
System.out.println(tFirstPoint);
```

or to:

```
System.out.println(new Point(100, 200));
```

3.2.12 A program that uses the class `Point`

A program that uses some of the material presented on the preceding pages is given in Figure 3.7.

3.3 The primitive type `char`

Before looking at the type `String`, we need briefly to consider the primitive type `char`. The values of this type are single characters, and so one character can be stored in a variable of this type. Previously, we have seen that Java uses a pair of double

```
// This program creates some points in 2D space.
// Barry Cornelius, 29 May 2000
import java.awt.Point;
public class SimplePoints
{
    public static void main(final String[] pArgs)
    {
        // here is sensible way of setting up a rectangle of points
        Point tPointSW = new Point(100,100);
        Point tPointNW = new Point(100,500);
        Point tPointNE = new Point(400,500);
        Point tPointSE = new Point(400,100);
        // here is another way of setting tPointNW to represent 100,500
        tPointNW = new Point(tPointSW.x, tPointSW.y + 400);
        // now a complicated way of setting tPointNE equal to 400,500
        tPointNE = new Point(tPointNW);
        tPointNE.translate(300,0);
        // and an even sillier way of setting tPointSE equal to 400,100
        tPointSE = new Point(0,0);
        tPointSE.move(400,100);
        System.out.println("SW point is at: " + tPointSW);
        System.out.println("NW point is at: " + tPointNW);
        System.out.println("NE point is at: " + tPointNE);
        System.out.println("SE point is at: " + tPointSE);
    }
}
```

Figure 3.7   A program creating some points in 2D space.

quotes to surround the characters of a string literal; a pair of single quotes is used to surround the character of a **character literal**. Here is an example:

```
char tCommandChar = 'a';
```

This statement declares a variable called `tCommandChar` to be of type `char` and uses an initializer to give the variable its initial value. The `'a'` is the character literal, i.e. a literal of the type `char`. The result is shown here:

tCommandChar

'a'

There are some characters that are difficult to represent in this way: these characters are called **non-graphic characters**. You can indicate that you want a character literal to represent a non-graphic character by using an **escape sequence**. A table of escape sequences is given in Figure 3.8.

We will not need most of these in this book. However, the table indicates that you also need to use an escape sequence if you want a character literal representing a single quote, a double quote or a backslash character. We will occasionally find these useful.

\b	backspace character
\f	formfeed character
\n	linefeed character
\r	carriage return character
\t	tab character
\'	single quote character
\"	double quote character
\\	backslash character
\n	the character whose octal value is n where $0 \leq n \leq 7$
\nn	the character whose octal value is nn where $0 \leq nn \leq 77$
\nnn	the character whose octal value is nnn where $0 \leq nnn \leq 377$
\u$nnnn$	a Unicode character — see Curio 3.7

Figure 3.8   A table of escape sequences.

For example, you can set up a variable containing a backslash character by using:

```
final char tBackslashChar = '\\';
```

If you want to know why escape sequences have also to be used for single quotes, double quotes and backslashes, see Curio 3.6.

3.4   The class String

3.4.1 An introduction to the class java.lang.String

Although a variable that is of the type char can be used to store a single character, the class String (from the package java.lang) is more useful as it can be used to represent a sequence of characters. We have met this class on two occasions already:

● In the previous chapter, we used a literal of type java.lang.String, e.g.:

```
"The sum of the two numbers is: "
```

This appeared in the statement:

```
System.out.print("The sum of the two numbers is: ");
```

● And, earlier in this chapter, the toString method (of the class java.awt.Point) returned a string, i.e. a value of type java.lang.String.

The class String is used a great deal when constructing Java programs, and so we will now look at it in more detail.

Earlier, when looking at the class java.awt.Point, we looked at declaring reference variables, creating an object, referring to the fields of an object, applying methods to an object, copying objects, garbage collection and outputting the value of an object. The ways in which these are performed are the same no matter what the class of the object. However, we will look at each of these again with an object of the class java.class.String in order to reinforce the various ideas.

The documentation for the class java.lang.String appears on the WWW pages starting at $API/java/lang/String.html. Some of this documentation also appears in Figure 3.9.

public String(String pString);

  Initializes the new String object to be a copy of the object pointed to by
  pString.

....

public char charAt(int pIndex);

  Returns the character at position pIndex of the target string. If pIndex
  is not in the range 0 to *length*−1 where *length* is the length of the string,
  a StringIndexOutOfBoundsException exception occurs.

public int compareTo(String pString);

  Compares the target string with the string pString. The method compares
  characters from left to right until a difference is found or the end of either string
  is reached. A value less than 0 is returned if the target string comes before
  pString; 0 is returned if it is the same as pString; and a value greater than 0
  is returned if it comes after pString.

public int compareTo(Object pObject);

  If pObject points to a String, a call of this method behaves like the compareTo
  with a String parameter. Otherwise, a ClassCastException exception occurs.

public String concat(String pString);

  Returns a string that is the concatenation of the target string and pString.

public int indexOf(String pString);
public int indexOf(String pString, int pFromIndex);

  Returns the position of the first occurrence of pString in the target string. If
  the second argument is omitted, the search starts from the beginning; otherwise
  it starts from position pFromIndex of the target string or from the beginning if
  pFromIndex is negative. If pString is not found, the value −1 is returned. This
  value is also returned if pFromIndex is greater than *length*−1, where *length* is
  the length of the string.

public int lastIndexOf(String pString);
public int lastIndexOf(String pString, int pFromIndex);

  Returns the position of the last occurrence of pString in the target string. If
  the second argument is omitted, or if the value of pFromIndex is too big, the
  search starts from the end of the target string; otherwise it starts from position
  pFromIndex of the target string. If pFromIndex is negative. or pString is not
  found, the value −1 is returned.

public int length();

  Returns the length of the target string.

public String replace(char pOldChar, char pNewChar);

  Returns the string formed by taking a copy of the target string replacing every
  occurrence of the character pOldChar by pNewChar.

public String substring(int pFromIndex);
public String substring(int pFromIndex, int pToIndex);

  Returns the string formed by taking a substring of the target string starting
  from position pFromIndex of the target string to the end of the target string.
  If the second argument is included, only characters up to but not including
  the character at position pToIndex are returned. If either pFromIndex and/or
  pToIndex is not in the range 0 to *length*−1 where *length* is the length of the
  string, a StringIndexOutOfBoundsException exception occurs.

public String toLowerCase();

  Returns the string formed by taking a copy of the target string replacing any
  upper-case letter by its lower-case equivalent.

Figure 3.9 *Continues on the next page.*

```
public String toUpperCase();
```
>   Returns the string formed by taking a copy of the target string replacing any lower-case letter by its upper-case equivalent.
```
public String trim();
```
>   Returns the string formed by taking a copy of the target string removing any *white space* characters from both ends of the string.

Figure 3.9   Constructors and methods of the `java.lang.String` class.

3.4.2 Using a reference variable to point to a `String` object

We can create a reference variable that can point to a `String` by a declaration such as:

```
java.lang.String tName;
```

This can be abbreviated to:

```
String tName;
```

When we were looking at the class `java.awt.Point`, we saw that we could only do this if we used an *import declaration*. However, any class of the package `java.lang` is automatically available to a program without the need for an import declaration. So you do not need to include:

```
import java.lang.String;
```

3.4.3 Creating an object of the class `String`

Having declared the reference variable, we can get it to refer to a `String` object by using an assignment statement where the right-hand side contains an expression that is a *class instance creation expression* that uses one of `String`'s *constructors*:

```
tName = new String("James Gosling");
```

As before, this class instance creation expression can instead appear as part of the variable's declaration:

```
String tName = new String("James Gosling");
```

So we now have a variable called `tName` that points to an object that has the sequence of characters `James Gosling`. This is illustrated here:

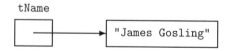

Although:

```
String tName = new String("James Gosling");
```

is the obvious way of creating a string object and making `tName` point to it, for strings there is an alternative syntax for the class instance creation expression. You can use

`"James Gosling"` instead of using `new String("James Gosling")` as in:

```
String tName = "James Gosling";
```

So you have a choice here: both forms of syntax can be used to create new string objects.

We have already seen this alternative syntax before in a statement like:

```
System.out.print("The sum of the two numbers is: ");
```

This statement causes a string object containing the string:

```
"The sum of the two numbers is: "
```

to be created and a reference to this string object is passed to the `print` method. This statement could instead be written as:

```
System.out.print(new String("The sum of the two numbers is:"));
```

but usually this is not done.

As with character literals, a string literal can include characters that are non-graphic characters. Once again, this is done by using one of the escape sequences given in Figure 3.8. An example is:

```
System.out.println("Glaring, Lister said: \"You really are a smeghead\".");
```

This would produce the output:

```
Glaring, Lister said: "You really are a smeghead".
```

We will sometimes need to represent a string that has no characters. The string literal `""` or the expression `new String("")` can be used. Such a string is called an **empty string**.

3.4.4 Referring to the characters of a `String` object

When we were looking at the class `java.awt.Point`, we saw that the designers of the class have decided that we should be allowed to access the x and y coordinates: they allow us to use the names `tFirstPoint.x` and `tFirstPoint.y` to access the x and y *field*s of the object pointed to by the `tFirstPoint` variable. We will find out in Chapter 11 that allowing direct access to the fields of an object is not usually desirable. In fact, there are only a few occasions where the classes of Java's *Core APIs* allow this: as we have just seen, one of these is with the fields of the class `java.awt.Point`. However, this is not possible with the class `java.lang.String`.

3.4.5 Applying methods to a `String` object

If we are unable to access the individual characters directly, is there some other way of accessing them? Well, the class `java.lang.String` comes with a large number of methods for manipulating strings. We will look at a few of these now, and look at some other ones later (in Section 6.5).

If you want to access an individual character of a string, you can use a method called charAt. Like the toString method introduced in Section 3.2.11, the charAt method is a *function*, i.e. it returns a value that is used in the evaluation of the expression (from which it has been called). The value that is returned is of type char.

You use an argument that is an int value to indicate the position of the character which you want to be returned. However, its value needs to be one less than the position of the character. This value is sometimes called the **index** of the character (within the string).

So if you want the first character of the string to be returned, you need an argument with the value 0:

```
final String tName = new String("James Gosling");
final char tFirstChar = tName.charAt(0);
System.out.println("The first character of the name is: " + tFirstChar);
```

In this example, the char value returned by the call of the charAt method is assigned to the tFirstChar variable. And then the println statement will output the line:

```
The first character of the name is: J
```

Another useful method of the String class is a method to find out how many characters there are in a string: it is an argumentless function called length (that returns a value of type int):

```
final String tName = new String("James Gosling");
final int tNameLength = tName.length();
final char tLastChar = tName.charAt(tNameLength -1);
System.out.println("The last character of the name is: " + tLastChar);
```

These statements will output:

```
The last character of the name is: g
```

As was explained earlier, the class java.lang.String includes a large number of methods that perform various operations on objects that are strings. A list of some of these methods is included in Figure 3.9. They are more formally documented in the *Method Detail* section of $API/java/lang/String.html. Most of the methods listed in Figure 3.9 appear in the examples given in this chapter.

3.4.6 The exception StringIndexOutOfBoundsException

Many of the methods mentioned in Figure 3.9 have an argument that is an integer that is the position of a character within a string. For example, the charAt method requires an argument that is the position of one of the characters of the string (to which charAt is being applied). If a string has 5 characters, you can only use an argument whose value is in the range 0 to 4. This method would not be very happy if you passed an argument of −1 or an argument of 5.

If you pass an argument that is invalid, the method charAt signifies that it cannot handle this situation. It does this by *throw*ing an *exception* called StringIndexOutOfBoundsException.

```
// This program causes a StringIndexOutOfBounds exception.
// Barry Cornelius, 29 May 2000
public class StringIndexTest
{
   public static void main(final String[] pArgs)
   {
      final String tName = new String("James");
      final char tChar = tName.charAt(5);
      System.out.println(tChar);
   }
}
```

Figure 3.10 A program which causes a `StringIndexOutOfBounds` exception.

An **exception** is an occurrence of an exceptional circumstance, a situation that does not normally occur. Unless we include additional code in the program that called charAt, the execution of the program will **crash**.

For example, the program given in Figure 3.10 crashes displaying the lines:

```
java.lang.StringIndexOutOfBoundsException: String index out of range: 5
        at java.lang.String.charAt(String.java)
        at StringIndexTest.main(StringIndexTest.java:6)
```

Note that this output not only indicates that a `StringIndexOutOfBoundsException` exception has occurred: it also displays the value (5) of the *index* that caused the problem, the method (charAt) where the exception occurred, the name of the file (StringIndexTest.java) in which the call of charAt appears, the number (6) of the line (of the file) at which the call appears, and the name of the method (main) which called charAt.

So, if you do write some code that causes a program to crash when it is executed, there is a lot of information in the output that you can use to detect where the error occurs in your program.

Instead of letting the program crash like this, we can include code in our program that will be executed when an exception occurs. Java has a statement called a *try statement* that is used to *handle exceptions*: we will look at try statements in Section 9.9.

Even after try statements have been introduced, we will not use them to deal with exceptions caused by bad programming. They will not be used to handle String-IndexOutOfBoundsException exceptions. Instead we should do sufficient testing of the program in order to try to ensure that such exceptions never occur.

Java divides exceptions into two categories: **checked exceptions** and **unchecked exceptions**. A StringIndexOutOfBoundsException is an unchecked exception, and the JLS says that a program can ignore any unchecked exceptions. Later, we will be writing code that can cause checked exceptions. For example, in Chapter 10, we will be producing code that reads values in from a file and, if the program attempts to read from a file that does not exist, a FileNotFoundException exception will occur. This is an example of a checked exception, and the JLS says that we must have code in our program that says what we want the program to do when one of these occurs. There are two things we can do: these are discussed in Section 4.3 and Section 9.9.

Here is a summary of all we currently need to know about exceptions: if we have written our program correctly, it should not be passing to charAt an argument that is invalid. If a program does this, charAt will generate a String-IndexOutOfBoundsException exception. This will cause the program to **crash**, because it has no code to handle a StringIndexOutOfBoundsException exception.

3.4.7 String objects are immutable

When we used the class java.awt.Point, we saw that it had methods that can be used to alter the value of the object to which the method is being applied. For example, in the following method invocation, the translate method alters the value of the object pointed to by tFirstPoint:

```
tFirstPoint.translate(50, 75);
```

Because of this, we described the class as a *mutable class*. However, the class java.lang.String is different: instead of a method altering the value of a string object, it will produce a new string object, leaving the original string object unchanged. The objects of the class are said to be **immutable** (which means that they cannot be changed). In this book, we will call a class like this an **immutable class**.

For example, consider:

```
String tToday = new String("2000-07-11");
tToday = tToday.replace('-', ':');
System.out.println(tToday);
```

First, a string object containing the string "2000-07-11" is created and tToday is made to point to it. Then the method replace is applied to the string object that is pointed to by tToday. This does not change that string object, but instead creates a new string object in which any occurrences of the '-' character are replaced by a ':' character. Then the value of tToday is changed. It is currently pointing to the first string object, and it is now altered to point to the new string object. There is now no variable pointing to the first string object: it is lost. Finally, the string that tToday points to is output by the call of the println method:

```
2000:07:11
```

3.4.8 Garbage collection of unwanted String objects

As with java.awt.Point, whenever you change the value of a reference variable so that it points to a new string, the previous string becomes lost unless there is at least one other reference variable pointing to it. Such lost strings are detected by the *garbage collector* and the space that they occupy becomes available for reuse later.

3.4.9 Outputting the value of a String object

We have already discussed the topic of outputting the value of a String object. In the previous chapter, the following example of outputting a String literal was given:

```
System.out.print("The sum of the two numbers is: ");
```

And in this chapter we have seen examples where the string to be output is pointed to by a reference variable. Another example of this is:

```
final String tName = new String("James Gosling");
System.out.println(tName);
```

3.4.10 String concatenation

Looking at Figure 3.9, you will see that the class java.lang.String has a method called concat that can be used for joining two strings together. Here is an example of its use:

```
final String tFirstName = new String("James");
final String tName = tFirstName.concat(" Gosling");
```

The variable tName now points to a string object containing the string "James Gosling".

However, the class java.lang.String is unusual because an operator is defined in the language specifically for the concatenation of the values of two objects of this class. As was mentioned earlier, there is a **string concatenation operator**: in an expression, a new string object can be formed from two existing string objects by using a + operator. Here is an example:

```
final String tFirstName = new String("James");
final String tSurname = new String("Gosling");
final String tName = tFirstName + tSurname;
```

The variable tName now points to a string object containing the string "JamesGosling". Perhaps that is not what we were after. So use this instead:

```
final String tName = tFirstName + " " + tSurname;
```

The string concatenation operators will produce a new string object containing a string that is the concatenation of the string pointed to by tFirstName, a string literal representing a space, and the string pointed to by tSurname. The variable tName now points to the string object containing the string "James Gosling".

As was mentioned in Section 2.10.5, the string concatenation operator is very flexible in that it will convert any operand (that is permitted) into a string. Here is an example:

```
final Point tFirstPoint = new Point(100, 200);
final String tLine = "The point has the value " + tFirstPoint;
System.out.println(tLine);
```

This will output:

```
The point has the value java.awt.Point[x=100,y=200]
```

If you have a long string literal, the string concatenation operator can be used to help in the layout of the text. For example, the statement:

```
System.out.println("Glaring, Lister said: \"You really are a smeghead\".");
```

can instead be written as:

```
System.out.println("Glaring, Lister said:" +
                   " \"You really are a smeghead\".");
```

3.4.11 A program that uses the methods of `java.lang.String`

Suppose we want a program that takes a name arranged as *FirstName Surname* and outputs it in the format *Surname, Initial* where *Initial* is the first letter of the *FirstName*. We will also suppose that the output must be displayed in upper-case. A program that does this for the name `James Gosling` is given in Figure 3.11.

```
// This program uses some of the methods of java.lang.String.
// Barry Cornelius, 29 May 2000
public class SimpleString
{
   public static void main(final String[] pArgs)
   {
      final String tName = new String("James Gosling");
      System.out.println(tName);
      final char tFirstChar = tName.charAt(0);
      final int tPositionOfSpace = tName.indexOf(" ");
      final String tSurname = tName.substring(tPositionOfSpace + 1);
      final String tLabel = tSurname + ", " + tFirstChar;
      final String tUpperLabel = tLabel.toUpperCase();
      System.out.println(tUpperLabel);
   }
}
```

Figure 3.11   A program that uses methods of `java.lang.String`.

The program first creates a string object containing the string `"James Gosling"`, makes `tName` point to it, and outputs the string pointed to by `tName`. It then uses `charAt` to extract the first character of the string object and puts this character into the variable `tFirstChar`. It then uses `indexOf` to locate the position of the space character in `"James Gosling"`, and this `int` value is stored in the variable `tPositionOfSpace`. It then uses `substring` to extract a substring of the string pointed to by `tName`: this is the substring starting at the position given by the value of `tPositionOfSpace + 1` and finishing at the end of the string pointed to by `tName`. A string object containing this substring is created (by the call of the method `substring`), and the variable `tSurname` is made to point to this string object. The program then creates another `String` object by the concatenation of the string held by `tSurname`, the string literal `", "` and the string formed from the single character in the variable `tFirstChar`. The variable `tLabel` is made to point to this new string object. The method `toUpperCase` is then applied to the string object pointed to by `tLabel`. This method produces a new string object that is the upper-case equivalent of the string object pointed to by `tLabel`, and a new variable called `tUpperLabel` is made to point to this new string object. Finally, the value of this string object is output.

The two `println`s of this program produce the following output:

```
James Gosling
GOSLING, J
```

3.5 The class `StringBuffer`

Because the methods of the class `String` create a new `String` object rather than reusing the same `String` object, it is not very efficient to use the methods of this class if you have to perform a large number of string operations. The class `StringBuffer` (from the `java.lang` package) should be used instead.

For example, it should be used if you wish to build up a string gradually by performing a lot of string manipulations. Here is an artificial example:

```
final StringBuffer tStringBuffer = new StringBuffer ("cosmos");
tStringBuffer.replace(1, 3, "at");         // catmos
tStringBuffer.delete(4, 6);                // catm
tStringBuffer.append("at");                // catmat
tStringBuffer.insert(3, " saw on the ");   // cat saw on the mat
tStringBuffer.insert(0, "the ");           // the cat saw on the mat
tStringBuffer.setCharAt(10, 't');          // the cat sat on the mat
final String tString = tStringBuffer.toString();
System.out.println(tString);
```

These statements use some of the methods of the `StringBuffer` class. Each method is changing the value of the `StringBuffer` object. The state of this object after the call of each method is indicated by the comment that appears after the call.

The class is formally documented at $API/java/lang/StringBuffer.html. Some of this documentation also appears in Figure 3.12.

```
public StringBuffer();
    Initializes the new StringBuffer object to be one with no characters and an
    initial capacity of 16 characters.
public StringBuffer(int pInitialCapacity);
    Initializes the new StringBuffer object to be one with no characters and an
    initial capacity of pInitialCapacity characters.
```

Figure 3.12 *Continues on the next page.*

```
public StringBuffer(String pString);
```
Initializes the new `StringBuffer` object to be one containing the characters of the string `pString`.
. . . .

```
public void append(...);
```
Appends to the target stringbuffer a textual representation of the argument which may be of any primitive type or any reference type.

```
public char charAt(int pIndex);
```
Returns the character at position `pIndex` of the target stringbuffer. If `pIndex` is not in the range 0 to *length*−1 where *length* is the length of the stringbuffer, a `StringIndexOutOfBoundsException` exception occurs.

```
public void delete(int pFromIndex, int pToIndex);
```
Removes characters from the target stringbuffer starting from position `pFromIndex` of the target stringbuffer up to but not including the character at position `pToIndex`. If `pFromIndex` is not in range, a `StringIndexOutOfBoundsException` exception occurs.

```
public void ensureCapacity(int pMinimumCapacity);
```
Ensures that the capacity of the target stringbuffer is at least `pMinimumCapacity` characters.

```
public void insert(int pIndex, ...);
```
Inserts at position `pIndex` of the target stringbuffer a textual representation of the second argument which may be of any primitive type or any reference type. If `pIndex` is not in the range 0 to *length* where *length* is the length of the stringbuffer, a `StringIndexOutOfBoundsException` exception occurs.

```
public int length();
```
Returns the length of the target stringbuffer.

```
public void replace(int pFromIndex, int pToIndex, String pString);
```
Replaces the characters of the target stringbuffer starting from position `pFromIndex` of the target stringbuffer up to but not including the character at position `pToIndex` by the string `pString`. This may result in a change to the length of the target stringbuffer. If `pFromIndex` is not in range, a `StringIndexOutOfBoundsException` exception occurs.

```
public void reverse();
```
Reverses the characters of the target stringbuffer.

```
public void setCharAt(int pIndex, char pNewChar);
```
Replaces the character of the target stringbuffer that is at position `pIndex` by the character `pNewChar`. If `pIndex` is not in the range 0 to *length*−1 where *length* is the length of the stringbuffer, a `StringIndexOutOfBoundsException` exception occurs.

```
public String substring(int pFromIndex);
public String substring(int pFromIndex, int pToIndex);
```
Returns the string formed by taking a substring of the target stringbuffer starting from position `pFromIndex` of the target stringbuffer to the end of the target stringbuffer. If the second argument is included, only characters up to but not including the character at position `pToIndex` are returned. If either `pFromIndex` and/or `pToIndex` is not in the range 0 to *length*−1 where *length* is the length of the stringbuffer, a `StringIndexOutOfBoundsException` exception occurs.

```
public String toString();
```
Returns the string formed from the characters of the target stringbuffer.

Figure 3.12 Constructors and methods of the `java.lang.StringBuffer` class.

```
// This program uses some of the methods of java.lang.StringBuffer.
// Barry Cornelius, 29 May 2000
public class SimpleStringBuffer
{
    public static void main(final String[] pArgs)
    {
        final String tName = new String("James Gosling");
        System.out.println(tName);
        final char tFirstChar = tName.charAt(0);
        final int tPositionOfSpace = tName.indexOf(" ");
        final StringBuffer tNewNameBuffer = new StringBuffer(tName);
        tNewNameBuffer.delete(0, tPositionOfSpace + 1);
        tNewNameBuffer.append(", ");
        tNewNameBuffer.append(tFirstChar);
        final String tLabel = tNewNameBuffer.toString();
        final String tUpperLabel = tLabel.toUpperCase();
        System.out.println(tUpperLabel);
    }
}
```

Figure 3.13 A program that uses methods of `java.lang.StringBuffer`.

Figure 3.13 contains some more code involving methods of the String-
Buffer class. The program `SimpleStringBuffer` solves the same problem as the
`SimpleString` program that was given in Figure 3.11.

3.6 Wrapper classes for the primitive types

It takes more time to access a value that is pointed to by a reference variable than it
takes to access the value of a variable that is of a primitive type. This is because for
a reference variable the computer will have to look to see what it is pointing at and
get the value of that object: look at Figure 3.14. So whenever possible it is sensible
to use a variable of a primitive type to represent a real-world object. However, the
structure of most real-world objects is complicated and so this will not be possible.

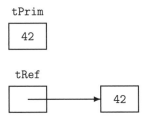

Figure 3.14 It is slower to access an object that is pointed to by a reference variable.

There are occasions when, even though the real-world object could be represented
by a variable of a primitive type, it is necessary or it is more useful to use a reference
variable. On these occasions you can use the **wrapper class**es that exist for each of

the primitive types:

primitive type	wrapper class
`boolean`	`java.lang.Boolean`
`char`	`java.lang.Character`
`byte`	`java.lang.Byte`
`short`	`java.lang.Short`
`int`	`java.lang.Integer`
`long`	`java.lang.Long`
`float`	`java.lang.Float`
`double`	`java.lang.Double`

For example, as well as the primitive type `int` there is also a reference type called `Integer`, and you can use either of these types to represent integral values.

You can construct an `Integer` object from an `int` as follows:

```
int tPrim = 42;
Integer tRef = new Integer(tPrim);
```

This produces the situation illustrated by Figure 3.14. The above class instance creation expression uses a constructor where the argument is of type `int`. Alternatively, an `Integer` object can be produced using a constructor that has a `String` argument:

```
String tStr = new String("27");
Integer tRef = new Integer(tStr);
```

This produces the situation shown in Figure 3.15.

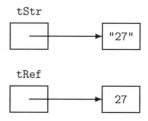

Figure 3.15   Creating an `Integer` object from a `String` object.

Having got a reference variable that points to an `Integer` object, it is possible to extract the numerical value as an `int` by using a method of the `Integer` class called `intValue`:

```
String tStr = new String("27");
Integer tRef = new Integer(tStr);
int tPrim = tRef.intValue();
```

You can find the documentation for these eight wrapper classes in the WWW pages for the `java.lang` package (whose index appears at $API/java/lang/package-frame.html). A list of those constants, constructors and methods of the classes `java.lang.Integer` and `java.lang.Double` that will be used in this book are given in Figure 3.16 and Figure 3.17.

Like the class `String`, these wrapper classes are *immutable class*es, which means that after you have created an object of one of these wrapper classes you are unable to change the value of the object.

Although it is appropriate to introduce these classes in this chapter about objects, it is difficult to justify their existence at this point: we will see a use of these wrapper classes in the next chapter.

```
public static final int MIN_VALUE;
```
> A constant whose value is equal to the minimum value of the type `int`.

```
public static final int MAX_VALUE;
```
> A constant whose value is equal to the maximum value of the type `int`.

....

```
public Integer(int pI);
```
> Initializes the new `Integer` object to contain an integer value equal to that of pI.

```
public Integer(String pS);
```
> Initializes the new `Integer` object to contain an integer value equal to that represented by the string pS. If this string contains whitespace characters, a `NumberFormatException` exception occurs.

....

```
public int intValue();
```
> Returns the integer value stored in the target object.

```
public static int parseInt(String pS);
```
> Returns the integer value represented by the string pS. If this string contains whitespace characters, a `NumberFormatException` exception occurs.

Figure 3.16 Constants, constructors and methods of the `java.lang.Integer` class.

```
public static final double MIN_VALUE;
```
> A constant whose value is equal to the minimum positive value of the type `double`.

```
public static final double MAX_VALUE;
```
> A constant whose value is equal to the maximum positive value of the type `double`.

....

```
public Double(double pD);
```
> Initializes the new `Double` object to contain a floating point value equal to that of pD.

```
public Double(String pS);
```
> Initializes the new `Double` object to contain a floating point value equal to that represented by the string pS. This string may start or end with whitespace characters.

....

```
public double doubleValue();
```
> Returns the floating point value stored in the target object.

```
public static double parseDouble(String pS);
```
> Returns the floating point value represented by the string pS. This string may start or end with whitespace characters.

Figure 3.17 Constants, constructors and methods of the `java.lang.Double` class.

Tips for programming and debugging

3.1   We have seen that you need a class instance creation expression in order to create a new object:

```
Point tPointSW = new Point(100, 100);
```

If you fail to include the new as in:

```
Point tPointSW = Point(100, 100);
```

you will get a compilation error such as:

```
SimplePoints.java:9: Method Point(int,int) was not found
                 in the class SimplePoints.
    Point tPointSW = Point(100, 100);
                     ^
1 error
```

3.2   It is very easy to forget that the positions of the characters of a `String` object are numbered from 0 to *length*−1 rather than from 1 to *length*. For example, it is tempting to use `charAt(1)` rather than `charAt(0)` to obtain the first character of a string. Such an error is called a **one-off error**.

3.3   If you forget that the methods of the class `java.lang.String` shown in Figure 3.9 return new string objects and instead think that they alter the object to which they are being applied, you may be tempted to use the following code:

```
String tToday = new String("2000-07-11");
tToday.replace('-', ':');
System.out.println(tToday);
```

This code outputs:

```
2000-07-11
```

Although the call of `replace` creates a new string object, the result of the call of `replace` is thrown away. Normally, the call of a *function* appears in an expression. However, here the call of the function appears as a statement. This is legal in Java; in other situations it may be that the function you have called performs a complicated and useful task but you do not want to store its result anywhere.

However, there are many functions in the Core APIs where it is nonsensical to throw away the result of the function. This applies to all of the methods of the class `java.lang.String`. It is unfortunate that Java's design allows the results of functions to be thrown away. With Java as it is, it is difficult for a programmer to detect when they have written nonsensical bits of code like the statements given above.

3.1 There are two books that give an annotated specification of Java's *Core APIs*. They are *The Java Class Libraries, Second Edition, Volume 1* and *The Java Class Libraries, Second Edition, Volume 2*. The first volume ([8]) covers the *package*s called `java.io`, `java.lang`, `java.math`, `java.net`, `java.text` and `java.util`, and the second volume ([9]) covers the packages called `java.applet`, `java.awt` and `java.beans`. Besides providing valuable information about the Core APIs and how to use them, these books are also useful for door-stops or pressing wild flowers! Volume 1 has 2080 pages, and Volume 2 has 1712 pages.

As these books were published in 1998, they cover the APIs of JDK 1.1. With the advent of the Java 2 Platform, in 1999 the same authors and publisher released a book ([10]) entitled *The Java Class Libraries: Second Edition, Volume 1: Supplement for the Java 2 Platform, Standard Edition v 1.2*. It has another 1200 pages! At the time of writing this book, there was no supplement for Volume 2. For more details, see [1].

3.2 The WWW pages defining the *Core APIs* are structured so that it is easy to find classes. If you want to look at the documentation for the class `java.`*SubPackageName*`.`*ClassName*, you will find it on the WWW page that is at $API/java/*SubPackageName*/*ClassName*.html. For example, the text of Curio 1.2 refers to the class `java.lang.Character`. The WWW pages for this class will be located at $API/java/lang/Character.html.

3.3 If you are using a computer that has an **integrated development environment** (*IDE*) for Java, you may find that the IDE has some way of viewing the documentation of the Core APIs.

3.4 Section 3.2.10 indicates that the garbage collector will reclaim the space occupied by an object that is no longer pointed to by any reference variables. So, suppose that `tFirstPoint` points to some object, e.g. by executing `tFirstPoint = new Point(100, 200);` If, later, the object pointed to by `tFirstPoint` is no longer needed, the assignment statement `tFirstPoint = null;` can be executed to indicate this. If a reference variable has the value `null`, this means that the variable is not pointing to an object. For more information about `null`, see Section 6.4. Having assigned `null` to `tFirstPoint`, the (100,200) object can be reclaimed by the garbage collector (provided no other reference variable is pointing to it). This technique of indicating that an object is no longer wanted is particularly useful if an unwanted object occupies a large amount of space.

3.5 Section 3.2.11 says that 'each class has access to a method called `toString`'. Often a class itself provides a method called `toString`. This is sensible because it knows what fields are possessed by each object of the class. However, if a class does not provide a method called `toString` a default method called `toString` is used. This is the `toString` method provided by the class

Object. As will be explained in Section 11.7, this is used because all classes are *derived* from the class Object. Section 11.7 also explains that Object's version of toString just returns a string consisting of the name of the class, followed by an @, followed by the *hashcode* of the object (given in hexadecimal notation).

3.6   In Section 3.3, when discussing escape sequences, it was pointed out that an escape sequence is needed if you wish to use a single quote, a double quote or a backslash character in a character literal (or in a string literal). In this chapter we have seen that each of these three characters has a special meaning in literals: a ' is used to mark the beginning and end of a character literal, a " is used for a similar purpose with string literals, and a \ is used to introduce an escape sequence.

The reason why an escape sequence has to be used when representing any of these characters will be illustrated by an example. Suppose you want a string to have the five characters a"+"b. You would need to use the string literal "a\"+\"b". If, instead, you wrote "a"+"b", this would be taken to be the concatenation of the two strings "a" and "b" (to produce the string "ab").

3.7   The Java programming language permits characters from the **Unicode** character set to appear in character literals and string literals. If you are familiar with **ISO 8859-1** or **ASCII**, you may be interested to know that Unicode includes ISO 8859-1 as a subset and that ISO 8859-1 in turn includes ASCII as a subset. It is possible to include a Unicode character in a literal by using a **Unicode escape**. This consists of \u followed by four hexadecimal digits that indicate the value of the Unicode character. For more details, see Chapter 3 of the JLS.

3.8   Section 3.4.6 distinguishes between an *unchecked exception* and a *checked exception*. You can easily detect from the WWW pages whether an exception is unchecked or checked. An unchecked exception is *derived* from the class java.lang.RunTimeException or from the class java.lang.Error. All other exceptions are checked exceptions.

3.9   Although the table in Figure 3.12 indicates that the methods append, delete, insert, replace and reverse are void methods, this is incorrect. They are all of type StringBuffer. Besides changing the target stringbuffer, each of these methods also returns a pointer to the target stringbuffer.

3.10 The methods replace and substring were introduced to StringBuffer at the release of the Java 2 Platform.

(**Exercises**)───

3.1   The grid reference system devised by the Ordnance Survey can be used to produce a unique reference for any point in Great Britain. The system divides Great Britain up into squares that are identified by two-letter codes (as shown

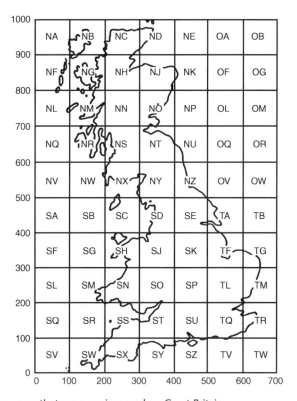

Figure 3.18 The squares that are superimposed on Great Britain.

in Figure 3.18). Each square is 100 kilometres by 100 kilometres. A unique grid reference for any point can be obtained by stating:

- the two-letter code of the square in which the point is located,

- the distance the point is east of the south-west corner of the square,

- the distance the point is north of the south-west corner of the square.

For example, Durham is located in the NZ square. The south-west corner of this square happens to be located somewhere in the wilds of Swaledale, one of the Yorkshire dales. Since Durham Cathedral is 27.3 kilometres east and 42.1 kilometres north of this point, its grid reference is NZ273421.

Write a program that declares a `String` variable, assigns to it the string `"NZ273421"`, and then uses the information in this object to output a line like:

```
The point NZ273421 is 27.3 kilometres east and 42.1 kilometres north
of the origin of the NZ square.
```

[Hint: in your solution, use the `substring` method five times. For example, with the string `"NZ273421"`, use `substring` first to produce the characters

"NZ"; then use it to obtain the characters "27"; then "3"; then "42"; and finally use it to obtain a string containing the last character, in this case, the string "1".]

3.2 Modify the program that you produced as a solution to Exercise 3.1 so that it causes a `StringIndexOutOfBoundsException`. Analyse the output produced when the program crashes to see if it correctly identifies the location of the error in your program.

3.3 At the University of Durham, an electronic mail address can be something like:

`Joe.Bloggs@durham.ac.uk`

However, if the person has more than one forename, their address will start with their initials, as in `J.A.Bloggs@durham.ac.uk` or `J.A.D.Bloggs@durham.ac.uk`. Write a program that declares a `String` variable, assigns to it the string `"J.A.D.Bloggs@durham.ac.uk"`, finds the person's surname from this object, and outputs it.

3.4 On a UNIX system a file may be located at:

`/users/dxy3fab/papers/fred.doc`

whereas on a Windows system the same file may be located at:

`C:\PAPERS\FRED.DOC`

Write a program that declares a `String` variable called `tFileName`, assigns the string literal `"/users/dxy3fab/papers/fred.doc"` to the variable, replaces the `/users/dxy3fab` by `C:`, replaces each occurrence of a `/` by `\`, translates all the letters into upper-case, and then outputs the result.
Reminder: if you want a character literal for a backslash character you will need to use one of the escape sequences (given in Figure 3.8), i.e. you will need to use `'\\'` rather than `'\'`.

Chapter 4

Reading values from the keyboard

The major deficiency of the programs of previous chapters is that they always perform the same task. What we need is some way of influencing the program while it is executing. The problem is that all of the variables get their values from values that are given in the text of the program. One way of affecting the task of a program is to get it to ask the user of the program for some of the values.

So in this chapter we look at how to read input from the keyboard. We will find that it is reasonably easy to read a string of characters from the keyboard. However, we will need to do some more work to turn a string of characters into a value of type int or a value of type double. This chapter also looks at how to cope with more than one value on a line of data.

4.1 The need for input

Most music boxes are very boring because they always play the same tune, whereas juke-boxes and CD-players are a lot more exciting because they have buttons that allow the *user* to choose which track to play! Similarly, programs would be really uninteresting if they did not accept some **input** from the person executing the program. What we need is some way of giving some of the values as a program is being executed. Such values are referred to as the **data** for the program, and most programming languages have facilities for reading values while a program is executing.

In days gone by, most of the input came from a person typing values at the keyboard into the terminal window which was used to run the program. Or the data would come from a file that had been created before the program started to run. And small amounts of data could also be passed on the command line used to run the program. However, these days a lot of the keyboard input is typed into dialog boxes of some graphical user interface (GUI) or the user gives their input in some other way such as using a mouse to choose one of several options. And some programs read their data from a WWW page. Each of these various ways of getting data into a program is useful.

Although programs that read their input from dialog boxes are more exciting to use, we need to understand a lot more Java in order to do this. So we defer getting data from a GUI until Chapter 13. To begin with, because it is a lot easier, we will look at how to get input from the keyboard.

4.2 Using `readLine` to read a string from the keyboard

In order to read from the keyboard, we need to create an `InputStreamReader` object that is associated with the keyboard. We can do this as follows:

```
InputStreamReader tInputStreamReader = new InputStreamReader(System.in);
```

where the class `InputStreamReader` is from the `java.io` package. However, for efficiency reasons, we ought to **buffer** the input that we get from the keyboard. To do this, we need to create a `BufferedReader` object from the `InputStreamReader` object:

```
BufferedReader tKeyboard = new BufferedReader(tInputStreamReader);
```

where the class `BufferedReader` is also from the `java.io` package. Having done that, whenever we want to read a line of characters from the keyboard, we can use `BufferedReader`'s `readLine` method:

```
String tLine = tKeyboard.readLine();
```

This initializer will cause `tLine` to point to a `String` object containing the line of characters.

```
// This program reads in a string and then displays it.
// Barry Cornelius, 2 June 2000
import java.io.BufferedReader;
import java.io.InputStreamReader;
import java.io.IOException;
public class StringInput
{
    public static void main(final String[] pArgs) throws IOException
    {
        final InputStreamReader tInputStreamReader =
                        new InputStreamReader(System.in);
        final BufferedReader tKeyboard =
                    new BufferedReader(tInputStreamReader);
        System.out.println("Please type your message:");
        final String tLine = tKeyboard.readLine();
        System.out.println("You typed in the following message:");
        System.out.println(tLine);
    }
}
```

Figure 4.1   A program that reads a string from the keyboard.

A complete program that reads in a string from the keyboard is given in Figure 4.1.
In this program we have used the statements:

```
final InputStreamReader tInputStreamReader =
                                new InputStreamReader(System.in);
final BufferedReader tKeyboard = new BufferedReader(tInputStreamReader);
final String tLine = tKeyboard.readLine();
```

However, there is no need for the intermediate variable called tInputStream-
Reader as its value is just passed as an argument to the constructor for Buffered-
Reader. So the above statements can be abbreviated to:

```
final BufferedReader tKeyboard =
            new BufferedReader(new InputStreamReader(System.in));
final String tLine = tKeyboard.readLine();
```

Although the assignment to tKeyboard should be executed only once, we need
to call readLine each time we wish to read a new line of data from the keyboard.
So, if we wanted to read another line of data, we would need to include another call
of readLine, e.g.:

```
final String tSecondLine = tKeyboard.readLine();
```

4.3 The exception `IOException`

Any program that does any input must say what it is going to do with any errors that
occur whilst reading the data: any errors will cause the exception IOException

(from the package `java.io`). Back in Section 3.4.6, we distinguished between two kinds of exception: unchecked exceptions and checked exceptions. Unchecked exceptions (like `StringIndexOutOfBoundsException`) are the kind of exceptions that we can ignore, whereas Java requires us to do something with any exceptions that are checked exceptions. And you have probably guessed by now: the exception `IOException` is a checked exception.

There are two ways in which we can satisfy Java's insistence that we say what we want to happen if a checked exception occurs. The program can either use a *try statement* to retain control or it can say that it is unable to handle the exception. We will look at try statements in Section 9.9, but, to begin with, we will just indicate that the method called `main` may cause an IOException but does not want to handle it. This is done by including a **throws clause** in the header of the method:

```
public static void main(final String[] pArgs) throws IOException
```

If we do this, then, if an IOException occurs when the main method of the program is executed, the program will *crash*: the Java interpreter will output an error message explaining that an IOException has occurred.

The simplified syntax diagram for a main method declaration that was given in Figure 1.3 does not mention a throws clause. A revised syntax diagram is given in Figure 4.2. This figure also includes a syntax declaration for a throws clause.

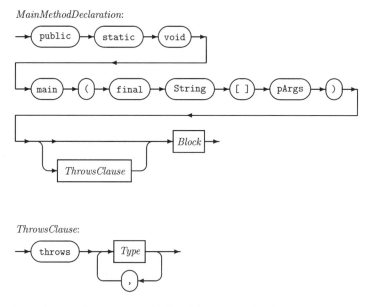

Figure 4.2   Revised syntax for a main method and the syntax of a throws clause.

4.4 More about import declarations

Because the `StringInput` program uses the classes `InputStreamReader`, `BufferedReader` and `IOException` from the `java.io` package, the program (given in Figure 4.1) contains import declarations for these classes:

```
import java.io.BufferedReader;
import java.io.InputStreamReader;
import java.io.IOException;
```

Each import declaration gives both the package name (e.g. `java.io`) and the name of the class (e.g. `BufferedReader`). Although all the classes that are imported into the `StringInput` program come from `java.io`, in general we may have to import many classes from different packages.

4.5 Flushing the output before reading

If a program requires some input from a user of the program, it is useful to output a message that **prompt**s the user for the input. For example, in the `StringInput` program, the user is prompted with the line:

```
Please type your message:
```

and then they type something on a separate line:

```
Hello Mum!
```

If you want the user to type on the same line as a prompt, you should use `print` instead of `println`. So, instead of the statements:

```
System.out.println("Please type your message:");
final String tLine = tKeyboard.readLine();
```

you could use:

```
System.out.print("Please type your message: ");
final String tLine = tKeyboard.readLine();
```

However, because output to `System.out` is buffered, it is output to the output device at times which are unknown to us. So, it is a good idea to **flush** the output stream before calling `readLine`. This is done by calling a method called `flush`:

```
System.out.print("Please type your message: ");
System.out.flush();
final String tLine = tKeyboard.readLine();
```

The use of `flush` will ensure that the program outputs the prompt:

```
Please type your message:
```

and then waits on the same line waiting for the user's input.

If the user types `Hello Mum!`, the screen will finish up looking like this:

```
Please type your message: Hello Mum!
```

With many implementations of Java, there is no need for a call of `flush`, as a call of `readLine` (on an input stream that is associated with the keyboard) will automatically call flush before reading characters from the keyboard. However, this is not always the case: so it is better to call flush as any superfluous flush is harmless.

4.6 Class methods and instance methods

Until now, we have applied a method to an object. Here are two examples of this:

```
tUpperName = tName.toUpperCase();
System.out.print(tUpperName);
```

The toUpperCase method is applied to the object pointed to by the variable tName, and the print method is applied to the object pointed to by the variable out (that is declared in the class System). In one of these cases, we are using a function, and in the other a void method is being used. However, in both cases, the method is being applied to some target object.

Sometimes we want to execute a method but there is no target object. For example, in mathematics, we may want to evaluate something like $\sqrt{x}$, the square root of x. In programming languages, it has been traditional to provide a function called sqrt with one parameter, and you could find out the value of $\sqrt{x}$ by writing something like sqrt(x) in a program. Here there is no target object to which to apply sqrt.

In the next chapter, we will find out that in Java there is a class that provides a number of standard mathematical functions like sqrt: it is a class called Math (belonging to the java.lang package). Normally, in a call of a method, the target variable is written on the left of the dot. When a function has no target object, the name of the class is written instead, as in:

```
y = Math.sqrt(x);
```

In Java, a method like sqrt is called a **class method** whereas the methods that are applied to objects (i.e. instances of a class) are called **instance method**s. In the WWW pages that document the APIs, you can see which methods are class methods because the header of the method contains the static keyword. For example, if you glance ahead to Figure 5.2, you will see that the description of sqrt starts with:

```
public static double sqrt(double pX);
```

So, besides being able to split methods into two kinds depending on whether they are functions or void methods, we can also distinguish between class methods and instance methods. This is illustrated by the table in Figure 4.3.

	functions	*void methods*
class methods	sqrt (Math) parseInt (Integer) parseDouble (Double)	main (StringInput)
instance methods	toString (Point) toUpperCase (String) intValue (Integer)	print (PrintStream) println (PrintStream) translate (Point)

Figure 4.3 Some examples of the various kinds of methods.

4.7 Reading a value of a primitive type

Suppose you would like to read a value into a variable whose type is one of the primitive types, say the type `int`. The *wrapper class* called `Integer` (from the `java.lang` package) has a *class method* called `parseInt` that can help you do this:

```
final String tFirstLine = tKeyboard.readLine();
final int tFirstInt = Integer.parseInt(tFirstLine);
```

First, call `readLine` to read in a line of characters and get `tFirstLine` to point to the `String` object created by `readLine`. Then use this string as an argument of a call of `parseInt`. The `parseInt` method examines the string that has been passed as an argument and returns the appropriate value of type `int`.

As indicated by the `static` keyword that appears in the documentation of the class `Integer` (either in Figure 3.16 or at $API/java/lang/Integer.html), this method is a *class method*. This means that it is not applied to a target object: the name of the class appears in the call in place of the target variable.

Since the `String` value is just an intermediate value, the above two statements could be abbreviated to:

```
final int tFirstInt = Integer.parseInt(tKeyboard.readLine());
```

However, we will refrain from doing this because it looks too cryptic!

Similar code can be produced for reading a floating point value, e.g. to read a floating point value into a `double` variable called `tSomeDouble`:

```
final String tAnotherLine = tKeyboard.readLine();
final double tSomeDouble = Double.parseDouble(tAnotherLine);
```

4.8 A program to read two numbers and find their sum

Suppose we want a program that reads in two numbers, finds the sum of the two numbers, and outputs this value. We can do this using the statements:

```
final String tFirstLine = tKeyboard.readLine();
final double tFirst = Double.parseDouble(tFirstLine);
final String tSecondLine = tKeyboard.readLine();
final double tSecond = Double.parseDouble(tSecondLine);
final double tSum = tFirst + tSecond;
```

However, the `SumProg` program given in Figure 4.4 chooses to use the same `String` variable (called `tLine`) twice:

```
String tLine = tKeyboard.readLine();
final double tFirst = Double.parseDouble(tLine);
tLine = tKeyboard.readLine();
final double tSecond = Double.parseDouble(tLine);
final double tSum = tFirst + tSecond;
```

```
// This program read in two numbers and displays their sum.
// Barry Cornelius, 2 June 2000
import java.io.BufferedReader;
import java.io.InputStreamReader;
import java.io.IOException;
public class SumProg
{
   public static void main(final String[] pArgs) throws IOException
   {
      final BufferedReader tKeyboard =
                   new BufferedReader(new InputStreamReader(System.in));
      System.out.print("Type in your first number: ");
      System.out.flush();
      String tLine = tKeyboard.readLine();
      final double tFirst = Double.parseDouble(tLine);
      System.out.print("Type in your second number: ");
      System.out.flush();
      tLine = tKeyboard.readLine();
      final double tSecond = Double.parseDouble(tLine);
      final double tSum = tFirst + tSecond;
      System.out.println("The sum of " + tFirst +
                   " and " + tSecond + " is " + tSum);
   }
}
```

Figure 4.4   A program that reads two numbers and finds their sum.

At the declaration of tLine, the tLine variable is made to point to a String object containing the first line of input. Later, an assignment statement is used to give tLine its second value: it is now pointing to the String object containing the second line of input.

So you can either use two separate String variables or you can use the same one twice. There is not much to choose between these two pieces of code.

When a statement is too long for it to appear on one line, it should be split at a convenient point. When discussing the layout of programs, Section 1.6.2 pointed out that a line can be split (and continued on the next line) at any point where a space is permitted. To make it more obvious that a line is continued on the next line, in this book we adopt the convention of splitting long lines immediately after an operator. There are two examples of this in the SumProg program (given in Figure 4.4): the assignment to tKeyboard is split immediately after the assignment operator and the argument of the call of println is split after one of the string concatenation operators.

4.9 The exception NumberFormatException

The SumProg program uses Double's parseDouble method:

```
Double.parseDouble(tLine)
```

to produce a `double` value from a string. It does this in the declaration:

```
final double tFirst = Double.parseDouble(tLine);
```

When it uses this method, the string that is passed to the method must contain characters that can be parsed into a value of type `double`. If the string is not valid, an unchecked exception called `NumberFormatException` occurs.

When we execute the `SumProg` program, it outputs the prompt:

```
Type in your first number:
```

If, at this point, we type `2p7` instead of `2.7`, the program will crash:

```
Type in your first number: 2p7
java.lang.NumberFormatException: 2p7
        at java.lang.Double.<init>(Double.java)
        at SumProg.main(SumProg.java:15)
```

Because `NumberFormatException` is an unchecked exception, Java does not require us to provide code to say what the program should do if the exception occurs. So we can forget about it, and hope that the users of our programs are good typists! However, if we want to make our programs more user-friendly, we need to allow for this possibility. We will return to this example when we look at *try statement*s in Section 9.9.

4.10 Removing whitespace before parsing

Consider the following statements again:

```
final String tFirstLine = tKeyboard.readLine();
final int tFirstInt = Integer.parseInt(tFirstLine);
```

You may think it to be cruel, but a `NumberFormatException` will be generated if the user types spaces (or some other *whitespace* characters) before or after the characters of the number that is then parsed using `parseInt`. So if, instead of typing `27`, the user types a space followed by `27` or `27` followed by a space, a NumberFormat-Exception exception will occur.

If you wish, your program can be more forgiving; it can use a method called `trim` that produces a new string in which whitespace characters have been removed from the start and from the end of the line that has been read:

```
String tFirstLine = tKeyboard.readLine();
tFirstLine = tFirstLine.trim();
final int tFirstInt = Integer.parseInt(tFirstLine);
```

The method `trim` is a method of the class `java.lang.String` (and it is mentioned in Figure 3.9).

Although `parseInt` generates a NumberFormatException exception, the `parseDouble` method is more lenient. If the string supplied as an argument to `parseDouble` starts or ends with *whitespace* characters, these will be ignored. These points are documented in the descriptions of `parseInt` and `parseDouble` that are given in the tables of Figure 3.16 and Figure 3.17.

4.11 Using `StringTokenizer` for more than one data item

So far we have assumed that each line of data only has one value. The package
`java.util` has a useful class called `StringTokenizer` that can be used if you
wish to have more than one item of data on a line. Suppose you are going to read
some details about a person, such as their age, their height and the number of children
that they have. Suppose you want to put all this data on one line of input. So the line
contains an `int`, followed by a `double`, followed by another `int`. For example:

```
42 1.85 2
```

We will now look at some code that can be used to read in these values.

First, use the `readLine` method to read in the line as a `String`:

```
final String tLine = tKeyboard.readLine();
```

Now the line can be broken up into individual items or **token**s by passing it to
`StringTokenizer`'s constructor:

```
final StringTokenizer tTokens = new StringTokenizer(tLine);
```

Unless we state otherwise, the string is broken up at any whitespace characters, which
is what we want. So the program now has a variable called `tTokens` that knows what
data items there are on the line.

The class `StringTokenizer` has a number of methods including the ones shown
in Figure 4.5 (or at $API/java/util/StringTokenizer.html).

```
public StringTokenizer(String pString);
    Initializes the new StringTokenizer object to be the tokens of the string
    pString where each token is separated (from the next token) by one or more
    whitespace characters.
public StringTokenizer(String pString, String pSeparators);
    Initializes the new StringTokenizer object to be the tokens of the string
    pString where each token is separated (from the next token) by one or more
    characters from the string pSeparators.
.............................................................................
public int countTokens();
    Returns the number of tokens left in the target. The number of tokens decreases
    by 1 each time the nextToken method is called.
public String nextToken();
    Returns the next token from the target. If there are no tokens left, an unchecked
    exception called NoSuchElementException occurs.
public boolean hasMoreTokens();
    Returns true if and only if there is another token left in the target.
```

Figure 4.5 Constructors and methods of the `java.util.StringTokenizer` class.

The program can use the `nextToken` method in order to get a string that contains
the text of the first data item on the line:

```
final String tAgeString = tTokens.nextToken();
```

This will be a string like `"42"`, and this can be converted into an `int` in the normal
way:

```
final int tAge = Integer.parseInt(tAgeString);
```

Using nextToken repeatedly, the program can obtain the remaining tokens that are known to the StringTokenizer object and process them:

```
final String tHeightString = tTokens.nextToken();
final double tHeight = Double.parseDouble(tHeightString);
final String tNumberOfChildrenString = tTokens.nextToken();
final int tNumberOfChildren = Integer.parseInt(tNumberOfChildrenString);
```

The complete program is shown in Figure 4.6.

```
// This program reads three values from the same line of input.
// Barry Cornelius, 2 June 2000
import java.io.BufferedReader;
import java.io.InputStreamReader;
import java.io.IOException;
import java.util.StringTokenizer;
public class OneLine
{
   public static void main(final String[] pArgs) throws IOException
   {
      final BufferedReader tKeyboard =
                  new BufferedReader(new InputStreamReader(System.in));
      System.out.println("Type age, height, and number of children");
      System.out.println("Separate the values by at least one space");
      final String tLine = tKeyboard.readLine();
      final StringTokenizer tTokens = new StringTokenizer(tLine);
      final String tAgeString = tTokens.nextToken();
      final int tAge = Integer.parseInt(tAgeString);
      final String tHeightString = tTokens.nextToken();
      final double tHeight = Double.parseDouble(tHeightString);
      final String tNumberOfChildrenString = tTokens.nextToken();
      final int tNumberOfChildren =
                  Integer.parseInt(tNumberOfChildrenString);
      System.out.println("Age is " + tAge + " and height is " + tHeight);
      System.out.println("Number of children is " + tNumberOfChildren);
   }
}
```

Figure 4.6   A program that reads three values from the same line of input.

4.12 Even more about import declarations

Perhaps the obvious order in which to list import declarations is to use alphabetical order, e.g.:

```
import java.awt.Point;
import java.io.BufferedReader;
import java.io.InputStreamReader;
import java.io.IOException;
import java.util.StringTokenizer;
```

However, it is probably more useful to list the import declarations so that the class names appear in alphabetical order no matter what package they come from, e.g.:

```
import java.io.BufferedReader;
import java.io.InputStreamReader;
import java.io.IOException;
import java.awt.Point;
import java.util.StringTokenizer;
```

This makes it a little easier for a reader to find out to which package a particular class belongs.

To help the reader even further, we will add extra spaces in import declarations so that the class names line up on their first character:

```
import java.io.    BufferedReader;
import java.io.    InputStreamReader;
import java.io.    IOException;
import java.awt.   Point;
import java.util.  StringTokenizer;
```

Although this style is not adopted elsewhere, it will be used in this book.

(4.13) Using a non-space separator between data items

Sometimes a data item uses characters other than spaces to separate the components of the data. For example, the string 2000-09-01 might be some data representing a date, or 400:500 might be data representing a point in 2D-space.

Suppose we want to read values like these into a program. This can easily be done using methods from the StringTokenizer class. All we need is some way of indicating that the separator between the values is not a whitespace character but is a - character or a : character. It so happens that the StringTokenizer class has a constructor which allows us to specify the character(s) that are to be used as a separator.

In the previous section, we used a constructor with one argument (that is the string containing the characters of the line):

```
final StringTokenizer tTokens = new StringTokenizer(tLine);
```

If we use this constructor, the string is broken up into *tokens* according to where the whitespace characters appear. If instead we use the constructor of String-Tokenizer that has two arguments, the string given as the second argument indicates the characters that can be used as a separator between the tokens. For example, when the data contains 400:500 it is appropriate to use:

```
final StringTokenizer tTokens = new StringTokenizer(tLine, ":");
```

A program using this constructor is given in Figure 4.7. The program first outputs a prompt:

```
Type in a point, e.g., 400:500
```

```
// This program reads a value of the class Point.
// Barry Cornelius, 2 June 2000
import java.io.    BufferedReader;
import java.io.    InputStreamReader;
import java.io.    IOException;
import java.awt.   Point;
import java.util.  StringTokenizer;
public class ReadAPoint
{
    public static void main(final String[] pArgs) throws IOException
    {
        final BufferedReader tKeyboard =
                       new BufferedReader(new InputStreamReader(System.in));
        System.out.println("Type in a point, e.g., 400:500");
        final String tLine = tKeyboard.readLine();
        final StringTokenizer tTokens = new StringTokenizer(tLine, ":");
        String tThisToken = tTokens.nextToken();
        final int x = new Integer(tThisToken).intValue();
        tThisToken = tTokens.nextToken();
        final int y = new Integer(tThisToken).intValue();
        final Point tPoint = new Point(x, y);
        System.out.println("The point is at: " + tPoint);
    }
}
```

Figure 4.7 A program that reads two values separated by a : character.

It uses `readLine` to read in a line such as:

```
400:500
```

It uses the `StringTokenizer` class to help it to create an object of the class `java.awt.Point`. It then produces output like:

```
The point is at: java.awt.Point[x=400,y=500]
```

Tips for programming and debugging

4.1   In Section 4.8, it was suggested that you can use the same `String` variable for each line of input. However, make sure you do not write:

```
String tLine = tKeyboard.readLine();
final double tFirst = Double.parseDouble(tLine);
String tLine = tKeyboard.readLine();
final double tSecond = Double.parseDouble(tLine);
final double tSum = tFirst + tSecond;
```

This is wrong because it declares `tLine` twice: if you do attempt this, the program will not compile. Instead, you need:

```
String tLine = tKeyboard.readLine();
final double tFirst = Double.parseDouble(tLine);
tLine = tKeyboard.readLine();
final double tSecond = Double.parseDouble(tLine);
final double tSum = tFirst + tSecond;
```

4.2   Having read a value into a variable, it is often useful to output the value of the variable. By checking the output that is produced, you can ensure that the program has correctly read its data. For example, here is part of the SumProg program (Figure 4.4) with some debugging statements added to it:

```
        ...
        System.out.print("Type in your first number: ");
        System.out.flush();
        String tLine = tKeyboard.readLine();
/**/    System.out.println("*** value of tLine is: " + tLine);
        final double tFirst = Double.parseDouble(tLine);
/**/    System.out.println("*** value of tFirst is: " + tFirst);
        ...
```

Curios, controversies and cover-ups

4.1   The syntax diagram for an import declaration (shown in Figure 3.3) only gives one possibility for the syntax. There is an alternative form of import declaration where lines like:

```
import java.io.BufferedReader;
import java.io.InputStreamReader;
import java.io.IOException;
```

can be abbreviated to:

```
import java.io.*;
```

This kind of import declaration (called a **type-import-on-demand declaration**) essentially gives the compiler that is compiling your code permission, when looking for a definition of a class, to look in the package java.io for the class.

In this book, we do not recommend this alternative form of an import declaration: we believe it to be a lazy cop-out. In its extreme form, you just put a list like this at the start of each file:

```
import java.awt.*;
import java.io.*;
import java.util.*;
```

and then you need not be bothered with import declarations. This is a bad programming practice: the list of import declarations is a good way of documenting from which package a class is being obtained.

4.2   When calling a method that is an *instance method*, the name of the target variable is given on the left-hand side of the dot that appears in the call. It was stated in Section 4.6 that, when a program calls a *class method*, the name of the target variable is replaced by the name of the class. Here is an example that has occurred many times in this chapter:

```
double tFirst = Double.parseDouble(tLine);
```

In the call of this class method, the name of a class precedes the dot. However, it is possible, instead, to call a class method using the name of a reference variable (of the appropriate class type) as in:

```
Double tSomeDouble = new Double(1.0);
double tFirst = tSomeDouble.parseDouble(tLine);
```

Although this seems not to be a useful facility, a need for it will be mentioned in Curio 19.1. In the meanwhile, forget about this possibility! It is a lot less confusing and a lot more helpful to use the name of the class (when calling a class method).

4.3   Instead of using `parseInt` or `parseDouble`, it is possible to use `intValue` or `doubleValue` instead. For example:

```
final String tLine = tKeyboard.readLine();
final Double tFirstDouble = new Double(tLine);
final double tFirst = tFirstDouble.doubleValue();
```

This can be abbreviated to:

```
final String tLine = tKeyboard.readLine();
final double tFirst = new Double(tLine).doubleValue();
```

When constructing a `Double` from a `String`, the constructor permits the string to start or end with whitespace characters. However, when constructing an `Integer` from a `String`, the constructor will produce a NumberFormat-Exception if the string starts or ends with whitespace characters. This behaviour is the same as that for `parseDouble` and `parseInt` (which was mentioned in Section 4.10).

4.4   In many ways, the use of `parseDouble` is a lot easier to understand than this use of the `doubleValue` method with an object of class `Double`. However, `Double`'s `parseDouble` and `Float`'s `parseFloat` were introduced to Java when the Java 2 Platform was released. So, in both JDK 1.0.2 and JDK 1.1, `java.lang.Double` does not have a method called `parseDouble`. If, for some reason, you have to use one of these earlier versions, you will have to use the `doubleValue` method with an object of class `Double`.

There is no such problem with `Integer`'s `parseInt`: this is available in all versions of Java.

4.5   It is curious that the various `parseXXX` methods were not all present at the start: they have slowly been added to Java. Even now there is no `parse-Boolean` for use with the primitive type `boolean` (which will be introduced in Section 6.13). For more details about the lack of `parseBoolean`, see Curio 6.7.

Exercises

4.1   Modify your solution to Exercise 3.1 so that it reads the grid reference from the keyboard. Test your program by executing it several times trying it with the following grid references:

```
NZ273421
NZ270410
NZ203408
NZ053048
```

4.2   Modify your solution to Exercise 3.3 so that it reads the electronic mail address from the keyboard. Test your program by executing it several times trying it with the following addresses:

```
Joe.Bloggs@durham.ac.uk
J.A.Bloggs@durham.ac.uk
J.A.D.Bloggs@durham.ac.uk
```

4.3   Modify the program given in Figure 4.6 so that it instead assumes that the data items on the input line are separated by a – character rather than by a space. For example, the data might contain:

```
42-1.85-2
```

Chapter 5

Using arithmetic expressions to represent formulae

It is time to have a detailed look at how operations can be performed on variables that hold numerical values. In this chapter, we will see that this can be done in two ways.

First, like as in algebra, there are various arithmetic operators that can be used on numerical values. In Java, we use symbols such as +, −, * and / for these operations. And, when these are used with parentheses to form subexpressions, quite complicated expressions can be formed.

The second way that Java offers for performing operations on numerical values is the same as what we used for strings: we can use methods from a class of Java's Core APIs. The methods are in a class called `java.lang.Math`. They can perform complicated operations such as finding the square root of a value, finding the sine of an angle, and so on.

The chapter finishes by looking at arithmetic expressions that involve values of the primitive type `char`.

5.1 Expressions and arithmetic expressions

We have already seen that expressions are used in a number of places in Java. For example, they are used as arguments in method invocations, and they are used on the right-hand side of the = of an assignment statement. Often, an expression is simple: it is just a literal, the name of a variable, or perhaps the call of a function. However, we sometimes need to construct complicated expressions. Here is an example of an assignment statement that has a complicated expression:

```
y = Math.log(Math.sin(x*x + 1.0) - 4.0*Math.atan(1.0)/10.0);
```

Such expressions are a combination of **operator**s (such as + and -) and **operands** (such as 1.0 and x).

In Java, there are two main kinds of expressions: **infix expression**s and **prefix expression**s. An infix expression is one that involves an operator placed in between two operands, whereas a prefix expression only has one operand. For example, in the expression -b + a/c, the -b is a prefix expression, the a/c is an infix expression, and the whole expression is an infix expression which has operands -b and a/c.

In this chapter, we will be considering expressions that have operands that are of numeric types. Such expressions are called **arithmetic expression**s.

We will look at five areas that you need to know about when constructing arithmetic expressions:

- Section 5.2 looks at the types of the operands and the type of an expression.
- Section 5.3 and Section 5.4 look at the operators that can be used.
- Section 5.5 looks at the operations that produce out-of-range values.
- Section 5.6 looks at the order of the application of the operators.
- Section 5.7 looks at the use of functions provided by the class java.lang.Math.

The text covering the first four of these will need careful reading in order to avoid their pitfalls!

5.2 The types of the operands and the type of an expression

Since the language Java has *strong typing*, there are rules about what can appear in an arithmetic expression. In order to apply the rules, you need to be aware of the types of the operands being used in an expression.

If a variable is used as an operand, the type of the operand is the same as that of the variable. If a numeric literal is used as an operand, the type of the operand depends on whether you write something like 2 or 2.0. Literals like 2 are of type int, whereas a literal like 2.0 is of type double.

The type of a prefix expression is the same as that of its operand.

If an infix expression uses two operands that are of the same type, the type of the infix expression is also of this type.

However, sometimes we will be producing infix expressions where one operand is of type int and the other is of type double. For example, suppose that a program has to calculate the cost of some oranges. We might have a int variable called tNumberOfOranges and a double variable called tPriceOfAnOrange. You can then use the infix expression tNumberOfOranges*tPriceOfAnOrange in order to calculate the cost of the oranges. In this situation, the value of the int operand is converted into a double. So the type of the infix expression is a double. This conversion process is known as **numeric promotion**. More detailed information about numeric promotion appears in Curio 5.1.

5.3 The operators that can be used

The following table indicates the symbols that can be used as **operator**s in an infix expression:

name of the operation	symbol
addition	+
subtraction	−
multiplication	*
division	/
remainder operation	%

and the following table indicates the symbols that can be used as operators in a prefix expression:

name of the operation	symbol
identity	+
negation	−

```
double d = 2.7;
int i = 20;
```

The following table assumes the existence of the above variables:

expression	value of expression	type of expression
i+10	30	int
i-10	10	int
i*10	200	int
i/10	2	int
i%10	0	int
d+10.0	12.7	double
d-10.0	−7.3	double
d*10.0	27.0	double
d/10.0	0.27	double
d%10.0	2.7	double
d+i	22.7	double
d-i	−17.3	double
d*i	54.0	double
d/i	0.135	double
d%i	2.7	double

Figure 5.1 A table giving the values of some arithmetic expressions.

Note that a * symbol is used to indicate multiplication. This symbol must always appear when multiplication is involved. Unlike mathematics, it is not possible in Java to use the juxtaposition of two operands to indicate multiplication, i.e. a formula such as *3x* must be written with a multiplication operator. Your choice between 3*x and 3.0*x depends on the type of x.

The table in Figure 5.1 gives some examples illustrating the use of these operators.

5.4 Cast operators

5.4.1 Using a cast from double to int

Section 5.2 pointed out that *numeric promotion* takes place when an infix expression has one int operand and one double operand, i.e. the int is automatically promoted to a double. In some situations, we may not wish for this conversion to happen: instead, you may want the value of the operand that is of type double to be converted to an int.

With some types, you can indicate that you wish an operand to behave as if it were of a different type by putting the name of the desired type within parentheses before the operand: this is called a **cast**.

Suppose a car park charges 10 pence for each hour or part of an hour:

```
final int tAmountperHour = 10;
```

And suppose that, in some way, a double variable finds out the number of hours a vehicle has been parked:

```
double tNumberOfHours = ...;
```

For example, if you have been parked for 3 hours and 15 minutes, this variable will have the value 3.25, and you will be expecting to pay a charge of 40 pence.

If the program calculates the charge using the expression:

```
tAmountPerHour*tNumberOfHours
```

numeric promotion will take place. For a time of $3\frac{1}{4}$ hours, this expression would have the value 32.5. However, finding the charge is not easy if the calculation is done using floating point arithmetic: it is more convenient to use ints:

```
int tCharge = tAmountPerHour*(int)tNumberOfHours;
```

The expression (int)tNumberOfHours is a *cast*. The result of this cast is the integer part of the value of tNumberOfHours, i.e. it produces the value that results from **round**ing the floating point value towards zero. Note that a cast works on a copy of the floating point value: it never alters the value of the variable being *cast*ed.

So if tNumberOfHours has the value 3.25 (or any value between 3 and 4), the expression (int)tNumberOfHours has the value 3.

In the car parking problem, this value is one less than what we want: so we might instead use:

```
int tCharge = tAmountPerHour*((int)tNumberOfHours + 1);
```

However, this unfairly penalizes someone who stays for an exact number of hours, e.g. for precisely 3 hours, and so we will add a fiddle factor (which effectively gives everyone about a minute's worth of free parking):

```
final double tFreeParkingPeriod = 0.01;
int tCharge =
    tAmountPerHour*((int)(tNumberOfHours - tFreeParkingPeriod) + 1);
```

We have seen that a cast is necessary to convert a `double` into an `int`: other casts with these two types are discussed in Curio 5.2.

5.4.2 Using a cast to find the `int` that is nearest to a `double`

Sometimes we are not interested in all of the decimal places of a floating point value: we are only interested in a ballpark figure. For example, suppose we want to obtain the whole number that is nearest to a `double` value. One way of doing this is to add 0.5 to the `double` value before using a cast to convert the value to type `int`.

For example, suppose we have a program that, after doing a lot of calculations, assigns to `tSpeedOfLight` some approximation to the value `2.99792458`. If we use:

```
System.out.println(tSpeedOfLight);
```

then it will output a value like:

```
2.99792458
```

If instead we use:

```
int tRoughSpeedOfLight = (int)(tSpeedOfLight + 0.5);
System.out.println(tRoughSpeedOfLight);
```

then it will output:

```
3
```

Another way of rounding a `double` value is given in Curio 5.3.

5.4.3 Obtaining a `double` correct to some number of decimal places

Perhaps, that is too crude an estimate. So, a variation on this is to obtain a `double` value that is correct to a certain number of decimal places. For example, suppose we want to output the value of `tSpeedOfLight` using three decimal places, i.e. we are aiming to output `2.998`. One way of doing this is to introduce a value that represents

10^3, i.e. 1000:

```
double tFactor = 1000.0;
int tDigitsOfSpeedOfLight = (int)(tSpeedOfLight*tFactor + 0.5);
double tApproxSpeedOfLight = tDigitsOfSpeedOfLight/tFactor;
System.out.println(tApproxSpeedOfLight);
```

5.5 Operations that produce out-of-range values

We now consider what happens if an operation produces a value which is too large or too small for the range of the type of the expression. If the result of an `int` or a `double` operation is too large in magnitude, the operation is said to **overflow**. If the result of a `double` operation is too small in magnitude, the operation is said to **underflow**.

We also have to consider other situations like dividing by zero. The rules are quite complicated, and the 10 rules given below are actually a simplification of the rules given in the JLS.

Before looking at these rules, it is useful to know that there are three special floating point values that can be produced by an operation that has operands of type `double`. They are called **minus infinity**, **plus infinity** and **Not-a-Number** (or **NaN**). Besides pointing out some of the situations in which these three special values are produced, the following rules also discuss what happens if one of these values is used in a subsequent operation.

We first look at two rules that apply for expressions that involve `int` values:

1. If the divisor of an `int` / operation or an `int` % operation has the value zero, an exception called `ArithmeticException` occurs. Like `StringIndexOut-OfBoundsException` (in Section 3.4.6), ArithmeticException is an unchecked exception. This means that Java does not require you to include code in your program to say what should happen if this exception occurs. As explained in Section 3.4.6, because our aim is to produce programs that do not cause unchecked exceptions, we will not include such code: so, if an ArithmeticException occurs, our program will crash.

2. If the result of an `int` operation is too large in magnitude (*overflow*), the value of the expression is some other integer value, a value that is one of the values of the type `int`. Other than noting that an `int` value is produced and its value is usually inappropriate for our needs, we need not really be too concerned with its actual numerical value. If you want to know the details, look at Curio 5.4.

The other eight rules are concerned with expressions that involve `double` values:

3. If an expression is a *cast* from `double` to `int` and the value of the `double` operand is a NaN, the value of the expression is the `int` value 0; if the value of the operand is smaller than -2147483648, the value of the expression is -2147483648; or if the value of the operand is larger than 2147483647, the value of the expression is 2147483647.

4. If an operand of a `double` operation is a NaN, the value of the expression will be a NaN.

5. If an operand of a `double` operation is *minus infinity* or *plus infinity*, the value of the expression is governed by other rules that are not covered here: see the JLS for more details.

6. If the values of both operands of a `double` / operation are zero, the value of the expression is a *NaN*.

7. If the divisor of a `double` / operation is zero, the value of the expression is either *minus infinity* or *plus infinity*. The one that is used depends on the signs of the operands.

8. If the divisor of a `double` % operation is zero, the value of the expression is a *NaN*.

9. If the result of a `double` operation is too large in magnitude (*overflow*), the value of the expression is either *minus infinity* or *plus infinity*. The one that is used depends on the signs of the operands.

10. If the result of a `double` operation is too small in magnitude (*underflow*), the value of the expression is the `double` value 0.0.

5.6 The order of the application of the operators

If an expression involves more than one operator, we need rules to define the order in which the operators are applied to the operands. These rules establish the **priority** (or the **precedence**) of the operators. The rules for Java are much the same as they are for conventional algebra.

One rule states that any sub-expressions within parentheses are performed first, then any casts are performed, and finally any multiplications and divisions are performed before any additions and subtractions. In fact, with the operators that have been introduced so far, four levels of priority can be identified:

Highest priority: the use of (and) to form subexpressions
                       the use of a cast
                       `*, /, %`
Lowest priority: `+, -`

Another rule defines what happens if two operators having the same priority occur within the same expression. For example, in what order are the operators of the expression x/y/z applied? If you are not convinced that it makes a difference, consider the value of 20.0/4.0/2.0. Is it *2.5* or *10.0*? In Java, the expression has the value *2.5*. This is because the second rule states that, in such situations, the operators are applied from left to right. So, for the Java expression x/y/z, the expression x/y is evaluated first and then that result is divided by z, i.e. x/y/z could instead be written as (x/y)/z. However, the same value is also produced by the expression x/(y*z), and in fact it is probably easier to understand a program if x/(y*z) is used rather than x/y/z.

5.7 The use of functions provided by `java.lang.Math`

The class `Math` from the package `java.lang` provides a number of **mathematical functions** and two **mathematical constants**. Figure 5.2 gives details about the two constants and some of the functions. They are more formally documented at $API/java/lang/Math.html.

```
public static final double E;
```
    A constant whose value is an approximation to the value of *e*.
```
public static final double PI;
```
    A constant whose value is an approximation to the value of π.

. . . .

```
public static int abs(int pX);
public static double abs(double pX);
```
    Returns the absolute value of `pX`.
```
public static double atan(double pX);
```
    Returns the arc tangent of `pX`.
```
public static double cos(double pX);
```
    Returns the cosine of `pX`.
```
public static double exp(double pX);
```
    Returns the value of *e* raised to the power of `pX`.
```
public static double log(double pX);
```
    Returns the natural logarithm (base *e*) of `pX`.
```
public static double pow(double pX, double pPower);
```
    Returns the value of `pX` raised to the power of `pPower`. An unchecked exception called `ArithmeticException` occurs if `pX` is zero and `pPower` is `<=` zero or if `pX` is `<=` zero and `pPower` is not a whole number.
```
public static double random();
```
    Returns a random number between 0.0 and 1.0.
```
public static long round(double pX);
```
    Returns the value of type `long` that is closest to the value of `pX`.
```
public static double sin(double pX);
```
    Returns the sine of `pX`.
```
public static double sqrt(double pX);
```
    Returns the square root of `pX`. If the value of `pX` is NaN or is less than zero, the function returns a NaN.
```
public static double tan(double pX);
```
    Returns the tan of `pX`.
```
public static double toDegrees(double pRadians);
```
    Returns the value of the angle `pRadians` (that is given in radians) converted to degrees.
```
public static double toRadians(double pDegrees);
```
    Returns the value of the angle `pDegrees` (that is given in degrees) converted to radians.

Figure 5.2 Constants and methods of the `java.lang.Math` class.

As was mentioned in Section 4.6, all of the functions of this class are *class methods*. In the documentation this is immediately obvious because the `static` keyword appears in the descriptions of each method.

So when you come to use one of these methods, there is no object to which to apply the method, instead, you just write the name of the class.

An example is:

```
y = Math.sqrt(x);
```

This assignment statement assigns to *y* the result of calculating $\sqrt{x}$, the square root of *x*.

If you look at Figure 5.2, you will see that the `pow` function is different from the other functions in that it has two arguments. So if you want to calculate the value of x^y and assign this value to a variable called `z`, you will need to write:

```
z = Math.pow(x, y);
```

Figure 5.3 contains a Java program illustrating calls of some of the functions of `java.lang.Math`. In this program, the variable `y` is assigned the value of:

$$\log_e \left(\sin(\sqrt{x^2 + 1}) - \frac{3}{10} \right)$$

Then, the variable `pi` is assigned a value which is an approximation to the value of the mathematical constant π.

Actually one of the two mathematical constants defined by `java.lang.Math` is an approximation to the value of π. In the declaration of `java.lang.Math`, it

```
// This program demonstrates the use of entities from java.lang.Math.
// Barry Cornelius, 2 June 2000
public class MathProg
{
    public static void main(final String[] pArgs)
    {
        final double x = 2.0;
        final double y = Math.log(Math.sin(Math.sqrt(x*x + 1.0)) - 0.3);
        System.out.println("The value of the complicated formula is: " + y);

        final double pi = 4.0*Math.atan(1.0);
        System.out.println("An approximation to the value of pi is: " + pi);

        System.out.println("Another approximation to pi is:  " + Math.PI);
    }
}
```

Figure 5.3   A program that demonstrates the use of entities from `java.lang.Math`.

appears as:

```
public static final double PI = 3.14159265358979323846;
```

So, in a program, you can refer to this constant by using Math.PI. The program in Figure 5.3 contains a use of Math.PI. The other constant in the class java.lang.Math is Math.E which is an approximation to the value of *e*.

Finally, note that, in this program, there is no import declaration:

```
import java.lang. Math;
```

As was explained in Section 3.4.2, you do not need an import declaration for any class that is in the java.lang package.

5.8 Solving other problems

5.8.1 Introduction

In this chapter, a lot of new material has been introduced, and it is the aim of this section to use this material in other examples to try to ensure that it has been understood. The SumProg program (that appeared in Figure 4.4) performed a trivial task, the addition of two numbers. Programs that solve slightly more complicated problems will now be introduced.

We first look at a program to convert temperatures in degrees Fahrenheit to degrees Celsius; and then at a program to solve a quadratic equation. It may be that solving quadratic equations does not interest you: if this is the case, you should ignore Section 5.8.3.

5.8.2 A temperature conversion problem

In the UK, there has been a gradual conversion from using temperatures expressed in degrees Fahrenheit to degrees Celsius (or Centigrade). Needless to say, in some countries, they seem to be quite happy with using Fahrenheit! In this section, we look at how to write a program to convert between the two systems.

First of all, here are some temperatures in the two systems:

32°F	0°C	freezing point of water
50°F	10°C	
68°F	20°C	
98.6°F	37.0°C	normal blood temperature
212°F	100°C	boiling point of water

A °C value can be obtained by subtracting 32 from the °F value, by multiplying this result by 5 and dividing the result of the multiplication by 9.

Suppose we want a program that reads in a temperature given in Fahrenheit and produces as output the corresponding value in Celsius. The program for this problem can have the following form:

1. Read the °F value.

2. Calculate the °C value from the formula $\frac{5}{9}$ (°F value − 32).

3. Output the °C value.

So, there are three actions that need to be performed, and they need to be performed in the above order. To produce Java statements for these actions, we need:

- variables in order to store the °F and °C values;
- an arithmetic expression which finds the value produced by the formula;
- an assignment statement to assign this value to the °C variable;
- appropriate input and output statements.

One possible program for this problem is given in Figure 5.4.

```java
// This program reads in a temperature given in degrees Fahrenheit
// and outputs the corresponding value in degrees Celsius.
// Barry Cornelius, 2 June 2000
import java.io. BufferedReader;
import java.io. InputStreamReader;
import java.io. IOException;
public class TemperatureConversion
{
    public static void main(final String[] pArgs) throws IOException
    {
        final BufferedReader tKeyboard =
                        new BufferedReader(new InputStreamReader(System.in));
        System.out.print("Type in a value in degrees Fahrenheit: ");
        System.out.flush();
        final String tLine = tKeyboard.readLine();
        final double tFahrenheit = Double.parseDouble(tLine);
        final double tCelsius = (tFahrenheit - 32.0)*5.0/9.0;
        System.out.println("In degrees Celsius, this is: " + tCelsius);
    }
}
```

Figure 5.4   A temperature conversion program.

Note that the names `tFahrenheit` and `tCelsius` have been chosen for the two variables. It is easier to understand a program when the name of each variable is connected with its purpose. So, these names should be used instead of names like `f` and `c` which, for example, could be something to do with a frequency *f* and the speed of light *c*. Even worse are names like `a` and `b`. When meaningless names are chosen, one has to hunt for the meaning of the program by looking at how each of the variables is used in the program.

Although temperatures are often given as whole numbers, the Temperature-Conversion program is more general since it allows temperatures that have a fractional part. So the variables tFahrenheit and tCelsius are of type double rather than of type int.

The TemperatureConversion program uses the Java expression:

```
(tFahrenheit - 32.0)*5.0/9.0
```

in order to represent the mathematical formula:

$$\frac{5}{9}(°\text{F value} - 32)$$

Other possibilities include:

```
5.0/9.0*(tFahrenheit - 32.0)
(tFahrenheit - 32.0)/9.0*5.0
5.0*(tFahrenheit - 32.0)/9.0
```

Note that the parentheses in these expressions are necessary. For example, the expression:

```
tFahrenheit-32.0*5.0/9.0
```

would produce the wrong value since it represents the formula:

$$°\text{F value} - \frac{32 \times 5}{9}$$

This is because, in Java, the priority of the / and * operators is higher than that of the - operator.

◊   ### 5.8.3 The quadratic equation problem

For this problem, the **quadratic equation**:

$$ax^2 + bx + c = 0$$

has to be solved given some values for a, b and c. Such an equation has two roots and these are given by the formula:

$$x = \frac{-b \pm \sqrt{b^2 - 4ac}}{2a}$$

We will assume for the time being that the equation has real roots (i.e. the roots are not complex, i.e. $b^2 \geq 4ac$) and that $a \neq 0$. These constraints will be lifted in Section 6.8.

The program for this problem can have the following form:

1. Read the values of a, b and c.

2. Calculate the two roots.

3. Output the two roots.

Often the **coefficient**s of the quadratic equation, i.e. *a*, *b* and *c*, will be whole numbers. However, the program will be more general if we allow coefficients that have fractional parts. In the program, three `double` variables with the names a, b and c can be used to store the values of these coefficients. Although the names a, b and c are not very meaningful, these are the names that are often used in mathematics for the names of the coefficients of a quadratic equation.

Although there are a lot of other details to be sorted out in order to produce the program, the major problem is producing Java expressions for the right-hand side of the formula, i.e. for both:

$$\frac{-b + \sqrt{b^2 - 4ac}}{2a}$$

and:

$$\frac{-b - \sqrt{b^2 - 4ac}}{2a}$$

An expression for the first one of these formulae will be now developed in stages.

The formula has the following structure:

$$\frac{X + Y}{Z}$$

which is written as `(X + Y)/Z` in Java. Note that the parentheses are necessary, for if `X + Y/Z` were used, this would have the same meaning as the formula:

$$X + \frac{Y}{Z}$$

since / has greater priority than +.

X is simply `-b`; so we now have `(-b + Y)/Z`. How about the *Y*? Well, *Y* is a complicated expression, namely, the square root of `b*b - 4.0*a*c`, i.e. `Math.sqrt(b*b - 4.0*a*c)`. This is *Y* sorted out. So, we now have:

`(-b + Math.sqrt(b*b - 4.0*a*c))/Z`

What is *Z*? It is 2*a*, which can be represented in Java by `2.0*a`. So we might try the expression `(-b + Math.sqrt(b*b - 4.0*a*c))/2.0*a`. But this is incorrect, because both / and * have equal priority. So if this expression were used, the computer would be instructed to calculate the value of:

$$\frac{-b + \sqrt{b^2 - 4ac}}{2} \times a$$

Instead, we need to indicate that the `2.0*a` is to be evaluated before the `/` takes place. This can be done by using the expression:

```
(-b + Math.sqrt(b*b - 4.0*a*c))/(2.0*a)
```

The program is now reasonably easy to write. It is shown in Figure 5.5.

```
// This program reads in the coefficients of a quadratic equation and
// outputs its two roots.   The equation is assumed to have real roots.
// Barry Cornelius, 2 June 2000
import java.io. BufferedReader;
import java.io. InputStreamReader;
import java.io. IOException;
public class QeSimple
{
    public static void main(final String[] pArgs) throws IOException
    {
        final BufferedReader tKeyboard =
                    new BufferedReader(new InputStreamReader(System.in));
        System.out.print("Type in the value of a: ");   System.out.flush();
        String tLine = tKeyboard.readLine();
        final double a = Double.parseDouble(tLine);
        System.out.print("Type in the value of b: ");   System.out.flush();
        tLine = tKeyboard.readLine();
        final double b = Double.parseDouble(tLine);
        System.out.print("Type in the value of c: ");   System.out.flush();
        tLine = tKeyboard.readLine();
        final double c = Double.parseDouble(tLine);
        final double tSqrtPart = Math.sqrt(b*b - 4.0*a*c);
        final double tRoot1 = (-b + tSqrtPart)/(2.0*a);
        final double tRoot2 = (-b - tSqrtPart)/(2.0*a);
        System.out.println("The roots of the quadratic equation are:");
        System.out.println(tRoot1 + " and " + tRoot2);
    }
}
```

Figure 5.5   A program for the quadratic equation problem.

Note that the program uses another variable (`tSqrtPart`) in order to avoid having to calculate the square root part of the formula twice. That is, the program uses:

```
tSqrtPart = Math.sqrt(b*b - 4.0*a*c);
tRoot1 = (-b + tSqrtPart)/(2.0*a);
tRoot2 = (-b - tSqrtPart)/(2.0*a);
```

rather than:

```
tRoot1 = (-b + Math.sqrt(b*b - 4.0*a*c))/(2.0*a);
tRoot2 = (-b - Math.sqrt(b*b - 4.0*a*c))/(2.0*a);
```

So, during the execution of the `QeSimple` program, the variable `tSqrtPart` is assigned a subsidiary value of the calculation. Such **temporary variables** should be introduced if it makes the resulting program easier to understand or if it avoids the value of some complicated expression being calculated more than once.

5.9 Expressions involving values of type `char`

In Java, each value of type `char` is represented (in the computer) by an integer value. The **coding** that is used is one known as *Unicode*. More details about Unicode are given in Curio 3.7.

Here are some of the codes that are used:

char	code	char	code	char	code
'0'	48	'A'	65	'a'	97
'1'	49	'B'	66	'b'	98
...	...	...	...	...	...
'9'	57	'Z'	90	'z'	122

So if a variable is assigned the value '2' as in:

```
char tChar = '2';
```

the location used for the variable contains the value 50.

The type `char` is another kind of whole number type. If you perform arithmetic with a value of type `char`, *numeric promotion* will take place on the value.

Consider the expression `tChar + 1` where the variable `tChar` is the one that was declared above. Because the other operand of this expression is an `int`, the `tChar` operand will be promoted to an `int`. So, the expression is of type `int`, and it has the value 51. Such an expression could be assigned to a variable of type `int` as in:

```
int tValue = tChar + 1;
```

in which case `tValue` would now have the value 51.

Or, if you want to assign to a `char` variable called `tNextChar` the `char` value associated with this value, you could use a cast as in:

```
char tNextChar = (char)(tChar + 1):
```

The variable `tNextChar` would now have the value '3'.

Suppose you know that a `char` variable has been assigned the `char` value for some digit, e.g.:

```
char tChar = '2';
```

Suppose that you want to assign the appropriate integer value, in this case, the value 2, to an `int` variable called `tDigit`. This could be done using:

```
int tDigit = tChar - 48;
```

It is better to write:

```
int tDigit = tChar - '0';
```

(because this has more meaning). Here both operands are of type char. As explained in Curio 5.1, in such situations, both operands are promoted to the type int. However, even better is to use the class method called digit that is provided by the class java.lang.Character. The method has two parameters: the value of type char and the base that is to be used. So, since we are assuming decimal notation in the above example, we can code it as:

```
int tDigit = Character.digit(tChar, 10);
```

Other details about this method are given at $API/java/lang/Character.html.

Tips for programming and debugging

5.1 Some programmers often add superfluous parentheses to a complicated expression in order to make it easier to understand. However, overdoing this can have the opposite effect.

5.2 Some programmers use different spacing in order to emphasize the different priority of the operators used in an expression. For example, they might use the expression a + b*c rather than a+b*c. The spaces on either side of the + and the lack of spaces around the * is an attempt to show the priorities of the operators, i.e. that the * has higher priority than the + operator. This idea is often used in this book.

5.3 If an int variable is being used for a value which is always less than 100, then, when you are outputting this value, it is sometimes useful for the output always to have two digits (even when the value is less than 10). This might occur if you have three variables called tYear, tMonth and tDay, and you want to output the values of these variables using a format like:

```
2000-08-07
```

One way of outputting the value of a variable like tMonth so that it always occupies two printing positions is to output the value of tMonth/10 followed by the value of tMonth%10. Although you might at first produce:

```
System.out.print(tMonth/10 + tMonth%10);
```

this does not have the desired effect (why not?). Instead, you need something like:

```
System.out.print("" + tMonth/10 + tMonth%10);
```

And to output a date using the above format you can use something like:

```
System.out.print(tYear + "-" + tMonth/10 + tMonth%10
                    + "-" + tDay/10 + tDay%10);
```

Although this solution to the problem looks amateurish, it is quite effective. The class NumberFormat from the java.text package provides more sophisticated solutions. For more details, see $API/java/text/NumberFormat.html.

Curios, controversies and cover-ups

5.1 As was explained in Section 5.2, when an arithmetic expression involves operands that are of different numeric types, **numeric promotion** takes place. The complete set of rules is as follows, and these rules are applied in the order given:

1. if an operand is of type double, the other operand is converted to a double;

2. if an operand is of type float, the other operand is converted to a float;

3. if an operand is of type long, the other operand is converted to a long;

4. any operand that is not of type int is converted to an int.

5.2 Suppose the variables i and j are of type int, and the variables d and e are of type double. As was explained in Section 5.4, a *cast* is necessary in the following assignment statement:

```
i = (int)d;
```

Although the following examples of casts are valid, they are a bit silly:

```
i = (int)j;
d = (double)e;
```

Even though a cast is not necessary in the following example, it may be useful to use a cast to document the change of type:

```
d = (double)i;
```

5.3 Section 5.4.2 gives one technique for finding the nearest int value to a double value (that is stored in the variable tSpeedOfLight). Another way is to use the method called round that is provided by the java.lang.Math class. Because this method produces a result of type long, a cast will be needed if you want to assign the result to an int:

```
int tRoughSpeedOfLight = (int)Math.round(tSpeedOfLight);
System.out.println(tRoughSpeedOfLight);
```

5.4 In order to understand what happens when the result of an int operation overflows, i.e. when the result is less than −2147483648 or bigger than 2147483647, it is necessary to know something about the way in which numbers are stored by a computer.

Usually, **decimal notation** is used by human beings for communicating numerical values. So the notation 217 is used for the value that is $(2 \times 10^2) + (1 \times 10^1) + (7 \times 10^0)$, which is $2 \times 100 + 1 \times 10 + 7 \times 1$. However, this is an inconvenient notation for computers to use. In a computer, it is easier to store numerical values using a notation which has two states, and so **binary notation** is used instead. So the value 217 is represented using the **bits (binary digits)** 11011001 because the value 217 is $1 \times 128 + 1 \times 64 + 1 \times 16 + 1 \times$

$8 + 1 \times 1$, i.e. $(1 \times 2^7) + (1 \times 2^6) + (0 \times 2^5) + (1 \times 2^4) + (1 \times 2^3) + (0 \times 2^2) + (0 \times 2^1) + (1 \times 2^0)$.

In Java, 32 bits are allocated for each value of type int. By using 32 bits, it means that there are 4294967296 possible bit patterns, from a bit pattern with 32 zeroes to a bit pattern with 32 ones. Just over half of these are used for negative int values and the others are positive values and the value zero. Here are the bit patterns that are used:

value	bit pattern
–2147483648	10000000000000000000000000000000
–2147483647	10000000000000000000000000000001
. . .	
–2	11111111111111111111111111111110
–1	11111111111111111111111111111111
0	00000000000000000000000000000000
1	00000000000000000000000000000001
2	00000000000000000000000000000010
. . .	
2147483646	01111111111111111111111111111110
2147483647	01111111111111111111111111111111

In this table, each bit pattern is given with 32 bits.

Having looked in some detail at how Java stores values of type int, we now look at what happens when a program performs an int operation that overflows. As in Exercise 2.2, suppose we have a program that performs a + operation on the values 2147483647 and 1:

2147483647	01111111111111111111111111111111
1	00000000000000000000000000000001

We would like this addition operation to produce the value 2147483648 but this value cannot be represented using the type int. The result of this operation is the bit pattern 10000000000000000000000000000000 which is the bit pattern that is used by ints for representing the value –2147483648. So this explains why, in Java, the result of adding the int values 2147483647 and 1 is the value –2147483648.

In general, when an int operation should produce a value that is less than –2147483648 or bigger than 2147483647, it will instead produce some other integer, the int value whose representation is given by the bottom 32 bits of the operation.

5.5 Figure 3.9 mentions the functions toDegrees and toRadians. These functions were new with the Java 2 Platform and so they are not available if you are using JDK 1.1 or JDK 1.0.2.

5.6 In Section 5.7, it was said that when evaluating something like $\sqrt{x}$ 'there is no object to which to apply the method'. However, in some object-oriented programming languages, all types are reference types: there are no primitive types. In these languages, all values are represented by objects, and in such languages, for $\sqrt{x}$ you would write an expression like:

```
new Double(x).sqrt()
```

but this is not Java. Instead, in Java, you write:

```
Math.sqrt(x)
```

Exercises

◇   **5.1**   What is the mathematical formula corresponding to the complicated Java expression given in Section 5.1?

5.2   Write a program that reads in the values of two `int`s and then outputs both the sum and the product of the two `int`s.
      Execute this program on the computer using the data:

```
27
42
```

Execute the program another three times using the following three pairs of values in the data:

2nd set:	−6	−3
3rd set:	214750	10000
4th set:	429500	10000

Some of these executions will produce the wrong answers. For each case, indicate why the abnormal behaviour occurs.

◇   **5.3**   Type in the quadratic equation program given in Figure 5.5. Execute this program on the computer using the data:

```
3.9
7.2
2.8
```

Execute the program another three times using the following values in the data:

2nd set:	1.0	6.0	9.0
3rd set:	3.9	2.7	2.8
4th set:	0.0	2.7	2.8

With the first set of data, the program produces the values −0.5568498241772898 and −1.2893040219765566. For the second set of data, it should output the value −3.0 twice. However, the third and fourth sets should both fail in some way. To be more specific, the third set should fail because the program will attempt to find the square root of a negative number and the fourth set should fail because the program will attempt to divide by a value that is zero. For these last two cases, explain the results produced by the Java interpreter.

5.4 Write a program that reads in the lengths, a, b and c, of the three sides of a triangle and then outputs these lengths together with the area of the triangle. Use the formula:

$$area = \sqrt{s(s-a)(s-b)(s-c)}$$

where:

$$s = \frac{a+b+c}{2}$$

Execute the program on the computer using the data:

```
5.0
12.0
13.0
```

The values 5.0, 12.0, 13.0 and 30.0 should be output.

5.5 Write a program that reads in a temperature given in degrees Celsius and then outputs the corresponding value in degrees Fahrenheit.

Test your program by executing it several times with a different value in the data.

5.6 Write a program that reads in the value of two integers representing a height in feet and inches, e.g.:

```
6
1
```

represents 6′ 1″ and then outputs the height in centimetres, e.g.:

```
6.0 feet and 1.0 inches is 185.42000000000002 centimetres
```

[Note: here are some useful conversion formulae: 1 foot is 12 inches, and 1 inch is 2.54 centimetres.]

◊ **5.7** Write a program that reads in an integer and then outputs the integer together with its square, cube and fourth power.

Test your program by executing it several times with a different value in the data.

5.8 Write a program that reads a number of minutes since midnight and then outputs the time in the form:

hours:minutes

Here are some examples of the output that your program should produce:

data	output
0	0:00
59	0:59
60	1:00
719	11:59
721	12:01
780	13:00
1439	23:59

Test your program by executing it several times with a different value in the range 0 to 1439 as input data.

[Hint: there is some useful information in Tip 5.3.]

◇ **5.9** Write a program that reads in the values of u, v, w and x and then outputs the values of the following four quantities:

$$(u + 2v)(3w + 4x)$$

$$e^{\frac{u}{v} - wx}$$

$$\tan \frac{u - v}{10}$$

$$\frac{u}{27v^{\frac{w}{x}}}$$

Execute the program on the computer using the values 11.6, 3.8, 2.1 and 0.9 in the data (for u, v, w and x). Your program should output the values: 190.08, 3.198338892539846, 0.989261536876605 and 0.019066274132472843. If you fail to get these values, check that you have used the correct formulae.

◇ **5.10** Suppose you are interested in how much money you have to repay each month for a mortgage. The monthly repayment figure is given by:

$$\frac{p \times \frac{r}{1200} \times \left(1 + \frac{r}{1200}\right)^{12t}}{\left(1 + \frac{r}{1200}\right)^{12t} - 1}$$

where p is the amount of the loan, r is the annual rate of interest (e.g. 5.5) and t is the number of years that you will be paying back the mortgage.

Write a program that reads in the values of p, r and t and then outputs the amount that has to be repaid each month. Ensure that your program rounds the amount to the nearest penny.

Execute the program in order to find the repayment amount for a loan of £75 000 taken over 25 years when the annual rate of interest is 5.5%. Although the formula produces the value 460.56561921110034, after rounding you should find that the monthly repayment is £460.57.

5.11 Write a program that reads in a whole number representing a temperature in degrees Fahrenheit and then outputs the whole number that is nearest to the corresponding value in degrees Celsius. Assume that the value in the data is greater than or equal to 32.

Here are some examples of the output that your program should produce:

data	output
32	0
50	10
51	11
52	11
53	12
54	12

Test your program by executing it several times with a different value in the data.

[Hint: one way of outputting the nearest whole number to a `double` value is described in Section 5.4.2.]

5.12 Write a program that uses the ideas of the program given in Figure 4.7 to read the x and y coordinates of the two points that are the SW and NE corners of a rectangle; creates four variables of class `Point` (of the package `java.awt`) that represent the SW, NW, NE and SE corners of the rectangle; and then calculates the length of the diagonal joining the NW and the SE corners.

Execute the program using the values `100:100` and `400:500` in the data. The value 500.0 should be output.

5.13 Write a program that reads a string containing a time in 24-hour format, e.g. `11:42:44`, and then outputs the number of seconds since midnight that this time is.

Here are some examples of the output that your program should produce:

data	output
00:00:00	0
00:59:59	3599
01:00:00	3600
11:59:00	43140
12:01:00	43260
13:00:00	46800
23:59:59	86399

Test your program by executing it several times with different times in the data.

Chapter 6

Using if statements to make decisions

Programs are very boring if they consist of a sequence of statements in which each statement of the sequence is always executed and is always executed once. Java has two kinds of statements that make programs more exciting! They are:

- conditional statements, which are used for making decisions

- looping statements, which are used to execute a group of statements a number of times

We will look at one of the forms of conditional statements, the *if statement*, in this chapter, and at one of the looping statements (the *for statement*) in the next chapter. The other forms of conditional and looping statements will be considered in Chapter 9.

In order to help the discussion of *if statements*, this chapter also introduces the primitive type `boolean`.

This chapter also contains an initial skirmish with the idea of *scope*.

6.1 The need for an if statement

Some employees get overtime pay if they have worked more than the normal number of hours. So if we have a payroll program, it should calculate and add in overtime pay if and only if the required number of hours has been worked. Programming languages provide conditional statements that can be used to decide at runtime whether to execute a sequence of statements or not.

In Java, the keyword `if` is used in a similar way to which it is used in English. For example, the sentence:

> if the bar is open, get me a beer; otherwise get me a coffee

has the same sort of meaning as the following piece of Java:

```
Drink tBeer, tCoffee, tDrink;
...
if (tBar.isOpen(tTimeNow))
{
    tDrink = tBeer;
}
else
{
    tDrink = tCoffee;
}
```

The syntax of an **if statement** is given in Figure 6.1. An if statement is in three parts. In the first part, there is a *BooleanExpression*. The second part consists of a *Statement*: we will refer to this *Statement* as the **then part** of the if statement. The final part of an if statement is optional: the *Statement* following an `else` will be called the **else part**.

Back in Section 2.1, we saw that the most important part of a program is its *Block*: this is the sequence of statements that are executed when we run the program. When

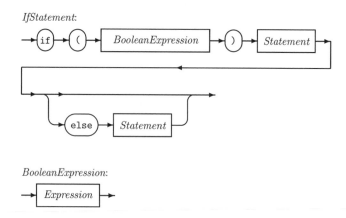

Figure 6.1   The syntax of an if statement.

programming in Java, we will find other situations where it will be useful to group statements together to form a *Block*. For example, we will often want a program to execute one sequence of statements if the condition of an if statement is true, and a different sequence if it is false. The syntax diagram for *Statement* given earlier (in Figure 2.2) was simplified: in the complete version shown in Figure 6.2, you can see that *Block* is one of the possibilities for a *Statement*, and so we can use a *Block* in the then part or the else part of an if statement.

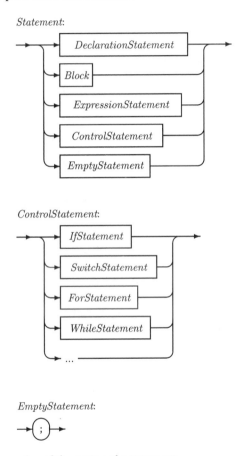

Figure 6.2   A complete version of the syntax of a statement.

In this book, for the reasons explained in Tip 6.2, we will always use a *Block* as the *Statement* in both the then part and the else part. So we will use if statements as if they have the syntax shown in Figure 6.3. This syntax is illustrated by the drinks example given earlier. The only time when this syntax will not be adopted is when we need a *cascaded if statement*: this kind of if statement will be introduced in Section 6.7.

We have seen that an *IfStatement* is defined in terms of one or more *Statements*. One (or more) of these *Statements* could itself be an *IfStatement*. Later, we will see examples where this in fact happens. A definition that is given in terms of itself is called a **recursive definition**.

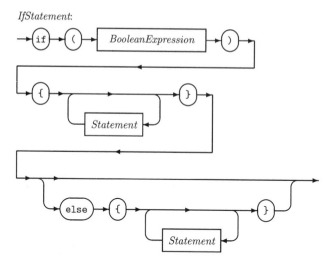

IfStatement:

Figure 6.3   The syntax that is normally used in this book.

6.2 Two examples comparing values of a primitive type

We will look at two programs: both programs will contain an if statement, one without an else part and the other with. The programs are given in Figure 6.4 and Figure 6.5. Both programs read in a value and output the square root of that value. And both programs use an if statement to ensure that they do not attempt to find the square root of a negative number.

Program Sqrt2 is a little more friendly, because it outputs a message if we do supply a negative number. To be more specific: in program Sqrt2, a choice is made as to whether to execute the two statements:

```
final double tSqrtX = Math.sqrt(x);
System.out.print("The square root of this value is: " + tSqrtX);
```

or the statement:

```
System.out.print("This value is negative");
```

This choice depends on the value of the expression:

```
x>=0.0
```

i.e. on whether the value of x is greater than or equal to zero.

This expression either has the value *true* or the value *false*. Such an expression is called a **condition**. It is a **boolean expression**, because it has the type boolean. There is more about the type boolean in Section 6.13.

If the value of the condition is *true*, the *then part* is executed (and the *else part* is ignored). Alternatively, if the value of the condition is *false*, the else part is executed (and the then part is ignored). One other thing: an if statement has no effect if the condition has the value *false* and there is no else part.

```
// This program reads in a value and outputs its square root.
// Barry Cornelius, 3 June 2000
import java.io. BufferedReader;
import java.io. InputStreamReader;
import java.io. IOException;
public class Sqrt1
{
    public static void main(final String[] pArgs) throws IOException
    {
        final BufferedReader tKeyboard =
                        new BufferedReader(new InputStreamReader(System.in));
        System.out.print("Type in a value: ");
        System.out.flush();
        final String tLine = tKeyboard.readLine();
        final double x = Double.parseDouble(tLine);
        if (x>=0.0)
        {
            final double tSqrtX = Math.sqrt(x);
            System.out.println("The square root of this value is: " + tSqrtX);
        }
    }
}
```

Figure 6.4 A program with an `if` that has no `else`.

```
// This program reads in a value and outputs its square root.
// It outputs an error message if the data value is negative.
// Barry Cornelius, 3 June 2000
import java.io. BufferedReader;
import java.io. InputStreamReader;
import java.io. IOException;
public class Sqrt2
{
    public static void main(final String[] pArgs) throws IOException
    {
        final BufferedReader tKeyboard =
                        new BufferedReader(new InputStreamReader(System.in));
        System.out.print("Type in a value: ");
        System.out.flush();
        final String tLine = tKeyboard.readLine();
        final double x = Double.parseDouble(tLine);
        if (x>=0.0)
        {
            final double tSqrtX = Math.sqrt(x);
            System.out.print("The square root of this value is: " + tSqrtX);
        }
        else
        {
            System.out.print("This value is negative");
        }
        System.out.println();
    }
}
```

Figure 6.5 A program with an `if` that does have an `else`.

When a boolean expression has operands whose types are the numeric types (such as int or double), the operator can be one of the six **relational operators**:

operator	meaning
==	is equal to
!=	is not equal to
<	is less than
<=	is less than or equal to
>	is greater than
>=	is greater than or equal to

If the operands are of different numeric types, *numeric promotion* will be used on one of the operands. As we are mainly using the types int and double, this means an int operand will be converted into a double if the other operand is a double. Having done this, either floating-point comparison or integer comparison is then used depending on the final types of the operands.

6.3 Comparing Point objects

Although all six relational operators may be used with values that are of a primitive type, only the == and != operators may be used with values that are of a *reference type*, i.e. with variables that point to some object. Suppose we have declared:

```
final Point tFirstPoint = new Point(100,200);
final Point tOtherPoint = tFirstPoint;
final Point tClonePoint = new Point(tFirstPoint);
```

This is a situation illustrated by the following diagram:

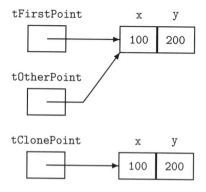

When the == operator is used between two reference variables, we are finding out whether they are pointing to the same object. So the boolean expression tFirstPoint==tOtherPoint has the value *true* whereas tFirstPoint==tClonePoint has the value *false*. So the following if statement outputs the string `"different objects"`:

```
if (tFirstPoint==tClonePoint)
{
    System.out.print("same objects");
}
else
{
    System.out.print("different objects");
}
```

Instead of finding out whether two reference variables are pointing to the same object, you may want to find out whether the values of the objects (to which they are pointing) are the same. You can often do this by using a method called equals. At the call of the equals method, one of the objects is used as the *target object* and the other object is passed as an argument:

```
if (tFirstPoint.equals(tClonePoint))
{
    System.out.print("same values");
}
else
{
    System.out.print("different values");
}
```

Given the variables declared earlier, this would output the string `"same values"`.

The text given above says '*You can often do this by using a method called* equals'. The word *often* is used because whether there is an appropriate equals method depends on the person who wrote the class: they need to provide a method called equals. Most of the classes of the Core APIs have a method called equals, and when we come to defining our own classes we will look at how to provide an appropriate equals method.

6.4 Reference variables may have the value null

The purpose of a reference variable is to point to some object (which will have been created using some class instance creation expression). However, later, we will find that occasionally it will be useful to be able to indicate that a reference variable is currently not pointing to an object. This can be done by assigning a special value to the reference variable. In a program, we can refer to this special value by using the symbol null:

```
tFirstPoint = null;
```

And you can use null with a == operator if you want to test whether a reference variable is currently not pointing to an object, e.g.:

```
if (tFirstPoint==null) ...
```

Or you can use ! = if you want to test whether a reference variable is pointing to an object, e.g.:

```
if (tFirstPoint!=null) ...
```

We will see real reasons for using null later.

6.5 Comparing String objects

The ideas about comparing Points and the use of null that were introduced in the last two sections apply to all objects including objects of the class String.

So, although it is tempting to use something:

```
String tCommand = tKeyboard.readLine();
if (tCommand=="quit") ...
```

to test whether the user has typed in a particular string, the use of == is wrong because of the reasons given in Section 6.3. Instead, the designers of the java.lang.String class have provided a method called equals that can be used to compare two strings:

```
String tCommand = tKeyboard.readLine();
if (tCommand.equals("quit")) ...
```

It is usually wrong to use == with two string objects: use equals instead.

If you want to check whether the line of data is empty (because the user of the program did not type any characters on the line), you can use a string literal representing the *empty string*:

```
String tCommand = tKeyboard.readLine();
if (tCommand.equals("")) ...
```

Back in Section 3.4.5, we met a number of methods provided by the class java.lang.String, and we have now met another one: equals. Besides equals, the class has other methods that deliver results of type boolean. They include equalsIgnoreCase, startsWith and endsWith. Details about these methods are given at $API/java/lang/String.html and in Figure 6.6.

Some of the possibilities with strings are shown by the StringCompare program that is given in Figure 6.7.

```
public boolean equals(Object pObject);
    Returns the value true if and only if the target string and the string pObject
    are the same sequence of characters.
public boolean equalsIgnoreCase(String pString);
    Returns the value true if and only if the target string and the string pString
    are the same sequence of characters when the case of any letters is ignored.
public boolean startsWith(String pString);
    Returns the value true if and only if the target string starts with the string
    pString.
public boolean endsWith(String pString);
    Returns the value true if and only if the target string ends with the string
    pString.
```

Figure 6.6 Methods of the java.lang.String class that return a boolean.

```java
// This program reads in strings and compares them.
// Barry Cornelius, 3 June 2000
import java.io. BufferedReader;
import java.io. InputStreamReader;
import java.io. IOException;
public class StringCompare
{
    public static void main(final String[] pArgs) throws IOException
    {
        final BufferedReader tKeyboard =
                    new BufferedReader(new InputStreamReader(System.in));
        System.out.print("Type in a string: ");
        System.out.flush();
        final String tFirstString = tKeyboard.readLine();
        System.out.print("Now type in another string: ");
        System.out.flush();
        final String tSecondString = tKeyboard.readLine();

        if (tFirstString==tSecondString)
        {
            System.out.println("The same string objects are being used");
        }
        else
        {
            System.out.println("Different string objects are being used");
        }

        if (tFirstString.equals(tSecondString))
        {
            System.out.println("The two strings have the same characters");
        }
        else
        {
            System.out.println("The two strings have different characters");
        }

        if (tFirstString.equalsIgnoreCase(tSecondString))
        {
            System.out.println("Ignoring case, they are the same string");
        }
        else
        {
            System.out.println("Even ignoring case, they are different");
        }
```

Figure 6.7   *Continues on the next page.*

```
if (tFirstString.startsWith("I love"))
{
    final String tObjectOfAffection = tFirstString.substring(6);
    System.out.println("You love" + tObjectOfAffection);
}

if (tFirstString.endsWith(tSecondString))
{
    System.out.println("The 1st string ends with the 2nd string");
}
        }
    }
```

Figure 6.7 A program illustrating some possibilities when comparing two strings.

6.6 Enquiring about characters

Having obtained a character value (e.g. by using `java.lang.String`'s `charAt` method), you may want to enquire about what kind of character it is. The class `java.lang.Character` provides some appropriate methods: details about these methods are given at $API/java/lang/Character.html and in Figure 6.8.

```
public static boolean isDigit(char pChar);
    Returns the value true if and only if the character pChar is a digit.
public static boolean isLetter(char pChar);
    Returns the value true if and only if the character pChar is a letter.
public static boolean isLowerCase(char pChar);
    Returns the value true if and only if the character pChar is a lower-case letter.
public static boolean isSpaceChar(char pChar);
    Returns the value true if and only if the character pChar is a space character.
public static boolean isUpperCase(char pChar);
    Returns the value true if and only if the character pChar is an upper-case letter.
public static boolean isWhiteSpace(char pChar);
    Returns the value true if and only if the character pChar is a whitespace character.
```

Figure 6.8 Methods of the `java.lang.Character` class.

Here is an example of the use of one of these methods:

```
final String tCommand = tKeyboard.readLine();
final char tFirstChar = tCommand.charAt(0);
if (Character.isLetter(tFirstChar)) ...
```

Here the then part will only be executed if the first character of the line is a letter. Note that all the methods mentioned in Figure 6.8 have declarations using the `static` keyword. So they are all class methods. This is reflected in how the methods are called (as is shown above in the call of `isLetter`).

6.7 Cascaded if statements

Suppose we wish to output an appropriate message depending on whether x>y, x==y or x<y. Here is one attempt:

```
if (x>y)
{
    System.out.print("x is bigger");
}
if (x==y)
{
    System.out.print("both the same");
}
if (x<y)
{
    System.out.print("y is bigger");
}
```

This is a bad way of doing the job. It is bad because three conditions will always be tested.

We should instead recognise that only one of them can be *true* – the three conditions are said to be **mutually exclusive**. The fact that they are mutually exclusive should be reflected in the program by using a **cascaded if statement**, an if statement that is formed from a cascade of if statements:

```
if (x>y)
{
    System.out.print("x is bigger");
}
else if (x==y)
{
    System.out.print("both the same");
}
else
{
    System.out.print("y is bigger");
}
```

Writing the code like this means that at most two conditions will be tested (and if x is greater than y, only one condition will be tested). If a condition is more likely to be true, it is usually best to put it as the first one to be tested.

◇ 6.8 Handling the special cases of a quadratic equation

When the quadratic equation problem was considered in Section 5.8.3, we ignored the difficulties that arise when a is zero or $b^2 < 4ac$. We now use if statements to cater for these special cases.

The new version of the program requires the following two steps to be executed:

1. Read coefficients into a, b and c.

2. If a is zero
   then Output an error message
   else Solve quadratic equation and output its roots.

The notation used in this informal description of the code of a program will be called **pseudo-code**. Further details about this notation appear in Curio 7.1.

In order to solve the subproblem *Solve quadratic equation and output its roots*, the program needs to distinguish between the three cases:

$b^2 > 4ac$,   i.e. real roots
$b^2 = 4ac$,   i.e. equal roots – there are two roots at $x = -b/2a$
$b^2 < 4ac$,   i.e. complex roots

As there are three mutually exclusive cases, it is appropriate to use a cascade of if statements. So, here is some pseudo-code for the subproblem *Solve quadratic equation and output its roots*:

1. Work out the value of the discriminant, $b^2 - 4ac$.

2. If the discriminant is zero
   then Deal with the equal roots case
   else If the discriminant is greater than zero
        then Deal with the real roots case
        else Deal with the complex roots case.

We will need a boolean expression in order to represent the condition *the discriminant is zero*. The obvious expression is:

```
tDiscriminant==0.0
```

However, because of the inaccuracies associated with the representation of double values, it is usual to avoid equality tests with double values. So instead of testing whether the discriminant is exactly equal to zero, we will test whether it is close to zero. By *close to zero*, we mean that its magnitude is small, say, less than 10^{-8}. This can be expressed in Java by the boolean expression:

```
Math.abs(tDiscriminant)<tCloseToZero
```

where tCloseToZero is a variable having the value 10^{-8}.

The Java code that evolves from the above pieces of pseudo-code is shown in Figure 6.9.

The outer if statement of this program is 32 lines long, and it is concerned with a number of unrelated tasks. In Chapter 8, we will look at a technique for producing code that results in the code appearing in chunks that are smaller and not so complicated. This will lead to programs that are a lot easier to understand.

```
// This program reads in the coefficients of a quadratic equation and
// outputs its two roots.  It may have real, complex, or equal roots.
// Barry Cornelius, 3 June 2000
import java.io. BufferedReader;
import java.io. InputStreamReader;
import java.io. IOException;
public class QeIfs
{
   public static void main(final String[] pArgs) throws IOException
   {
      final double tCloseToZero = 1.0E-8;
      final BufferedReader tKeyboard =
                  new BufferedReader(new InputStreamReader(System.in));
      System.out.print("Type in the value of a: ");
      System.out.flush();
      String tLine = tKeyboard.readLine();
      final double a = Double.parseDouble(tLine);
      System.out.print("Type in the value of b: ");
      System.out.flush();
      tLine = tKeyboard.readLine();
      final double b = Double.parseDouble(tLine);
      System.out.print("Type in the value of c: ");
      System.out.flush();
      tLine = tKeyboard.readLine();
      final double c = Double.parseDouble(tLine);
      if (Math.abs(a)<tCloseToZero)
      {
         System.out.println("The equation is not a quadratic equation");
      }
      else
      {
         final double tDiscriminant = b*b - 4.0*a*c;
         if (Math.abs(tDiscriminant)<tCloseToZero)
         {
            // deal with equal roots
            System.out.print("The quadratic equation has two roots at: ");
            System.out.println(-b/(2.0*a));
         }
         else if (tDiscriminant>0.0)
         {
            // deal with real roots
            final double tSqrtPart = Math.sqrt(tDiscriminant);
            final double tRoot1 = (-b + tSqrtPart)/(2.0*a);
            final double tRoot2 = (-b - tSqrtPart)/(2.0*a);
            System.out.print("Quadratic has real roots at: ");
            System.out.println(tRoot1 + " and " + tRoot2);
         }
```

Figure 6.9 *Continues on the next page.*

```
            else
            {
                // deal with complex roots
                final double tReal = -b/(2.0*a);
                final double tImag = Math.abs(Math.sqrt(-tDiscriminant)/(2.0*a));
                System.out.println("Quadratic has complex roots at: ");
                System.out.println("    " + tReal + "+I*" + tImag);
                System.out.println("and " + tReal + "-I*" + tImag);
            }
        }
    }
}
```

Figure 6.9 Dealing with the special cases of a quadratic equation.

6.9 More about the layout of programs

Note the use of indenting in the QeIfs program. As far as the compiler is concerned, all the indenting is ignored. The objective of the indenting is to ensure that the structure of the program is immediately obvious to a (human) reader without them having to analyse the language constructs that are being used. In this way, programs are much easier to read, understand and maintain.

The actual method of indenting is either one of personal preference or one used by your company. In this book, the indenting style places both the { and the } of a then part under the if and indents the statements that appear in between. If there is an else part, its else, its { and its } are all placed under the if, and the statements that appear in the else part are indented. For a cascaded if statement, the final else and all of the intermediate occurrences of else if are placed under the opening if.

There is another common style of indenting if statements which is different from that used in this book. Examples illustrating this alternative style are shown in Curio 6.6.

Note that indenting by one or two columns is probably insufficient to show the structure of a program – you should indent by three or four columns. If you indent by more than this, you may find yourself typing text off the right-hand side of the window! This will be inconvenient!

6.10 The scope of the identifier of a variable

Consider the program given in Figure 6.10. There are three declarations of tValue in this program. Whenever you declare an identifier, a new variable is introduced. So, in this program, there are three variables called tValue.

The text in which you are allowed to refer to a particular identifier is called the **scope** of the identifier. For an identifier that is used for a variable, the scope runs from the declaration of the variable to the end of the block in which the variable declaration appears. The variable is said to be a **local variable** of that block.

```
// This program illustrates the scope of the identifier of a variable.
// Barry Cornelius, 3 June 2000
public class VariableScope
{
    public static void main(final String[] pArgs)
    {
        System.out.println("start of program");
        int tCheck = 1;                                              /*C*/
        System.out.println("tCheck is: " + tCheck);                 /*C*/
        if (tCheck==1)                                              /*C*/
        {                                                          /*C*/
            System.out.println("start of then part");              /*C*/
            int tValue = 42;                              /*T*/     /*C*/
            System.out.println("tValue is: " + tValue);   /*T*/     /*C*/
            System.out.println("end of then part");       /*T*/     /*C*/
        }                                                          /*C*/
        else                                                       /*C*/
        {                                                          /*C*/
            System.out.println("start of else part");              /*C*/
            int tValue = 27;                              /*E*/     /*C*/
            System.out.println("tValue is: " + tValue);   /*E*/     /*C*/
            System.out.println("end of else part");       /*E*/     /*C*/
        }                                                          /*C*/
        System.out.println("after the if statement");              /*C*/
        int tValue = 0;                                   /*O*/     /*C*/
        System.out.println("tValue is: " + tValue);       /*O*/     /*C*/
        System.out.println("end of program");             /*O*/     /*C*/
    }
}
```

Figure 6.10   This program illustrates the scope of the identifier of a variable.

For an example, consider the tValue variable declared in the then part of the
VariableScope program. This variable is a *local variable* of the block that forms
the then part. The scope of this variable are the three lines that have been marked
with the /*T*/ comment. Similarly, the else part also has a local variable called
tValue. The scope of this tValue and the outer tValue are indicated by the
/*E*/ and /*O*/ comments. And the scope of the tCheck variable is indicated by
/*C*/ comments.

In this section, we have looked at the scope of identifiers that are declared by
variable declarations. We will look at the scope of other kinds of identifiers later.
There are some other comments about the scope of an identifier declared in an
if statement in Tip 6.3 and Tip 6.4.

6.11 More about boolean expressions

The boolean expressions given in this book so far have just compared one value with
another value. For this, we have been using the six relational operators. However,

it is often necessary to construct boolean expressions that involve more than one condition. This is done using the **logical operator**s: they are `&&` meaning *and*, `||` meaning *or* and `!` meaning *not*.

Here is an example involving the `&&` operator. Suppose we want to output a message if a program is being used on Christmas Day:

```
if (tDayOfMonth==25 && tMonthNumber==12)
{
    tNumberOfSadPeople++;
    System.out.println("Merry Christmas");
}
```

The then part will only be executed if the conditions `tDayOfMonth==25` and `tMonthNumber==12` both have the value *true*.

The boolean expression involving `==`, `&&` and `==` has been written without any additional parentheses. This is because the `==` operator has a higher priority than `&&`.

A simplified version of the rules for the priority of the operators was given earlier (in Section 5.6). We now give a more complete table of the priority of operators. There are now ten levels of priority:

Highest priority:	the use of (and) to form subexpressions
	`!`, the use of a cast
	`*`, `/`, `%`
	`+`, `-`
	`<`, `<=`, `>`, `>=`
	`==`, `!=`
	`&`
	`|`
	`&&`
Lowest priority:	`||`

Details about the `&` and `|` operators are given in Section 6.12.

If you are unsure about the priority of the operators `==` and `&&`, you may write the first line of the above if statement as:

```
if ((tDayOfMonth==25) && (tMonthNumber==12))
```

However, these additional parentheses are unnecessary.

Here is another example. Suppose that there are two variables, `tFreezing` and `tBoiling`, which contain the freezing point and the boiling point of some liquid. And suppose we want to test whether a temperature lies within this range. In mathematics, this condition could be expressed by the formula:

$$freezing < temperature < boiling$$

and for this reason you might be tempted to write:

```
if (tFreezing<tTemperature<tBoiling)
{
    ...
}
```

However, Java does not allow this sort of comparison. Instead we must write:

```
if (tTemperature>tFreezing && tTemperature<tBoiling)
{
    . . .
}
```

All the examples so far have illustrated the use of the && operator. Here is an example involving the use of the || operator. It is concerned with deciding whether a year is a leap year. We need to know that:

> Any year whose number is a multiple of 4 is a leap year, except that a year whose number is also a multiple of 100 but not of 400 is not a leap year.

Thus:

1900	not leap
1996	leap
1999	not leap
2000	leap
2001	not leap

The above rule for leap years can also be expressed in the following way:

> A year is a leap year if its number is *either* a multiple of 400 *or* a multiple of 4 but not of 100.

We can test whether an expression n is a multiple of d, i.e. is exactly divisible by d, by the boolean expression n%d==0. This is finding out whether the remainder of the division of n by d is zero. We can write this without parentheses because a % operator has a higher priority than an == operator. So, the above rule can be expressed in Java by:

```
if (tYear%400==0 || tYear%4==0 && tYear%100!=0)
{
    System.out.print("leap")
}
else
{
    System.out.print("not leap")
}
```

Note that this boolean expression uses the fact that an && operator has a higher priority than an || operator. So, although the first line could instead be written as:

```
if ((tYear%400==0) || (tYear%4==0 && tYear%100!=0))
```

these additional parentheses are unnecessary. However, as was pointed out in Tip 5.1, programmers often add superfluous parentheses to a complicated expression in order to make it easier to understand.

6.12 Short-circuit and full evaluation

In Java, boolean expressions containing the && and || operators are evaluated using **short-circuit evaluation**. This means that the subconditions of a boolean expression are evaluated from left to right only as far as is necessary in order to determine the value of the boolean expression.

So, the boolean expression b && c is evaluated in the following way:

1. Find the value of the subcondition b.

2. If it has the value *false*
   then The boolean expression has the value *false*
   else The boolean expression has the value of c.

Similarly, the boolean expression b || c is evaluated as follows:

1. Find the value of the subcondition b.

2. If it has the value *true*
   then The boolean expression has the value *true*
   else The boolean expression has the value of c.

Besides && and ||, Java also has two other *logical operators*, & and |. With these two operators, both operands are always evaluated. This is called **full evaluation**.

Consider the following fragment of Java code:

```
int tFirst = ...;
int tSecond = ...;
if (tSecond!=0 && tFirst%tSecond==0)
{
    System.out.println("The first value is a multiple of the second value");
}
```

Here the left operand of the && operator determines whether tSecond is non-zero, and, because a && operator is being used, the right operand is only evaluated if tSecond is non-zero.

Suppose a & operator is used instead:

```
...
if (tSecond!=0 & tFirst%tSecond==0)
...
```

Now, both operands will always be evaluated. If tSecond were to be zero, this would lead to an attempt to find the remainder of a division by zero.

Although in this book we will use && and || in preference to & and |, there are few occasions where the code is written so as to make use of the fact that short-circuit evaluation is being used.

6.13 Variables of the primitive type `boolean`

The type `boolean` is one of the primitive types of Java. It is a type that has only two values, *false* and *true*. Variables can be declared to be of this type in the usual way:

```
boolean tIsInDebugMode, tIsLeap, tHasElectricWindows;
```

Often `boolean` variables have names containing `Is` or `Has`.

We can assign values to such variables by means of assignment statements. This is often done using one of the literals *false* or *true*:

```
tIsInDebugMode = true;
```

However, the right-hand side can be a lot more complicated because, as we have already seen, the language has quite extensive facilities for writing expressions of type `boolean`:

```
tIsLeap = (tYear%400==0) || (tYear%4==0 && tYear%100!=0);
```

Such an assignment statement is a lot better than the following rather verbose equivalent:

```
if ((tYear%400==0) || (tYear%4==0 && tYear%100!=0))
{
    tIsLeap = true;
}
else
{
    tIsLeap = false;
}
```

Note also that the forms:

```
if (tIsLeap==true)
if (tIsLeap==false)
```

are usually written as:

```
if (tIsLeap)
if (! tIsLeap)
```

Here the `!` is the not operator. It is being applied to the boolean variable `tIsLeap`. So `! tIsLeap` has the value *true* if and only if `tIsLeap` has the value *false*.

Tips for programming and debugging

6.1   Although it may be tempting to use = to test whether two operands have the same value:

```
if (tDayOfMonth=25)
```

this is incorrect: the == operator has to be used. In Java, the = operator is used for assignment. The above error will be detected at compilation time: it will give an error message like:

```
Incompatible type for if. Can't convert int to boolean.
```

However, the use of = in this context is not always illegal. For example:

```
if (tIsLeap = (tYear%400==0) || (tYear%4==0 && tYear%100!=0))
```

is valid in Java: it assigns the value to the variable `tIsLeap` and then that value is used as the value of the boolean expression. Although the use of an assignment as an operand of an expression is allowed by Java, in this book, an assignment will always be used as a statement:

```java
tIsLeap = (tYear%400==0) || (tYear%4==0 && tYear%100!=0);
if (tIsLeap)
```

It is believed that such code is easier to understand.

6.2 In this book, both the then part and the else part will be written as blocks, i.e. both will start with a { symbol and end with a } symbol. This will be done even when either or both parts contain only one statement. There are a number of problems that arise if you do not do this.

Here is a legal if statement:

```java
if (a==0)
    if (b==0)
        System.out.println("a==0 and b==0");
    else
        System.out.println("a==0 and b!=0");
else
    System.out.println("a!=0");
```

But how about this:

```java
if (a==0)
    if (b==0)
        System.out.println("a==0 and b==0");
else
    System.out.println("a!=0");
```

To which `if` is this `else` matched? This is called the **dangling else** problem. In Java, the above is valid, but the indenting is misleading: an else part is matched to the nearest unmatched then part. So the Java compiler will interpret the above as if the programmer had written:

```java
if (a==0)
    if (b==0)
        System.out.println("a==0 and b==0");
    else
        System.out.println("a!=0");
```

which is not what was intended.

Suppose now we have the following if statement:

```java
if (a==0)
    if (b==0)
        System.out.println("a==0 and b==0");
    else
        System.out.println("a==0 and b!=0");
System.out.println("after the outer if");
```

Suppose that the case when a=0 and b!=0 should never occur, and so we have been asked to alter this code so that it outputs another line if this ever occurs. When maintaining code, it is easy to forget to add the { and } brackets when adding another statement to a then/else part that currently only has one statement. We may be tempted to produce:

```
if (a==0)
    if (b==0)
        System.out.println("a==0 and b==0");
    else
        System.out.println("a==0 and b!=0");
        System.out.println("ERROR: THIS SHOULD NOT OCCUR");
System.out.println("after the outer if");
```

Although indenting may convince us this is right, the above is equivalent to:

```
if (a==0)
    if (b==0)
        System.out.println("a==0 and b==0");
    else
        System.out.println("a==0 and b!=0");
System.out.println("ERROR: THIS SHOULD NOT OCCUR");
System.out.println("after the outer if");
```

Always writing then parts and else parts as blocks (even when they contain only one statement) avoids problems like these.

6.3   You will get a compilation error if you declare a variable in the then part or the else part of an if statement and then try to refer to this variable in a statement that follows the if statement. This is because the variable is now not in *scope*.

For example, suppose a line of data either contains data about a circle or a rectangle. You might write code like:

```
final String tLine = tKeyboard.readLine();
final StringTokenizer tTokens = new StringTokenizer(tLine);
if (tTokens.countTokens()==1)
{
    final char tShape = 'c';
    final String tRadiusString = tTokens.nextToken();
    final int tRadius = Integer.parseInt(tRadiusString);
}
else
{
    final char tShape = 'r';
    final String tWidthString = tTokens.nextToken();
    final int tWidth = Integer.parseInt(tWidthString);
    final String tHeightString = tTokens.nextToken();
    final int tHeight = Integer.parseInt(tHeightString);
}
```

```
...
if (tShape=='c')
{
    System.out.println("circle with radius " + tRadius);
}
else
{
    System.out.println("rectangle of size " + tWidth + " " + tHeight);
}
```

This code introduces two different variables called tShape. And because tRadius and the first tShape are declared in the block that is the then part, they can only be used in this block. So the attempts to use tRadius and tShape after the if statement produce compilation errors. Similar points apply to the variables declared in the else part.

To avoid this, the above code needs to be written as follows:

```
char tShape;
int tRadius = 0;
int tWidth = 0;
int tHeight = 0;
if (tTokens.countTokens()==1)
{
    tShape = 'c';
    final String tRadiusString = tTokens.nextToken();
    tRadius = Integer.parseInt(tRadiusString);
}
else
{
    tShape = 'r';
    final String tWidthString = tTokens.nextToken();
    tWidth = Integer.parseInt(tWidthString);
    final String tHeightString = tTokens.nextToken();
    tHeight = Integer.parseInt(tHeightString);
}
...
if (tShape=='c')
{
    System.out.println("circle with radius " + tRadius);
}
else
{
    System.out.println("rectangle of size " + tWidth + " " + tHeight);
}
```

Because the then part of the first if statement assigns a value to tRadius and the else part does not, it is necessary to assign a value to tRadius before this if statement. If you fail to do this, you will get a compilation error message like:

```
Variable tRadius may not have been initialized
```

if the program subsequently tries to use tRadius. With the above code, this compilation error will occur for the statement:

```
System.out.println("circle with radius " + tRadius);
```

A similar comment applies for both the tWidth and tHeight variables. However, the tShape variable is different. As it is assigned a value by both the then part and the else part, it does not need to be given a value before the execution of the first if statement.

6.4 Consider the following code:

```
int tValue;
...
if (... )
{
    int tValue;
    ...
```

Here there are two possibilities. First, you do want two variables, in which case using the same name is confusing: it would be better to use variables with different names. The other possibility is that the redeclaration is a mistake; you only want one variable called tValue.

Unlike other programming languages, Java does not allow you to write the above code: the above will lead to a compilation error. So, although the scope of any variable declared in the then part of an if statement is the text from the declaration to the end of the then part, in Java it is not possible for a statement preceding the if statement to declare a variable of the same name.

6.5 Mistakes are often made when a boolean expression contains subconditions (combined using the && or the || operator) and also contains uses of the != operator. For example, consider the following if statement:

```
if (tNumberOfPeople!=0 && tNumberOfSeatsLeft!=0)
{

    statement-sequence-1

}
else
{

    statement-sequence-2

}
```

The usual mistake is to write && when || is intended (or vice versa). So, in this example, is it right to write:

```
if (tNumberOfPeople!=0 && tNumberOfSeatsLeft!=0)
```

or do we really need:

```
if (tNumberOfPeople!=0 || tNumberOfSeatsLeft!=0)
```

Such complex conditions are easier to understand if they are re-coded so as to make the condition *more positive*. Often this can be achieved by *not*ing the condition and interchanging the two statement sequences.

De Morgan's laws can be used to *not* a condition. These laws state that:

1. $!(p||q)$ is the same as $(!p) \&\& (!q)$
2. $!(p\&\&q)$ is the same as $(!p) || (!q)$

In the if statement given earlier, we are *and*ing the subconditions `tNumberOfPeople!=0` and `tNumberOfSeatsLeft!=0`. According to the second law, *not*ing an *and*ed condition can also be achieved by *or*ing the results of *not*ing each subcondition. Thus, instead of using the above if statement, we can interchange the order of the then part and else part and use `||` with the subconditions `tNumberOfPeople==0` and `tNumberOfSeatsLeft==0`. So, the above if statement can be rewritten as:

```
if (tNumberOfPeople==0 || tNumberOfSeatsLeft==0)
{

    statement-sequence-2

}
else
{

    statement-sequence-1

}
```

If it is rewritten in this way, the if statement will be a lot easier to understand, and we are more likely to get it right.

6.6   In order to employ the technique of Tip 6.5, it is necessary for the if statement to have both a then part and an else part. So, what can we do if an if statement with a complex condition has no else part? For example:

```
if (tNumberOfPeople!=0 && tNumberOfSeatsLeft!=0)
{

    statement-sequence

}
```

Well, this statement might be easier to understand if it is rewritten as:

```
if (tNumberOfPeople==0 || tNumberOfSeatsLeft==0)
{
    // do nothing
}
```

```
else
{

    statement-sequence

}
```

6.7 In an if statement it is better to have a short then part and a long else part. Consider the program given in Figure 6.9. The outer if statement of this program is:

```
if (Math.abs(a)<tCloseToZero)
{
    System.out.println("The equation is not a quadratic equation");
}
else
{

    25 lines of code

}
```

So the then part is short and the else part is long. This statement is easier to read than:

```
if (Math.abs(a)>=tCloseToZero)
{

    25 lines of code

}
else
{
    System.out.println("The equation is not a quadratic equation");
}
```

6.8 The effect of any debugging statements can easily be switched on or off by embedding them in an if statement:

```
        ...
        final double tSqrtPart = Math.sqrt(tDiscriminant);
/**/    if (tIsInDebugMode)
/**/    {
/**/        System.out.println("*** value of tSqrtPart is: " + tSqrtPart);
/**/    }
        final double tRoot1 = (-b + tSqrtPart)/(2.0*a);
        ...
```

where tIsInDebugMode is a boolean variable. For example, it could be a variable that has been given the value *true*:

```
/**/    final boolean tIsInDebugMode = true;
```

6.9 If a program containing an if statement crashes (or fails in some other way), it may be useful to add debugging statements at the start of the *then part* and at the start of the *else part* (if it exists). This will help to confirm the path taken by the execution of a program.

Curios, controversies and cover-ups

6.1 The type boolean is named after George Boole, a 19th-century mathematician and logician. Although born in Lincoln (England), he spent his later years in Queen's College, Cork in Ireland. De Morgan's laws are named after Augustus De Morgan, another 19th-century mathematician and logician. He was born in India, but spent most of his life in England at the University of Cambridge and at UCL in London.

6.2 Although Section 6.2 says that the six operators <, <=, >, >=, == and != are all relational operators, this is strictly incorrect: only four of them are. The operators == and != are not relational operators: in the JLS, they are called **equality operators**. Besides the above four, there is one other relational operator: the instanceof operator. This operator will not be introduced until Curio 11.9.

6.3 Although C and C++ allow the condition of an if statement to be an arithmetic expression, this is not permitted in Java: the condition must be a boolean expression.

6.4 When a class provides a method called equals, the method should be *symmetric*, i.e. the value of a.equals(b) should always be the same as the value of b.equals(a).

6.5 Although a class often provides a method called equals, it is not usual to provide a notequals method. Instead of writing a.notequals(b), you could use the ! operator with a.equals(b), i.e.:

```
if (! a.equals(b))
```

6.6 In Section 6.9, you were recommended to use a particular style for the layout of if statements. An alternative style for the layout of if statements is shown by:

```
if (x>=0.0) {
    final double tSqrtX = Math.sqrt(x);
    System.out.print("The square root of this value is: " + tSqrtX);
} else   {
    System.out.print("This value is negative");
}
```

And here is an alternative style for the layout of a cascaded if statement:

```
if (x>y) {
    System.out.print("x is bigger");
} else if (x==y) {
    System.out.print("both the same");
} else {
    System.out.print("y is bigger");
}
```

6.7 Because of your experience of using `parseInt` and `parseDouble`, you may be tempted to use:

```
final String tAnswerString = tKeyboard.readLine();
final boolean tAnswer = Boolean.parseBoolean(tAnswerString);
```

in order to read a value of type `boolean`. However, the wrapper class `Boolean` (from the `java.lang` package) does not have a method called `parseBoolean`. Instead, it is possible to use `Boolean`'s `booleanValue` method:

```
final String tAnswerString = tKeyboard.readLine();
final Boolean tAnswerBoolean = new Boolean(tAnswerString);
final boolean tAnswer = tAnswerBoolean.booleanValue();
```

This can be abbreviated to:

```
final String tAnswerString = tKeyboard.readLine();
final boolean tAnswer = new Boolean(tAnswerString).booleanValue();
```

The `boolean` variable `tAnswer` will be assigned the value *true* if the string pointed to by `tAnswerString` is equal (ignoring case) to the string `"true"`. For all other strings (including strings containing any whitespace characters), it will have the value *false*.

Exercises

6.1 Modify your solution to Exercise 4.2 so that your program also outputs whether the person has a University of Durham e-mail address, i.e. an address ending in `@durham.ac.uk`.

◊ **6.2** Type in the `QeIfs` program given in Figure 6.9. Demonstrate that it distinguishes between the various kinds of quadratic equation by executing it several times with different values for a, b and c. Establish what happens for each of the sets of data given in Exercise 5.3. The third set of data should now produce the values $-0.3461538461538462 \pm 0.7733862118900345i$.

6.3 Modify your solution to Exercise 5.8 so that it outputs the time in terms of the 12-hour clock rather than the 24-hour clock. Here are some examples of what your program should produce:

data	output
1	12:01 a.m.
59	12:59 a.m.
60	1:00 a.m.
719	11:59 a.m.
721	12:01 p.m.
780	1:00 p.m.
1439	11:59 p.m.

Test your program using various values in the range 0 to 1439. In particular, use values that are close to where there should be a change in the program's behaviour. Some of these values are given in the above table.

6.4 An angle lying between 0 degrees and 360 degrees belongs to the first quadrant if its value is less than 90, to the second quadrant if its value lies between 90 and 180, to the third quadrant if it is between 180 and 270, or to the fourth quadrant if it is greater than 270. Write a program that reads in an integer representing an angle in degrees and then outputs a message stating which quadrant the angle is in. If the angle's value is 0, 180 or 360, the program should state that the angle coincides with the *x*-axis; or if it is 90 or 270 that it coincides with the *y*-axis. Make sure the program outputs an error message if the value in the data is outside the range 0 to 360.

6.5 Three integers can be used to represent a date. For example, the integers 2000, 11 and 4 can be used to represent the date of 4 November 2000. Write a program that reads in three integers, y, m and d, that are given on separate lines of the data. The program should then calculate the appropriate day of the week by using Zeller's congruence:

$$z = (700 + (26a - 2) \div 10 + d + b + b \div 4 + c \div 4 - 2c) \bmod 7$$

where the values of a, b and c are given by the table:

	if $m \leq 2$	if $m \geq 3$
$a =$	$m + 10$	$m - 2$
$b =$	$(y - 1) \bmod 100$	$y \bmod 100$
$c =$	$(y - 1) \div 100$	$y \div 100$

The notation $i \div j$ means the whole number division of i by j, and the notation $i \bmod j$ means the remainder of the whole number division of i by j. Your program should output the value of z. This will be in the range 0 to 6 where 0 means *Sunday*, 1 means *Monday*, and so on. Execute your program several times choosing dates such as the date on which you were born, today's date and the date of Christmas Day this year. Check that the answers that the program produces are correct.

[Note: the above formula is only appropriate for the Gregorian calendar. This calendar is mainly the work of a Jesuit mathematician and astronomer called Christopher Clavius. However, it is named after Pope Gregory XIII, who, on 24 February 1582, issued a papal bull abolishing the Julian calendar in all Catholic countries. Italy, Poland, Portugal and Spain adopted the calendar in 1582. To get the calendar right, 10 days had to be dropped, and so 4 October was followed by 15 October. The calendar was adopted by other countries at different times. For example, in the UK (and the USA), it was not adopted until 1752 when 11 days were lost between 2 and 14 September. Zeller's congruence was devised by a Reverend Zeller. For more information about calendars, see Claus Tøndering's WWW page at http://www.tondering.dk/claus/calendar.html.]

6.6 In the UK, the postage rate that applies for sending a letter by first class post depends on the weight of the letter. Currently, the first four steps of the scale are:

weight	postage rate
up to 60g	26p
up to 100g	39p
up to 150g	49p
up to 200g	60p

Write a program that reads in a weight and then outputs the appropriate postage rate. Your program should assume the weight is an integer. Ensure that your program does something sensible if a value outside the range 0 to 200 is supplied in the data.

[Hint: you should not use the && or & operators in your program.]

◇ **6.7** Suppose that the coefficients a, b and c of a quadratic equation are such that b^2 is very much greater than $4ac$. If the two roots are calculated using the formula:

$$x = \frac{-b \pm \sqrt{b^2 - 4ac}}{2a}$$

one of these calculations will involve forming the difference of two nearly equal numbers (since $\sqrt{b^2 - 4ac} \simeq |b|$). Modify the QeSimple program given in Figure 5.5 so that it calculates x_1 using the formula $x_1 = (-b + \sqrt{b^2 - 4ac})/2a$ if $b < 0$ and the formula $x_1 = (-b - \sqrt{b^2 - 4ac})/2a$ if $b > 0$. The program then calculates x_2 from the formula $x_2 = c/x_1$. Use this program to calculate the roots of the equation $x^2 - 200x + 5 = 0$. Compare these answers with those produced by the QeSimple program.

6.8 A line of data consists of two words which are separated by a space. Write a program that reads these words and outputs a line indicating the lexicographical ordering of the words.

Here are some examples of the output that your program should produce:

data	output
bored bread	bored comes before bread
bred bread	bred comes after bread
bord bord	bord is the same as bord
bord bourd	bord comes before bourd
a i	a comes before i

Here are some hints about how you can code the program:

1. Use an object of the class `java.util.StringTokenizer` (mentioned in Section 4.11) to help you parse the data.

2. Use `countTokens` (mentioned in Figure 4.5) to check whether there are two words. If there are not exactly two words, the program should output an error message and not complete the next two steps.

3. Use `compareTo` (mentioned in Figure 3.9) to compare the strings.

4. Use a cascaded if statement to cope with the values that `compareTo` can return.

6.9 The **Fujita Tornado Scale** was devised by Theodore Fujita and Allen Pearson in 1971. It classifies tornadoes according to how much damage they cause:

force	description	speed (in mph)
F0	light	40–72
F1	moderate	73–112
F2	considerable	113–157
F3	severe	158–206
F4	devastating	207–260
F5	incredible	261–318

Write a program that reads in an integer representing a speed in miles per hour and then outputs the appropriate *force* and *description*. Ensure that your program does something sensible if a value outside the range 40 to 318 is supplied in the data.

[Hint: you should not use the && or & operators in your program.]

6.10 Write a program that reads a number of minutes since midnight and then outputs whether the time is in the morning, the afternoon, the evening or is during the night. Here are some examples of what your program should output:

data	output
1	Good night
450	Good morning
900	Good afternoon
1080	Good evening

Test your program using various values in the range 0 to 1439.

[Note: you can suppose that *morning* starts at 5 a.m. (which is 300 minutes past midnight), that *afternoon* starts at 12.01 p.m. (which is at 721 minutes), that *evening* starts at 6 p.m. (1080 minutes) and that *night* starts at 10 p.m. (1320 minutes).]

6.11 Write a program that reads in two grid references. It then finds out whether both grid references are in the same square (i.e. both grid references start with the same first two letters). If this is the case, it determines the distance (in kilometres) between the two points; otherwise it outputs the string `"Too hard!"`.

[Note: there is some background information about grid references in Exercise 3.1.]

Chapter 7

Using for statements to repeat statements

Programs often need to do the same task more than once using different data each time. Java has three statements that can be used for repeating a statement: they are the *for statement*, the *while statement* and the *do statement*. In this chapter we will look at the *for statement*: the other two looping statements will be considered in Chapter 9.

7.1 The need for a for statement

Not so many people these days know much about knitting patterns. The patterns have to use a complicated language to try to ensure that there is no ambiguity in the instructions that are used for producing the desired end-product. Here is a typical instruction:

(P.1, K.1) 6 times

It happens to be taken from a knitting pattern for making bootees for a baby.

In just the same way that knitting patterns use a notation to indicate that a group of instructions is to be repeated a certain number of times, in a program we may want to indicate that a group of statements is to be repeated a certain number of times. For this, Java has a *for statement*. The Java equivalent of the above knitting instruction is:

```
final KnittingMachine tKnittingMachine = new KnittingMachine();
final int tNumberStitches = 6;
for (int tStitchNumber = 1; tStitchNumber<=tNumberStitches; tStitchNumber++)
{
    tKnittingMachine.purl(1);
    tKnittingMachine.knit(1);
}
```

7.2 The *ForBody* part of a for statement

The syntax of a **for statement** is shown in Figure 7.1. The main part of the for statement is the *ForBody* that appears after the) symbol. When a for statement is executed, it is this *ForBody* that is repeatedly executed.

As you can see from one of the syntax diagrams in Figure 7.1, the *ForBody* is a *Statement*. Earlier, in Figure 6.2, we saw that a *Statement* has many different forms: the one that is most often used with a for statement is the *Block*. However, for similar reasons to those given in Tip 6.2, in this book we will *always* use a *Block* for the *ForBody* (even when only one statement is inside the *Block*).

Note that a *ForStatement* is defined in terms of a *ForBody* which is a *Statement*; that this *Statement* is often a *Block*, i.e. a sequence of *Statements*; and that one (or more) of these *Statements* could itself be a *ForStatement*. So a for statement's body may contain a statement that is itself a for statement. Later, we will see examples where this in fact happens. So, like the definition of an if statement, the definition of a for statement is a *recursive definition*.

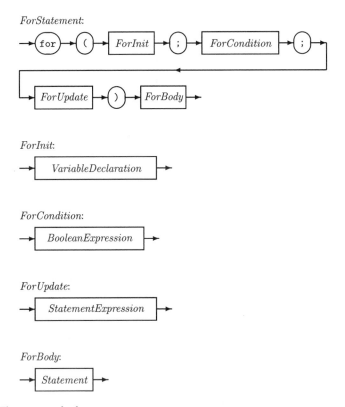

Figure 7.1   The syntax of a for statement.

7.3 The *ForInit, ForCondition* and *ForUpdate* parts

Preceding the *ForBody*, a for statement has some code within parentheses containing the *ForInit, ForCondition* and the *ForUpdate* parts. Although not mentioned in the syntax diagram shown in Figure 7.1, the *ForInit* part can be several *StatementExpressions* or a *VariableDeclaration*, and the *ForUpdate* part can be several *StatementExpressions*. Because of this flexibility, it is possible to produce for statements that do all sorts of wonderful things.

However, in this book, we will use for statements for a specific purpose: a for statement will be used to execute the *ForBody* many times giving a variable a different value just before each execution of the *ForBody*. So the *ForInit, ForCondition* and the *ForUpdate* parts of a for statement will be used to give this variable its values. This variable will be called the **control variable**.

So, as indicated in Figure 7.1, in this book the *ForInit* part will always be a *VariableDeclaration*. We will use this variable declaration to declare the control variable and to give the variable its initial value. So this variable declaration will always have an initializer.

Each time around the loop, before executing the *ForBody*, the value of the boolean expression of the *ForCondition* part is checked, and the loop terminates if it has the value *false*. We will use the boolean expression to check whether the control variable has reached a particular value.

A single *StatementExpression* will be used for the *ForUpdate* part. Each time, after the *ForBody* has been executed, this *StatementExpression* will be evaluated. This is the part of the for statement that we will use to change the value of the control variable, and, normally, it will be used to increase the value of the control variable by 1.

All these rules about how a for statement is executed are summarized by the diagram given in Figure 7.2. In this book, such a diagram will be called an **execution diagram**.

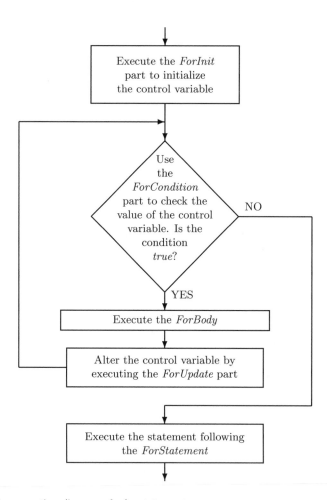

Figure 7.2   The execution diagram of a for statement.

7.4 The scope of a control variable

Back in Section 6.10, we discussed the *scope* of variables. For any variable, this is the portion of text in which you can use the variable. For a control variable, i.e. a variable that is declared in the *ForInit* part, the scope is the text of the for statement. Because of this, it is not possible to use this variable in code that appears after the for statement. There are some other comments about the scope of a control variable in Tip 7.8.

However, apart from the scope restriction, the control variable is just like any other variable. Having said that, the statements of the *ForBody* should not attempt to alter its value. This is considered to be bad programming practice.

So, back to the knitting pattern program: perhaps we ought to get the program to output the stitch number each time it goes round the loop. We can do this as follows:

```
final KnittingMachine tKnittingMachine = new KnittingMachine();
final int tNumberStitches = 6;
for (int tStitchNumber = 1; tStitchNumber<=tNumberStitches; tStitchNumber++)
{
    System.out.println("Stitch number " + tStitchNumber);
    tKnittingMachine.purl(1);
    tKnittingMachine.knit(1);
}
```

7.5 Handling more than one temperature conversion

Perhaps we have written a useful program and we now want to execute it with more than one set of data. We can do this by putting the statements of this program inside a for statement.

For example, the temperature conversion program given in Figure 5.4 only converts *one* temperature from Fahrenheit to Celsius and it may be that we have several such temperatures that need to be converted. One way of doing this is to include at the start of the data an integer that states the number of data values that we have. The program first reads this integer value and this lets the program know how many times to go round the loop.

Using *pseudo-code* (introduced in Section 6.8), the program can have the following steps:

1. Read in the value of tNumberOfTemperatures.

2. tNumberOfTemperatures times

   loop $\begin{cases} \text{1. Read in the °F value.} \\ \text{2. Calculate the °C value from the} \\ \quad\text{formula } \frac{5}{9} \text{ (°F value} - 32\text{).} \\ \text{3. Output the °C value.} \end{cases}$

The corresponding Java code for the program is shown in Figure 7.3.

```
// This program reads in a temperature in degrees Fahrenheit
// and outputs the corresponding value in degrees Celsius.
// Barry Cornelius, 3 June 2000
import java.io. BufferedReader;
import java.io. InputStreamReader;
import java.io. IOException;
public class TempFor
{
    public static void main(final String[] pArgs) throws IOException
    {
        final BufferedReader tKeyboard =
                    new BufferedReader(new InputStreamReader(System.in));
        System.out.print("How many temperatures are there to convert? ");
        System.out.flush();
        String tLine = tKeyboard.readLine();
        final int tNumberOfTemperatures = Integer.parseInt(tLine);
        for (int tTemperatureNumber = 1;
                tTemperatureNumber<=tNumberOfTemperatures;
                tTemperatureNumber++)
        {
            System.out.print("Type in a value in degrees Fahrenheit: ");
            System.out.flush();
            tLine = tKeyboard.readLine();
            final double tFahrenheit = Double.parseDouble(tLine);
            final double tCelsius = (tFahrenheit - 32.0)*5.0/9.0;
            System.out.println("In degrees Celsius, this is: " + tCelsius);
        }
    }
}
```

Figure 7.3   Handling more than one temperature conversion.

The data for the program might be:

```
3
32.0
98.6
212.0
```

Or, if you only had one temperature to convert, the data would look like:

```
1
68.0
```

The data could even be:

```
0
```

This last example warrants some further explanation. The value 0 will be read and stored in the variable tNumberOfTemperatures. So, the for statement effectively becomes:

```
for (int tTemperatureNumber = 1; tTemperatureNumber<=0; tTemperatureNumber++)
{
    System.out.print("Type in a value in degrees Fahrenheit: ");
    ...
    System.out.println("In degrees Celsius,this is: " + tCelsius);
}
```

Here the boolean expression (tTemperatureNumber<=0) has the value *false* the first time it is evaluated. If you look at the execution diagram (Figure 7.2), you will see that very little happens when such a for statement is executed: the control variable (tTemperatureNumber) is created and assigned the value of its initializer (i.e. the value 1), and, because the value of the boolean expression is *false*, the for statement is then terminated. So, in such a situation, the *ForBody* does not get executed.

7.6 Stepping by a value other than 1

It is normally the case that we want a control variable to increase by 1 each time a loop is executed. However, there are occasions when some other increment is required. If you look at the execution diagram (in Figure 7.2), you will see that the part of the for statement that is responsible for updating the control variable is the *ForUpdate* part. Looking at the syntax diagram (in Figure 7.1), you will see that the *ForUpdate* part is a *StatementExpression*. Figure 2.2 reveals that there are three main variants of a *StatementExpression*. Although a *ForUpdate* is seldom a *MethodInvocation*, and is sometimes an *Assignment*, it is usually an *IncrementDecrementExpression*.

Section 2.7 explains that an *IncrementDecrementExpression* uses an *increment operator* or a *decrement operator*. So far we have used an increment operator like tTemperatureNumber++ in order to increase the value of the control variable by 1.

In the Countdown program in Figure 7.4, the for statement has a *ForUpdate* part which is an *IncrementDecrementExpression* that uses a *decrement operator* to decrease the value of the control variable by 1:

```
for (int tSecondsToGo = 10; tSecondsToGo>=1; tSecondsToGo--)
{
    System.out.print(tSecondsToGo + " ");
    Thread.sleep(1000);
}
```

The sleep method from the class java.lang.Thread can be used to pause the execution of a program. This delay lasts for the amount of time in milliseconds passed as an argument to sleep. Thus, the call Thread.sleep(1000) will pause the execution for 1000 milliseconds, i.e. 1 second. The call of sleep may cause the checked exception java.lang.InterruptedException and, for this reason, the main method of the Countdown program has a *throws clause*.

The Countdown program outputs:

```
10 seconds to Lift Off: 10 9 8 7 6 5 4 3 2 1 Lift Off
```

```
// This program simulates a count down from 10 to 0.
// Barry Cornelius, 3 June 2000
public class Countdown
{
   public static void main(final String[] pArgs) throws InterruptedException
   {
      System.out.print("10 seconds to Lift Off: ");
      for (int tSecondsToGo = 10; tSecondsToGo>=1; tSecondsToGo--)
      {
         System.out.print(tSecondsToGo + " ");
         Thread.sleep(1000);
      }
      System.out.println("Lift Off");
   }
}
```

Figure 7.4 An example where the control variable is stepped by −1.

Another example where the control variable is decreased by 1 each time is given in Figure 7.5. In this program, a string is read in; then the length of the string is determined using the method `length` from the class `java.lang.String`; and then there is a for statement which outputs each character of the string but in reverse order starting with the last one and finishing up with first one. The program uses the

```
// This program reads in a string and outputs it backwards.
// Barry Cornelius, 3 June 2000
import java.io. BufferedReader;
import java.io. InputStreamReader;
import java.io. IOException;
public class StringBackwards
{
   public static void main(final String[] pArgs) throws IOException
   {
      final BufferedReader tKeyboard =
                     new BufferedReader(new InputStreamReader(System.in));
      System.out.print("Type in a string: ");
      System.out.flush();
      final String tInputString = tKeyboard.readLine();
      System.out.print("And here is it backwards: ");
      final int tStringLength = tInputString.length();
      for (int tCharNumber = tStringLength - 1;
                tCharNumber>=0; tCharNumber--)
      {
         System.out.print(tInputString.charAt(tCharNumber));
      }
      System.out.println();
   }
}
```

Figure 7.5 Stepping backwards through the characters of a string.

method called charAt to get hold of a particular character of the string. As was mentioned in Section 3.4.5, the int argument that is passed to charAt needs to be one less than the position: this means that you use an argument of 0 to get the first character, 1 to get the second character, and so on.

7.7 Using a loop to form a sum

One of the common uses of a for statement is to find the sum of a set of numbers. Suppose that a program is required that finds the average number of votes cast for the candidates of an election. So, the data for the program consists of the number of votes obtained by each of the candidates. And we will precede these values with an integer which indicates how many candidates there are in the election. For example the data might contain:

```
5
12
6
8
5
3
```

where the purpose of the first 5 is to indicate that there are five numbers following.

The problem can be solved by a program containing code for the following four subproblems:

1. Read in the value of tNumberOfCandidates.

2. Read in each number of votes, adding them into tTotalVotes.

3. Compute tAverage from tTotalVotes and tNumberOfCandidates.

4. Output tAverage.

The second subproblem needs further development:

1. Read in the value of tNumberOfCandidates.

2. Read in each number of votes, adding them into tTotalVotes.
   ‖ 1. Put the variable tTotalVotes equal to zero.
   ‖ 2. tNumberOfCandidates times loop
       { 1. Read in a number.
         2. Add it into tTotalVotes. }

3. Compute tAverage from tTotalVotes and tNumberOfCandidates.

4. Output tAverage.

An explanation of the notation used in this pseudo-code appears in Curio 7.1.

```
// This program reads in the number of votes obtained by each
// candidate in an election.  It then outputs the average of the
// number of votes obtained by the candidates.
// Barry Cornelius, 3 June 2000
import java.io. BufferedReader;
import java.io. InputStreamReader;
import java.io. IOException;
public class AvSimple
{
    public static void main(final String[] pArgs) throws IOException
    {
        final BufferedReader tKeyboard =
                    new BufferedReader(new InputStreamReader(System.in));
        System.out.print("How many candidates are there? ");
        System.out.flush();
        String tLine = tKeyboard.readLine();
        final int tNumberOfCandidates = Integer.parseInt(tLine);
        int tTotalVotes = 0;
        for (int tCandidateNumber = 1;
                tCandidateNumber<=tNumberOfCandidates; tCandidateNumber++)
        {
            System.out.println("Candidate number: " + tCandidateNumber);
            System.out.print("Type in number of votes for this candidate: ");
            System.out.flush();
            tLine = tKeyboard.readLine();
            final int tNumberOfVotes = Integer.parseInt(tLine);
            tTotalVotes += tNumberOfVotes;
        }
        final double tAverage = (double)tTotalVotes/tNumberOfCandidates;
        System.out.println("Average number of votes scored is: " + tAverage);
    }
}
```

Figure 7.6   Using a loop to form a sum.

Having produced the above pseudo-code for the problem, we can now write the code for the program to solve the problem. The AvSimple program is given in Figure 7.6.

The pseudo-code says that the program should read in the number of votes and then add that value into the tTotalVotes variable. This can be done by the assignment statement:

```
tTotalVotes += tNumberOfVotes;
```

Each time round the loop, the program is adding a new value into tTotalVotes. So, the sum of the number of votes is gradually being accumulated in the variable tTotalVotes.

The program declares tTotalVotes in the following way:

```
int tTotalVotes = 0;
```

Note that this declaration includes an initializer that gives the variable its initial value. Since we are forming a sum, the initial value of this variable is 0. It is quite common for programmers to forget to initialize variables like tTotalVotes. So, what would happen if we declared tTotalVotes but failed to initialize it?

```
int tTotalVotes;
```

With the Java programming language, our program would fail to compile (at the point where we use tTotalVotes) because, as mentioned earlier, it is not valid to use a *local variable* unless that variable has been given a value. The Java 2 SDK's compiler will give a compilation error such as:

```
AvSimple.java:28: Variable tTotalVotes may not have been initialized.
```

The purpose of the program is to output the average number of votes as a double value. In order to calculate the average, the program divides the value of tTotalVotes by the value of tNumberOfCandidates. We may be tempted to do this using:

```
final double tAverage = tTotalVotes/tNumberOfCandidates;
```

However, the variables tTotalVotes and tNumberOfCandidates are both of type int, and therefore this division will be done using integer division. For example, if tTotalVotes has the value 34 and tNumberOfCandidates has the value 5, the result of the division will be the int value 6. Instead, we probably would prefer to produce 6.8, i.e. a result of type double. We can do this if we *cast* one (or both) of the operands:

```
final double tAverage = (double)tTotalVotes/tNumberOfCandidates;
```

If we use this statement, then in our example the value 34.0 will be divided by 5 giving 6.8.

7.8 Using an if statement inside a for statement

Inside the *ForBody*, the statements may be any of the possible forms of statement. We look now at an example where one of the statements of the *Block* is an if statement.

This time, the problem is to read in a string of characters and only output those characters that are vowels: this means that the program should only output the a, A, e, E, i, I, o, O, u and U characters. A program that solves this problem is given in Figure 7.7.

If, when prompted, the user types:

```
The kitten sat on the mat.
```

this program will output:

```
Here are the vowels of this string: eieaoea
```

7.9 Using a for statement inside a for statement

The following statements output a row of five stars to the screen:

```
System.out.println("*****");
```

```
// This program reads in a string and outputs the characters that are vowels.
// Barry Cornelius, 3 June 2000
import java.io. BufferedReader;
import java.io. InputStreamReader;
import java.io. IOException;
public class StringVowels
{
    public static void main(final String[] pArgs) throws IOException
    {
        final BufferedReader tKeyboard =
                    new BufferedReader(new InputStreamReader(System.in));
        System.out.print("Type in a string: ");
        System.out.flush();
        final String tInputString = tKeyboard.readLine();
        System.out.print("Here are the vowels of this string: ");
        final int tStringLength = tInputString.length();
        for (int tCharNumber = 0; tCharNumber<tStringLength; tCharNumber++)
        {
            final char tChar = tInputString.charAt(tCharNumber);
            final char tLowerChar = Character.toLowerCase(tChar);
            if (tLowerChar=='a' || tLowerChar=='e' || tLowerChar=='i' ||
                            tLowerChar=='o' || tLowerChar=='u')
            {
                System.out.print(tChar);
            }
        }
        System.out.println();
    }
}
```

Figure 7.7 Using an if statement inside a for statement.

Here the number of stars that are output is fixed. If we want more control over the number of stars that are printed, we could use:

```
final int tNumberOfStars = 5;
for (int tColNumber = 1; tColNumber<=tNumberOfStars; tColNumber++)
{
    System.out.print('*');
}
System.out.println();
```

This loop is executed tNumberOfStars times, and each time round the loop a * is output.

It is important to use System.out.print('*') rather than System.out. println('*') inside the loop. If instead we used System.out.println('*'):

```
for (int tColNumber = 1; tColNumber<=tNumberOfStars; tColNumber++)
{
    System.out.println('*');
}
```

then each output of a star would be followed by a move to a new line. Thus, we would obtain tNumberOfStars lines of output each containing one star.

Suppose now that, instead of just outputting one row of stars, we want instead a *square of stars*, e.g.:

```
*****
*****
*****
*****
*****
```

We have seen that the statements:

```
for (int tColNumber = 1; tColNumber<=tNumberOfStars; tColNumber++)
{
    System.out.print('*');
}
System.out.println();
```

will output one row of stars. So, in order to output several rows of stars, the above statements need to be executed several times.

For example, if we had wanted two rows of stars we could use:

```
for (int tRowNumber = 1; tRowNumber<=2; tRowNumber++)
{
    for (int tColNumber = 1; tColNumber<=tNumberOfStars; tColNumber++)
    {
        System.out.print('*');
    }
    System.out.println();
}
```

This would produce the output:

```
*****
*****
```

However, we want a *square* of stars. So in fact the statements should not be executed twice: instead, they should be executed tNumberOfStars times:

```
final int tNumberOfStars = 5;
for (int tRowNumber = 1; tRowNumber<=tNumberOfStars; tRowNumber++)
{
    for (int tColNumber = 1; tColNumber<=tNumberOfStars; tColNumber++)
    {
        System.out.print('*');
    }
    System.out.println();
}
```

The **inner loop** is said to be **nested** inside the **outer loop**. So this kind of loop is called a **nested for loop**.

Here is another example: this time we will suppose that a *triangle of stars* is required, e.g.:

```
*
* *
* * *
* * * *
* * * * *
```

How are we to output this pattern? Note that on the first line one star is to be output; on the second line two stars are output; and so on. So the number of stars that are output is determined by the line number. It so happens that in the code fragments given above we have a variable (tRowNumber) which is increased by 1 each time the output moves on to a new line. So instead of repeating the inner loop tNumberOfStars times we need to repeat it tRowNumber times:

```
final int tNumberOfStars = 5;
for (int tRowNumber = 1; tRowNumber<=tNumberOfStars; tRowNumber++)
{
    for (int tColNumber = 1; tColNumber<=tRowNumber; tColNumber++)
    {
        System.out.print('*');
    }
    System.out.println();
}
```

In this section we have looked at examples of Java code where there is an inner loop inside an outer loop. We will see more examples like this later.

Tips for programming and debugging

7.1 In your keenness to ensure that each statement ends in a semicolon, you may be tempted to write:

```
for (int tStitchNumber = 1;
        tStitchNumber<=tNumberStitches; tStitchNumber++);
{
    tKnittingMachine.purl(1);
    tKnittingMachine.knit(1);
}
```

Here a semicolon has been typed at the end of the line containing the) symbol. This code introduces an **empty statement** after the) symbol, i.e. the body of the for statement is an empty statement. So each time round the loop of the for statement an empty statement will be executed. The statements that you wanted to be executed several times (the statements that appear within the { and the } symbols) will be executed only once (after the for statement has finished). An error like this is difficult to detect.

7.2   It is a common error to have a for statement that loops one too many times or that loops one too few times. (This is another example of a *one-off error*.) It does not help that Java has so many ways in which a for statement can be written. For example, if we want a loop that loops four times and we want a control variable that increases by 1 each time, all of the following are possible candidates for the for statement:

```
for (int tCount = 0; tCount<4;  tCount++) { ... }
for (int tCount = 0; tCount<=3; tCount++) { ... }
for (int tCount = 1; tCount<5;  tCount++) { ... }
for (int tCount = 1; tCount<=4; tCount++) { ... }
```

Well, sometimes it will be obvious whether you want to start from 0 or 1, in which case we are down to two possibilities, and these depend on whether you prefer the condition to be a < condition or a <= condition. This book recommends you use < when it is appropriate for the control variable to start from 0 and <= when the control variable starts from 1. With the above examples, you would choose either the first or the last example. If you do this, the value to the right of the < or the <= will be the number of times the loop is to be executed.

7.3   Given the freedom that Java gives us when writing for statements, it is easy to write for statements that loop for a long time:

```
for (int tCount = 0; tCount<4; tCount--) { ... }
for (int tCount = 4; tCount>0; tCount++) { ... }
```

This seems to get the program into an **infinite loop**, a loop that will continue for ever. In the above two examples, it has occurred because we have used tCount-- where we should have used tCount++, or vice-versa.

Even though both of the above two loops will continue for a long time, they are not actually infinite loops. With the second example, tCount is being increased by 1 each time; eventually tCount will reach the value 2147483647; then it will be incremented and get the value −2147483648; and then the condition tCount>0 will have the value *false*. Even though this loop does not create an infinite loop, it will take a long time to execute.

We could also produce this sort of loop if we use the wrong variable in one of the parts between the parentheses. For example, we might have:

```
for (int tCount = 1; tWrongVariable<=4; tCount++) { ... }
```

or:

```
for (int tCount = 1; tCount<=4; tWrongVariable++) { ... }
```

instead of:

```
for (int tCount = 1; tCount<=4; tCount++) { ... }
```

Details about how to get a program out of this sort of loop are given in the next tip.

7.4   Having just learned about the for statement, it will now be easy to write programs that get stuck in a loop. When using the Java 2 SDK's interpreter, you can abort the execution of the program by pressing **Ctrl/C** in the window used to run the java command. In order to press Ctrl/C, you need to hold down the Control key, press the C key, and then release the Control key.

7.5 Equally as embarrassing as getting a program into an infinite loop is writing code that does not do anything. Examples are:

```
for (int tCount = 1; tCount>=4; tCount++) { ... }
for (int tCount = 4; tCount<=1; tCount--) { ... }
```

Although it is never sensible to write these for statements, it is not *always* wrong to loop zero times: there are some occasions where we do want a for statement to do this.

7.6 Sometimes an execution error occurs during the execution of a for statement, and it is not immediately obvious as to which particular execution of the block of the for statement is causing the error to occur. In such a situation, it may be helpful to add to the block debugging statements that output the value of the control variable. Here is an example taken from the TempFor program (Figure 7.3):

```
for (int tTemperatureNumber = 1;
          tTemperatureNumber<=tNumberOfTemperatures;
          tTemperatureNumber++)
{
/**/    System.out.print("*** value of tTemperatureNumber is: ");
/**/    System.out.println(tTemperatureNumber);
        System.out.print("Type in a value in degrees Fahrenheit: ");
        ...
```

As has already been mentioned, there are circumstances in which it is possible for the block of a for statement not to be executed at all. If the output of the program contains no output from these debugging statements, you know that this has in fact occurred. Similarly, when you inadvertently write loops that loop forever, this will become obvious if the value of the control variable is output by the statements of the loop.

7.7 In Section 7.7, it was pointed out that we need to include a cast in the AvSimple program (given in Figure 7.6), i.e. because we want a floating-point division, we need:

```
final double tAverage = (double)tTotalVotes/tNumberOfCandidates;
```

rather than:

```
final double tAverage = tTotalVotes/tNumberOfCandidates;
```

It is easy to forget a cast like this one, in which case integer division will be used instead of floating-point division. This will lead to tAverage being assigned an inappropriate value. Although it is obvious in a small program like this one as to where the wrong value is being generated, when this statement is in the middle of a long sequence of statements, it may not be obvious as to which statement is causing the problem. Part of the problem is that the statement:

```
final double tAverage = tTotalVotes/tNumberOfCandidates;
```

does not look as if it is inappropriate!

And the definition of Java does not help: the above assignment statement is legal because, in Java, an `int` is assignment compatible with a `double`. If this were not the case, the above would not compile, and you would be forced to choose between:

```
final double tAverage = (double) (tTotalVotes/tNumberOfCandidates);
```

and:

```
final double tAverage = (double) tTotalVotes/tNumberOfCandidates;
```

Some people argue that being able to assign `int`s to `double`s is a deficiency of the design of Java.

7.8 Consider the following code:

```
int tValue;

...

for (int tValue = 1; ... )
{

    ...

}
```

If this code is what you intended to write, using the same name is confusing: it would be better to use variables with different names. Java does not allow you to write the above code: the above will lead to a compilation error. So, although the scope of any variable declared in the *ForInit* part of a for statement is the text from the declaration to the end of the for statement, in Java it is not possible for a statement preceding the for statement to declare a variable that has the same name as that of the control variable.

Curios, controversies and cover-ups

7.1 In Section 6.8, Section 7.5 and Section 7.7, a notation called **pseudo-code** has been used to present an informal notation for the steps to be executed by a piece of code. In pseudo-code, a problem is divided up into a number of subproblems:

    1. subproblem
    2. subproblem
       ...
    n. subproblem

Each of these subproblems is to be solved in turn. The notation:

$$\text{problem} \left\|\begin{array}{l} \textbf{1. } \text{subproblem} \\ \textbf{2. } \text{subproblem} \\ \quad ... \\ \textit{n. } \text{subproblem} \end{array}\right.$$

means that the problem stated to the left is solved by the subproblems given to the right. And the notation:

$$\text{loop } m \text{ times} \begin{cases} \textbf{1. } \text{subproblem} \\ \textbf{2. } \text{subproblem} \\ \quad \cdots \\ \textbf{\textit{n}. } \text{subproblem} \end{cases}$$

indicates that the code for the n subproblems that are inside the loop is to be executed m times.

7.2   Consider the tFahrenheit and tCelsius variables of the TempFor program that was given in Figure 7.3. Because these variables are only used inside the loop, they have been declared within the block of the for statement:

```
for (int tTemperatureNumber = 1; ... )
{

   ...

   final double tFahrenheit = Double.parseDouble(tLine);
   final double tCelsius = (tFahrenheit - 32.0)*5.0/9.0;
   System.out.println("..." + tCelsius);
}
```

So, each time the block is executed, the variables tFahrenheit and tCelsius are created and their initializers give them their initial values. The value of tFahrenheit is used to give tCelsius a value, and then the value of tCelsius is output. At the end of each execution of the block of the loop, these two variables are destroyed (because they are *local variables* of the block). Note that the same variables do not get reused: instead two new variables get created each time the loop is executed. So, each incarnation of each variable is only assigned one value: for this reason, they can be declared to be final.

Alternatively, the two variables can be declared outside the loop:

```
double tFahrenheit;
double tCelsius;
for (int tTemperatureNumber = 1; ... )
{

   ...

   tFahrenheit = Double.parseDouble(tLine);
   tCelsius = (tFahrenheit - 32.0)*5.0/9.0;
   System.out.println("..." + tCelsius);
}
```

Here it is inappropriate to use final as the two variables get new values assigned to them each time the loop is executed.

Some people argue that variables like this should be declared outside the loop only if it is necessary to do this, i.e. if it is necessary to retain the value of the variable from one execution of the block of the for statement to the next (as is the case with the `tTotalVotes` variable of the `AvSimple` program (shown in Figure 7.6)). However, others argue that declaring variables inside a loop leads to code that is more difficult to understand.

7.1 In Exercise 5.4, you were asked to write a program to calculate the area of a triangle. Now write a program that can handle more than one triangle. Use an integer at the start of the data to indicate how many triangles there are, and insist that the user types each set of three values on a separate line.
Execute this program with the data:

```
3
5.0   12.0   13.0
2.1    3.2    5.2
1.0    1.0    1.0
```

Execute the program again with the data:

```
0
```

7.2 In Section 7.9, we looked at outputting a *triangle of stars*. Suppose that a triangle like the following triangle is required instead:

```
    *
   **
  ***
 ****
*****
```

Although the number of stars on each line is the same as it was before, the stars have to be preceded by some spaces:

line number	number of spaces required
1	4
2	3
3	2
4	1
5	0

Write a program that reads in a size (e.g. 5), and then outputs the appropriate triangle.

7.3 Write a program to calculate and output a table giving the Centigrade (or Celsius) equivalent of the Fahrenheit temperatures in the range 175°F to 525°F at steps of 25°F. Your output should give the Centigrade equivalent rounded to the nearest 10°C.
In the UK, such tables often appear in cookery books and the following figures are the most popular choices given in a small sample of cookery books:

°F	°C		°F	°C
175	80		375	190
200	100		400	200
225	110		425	220
250	120		450	230
275	140		475	240
300	150		500	260
325	160		525	270
350	180			

You should find that your output contains two °C values that are different.

7.4 Write a program that produces a table of values of $\sin x$ and $\cos x$ for values of x between -90 degrees and 90 degrees in steps of 10 degrees. [Note: 180 degrees is equal to π radians.]

7.5 Carl Gauss, a German mathematician (who lived from 1777–1855), devised an algorithm which determines the day, d, and the month, m, on which Easter Sunday occurs in the year, y. The algorithm requires the values in the last two columns of the following table to be calculated. Each value is either the (integer) quotient or the remainder of a whole number division.

dividend	divisor	quotient	remainder
y	19	—	a
y	100	b	c
b	4	z	e
$8b + 13$	25	g	—
$19a + b - z - g + 15$	30	—	h
$a + 11h$	319	u	—
c	4	i	k
$2e + 2i - k - h + u + 32$	7	—	x
$h - u + x + 90$	25	m	—
$h - u + x + m + 19$	32	—	d

For example, if y is equal to 2001, the above calculations lead to $a = 6$, $b = 20$, $c = 1$, $z = 5$, $e = 0, \ldots, m = 4$ and $d = 15$, i.e. April 15th. Write a program that outputs the values of m and d for all the years in the range 1997 to 2006. You should obtain the following values:

y	m	d		y	m	d
1997	3	30		2002	3	31
1998	4	12		2003	4	20
1999	4	4		2004	4	11
2000	4	23		2005	3	27
2001	4	15		2006	4	16

7.6 Write a program that uses a **for** statement to output the values of $1!$, $2!$, $3!, \ldots, 11!$ and $12!$. The value $k!$ (k *factorial*) is the product of the first k integers, i.e. $1 \times 2 \times 3 \times \ldots \times k$. In your program, use an int to represent the value of $k!$.

[Hint: your program should only contain one loop: you may think that you need a loop inside this loop. However, this is unnecessary: the value to be output on, say, the fifth execution of the loop is five times the value that was output on the fourth execution of the loop.]

7.7 A standard class return fare for the journey by train and hovercraft from London to Paris is normally £80.00. However, special rates apply for children and for adults aged 65 or over:

age	cost
16–64	£80.00
65 or more	£52.60
12–15	£55.00
4–11	£40.20
under 4	free

Suppose that it is required to find the total cost for a family. Write a program that first reads in the number of people in the family, then reads in the ages of each member of the family, and then calculates the total cost of the tickets.

Use this program to calculate the cost for six people that have the ages 36, 40, 65, 11, 12 and 16. You should find that the cost is £387.80.

7.8 Some data consists of an integer n followed by n integer values. Write a program that reads this data and then outputs three numbers which are the numbers of values that are positive, zero and negative.

◇ 7.9 Given data containing the x and y coordinates of n points, the straight line that best fits these points (using the method of *least squares*) is:

$$y = a + bx$$

where:

$$b = \frac{n \sum_{i=1}^{n} x_i y_i - \sum_{i=1}^{n} x_i \sum_{i=1}^{n} y_i}{n \sum_{i=1}^{n} x_i^2 - \left(\sum_{i=1}^{n} x_i \right)^2}$$

and:

$$a = \frac{\sum_{i=1}^{n} y_i - b \sum_{i=1}^{n} x_i}{n}$$

Write a program that reads in the coordinates of n points and then outputs the values of a and b for the straight line that best fits the points. [Hint: as the coordinates are read in, the various sums can be built up in variables called tSumX, tSumY, tSumXY and tSumXX.] The number of points, n, is given as an integer which precedes the rest of the data.

Execute your program using the seven points (0.0, 0.0), (0.5, 2.0), (1.0, 3.0), (1.5, 5.0), (2.0, 8.0), (2.5, 11.5) and (3.0, 15.0). You should find that the straight line that best fits the points is approximately:

$$y = -1.036 + 4.929x$$

◇   **7.10** The mathematical constant π can be computed from the formula:

$$\frac{2}{\pi} = \frac{\sqrt{2}}{2} \times \frac{\sqrt{2+\sqrt{2}}}{2} \times \frac{\sqrt{2+\sqrt{2+\sqrt{2}}}}{2} \times \cdots$$

This formula was discovered by a 16th-century French mathematician called Franciscus Vieta. Write a program that reads in an integer n and then outputs the value of π that is obtained by using the first n products of the formula. If you supply the value 7 in the data, your program should output the value 3.141513801144301.

7.11 The next term in the sequence of integers:

0   1   1   2   3   5   8   13   21   ...

is obtained from the sum of the previous two terms. Such a sequence is called a Fibonacci sequence. It is named after an Italian mathematician called Fibonacci who published a work on this topic in 1202.

The particular sequence obtained depends on the values of the first two terms of the sequence. Write a program that reads in the values of the first two terms and then outputs each of the first 18 terms of the chosen sequence.

7.12 The mathematical constant π can be computed from the formula:

$$\frac{\pi}{2} = \frac{2}{1} \times \frac{2}{3} \times \frac{4}{3} \times \frac{4}{5} \times \frac{6}{5} \times \frac{6}{7} \times \cdots$$

This formula was discovered by a 17th-century English mathematician called John Wallis. Write a program that reads in an integer n and then computes π from the formula by multiplying the first n fractions of the right-hand side of the formula. If you execute your program with the value 20 in the data, it should produce the value 3.067703806643497. Note that this formula does not produce a very accurate value for π.

7.13 Write a program that outputs the calendar for a month in the following format:

```
S   M  Tu   W  Th   F   S
                         1
 2   3   4   5   6   7   8
 9  10  11  12  13  14  15
16  17  18  19  20  21  22
23  24  25  26  27  28  29
30
```

Arrange for the program always to produce seven lines of output even if some of the last few lines are empty.

The data for the program should consist of the number of days in the month and the number of the day in the week on which the month starts. Assuming 0 means *Sunday*, 1 means *Monday*, ..., the values 30 and 6 need to be supplied to get the above output.

7.14 Write a program that reads in a sentence like:

```
The mouse was caught in a clothes peg.
```

and then outputs it with the letters of alternate words in reverse order, e.g.:

```
The esuom was thguac in a clothes gep.
```

7.15 International Standard Book Numbers (ISBNs) can be used to identify a book uniquely. For example, the second edition ([19]) of the book *The Java Language Specification* by Gosling, Joy, Steele and Bracha has the ISBN 0-201-31008-2. There are four parts to an ISBN: country of origin, publisher, book number, and a check character. These four parts can be separated by hyphens or spaces; and there are always exactly 13 characters in an ISBN.

The check character is present in order to ensure that an ISBN has been given correctly. The method by which it is calculated is defined by ISO Standard 2108 ([25]). As an example, consider the calculation of the check character for the above book. Start with the first nine digits, i.e. 020131008. Multiply the ith digit of this number by $(11 - i)$:

$$
\begin{array}{ccccccccc}
0 & 2 & 0 & 1 & 3 & 1 & 0 & 0 & 8 \\
10 & 9 & 8 & 7 & 6 & 5 & 4 & 3 & 2 \\
0 & 18 & 0 & 7 & 18 & 5 & 0 & 0 & 16
\end{array}
$$

Now, add these nine products together: $0 + 18 + 0 + 7 + 18 + 5 + 0 + 0 + 16 = 64$. Next, find the remainder when this value is divided by 11. In this example, 64 mod 11 is equal to 9. Finally:

> if the remainder is 0, the check character is 0,
> if the remainder is 1, the check character is X,
> otherwise, it is the digit equal to (11–remainder).

So, for the above book, the check character is $11 - 9$, i.e. 2.

Write a program that reads in an ISBN and determines whether the check character for the ISBN is correct. Assume that the rest of the ISBN has been correctly given.

[Hint: your program will need to convert between chars and ints. There are details about how to do this in Section 5.9.]

Test your program by executing it several times, each time using one of the following strings in the data:

```
0-201-31008-2
3-540-15078-1
0-13-161654-4
0-580-06624-X
1-56592-184-4
1-91-374200-0
0-201-71107-9
0-7897-1627-5
```

Only one of these is illegal – which one?

7.16 A line of data contains two words which are separated by a space. Assume that the two words are of equal length. Write a program that outputs how many characters in the corresponding positions of the two words are the same.

For example, given the data:

```
bored bread
```

your program should output the value 2. And, given the data:

```
a b
```

it should output the value 0.

7.17 A word is said to be a **palindrome** if it is spelt the same forwards as backwards. Some examples are mum, noon and madam. Write a program that reads in a line containing a single word and then determines whether or not it is a palindrome.

7.18 Write a program that reads a line of words and then outputs the words coded in the following way:

> Assume that the ith letter of the message is an upper-case letter. Instead of outputting this letter, output the letter which appears in the alphabet i letters on from this letter. The letters of the alphabet should be treated cyclically (i.e. Z is followed by A). Any lower-case letter in the message should be coded as if it were the corresponding upper-case letter. Any other characters in the message should be output unchanged.

Given the data End of term party, your program should output FPG SK ZLZV ZLDGM.

[Hint: your program will need to convert between chars and ints. There are details about how to do this in Section 5.9.]

Chapter 8

Using methods to organize programs

The programs you are writing are starting to get large in size. They are becoming monolithic and unwieldly. For this reason, they are becoming difficult to understand.

The pseudo-code notation enables the solution to a problem to be expressed as the solution to a number of subproblems. However, the code that is appropriate for each of these subproblems may itself be quite complicated. What we want is some way of hiding the detail. Most programming languages have a construct that can be used for this purpose. In the Java programming language, the construct is called a *method declaration*.

8.1 The need for methods

Have another look at the program AvSimple given in Figure 7.6. It does the fairly simple task of finding the average vote scored by a set of candidates in an election. When we execute this program, we enter into a dialogue with the computer: it asks us for some information; we supply the information; and it computes some results.

Suppose we now decide to make the dialogue that appears on the screen a bit easier to read. Suppose that this is to be done by dividing the output into sections, each section being separated by a line of hyphens. The sort of output that could be produced is shown in Figure 8.1.

```
-----------------------------------------------------------------
How many candidates are there? 3
-----------------------------------------------------------------
Candidate number: 1
Type in the number of votes for this candidate: 27
-----------------------------------------------------------------
Candidate number: 2
Type in the number of votes for this candidate: 42
-----------------------------------------------------------------
Candidate number: 3
Type in the number of votes for this candidate: 3
-----------------------------------------------------------------
Average number of votes scored is: 24.0
-----------------------------------------------------------------
```

Figure 8.1 The new form of output from the average program.

One way of outputting a line of hyphens is by executing the statements:

```
for (int tColNumber = 1; tColNumber<=tNumberOfCols; tColNumber++)
{
    System.out.print('-');
}
System.out.println();
```

where tNumberOfCols is a constant having some value, say, 65. So, in order to produce output like that given in Figure 8.1, the above statements could be inserted at appropriate points in the program given in Figure 7.6. The resulting program (Av0Subs) is given in Figure 8.2.

```
// This program processes the votes of candidates obtained in an election.
// The output is divided in sections by outputting lines of hyphens.
// The code for doing this appears several times.
// Barry Cornelius, 4 June 2000
import java.io. BufferedReader;
import java.io. InputStreamReader;
import java.io. IOException;
```

Figure 8.2 *Continues on the next page.*

```
public class AvOSubs
{
    public static void main(final String[] pArgs) throws IOException
    {
        final int tNumberOfCols = 65;
        final BufferedReader tKeyboard =
                        new BufferedReader(new InputStreamReader(System.in));
        for (int tColNumber = 1; tColNumber<=tNumberOfCols; tColNumber++)
        {
            System.out.print('-');
        }
        System.out.println();
        System.out.print("How many candidates are there? ");
        System.out.flush();
        String tLine = tKeyboard.readLine();
        final int tNumberOfCandidates = Integer.parseInt(tLine);
        int tTotalVotes = 0;
        for (int tCandidateNumber = 1;
                    tCandidateNumber<=tNumberOfCandidates; tCandidateNumber++)
        {
            for (int tColNumber = 1; tColNumber<=tNumberOfCols; tColNumber++)
            {
                System.out.print('-');
            }
            System.out.println();
            System.out.println("Candidate number: " + tCandidateNumber);
            System.out.print("Type in number of votes for this candidate: ");
            System.out.flush();
            tLine = tKeyboard.readLine();
            final int tNumberOfVotes = Integer.parseInt(tLine);
            tTotalVotes += tNumberOfVotes;
        }
        for (int tColNumber = 1; tColNumber<=tNumberOfCols; tColNumber++)
        {
            System.out.print('-');
        }
        System.out.println();
        final double tAverage = (double)tTotalVotes/tNumberOfCandidates;
        System.out.println("Average number of votes scored is: " + tAverage);
        for (int tColNumber = 1; tColNumber<=tNumberOfCols; tColNumber++)
        {
            System.out.print('-');
        }
        System.out.println();
    }
}
```

Figure 8.2   The drawing-a-line code clutters up the program.

There is a major weakness with this program: the code that we are using for outputting a line of hyphens appears four times. And this makes the program more difficult to understand, because the code for outputting a line of hyphens is cluttering up the rest of the program. It also makes the program more difficult to maintain: if we had to change the hyphen to some other character, there are numerous occurrences of this code to find and change. It would be very easy to miss one of the occurrences.

The program is in fact composed of two quite separate activities: one of these is the task to output a line of hyphens and the other is the main task of the program, i.e. finding the average vote. What we want is some way of splitting the code up so that the statements for these two tasks are not intermingled.

Here is how we do this: when a set of statements can be regarded as solving a **subproblem**, it should be coded as a **method**. In its simplest form, a **method declaration** is a construct that just gives a name to a set of statements.

So, we should put all the detail of outputting a line of hyphens in a method declaration. This results in the Av1Sub program shown in Figure 8.3.

In the Av1Sub program, the details of how a line is drawn has been hidden away in a **subsidiary method** called iDrawLine. These details are irrelevant to the block of the main method. So the reader of the program can now read the block of the main method without being distracted by the details of how lines are drawn.

Hopefully, you will agree that this program is a lot easier to understand than the one which does not use the iDrawLine method.

8.2 Method declarations

We have just found out that one way of giving a part of a program a name is to turn it into a method. Thus, in program Av1Sub, the block:

```
{
    final int tNumberOfCols = 65;
    for (int tColNumber = 1; tColNumber<=tNumberOfCols; tColNumber++)
    {
        System.out.print('-');
    }
    System.out.println();
}
```

has been given the name iDrawLine.

From the syntax diagrams given in Figure 8.4 you can see that the above block is the *MethodBody* part of a method declaration and that the first line of iDrawLine's method declaration:

```
private static void iDrawLine()
```

is the *MethodHeader* part. As, to begin with, we will just be using methods for subsidiary pieces of work, we will declare them using private and static.

```java
// This program processes the votes of candidates obtained in an election.
// The output is divided in sections by outputting lines of hyphens.
// The program uses a method for outputting the line of hyphens.
// Barry Cornelius, 4 June 2000
import java.io. BufferedReader;
import java.io. InputStreamReader;
import java.io. IOException;
public class Av1Sub
{
    public static void main(final String[] pArgs) throws IOException
    {
        final BufferedReader tKeyboard =
                    new BufferedReader(new InputStreamReader(System.in));
        iDrawLine();
        System.out.print("How many candidates are there? ");
        System.out.flush();
        String tLine = tKeyboard.readLine();
        final int tNumberOfCandidates = Integer.parseInt(tLine);
        int tTotalVotes = 0;
        for (int tCandidateNumber = 1;
                tCandidateNumber<=tNumberOfCandidates; tCandidateNumber++)
        {
            iDrawLine();
            System.out.println("Candidate number: " + tCandidateNumber);
            System.out.print("Type in number of votes for this candidate: ");
            System.out.flush();
            tLine = tKeyboard.readLine();
            final int tNumberOfVotes = Integer.parseInt(tLine);
            tTotalVotes += tNumberOfVotes;
        }
        iDrawLine();
        final double tAverage = (double)tTotalVotes/tNumberOfCandidates;
        System.out.println("Average number of votes scored is: " + tAverage);
        iDrawLine();
    }

    private static void iDrawLine()
    {
        final int tNumberOfCols = 65;
        for (int tColNumber = 1; tColNumber<=tNumberOfCols; tColNumber++)
        {
            System.out.print('-');
        }
        System.out.println();
    }
}
```

Figure 8.3 The drawing-a-line code is hidden away in a subsidiary method.

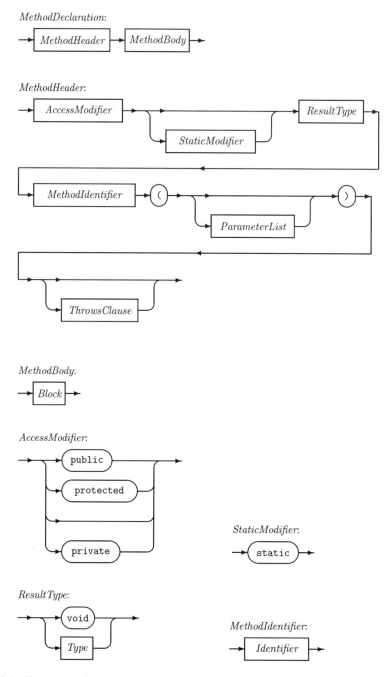

Figure 8.4   The syntax of a method declaration.

If you look at the syntax diagram for *MethodHeader*, you will see that, besides `private static`, there are other possibilities, e.g.:

- using `public` instead of `private`;
- omitting `static`.

The meaning of `private static` and the consideration of these other possibilities will be left until the chapter in which we declare our own classes (Chapter 11).

In the method header, the name of the method is preceded by the method's *ResultType*. To begin with, we will declare methods that do some work but which do not return a result: this is indicated by using the `void` keyword instead of a type. We look at declaring methods that return results later in this chapter (in Section 8.8).

This method is just being used for a subsidiary part of the work of the main method. Later, when we look at providing our own classes, we will be providing methods for other people to call. To distinguish between these two kinds of methods, in this book a prefix will be used in the identifiers of methods that are just subsidiary methods. So, as well as using a prefix of `t` (meaning *temporary*) for naming local variables, it is suggested that you use a prefix of `i` (meaning **internal**) when naming subsidiary methods. So this method will be called `iDrawLine` rather than `drawLine`. When you look at a call of `iDrawLine`, you will immediately know from the prefix in its name that this method is declared as part of this class: it is an *internal* method of the class.

At the end of the *MethodHeader*, there is an optional *ParameterList* and an optional *ThrowsClause*. We will look at these later in this chapter.

All the programs we have looked at so far have just contained the declaration of a method called `main`. The main method declaration is another example of a method declaration. Most of the programs we will write, from now on, will contain several method declarations as well as the main method declaration. These method declarations can be declared in any order. Some people prefer to put the main method declaration first; others prefer to put it last. Some people prefer to put the declarations in alphabetical order, whereas others prefer to group related methods together.

It is recommended that you separate method declarations by one or two blank lines. This will make it easier to find the various methods of a program.

8.3 Method invocations

The only difference between the statements of the main method of the `AvSimple` program (given in Figure 7.6) and those of the `Av1Sub` program (given in Figure 8.3) is that `Av1Sub`'s main method has four additional statements each of which is:

```
iDrawLine();
```

Such a statement is a **method invocation** or a **call**.

When a call is executed, the statements contained in the method declaration get executed. Having finished these statements, execution returns to the statement following the call.

Consider the Av1Sub program again. It is shown in Figure 8.3. When a program is executed, the first statement that will get executed is the first statement of the block of the main method. With Av1Sub, this is the statement:

```
final BufferedReader tKeyboard =
                new BufferedReader(new InputStreamReader(System.in));
```

The next statement is:

```
iDrawLine();
```

As this is a call of the method iDrawLine, execution is transferred to the statements of this method and these are then executed in turn. So, the following statements are executed:

```
final int tNumberOfCols = 65;
for (int tColNumber = 1; tColNumber<=tNumberOfCols; tColNumber++)
{
    System.out.print('-');
}
System.out.println();
```

Having executed these statements, the execution returns to the point from which the method was called and executes the statement following the call. This is the statement:

```
System.out.print("How many candidates are there? ");
```

There are three other calls of iDrawLine in the program and, at each call, the block of the method is executed and then the statement following the call is executed.

8.4 The use of methods for procedural abstraction

So far, we have seen a method being used when a piece of code occurred more than once in a program. Instead of writing the code down several times, it was put into a method. We saw that this made the block of the main method a lot clearer. However, methods are not just used to avoid duplications of code: any set of statements that can be regarded as solving a subproblem can be coded as a method.

Indeed, it is usually found that the effort entailed in developing a complicated piece of code is considerably reduced if subsidiary parts are put into methods. It makes the code a lot easier to understand. And because of this, it is easier to change the program, i.e. the program will be more maintainable. The technique of hiding detail in methods is called **procedural abstraction**.

In older programming languages, procedural abstraction is the only mechanism for breaking down a problem into manageable subproblems. Later, it was discovered that establishing what real-world objects need to be represented (*data abstraction*) plays a valuable part in the construction of programs. So later programming languages have constructs that allow the data abstraction to be expressed: as we will see later, this is the main role of interfaces and classes in Java.

8.5 The need for methods with parameters

A method can often be a lot more useful if we can vary its action from one call to another. We can do this by adding *parameters* to a method.

Here, again, is the code of the iDrawLine method:

```
private static void iDrawLine()
{
    final int tNumberOfCols = 65;
    for (int tColNumber = 1; tColNumber<=tNumberOfCols; tColNumber++)
    {
        System.out.print('-');
    }
    System.out.println();
}
```

Suppose that we want to allow the possibility of outputting a different number of hyphens each time the method is called.

We can do this by making the length of the line a **parameter** of the method:

```
private static void iDrawLine(int pNumberOfCols)
{
    for (int tColNumber = 1; tColNumber<=pNumberOfCols; tColNumber++)
    {
        System.out.print('-');
    }
    System.out.println();
}
```

and at each call of the method we include within parentheses the value of the length of the line that is required at that call.

Here are some examples of calls of the new version of the iDrawLine method:

```
iDrawLine(65);
final int tLength = Integer.parseInt(tLine);
iDrawLine(tLength);
iDrawLine(tLength/2);
```

So far, in this book, we have suggested the use of t and i prefixes for the names of local variables and internal methods. It is now suggested that you use a p prefix for any variables that are those of parameters. So, when examining a piece of code containing the use of the pNumberOfCols variable, the p prefix immediately points out to you where the variable is declared.

8.6 Distinguishing between parameters and arguments

The text that occurs within the parentheses of the method header gives a list of the **parameters** (or the **formal parameters**); and the text used in the call is a list of the **arguments** (or the **actual arguments**). So, this new version of the method iDrawLine has one parameter called pNumberOfCols, and in the last call of iDrawLine given above tLength/2 is the argument.

There are rules that govern the correspondence between parameters and arguments. One rule says that each call must have the same number of arguments as there are parameters in the declaration of the method. Another rule says that each argument must be an expression whose type is *assignment compatible* with the type of the parameter. For details about what is meant by *assignment compatible*, refer back to Section 2.6. For more details about parameter compatibility, see Curio 8.1.

It may be useful to modify iDrawLine so that the character that is output can be varied instead of always being a hyphen. This can be done by including another parameter:

```
private static void iAnotherDrawLine(int pNumberOfCols, char pCharToOutput)
{
    for (int tColNumber = 1; tColNumber<=pNumberOfCols; tColNumber++)
    {
        System.out.print(pCharToOutput);
    }
    System.out.println();
}
```

As there are now two parameters, each call of the iAnotherDrawLine method will need two arguments. For example, the call iAnotherDrawLine(65, '-') outputs a line containing 65 hyphens. And the call iAnotherDrawLine(1, '=') outputs a line containing one equals sign. Note that the call iAnotherDrawLine(0, '-') has the effect of outputting an empty line.

Section 8.2 chose not to give the syntax of the parameters part of a method header. This is given in Figure 8.5. The use of the optional final and [] parts of a *Parameter* are discussed in Section 8.7 and Curio 15.1.

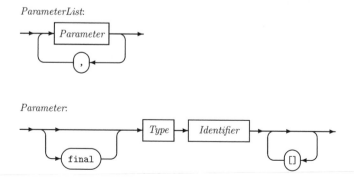

Figure 8.5 The syntax of a parameter list.

8.7 The scope of a parameter

The *scope* of an identifier that is a parameter is the code of its associated method declaration. This means that it is only possible to refer to the parameter pNumberOfCols within the code of the declaration of the method iDrawLine.

What happens when we call a method that has parameters? For each parameter, a variable that is local to the block of the method is created. Prior to executing the block of the method, the local variable is assigned the value of the argument. For example, if the execution gets to the call:

```
iDrawLine(tLength);
```

then, prior to executing the block of method iDrawLine, a local variable for the parameter pNumberOfCols is created and assigned the value of the expression tLength:

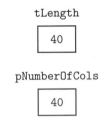

tLength

40

pNumberOfCols

40

Any references to pNumberOfCols within the block are references to this local variable.

Because pNumberOfCols is a local variable of this method, it is possible for the statements of the block of the method to assign a new value to pNumberOfCols. However, if this were to happen, it is only pNumberOfCols that gets changed: the value of the tLength variable remains unchanged.

On most occasions, the statements of the block of a method will not be assigning any values to a parameter. This can be (and should be) documented by using the final keyword. So a better version of iDrawLine is:

```
private static void iDrawLine(final int pNumberOfCols)
{
    for (int tColNumber = 1; tColNumber<=pNumberOfCols; tColNumber++)
    {
        System.out.print('-');
    }
    System.out.println();
}
```

For this reason, in this book most parameters will be qualified with the final keyword.

8.8 Providing our own functions

So far in this chapter, we have looked at methods that are *void methods*. Whereas a call of a void method just executes a group of statements, a call of a **function** executes a group of statements that returns a value to the point of call. We have already seen that the call of a void method is a kind of statement. A **function call**, however, usually appears as an operand in an expression, and the value returned by the function is used in the calculation of the value of the expression.

Suppose a function is required which returns the larger of two double values. We could call the function maximum and could supply the two values as arguments of the function call. Such a function could be called in the following situation:

```
tHalfMax = maximum(p,q)/2.0;
```

And here is a suitable function declaration:

```
private static double maximum(final double x, final double y)
{
    double tResult;
    if (x>y)
    {
        tResult = x;
    }
    else
    {
        tResult = y;
    }
    return tResult;
}
```

The statement tResult = x; gets executed if the value of x is greater than the value of y; otherwise tResult = y; gets executed. The value of the variable tResult is then used in a **return statement**.

A function must have at least one return statement. The return keyword of a return statement is followed by an expression, and it is the value of this expression that is returned by the function. The execution of the return statement causes an immediate exit from the function.

So, the above function declaration could alternatively be written as:

```
private static double maximum(final double x, final double y)
{
    if (x>y)
    {
        return x;
    }
    else
    {
        return y;
    }
}
```

The important thing is that when the block of a function is executed, a return statement must eventually be executed no matter which route is taken through the block. However, many people have reservations about using more than one return statement – see Tip 8.1.

At the point where the header of the declaration of a void method would include the symbol void, a function declaration specifies the type of the value that is to be returned by the function. This type is known as the **result type** of the function.

For the above function, the header contains double, and so the value returned by a call of maximum will be of type double.

The expression used in a return statement must have a type that is *assignment compatible* with the result type of the function. In the examples given above, the return statement contains an expression which is simply the name of a variable (that is of type double). This expression is therefore of the right type (because the result type of maximum is also the type double).

8.9 Differences between a void method and a function

We have now seen two different ways in which a programmer can give a name to a group of statements. It can be done either by declaring a void method or by declaring a function. In this section, the major differences between void methods and functions will be re-stated.

One of the main differences occurs in their use: a call of a function *normally* appears as an operand in an expression, whereas a call of a void method is one of the possible forms of statement. The word *normally* has been used because it is possible for a function call to be a statement, i.e. for a function to be called just like a void method. For more details, see Tip 8.2.

Because a function is called from an expression, the function must indicate the value that is to be used in the expression. This is done by including in the block of a function a return statement that contains the expression whose value is to be returned. There is one other difference: the header of a function contains the type of the value being returned by the function whereas the header of a void method contains the symbol void.

Even though there are these significant differences, void methods and functions do have a lot in common.

8.10 Parameters which are of a reference type

Section 8.6 and Section 8.7 described parameter passing for a parameter that is of a primitive type. We saw that (for each parameter) a local variable gets created in which is stored a copy of the argument. The mechanism of using a local variable also applies if a parameter is of a reference type. However, because a value that is of a reference type is a pointer, you get a different effect.

In Section 3.2.11, we used:

```
System.out.println(tFirstPoint);
```

to output the value of a `Point` object. We obtained output like:

```
java.awt.Point[x=100,y=200]
```

Suppose we want to improve on the format that is used in the output. We could write a function that has a parameter of type `Point` and get it to return a `String` containing the characters that we want to be output. Here is a possible function:

```
private static String iGetStringFromPoint(Point pPoint)
{
    return pPoint.x + ":" + pPoint.y;
}
```

We could call it as follows:

```
Point tFirstPoint = new Point(100, 200);
System.out.println(iGetStringFromPoint(tFirstPoint));
```

This would output:

```
100:200
```

When the `iGetStringFromPoint` method is called, first a local variable called `pPoint` is created; and then it is assigned the value of the argument. At the above call, it is assigned the value of `tFirstPoint`:

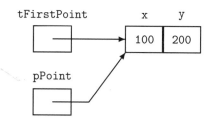

If the block of `iGetStringFromPoint` were to assign a new value to `pPoint`, e.g.:

```
private static String iGetStringFromPoint(Point pPoint)
{
    pPoint = new Point(200, 300);
    return pPoint.x + ":" + pPoint.y;
}
```

this assignment statement would not change the value of `tFirstPoint`: only the value of `pPoint` would be changed. Here is a diagram showing the situation which would result from this assignment statement:

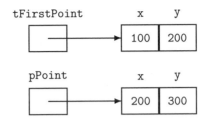

However, our method does not assign a new value to pPoint: it is useful to document this. As usual, this is done using the final keyword:

```
private static String iGetStringFromPoint(final Point pPoint)
{
    return pPoint.x + ":" + pPoint.y;
}
```

If we use this method declaration, it is not possible to change the value of pPoint. It means that we know that pPoint is pointing to the same object as tFirstPoint throughout the execution of the method:

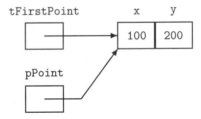

In Section 3.2.7, we found that it is still possible to change the value of an object even when its reference variable is declared to be final. Similiarly, when a parameter that is of a reference type is described to be final, it is still possible for the method to change the value of the object that is pointed to by the parameter. For example, the block of this latest version of iGetStringFromPoint could be changed to include the execution of the assignment statement:

```
pPoint.x = 500;
```

or the method call:

```
pPoint.translate(200, 300);
```

If it were to execute both of these in turn, you would finish up with the following situation:

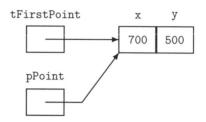

So, although the final keyword guarantees to the reader of the method declaration that pPoint will always be pointing to the same object as tFirstPoint, there
is no way in Java of saying that you do not want the object (to which the argument
tFirstPoint is pointing) to be altered by the method.

8.11 Identifying other subproblems of the Av1Sub program

There are still many other parts of the main method of the Av1Sub program (given in
Figure 8.3) that are given in a lot of detail. In order to understand the essence of the
tasks being performed by the main method there is no need to understand the detail
of these parts. You are only interested in *what* they do rather than in *how* they do it.
For this reason, it would be better if these parts were also hidden away in subsidiary
methods.

For example, consider the task of obtaining the number of votes that have been
scored by a particular candidate. In order to understand the program we need
not be bothered about how this is done: our only concern is that the variable
tNumberOfVotes is assigned an appropriate value.

The task could be carried out by the statements:

```
tLine = tKeyboard.readLine();
final int tNumberOfVotes = Integer.parseInt(tLine);
```

or by the statements:

```
System.out.print("Type in the number of votes for this candidate: ");
System.out.flush();
tLine = tKeyboard.readLine();
final int tNumberOfVotes = Integer.parseInt(tLine);
```

The statements that are actually included in the Av1Sub program are:

```
System.out.println("Candidate number: " + tCandidateNumber);
System.out.print("Type in the number of votes for this candidate: ");
System.out.flush();
tLine = tKeyboard.readLine();
final int tNumberOfVotes = Integer.parseInt(tLine);
```

Another possibility would be to display a new window containing a box; wait until the user types something in the box; read the value within the box; and then remove the window. (The details of how to do this will be given in Chapter 13.)

So far, four possibilities have been given for the task of finding the value of `tNumberOfVotes`. We could give more. But all of this is detail as far as the reader of the main method is concerned. In order to understand the main method, he/she is not interested in *how* this task is being done: instead the reader is only concerned with *what* is actually being achieved.

So the detail of this task ought to be hidden away in a subsidiary method and the statements that appear in the block of the main method ought to be replaced by a call of the method.

For example, we could replace the above statements by:

```
final int tNumberOfVotes = iObtainNumberOfVotes(tCandidateNumber);
```

Such a call conveys in its name all that a reader of the block of the main method needs to know if he/she wishes to understand the task being performed by this part of the main method.

Figure 8.6 gives a version of the `AvSimple` program in which a number of subproblems have been coded as subsidiary methods. The `Av4Subs` program is better than the `AvSimple` program because the block of its main method is uncluttered by detail and so it is a lot easier to understand. Note: some aspects of this program will be discussed in Section 8.12 and Section 8.13.

```
// This program processes the votes of candidates obtained in an election.
// Besides the main method, the program declares four subsidiary methods
// to represent four subproblems.
// Barry Cornelius, 4 June 2000
import java.io. BufferedReader;
import java.io. InputStreamReader;
import java.io. IOException;
public class Av4Subs
{
    private static final BufferedReader iKeyboard =
                        new BufferedReader(new InputStreamReader(System.in));
    public static void main(final String[] pArgs) throws IOException
    {
        iDrawLine();
        final int tNumberOfCandidates = iObtainNumberOfCandidates();
        int tTotalVotes = 0;
        for (int tCandidateNumber = 1;
                tCandidateNumber<=tNumberOfCandidates; tCandidateNumber++)
        {
            iDrawLine();
            final int tNumberOfVotes = iObtainNumberOfVotes(tCandidateNumber);
            tTotalVotes += tNumberOfVotes;
        }
```

Figure 8.6 *Continues on the next page.*

```
            iDrawLine();
            iOutputAverageNumberOfVotes(tTotalVotes, tNumberOfCandidates);
            iDrawLine();
        }

        private static void iDrawLine()
        {
            final int tNumberOfCols = 65;
            for (int tColNumber = 1; tColNumber<=tNumberOfCols; tColNumber++)
            {
                System.out.print('-');
            }
            System.out.println();
        }

        private static int iObtainNumberOfCandidates() throws IOException
        {
            System.out.print("How many candidates are there? ");
            System.out.flush();
            final String tLine = iKeyboard.readLine();
            return Integer.parseInt(tLine);
        }

        private static int iObtainNumberOfVotes(final int pCandidateNumber)
                                                          throws IOException
        {
            System.out.println("Candidate number: " + pCandidateNumber);
            System.out.print("Type in number of votes for this candidate: ");
            System.out.flush();
            final String tLine = iKeyboard.readLine();
            return Integer.parseInt(tLine);
        }

        private static void iOutputAverageNumberOfVotes(
                        final int pTotalVotes, final int pNumberOfCandidates)
        {
            final double tAverage = (double)pTotalVotes/pNumberOfCandidates;
            System.out.println("Average number of votes scored is: " + tAverage);
        }
    }
```

Figure 8.6   Using subsidiary methods to reflect the subproblems of a problem.

8.12 Class variables and their scope

Having decided to use one or more subsidiary methods, it is likely to be the case
that some variables will need to be accessed from both the main method and from
subsidiary methods. This can be done in two ways:

- For some variables, it is appropriate to pass the variable as an argument of the method. In the Av4Subs program, the value of the tCandidateNumber variable is communicated to the method iObtainNumberOfVotes by passing it as an argument of the call of the method.

- For other variables, it will be more appropriate to make the variable a *field* of the program's class declaration. In the Av4Subs program, this has been done for the variable iKeyboard. Such a variable is called a **class variable**. Since this variable is an internal aspect of the task being performed by the program class, an i prefix will be used, and in the variable's declaration it will be marked as private and static.

The scope of a class variable is the text of the class declaration in which it is declared. This means that we can refer to the variable iKeyboard in any of the methods of the program class, i.e. in the text of the main method and all of the subsidiary methods. In the Av4Subs program, it is only necessary to access this variable from the two methods that read lines from the keyboard, i.e. the methods iObtainNumberOfCandidates and iObtainNumberOfVotess.

It may be tempting to change many of the variables of a main method into class variables. However, whenever possible, it is best to declare variables to be local to a method. In particular, local variables should be used for counting variables, control variables, summing variables and other kinds of temporary variables. Only variables that form part of the specification of the problem that the program is solving should be declared as fields of its class declaration.

8.13 Handling IOException in a method

Back in Section 4.2, it was pointed out that Java requires us to indicate what we want to happen when any *checked exception* occurs. At the time, we were looking at how the main method could read data from the keyboard. In such situations, there may be an exception called IOException. Because IOException is one of the checked exceptions, we needed to do something with it if it occurred; as we did not wish to *handle* the exception, we added a *throws clause* to the main method's header:

```
public static void main(final String[] pArgs) throws IOException
```

The statements that read from the keyboard have now been moved from the main method to subsidiary methods, e.g. iObtainNumberOfCandidates. So, because an IOException may occur when the statements of this method are being executed, the header of this method is:

```
private static int iObtainNumberOfCandidates() throws IOException
```

The inclusion of this throws clause in this method header effectively says: 'an IOException may occur whilst this method is being executed; I do not have code to handle it; I'll leave it to the caller of the method to handle the exception'.

The call of iObtainNumberOfCandidates appears in one of the statements of the main method:

```
final int tNumberOfCandidates = iObtainNumberOfCandidates();
```

We have just noted that iObtainNumberOfCandidates has deferred handling of IOException to the caller. Because the main method is also unwilling to do anything with an IOException if it occurs, this must also be documented in its header:

```
public static void main(final String[] pArgs) throws IOException
```

In Section 9.9, we will look at how we can use a try statement to retain control when an exception occurs, but until then we will document any method's inability to handle a checked exception by using a throws clause.

8.14 Method overloading

Back in Section 2.10.3, the term *method overloading* was introduced to explain the possibility of a class having several declarations of methods called print (and println).

The **signature** of a method consists of a method's name together with the number and the types of the parameters. A class declaration can have several methods that have the same name but which have different signatures.

So, **method overloading** occurs when a class declaration has several methods having the same name but which can be distinguished by the types of their parameters. Here is an example where the name maximum is declared twice:

```
private static double maximum(final double x, final double y)
{
    if (x>y)
    {
        return x;
    }
    else
    {
        return y;
    }
}
private static String maximum(final String x, final String y)
{
    if (x.compareTo(y)>0)
    {
        return x;
    }
    else
    {
        return y;
    }
}
```

At a call of maximum, the compiler looks at the arguments of the call to see which maximum is being used.

8.15 Reworking the ReadAPoint program to use methods

In Section 4.13, we used the StringTokenizer class to enable us to read in a value of class Point. The code to obtain a value of a class (e.g. a value of class Point) from a String (e.g. "400:500") forms a very useful set of statements. If we are going to do a lot of reading of Points, it would be useful to provide a method for this task.

```
// This program uses methods when reading/writing a value of the class Point.
// Barry Cornelius, 4 June 2000
import java.io.    BufferedReader;
import java.io.    InputStreamReader;
import java.io.    IOException;
import java.awt.   Point;
import java.util.  StringTokenizer;
public class ReadAPointUsingMethods
{
    public static void main(final String[] pArgs) throws IOException
    {
        final BufferedReader tKeyboard =
                        new BufferedReader(new InputStreamReader(System.in));
        System.out.println("Type in a point, e.g., 400:500");
        final String tLine = tKeyboard.readLine();
        final Point tPoint = iGetPointFromString(tLine);
        System.out.println("The point is at: " + iGetStringFromPoint(tPoint));
    }

    private static Point iGetPointFromString(final String pString)
    {
        final StringTokenizer tTokens = new StringTokenizer(pString, ":");
        String tThisToken = tTokens.nextToken();
        final int x = Integer.parseInt(tThisToken);
        tThisToken = tTokens.nextToken();
        final int y = Integer.parseInt(tThisToken);
        return new Point(x, y);
    }

    private static String iGetStringFromPoint(final Point pPoint)
    {
        return pPoint.x + ":" + pPoint.y;
    }
}
```

Figure 8.7   Using subsidiary methods to improve the ReadAPoint program.

So, here is a method declaration for producing a value of class `Point` from a `String`:

```
private static Point iGetPointFromString(final String pString)
{
    final StringTokenizer tTokens = new StringTokenizer(pString, ":");
    String tThisToken = tTokens.nextToken();
    final int x = Integer.parseInt(tThisToken);
    tThisToken = tTokens.nextToken();
    final int y = Integer.parseInt(tThisToken);
    return new Point(x, y);
}
```

When we come to designing our own classes (from Chapter 11 onwards), it will be suggested that you always provide a *constructor* that constructs a value of a class from a `String` and a method that provides a `String` from a value of the class. Both of these are very useful.

Figure 8.7 illustrates how the above method together with the `iGetStringFrom-Point` method from Section 8.10 can be used to improve the `ReadAPoint` program that was given in Figure 4.7.

8.16 Using methods recursively

8.16.1 Recursive definitions

Imagine that this is an apple tree:

And that this is another, slightly bigger, tree:

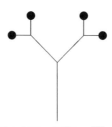

We can define such a tree in the following way:

> An apple tree consists of a trunk and two branches. If we are at the leaves of the tree, there is an apple at the end of each branch; otherwise, each branch is in fact the trunk of a smaller apple tree.

Note that this definition is given in terms of a *smaller apple tree*, i.e. the definition of an apple tree is worded in terms of itself. Earlier, we referred to this as a *recursive definition*.

We first met recursive definitions in Section 6.1. In that section, we noted that any statement in the then part or the else part of an if statement may itself be a if statement. There are, in fact, many places where the syntax of Java is given recursively. For example, the syntax diagram for a *Statement* states it can be an assignment statement, an if statement, a switch statement, a for statement, and so on. Each of the diagrams for if statement, switch statement and for statement refers to *Statement*. The syntax of a *Statement* is therefore given in terms of itself.

In this chapter, we have seen that methods are used to define a sequence of actions. Sometimes, it is useful to define a method in terms of itself. Such a method is called a **recursive method**. In the next few sections, we look at some examples of **recursive functions**.

8.16.2 Using a recursive function for factorial

In Exercise 7.6, you were asked to produce some code to calculate the value of $n!$ (*n factorial*), the product of the first n integers. Suppose that a function is required that returns the value of:

$$n! \equiv \textbf{if } n = 0 \textbf{ then } 1 \textbf{ else } n \times (n-1) \times \cdots \times 3 \times 2 \times 1$$

It is easy to see that:

$$fac(n) \equiv \textbf{if } n = 0 \textbf{ then } 1 \textbf{ else } n \times fac(n-1)$$

and it is this observation that leads to a simple recursive function for factorial:

```
private static int fac(final int n)
{
    if (n==0)
    {
        return 1;
    }
    else
    {
        return n*fac(n-1);
    }
}
```

This is a recursive function because the block of `fac` contains a call of `fac`.

8.16.3 Evaluating a call of the recursive factorial function

We now look at what happens if a program contains a call of fac, e.g.:

```
System.out.println(fac(3));
```

The call of println needs to know the value of fac(3), so the function fac is entered with n equal to 3. As there will be several calls of fac, we will number them. This first call will be referred to as the call at *level 1*. Since n is a parameter, a local variable for n will be created – we will call it n_1 – and it will be assigned the value 3. The program then executes the block of the function:

```
if (n₁==0)   return 1;   else   return n₁*fac(n₁-1);
```

The else part is obeyed – this is a return statement, whose expression has to be evaluated. Although it is straightforward to evaluate the n_1 part of the expression, the evaluation of fac(n_1-1) requires a call of the function fac. So, the evaluation of this expression is suspended until a value for fac(n_1-1) has been found.

We now look at this new call of fac. Since fac has a parameter called n, a new variable, n_2, is created and it is assigned the value of the argument:

$$n_2 = n_1 - 1, \text{i.e. } n_2 = 2$$

The block of the function is executed:

```
if (n₂==0)   return 1;   else   return n₂*fac(n₂-1);
```

Again the execution of the else part leads to another call of fac:

$$n_3 = n_2 - 1, \text{i.e. } n_3 = 1$$

```
if (n₃==0)   return 1;   else   return n₃*fac(n₃-1);
```

Once more the else part is executed, and the program enters fac for the fourth time:

$$n_4 = n_3 - 1, \text{i.e. } n_4 = 0$$

```
if (n₄==0)   return 1;   else   return n₄*fac(n₄-1);
```

As n_4 is 0, the then part is executed and this means that the value 1 is returned.

So the program returns to the point of call that led to entering fac for the fourth time. This call occurred when evaluating n_3 * fac(n_3-1). So it is now able to complete the evaluation of this expression – it is in fact equal to 1×1, i.e. 1. So the value 1 is returned.

Again the return causes the program to return to the point which led to this call of fac. This occurred in the middle of evaluating n_2 * fac(n_2-1). This evaluates to 2×1 and so 2 is returned.

We then return to the evaluation of n_1 * fac(n_1-1) which gives 3×2, i.e. 6. The program returns to the point where fac was called for the first time, and this was in the call of println. So ultimately the value 6 will be output.

8.16.4 Characteristics of recursive methods

A recursive method will recurse indefinitely unless it is coded properly:

- There must be at least one possible call of the method that does not lead to a recursive call. In the case of `fac`, the call `fac(0)` will not lead to a recursive call.

- All other calls of the method must eventually lead to a call that is not recursive. In the case of `fac`, it is *obvious* that any other call of `fac` eventually leads to the call `fac(0)` as the parameter is decreased by 1 at each recursive call.

8.16.5 To recurse or not to recurse!

As this is the first example of a recursive method, the evaluation of a typical call has been presented in a lot of detail. As you can see, a recursive call often leads to a number of other calls of the same method. At each call, a certain amount of time is required to call the method, to acquire the space for its local variables(s), and finally to leave the method. With some recursive methods, the overhead involved in performing all the calls can dominate the time taken to perform the method's task.

Quite often, the same task can be coded using a non-recursive method. For example, it would be easy to produce a non-recursive function for calculating a factorial:

```
private static int fac(final int n)
{
    int tProduct = 1;
    for (int tInt = 1; tInt<=n; tInt++)
    {
        tProduct *= tInt;
    }
    return tProduct;
}
```

This function is a much more efficient way to calculate n!, because it takes less time and less storage.

It was just as easy to write the non-recursive function for `fac` as it was to write the recursive function. This is usually the case for most simple numerical problems: the non-recursive method is easy to write and is more efficient. However, for non-numerical problems, a non-recursive method is often much more complex. And the additional computer time and storage required when executing a recursive method is a good investment because usually it is less obscure to write and hence it can be written and debugged more quickly. This trade-off between program complexity and runtime efficiency often occurs in computing.

8.16.6 Using a recursive function for a Fibonacci sequence

Fibonacci sequences were mentioned in Exercise 7.11. Suppose a Fibonacci sequence has as its first two terms the values 0 and 1. So the sequence is:

```
0   1   1   2   3   5   8   13   21   ...
```

There is an obvious relationship between the terms of the sequence:

$$fib(n) \equiv \textbf{if } n \leq 1 \textbf{ then } n \textbf{ else } fib(n-1) + fib(n-2)$$

where the 0 in the sequence is defined to be the zeroth term of the sequence. This leads to the immediate formulation of a recursive function that can be used to calculate the nth member of the sequence:

```
private static int fib(final int n)
{
    if (n<=1)
    {
        return n;
    }
    else
    {
        return fib(n-1) + fib(n-2);
    }
}
```

No other function for `fib` could be as easy to derive as this one.

But what an inefficient beast it is! Figure 8.8 contains a diagram showing the calls that are made in order to calculate the value of `fib(5)`. It makes another 14 calls of `fib`, and many of these calls are the same as calls that have already been made. Thus, there is a lot of duplicated work, e.g. `fib(1)` has to be evaluated five times.

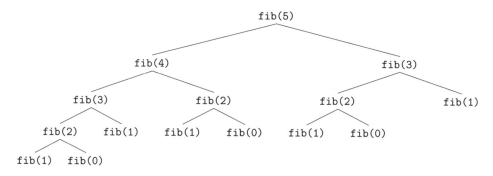

Figure 8.8   The calls involved in evaluating fib (5).

A non-recursive function can be derived after a bit more work:

```
private static int fib(final int n)
{
    if (n<=1)
    {
        return n;
    }
    else
    {
```

```
    int tLastTerm = 0;
    int tNewTerm = 1;
    for (int tTermNumber = 2; tTermNumber<=n; tTermNumber++)
    {
        final int tLastButOneTerm = tLastTerm;
        tLastTerm = tNewTerm;
        tNewTerm = tLastButOneTerm + tLastTerm;
    }
    return tNewTerm;
  }
}
```

Although the non-recursive function is a lot faster than the recursive function, it is more complicated.

8.16.7 When is it natural to use recursion?

Have problems that lend themselves to recursion anything in common? Why are fac and fib so easy to express recursively? In each of these methods, the solution is defined in terms of subproblem(s) that are very similar to the original problem:

problem	subproblem(s)
fac(n)	fac(n-1)
fib(n)	fib(n-1), fib(n-2)

So, if a problem can be related to subproblems that are similar to the original problem, it is natural to use a recursive definition.

8.16.8 Other points about recursion

The examples that have been used in the previous sections have involved the block of a method calling itself – this is known as **direct recursion**. If a method p calls method q, and q calls p, **indirect recursion** is taking place.

In this chapter, all the examples of recursive methods have been examples of recursive functions. It is also possible to have void methods that are recursive.

Tips for programming and debugging

8.1   The declaration of a function (or a void method) is often difficult to understand if there are lots of return statements scattered all over the text of the block of the method declaration. The declaration may be easier to understand if the code of its block is rewritten so that one of the following occurs:

⬤ there is just one return statement at the end of the block;

⬤ the last statement of the block is an if statement or a switch statement, and there is a return statement at the end of each arm of this statement;

- the block consists of a sequence of if statements (each of which has no else part and a then part ending in a return statement) followed by a sequence of statements (not containing return statements), followed by a return statement;

- there are just two return statements, one occurring somewhere in the block and the other one appearing at its end.

However, some people regard it as bad programming practice to use a return statement other than at the end of the block of a method declaration. In this book, we do not adopt this point of view.

8.2   Normally, the call of a function appears in an expression. For example, it might be used on the right-hand side of an assignment or as an argument of a call of a method. However, it is also possible to use the call as a statement. This could be useful if the function performs a complicated and useful task but you do not want to store its result anywhere.

However, it is the view of this book that this is not a good bit of programming language design. As was explained in Tip 3.3, because you can call a function as if it were a void method, you can mistakenly do this and not get the behaviour that you intended.

8.3   It is possible for a statement of the block of a method to assign a value to a *class variable* of the class in which the method is declared. This is referred to as a **side effect** of the method. Since the whole purpose of a method that is a function is to produce a value, it may be argued to be inappropriate for a function to generate other values that have an effect outside the function – you could call it *moonlighting*! So, it is usually considered bad programming practice for a function to alter the value of a class variable.

8.4   If you are confused as to where in the code your program is going wrong, it can often be useful to add debugging statements to each method which will help to identify when methods are entered and left. It can also be useful to include, at the start of a method, debugging statements that output the values of any parameters. The output that is produced can be checked to ensure that the correct values are being passed to the method. For example, method `iOutput-AverageNumberOfVotes` of the `Av4Subs` program could be altered to:

```
        private static void iOutputAverageNumberOfVotes(
                final int pTotalVotes, final int pNumberOfCandidates)
          {
/**/      System.out.println("*** enter iOutputAverageNumberOfVotes");
/**/      System.out.println("*** pTotalVotes: " + pTotalVotes);
/**/      System.out.println("*** pNumberOfCandidates: " +
/**/                                    pNumberOfCandidates);
          final double tAverage =
                          (double)pTotalVotes/pNumberOfCandidates;
          System.out.println("Average number of votes scored is: " +
                          tAverage);
/**/      System.out.println("*** leave iOutputAverageNumberOfVotes");
          }
```

If a method is being called several times and a crash occurs during the execution of the method, this output may be useful for detecting which call is causing problems.

8.5 Guidelines for coding recursive methods (so that they do not recurse indefinitely) were given in Section 8.16.4. If you fail to follow these guidelines, your program will crash with a `StackOverflowError` exception, and you will get a large amount of output identifying the large number of calls that were active when the execution ran out of memory.

Curios, controversies and cover-ups

8.1 In Section 8.6, it was said that the type of the argument of a call must be *assignment compatible* with the type of the parameter. This is not strictly correct. With assignments, it is possible to assign a constant expression of type `int` to a variable of type `byte`, `short` or `char`. However, it is not possible to use a constant expression of type `int` as an argument for a parameter which is of one of these types.

8.2 Usually, the execution of a void method will be terminated when the last statement of its block has been executed. It can also be terminated by executing a return statement:

```
return;
```

anywhere within the block. Note that there is no expression after the `return` when a return statement appears in the block of a void method. In this book, there are no occurrences of this form of return statement.

As mentioned in Tip 8.1, some people regard it as bad programming practice to use a return statement other than at the end of the block of a method declaration. They would therefore see no role for this form of return statement.

8.3 Like C and C++, Java has one **ternary operator**. As the name *ternary* implies, this is an operator that takes three operands. It is used to form a **conditional expression**. Here is the `maximum` function (from Section 8.8) coded using a conditional expression:

```
private static double maximum(final double x, final double y)
{
    return (x>y)?x:y;
}
```

The `?:` operator has a priority that is lower than the `||` operator. This book does not use the `?:` operator because the resulting code is not particularly easy to understand.

8.4 Traditionally, in programming languages, there have been three ways by which a method can affect the environment in which it is called:

1. a method can be a function and so it returns some value;

2. a method alters the value of some variable that is declared elsewhere in the program;

3. the method construct has some mechanism for changing the value of a variable that is passed as an argument.

Although Java has the first two mechanisms (and these were discussed in Section 8.8 and Section 8.12), it does not have the third.

Here is an example of the third mechanism. Suppose you want to write a method that calculates the values of the two roots of a quadratic equation. In some programming languages, you would write a method with a header which looks something like:

```
private static void iSolve(final double a,
                           final double b, final double c,
                           result double x, result double y)
```

where `result` is a keyword of the language indicating that these are result parameters. Although this feature is present in many programming languages, it is debatable as to whether it is a good piece of programming language design.

And the above is not Java. So what can be done in Java? There are a number of possibilities. The first mimics the above. In Section 8.10, it was mentioned that it is possible for a method to change the value of an object pointed to by a reference variable that is passed as an argument to a method. So if you have a class that acts as a **holder** for a value you could use that. We would need the caller to create the object, then call the method that changes the object's value, and then look at the value of the object.

Although an object of a wrapper class such as `java.lang.Double` seems to be the obvious class to use, this does not work in practice because `Double` objects are *immutable*, i.e. it is not possible to change the value of an object of this class once the object has been created.

Instead, you could create your own class: this is a topic that will be discussed in Chapter 11.

In the meanwhile, (provided you have an implementation of the Java 2 Platform) you could use the holder classes of the package `org.omg.CORBA`. Although this package is primarily provided to enable a program to work with objects running in another program probably on a different computer, it includes holder classes for all of the primitive types and for the type `String`. Each of these classes has one field called `value`. Using:

```
import org.omg.CORBA.DoubleHolder;
```

the above heading would become:

```
private static void iSolve(final double a,
                           final double b, final double c,
                           final DoubleHolder x, final DoubleHolder y)
```

Given this header, the method can assign appropriate values to x.value and y.value, and the caller can use code like:

```
final DoubleHolder tRoot1 = new DoubleHolder();
final DoubleHolder tRoot2 = new DoubleHolder();
iSolve(a, b, c, tRoot1, tRoot2);
System.out.println(tRoot1.value);
System.out.println(tRoot2.value);
```

Having said all that, this is a very ugly botch.

It is not the real way in which you should solve this problem. Instead, you should realize that the two roots form an object of your problem, and therefore you could have a class that represents this. In Chapter 11, we will learn how to create such a class. Having declared such a class, e.g. one called Roots, the header of the method can be written as:

```
private static Roots iSolve(final double a,
                            final double b, final double c)
```

But the best solution is not to introduce a class for the roots but one for quadratic equations. If the class is called Qe, it could be used as follows:

```
final Qe tQe = new Qe(a, b, c);
final double x1 = tQe.getRoot1();
final double x2 = tQe.getRoot2();
```

However, such a solution awaits the material in the chapter on creating classes (Chapter 11). And, in a later chapter, this particular problem is set as an exercise (Exercise 12.11).

Exercises

8.1 In Section 8.5 and Section 8.6, methods for drawing a line were defined. Write a program that contains a main method and three declarations called iDrawLine:

```
private static void iDrawLine()
{
    ...
}
private static void iDrawLine(final int pNumberOfCols)
{
    ...
}
private static void iDrawLine(final int pNumberOfCols,
                              final char pCharToOutput)
```

```
{
    for (int tColNumber = 1; tColNumber<=pNumberOfCols; tColNumber++)
    {
        System.out.print(pCharToOutput);
    }
    System.out.println();
}
```

This is permitted because (as explained in Section 8.14) Java allows *method overloading*.

The block of the first two `iDrawLine` method declarations should both just consist of one statement: an appropriate call of the third `iDrawLine` method. The main program should consist of calls of the three methods that test the methods.

8.2   Modify your solution to Exercise 8.1 so that it also contains a fourth method called `iDrawLine`. This method has a `String` instead of a `char` and has a third parameter which is the number of lines that are to be output. So the call:

```
iDrawLine(5, ".:!", 2);
```

produces the output:

```
.:!.:!.:!.:!.:!
.:!.:!.:!.:!.:!
```

8.3   April, June, September and November are months with 30 days; all the other months, except February, have 31 days. February has 29 days in leap years and 28 days in non-leap years.

Write a program which reads in three integers representing a date, i.e. a year, a month and a day. You can assume that the three integers are on separate lines of the data. The program should then check that the integers constitute a valid date of the 21st century. Some examples are given in the following table:

year	month	day	output
1999	12	31	invalid
2000	11	16	valid
2000	11	31	invalid
2000	11	0	invalid
2000	13	0	invalid
2000	0	16	invalid

Important: identify the subproblems of the problem to be solved, and use a separate method for each subproblem.

8.4   Write a program which reads in two integers, *year* and *month*, which represent a year and a month. You can assume that the two integers are on separate lines of the data. The program should then output the calendar for the month in the following format:

```
S   M Tu  W Th  F   S
                    1
2   3   4   5   6   7   8
9  10  11  12  13  14  15
16  17  18  19  20  21  22
23  24  25  26  27  28  29
30
```

This problem divides into the following subproblems:

1. reading in the values of *year* and *month*;

2. finding out the day of the week on which the month starts;

3. finding out how many days there are in the month;

4. outputting the calendar.

Zeller's congruence can be used to do subproblem (2) – it was mentioned in Exercise 6.5; subproblem (3) formed part of Exercise 8.3; and subproblem (4) was tackled by Exercise 7.13.

   Important: use a separate method for each of these subproblems.

8.5 Write a program which calculates the value of:

$$1 - \frac{1}{2} + \frac{1}{3} - \frac{1}{4} + \frac{1}{5} - \frac{1}{6} + \cdots + \frac{1}{499} - \frac{1}{500}$$

in several different ways:

1. adding the terms in one at a time from left to right;

2. adding the terms in one at a time from right to left;

3. subtracting the sum of the negative terms from the sum of the positive terms using the terms from left to right;

4. subtracting the sum of the negative terms from the sum of the positive terms using the terms from right to left.

Important: use a separate method for each method of evaluation.

8.6 Modify your solution to Exercise 7.5 so that the code that uses the Gauss algorithm to calculate the date of Easter Sunday is hidden away in a function (called `iGetDateOfEaster`). The function should have one parameter, the year number, and it should return a `String` containing the date in the format illustrated by `"2001-4-15"`.

   Write another function (called `iTransformDate`) which has one parameter, a `String` like `"2001-4-15"`, and which returns a `String` containing a date in the more friendly format illustrated by `"15th April 2001"`.

   Write a main method that reads in a year number; calls the function to find the date of Easter Sunday; calls the function to produce the `String` in the more friendly format; and then outputs that `String`.

Test your program by outputting the date of Easter Sunday for all the years in the range 1997 to 2006. Check your output with the information given in Exercise 7.5.

8.7 Write a declaration for a function that determines whether a year is a leap year. The function should have one `int` parameter (representing a year) and should return a value of type `boolean`. It should return the value *true* if and only if the year is a leap year. [Note: the details about which years are leap years appear in Section 6.11.]

Use this function in a program that outputs which of the years 1995 to 2006 are leap years.

◇ **8.8** The binomial coefficient $c(n, k)$ has the value:

$$\begin{array}{ll} \frac{n(n-1)(n-2)...(n-k+1)}{k(k-1)(k-2)...(1)} & 1 \le k \le n \\ 1 & k = 0 \\ \text{undefined} & k > n \end{array}$$

For example:

$$c(4, 0) = 1$$
$$c(10, 4) = \frac{10 \times 9 \times 8 \times 7}{4 \times 3 \times 2 \times 1} = 210$$

Write a declaration for a function that has the header:

```
private static int iGetBinCoeff(final int n, final int k)
```

where the function should return the value of $c(n, k)$ if it is defined; otherwise it should return the value 0.

Test `iGetBinCoeff` using numerous values of n and k. Here are some binary coefficients:

		k							
n	0	1	2	3	4	5	6	...
0	1							...
1	1	1						...
2	1	2	1					...
3	1	3	3	1				...
4	1	4	6	4	1			...
5	1	5	10	10	5	1		...
6	1	6	15	20	15	6	1	...
...	...	...	...	...	...	...	...	...

[Hint: if you code `iGetBinCoeff` using `int` arithmetic, you are likely to write code that overflows even for values of n and k that are not very big. It is probably easier for `iGetBinCoeff` to work using `double` arithmetic before rounding its final value to a `int`.]

8.9   All the data we provide is read using a statement like:

```
String tLine = tKeyboard.readLine();
```

If we make a typing error when typing the line, this will probably cause a problem. One improvement would be to allow the user to type some special character, say the @ character, which means 'ignore everything I have typed so far'. So we could type:

```
She loves you@She loves you not@She loves you
```

with the intention that only the characters following the last @ would be retained.

Write a method called iMassageString that can be used as follows:

```
tLine = iMassageString(tLine);
```

i.e. write a method declaration that has the header:

```
private static String iMassageString(final String pString)
```

Include this method declaration in a program that has a main method that tests the use of iMassageString.

8.10 Suppose you are unhappy with having to use @ as the *cancel character*. Add another method called iMassageString to the program you produced for Exercise 8.9. This new method has an additional parameter which is of type char and this character is to be used for the *cancel character*. Alter the block of the original iMassageString method so that the only statement it now has is one that calls the new iMassageString method.

Modify your test program so that it tests the use of both methods.

8.11 Write a declaration for a function (called iSumOfDigits) that returns the sum of the digits of a non-negative integer. For example, if it is passed the value 103, it should return the value 4. The code of the function declaration should use recursion.

Write a main method that reads in an integer, calls the function to find the sum of its digits, and then outputs this sum.

8.12 One particular recursive function that has attracted a lot of attention is a function known as **Ackermann's function**:

```
private static int iAck(final int m, final int n)
{
    if (m==0)
    {
        return n + 1;
    }
    else if (n==0)
    {
        return iAck(m - 1, 1);
    }
```

```
    else
    {
        return iAck(m - 1, iAck(m, n - 1));
    }
}
```

This is a simplification of a function devised in 1928 by a German mathematical logician called Wilhelm Ackermann. Since then it has become infamous because it looks fairly simple:

m	n 0	1	2	3	4	5	6	7	...
0	1	2	3	4	5	6	7	8	...
1	2	3	4	5	6	7	8	9	...
2	3	5	7	9	11	13	15	17	...
...	...	...	...	...	...	...	...	...	...

and yet it leads to some amazingly complex calculations. For example, the calculation of iAck(2,2) requires 27 recursive calls of iAck in order to produce the value 7.

Type in the function declaration and write a program that produces a table like the one given above.

What are the values of iAck(3,n) for values of n in the range 0 to 9?

You may find your computer straining a bit if you try to evaluate iAck(3,n) if $n > 7$ or iAck(4,n) if $n > 0$ or iAck(m, n) if $m > 4$. This is not unreasonable as the calculation of iAck(3,6), for example, requires 172233 calls of iAck and at the deepest call of the method there are 1017 other active calls.

8.13 Suppose that we have found the quotient and remainder resulting from the whole number division of a non-negative integer n by 8. Suppose that we repeat this process on the quotient, and that this process is then repeatedly executed until a quotient equal to 0 is obtained. The remainders that are produced by this technique can be used to form the base-8 representation of the integer n (i.e. the value of n in octal).

For example, here is what happens if the technique is applied when n has the value 41679:

number	*quotient*	*remainder*
41679	5209	7
5209	651	1
651	81	3
81	10	1
10	1	2
1	0	1

So the base-8 representation of 41679 is 121317.

Write a declaration for a recursive method iToOctalString that has the header:

```
private static String iToOctalString(final int pValue)
```

The method should return the base-8 representation of the int value that is passed as an argument. [Hint: the block of iToOctalString should first find the quotient and remainder of the division; then it should use a recursive call of iToOctalString that returns the digits of the quotient.]

Test the method by including it in a program that outputs the base-8 representation of the values 0 to 65.

8.14 If you have completed the previous exercise, then it is easy to modify your solution to use any base in the range 2 to 10. Write a declaration for a method that has the header:

```
private static String iToBaseString(final int pValue, final int pBase)
```

Test the method by including it in a program that outputs a table of the values 0 to 20 in bases 2 to 10.

8.15 Look back at your solutions to the exercises of the previous chapters and identify code that could usefully be hidden away in a method.

Chapter 9

Using other forms of control statements

In earlier chapters, we have looked at a construct, the *for statement*, for allowing a piece of code to be executed many times, and a construct, the *if statement*, for making decisions. In this chapter, we will look at other ways of controlling the flow through a program.

We will look at one other decision-making construct, the *switch statement*, and at two other statements for looping, the *while statement* and the *do statement*.

We will also see how we can use a *try statement* to handle exceptions.

By the end of this chapter, you will know about all the statements that can be used to control the flow of a Java program.

9.1 Deterministic and non-deterministic loops

Most programming languages provide constructs to allow two kinds of looping, called *deterministic loops* and *non-deterministic loops*. In a **deterministic loop**, the body of the loop is repeated a pre-determined number of times, whereas, in a **non-deterministic loop**, some situation arises during one of the executions of the body of the loop which is the cue for the loop to be terminated.

Java has three looping constructs. The for statement is normally used to construct deterministic loops, whereas the other two looping constructs (the *while statement* and the *do statement*) are used to construct non-deterministic loops. In the first part of this chapter, we will use an example to illustrate the difference between these two kinds of loops, and at the same time introduce *while statements* and *do statements*.

Suppose we have values which are a set of monthly rainfall figures and that these values are preceded by a number stating how many months there are. For example, the data might be:

```
3
2.7
0.5
4.2
```

Suppose we want a program that finds the sum of these rainfall figures.

The program can first read in the value that indicates how many rainfall figures there are:

```
String tLine = tKeyboard.readLine();
final int tNumberOfMonths = Integer.parseInt(tLine);
```

Then it can read each of the rainfall figures by using a readLine call that is inside a loop. Now the program knows (prior to executing this loop) the number of times the body of this loop is to be executed – it is given by the value of the variable tNumberOfMonths. This is therefore a *deterministic loop* according to the jargon given above.

So, in Java, the appropriate construct to use is a for statement. The following code can be used:

```
String tLine = tKeyboard.readLine();
final int tNumberOfMonths = Integer.parseInt(tLine);
double tRainfallSum = 0.0;
for (int tMonthNumber = 1; tMonthNumber<=tNumberOfMonths; tMonthNumber++)
{
    tLine = tKeyboard.readLine();
    final double tFigureForAMonth = Double.parseDouble(tLine);
    tRainfallSum += tFigureForAMonth;
}
System.out.println("The sum of the rainfall figures is: " + tRainfallSum);
```

However, if you have a lot of data, it can be very inconvenient to have to count how many data values there are. One way of avoiding this is to follow the data values by a **sentinel value** (also known as a **rogue value**) rather than precede the values with a count. The sentinel value needs to be a value that cannot be part of the real data. For example, in the rainfall problem, a negative value can be put at the end of the rainfall figures (instead of preceding the values by an integer which indicates how many values there are).

So, instead of using the data given above, we could use data like:

```
2.7
0.5
4.2
-1.0
```

As each value is read in, it will have to be checked to see whether it is the sentinel value. If it is, we know that the loop has to be finished. Thus, we have the situation described above as a *non-deterministic loop*.

For a non-deterministic loop, in Java we have a choice as to whether the loop is represented by a while statement, a while with a break, or a do statement. We now look at each of these.

9.2　Using while statements

The code that results from using a **while statement** for the rainfall figures problem is:

```
double tRainfallSum = 0.0;
String tLine = tKeyboard.readLine();
double tFigureForAMonth = Double.parseDouble(tLine);
while (tFigureForAMonth>=0.0)
{
    tRainfallSum += tFigureForAMonth;
    tLine = tKeyboard.readLine();
    tFigureForAMonth = Double.parseDouble(tLine);
}
// tFigureForAMonth<0.0
System.out.println("The sum of the rainfall figures is: " + tRainfallSum);
```

A while statement is coded using a *BooleanExpression* and a *Statement*. Although the syntax of a while statement (shown in Figure 9.1) allows any statement to appear

WhileStatement:

Figure 9.1　The syntax of a while statement.

in the body of a while statement, in this book we will always use a *Statement* that is a *Block*.

When a while statement is executed, the *BooleanExpression* is evaluated first. If it has the value *true*, the *Statement* is executed and then the *BooleanExpression* is tested again. Provided the expression has the value *true*, the *Statement* will be executed again, and then the *BooleanExpression* will be re-evaluated. In this way, the *Statement* is repeatedly executed. However, each time before it is executed, the *BooleanExpression* is re-evaluated. At some point it should have the value *false*. The execution of the while statement finishes when this happens.

All this long-winded description of the meaning of a while statement is summarized by the execution diagram given in Figure 9.2.

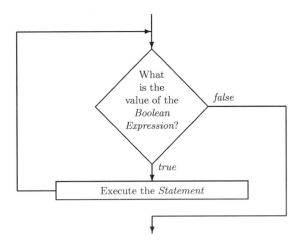

Figure 9.2   The execution diagram of a while statement.

9.3 Stay conditions and quit conditions

The condition that is given after the `while` is the condition that is used to decide whether to execute the loop again. In the book, this condition will be referred to as the **stay condition**. In the above example of a while statement, it is:

```
tFigureForAMonth>=0.0
```

The program executes the loop again if this condition is true. However, if `tFigureForAMonth` has a value less than zero, the loop is terminated. The condition `tFigureForAMonth<0.0` will be referred to as the **quit condition**. It is useful to put a comment containing this quit condition on the line immediately following the while statement.

Sometimes the quit condition is easier to produce than the stay condition. Since it is the *not* of the quit condition, the stay condition can then be derived from the quit condition using De Morgan's laws – see Tip 6.5.

Here is a slightly more involved example. Suppose we want to keep reading numbers so long as they are in the range 0.0 to 99.0. Here is some code for this example:

```
double tSum = 0.0;
String tLine = tKeyboard.readLine();
double tNumber = Double.parseDouble(tLine);
while (tNumber>=0.0 && tNumber<=99.0)
{
    tSum += tNumber;
    tLine = tKeyboard.readLine();
    tNumber = Double.parseDouble(tLine);
}
// tNumber<0.0 || tNumber>99.0
System.out.println("The sum of the figures is: " + tSum);
```

Although in the rainfall figures problem we can use a negative value as a sentinel value, in other situations all possible numerical values may be legitimate values of the data. Instead, we could use some non-numeric value in the data such as end or **** or even an empty line.

So, suppose we terminate the data with a line that just contains the string end. We want to keep reading lines so long as the line that has just been read does not contain the string end. We can use the function equals (from java.lang.String) to check the contents of a line:

```
tLine.equals("end")
```

We will have to *not* the result:

```
! tLine.equals("end")
```

if we want to check whether a line does not contain this string:

```
double tSum = 0.0;
String tLine = tKeyboard.readLine();
while ( ! tLine.equals("end") )
{
    final double tNumber = Double.parseDouble(tLine);
    tSum += tNumber;
    tLine = tKeyboard.readLine();
}
// tLine.equals("end")
System.out.println("The sum of the figures is: " + tSum);
```

9.4) Using a break statement to exit a while loop

In all of the examples of while statements given above, the statement(s) to read a new value from the keyboard appear twice: they occur before the loop and they also occur as the last task to be performed in the body of the loop. The first example (given in Section 9.2) could instead be written in the following way:

```
double tRainfallSum = 0.0;
while (true)
{
   final String tLine = tKeyboard.readLine();
   final double tFigureForAMonth = Double.parseDouble(tLine);
   if (tFigureForAMonth<0.0)
   {
      break;
   }
   tRainfallSum += tFigureForAMonth;
}
System.out.println("The sum of the rainfall figures is: " + tRainfallSum);
```

The use of `true` as the boolean expression of this while statement effectively creates an infinite loop for which the only escape is to execute its **break statement**. In Java, if a break statement of a looping statement is executed, the looping statement is immediately terminated.

With this kind of while statement, only the first *half* of the body of the loop is executed on the last execution of the body of the loop. For this reason, such a loop is sometimes called an $n + \frac{1}{2}$ **times loop**.

We have already noted that, in the code given in Section 9.2, the code to read a new value is duplicated. Although one of the advantages of using an $n + \frac{1}{2}$ times loop is that it avoids this duplication, the duplication could also have been avoided by putting the code into a method. Another advantage of using an $n + \frac{1}{2}$ times loop is that the boolean expression used to decide whether to leave an $n + \frac{1}{2}$ times loop is a quit condition (which often makes the loop easier to understand).

9.5 Using do statements

So far, this chapter has presented two ways in which while statements can be used to code non-deterministic loops. In the Java programming language, such loops can instead be coded using a **do statement**. Here is some code for the rainfall figures problem that uses a do statement instead:

```
double tRainfallSum = 0.0;
double tFigureForAMonth;
do
{
   final String tLine = tKeyboard.readLine();
   tFigureForAMonth = Double.parseDouble(tLine);
   if (tFigureForAMonth>=0.0)
   {
      tRainfallSum += tFigureForAMonth;
   }
} while (tFigureForAMonth>=0.0);
// tFigureForAMonth<0.0
System.out.println("The sum of the rainfall figures is: " + tRainfallSum);
```

Inside the body of the loop, the program does two things: it reads in a new rainfall figure, and then it adds this rainfall figure into the sum provided the rainfall figure is not negative. The program keeps doing these two statements so long as the rainfall figure is positive. Like the while statement, the boolean expression of a do statement is the condition for staying in the loop. So, once again, to aid understanding, the quit condition can be included in a comment after the do statement.

The syntax and execution diagrams for the do statement are given below.

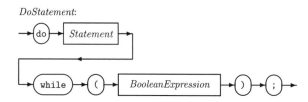

Figure 9.3 The syntax of a do statement.

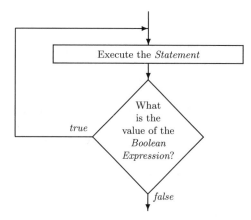

Figure 9.4 The execution diagram of a do statement.

You can see that a do statement is, in many ways, similar to a while statement. Both are coded using a *BooleanExpression* and a *Statement*. There are, however, two important differences:

1. The testing of the *BooleanExpression* is done at the start of the loop for a while statement and at the end of the loop for a do statement.

2. From this, it follows that the body of a do statement is always executed at least once. However, because the *BooleanExpression* of a while statement is tested before the *Statement* is executed, the *Statement* of a while statement will not be executed at all if the first evaluation of the *BooleanExpression* produces the value *false*.

9.6 Choosing between while statements and do statements

It is possible to write a looping statement (i.e. a for, a while or a do) that contains several break statements, and the looping statement will terminate when any one of these break statements is executed. However, the code becomes a lot harder to understand if there are a lot of break statements in a looping statement. For this reason, some people argue that it is best never to use break statements. If you are going to use break statements, it is better programming practice to have just one break statement within a while (true) statement (to form an $n + \frac{1}{2}$ times loop).

As far as choosing between a while statement and a do statement is concerned, people often write code using a do statement forgetting that there may be occasions when the *Statement* of the loop ought not to be executed. Unless you are really really certain that the body of the loop has always to be executed at least once, you should code a non-deterministic loop as a while statement rather than as a do statement. In this book, there are few uses of the do statement.

9.7 Exiting from a program

Sometimes a program detects that something really weird has happened, and that it is not in a position to continue. What we really would like to do is to abort the execution of the program. In Java, if a program calls the method exit of the class java.lang.System, the execution of the program is immediately terminated. For example:

```
System.exit(1);
```

The value of the argument (in this example, the value 1) is passed to the environment from which the Java program was started. For details about how you could use this value, see Curio 9.2.

The exit method should only be called as part of some code which is executed when something untoward has happened: it should not form part of the code that is normally executed when a program is executed.

9.8 Checking the values supplied in the data

It is very easy to make mistakes when typing data at a keyboard. Programs can help by being lenient if a user has typed invalid characters. We now look at some techniques that can be used by a program in order to check that the supplied data values are appropriate.

We will look at the Av4Subs program given in Figure 8.6. This program contains the statement:

```
final int tNumberOfCandidates = iObtainNumberOfCandidates();
```

where the block of the iObtainNumberOfCandidates function contains:

```
System.out.print("How many candidates are there? ");
System.out.flush();
final String tLine = iKeyboard.readLine();
return Integer.parseInt(tLine);
```

It may be that a user of this program inadvertently types in one or more non-numerical characters. If this happens, an exception occurs. This is because the body of parseInt is unable to parse the string passed in its argument, i.e. the string to which the variable tLine is pointing. So, although the call of readLine succeeds, the call of parseInt leads to an exception. It will be a NumberFormatException exception (from the java.lang package): this exception was mentioned in Section 4.9.

For example, if the user types 5u instead of 57, the program will crash with the following output:

```
How many candidates are there? 5u
Exception in thread "main" java.lang.NumberFormatException: 5u
        at java.lang.Integer.parseInt(Integer.java:418)
        at java.lang.Integer.parseInt(Integer.java:458)
        at Av4Subs.iObtainNumberOfCandidates(Av4Subs.java:47)
        at Av4Subs.main(Av4Subs.java:17)
```

Because NumberFormatException is an unchecked exception, there is no obligation on the programmer to provide code indicating what should happen if the exception occurs. However, we may wish to provide code to handle the exception if we would like the program to be more user-friendly. So we wish to handle any exception that is a NumberFormatException exception. In Java, a program can do this by using a *try statement*.

9.9 Using try statements

As you can see from Figure 9.5, the syntax of a **try statement** has many possibilities. However, to begin with, we will look at a simple example.

What should the above code do if the user types in invalid characters? We might want to abort the execution of the program. So, we could alter the block of iObtainNumberOfCandidates so that it contains:

```
int tNumberOfCandidates = 0;
try
{
   System.out.print("How many candidates are there? ");
   System.out.flush();
   final String tLine = iKeyboard.readLine();
   tNumberOfCandidates = Integer.parseInt(tLine);
}
catch(final NumberFormatException pNumberFormatException)
{
   System.out.println("You pressed a non-digit character");
   System.exit(1);
}
return tNumberOfCandidates;
```

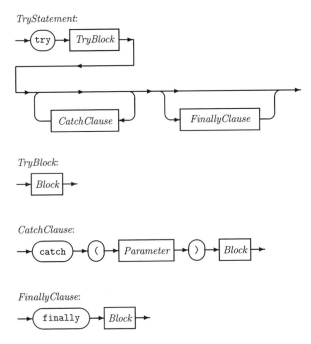

Figure 9.5 The syntax of a try statement.

The above code contains a try statement that has a **catch clause** for any Number-FormatException exceptions. When the try statement is executed, the statements of its try block are executed. In the above example, they are the statements:

```
System.out.print("How many candidates are there? ");
System.out.flush();
final String tLine = iKeyboard.readLine();
tNumberOfCandidates = Integer.parseInt(tLine);
```

If a NumberFormatException exception occurs while this try block is being executed, control is transferred to the statements of the NumberFormatException catch clause:

```
System.out.println("You pressed a non-digit character");
System.exit(1);
```

By the way, a catch clause is often called an **exception handler**.

So, if the user types an invalid character:

```
How many candidates are there? 5u
```

the call of parseInt will throw a NumberFormatException exception. This will be handled by the catch clause which outputs the own error message:

```
You pressed a non-digit character
```

and then the execution of System.exit(1) will cause the program to terminate.

Outputting your own error message is a lot better than a program crashing with messages about exceptions. However, aborting the program is not particularly friendly to the user. It would be better to ask the user for the value again. You can code this in several ways. Here is one way:

```
int tNumberOfCandidates;
System.out.print("How many candidates are there? ");
System.out.flush();
while (true)
{
    try
    {
        final String tLine = iKeyboard.readLine();
        tNumberOfCandidates = Integer.parseInt(tLine);
        break;
    }
    catch(final NumberFormatException pNumberFormatException)
    {
        System.out.println("You pressed a non-digit character");
        System.out.print("Please type in the number of candidates again: ");
        System.out.flush();
    }
}
return tNumberOfCandidates;
```

Here the try statement is inside a `while (true)` statement. If a `NumberFormat-Exception` exception does not occur while the statements of the try block are being executed, the break statement at the end of the try block causes the while statement to be left.

The above code forms a useful skeleton of code for reading a value without crashing if the user types inappropriate characters. A commonly used way of putting statements together is called a **pattern**. Other patterns will be pointed out later.

9.10 The catch clause of a try statement

A catch clause of a try statement signifies through the type of its parameter the kind of exception that it can handle. For example, because the catch clause of the above try statement has a parameter of the type `NumberFormatException`, that catch clause will only be executed if a `NumberFormatException` occurs (while executing the try block).

In the examples of try statements given above, there is only *one* catch clause. As you can see from the syntax diagram (given in Figure 9.5), a try statement may include zero or more catch clauses. So, if a try block can cause more than one kind of exception, we can provide different catch clauses, one for each kind of exception. See Curio 9.3 if you wish to provide a catch clause that handles any kind of exception.

The syntax diagram implies you can have a try statement that simply consists of `try` followed by a try block (without any catch clauses or a finally clause). However, this syntax diagram simplifies the true syntax: Java requires a try statement *either* to have one or more catch clauses *or* to have a finally clause *or* to have both. We will look at a try statement that has a finally clause in Section 10.12.

When an exception occurs, a pointer to an object is passed from where the exception occurred to the handler. In the above example, this object will be of the class NumberFormatException. This object is accessible within the block of the catch clause by using the parameter of the catch clause (i.e. by using pNumberFormat-Exception in the above code). The information that is contained in this object depends on the kind of exception. Some details are provided in Curio 9.4. Although the syntax of a catch clause requires us to provide the parameter, often we will not refer to this parameter in the block of the catch clause. This is true in the examples given above.

9.11 Further checking of the values in the data

In the program Av4Subs, the variable tNumberOfCandidates should be greater than 0, and so the program could check whether the value that is typed is in fact greater than 0. Also, it would probably be an error if some unreasonably high value is typed. Of course, it is a matter of judgement as to what constitutes a high value. We will suppose that there are not more than 50 candidates. These further checks are tested in the following code:

```
final int tMaxNumberOfCandidates = 50;
int tNumberOfCandidates;
System.out.print("How many candidates are there? ");
System.out.flush();
while (true)
{
   try
   {
      final String tLine = iKeyboard.readLine();
      tNumberOfCandidates = Integer.parseInt(tLine);
      if (tNumberOfCandidates>=1 &&
          tNumberOfCandidates<=tMaxNumberOfCandidates)
      {
         break;
      }
      System.out.println("This is not a value in the range 1 to " +
                      tMaxNumberOfCandidates);
   }
   catch(final NumberFormatException pNumberFormatException)
   {
      System.out.println("You pressed a non-digit character");
   }
   System.out.print("Please type in the number of candidates again: ");
   System.out.flush();
}
return tNumberOfCandidates;
```

9.12 The proper use of exceptions

Although the try statement is a useful statement, an exception should, as its name suggests, be used only for handling exceptional circumstances. If there is appropriate code that can be written which does not use exceptions, it is probably preferable to use that code.

For example, suppose we have written a program that plays a game sometimes known as *Hangman*. In this game, the program chooses a string and the user of the program has to guess the string. Suppose we allow the user to keep choosing numbers, and each time the user chooses a number we tell him/her what character is at that position in the string. We could code a part of this problem using:

```
final int tCharNumber = Integer.parseInt(tLine);
final int tCharAtIndex = tCharNumber - 1;
try
{
    final char tChar = tString.charAt(tCharAtIndex);
    System.out.println("The character at that position is: " + tChar);
}
catch(final StringIndexOutOfBoundsException pStringIndexOutOfBoundsException)
{
    System.out.println("That character does not exist");
}
```

However, many people argue that this is an inappropriate use of exceptions. Instead, we could use:

```
final int tMaxCharAtIndex = tString.length() - 1;
...
final int tCharNumber = Integer.parseInt(tLine);
final int tCharAtIndex = tCharNumber - 1;
if (tCharAtIndex>=0 && tCharAtIndex<=tMaxCharAtIndex)
{
    final char tChar = tString.charAt(tCharAtIndex);
    System.out.println("The character at that position is: " + tChar);
}
else
{
    System.out.println("That character does not exist");
}
```

There is more information about exceptions and their use/misuse in Section 21.1.

9.13 Using switch statements

An if statement provides a way of choosing which of two pieces of code to execute – the choice is based upon the value of a boolean expression. If we arrange several if statements in the form of a cascade (as was done in Section 6.7), we can choose to execute one of several pieces of code. A **switch statement** provides an alternative mechanism which can sometimes be used to do this.

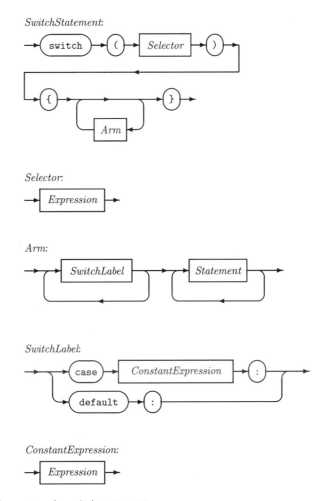

Figure 9.6 The syntax of a switch statement.

The syntax diagrams for a switch statement are given in Figure 9.6. An example will help in the explanation of some of their mysteries:

```
int tDayNumber;
int tWeekNumber;
...
switch (tDayNumber)
{
    case 2:
    case 3:
```

```
case 4:
case 5:
case 6:
{
    iGotoWork();
    iWork();
    iGoHome();
    iWatchTV();
    iGotoThePub();
}
break;
case 7:
{
    // do nothing
}
break;
case 1:
{
    iReadRatherHeavySundayNewspaper();
    if (tWeekNumber%2==0)
    {
        iWashCar();
    }
}
break;
}
```

There are usually several arms to a switch statement. Each **arm** consists of one or more switch labels followed by one or more *Statements*; and each **switch label** is introduced by the case (or the default) keyword. In this book, for an *Arm*, we will use the syntax given by the diagram in Figure 9.7 instead of that given in Figure 9.6. The reasons for doing this are given in Curio 9.5. Preceding the first arm, there is an expression – it is given within the parentheses that follow the switch keyword. In this book, this expression will be called the **selector**.

Arm:

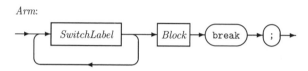

Figure 9.7   The syntax that is used in this book for an *Arm*.

What happens when a switch statement is executed? First, the value of the selector is obtained; and then a sequence of statements is executed. The sequence that gets chosen comprises the statements following a label that has a value equal to the value of the selector.

In the above example, if tDayNumber has a value in the range 2 to 6, the block containing the following sequence of statements is executed:

```
iGotoWork();
iWork();
iGoHome();
iWatchTV();
iGotoThePub();
```

and then a break statement is executed. Earlier (in Section 9.4), we saw a break state-ment being used to terminate the execution of a while statement. When a break state-ment of a switch statement is executed, the switch statement is exited.

If instead tDayNumber is equal to 7, very little happens. Following the label:

```
case 7:
```

is an empty block and a break statement (which causes control to leave the switch statement).

Finally, if tDayNumber happens to have the value 1, the following two statements are executed:

```
iReadRatherHeavySundayNewspaper();
if (tWeekNumber%2==0)
{
    iWashCar();
}
```

and then a break statement is executed.

9.14 The default part of a switch statement

We now consider what happens if the selector does not have a value that is the same as any of the labels.

If there is a **default part** to the switch statement, the statements following the default label are executed. For example, the last part of the above switch statement could be altered to:

```
    ...
    case 1:
    {
        iReadRatherHeavySundayNewspaper();
        if (tWeekNumber%2==0)
        {
            iWashCar();
        }
    }
    break;
```

```
default:
{
    System.out.println("tDayNumber is out of range");
    System.out.println("It has the value: " + tDayNumber);
    System.exit(1);
}
break;
}
```

In this way, an error message would be output if tDayNumber has a value less than 1 or greater than 7.

If the value of the selector does not equal any of the labels and there is no default part, control ignores the switch statement and moves to the statement following the switch statement.

9.15 Some other points about switch statements

Although the revised syntax for an *Arm* (that was given in Figure 9.7) implies that an *Arm* must end in a break statement, an examination of the real syntax for an *Arm* (given in Figure 9.6) shows that this is not the case. If the statements of an arm are being executed and the arm does not end in a break statement, the switch statement is not left: instead control passes to the first statement of the next arm. If you think that your code requires this feature, this book would recommend you to think again: rewrite the code to avoid using this feature. However, if you *must* use it, its use ought to be documented: see Tip 9.5.

Here are some other points about switch statements:

- The selector must be of the type char, byte, short or int.
- The labels must be of a type that is *assignment compatible* with the type of the selector.
- The labels must have different values.

Tips for programming and debugging

9.1   When looking at if statements in Chapter 6, you were warned (in Tip 6.5) that mistakes are often made when a boolean expression contains subconditions (combined using && or ||) and also contains uses of the != operator. Actually, such mistakes usually occur when the complex boolean expression is the stay condition of a while statement or a do statement. You are less likely to make such a mistake if you also write down the quit condition in a comment immediately after the while statement – see Section 9.3. By using De Morgan's laws (given in Tip 6.5), you can then check that the stay condition and the quit condition correspond, i.e. that one is the *not* of the other.

9.2   In Tip 7.3, we saw that it is possible to write for statements that seem to get into an **infinite loop**. However, it is probably more likely that an incorrect while statement (or an incorrect do statement) is the cause of an infinite loop. For example, an infinite loop will occur if none of the statements in the body of a while statement alters the value of at least one of the variables of the boolean expression (that controls the while statement).

For example, consider the following:

```
double tRainfallSum = 0.0;
String tLine = tKeyboard.readLine();
double tFigureForAMonth = Double.parseDouble(tLine);
while (tFigureForAMonth>=0.0)
{
    tRainfallSum += tFigureForAMonth;
}
// tFigureForAMonth<0.0
System.out.println("The sum of the rainfall figures is: " +
                   tRainfallSum);
```

Here we have forgotten to put in the loop the statements that read in another rainfall figure. Consequently, tFigureForAMonth, the only variable that appears in the stay condition, never gets its value changed. Hence, if the first value in the data is not negative, the program enters the loop and fails to exit from it.

Details about how to get a program out of an infinite loop were given in Tip 7.4.

9.3   It may be that the output at the point where a program is going wrong disappears off the top of the screen because the program produces lots more output before it finishes. If you want to see this output, you could temporarily add a call of System.exit at an appropriate point of the program, and this would cause the program to finish early.

9.4   It is fairly easy to forget the break statement that normally appears at the end of an arm of a switch statement. And you may be baffled by what your program is doing when you execute it if you inadvertently forget a break statement. As explained in Section 9.13, control falls through to the first statement of the next arm. The easiest way of avoiding this mess is to get into the habit of typing the code in the following order: first type the switch label(s), then the {, then the }, then the line containing break, and then the statements that come between the { and } symbols.

9.5   In Section 9.13, it was recommended that you always have a break statement at the end of each arm of a switch statement. If you find it is necessary to ignore this recommendation, you should help the reader of your code by using a comment to document this. For example:

```
switch (...)
{
    case 1:
    {
        ...
    }
    // falls through
    case 2:
    {
        ...
    }
    break;
    ...
}
```

However, the use of this feature can usually be avoided. In the above example, you could instead use:

```
switch (...)
{
    case 1:
    {
        ...
        iCommonCode();
    }
    break;
    case 2:
    {
        iCommonCode();
    }
    break;
    ...
}
```

where the method iCommonCode contains the code that is common to both arms.

9.6 You will get a compilation error if you attempt to write code like:

```
case 2:
{
    ...
    return tNumberOfCandidates;
}
break;
```

You will need to remove the break statement as the compiler will complain that this statement cannot be executed (because it is preceded by a return statement).

9.7 Tip 6.3 pointed out that it is not possible to use any variables declared in the then part or the else part of an if statement in the statements that follow the if statement. And Section 7.4 pointed out that it is not possible to use any variables declared in the body of a for statement in the statements that follow the for statement. In the same way, the scope of any variable declared in the try block of a try statement is the text of the try block.

Curios, controversies and cover-ups

9.1 In C and C++, it has been traditional to set up an $n + \frac{1}{2}$ times loop using:

```
for (;;)
{
    ... // use a break statement to quit the infinite loop
}
```

Although this is also legal in Java, the following is probably easier to understand:

```
while (true)
{
    ... // use a break statement to quit the infinite loop
}
```

9.2 As was explained in Section 9.7, the execution of a call of the method `exit` of the class `java.lang.System` causes the immediate termination of the program. Here is an example of a call:

```
System.exit(1);
```

It is possible for the environment running the Java program to find out the value of the argument that was passed in the call of `exit`. If the Java program is being used in an MS-DOS window, this can be done by looking at the value of the `ERRORLEVEL` environment variable. If Java is being used in a UNIX environment, the value that was passed can be found from the `$?` variable if the Bourne shell (or one of its derivatives) is being used or from the `$status` variable if you are using the C shell (or one of its derivatives).

9.3 Because all Exception classes are *derived* from the class `Exception`, you can use a try statement with the following catch clause if you want to catch any exception that occurs when its try block is being executed:

```
catch(final Exception pException)
{
    ...
}
```

If, instead, you want to handle `NumberFormatExceptions` in one way and to handle all other kinds of exceptions in some other way, you can use a try statement with the following catch clauses. Note that the order of these catch clauses is important.

```
catch(final NumberFormatException pNumberFormatException)
{
    ...
}
catch(final Exception pException)
{
    ...
}
```

9.4 Section 9.10 only gave a few details about the `Exception` object that is passed to the catch clause. There are several methods that can be applied to this object. They include `getMessage`, `toString` and `printStackTrace`.

The `getMessage` method returns a `String` that describes something about what caused the exception. For example, for a `NumberFormat-Exception` exception, it is the string that was passed to `parseInt` (for example). And for a `StringIndexOutOfBoundsException` exception, it is a string formed from the `int` that was passed to `charAt` (for example). The `toString` method returns a `String` that contains the name of the exception (such as `java.lang.NumberFormatException`) followed by a colon, followed by a space, followed by the result of calling `getMessage`. Finally, the `printStackTrace` method outputs a line containing the string produced by calling `toString` followed by lines giving a trace of how the execution got to the point where the exception occurred. So, as an example, here is how you might call `printStackTrace`:

```
catch(final NumberFormatException pNumberFormatException)
{
    pNumberFormatException.printStackTrace();
}
```

9.5 Suppose, in one arm of a switch statement, you need a temporary variable to point to a line of data. Suppose you wish to do a similar thing in another arm of the switch statement. The following code is illegal because it attempts to declare the variable `tName` twice in the block that forms the body of the do statement:

```
do
{
    switch (tCommandLetter)
    {
        case 'o':
            final String tName = tKeyboard.readLine();
            ...
            break;
        case 'r':
            final String tName = tKeyboard.readLine();
            ...
```

```
            break;
        ...

    }

}
```

You could instead use one `tName` variable:

```
do
{
    String tName = null;
    switch (tCommandLetter)
    {
        case 'o':
            tName = tKeyboard.readLine();

            ...

            break;
        case 'r':
            tName = tKeyboard.readLine();

            ...

            break;

        ...

    }

}
```

However, this is not a good idea because it makes the scope of `tName` wider than we need.

Because, in this book, we recommend that a block is always used after a switch label, the above problem does not arise. So this book recommends you to use something like:

```
do
{
    switch (tCommandLetter)
    {
        case 'o':
        {
            final String tName = tKeyboard.readLine();

            ...

            break;
        }
        case 'r':
        {
            final String tName = tKeyboard.readLine();

            ...

            break;
        }

        ...

    }

}
```

However, instead of putting the break statement as the last statement of the block, in this book we recommend that it is put after the block. This is because it is thought that it might be easier to notice when the break statement has inadvertently been left out:

```
do
{
    switch (tCommandLetter)
    {
        case 'o':
        {
            final String tName = tKeyboard.readLine();
            ...
        }
        break;
        case 'r':
        {
            final String tName = tKeyboard.readLine();
            ...
        }
        break;
        ...
    }
}
```

9.6 Java also has a continue statement: this is used to transfer control to the end of the current iteration of a looping statement. A continue statement may include a label and, if this is the case, control skips to the end of the current iteration of the loop that has this label.

We have already seen two uses of a break statement: to leave a while statement early and to leave a switch statement. It is possible for a break statement to include a label, and this label indicates that it is the statement with that label that is to be left:

```
input_loop:
    while (...)
    {
        ...
        while (...)
        {
            ...
            break input_loop;
            ...
        }
        ...
    }
```

Many people argue that the use of continue statements or break statements that have labels produces programs that are hard to understand. In this book, such statements are not used.

Exercises

9.1 In Exercise 7.7, the first item of the data was the number of people in the family. Modify your solution to this exercise so that, instead, a negative value is used to indicate the end of the data. Test your program for the same group of people mentioned in Exercise 7.7.

9.2 Write a program that reads in two integers and then outputs the sum and difference of the two integers. The program should do this repeatedly, stopping when both values are zero. Do not output the sum and difference of the two zero values.

9.3 Write a program that reads in an integer value n, followed by n lists of positive double numbers, each list being terminated by a negative number. After each list has been read, output the average of the numbers in the list.

For example, the data could have the values:

```
3
1.3
2.7
-1.0
1.3
-2.0
1.3
2.7
-1.0
```

The 3 at the start of the data means that the data contains three lists. The first list contains the values 1.3 and 2.7; the second list has one value, the value being 1.3; and the third list contains the values 1.3 and 2.7.

9.4 The greatest common divisor (GCD) of a pair of integers m and n is defined to be the largest integer that exactly divides both m and n. Back in about 300 BC, Euclid, a geometrician from Alexandria, devised the following algorithm for finding the GCD:

    1. Start with the pair of integers (m, n).

    loop while the $\Big\{$ **1.** Using the notation (m, n) to refer to
    2. second value of the   the pair, calculate the remainder r of
    pair is non-zero   the whole number division of m by n.
                     2. Replace the pair (m, n) by (n, r).

    3. The GCD is equal to the first value of the pair.

For example, if the pair is *(2772,714)*, the algorithm produces the following results:

$$GCD(2772, 714) = GCD(714, 630) = GCD(630, 84)$$
$$= GCD(84, 42)   = GCD(42, 0)   = 42$$

Write a (non-recursive) function declaration that returns the greatest common divisor of the two integer values that are passed as parameters.

Write a program that reads in two integer values, calls the function to find the greatest common divisor of the two values, and then outputs the value returned by the function.

◇   **9.5**   Write a function declaration that returns the sine of the angle (given in radians) that is supplied as a parameter. Both the type of the parameter and the result type should be the type `double`. Use the following series in order to compute the value of sin x:

$$\sin x = x - \frac{x^3}{3!} + \frac{x^5}{5!} - \frac{x^7}{7!} + \cdots$$

[Hint: the term of the series involving x^n can be calculated by multiplying the previous term of the series by:

$$-\frac{x^2}{n \times (n-1)}$$

Note that it is not necessary to calculate the value of $n!$ each time round the loop.]

Terms of the series should be used as far as a term whose absolute value is less than 0.000 05. This final term should be included in the sum.

This series should only be used if the value of x is in the range $0 \le x \le \frac{\pi}{2}$. If the value of the parameter is not in this range, a value in the range should be produced by using the identities:

$$\sin x \equiv \sin(\pi - x) \qquad \frac{\pi}{2} \le x \le \pi$$
$$\sin x \equiv -\sin(2\pi - x) \qquad \pi \le x \le 2\pi$$
$$\sin x \equiv \sin(x - 2\pi) \qquad x \ge 2\pi$$

[Hint: you should write the function so that it is *self-contained*. It should also not do any input or output.]

If, you are using an early version of Java, provide a function declaration called `toRadians` that returns an appropriate value in radians given a parameter that is an angle in degrees. [Note: π radians is equal to 180 degrees.] If, instead, you are using the Java 2 Platform, there is no need to provide this function as the class `java.lang.Math` provides a method called `toRadians` (as explained in Figure 5.2).

Now write a program that reads in an angle given in degrees and then outputs the sine of that angle. The program should also output the value of sin x that is given by the function `sin` of the class `java.lang.Math`.

Here are some examples of the values that should be produced by your program:

a	$\sin x$
0.0	0.0000
30.0	0.5000
45.0	0.7071
60.0	0.8660
90.0	1.0000

◇ **9.6** If x_0 is an approximation to $\sqrt{a}$, then a better approximation is:

$$x_1 = \frac{1}{2}\left(x_0 + \frac{a}{x_0}\right)$$

This can be repeated with x_1 in place of x_0 to obtain a new approximation:

$$x_2 = \frac{1}{2}\left(x_1 + \frac{a}{x_1}\right)$$

Thus, this method can be generalized as:

$$x_n = \frac{1}{2}\left(x_{n-1} + \frac{a}{x_{n-1}}\right) \qquad n = 1, 2, \ldots$$

i.e. from x_0 we are generating a sequence of numbers $x_1, x_2, \ldots$ which, it is claimed, are gradually converging to $\sqrt{a}$. It is possible to use the value $\frac{a}{2}$ as the value of x_0. This method is an application of Newton–Raphson iteration.

Write a function declaration that returns the square root of the value that is supplied as a parameter. Both the type of the parameter and the result type should be the type `double`. Use the method given above in order to find the square root. You should stop finding further approximations when the difference between consecutive approximations is less than 0.00005 in modulus.

Use this function in a program whose main method reads in a value and then outputs the square root of that value. The main method should also output the value that is given by the function `sqrt` of the class `java.lang.Math`.

[Hint: you should write the function so that it is *self-contained*. It should also not do any input or output. However, to begin with, you may find it useful for the function to output each of the approximations that it generates.]

◇ **9.7** Modify your solution to Exercise 6.4 so that it uses switch statements rather than if statements.

9.8 In Exercise 7.6, you were asked to produce some code to calculate the value of $n!$ (*n factorial*), the product of the first n integers. If `int` arithmetic is used, it is only possible to find the values of $0!$, $1!$, $\ldots$, $12!$ because overflow will occur if n is greater than 12. [Note: the value of $0!$ is defined to be equal to 1.]

Write a declaration for a function that has one parameter n which returns the value of n factorial. However, if the value of n is less than 0 or greater than 12, the function should return the value -1. The block of your function declaration should simply consist of a switch statement (having 14 arms) that decides which one of the values 1, 1, 2, 6, 24, 120, 720, 5040, 40320, 362880, 3628800, 39916800, 479001600 and −1 to return.

Write a main method that uses a for statement to output the values of 0!, 1!, 2!, ..., 11! and 12!. Each time round the loop, a statement of the loop should call your factorial function and output the value it returns.

9.9 Modify your solution to Exercise 8.4 so that it also outputs a heading giving the name of the month and the number of the year:

```
      June 2002
  S  M Tu  W Th  F  S
                    1
  2  3  4  5  6  7  8
  9 10 11 12 13 14 15
 16 17 18 19 20 21 22
 23 24 25 26 27 28 29
 30
```

9.10 Modify your solution to Exercise 9.4 so that it uses a recursive function to find the greatest common divisor.

Chapter 10

Reading from and writing to files

....

In this chapter, we will investigate various methods by which we can get a program to read from a file or write to a file.

One of these methods does not really require any change to a program. We just use the facilities of the operating system (being used to run the Java program) in order to *redirect* the input and/or the output so that it comes from and/or it is written to a file.

Although this is useful in some situations, in others we will not want to do this. So the chapter also looks at how the `FileReader` and `FileWriter` classes can be used instead of using the `System.in` and `System.out` variables.

The chapter concludes by showing how a *finally clause* of a try statement can be used to ensure that a resource (such as opening a file) is properly dealt with (such as closing the file) when you have finished using it.

10.1 Some reasons for using file input/output

If a program has to read a lot of data, it will be inconvenient to have to type it all in at the keyboard. It will be *very* inconvenient if we have to do this several times, doing it each time we make a modification to the program as we debug it. Similarly, we may want to save the output from the execution of a program in a file.

In this chapter, we look at ways in which we can read data from a file and write the output to a file.

10.2 Using redirection

With many operating systems, it is possible to say to the operating system: 'I know this program says it wants to read its input from the keyboard: however, instead, I would like you to get the input from this file'. With both UNIX and MS-DOS, it is done by a process known as **redirection** of the **standard input**.

For example, with this UNIX/MS-DOS command line:

```
java fred <fred.data
```

the "`<fred.data`" part causes the Java interpreter to get all its keyboard input from the file `fred.data`. Similarly, "`>fred.op`" can be used on a command line to send all the output that normally goes to the screen to a file called `fred.op` instead. This is called the **redirection** of the **standard output**.

When you come to run a program, you can choose whether you want to use either form of redirection. Both forms can be used at the same time as in:

```
java fred <fred.data >fred.op
```

Such a program is sometimes called a **filter**.

So, when you come to run the program, you can choose which files to use. This is very convenient if you have to run your program with several sets of data generating a set of results for each set of data. You can do this by using different files on the command lines, e.g.:

```
java fred <fred01.data >fred01.op
java fred <fred02.data >fred02.op
```

10.3 A redirection example: `SumFilter`

To illustrate these ideas, consider the `SumProg` program (given in Figure 4.4) again: this is the program that reads two values (of type `double`) and outputs their sum. Previously, we read the data from the keyboard and wrote the results to the screen. However, suppose instead we want to read the data from a file and to send the output to another file.

Unlike the `SumProg` program, it makes no sense to output a prompt. So the program reduces to the `SumFilter` program shown in Figure 10.1.

```
// This program read in two numbers and displays their sum.
// Barry Cornelius, 17 June 2000
import java.io. BufferedReader;
import java.io. InputStreamReader;
import java.io. IOException;
public class SumFilter
{
    public static void main(final String[] pArgs) throws IOException
    {
        final BufferedReader tKeyboard =
                    new BufferedReader(new InputStreamReader(System.in));
        String tLine = tKeyboard.readLine();
        final double tFirst = Double.parseDouble(tLine);
        tLine = tKeyboard.readLine();
        final double tSecond = Double.parseDouble(tLine);
        final double tSum = tFirst + tSecond;
        System.out.println("The sum of " + tFirst +
                    " and " + tSecond + " is " + tSum);
    }
}
```

Figure 10.1   A reduced form of SumProg suitable for use as a filter.

Suppose we have compiled the program in the file SumFilter.java and that we have used a text editor to create the file SumFilter.data. Suppose that this file contains the two lines:

```
2.7
4.2
```

Then, after executing the UNIX/MS-DOS command line:

```
java SumFilter <SumFilter.data >SumFilter.op
```

a file called SumFilter.op will have been created, and it will contain the line:

```
The sum of 2.7 and 4.2 is 6.9
```

The file will be created if it does not exist and will be overwritten if it already exists.

10.4 Another redirection example: `CopyFilter`

One useful program that manipulates files is a program that copies from one file to another file. This program can keep reading lines writing each line to the output until there are no more lines left. If we have redirected both the standard input and the standard output, the program will be copying from one file to another.

How does the program detect when it has reached the end of the input? Well, if it is using readLine to read each line, then, looking at $API/java/io/BufferedReader.html#readLine(), you can see that readLine returns the value `null` if there are no more lines in the input. A program to do this task is given in Figure 10.2.

```
// This program read in lines and displays them.
// Barry Cornelius, 17 June 2000
import java.io. BufferedReader;
import java.io. InputStreamReader;
import java.io. IOException;
public class CopyFilter
{
   public static void main(final String[] pArgs) throws IOException
   {
      final BufferedReader tKeyboard =
                    new BufferedReader(new InputStreamReader(System.in));
      while (true)
      {
         final String tLine = tKeyboard.readLine();
         if (tLine==null)
         {
            break;
         }
         System.out.println(tLine);
      }
   }
}
```

Figure 10.2   A filter to read lines and write them out.

Assuming the file `CopyFilter.data` already exists, its contents can be copied to the file `CopyFilter.op` by the command line:

```
java CopyFilter <CopyFilter.data >CopyFilter.op
```

10.5 Other filter programs

Although the `CopyFilter` performs a reasonably useful task, it does not do much to the input. By adding other instructions to a program like this, we can produce a whole range of programs that do useful tasks. As was mentioned earlier, these programs are called *filters*. UNIX abounds with such programs: examples are `grep`, `uniq`, `sort`, `sed`, and so on. Some of these are set as exercises for this chapter: see Exercises 10.1, 10.2, 10.3, 10.12 and 10.13.

10.6 A program to remove debugging statements

We do not have to do much to get the `CopyFilter` program to do something more useful. The `UnDebugFilter` program in Figure 10.3 is a program that removes debugging statements from a Java program. The program sits in a loop reading a line

```
// This program reads in lines and displays them.
// However, any debugging statements are removed.
// Barry Cornelius, 17 June 2000
import java.io. BufferedReader;
import java.io. InputStreamReader;
import java.io. IOException;
public class UnDebugFilter
{
    public static void main(final String[] pArgs) throws IOException
    {
        final BufferedReader tKeyboard =
                    new BufferedReader(new InputStreamReader(System.in));
        while (true)
        {
            final String tLine = tKeyboard.readLine();
            if (tLine==null)
            {
                break;
            }
            if ( ! tLine.startsWith("/**/") )
            {
                System.out.println(tLine);
            }
        }
    }
}
```

Figure 10.3   A filter to remove debugging statements.

from its input and then checking whether the first four characters of the line contain the characters `"/**/"`. This is the way in which the programs of this book signify that a line contains a debugging statement. The program outputs the line provided that the line does not start with these characters. It does this by checking each line using the condition:

```
! tLine.startsWith("/**/")
```

Here we are *not*ing the result of calling `String`'s `startsWith` function.
   The program can be executed by a command line like:

```
java UnDebugFilter.java <OriginalProgram.java >NewProgram.java
```

10.7 Getting a program to do I/O with a file

So far we have cheated: by using redirection, we have colluded with the underlying operating system to achieve our goal of reading from and/or writing to a file. Although this is a satisfactory solution for some situations, it is inappropriate for others. For example, we may not want all the data to come from one source: we may want to read some data from the keyboard and to read other data from a file, or from several files. So we now look at how we can get a program itself to do input/output (**I/O**) with a file.

10.8 A file I/O example: SumFixed

A program which is in some ways equivalent to SumFilter (of Figure 10.1) is the SumFixed program given in Figure 10.4. Unlike the SumFilter program, this program is run in the usual way, i.e.:

```
java SumFixed
```

Instead of the InputStreamReader class that we have used for reading from the keyboard, this program passes the name of an input file as an argument of a constructor of the class FileReader.

And, instead of using System.out for output, this program writes its output to a file: the name of the output file is passed as an argument of a constructor of the class FileWriter. To make the writing to the file more efficient, the program

```java
// This program reads in two numbers from the file SumFixed.data
// and outputs their sum to the file SumFixed.op.
// Barry Cornelius, 17 June 2000
import java.io. BufferedReader;
import java.io. BufferedWriter;
import java.io. FileReader;
import java.io. FileWriter;
import java.io. IOException;
import java.io. PrintWriter;
public class SumFixed
{
    public static void main(final String[] pArgs) throws IOException
    {
        final BufferedReader tInputHandle =
                    new BufferedReader(new FileReader("SumFixed.data"));
        String tLine = tInputHandle.readLine();
        final double tFirst = Double.parseDouble(tLine);
        tLine = tInputHandle.readLine();
        final double tSecond = Double.parseDouble(tLine);
        final double tSum = tFirst + tSecond;
        final PrintWriter tOutputHandle =
            new PrintWriter(new BufferedWriter(new FileWriter("SumFixed.op")));
        tOutputHandle.println("The sum of " + tFirst +
                            " and " + tSecond + " is " + tSum);
        tOutputHandle.close();
    }
}
```

Figure 10.4 SumFixed is a version of SumProg that reads and writes to fixed files.

performs the output using an object of the class `BufferedWriter`. Because of this buffering, we need to apply `close` to `tOutputHandle` when we have finished using it. This method arranges for any characters currently in the buffer to be written to the file before it closes the file. In order to be able to use familiar methods like `print` and `println`, the program constructs a `PrintWriter` object from this `BufferedWriter` object, and applies `println` to the `PrintWriter` object.

10.9 Getting the names of files from the keyboard

With the `SumFixed` program, the names of the input and output files are fixed in the text of the program. Although there are occasions when it is useful to do this, there are other occasions where you will want to choose the names of the files when you run the program.

We could do this by reading the names of the files from the keyboard. The `CopyReadNames` program (in Figure 10.5) first reads two lines (containing the two filenames) from the keyboard, and then it calls a method (`iCopyFile`) that copies lines from the first file to the second.

10.10 Checking whether a file exists

Although a `FileWriter` constructor will create an output file if the file does not already exist, a `FileReader` constructor will give a `FileNotFoundException` exception if the input file does not exist. We could put the attempt to open the input file in a try statement that is enclosed by a `while (true)` statement:

```
BufferedReader tInputHandle = null;
while (true)
{
    System.out.print("Type in the name of the input file: ");
    System.out.flush();
    final String tInputFilename = tKeyboard.readLine();
    try
    {
        tInputHandle = new BufferedReader(new FileReader(tInputFilename));
        break;
    }
    catch(final FileNotFoundException pFileNotFoundException)
    {
        System.out.println("The file " + tInputFilename + " does not exist");
    }
}
```

Here we have used `FileReader`'s constructor to open a file with the given name, and then the program recovers if a FileNotFoundException occurs.

```java
// This program reads in two filenames from the keyboard
// and then copies lines from the first file to the second.
// Barry Cornelius, 17 June 2000
import java.io. BufferedReader;
import java.io. BufferedWriter;
import java.io. FileReader;
import java.io. FileWriter;
import java.io. InputStreamReader;
import java.io. IOException;
import java.io. PrintWriter;
public class CopyReadNames
{
   public static void main(final String[] pArgs) throws IOException
   {
      final BufferedReader tKeyboard =
                  new BufferedReader(new InputStreamReader(System.in));
      System.out.print("Type in the name of the input file: ");
      System.out.flush();
      final String tInputFilename = tKeyboard.readLine();
      System.out.print("Type in the name of the output file: ");
      System.out.flush();
      final String tOutputFilename = tKeyboard.readLine();
      iCopyFile(tInputFilename, tOutputFilename);
   }

   private static void iCopyFile(final String pInputFilename,
                                 final String pOutputFilename)
                                            throws IOException
   {
      final BufferedReader tInputHandle =
                  new BufferedReader(new FileReader(pInputFilename));
      final PrintWriter tOutputHandle =
        new PrintWriter(new BufferedWriter(new FileWriter(pOutputFilename)));
      while (true)
      {
         final String tLine = tInputHandle.readLine();
         if (tLine==null)
         {
            break;
         }
         tOutputHandle.println(tLine);
      }
      tOutputHandle.close();
   }
}
```

Figure 10.5   A program that reads the names of the two files from the keyboard.

In Section 9.12, it was suggested that exceptions should not be used if other appropriate code can be used instead. It so happens that the class `java.io.File` has methods that can be used to check whether a file exists.

The class `File` from the package `java.io` can be used to represent real-world objects each of which is intended to be a file or a directory. For more details look at $API/java/io/File.html, or look at Figure 10.6. The class has a number of constructors, one of which takes one argument, a `String`, and it constructs an object for a file/directory that has that name.

```
public File(String pString);
```
Initializes the new `File` object so that it refers to the full filename (including the path) of the file or directory given by the value of `pString`.

....

```
public boolean canRead();
```
Returns the value *true* if and only if the target represents a file/directory that exists and can be read.

```
public boolean canWrite();
```
Returns the value *true* if and only if the target represents a file/directory that exists and can be written to.

```
public boolean delete();
```
Deletes the file/directory represented by the target returning the value *true* if and only if it can be created. Note: a directory cannot be deleted if it contains files.

```
public boolean equals(Object pObject);
```
Returns the value *true* if and only if the target has the same value as `pObject`.

```
public boolean exists();
```
Returns the value *true* if and only if the target represents a file/directory that exists.

```
public boolean isDirectory();
```
Returns the value *true* if and only if the target represents a directory.

```
public boolean isFile();
```
Returns the value *true* if and only if the target represents a *normal file*.

```
public long length();
```
Returns the length of the file represented by the target.

```
public boolean mkdir();
```
Creates the directory represented by the target returning the value *true* if and only if it can be created.

```
public boolean mkdirs();
```
Creates the directory represented by the target (creating any necessary parent directories) returning the value *true* if and only if all these directories can be created.

```
public boolean renameTo(File pFile);
```
Renames the file/directory specified by the target to the name of the object `pFile` returning the value *true* if and only if it can be renamed.

```
public String toString();
```
Returns a string representation of the target.

Figure 10.6 Constructors and methods of the `java.io.File` class.

The class has a method called `exists` that can be used to test whether a file exists. However, even if a file exists, it may be that the file is protected so that we cannot read it. So, this class also has a method called `canRead` that can be used to check whether a file exists and can be read. It also has a method called `canWrite` that can be used to check whether a file exists and can be written to.

The `CopyReadAndCheckNames` program (in Figure 10.7) uses these methods to see if the two names typed by the user are the names of files that can be used.

```java
// This program reads in two filenames from the keyboard, checks whether
// they can be used, and then copies lines from the first file to the second.
// Barry Cornelius, 17 June 2000
import java.io. BufferedReader;
import java.io. BufferedWriter;
import java.io. File;
import java.io. FileReader;
import java.io. FileWriter;
import java.io. InputStreamReader;
import java.io. IOException;
import java.io. PrintWriter;
public class CopyReadAndCheckNames
{
    public static void main(final String[] pArgs) throws IOException
    {
        final BufferedReader tKeyboard =
                    new BufferedReader(new InputStreamReader(System.in));
        final String tInputFilename = iGetInputFilename(tKeyboard);
        final String tOutputFilename = iGetOutputFilename(tKeyboard);
        iCopyFile(tInputFilename, tOutputFilename);
    }
    private static String iGetInputFilename(final BufferedReader pKeyboard)
                                                        throws IOException
    {
        String tInputFilename = null;
        while (true)
        {
            System.out.print("Type in the name of the input file: ");
            System.out.flush();
            tInputFilename = pKeyboard.readLine();
            final File tInputFile = new File(tInputFilename);
            if ( ! tInputFile.exists() )
            {
                System.out.println(tInputFilename + " does not exist");
            }
            else if ( ! tInputFile.canRead() )
            {
                System.out.println(tInputFilename + " exists but is unreadable");
            }
```

Figure 10.7 *Continues on the next page.*

```
            else
            {
                break;
            }
        }
    }
    return tInputFilename;
}
private static String iGetOutputFilename(final BufferedReader pKeyboard)
                                                        throws IOException
{
    String tOutputFilename = null;
    while (true)
    {
        System.out.print("Type in the name of the output file: ");
        System.out.flush();
        tOutputFilename = pKeyboard.readLine();
        final File tOutputFile = new File(tOutputFilename);
        if ( ! tOutputFile.exists() )
        {
            break;
        }
        else if ( ! tOutputFile.canWrite() )
        {
            System.out.println(tOutputFilename + " cannot be written");
        }
        else
        {
            System.out.print("OK to overwrite " + tOutputFilename + "? ");
            System.out.flush();
            final String tReply = pKeyboard.readLine();
            if (tReply.charAt(0)=='y')
            {
                break;
            }
        }
    }
    return tOutputFilename;
}
private static void iCopyFile(final String pInputFilename,
                             final String pOutputFilename)
                                        throws IOException
{
        ... same as in Figure 10.5
    }
}
```

Figure 10.7 A program that checks whether files suggested by the user can be used.

(10.11) Getting the names of files from the command line

Often when you run a program, you pass additional information as part of the command line used to run the program. For example, the UNIX command to copy a file is called cp, but when we use it we do not just type the command line:

```
cp
```

Instead, we pass it two arguments, e.g.:

```
cp fred bert
```

We now look at how we can do a similar thing with a program written in Java. The best we can do is to use a command line like:

```
java CopyArgs fred bert
```

All of the programs we have written have had a main method whose header is:

```
public static void main(final String[] pArgs)
```

We can obtain the strings passed on the **command line** by accessing the variable called pArgs. This is an *array*. We will consider the topic of arrays in detail in Chapter 15. However, all we need to know for the time being is:

- the first **command line argument** (i.e. fred in the above example) can be obtained using the pArgs[0] variable, i.e. pArgs[0] is a reference variable pointing to a String object containing the string "fred";
- the second command line argument can be obtained using the pArgs[1] variable;
- pArgs[0] and pArgs[1] are called the **element**s of the array object that is pointed to by pArgs;
- although a program can change the values of elements such as pArgs[0], the value of pArgs cannot be changed because it is marked as final;
- the number of command line arguments can be found from the size of the array object;
- the size of the array object to which pArgs points can be obtained using pArgs.length;
- when using an element such as pArgs[0], the expression within the square brackets is called the **index**; it may be any expression of type int (or short, or byte or char);
- if an index has a value that is not within the range 0 to pArgs.length-1, an unchecked exception called ArrayIndexOutOfBoundsException will occur.

So if the command line is:

```
java CopyArgs fred bert
```

then:

- pArgs[0] is a reference variable pointing to a String object having the value "fred";
- pArgs[1] is also of type String and points to "bert";
- pArgs.length is of type int and has the value 2.

The CopyArgs program (in Figure 10.8) uses the values of the first two arguments as the names of the files to be used. It looks at the value of pArgs.length to check whether the user supplied two arguments on the command line. If this does not have the value 2, the program outputs an error message, and exits. Otherwise, it copies from the file whose name is given as the first argument to the file whose name is given as the second argument.

Unlike the program given in Figure 10.7, this program does not include code to check whether the files exist.

```
// This program obtain two filenames from the command line
// and then copies lines from the first file to the second.
// Barry Cornelius, 17 June 2000
import java.io. BufferedReader;
import java.io. BufferedWriter;
import java.io. FileReader;
import java.io. FileWriter;
import java.io. IOException;
import java.io. PrintWriter;
public class CopyArgs
{
   public static void main(final String[] pArgs) throws IOException
   {
      if (pArgs.length!=2)
      {
         System.out.println("Usage: java CopyArgs inputname outputname");
         System.exit(1);
      }
      iCopyFile(pArgs[0], pArgs[1]);
   }

   private static void iCopyFile(final String pInputFilename,
                                 final String pOutputFilename)
                                          throws IOException
   {
      ... same as in Figure 10.5
   }
}
```

Figure 10.8   A program that reads the names of two files from the command line.

(10.12) And finally

Suppose a program opens an output file and it is writing useful information to the output file. Suppose something strange occurs and we want to cease execution of the program. If the program immediately calls System.exit, the final few lines of the information being written to the file may be lost (because the output to the file is buffered).

A rather artificial example is shown in the Copy2Closes program given in Figure 10.9. Here the iCopyFileStopEmpty method keeps reading lines from a file and writing them to an output file. However, (for some reason) it is intended that no lines of this input file should be empty. So, if tLine.length() has the value zero, the iCopyFileStopEmpty method is left: no more lines of the input are to be examined.

If we just code this as:

```
if (tLine.length()==0)
{
    return false;
}
```

the final few lines that were generated (by the calls of println) may not have been written to the output file. Instead, the Copy2Closes program contains:

```
if (tLine.length()==0)
{
    tOutputHandle.close();
    return false;
}
```

So this method now has two occurrences of the code to close the file. One of these is for the abnormal situation described above; the other is for normal execution, the code being given at the end of the method:

```
tOutputHandle.close();
return true;
```

```
// This program obtain two filenames from the command line
// and then copies lines from the first file to the second.
// The execution is aborted if a line of the input file is empty.
// The code to close the file appears in two places.
// Barry Cornelius, 17 June 2000
import java.io. BufferedReader;
import java.io. BufferedWriter;
import java.io. FileReader;
```

Figure 10.9   *Continues on the next page.*

```
import java.io. FileWriter;
import java.io. IOException;
import java.io. PrintWriter;
public class Copy2Closes
{
   public static void main(final String[] pArgs) throws IOException
   {
      if (pArgs.length!=2)
      {
         System.out.println("Usage: java Copy2Closes inputname outputname");
         System.exit(1);
      }
      final boolean tSuccessfulCopy = iCopyFileStopEmpty(pArgs[0], pArgs[1]);
      if ( ! tSuccessfulCopy )
      {
         System.out.println("Error: there was a blank line in " + pArgs[0]);
      }
   }

   private static boolean iCopyFileStopEmpty(final String pInputFilename,
                                    final String pOutputFilename)
                                                      throws IOException
   {
      final BufferedReader tInputHandle =
                  new BufferedReader(new FileReader(pInputFilename));
      final PrintWriter tOutputHandle =
        new PrintWriter(new BufferedWriter(new FileWriter(pOutputFilename)));
      while (true)
      {
         final String tLine = tInputHandle.readLine();
         if (tLine==null)
         {
            break;
         }
         if (tLine.length()==0)
         {
            tOutputHandle.close();
            return false;
         }
         tOutputHandle.println(tLine);
      }
      tOutputHandle.close();
      return true;
   }
}
```

Figure 10.9 A program that has two calls of close.

Rather than duplicating the code for closing a file, it is better for this code to appear in a finally clause. In outline, the code is:

```
try
{
    tOutputHandle = ... ;         // open the file
    ...
    if an untoward situation occurs
    {
        return false;
    }
    ...
}
finally
{
    tOutputHandle.close();
}
return true;
```

The finally clause will be executed no matter what happens during the execution of the try block. So even if a return statement appearing inside a try block is executed, the finally clause will be executed immediately before control is transferred to the point of call (of the method containing the try block).

The actual code is shown in the CopyFinally program (given in Figure 10.10).

Note that this example of a try statement just has a try block and a finally clause: it does not have any catch clauses. So the try statement is not being used to handle exceptions. Instead, by using a try statement with a finally clause, we can ensure that a sequence of statements (those given in the finally clause) are always executed.

```
// This program obtain two filenames from the command line
// and then copies lines from the first file to the second.
// The execution is aborted if a line of the input file is empty.
// A finally clause is used to ensure the output file is closed.
// Barry Cornelius, 17 June 2000
import java.io. BufferedReader;
import java.io. BufferedWriter;
import java.io. FileReader;
import java.io. FileWriter;
import java.io. IOException;
import java.io. PrintWriter;
public class CopyFinally
{
```

Figure 10.10 *Continues on the next page.*

```
public static void main(final String[] pArgs) throws IOException
{
   if (pArgs.length!=2)
   {
      System.out.println("Usage: java CopyFinally inputname outputname");
      System.exit(1);
   }
   final boolean tSuccessfulCopy = iCopyFileStopEmpty(pArgs[0], pArgs[1]);
   if ( ! tSuccessfulCopy )
   {
      System.out.println("Error: there was a blank line in " + pArgs[0]);
   }
}

private static boolean iCopyFileStopEmpty(final String pInputFilename,
                                final String pOutputFilename)
                                                   throws IOException
{
   PrintWriter tOutputHandle = null;
   try
   {
      tOutputHandle = new PrintWriter(
                  new BufferedWriter(new FileWriter(pOutputFilename)));
      final BufferedReader tInputHandle =
                  new BufferedReader(new FileReader(pInputFilename));
      while (true)
      {
         final String tLine = tInputHandle.readLine();
         if (tLine==null)
         {
            break;
         }
         if (tLine.length()==0)
         {
            return false;
         }
         tOutputHandle.println(tLine);
      }
   }
   finally
   {
      tOutputHandle.close();
   }
   return true;
}
}
```

Figure 10.10 A program that uses a `finally` clause to close the file.

The above code generalizes in the following way. Suppose a method contains the code:

```
try
{
    create some resource
    use the resource
    either  1. an exception occurs
        or  2. or the code executes a return statement
        or  3. all of the statements of the try block are executed
}
catch(final SomeException pSomeException)
{
    some exception handler
}
finally
{
    ...
}
```

The crucial point is that the code given in the finally clause will always be executed. Given the above outline, there are three situations to be discussed:

- if the try block's execution results in a SomeException exception, the exception handler is executed and then the finally clause is executed;

- if the try block's execution results in the execution of a return statement, its expression (if it has one) is evaluated, the finally clause is executed, and the return to the point of call of the method is then performed;

- if all of the statements of the try block are executed, then, following its execution, the finally clause is executed.

For details of the syntax of a try statement that has a finally clause, refer back to Figure 9.5.

Tips for programming and debugging

10.1   The class java.lang.String has a method called length that can be used to find the length of a string. For example:

```
final String tName = "java";
final int tNameLength = tName.length():
```

assigns the value 4 to tNameLength.

The number of *element*s in an *array* can be determined using length. For example, if we use the command line:

```
java Prog tom dick harry
```

to run a program called `Prog` (which is in the file `Prog.java`) then, if the program contains:

```
int tNumberOfArguments = pArgs.length;
```

the variable `tNumberOfArguments` is assigned the value 3.

Do not confuse these two different uses of the name `length`. Note that, in one of these uses, `length` is the name of a method and so it is followed by `()` whereas when used with an array it is not the name of a method and so there are no parentheses.

Curios, controversies and cover-ups

10.1 The class `FileNotFoundException` is a *subclass* of the class `IOException`.

Exercises

10.1 UNIX has a word count program called wc. Write a *filter* that mimics some aspects of wc. When the program is run:

```
java wc <somefilename
```

it should output one line to the standard output giving some details about the file attached to the standard input. It should say something like:

```
120 lines, 317 words, 4154 characters
```

In order to do this, your program will need to keep track of the number of lines in the file, the number of *words* in the file and the number of characters in the file. Getting a true value for the number of words on each line is quite tricky. Although the class `BreakIterator` of the package `java.text` can help to do this, for the purpose of this exercise you can cheat: first use `StringTokenizer` on the line and then use `countTokens`.

10.2 UNIX has a concatenate program called `cat` that can be used to combine files. Write a program that mimics some aspects of the `cat` command. When the program is run:

```
java cat fn1 fn2 fn3 ... fnN
```

it should output the contents of each of the files fn1, fn2, fn3, ..., fnN to the standard output.

10.3 UNIX has a program called `grep` that, in its simplest form, can be used to search a file looking for a particular string. The program outlines the lines of the file containing the string. Write a program that mimics some of the behaviour of `grep`, i.e. given the command line:

```
java grep str fn
```

it should output the lines of the file fn that contains the string `str`.

10.4 Modify the program produced in the previous exercise so that it can also handle the following cases:

```
java grep -i str fn
java grep -n str fn
java grep -in str fn
java grep -ni str fn
```

where the i option means output the line even if the case of letters does not agree and the n option means output the line number as well as the line, e.g.:

```
java grep -in Java publicity.txt
```

might produce:

```
27: and the Java programming language is wonderful
42: a popular place called Bandung on the island of JAVA
```

10.5 Write a program that reads the lines of a file and outputs the number of empty lines that are present in the file. The program should obtain the name of the file from the command line.

10.6 Write a program that reads in the characters of a file and outputs the *coding* of each character to another file. The *coding* of a character is the integer value of the bit pattern that is used to represent that character. There are details about how to obtain this value in Section 5.9.

   The program should obtain the names of the files from the command line. It should start a new line of output whenever it has processed all the characters that appear on a line or it has output 15 values on a line.

10.7 Produce a program called UnDebug that is like the program UnDebugFilter (that was given in Figure 10.3) except that for UnDebug:

   ● the program looks at the two arguments given on the command line and uses the first argument as the name of the original file and uses the second argument as the name of the new file;

   ● it outputs an error message if the file named as the input file does not exist;

   ● when producing the line of the output that contains the public class line, the program writes a name on the public class line that is appropriate for the output file.

10.8 Modify the CopyArgs program (given in Figure 10.8) so that it checks whether it can read from the input file and whether it can write to the output file. The program should output an appropriate error message if this is not the case.

10.9 Write a program (called MyRename) that renames a file. The program should obtain the names of the two files from the command line used to execute the program. The program should output an error message either if the file to be renamed does not exist or if a file with the new name already exists.

   [Hint: there are details about a method called renameTo in Figure 10.6.]

10.10 Write a program (called `ExcDebugFilter`) that is similar to the `UnDebug-Filter` program (given in Figure 10.3). However, instead of discarding a line that contains a debugging statement, it writes a line to the output that contains the three characters `"// "` followed by the debugging statement. In this way, the text of the debugging statement appears after a `//` comment. So if the input contains:

```
       tFirst = 2.7;
/**/   System.out.println("*** value of tFirst is: " + tFirst);
       tSecond = 4.2;
/**/   System.out.println("*** value of tSecond is: " + tSecond);
/**/   System.out.println("*** about to do the addition");
       tSum = tFirst + tSecond;
```

it writes the following lines to the output:

```
       tFirst = 2.7;
// /**/   System.out.println("*** value of tFirst is: " + tFirst);
       tSecond = 4.2;
// /**/   System.out.println("*** value of tSecond is: " + tSecond);
// /**/   System.out.println("*** about to do the addition");
       tSum = tFirst + tSecond;
```

10.11 Write a program (called `IncDebugFilter`) that performs the opposite task of that performed by program `ExcDebugFilter`: it removes the three characters (i.e. `"// "`) that were added by `ExcDebugFilter`.

10.12 Write a program (called `MaxLength`) that reads in the lines of a file and outputs some details about the line of the file that has the largest number of characters. The details should include:

- the length of the line;
- the number of occurrences of this length of line in the file;
- the line number of the first occurrence of a line of this length;
- the line number of the last occurrence of a line of this length.

The program should obtain the name of the file from the command line.

10.13 Write a program (called `uniq`) that reads from one file and writes to another file. The contents of the output file should be the same as that of the input file except that any line of the input file that is the same as the previous line of the input file should not be written to the output file. The program should obtain the names of these files from the command line.

For example, if the file `names.sorted` contains:

```
Ambrose, Adam
Best, Susan
Best, Susan
Jackson, Mark
```

```
Smith, Rebecca
Smith, Rebecca
Smith, Rebecca
Wilson, John
```

the command line:

```
java uniq names.sorted names.uniq
```

should write the following lines to the file names.uniq:

```
Ambrose, Adam
Best, Susan
Jackson, Mark
Smith, Rebecca
Wilson, John
```

10.14 Write a program that reads in one of the hands of a deal for a game of *Bridge*. The program should output the number of *points* that the hand contains together with the number of *voids*. The number of points in a hand is obtained in the following way: 4 points are allocated for each *Ace*, 3 points for each *King*, 2 points for each *Queen*, and 1 point for each *Jack*. A *void* is a suit in which the hand has no cards.

The data for this program is given in the following form:

```
S A 8 7 2
H Q 10 8 6 3 2
D
C A K J
```

where the letters S, H, D and C refer to spades, hearts, diamonds and clubs. Your program should output that this hand has 14 points and 1 void, whereas the hand:

```
S
H
D A K Q J 10 9 8 7 6 5 4 3 2
C
```

has 10 points and 3 voids.

Assume that the data for the program has been given correctly.

Chapter 11

Using interfaces and classes to produce new types

We will want to represent real-world objects that are not catered for by the APIs. So there is a need for us to produce our own classes (to represent these real-world objects). In this chapter, we will find out how to write our own *class declarations*. Towards the end of the chapter, the *interface declaration* is introduced.

An interface declaration allows us to concentrate on *what* is to be provided. Having declared an interface, we can then produce a class declaration that gives the details of *how* that interface is to be realized.

11.1 Using classes to represent real-world objects

11.1.1 Representing real-world objects in a program

Whenever we are designing a computer program, we need to find ways of representing situations that occur in the real world. As was explained in Section 1.1.6 and Section 3.1.1, one way of achieving this is to represent in our program, in some way, the objects that occur in the real world.

Some real-world objects can be represented by values that are of a primitive type:

- exchange rates (e.g. the US dollar/UK pound exchange rate) by a `double`;
- air temperatures by an `int`;
- speeds of a vehicle – by an `int` in normal conversations but by a `double` if you have been caught speeding!
- . . .

However, most real-world objects are more complex, and for these we can use Java's class types.

11.1.2 Using classes from Java's Core APIs

So far, we have been using classes from Java's Core APIs to represent more complex objects:

- `String` (from `java.lang`) for a sequence of characters;
- `Point` (from `java.awt`) for a point in two-dimensional space;
- . . .

However, there are a large number of classes that we have not looked at. This will be very obvious to you if you have access to the WWW pages that document the Core APIs. Examples are:

- `Date` (from `java.util`) for representing date-and-time values;
- `URL` (from `java.net`) to represent the URLs (Uniform Resource Locators) used when accessing WWW pages;
- . . .

In Java's Core APIs, there are hundreds of such classes, and so we will not list them all! These classes cover such areas as:

- reading from and writing to files, and other devices;
- producing a graphical user interface, such as:
  - creating new windows on the screen,
  - putting menus and buttons on the screen,
  - reacting to the selection of an item from a menu,

- reacting to the click of a button,

- ...

- writing programs in *thread*s that run in parallel with one another;
- representing collections of data both within the program or in a database;
- invoking methods of objects of Java programs running on other computers;
- writing applets (programs that run when someone visits a WWW page);
- communicating with the Internet in various ways;
- ...

Although this book will introduce some of these other APIs later, it is time to see how we can create our own classes.

11.1.3 Why do we need to produce our own classes?

We cannot just rely on others to produce all the classes we need: we have to do some of this work ourselves. This is because some of the real-world objects that we will want to represent will be specific to whatever we are doing. We may need to represent people, bank accounts, grid references, ISBNs, audio CDs, and so on. In each case, it is the person for whom you are writing the program that causes you to choose some particular representation of the real-world object: the representation is something you choose after having discussions with members of the company you work for, the customer you are writing the program for, or sometimes ourselves.

11.1.4 Object-oriented analysis and object-oriented design

Although the previous section refers to some real-world objects which it may be useful to represent in a program, for anything other than trivial problems, it is not often easy to decide what objects it would be useful for the program to have (to produce a satisfactory program for the problem).

This is all part of **object-oriented analysis** and **object-oriented design**. However, these are not topics which we will spend much time on in this book. This is not because OOA and OOD are not important: it is just that a full treatment of these topics would require a much bigger book and a superficial treatment would not be useful.

Another reason why we are ducking the issues of OOA and OOD is that there are many ways in which these tasks can be accomplished. Recently, a (temporary?) consensus has been reached on how systems can be described: the *Unified Modeling Language (UML)* has been produced. It is called *Unified* because it is the coming together of a number of different techniques. We will look at its notation for class diagrams in the next chapter.

But in this book we cheat as we will avoid the issues of OOA and OOD: in the exercises, you will usually be told what objects need to be produced.

11.2 Representing dates in a program

For the first example of a class declaration, we will look at how we might represent a date. We are looking long term here: we think that in many of the programs we write in the future we will need to store dates. And so we want to do some ground-work: we will build a `Date` that we will subsequently be able to use in any programs that need dates. Although there are classes called `Date` and `Calendar` in the package `java.util` that can be used to represent dates, for the purpose of this chapter it is useful to pretend that these do not exist!

Remember that there are two main characteristics to a type:

● a type has a set of values associated with it;
● a type has a set of operations that are permitted on these values.

So when we are choosing how to represent something (e.g. dates) we need to consider these two characteristics.

What values do dates have? Well, we normally think of a date as consisting of three parts, a year, a month and a day. For example, the values 2000, 9, 22 might represent the 22nd day of September in AD 2000. So, here we are using three integers for values that are dates. Note that not all of the triplets are used. For example, the second integer (the month) must be in the range 1 to 12 and there are some weird rules (that were given in Exercise 8.3) governing what the third value (the day) can be.

What operations do we want to perform on dates? Well, we will want to construct dates, to copy dates, to compare two dates, to get the year, month and day parts of a date, to perform input-output operations for values that are dates, and so on.

In this chapter, we will eventually introduce an *interface* that defines the type `Date` and a *class* called `DateImpl` that implements this interface. We will get to this goal in stages producing a number of different class declarations that gradually get better; the final version uses an interface as well as a class: it appears in Section 11.12.

11.3 Stage A: a simple version of the class `Date`

To begin with, we will produce a **class declaration** that is just able to represent values that are dates. It is shown in the top half of Figure 11.1.

This class declaration says that each object of this class will have three `int`s: they will be used to represent the year, month and day parts of a date. These three variables are called the **fields** of the class.

The class declaration for the class `Date` (i.e. the first 8 lines of Figure 11.1) needs to be stored in the file `Date.java`. The remaining 15 lines of Figure 11.1 give a program that uses the class `Date`. It is called `NoelProg`, and so these lines need to be stored in the file `NoelProg.java`.

```
// A simple class for representing values that are dates.
// Barry Cornelius, 19 June 2000
public class Date
{
   public int year;
   public int month;
   public int day;
}
```
....
```
// This program creates an object of the class Date
// and then sets its fields to represent Christmas Day 2000.
// Barry Cornelius, 19 June 2000
public class NoelProg
{
   public static void main(final String[] pArgs)
   {
      final Date tNoelDate = new Date();
      tNoelDate.year = 2000;
      tNoelDate.month = 12;
      tNoelDate.day = 25;
      System.out.println(tNoelDate.year + "-" +
                         tNoelDate.month + "-" + tNoelDate.day);
   }
}
```

Figure 11.1   Stage A: a simple version of class Date that is used by NoelProg.

When we want to execute the NoelProg program, we first have to compile the two pieces of Java source code:

```
javac Date.java
javac NoelProg.java
```

This produces the files Date.class and NoelProg.class. Since it is the file NoelProg.java that contains the main method, we can execute the program by typing:

```
java NoelProg
```

What does the NoelProg program do? The first statement:

```
final Date tNoelDate = new Date();
```

is a declaration. The left-hand side establishes a reference variable called tNoel-Date. The initializer on the right-hand side is a *class instance creation expression*:

```
new Date()
```

This creates an object (of the class Date) that is just big enough to hold the fields of the class, i.e. the three fields called year, month and day.

Each field will be initialized to a value which depends on the type of the field. The **default initial value**s are listed in Figure 11.2. As the three fields of the class Date have the type int, they will be initialized to zero. The above declaration causes

type	default value
boolean	false
char	'\000'
byte	(byte)0
short	(short)0
int	0
long	0L
float	0.0F
double	0.0
any reference type	null

Figure 11.2   The initial value of a field.

tNoelDate to be assigned a value that points to this object:

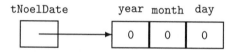

Following the declaration of tNoelDate, there are three assignment statements that assign values to each of these three fields. For example:

```
tNoelDate.year = 2000;
```

puts a value in the year field of tNoelDate. Here the dot notation introduced in Section 3.2.5 is being used. Although it is possible to assign values to the year, month and day fields that do not represent a date, we will ignore this deficiency for the time being.

The result of executing these assignment statements is:

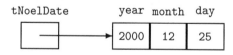

The last statement of the program looks at the values of the three fields and, as a result, it outputs the line:

```
2000-12-25
```

Here is some jargon: a piece of code that uses another class is said to be a **client** of the class. So the program NoelProg is a *client* of the class Date.

Although this is exciting because we have declared this class ourselves, there is nothing new about the way in which we are using the class. It is much like what we did with the class Point in Section 3.2. And, because the class declaration provides no means for performing operations on Date values, there will be little that we can do with these values.

11.4 Stage B: a constructor and a method declaration

11.4.1 Stage B1: adding a constructor declaration

The three assignment statements in the `NoelProg` program (shown in Figure 11.1) ensure that the `Date` object has the values that we want it to have. When we create an object, we will frequently want to assign values to all of the fields of the object. For this reason, the Java programming language allows a class to have *constructors*.

With a class to represent dates, an obvious constructor is one that creates a date object from three integers:

```
final Date tNoelDate = new Date(2000, 12, 25);
```

Here the class instance creation expression uses a constructor that has three `int` arguments. A client can only use this constructor if the class declaration for `Date` has a **constructor declaration** that has three `int` arguments. Here is the one that appears in Figure 11.3:

```
public Date(final int pYear, final int pMonth, final int pDay)
{
    year = pYear;
    month = pMonth;
    day = pDay;
}
```

In many ways, a constructor looks like a method declaration. However, there are two differences: there is no result type and the declaration has the same name as the class.

So, when the declaration:

```
final Date tNoelDate = new Date(2000, 12, 25);
```

is executed, first the object is constructed with *default initial values*, and then the constructor is executed. So, local variables called `pYear`, `pMonth` and `pDay` are created; the values 2000, 12, 25 are assigned to `pYear`, `pMonth` and `pDay`; and then the block of the constructor leads to the following statements being executed:

```
year = 2000;
month = 12;
day = 25;
```

A constructor can refer to the fields of the object being initialized by using the names of the fields. So these statements result in the fields of the object having their values changed. After the constructor of the class instance creation expression has finished executing, the final act of `tNoelDate`'s declaration is to make `tNoelDate` point to the object that has just been created by the class instance creation expression.

After the declaration of `tNoelDate`, the `NoelProg` program executes:

```
tNoelDate.day++;
```

This statement increases the value of the `day` field of this object by 1.

```
// A class for dates that has an output method for dates and a constructor.
// Barry Cornelius, 19 June 2000
public class Date
{
    public int year;
    public int month;
    public int day;
    public Date(final int pYear, final int pMonth, final int pDay)
    {
        year = pYear;
        month = pMonth;
        day = pDay;
    }
    public void display()
    {
        System.out.println(year + "-" + month/10 + month%10 +
                                "-" + day/10 + day%10);
    }
}
```
....
```
// This program creates an object of class Date representing Christmas Day
// 2000, then moves the day field on by 1, and then outputs the new date.
// Barry Cornelius, 19 June 2000
public class NoelProg
{
    public static void main(final String[] pArgs)
    {
        final Date tNoelDate = new Date(2000, 12, 25);
        tNoelDate.day++;
        tNoelDate.display();
    }
}
```

Figure 11.3   Stage B: adding a constructor and a method declaration to Date.

11.4.2 Stage B2: using a method to display the value of an object

The first NoelProg program (that was given in Figure 11.1) outputs the value of a
Date object by using:

```
System.out.println(tNoelDate.year + "-" +
                    tNoelDate.month + "-" + tNoelDate.day);
```

Displaying the value of an object is a common task, and:

◉ to save us from writing the above code each time we want to output a date;
◉ to ensure that we get consistent output;

it is useful to put the code for outputting a date into a method.

The class declaration for Date in Figure 11.3 includes a method declaration for a
method called display. So when the NoelProg program executes the statement:

```
tNoelDate.display();
```

the method called `display` will get called, and it will be applied to the object pointed to by the `tNoelDate` variable. When the block of `display` is executed, i.e. when the statement:

```
System.out.println(year + "-" + month/10 + month%10 +
                   "-" + day/10 + day%10);
```

is executed, the references to `year`, `month` and `day` are references to the `year`, `month` and `day` fields of `tNoelDate`. As mentioned in Tip 5.3, the uses of `/10` and `%10` ensure that two digits are always output for the month and day values.

The call of this method will output the line:

```
2000-12-26
```

11.5 Grouping fields and methods together

The class declaration for `Date` (in Figure 11.3) not only has the declaration of three fields (`year`, `month` and `day`): it also has the declaration of a method (`display`). Earlier, it was suggested that the two main characteristics of a type are a set of values and some operations to perform on those values. So, one of the major attractions of a class declaration is that it allows us to group together:

- fields to implement the values of a type;
- methods to implement the operations of a type.

The fields and methods are sometimes referred to as the **members** of the class. The syntax of a **class declaration** is given in Figure 11.4. Besides the declarations of fields and methods, these diagrams also confirm that a class body may contain constructor declarations. The syntax of a **field declaration** is given in Figure 11.5.

11.6 Stage C: providing access methods and `toString`

11.6.1 Stage C1: hiding the fields and accessing them using methods

With the class declaration for a date given in Figure 11.3, the fields of an object are directly accessible from a client, i.e. a program like `NoelProg` can refer to the `day` field of the object pointed to by `tNoelDate` by using `tNoelDate.day`. It can do this because, in the class declaration (given in Figure 11.3), the fields have a `public` modifier, e.g.:

```
public int day;
```

Back in the real world, when you want to get off a bus, you usually indicate this by signalling to the bus driver in some way, e.g. by pressing a button that rings a bell. Giving everyone a brake pedal would not be a good idea! In the same way, it is unusual to expose the fields of an object to a client. Instead of making a field `public`, we will make it `private` and usually we will provide some methods to allow access to the field. Such methods are called **access methods**.

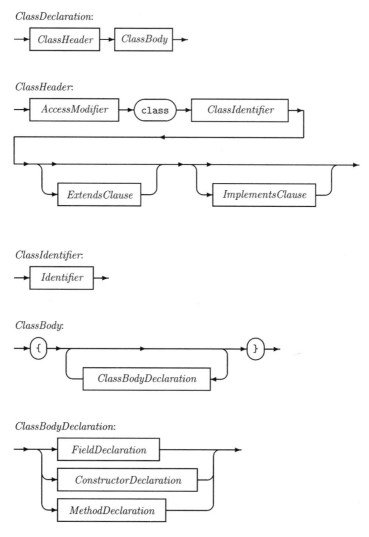

ClassDeclaration:

ClassHeader:

ClassIdentifier:

ClassBody:

ClassBodyDeclaration:

Figure 11.4 The syntax of a class declaration.

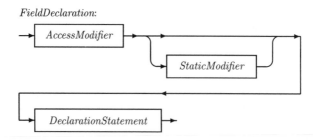

FieldDeclaration:

Figure 11.5 The syntax of a field declaration.

So in the class declaration for Date given in Figure 11.6, the three fields for year, month and day have been made `private`:

```
private int iYear;
private int iMonth;
private int iDay;
```

```
// A class for dates that hides the fields and provides access methods.
// Barry Cornelius, 19 June 2000
public class Date
{
   private int iYear;
   private int iMonth;
   private int iDay;
   public Date(final int pYear, final int pMonth, final int pDay)
   {
      iYear = pYear;
      iMonth = pMonth;
      iDay = pDay;
   }
   public int getYear()
   {
      return iYear;
   }
   public int getMonth()
   {
      return iMonth;
   }
   public int getDay()
   {
      return iDay;
   }
   public void setYear(final int pYear)
   {
      iYear = pYear;
   }
   public void setMonth(final int pMonth)
   {
      iMonth = pMonth;
   }
   public void setDay(final int pDay)
   {
      iDay = pDay;
   }
   public String toString()
   {
      return iYear + "-" + iMonth/10 + iMonth%10 + "-" + iDay/10 + iDay%10;
   }
}
```

Figure 11.6   Stage C: providing access methods and the `toString` method.

```
// This program creates an object of class Date representing Christmas Day
// 2000, then moves the day field on by 1, and then outputs the new date.
// Barry Cornelius, 19 June 2000
public class NoelProg
{
    public static void main(final String[] pArgs)
    {
        final Date tNoelDate = new Date(2000, 12, 25);
        final int tDay = tNoelDate.getDay();
        tNoelDate.setDay(tDay + 1);
        System.out.println(tNoelDate.toString());
        System.out.println(tNoelDate);
    }
}
```

Figure 11.7   Stage C: NoelProg modified to use access methods and toString.

At the same time, the names of these fields have been changed. Back in Section 8.2 and Section 8.12, an i prefix was used in the names of methods and variables belonging to the program class that were internal methods and internal variables of the program class. More generally, for any class, the i prefix will be used for entities that are *internal* to the class. You can also remember the meaning of i because it is also a letter of the words h*i*dden and pr*i*vate.

The class declaration (in Figure 11.6) also provides six access methods called getYear, getMonth, getDay, setYear, setMonth and setDay. Two of these are used by the NoelProg program (given in Figure 11.7). When the program calls getDay as in tNoelDate.getDay(), the block of getDay will execute the statement:

```
return iDay;
```

So the value of the iDay field of the object that is the target of the method invocation is returned. In the case of the NoelProg program, getDay is being applied to the object pointed to by tNoelDate, and so the method returns the value of its iDay field, i.e. 25 gets returned.

In the next statement, the program executes:

```
tNoelDate.setDay(tDay + 1);
```

So pDay (the parameter of setDay) is assigned the value 26 and this value is used in the block of setDay to change iDay to 26. Once again, the object pointed to by tNoelDate is the target of this call and so it is this object's iDay field that is changed to 26.

The technique of hiding fields behind access methods is an important one. It is called **data encapsulation** (or **information hiding**). If you look at the WWW pages for the Core APIs you will find very few classes that have public fields. Possibly the only ones are in the classes java.awt.Point and java.awt.Rectangle.

11.6.2 Stage C2: using `toString` instead of `display`

Although in Stage B2, we found it useful to introduce a method (`display`) which uses `println` to display the value of a date object, when writing Java programs, it is more usual:

- for a class to declare a method (called `toString`) that returns a string that is some textual representation of the value;
- for a client to do whatever it wants with the string, e.g. one possibility being to call `print` or `println` to output the string.

So, instead of having a method called `display` that calls `println`, the class `Date` in Figure 11.6 declares a method called `toString` that just returns a string. In the `NoelProg` program, the result of the call of `toString` is passed as an argument to `println`:

```
System.out.println(tNoelDate.toString());
```

When `toString` gets called, it just executes:

```
return iYear + "-" + iMonth/10 + iMonth%10 + "-" + iDay/10 + iDay%10;
```

You can see that the result type of `toString` is the type `String`. So the execution of this return statement forms a string consisting of the concatenation of the `iYear` field of `tNoelDate`, a hyphen, the two digits of the `iMonth` field of `tNoelDate`, another hyphen, and the two digits of the `iDay` field of `tNoelDate`, e.g. `"2000-12-25"`. This is the string that `NoelProg` passes as an argument to `println`.

It is usual to call this method `toString`. The reason for this is that the statement:

```
System.out.println(tNoelDate.toString());
```

can be abbreviated to:

```
System.out.println(tNoelDate);
```

This is because both `print` and `println` are defined so that if a variable of a reference type is passed as an argument then that type's `toString` method is called (as was mentioned back in Section 3.2.11 when objects were introduced).

11.7 Using the default version of `toString`

If you provide a class declaration but fail to provide a `toString` method, it is still possible for a program to apply the `toString` method to an object of the class. For example, if the `toString` declaration of `Date`'s declaration is removed, the `NoelProg` program given in Figure 11.7 is still a valid program. When it is run, the program will execute the `toString` method of a class called `Object`. The two calls of `println` would then produce output that is something like:

```
Date@80cb419
Date@80cb419
```

This is the name of the class, followed by an @, followed by the *hashcode* of the object (given in the hexadecimal notation). We look again at hashcodes in Section 11.11.2.

One of the key aspects of an object-oriented programming language such as Java is *inheritance*. This is a topic which will be described briefly in Section 13.3 and more fully in Chapter 19. What we need to know at this stage is that a class is *derived*, by default, from a class called `Object` (belonging to the package `java.lang`). It is said to be a *subclass* of the class `Object`. This means that, if a program applies a method to an object, and the class of the object does not provide the method, but it is provided by the class `Object`, then `Object`'s method will be called. The WWW page $API/java/lang/Object.html contains a list of the methods provided by the class `Object`: they are `clone`, `equals`, `finalize`, `getClass`, `hashCode`, `notify`, `notifyAll`, `toString` and `wait`. In this chapter, we consider `toString`, `equals`, `getClass` and `hashCode`: we will look at some of the other methods in later chapters.

On `Object`'s WWW page, i.e. at $API/java/lang/Object.html#toString(), it says:

> In general, the `toString` method returns a string that *textually represents* this object. The result should be a concise but informative representation that is easy for a person to read. It is recommended that all subclasses override this method.

And this is exactly what is happening in Figure 11.6: the definition of `toString` given in the class declaration for `Date` *overrides* the one given in `Object`. *Method overriding*, which is different from the idea of *method overloading* (which was introduced in Section 8.14), will be considered in more detail in Section 19.2.4.

11.8 Stage D: class variables and class methods

If a class declaration includes a field, every object that is of this class will include this field. Such a field is called an **instance variable**. In Section 8.12, we found out that it is possible to have a field that is associated with the class rather than with each object of the class. Such a field is called a **class variable**, and it is indicated by using a `static` modifier.

A superficial example would be a class declaration that has a field that is used to count how many times methods of the class have been called:

```
private static int iNumberOfCalls = 0;
```

In order for this to work, we would need to add the statement:

```
iNumberOfCalls++:
```

to each of the methods of the class. Such a class declaration is shown in Figure 11.8.

In Section 4.6, a distinction was made between *instance methods* and *class methods*. A method that can be applied to any object of its class is called an *instance method*. It is also possible for a class to have standalone methods: such a method is called a *class method*. So we could add to the `Date` declaration a method that returns the

```
// A class for dates that demonstrates a class variable and a class method.
// Barry Cornelius, 19 June 2000
import java.util. StringTokenizer;
public class Date
{
    private static int iNumberOfCalls = 0;
    private int iYear;
    private int iMonth;
    private int iDay;
    public static int getNumberOfCalls()
    {
        return iNumberOfCalls;
    }
    public Date(final int pYear, final int pMonth, final int pDay)
    {
        iNumberOfCalls++;
        iYear = pYear;
        iMonth = pMonth;
        iDay = pDay;
    }
    public int getYear()
    {
        iNumberOfCalls++;
        return iYear;
    }
    public int getMonth()
    {
        iNumberOfCalls++;
        return iMonth;
    }
    public int getDay()
    {
        iNumberOfCalls++;
        return iDay;
    }
    public void setYear(final int pYear)
    {
        iNumberOfCalls++;
        iYear = pYear;
    }
    public void setMonth(final int pMonth)
    {
        iNumberOfCalls++;
        iMonth = pMonth;
    }
```

Figure 11.8 *Continues on the next page.*

```
public void setDay(final int pDay)
{
   iNumberOfCalls++;
   iDay = pDay;
}
public String toString()
{
   iNumberOfCalls++;
   return iYear + "-" + iMonth/10 + iMonth%10 + "-" + iDay/10 + iDay%10;
}
}
```

Figure 11.8 Stage D: adding a class variable and class methods to Date.

value of the class variable iNumberOfCalls, i.e. that returns the number of times methods of the class have been called:

```
public static int getNumberOfCalls()
{
   return iNumberOfCalls;
}
```

As was mentioned in Section 4.6, a class method is called by putting the name of the class on the left of the dot as in Date.getNumberOfCalls(). An example of a call of this method is shown in the NoelProg program given in Figure 11.9. It outputs the value 7.

```
// This program creates objects of the version of the class Date that keeps
// track of the number of calls of its methods.
// Barry Cornelius, 19 June 2000
public class NoelProg
{
   public static void main(final String[] pArgs)
   {
      final Date tNoelDate = new Date(2000, 12, 25);     // 1
      final int tDay = tNoelDate.getDay();               // 2
      tNoelDate.setDay(tDay + 1);                        // 3
      System.out.println(tNoelDate.toString());          // 4
      System.out.println(tNoelDate);                     // 5
      final Date tAnotherDate = new Date(2001, 12, 25);  // 6
      System.out.println(tAnotherDate);                  // 7
      System.out.println("number of calls is: " + Date.getNumberOfCalls());
   }
}
```

Figure 11.9 Stage D: using Date's class method in NoelProg.

As a class method is not applied to an instance of a class, it does not make sense to refer to non-static members (e.g. `iDay` and `toString`) in the block of the method of a class method (e.g. `getNumberOfCalls`). Any attempt to do this produces a compilation error like *Can't make a static reference to nonstatic variable iDay in class Date.*

If it is appropriate for a class to have a constant associated with it, you can use a class variable whose declaration includes the `final` modifier. In Section 5.7, we saw that the class `java.lang.Math` includes:

```
public static final double PI = 3.14159265358979323846;
```

11.9 Stage E: constructors, `equals` and client methods

11.9.1 Stage E1: providing a constructor to convert a `String`

Although we have a means of outputting the value of a date object, we currently have no means of reading a textual representation of a date from the keyboard or from a file. Obviously, we could use `readLine` to read a textual representation of a date and store it in a string. What we then need is a way of parsing the string and forming an appropriate `Date` object. So instead of initializing a date from three integers, we are wishing to initialize it from a string.

The class declaration in Figure 11.10 not only provides the usual constructor to initialize a date from three `ints`, but it also has three other constructors including one which initializes a date from a `String`. This constructor could be used as follows:

```
Date tTodaysDate = new Date("2000-09-26");
```

The code for this constructor (which is given in Figure 11.10) uses `StringTokenizer` to obtain the various parts of the date. It uses a try statement to ensure that the constructor does not crash if the client provides an inappropriate string. The try statement has a catch clause that has a parameter of type `Exception`. As mentioned in Curio 9.3, choosing this type will ensure that *any* exception will be caught. In practice, it will catch `NoSuchElementException` if the client supplies a date that does not have at least three parts or a `NumberFormatException` if the client supplies a year, month or day that does not consist solely of digits.

What should this catch clause do, i.e. what do we want to happen if a client passes an inappropriate string to this constructor? We could output an error message and then abort the execution of the program:

```
catch (final Exception pException)
{
    System.out.println("Date constructor has an inappropriate string.");
    System.out.println("The string is: " + pDateString);
    System.exit(1);
}
```

However, this is not particularly helpful. Instead, we could allow the program to

```
// A class for dates providing other constructors and an equals method.
// Barry Cornelius, 19 June 2000
import java.util. StringTokenizer;
public class Date
{
   private int iYear;
   private int iMonth;
   private int iDay;
   public Date()
   {
      this(1970, 1, 1);
   }
   public Date(final Date pDate)
   {
      this(pDate.iYear, pDate.iMonth, pDate.iDay);
   }
   public Date(final int pYear, final int pMonth, final int pDay)
   {
      iYear = pYear;
      iMonth = pMonth;
      iDay = pDay;
   }
   public Date(final String pDateString)
   {
      try
      {
         final StringTokenizer tTokens =
                                  new StringTokenizer(pDateString, "-");
         final String tYearString = tTokens.nextToken();
         iYear = Integer.parseInt(tYearString);
         final String tMonthString = tTokens.nextToken();
         iMonth = Integer.parseInt(tMonthString);
         final String tDayString = tTokens.nextToken();
         iDay = Integer.parseInt(tDayString);
      }
      catch(final Exception pException)
      {
         iYear = 1970;
         iMonth = 1;
         iDay = 1;
         throw new IllegalArgumentException();
      }
   }
   public int getYear()
   {
      return iYear;
   }
```

Figure 11.10   *Continues on the next page.*

```
    public int getMonth()
    {
        return iMonth;
    }
    public int getDay()
    {
        return iDay;
    }
    public void setYear(final int pYear)
    {
        iYear = pYear;
    }
    public void setMonth(final int pMonth)
    {
        iMonth = pMonth;
    }
    public void setDay(final int pDay)
    {
        iDay = pDay;
    }
    public boolean equals(final Date pDate)
    {
        return iYear==pDate.iYear && iMonth==pDate.iMonth && iDay==pDate.iDay;
    }
    public String toString()
    {
        return iYear + "-" + iMonth/10 + iMonth%10 + "-" + iDay/10 + iDay%10;
    }
}
```

Figure 11.10   Stage E: adding other constructors and an `equals` method to `Date`.

carry on after initializing the `Date` object to some arbitrary `Date` value:

```
catch (final Exception pException)
{
    iYear = 1970;
    iMonth = 1;
    iDay = 1;
}
```

However, to do this without warning the client is confusing.

It so happens that an exception called `IllegalArgumentException` is provided by the `java.lang` package. So when a client uses the `Date` constructor with an inappropriate string, we could arrange for the constructor to throw an `IllegalArgumentException` exception. The code in Figure 11.10 does this, i.e. the catch clause ends with:

```
throw new IllegalArgumentException();
```

Here we are creating an object of the class `IllegalArgumentException` and using the object in a **throw statement**. As you might expect, the execution of a throw statement causes an exception to occur; in this case, an `IllegalArgumentException` exception occurs. The throw statement is discussed more thoroughly in Section 21.1.

Before throwing an exception, a constructor ought to ensure that the object being constructed has some valid value. In the `Date` class (shown in Figure 11.10), the constructor arranges for the object to have the date `1970-01-01` before throwing the `IllegalArgumentException` exception.

Even though this constructor may cause an `IllegalArgumentException` exception to occur, this does not have to be documented in the header of the constructor, i.e. we do not have to provide a throws clause:

```
public Date(final String pDateString) throws IllegalArgumentException
```

This is because the `IllegalArgumentException` exception is an unchecked exception.

Note that the textual representation of a date that is assumed by this constructor has the same format as that produced by `toString`. This means that if you were to use `toString` and `println` to output a date to a file, you would be able to read this in (perhaps in some other program) and construct an appropriate date using `readLine` and this new constructor.

In general, it is useful for you to arrange for the string that is produced by the `toString` of a class to be parseable by a constructor of the class.

This new constructor is used in the `NoelProg` program (given in Figure 11.11). This program uses `readLine` to read a string and then makes `tOtherDateString` point to it. Then the variable `tOtherDate` is made to point to a `Date` object created by passing this string as an argument to the constructor.

Although this constructor can throw an `IllegalArgumentException` exception, a client such as `NoelProg` is not forced to document what should happen if this exception occurs because `IllegalArgumentException` is an unchecked exception. If the string that is read by `readLine` is inappropriate, the `NoelProg` program will crash with an `IllegalArgumentException` exception.

Earlier (in Section 8.14), we saw that a class declaration can have several method declarations each having the same name provided the types of the parameters of each declaration are different (*method overloading*). In the same way, a class declaration can provide several constructors so long as the types of the parameters of each constructor are different.

11.9.2 Stage E2: providing a no-arg constructor

When we first provided a class declaration for `Date` (back in Figure 11.1), the class declaration did not have a constructor declaration. However, the `NoelProg` program given in Figure 11.1 assumes that one exists. The explanation for this is: if a class does not declare a constructor, a **default no-arg constructor** is magically available. So this is what is used by the `NoelProg` program shown in Figure 11.1. However, if a class has at least one constructor that has parameters, there is no default no-arg constructor.

```
// This program uses two new constructors of the class Date.   One of these
// has a parameter of type String; the other has a parameter of type Date.
// The program also shows the use of both the == operator and Date's equals
// method being applied to Date objects.   And the program also shows the use
// of a subsidiary method that has a Date parameter.
// Barry Cornelius, 19 June 2000
import java.io. BufferedReader;
import java.io. InputStreamReader;
import java.io. IOException;
public class NoelProg
{
    public static void main(final String[] pArgs) throws IOException
    {
        // use the constructor that has three parameters of type int
        final Date tNoelDate = new Date(2000, 12, 25);
        System.out.println("tNoelDate is: " + tNoelDate);
        // read a String and use the constructor that has a String parameter
        final BufferedReader tKeyboard =
                    new BufferedReader(new InputStreamReader(System.in));
        System.out.print("Type in the date, e.g., 2000-12-25: ");
        System.out.flush();
        final String tOtherDateString = tKeyboard.readLine();
        final Date tOtherDate = new Date(tOtherDateString);
        System.out.println("tOtherDate is: " + tOtherDate);
        // compare tNoelDate and tOtherDate using == and Date's equals method
        System.out.println("tUsingOperator: " + (tNoelDate==tOtherDate));
        System.out.println("tNoelDate.equals: " +
                                        tNoelDate.equals(tOtherDate));
        System.out.println("tOtherDate.equals: " +
                                        tOtherDate.equals(tNoelDate));
        // use the constructor that has a parameter of type Date
        final Date tHappyDate = new Date(tNoelDate);
        System.out.println("tHappyDate is: " + tHappyDate);
        // compare tNoelDate and tHappyDate using == and Date's equals method
        System.out.println("tUsingOperator: " + (tNoelDate==tHappyDate));
        System.out.println("tNoelDate.equals: " +
                                        tNoelDate.equals(tHappyDate));
        System.out.println("tHappyDate.equals: " +
                                        tHappyDate.equals(tNoelDate));
        // use the isLeap function on the three Date variables
        System.out.println("tNoelDate.iIsLeap: " + iIsLeap(tNoelDate));
        System.out.println("tOtherDate.iIsLeap: " + iIsLeap(tOtherDate));
        System.out.println("tHappyDate.iIsLeap: " + iIsLeap(tHappyDate));
    }

    private static boolean iIsLeap(final Date pDate)
    {
        final int tYear = pDate.getYear();
        return (tYear%400==0) || (tYear%4==0 && tYear%100!=0);
    }
}
```

Figure 11.11   Stage E: `NoelProg` modified to use other constructors and `equals`.

So, if a class has one or more constructors, you must declare a constructor that has no parameters if you want clients to be able to use such a constructor; otherwise, it will not be available. In other areas of Java, such as *JavaBeans*, it is useful for a class to have a **no-arg constructor**.

11.9.3 Stage E3: using one constructor in the body of another

The class declaration for `Date` that was given in Figure 11.10 also contains the following *no-arg constructor*:

```
public Date()
{
    this(1970, 1, 1);
}
```

This constructor would get used for the following declaration:

```
Date tDate = new Date();
```

The body of this constructor contains some magic: the `this(1970, 1, 1)` is a call of a constructor. When `this` is used like this, it means 'use the constructor of this class declaration that matches the arguments following the `this`'. So since the `1970, 1, 1` are three `int`s, the `this(1970, 1, 1)` leads to a call of the constructor that has three `int`s as parameters. If you use `this` in this way, the `this` call must appear as the first statement of the constructor.

By this means, you can provide a constructor that has no arguments in order to initialize an object with default values (that you can choose).

The syntax of a constructor declaration is shown in Figure 11.12.

11.9.4 Stage E4: providing a constructor for cloning an object

Section 3.2.9 mentioned that the classes of the Core APIs use two different ways of producing a copy of an object: a class sometimes provides a method called `clone` or it provides a suitable constructor. Getting the code of a `clone` method completely right is difficult: there is more about this in Curio 11.7. Instead, we will provide `Date` with a constructor that can be used for cloning.

We can provide an existing `Date` object as an argument to a constructor and use its values to initialize the new object. Here is how the constructor could be coded:

```
public Date(final Date pDate)
{
    iYear = pDate.iYear;
    iMonth = pDate.iMonth;
    iDay = pDate.iDay;
}
```

Another way of coding this constructor is shown in the class declaration in

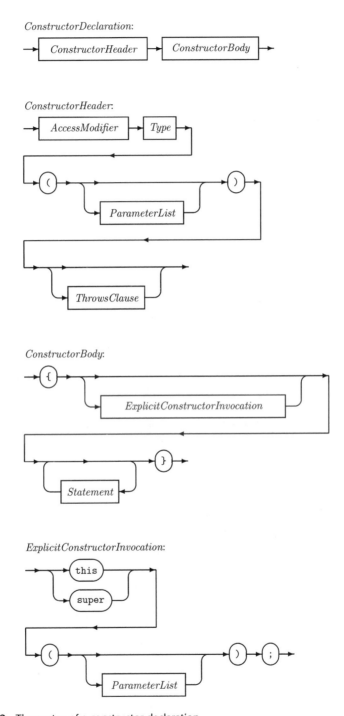

Figure 11.12 The syntax of a constructor declaration.

Figure 11.10:

```
public Date(final Date pDate)
{
    this(pDate.iYear, pDate.iMonth, pDate.iDay);
}
```

An example of how this constructor can be used is given in Figure 11.11. In the earlier part of the program, a Date object has been created using one of the other constructors:

```
final Date tNoelDate = new Date(2000, 12, 25);
```

Later, this reference variable is passed as an argument to the new constructor:

```
final Date tHappyDate = new Date(tNoelDate);
```

We finish up with two reference variables pointing to two different objects that have the same value.

11.9.5 Stage E5: defining a method called `equals`

If a client uses Date variables, using == on these variables only determines whether they are pointing to the same object. However, if a class declares an appropriate method called equals, a client can determine whether the dates are the same. Whenever you declare a class, it is important to declare a method called equals. This is done by the version of the class Date that is given in Figure 11.10.

Important note: although this version of equals is sufficient for some circumstances, it is not recommended: a better version of equals will be given in Section 11.11.1.

The NoelProg program (in Figure 11.11) evaluates tNoelDate==tOtherDate. This will deliver *false* because tNoelDate and tOtherDate point to different Date objects.

The program also evaluates tNoelDate.equals(tOtherDate). This invokes the equals method of the class Date. Because the argument of the call is tOtherDate, the variable pDate points to the same object as tOtherDate. So, when the block (of equals) evaluates iYear==pDate.iYear, it is effectively evaluating iYear==tOtherDate.iYear. Now the target of the call of equals is tNoelDate and so the iYear (on the left-hand side of the ==) is a reference to tNoelDate's iYear. So the complicated boolean expression (in the block of equals) finds out whether the iYear, iMonth and iDay fields of the object pointed to by tNoelDate have the same values as those of the object pointed to by tOtherDate, and only delivers *true* if they do have the same values.

If we declare a class and fail to declare a method called equals, the equals method can still be applied to an object of the class because the class java.lang.Object has a method called equals (as was mentioned in Section 11.7). However, Object's equals will just tell you whether the target and the argument point to the same objects (i.e. it does the same as ==): it will not compare the values of the two objects.

11.9.6 Stage E6: providing client methods that work on Dates

If a class fails to provide all the methods that we would like it to provide, we can provide our own methods in the client. To demonstrate this, the NoelProg program (in Figure 11.11) contains a declaration for a function called iIsLeap that it uses to determine whether a date is in a leap year. This function has a parameter of the class Date.

(11.10) Some more details about the class Object

In previous chapters, when we have declared a reference variable of some class type, we have done this in order to be able to point to an object of this class. However, when we look at inheritance in Chapter 19, we will find that a reference variable can point to an object of the class or to any object *of any of its subclasses*. In Section 11.7, it was mentioned that all classes are *derived* from the class Object. Because of this, a reference variable of type Object can point to any object of any class.

At one point in the execution of a program, it could be pointing to a Date; then later it could be pointing to a String; then to a Point; and so on:

```
Object tObject;
...
tObject = new Date(2000, 12, 25);
...
tObject = new String("hello there");
...
tObject = new Point(100, 200);
...
```

Even if a variable (of some class) is pointing to an object that is of a subclass (of that class), you cannot use methods of the subclass on the variable. So the following use of getYear produces a compilation error because tObject's type, i.e. Object, does not have a method called getYear:

```
Object tObject;
...
tObject = new Date(2000, 12, 25);
int tYear = tObject.getYear();
...
```

In fact, there is not much you can do with a reference variable of type Object, unless you use a **cast**. When we first used casts back in Section 5.4, we used them to convert a value from one primitive type to another. What happens when a cast is used with reference types? Suppose we have a variable tSomeClass of the class type SomeClass, and we know that it is pointing to an object of some other class type (say D). Suppose we would really like to refer to a value of that class. The cast (D) tSomeClass gives us the value of type D. Because we are now referring to a value that is of class D, a subclass of SomeClass, this kind of cast is called a **downcast**. Here are some examples of downcasts:

```
Object tObject;
...
tObject = new Date(2000, 12, 25);
Date tDate = (Date)tObject;
int tYear = tDate.getYear();
...
tObject = new String("hello there");
System.out.println(((String)tObject).toUpperCase());
...
tObject = new Point(100, 200);
int tX = ((Point)tObject).x;
...
```

So why would you want to work with a reference variable of type Object? Well, one important reason will occur when we look at forming collections of data: for example, we may be wanting to represent a collection of dates, a collection of strings, a collection of points, and so on. Java has a number of useful classes that can be used to manipulate collections. So as to make these classes generally useful, the methods of these classes are written in terms of the type Object. For example:

```
public boolean add(Object pObject);
public     void add(int pIndex, Object pObject);
public boolean contains(Object pObject);
public  Object get(int pIndex);
public boolean remove(Object pObject);
public  Object remove(int pIndex);
```

These are the methods that can be used to perform operations on one kind of collection (a *list*). We will look at these collection classes in Chapter 14 and Chapter 17.

11.11 Stage F: modifying Date to work with collections

11.11.1 Stage F1: modifying equals to work with collections

These collection classes are wonderful because they allow us to create dynamically growing collections of objects. But the person who wrote the code of the methods of these collection classes was not in a position to know what sort of objects you would be storing in a collection. When you call a method like contains (that finds out whether an object is in a collection), behind the scenes contains will call a method with the header:

```
public boolean equals(Object pObject);
```

Now, if you are storing Dates in the collection, and if in the class Date you have declared equals with a parameter of type Date:

```
public boolean equals(final Date pDate);
```

this equals will not be called (because the type of the parameter is different). Instead, the method called equals from the class Object will be called: as explained earlier this returns *true* if and only if the target and the argument point to the same object (and not if the two objects have the same values). This would be an inappropriate method to be used by contains.

We now look at how we can overcome this problem. As shown in Figure 11.10, the class declaration for Date has the method declaration:

```
public boolean equals(final Date pDate)
{
    return iYear==pDate.iYear && iMonth==pDate.iMonth && iDay==pDate.iDay;
}
```

In future, we will instead use the following method declaration:

```
public boolean equals(final Object pObject)
{
    if ( pObject==null || getClass()!=pObject.getClass() )
    {
        return false;
    }
    final Date tDate = (Date)pObject;
    return iYear==tDate.iYear && iMonth==tDate.iMonth && iDay==tDate.iDay;
}
```

This code uses a method called getClass (which is declared in the class java.lang.Object). This is a method that returns a value of type java.lang.Class, a value that describes the class of its target. In the above code for equals, the getClass method is called twice:

```
pObject==null || getClass()!=pObject.getClass()
```

In the second call, the target of the call of getClass is pObject. So the value that is returned is the class of the object to which pObject is pointing.

In the first call, there is no explicit target. We have seen that, when iYear appears without a target within the code of the equals method, the target is the object to which equals is being applied, i.e. it uses the iYear field of the target of equals. Similarly, when getClass is called without a target (from the equals method), it will be applied to whatever object is the target of the call of equals. So the first call of getClass is finding out the class of the object to which equals is being applied.

Since the equals method appears in a class called Date, you would think that the target of the equals method must be an object of class Date, and so this kind of call of getClass will always return the class Date. However, we will find out later (in Chapter 19) that, in some circumstances, it will return a value that is a *subclass* of the class Date.

So, if subclasses are not involved, this part of the code is checking to see whether the parameter pObject is pointing to an object of the class Date.

This method declaration for equals *overrides* the public boolean equals (Object pObject) that is declared in the class java.lang.Object. A class declaration containing this new version of equals is given in Figure 11.13.

```
// A class for dates that provides hashCode and a better version of equals.
// Barry Cornelius, 19 June 2000
import java.util. StringTokenizer;
public class Date
{
    private int iYear;
    private int iMonth;
    private int iDay;
    public Date()
    {
        this(1970, 1, 1);
    }
    public Date(final Date pDate)
    {
        this(pDate.iYear, pDate.iMonth, pDate.iDay);
    }
    public Date(final int pYear, final int pMonth, final int pDay)
    {
        iYear = pYear;  iMonth = pMonth;   iDay = pDay;
    }
    public Date(final String pDateString)
    {
        try
        {
            final StringTokenizer tTokens =
                            new StringTokenizer(pDateString, "-");
            final String tYearString = tTokens.nextToken();
            iYear = Integer.parseInt(tYearString);
            final String tMonthString = tTokens.nextToken();
            iMonth = Integer.parseInt(tMonthString);
            final String tDayString = tTokens.nextToken();
            iDay = Integer.parseInt(tDayString);
        }
        catch(final Exception pException)
        {
            iYear = 1970;  iMonth = 1;   iDay = 1;
            throw new IllegalArgumentException();
        }
    }
}
```

Figure 11.13 *Continues on the next page.*

```java
    public int getYear()
    {
        return iYear;
    }
    public int getMonth()
    {
        return iMonth;
    }
    public int getDay()
    {
        return iDay;
    }
    public void setYear(final int pYear)
    {
        iYear = pYear;
    }
    public void setMonth(final int pMonth)
    {
        iMonth = pMonth;
    }
    public void setDay(final int pDay)
    {
        iDay = pDay;
    }
    public boolean equals(final Object pObject)
    {
        if ( pObject==null || getClass()!=pObject.getClass() )
        {
            return false;
        }
        final Date tDate = (Date)pObject;
        return iYear==tDate.iYear && iMonth==tDate.iMonth && iDay==tDate.iDay;
    }
    public int hashCode()
    {
        return 0;
    }
    public String toString()
    {
        return iYear + "-" + iMonth/10 + iMonth%10 + "-" + iDay/10 + iDay%10;
    }
}
```

Figure 11.13   Stage F: the Date class modified so that it will work with collections.

11.11.2 Stage F2: providing hashCode (to work with collections)

You can imagine that when checking whether a collection contains a particular object it can be quite time-consuming to use equals on each of the objects of the collection in turn. So, some of these collection classes use clever techniques in order to reduce the number of items of the collection that need to be checked. Some of these techniques require there to be an integer (called a **hashcode**) associated with each of the possible values that can be stored in the collection. And to speed up the execution of methods like `contains`, the objects in the collection are arranged so that the ones that have the same hashcode are kept together, and so only these have to be checked.

In order to support this, the class `java.lang.Object` has a method called `hashCode`:

```
public int hashCode();
```

When this `hashCode` method is applied to a target object, the integer that is returned is one that is unique for that object. So, even if two objects have the same value, this method will return different values.

For this reason, `Object`'s `hashCode` method is inappropriate. What we need to do is to provide our own version of `hashCode` that *overrides* the one provided by `Object`. The WWW page $API/java/lang/Object.html#hashCode() says:

> The general contract of `hashCode` is:
>
> ⬤ Whenever it is invoked on the same object more than once during an execution of a Java application, the `hashCode` method must consistently return the same integer, provided no information used in equals comparisons on the object is modified. This integer need not remain consistent from one execution of an application to another execution of the same application.
>
> ⬤ If two objects are equal according to the `equals(Object)` method, then calling the `hashCode` method on each of the two objects must produce the same integer result.
>
> ⬤ It is not required that if two objects are unequal according to the `equals(Object)` method, then calling the `hashCode` method on each of the two objects must produce distinct integer results. However, the programmer should be aware that producing distinct integer results for unequal objects may improve the performance of hashtables.

The full implications of these three rules are not particularly easy to understand. So to begin with we will provide the following `hashCode` function:

```
public int hashCode()
{
    return 0;
}
```

When this function is called, it always returns the same value, and so this `hashCode` function satisfies the first two rules. What the third rule is saying is that we may get poor execution speeds by choosing this `hashCode` function. However, there are some subtle points that need to be considered if you want to provide a more sophisticated form of hashCode. So we will leave this until Section 17.4 when we look at a collection class that actually uses the hashCode function. In Section 17.4, we will also consider the better performance that can be achieved by choosing a better hashCode function.

Here is a summary of the above discussion. Some of the collection classes use hashCode. If a class declaration fails to override hashCode, some methods of those collection classes will not produce the results we would expect to get (and these bugs will often be difficult to detect). However, if a class declaration provides:

```
public int hashCode()
{
    return 0;
}
```

it will be used by some of the methods of these collection classes, but these methods may perform more slowly than a class that has a more sophisticated hashCode.

11.12 Stage G: using an interface as well as a class

11.12.1 Stage G1: introducing interface declarations

If you look at any of the class declarations for Date that have been provided in this chapter, you will find that the text of the class declaration is being provided for two distinct purposes:

- The text of the headers of the public methods (together with the names of any public fields) gives information as to *what* services are offered by the class.
- The text of the blocks of the public methods together with the text of the private members gives the details of *how* those services are provided.

Only the first of these is normally of interest to those people wishing to find out whether a particular class satisfies their needs.

The Java programming language provides a means by which we can make the *what* more obvious: it is the *interface declaration*.

11.12.2 Stage G2: providing an interface declaration called Date

An **interface declaration** is a construct that gives a list of related methods (and/or constants). For dates, we can provide an interface called Date: it appears in Figure 11.14. Earlier we said that a type provides a set of values and a set of operations (that are permitted on those values). The interface declaration is the ideal construct for documenting the set of operations for a type. Note that an interface does not mention constructors. The syntax of an interface declaration is given in Figure 11.15.

```
// A type to represent a date.
// Barry Cornelius, 19 June 2000
public interface Date
{
    // return the Year part of the target date
    public int getYear();

    // return the Month part of the target date
    public int getMonth();

    // return the Day part of the target date
    public int getDay();

    // set the Year part of the target date to pYear
    public void setYear(int pYear);

    // set the Month part of the target date to pMonth
    public void setMonth(int pMonth);

    // set the Day part of the target date to pDay
    public void setDay(int pDay);

    // return true if and only if the target is the same date as pObject
    public boolean equals(Object pObject);

    // return the hashcode for the value of the target date
    public int hashCode();

    // return a textual representation of the target date
    public String toString();
}
```

Figure 11.14   Stage G: the `Date` interface.

The text for an interface called `Date` (such as the one given in Figure 11.14) has to be stored in a file called `Date.java`. It can be compiled in the usual way:

```
javac Date.java
```

This command will produce a file called `Date.class`.

11.12.3 Stage G3: providing a class to implement an interface

The only way in which an interface can be used is to provide a class that implements the interface. We can do this by a class declaration that contains an **implements clause**:

```
public class DateImpl implements Date
{
    ...
}
```

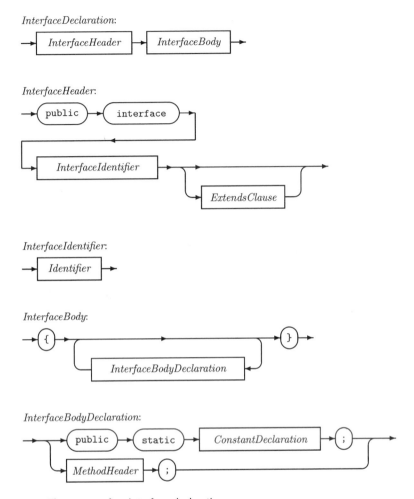

Figure 11.15 The syntax of an interface declaration.

where the rest of this class declaration is almost the same as the previous class declarations (of this chapter). The complete class declaration is shown in Figure 11.16.

A syntax diagram for an implements clause is shown in Figure 11.17.

If a class declaration has an implements clause, it must at least include declarations for each method that is declared in the interface. When this class is compiled using the command:

```
javac DateImpl.java
```

the compiler will look at the file `Date.class` to see whether the class `DateImpl` does in fact implement the `Date` interface.

In this book, we will normally use a name like *XXX*Impl for a class that implements the *XXX* interface.

```
// A class that implements the Date interface.
// Barry Cornelius, 19 June 2000
import java.util. StringTokenizer;
public class DateImpl implements Date
{
    private int iYear;
    private int iMonth;
    private int iDay;
    public DateImpl()
    {
        this(1970, 1, 1);
    }
    public DateImpl(final Date pDate)
    {
        final DateImpl tDateImpl = (DateImpl)pDate;
        iYear = tDateImpl.iYear;
        iMonth = tDateImpl.iMonth;
        iDay = tDateImpl.iDay;
    }
    public DateImpl(final int pYear, final int pMonth, final int pDay)
    {
        iYear = pYear;
        iMonth = pMonth;
        iDay = pDay;
    }
    public DateImpl(final String pDateString)
    {
        try
        {
            final StringTokenizer tTokens =
                                new StringTokenizer(pDateString, "-");
            final String tYearString = tTokens.nextToken();
            iYear = Integer.parseInt(tYearString);
            final String tMonthString = tTokens.nextToken();
            iMonth = Integer.parseInt(tMonthString);
            final String tDayString = tTokens.nextToken();
            iDay = Integer.parseInt(tDayString);
        }
        catch(final Exception pException)
        {
            iYear = 1970;
            iMonth = 1;
            iDay = 1;
            throw new IllegalArgumentException();
        }
    }
```

Figure 11.16 *Continues on the next page.*

```
public int getYear()
{
    return iYear;
}
public int getMonth()
{
    return iMonth;
}
public int getDay()
{
    return iDay;
}
public void setYear(final int pYear)
{
    iYear = pYear;
}
public void setMonth(final int pMonth)
{
    iMonth = pMonth;
}
public void setDay(final int pDay)
{
    iDay = pDay;
}
public boolean equals(final Object pObject)
{
    if ( pObject==null || getClass()!=pObject.getClass() )
    {
        return false;
    }
    final DateImpl tDateImpl = (DateImpl)pObject;
    return iYear==tDateImpl.iYear &&
            iMonth==tDateImpl.iMonth && iDay==tDateImpl.iDay;
}
public int hashCode()
{
    return 0;
}
public String toString()
{
    return iYear + "-" + iMonth/10 + iMonth%10 + "-" + iDay/10 + iDay%10;
}
}
```

Figure 11.16 Stage G: the `DateImpl` class implements the `Date` interface.

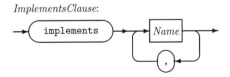

Implements Clause:

Figure 11.17 The syntax of an implements clause.

This book recommends you to use the `final` keyword for documenting those parameters of a method that do not have their value changed by the method. However, it is inappropriate for the headers of the interface declaration to include the `final` keyword: only the headers of the method declarations appearing in the class declaration should include `final`. This is because it is not a property of the interface: it is a detail of the implementation of the interface.

11.12.4 Stage G4: using an interface (and an associated class)

The code of a client should use the interface (rather than the class) whenever possible. So:

- reference variables should be declared to be of the interface type `Date` rather than of the class type `DateImpl`:

  ```
  Date tDate;
  ```

- parameters of any methods (of the client) should be declared to be of the interface type `Date` rather than of the class type `DateImpl`:

  ```
  public boolean iIsLeap(final Date pDate)
  ```

The only time we have to use the class type (`DateImpl`) is when we want to create an object:

```
Date tDate = new DateImpl(2000, 12, 25);
```

This creates an object of class `DateImpl` and makes the reference variable `tDate` (which is of the interface type `Date`) point to it. A variable that is of an interface type may point to any object that is of a class that implements that interface.

Figure 11.18 contains the `NoelProg` program of Figure 11.11 reworked to use the `Date` interface and the `DateImpl` class.

11.12.5 Stage G5: a different class implementing the same interface

By writing in terms of the interface (i.e. `Date`), it means that there are few references in our code to the particular implementation (i.e. `DateImpl`) that we are using. What we are doing is distinguishing in the code of the client the parts of the client that are independent of the implementation from those that are dependent on the implementation.

If this approach is followed, it means that if at a later date some other class is produced that is *better* at implementing the interface then only the small number of lines that refer to `DateImpl` need to be changed.

For example, Figure 11.19 contains another class (`DateImplY`) that implements the `Date` interface. Instead of storing three `int` values to represent a date, this class uses just one `int` that contains the value $416y + 32m + d$ where y, m and d are the year, month and day parts of a date.

Because both `DateImpl` and `DateImplY` say that they implement the `Date` interface, it is easy to change a client of `Date` to use `DateImplY` instead of `DateImpl`. The only change we need to make to the client given in Figure 11.18 is to change

```java
// This program uses the Date interface and the DateImpl class.
// Barry Cornelius, 19 June 2000
import java.io. BufferedReader;
import java.io. InputStreamReader;
import java.io. IOException;
public class NoelProg
{
    public static void main(final String[] pArgs) throws IOException
    {
        // use the constructor that has three parameters of type int
        final Date tNoelDate = new DateImpl(2000, 12, 25);
        System.out.println("tNoelDate is: " + tNoelDate);
        // read a String and use the constructor that has a String parameter
        final BufferedReader tKeyboard =
                    new BufferedReader(new InputStreamReader(System.in));
        System.out.print("Type in the date, e.g., 2000-12-25: ");
        System.out.flush();
        final String tOtherDateString = tKeyboard.readLine();
        final Date tOtherDate = new DateImpl(tOtherDateString);
        System.out.println("tOtherDate is: " + tOtherDate);
        // compare tNoelDate and tOtherDate using == and Date's equals method
        System.out.println("tUsingOperator: " + (tNoelDate==tOtherDate));
        System.out.println("tNoelDate.equals: " +
                                        tNoelDate.equals(tOtherDate));
        System.out.println("tOtherDate.equals: " +
                                        tOtherDate.equals(tNoelDate));
        // use the constructor that has a parameter of type Date
        final Date tHappyDate = new DateImpl(tNoelDate);
        System.out.println("tHappyDate is: " + tHappyDate);
        // compare tNoelDate and tHappyDate using == and Date's equals method
        System.out.println("tUsingOperator: " + (tNoelDate==tHappyDate));
        System.out.println("tNoelDate.equals: " +
                                        tNoelDate.equals(tHappyDate));
        System.out.println("tHappyDate.equals: " +
                                        tHappyDate.equals(tNoelDate));
        // use the isLeap function on the three Date variables
        System.out.println("tNoelDate.iIsLeap: " + iIsLeap(tNoelDate));
        System.out.println("tOtherDate.iIsLeap: " + iIsLeap(tOtherDate));
        System.out.println("tHappyDate.iIsLeap: " + iIsLeap(tHappyDate));
    }
    private static boolean iIsLeap(final Date pDate)
    {
        final int tYear = pDate.getYear();
        return (tYear%400==0) || (tYear%4==0 && tYear%100!=0);
    }
}
```

Figure 11.18   Stage G: using `Date` and `DateImpl` in the `NoelProg` program.

```java
// A class that implements the Date interface.
// Barry Cornelius, 19 June 2000
import java.util. StringTokenizer;
public class DateImplY implements Date
{
    private int iNumberOfDays;
    public DateImplY()
    {
        this(1970, 1, 1);
    }
    public DateImplY(final Date pDate)
    {
        final DateImplY tDateImplY = (DateImplY)pDate;
        iNumberOfDays = tDateImplY.iNumberOfDays;
    }
    public DateImplY(final int pYear, final int pMonth, final int pDay)
    {
        iNumberOfDays = pYear*416 + pMonth*32 + pDay;
    }
    public DateImplY(final String pDateString)
    {
        try
        {
            final StringTokenizer tTokens =
                                new StringTokenizer(pDateString, "-");
            final String tYearString = tTokens.nextToken();
            final int tYear = Integer.parseInt(tYearString);
            final String tMonthString = tTokens.nextToken();
            final int tMonth = Integer.parseInt(tMonthString);
            final String tDayString = tTokens.nextToken();
            final int tDay = Integer.parseInt(tDayString);
            iNumberOfDays = tYear*416 + tMonth*32 + tDay;
        }
        catch(final Exception pException)
        {
            iNumberOfDays = 1970*416 + 1*32 + 1;
            throw new IllegalArgumentException();
        }
    }
    public int getYear()
    {
        return iNumberOfDays/416;
    }
    public int getMonth()
    {
        return iNumberOfDays%416/32;
    }
```

Figure 11.19 *Continues on the next page.*

```
      public int getDay()
      {
          return iNumberOfDays%32;
      }
      public void setYear(final int pYear)
      {
          iNumberOfDays = pYear*416 + iNumberOfDays%416;
      }
      public void setMonth(final int pMonth)
      {
          iNumberOfDays = iNumberOfDays/416*416 + pMonth*32 + iNumberOfDays%32;
      }
      public void setDay(final int pDay)
      {
          iNumberOfDays = iNumberOfDays/32*32 + pDay;
      }
      public boolean equals(final Object pObject)
      {
          if ( pObject==null || getClass()!=pObject.getClass() )
          {
              return false;
          }
          return iNumberOfDays==((DateImplY)pObject).iNumberOfDays;
      }
      public int hashCode()
      {
          return 0;
      }
      public String toString()
      {
          final int tYear = getYear();
          final int tMonth = getMonth();
          final int tDay = getDay();
          return tYear + "-" + tMonth/10 + tMonth%10 + "-" + tDay/10 + tDay%10;
      }
  }
```

Figure 11.19 Stage G: the DateImplY class also implements the Date interface.

the three uses of constructors of the DateImpl class to use constructors of the DateImplY class instead.

(11.13) The role of interfaces and classes

In this chapter, we have come a long way. We started by writing a class declaration for Date. We did this because we were already familiar with *using* classes. However, it is sometimes better:

1. first to design an interface;

2. then to produce a class that implements that interface;

3. then to write clients in terms of the interface.

Why? Introducing an interface is preferable because:

- an interface declaration provides a clearer statement than a class declaration as to the contract (between the client and the supplier);

- writing the client in terms of an interface means that there is less work involved if you want to switch to a different implementation of a class.

For more details, see the articles mentioned in Curio 11.18.

In this chapter, because we were exploring possibilities, we took a long time to get to the final version: an interface for a `Date` and a class (`DateImpl`) that implements that interface. These are shown in Figure 11.14 and in Figure 11.16. In the chapters that follow, we will often do things differently: the interface will be defined first, and then we will produce a class (or several classes) that implement the interface.

Tips for programming and debugging

11.1   Each member of a class is either a field or a method. Each is described using a `private` or a `public` modifier. When an object is created (using a class instance creation expression), space is created so that the object has its own personal copy of each member of the class. It ceases to exist only when no reference variables point to the object. The names of the private members of a class may be referred to anywhere within the body of the class declaration, i.e. the *scope* of a private member is the text of its class declaration.

Contrast this with a variable whose declaration appears within a method. This variable only exists when the method is being executed: it comes into existence at the start of the execution of the block in which it is declared, and it ceases to exist at the end of the execution of that block. The scope of such a variable is from its declaration until the end of the block in which it is declared.

So it does not make sense to try and use a `private`/`public` modifier with a variable declared within a method as these variables are not part of an object: they are just temporary variables of the method.

11.2   The `NoelProg` program (given in Figure 11.7) uses:

```
final int tDay = tNoelDate.getDay();
tNoelDate.setDay(tDay + 1);
```

Because this version of the class `Date` (given in Figure 11.6) has `iDay` marked as `private`, a client can no longer contain statements like:

```
tNoelDate.iDay++;
```

Any attempt to access a private field of a class produces a compilation error like:

```
Variable iDay in class Date not accessible from class NoelProg.
```

11.3 Suppose a class fails to include an implements clause, i.e. it has:

```
public class DateImpl
```

instead of:

```
public class DateImpl implements Date
```

Suppose a client uses `Date` and `DateImpl`, e.g. in a declaration like:

```
final Date tNoelDate = new DateImpl(2000, 12, 25);
```

Then, when you compile the client, you will get an error message like:

```
Incompatible type for declaration.
Explicit cast needed to convert DateImpl to Date.
```

11.4 If a class says that it implements an interface, it must declare every method that is mentioned in the interface. If it fails to declare one of the methods, or if it declares the method with inappropriate parameters, then, when you attempt to compile the class, you will get an error message like:

```
Class DateImpl must be declared abstract.
It does not define void setYear(int) from interface Date.
```

11.5 If, in a class declaration, you wish to override the methods called `equals` and `hashCode` (that are provided by the class `java.lang.Object`), it is important to get the headers of the method declarations correct, i.e. you need:

```
public boolean equals(Object pObject);
public int hashCode();
```

For example, if you provide:

```
public int hashcode()
{
    return 0;
}
```

then, because the name of this method has been spelt with a lower-case c, this method declaration is not overriding the `hashCode` method of `java.lang.Object`. If your use of the `hashCode` method is an indirect use (e.g. by using `contains` of the `List` interface), you may find it very difficult to detect this error.

It could be argued that this is a poor piece of programming language design. Some languages such as Eiffel require you to indicate that a method declaration is overriding another declaration. For example, Java might have required you to use an `overrides` keyword as in:

```
public int hashCode() overrides
{
    return 0;
}
```

The `overrides` would be required because this method declaration is in a class that is derived from the class `java.lang.Object`, and `Object` has a method called `hashCode`. So, the declaration:

```
public int hashCode()
{
    return 0;
}
```

would produce a compilation error because the `overrides` keyword has been left out. And the misspelling of `hashCode` in the declaration:

```
public int hashcode() overrides
{
    return 0;
}
```

would be detected. This would not compile because `Object` does not have a method called `hashcode`. However, all of this is wishful thinking: it is not Java!

If you suspect that a method you think you are overriding is not being executed, you will be able to determine whether this is the case by adding a `println` to the block of the method.

11.6   The `NoelProg` program given in Figure 11.18 contains the statement:

```
System.out.println("tUsingOperator: " + (tNoelDate==tOtherDate));
```

The parentheses around the boolean expression cannot be omitted: they are required because the `==` operator has lower priority than the `+` operator: for more details, refer back to Section 6.11.

11.7   Having compiled the `Date` interface, the `DateImpl` class and the `Noel-Prog` class, it is appropriate to try to execute the `NoelProg` class using the command:

```
java NoelProg
```

This is because it has a method called `main`. However, it makes no sense to try and run a class like `DateImpl`. If you attempt to do this:

```
java DateImpl
```

the Java interpreter will output an error message like:

```
In class DateImpl: void main(String argv[]) is not defined.
```

11.8   Some people suggest adding a method called `main` to every class. This can be used for code that tests the methods of the class. The output from this testing can be stored in a file. If, later, the code of one (or more) of these methods is changed, the `main` method can be run again, and the output from this run can be checked with the output that is in the file. This is known as **regression testing**.

Curios, controversies and cover-ups

11.1 The `NoelProg` program (given in Figure 11.18) uses the `Date` interface and the `DateImpl` class. When we have wanted to use some class in programs of earlier chapters, we have had to use an import declaration to say in which package the class is declared. If you use class U in a class C and you do not have an import declaration for class U within the file containing class C, the compiler assumes that the class U belongs to the **default package**. The Java 2 SDK will look in the current directory in order to find classes of the default package. The topic of *packages* is considered in more detail in Section 21.4.

For an example, consider the first `NoelProg` program (given in Figure 11.1). It uses a class called `Date`. This must be a class of the *default package*, i.e. a class stored in the current directory, because there is no import declaration for `Date`. If, for example, the `NoelProg` program wanted instead to use the class `Date` from the package `java.util`, it would need the import declaration:

```
import java.util.Date;
```

11.2 The name *constructor* seems to be inappropriate. First, an object is created; then the fields are assigned their default initial values (given in Figure 11.2); and then the *constructor* is executed. A more appropriate name would be *re-initializer*.

11.3 Instead of using an `i` prefix when naming a private field, some programmers use the underscore character either as a prefix or as a suffix. For example:

```
private int _year;
private int _month;
private int _day;
public DateImpl(final int year, final int month, final int day)
{
    _year = year;
    _month = month;
    _day = day;
}
...
public void setYear(final int year)
{
    _year = year;
}
```

11.4 If you were to choose not to use an i prefix for private fields:

```
private int year;
private int month;
private int day;
```

then it is possible to write the constructor as:

```
public DateImpl(final int year, final int month, final int day)
{
    this.year = year;
    this.month = month;
    this.day = day;
}
```

Within this constructor, year is the name of the first parameter of the constructor. So how will we be able to refer to the field called year? Within a class declaration, this can be used to refer to the object that is the *target*. So, as shown above, it is possible to refer to one of the fields of the class using the notation this.*fieldname*.

Another example is:

```
public void setYear(final int year)
{
    this.year = year;
}
```

Not only can this be used in this way with fields, it can also be used with methods. For example, the equals method given in Figure 11.16 uses:

```
if ( pObject==null || getClass()!=pObject.getClass() )
```

This could alternatively be written as:

```
if ( pObject==null || this.getClass()!=pObject.getClass() )
```

The Java programming language uses the this keyword in two different ways. Here, we have seen how it can be used in a class declaration to access a member of the class, and in Section 11.9.3 it was used in a constructor to call another constructor of the same class.

11.5 In Section 11.6.1, methods like getYear and setYear were described as *access methods*. There is not much consistency on the jargon that is used:

- Some authors describe the get methods as **selectors**; others call them **accessors**.

- Some authors describe the set methods as **mutators**; others call them **modifiers**.

In other areas of Java, such as *JavaBeans*, it is important for these methods to have names beginning with get and set.

11.6 Although get and set methods are often used, not everyone agrees with this technique. Allen Holub says that 'get and set functions are evil. (They're just elaborate ways to make the data public.)' For more details, see his article ([23]) entitled 'Building user interfaces for object-oriented systems, Part 1'.

11.7 In Section 11.9.4, a constructor was provided for cloning an object of the class `Date`. Its use was demonstrated using the example:

```
final Date tHappyDate = new Date(tNoelDate);
```

It was stated that an alternative approach would be to provide a method called `clone`, with the idea that this method could be used in the following way:

```
final Date tHappyDate = tNoelDate.clone();
```

Although it may seem to be reasonably easy to provide a `clone` method:

```
public Date clone()
{
    return new Date(iYear, iMonth, iDay);
}
```

such a method is not recommended. It is confusing to provide such a method, because in situations involving inheritance, the `clone` method needs to be more sophisticated than this, and it is preferable to provide a method that overrides the `clone` method of the class `java.lang.Object`. It is not easy to do this properly! It will be tackled in Section 19.8.

11.8 Section 11.11.1 shows how to introduce an `equals` method that overrides the one given in the class `java.lang.Object`. There are rules about what such an `equals` method should do. For more details about its contract, see the details about `equals` at the WWW page $API/java/lang/Object.html#equals(java.lang.Object).

11.9 The version of `equals` presented in Section 11.11.1 is written in terms of a method called `getClass`. When providing a proper version of `equals` (for some class, e.g. the class X), many authors use code for `equals` that has the following form:

```
public boolean equals(final Object pObject)
{
    if ( ! (pObject instanceof X) )
    {
        return false;
    }
    return ... ;
}
```

(where X is the name of the class). So here the `instanceof` operator is being used instead of calling `getClass` twice.

Although in many situations the `getClass` code and the `instanceof` code provide the same result, in some cases involving *inheritance* they produce a different result. This book recommends that you use `getClass` as this works in all situations. A full discussion of this topic will be left until Curio 19.6.

11.10 At runtime, both the `getClass` method (used by the version of `equals` presented in Section 11.11.1) and the `instanceof` operator mentioned in Curio 11.9 determine the type of an object. This actually takes some time to evaluate. One of the reasons we made the parameter of `equals` to be of the class `Object` is to enable us to store values of the class `DateImpl` in a collection. However, on many occasions, the argument's type will be of the interface type `Date`. Vjeksoslav Nesek has pointed out that it may be appropriate to provide two declarations for `equals`, one which has a parameter of type `Object` and the other having a parameter of type `Date`.

11.11 In Section 11.11.2, it was explained that the class `java.lang.Object` has a method called `hashCode` which returns an integer that is unique for the object to which the method is being applied. Often this value is derived from the runtime address of the object.

11.12 In this chapter, each member of a class has been described as either `private` or `public`. Figure 8.4 shows that an *access modifier* can be either `private`, `public` or `protected` or it can be missing. The term **package access** is often used to refer to the access that applies when there is no access modifier. Curio 19.2 looks at *protected access* and *package access*.

11.13 Because all members of an interface must be `public`, it is possible to leave out the access modifier for a method header of an interface (as this is the default). In Curio 11.12, it was pointed out that, when a member of a class has no access modifier, there is *package access* to the member. Because the defaults are different, this book recommends you to include the `public` modifier for the method headers of an interface. This contravenes the advice given in the JLS which says 'It is permitted, but strongly discouraged as a matter of style, to redundantly specify the `public` modifier for interface methods'.

11.14 The `NoelProg` program given in Figure 11.18 prompts the user in the following way:

```
System.out.print("Type in the date, e.g., 2000-12-25: ");
```

Here the client is showing that it knows how dates are textually represented by the `DateImpl` class. Really it is showing more awareness than it should do. This can be avoided by using the following prompt instead:

```
System.out.print("Type in the date, e.g., " +
                new DateImpl(2000,12,25) + ": ");
```

This code assumes that the `toString` method of the `DateImpl` class adopts the same textual representation. However, this is a practice that is recommended by this book.

11.15 In this book, most classes will have methods called `equals`, `hashCode`, `toString`, a constructor that constructs an object from a `String`, a constructor that clones an existing object of the class, a constructor that has no parameters, together with appropriate access methods.

In some ways, a class is poorly constructed unless it has all of these. Riel introduces the idea of the **minimal public interface**. He says: 'If the classes that a developer designs and implements are to be reused by other developers in other applications, it is often useful to provide a common minimal public interface. This minimal public interface consists of functionality that can be reasonably expected from each and every class.' For more details about this, look at a book ([28]) entitled *Object-Oriented Design Heuristics* by Arthur Riel.

Bill Venners has also written an article ([48]) on the topic of minimal public interfaces. The article is entitled 'The canonical object idiom'.

11.16 It is useful to adopt a standard order for the various members of a class. Possible orders include:

- first fields, then constructors, then methods;
- first private members, then constructors and then public members;
- first constructors, then public members and then private members;
- first fields, then constructors, then mutators, then selectors, ...

11.17 Whenever we have wanted to find out the details about a class of one of Java's Core APIs, we have looked at the WWW pages that document the class. By using the javadoc tool (that comes with the Java 2 SDK), we can generate WWW pages for our own interfaces and classes. By this means, we can automatically generate the documentation for them. Details of how to do this are given in Appendix C.

11.18 On the WWW at [16], you will find a document entitled 'ChiMu OO and Java Development: Guidelines and Resources'. In this document, Mark Fussell says:

> Use interfaces as the glue throughout your code instead of classes: define interfaces to describe the exterior of objects (i.e. their Type) and type all variables, parameters, and return values to interfaces. The most important reason to do this is that interfaces focus on the client's needs: interfaces define what functionality a client will receive from an Object without coupling the client to the Object's implementation. This is one of the core concepts to OO.

One of the areas where some useful work was done in the 1990s on understanding how complex systems are built was in recognizing the importance of the use of *patterns*. Currently, the principal book ([17]) in this area is *Design Patterns: Elements of Reusable Object-Oriented Software* by Erich Gamma, Richard Helm, Ralph Johnson and John Vlissides. These four people are affectionately known as the *Gang of Four* (or *GoF*). In their book, they say:

> This ... leads to the following principle of reusable object-oriented design:

> *Program to an interface, not an implementation.*

Don't declare variables to be instances of particular concrete classes. Instead, commit only to an interface defined by an abstract class [or an interface in Java]. You will find this to be a common theme of the design patterns in this book.

In the book *UML Distilled* ([15]), Martin Fowler writes:

Programming languages [other than Java] use a single construct, the class, which contains both interface and implementation. When you subclass, you inherit both. Using the interface as a separate construct is rarely used, which is a shame.

Exercises ───

11.1 Several of the programs in this chapter contain a constructor to construct a date from a string. For example, the DateImpl class given in Figure 11.16 contains a constructor with the header:

```
public DateImpl(final String pDateString)
```

This constructor expects the string pDateString to be in three parts, where the parts are separated by a hyphen and each part consists of an integer value. Although the constructor detects when pDateString has less than three parts, it does not detect when pDateString has more than three parts. Improve this constructor by using a call of StringTokenizer's countTokens to ensure that pDateString has exactly three parts.

11.2 Make the changes to the NoelProg program that are described in Curio 11.14.

11.3 Details about International Standard Book Numbers were given in Exercise 7.15. Produce an interface called ISBN and a class called ISBNImpl that can be used to represent an ISBN. Internally, the class should use a char, a String, another String and another char for the country, publisher, book-number and check-character values.

The interface should provide:

● four get methods that return these four values;

● methods called equals, hashCode and toString (that have their usual meanings);

● a method called isValid that returns *true* if the check–character is correct – the details of how to check this character are given in Exercise 7.15.

Besides declarations for each of these methods, the class should also have a constructor that can be used when creating an ISBNImpl object from a string, and a constructor that can be used when creating an ISBNImpl object from an ISBN object that already exists.

Redo Exercise 7.15 so that it uses the constructor, the isValid method, and the toString method.

11.4   Although the package `java.awt` has a class called `Point`, the aim of this exercise is to write your own interface and class declarations to represent a point in two-dimensional space.

Produce an interface declaration called `MyPoint` that can be used to represent a point in two-dimensional space. The interface should have two methods (called `getX` and `getY`) that return the *x* and *y* coordinates, two methods (called `setX` and `setY`) that set the *x* and *y* coordinates, a method called `equals`, a method called `hashCode`, and a method called `toString`.

Produce a class declaration called `MyPointImpl` that implements the `MyPoint` interface. The class should have two private fields: the *x* coordinate (an `int`) and the *y* coordinate (an `int`). The class declaration should also contain appropriate constructor(s), and declarations for the methods that implement the interface.

Test your interface and class declarations using the following program:

```
public class MyPointImplProg
{
    public static void main(final String[] pArgs)
    {
        final MyPoint tDurham = new MyPointImpl(273, 421);
        System.out.println(tDurham);
        final int tX = tDurham.getX();
        System.out.println("tX is " + tX);
        final int tY = tDurham.getY();
        System.out.println("tY is " + tY);
        final MyPoint tSwaleDale = new MyPointImpl();
        System.out.println(tSwaleDale + " " + tDurham);
        System.out.println("tSwaleDale is same as tDurham is " +
                           tSwaleDale.equals(tDurham));
        final MyPoint tUniversity = new MyPointImpl(273, 421);
        System.out.println(tUniversity);
        System.out.println("tUniversity is same as tDurham is " +
                           tUniversity.equals(tDurham));
    }
}
```

11.5   Produce an interface called `Angle` and a class called `AngleImpl` that can be used to represent a value that is a longitude or a latitude. Such a value has three numerical parts called degrees, minutes and seconds (where there are 60 seconds to a minute and 60 minutes to a degree) and a direction character which is either E or W for a longitude and N or S for a latitude.

The interface should provide:

- four get methods that return the degrees, minutes, seconds and direction parts of an object;
- four set methods that can be used to change one of these parts;

- methods called equals, hashCode and toString (that have their usual meanings);
- a method called getDistance that returns an int that is the distance from the meridian measured in seconds. The value that is returned should be positive if the direction is either E or N; otherwise, it should be negative. The magnitude of the value that is returned should be the value of $degrees \times 3600 + minutes \times 60 + seconds$.

Besides declarations for each of these methods, the class should also have a constructor that can create an angle from three ints and a char. It should also have a constructor that creates an angle from a String. As mentioned in the text, the format of the string that is accepted by this constructor should be the same as that produced by the toString method of the class. And it should provide a constructor that can be used when creating an AngleImpl object from an Angle object that already exists.

Write a program called AngleImplProg to test this interface and class.

Chapter 12

Looking at other examples of interfaces and classes

Although a lot of information about interfaces and classes was presented in the previous chapter, only one example was given. In this chapter, several other examples are given. It turns out that there are four main ways in which class declarations are used, and an example is given of each category.

When there is a *natural order* to the values of a type, it is useful to provide a method for finding out whether one value comes before another value. In this chapter, we look at implementing an interface called `Comparable` and providing a `compareTo` method.

When developing a program that is composed of several *compilation units* (each one of which contains an interface declaration or a class declaration), it is useful to draw a *class diagram* that indicates the dependencies between these units. Not only does this help in understanding the relationship between the units, it also helps in trying to establish what needs to be re-compiled and re-tested when one of the units is changed. The chapter ends by looking at ways of reducing the dependencies between the units.

12.1 A classification of the different uses of classes

In the last chapter, a class declaration was used to produce a new type, a type where each value is a date. Although producing a new type is an important use of class declarations, there are other ways in which they can be used.

It is possible to produce a **classification** identifying four main categories of use of class declarations. Here are the first two categories:

1. A class declaration can be used to group together a number of related constants.

2. A class declaration can be used to group together a number of related methods.

In practice, some class declarations are a hybrid of these two categories. An obvious example is the class `java.lang.Math` which, besides declaring a large number of methods, also declares two constants (called `PI` and `E`). See Curio 12.1. Another example of each of these categories of use of a class declaration will be given in Section 12.2 and Section 12.3.

And, as we discovered in the previous chapter, a class declaration can be used to produce a new type. The values of the type can be modelled using the private variables of the class declaration, and the operations can be modelled by the public methods of the class declaration. It is sometimes useful to distinguish between situations where a client is likely to create many objects of the class from those where only one object is created. For example, suppose you are modelling a library, then a client is likely to create many instances of the class `Book` whereas you probably only want one instance of the class `Library`. So the other two main categories of use of class declarations are as follows:

3. A class declaration can be used to produce a new type where a client creates only one instance of the class. An example of this use of a class declaration will be given in Section 12.4.

4. A class declaration can be used to produce a new type where the client is expected to create many instances. Many of the classes of Java's Core APIs fall into this category (e.g. the class `java.lang.String`). The class declaration for `Date` given in Chapter 11 also falls into this category. Another example will be given in Section 12.5.

Do the following appear?	Grouping related constants	Grouping related methods	Only one instance of a class	Many instances of a class
public constructors	no	no	yes	yes
public constants	yes	no	maybe	maybe
public variables	no	no	no	no
public instance methods	no	no	yes	yes
public class methods	no	yes	maybe	maybe
private variables	no	no	yes	yes
private methods	no	maybe	maybe	maybe

Figure 12.1 Characteristics of the four categories of use of class declarations.

The table in Figure 12.1 identifies some of the characteristics of these four categories of use.

In practice, however, some class declarations do not fall into any of the above categories, and some are hybrids.

12.2 Grouping together related constants

The classification of the different uses of class declarations given above indicates that a class declaration is sometimes used to group together **related constants**. For example, we could declare a class declaration that provides identifiers for common mathematical constants. A possible class declaration is given in Figure 12.2.

```
// A class that provides identifiers for some mathematical constants.
// Barry Cornelius, 19 June 2000
public class MathsConstants
{
    public static final double pi     = 3.14159265358979;
    public static final double e      = 2.71828182845904;
    public static final double sqrt2  = 1.41421356237309;
    public static final double loge10 = 2.30258509299404;
    public static final double log10e = 0.434294481903252;
}
```

Figure 12.2 The MathsConstants class provides some mathematical constants.

As there is no intention of creating an instance of this class, the class declaration does not have any constructors. See Curio 12.2. And it does not have any private variables. This agrees with the characteristics given in Figure 12.1.

A client can refer to a constant of this class in the usual way. For example:

```
double tValue = 0.5*MathsConstants.sqrt2;
```

12.3 Grouping together related methods

A class declaration can also be used to group together a number of **related methods**. For example, we could devise our own class declaration containing some mathematical functions – say, a class called Math. If we are mathematical geniuses, we could set out to rival the Math class of the java.lang package!

If you have done Exercise 9.5 and Exercise 9.6, you will already have declarations for functions that calculate approximations to $sin(x)$ and $sqrt(x)$. Suppose we want a class declaration containing these two method declarations. A skeleton of such a class declaration is given in Figure 12.3.

```
// A class that provides declarations for the mathematical functions:
//    sin, sqrt
// Barry Cornelius, 19 June 2000
public class Math
{
    public static double sin(final double x)
    {
        ...
    }
    public static double sqrt(final double x)
    {
        ...
    }
}
```

Figure 12.3   The Math class provides some mathematical functions.

Note that this class declaration only contains declarations of *class methods* (marked as being public and static): it does not have any private variables and it does not have any constructors. These are the hallmarks of a class declaration that belongs to category 2.

A client can refer to one of these methods as follows:

```
double tSinOne = Math.sin(1.0);
```

12.4 Producing a new type: only one instance

In Java, the code that you need in order to read a value of a primitive type from the keyboard is not easy to understand. An example is:

```
final BufferedReader tKeyboard =
            new BufferedReader(new InputStreamReader(System.in));
final String tAnotherLine = tKeyboard.readLine();
final int tAge = Integer.parseInt(tAnotherLine);
```

So, many authors of books that teach Java provide their own class to simplify the reading of values from the keyboard. A class declaration for a class called KeyboardInput appears in Figure 12.4. When a client creates an object of this class:

```
final KeyboardInput tKeyboardInput = new KeyboardInput();
```

one of the fields (iKeyboard) of the KeyboardInput object is initialized using the complicated code that associates a variable with the keyboard. And when the client executes:

```
final int tAge = tKeyboardInput.nextInt();
```

the code of the nextInt method can read in a string and produce an int from it.

```java
// A class that helps reads values of a primitive type from the keyboard.
// Barry Cornelius, 19 June 2000
import java.io.   BufferedReader;
import java.io.   InputStreamReader;
import java.util. StringTokenizer;
public class KeyboardInput
{
   private final BufferedReader iKeyboard =
         new BufferedReader(new InputStreamReader(System.in));
   private StringTokenizer iTokens = null;

   public KeyboardInput()
   {
   }

   // return MAX_VALUE if an integer cannot be read
   public int nextInt()
   {
      try
      {
         final String tTokenString = iGetToken();
         return Integer.parseInt(tTokenString);
      }
      catch(final Exception pException)
      {
         return Integer.MAX_VALUE;
      }
   }

   // return MAX_VALUE if a double cannot be read
   public double nextDouble()
   {
      try
      {
         final String tTokenString = iGetToken();
         return Double.parseDouble(tTokenString);
      }
      catch(final Exception pException)
      {
         return Double.MAX_VALUE;
      }
   }

   private String iGetToken() throws Exception
   {
      while ( iTokens==null || ! iTokens.hasMoreTokens() )
      {
         final String tLine = iKeyboard.readLine();
         iTokens = new StringTokenizer(tLine);
      }
      // iTokens!=null && iTokens.hasMoreTokens()
      return iTokens.nextToken();
   }
}
```

Figure 12.4 The `KeyboardInput` class is useful for reading primitive values.

```
// This program read in two numbers and displays their sum.
// Barry Cornelius, 19 June 2000
public class KeyboardInputProg
{
    public static void main(final String[] pArgs)
    {
        final KeyboardInput tKeyboardInput = new KeyboardInput();
        System.out.print("Type in your first number: ");
        System.out.flush();
        final double tFirst = tKeyboardInput.nextDouble();
        System.out.print("Type in your second number: ");
        System.out.flush();
        final double tSecond = tKeyboardInput.nextDouble();
        final double tSum = tFirst + tSecond;
        System.out.println("The sum of " + tFirst +
                           " and " + tSecond + " is " + tSum);
    }
}
```

Figure 12.5   The `KeyboardInputProg` program shows uses of `KeyboardInput`.

A program that uses this class is given in Figure 12.5 – it is a rewrite of the `SumProg` program that appeared in Figure 4.4. Note that, unlike the `SumProg` program, the `KeyboardInputProg` program does not have to handle any `IOExceptions`: instead, any occurrences of this exception (and any occurrences of `NumberFormatException`) are handled by the methods of the `KeyboardInput` class.

The class declaration for `KeyboardInput` (given in Figure 12.4) is unlike those of categories 1 and 2: it is a proper class declaration in that it has a constructor (which we are using to create an object of this class). But it is a little different from class declarations like `Date` or `java.lang.String`, as we intend to create **only one instance** of this class. Because this class hides access to the computer's keyboard, producing more than one instance of this class would probably cause a problem. See Curio 12.3 and Curio 12.4.

12.5) Producing a new type: many instances

12.5.1 `Person` (like `Date`) belongs to category 4

In the previous chapter, we looked at a class declaration that can be used to represent dates. Such a class falls into the fourth category. We now suppose that we will be writing programs that manipulate objects that represent people. As the programs will be creating **many instances** of the type for representing people, this is another class that belongs to the fourth category.

In the previous chapter, it was suggested that, when introducing a new class, you should first produce an interface and then produce a class that implements this interface. Although we may be lazy and not do this for classes that fall into categories 1, 2 and 3, it is desirable to do this when the class belongs to category 4.

12.5.2 Modelling a person and defining an interface

How are we to represent a person? We can store all sorts of details about a person. However, in this book, to keep things simple a person will be represented by their name, their date of birth, their phone number and their height.

An interface declaration for a `Person` is shown in Figure 12.6. It defines the operations that are going to be provided. Except for the occurrence of the clause `extends Comparable` (which we will look at later), there are no surprises

```java
// A type to represent a person.
// Barry Cornelius, 18 June 2000
public interface Person extends Comparable
{
    // return the Name part of the target person
    public String getName();

    // return the DateOfBirth part of the target person
    public Date getDateOfBirth();

    // return the PhoneNumber part of the target person
    public String getPhoneNumber();

    // return the Height part of the target person
    public double getHeight();

    // set the Name part of the target person to pName
    public void setName(String pName);

    // set the DateOfBirth part of the target person to pDateOfBirth
    public void setDateOfBirth(Date pDateOfBirth);

    // set the PhoneNumber part of the target person to pPhoneNumber
    public void setPhoneNumber(String pPhoneNumber);

    // set the Height part of the target person to pHeight
    public void setHeight(double pHeight);

    // return true if and only if the target is the same person as pObject
    public boolean equals(Object pObject);

    // return the hashcode for the value of the target person
    public int hashCode();

    // return a textual representation of the target person
    public String toString();
}
```

Figure 12.6 The `Person` interface.

here:

- four get methods to get the current values of the name, date of birth, phone number and height of a `Person` object;
- four set methods to set these values;
- three methods called `equals`, `hashCode` and `toString`.

12.5.3 Representing the values of the type

A class (called `PersonImpl`) that implements this interface is shown in Figure 12.7. This class declaration has four fields:

```
private String iName;
private Date iDateOfBirth;
private String iPhoneNumber;
private double iHeight;
```

```
// A class that implements the Person interface.
// Barry Cornelius, 19 June 2000
import java.util. StringTokenizer;
public class PersonImpl implements Person
{
    private String iName;
    private Date iDateOfBirth;
    private String iPhoneNumber;
    private double iHeight;
    public PersonImpl()
    {
        this("", new DateImpl(), "", 0.0);
    }
    public PersonImpl(final Person pPerson)
    {
        final PersonImpl tPersonImpl = (PersonImpl)pPerson;
        iName = tPersonImpl.iName;
        iDateOfBirth = new DateImpl(tPersonImpl.iDateOfBirth);
        iPhoneNumber = tPersonImpl.iPhoneNumber;
        iHeight = tPersonImpl.iHeight;
    }
    public PersonImpl(final String pName, final Date pDateOfBirth,
                      final String pPhoneNumber, final double pHeight)
    {
        iName = pName;
        iDateOfBirth = new DateImpl(pDateOfBirth);
        iPhoneNumber = pPhoneNumber;
        iHeight = pHeight;
    }
```

Figure 12.7 *Continues on the next page.*

```java
public PersonImpl(final String pPersonString)
{
   try
   {
      final StringTokenizer tTokens =
                  new StringTokenizer(pPersonString, "%");
      iName = tTokens.nextToken();
      final String tDateOfBirthString = tTokens.nextToken();
      iDateOfBirth = new DateImpl(tDateOfBirthString);
      iPhoneNumber = tTokens.nextToken();
      String tHeightString = tTokens.nextToken();
      if (tHeightString.equals(""))
      {
         tHeightString = "0.0";
      }
      iHeight = Double.parseDouble(tHeightString);
   }
   catch(final Exception pException)
   {
      iName = "";
      iDateOfBirth = new DateImpl();
      iPhoneNumber = "";
      iHeight = 0.0;
      throw new IllegalArgumentException();
   }
}
public String getName()
{
   return iName;
}
public Date getDateOfBirth()
{
   return new DateImpl(iDateOfBirth);
}
public String getPhoneNumber()
{
   return iPhoneNumber;
}
public double getHeight()
{
   return iHeight;
}
```

Figure 12.7 *Continues on the next page.*

```
public void setName(final String pName)
{
    iName = pName;
}
public void setDateOfBirth(final Date pDateOfBirth)
{
    iDateOfBirth = new DateImpl(pDateOfBirth);
}
public void setPhoneNumber(final String pPhoneNumber)
{
    iPhoneNumber = pPhoneNumber;
}
public void setHeight(final double pHeight)
{
    iHeight = pHeight;
}
public boolean equals(final Object pObject)
{
    if ( pObject==null || getClass()!=pObject.getClass() )
    {
        return false;
    }
    return iName.equals(((PersonImpl)pObject).iName);
}
public int hashCode()
{
    return 0;
}
public int compareTo(final Object pObject)
{
    final PersonImpl tPersonImpl = (PersonImpl)pObject;
    return iName.compareTo(tPersonImpl.iName);
}
public String toString()
{
    return iName + "%" + iDateOfBirth + "%" + iPhoneNumber + "%" + iHeight;
}
}
```

Figure 12.7 The `PersonImpl` class.

So, a field of the class `java.lang.String` is being used to represent the name of a person. This is cheating. We ought to choose a type that enables us to distinguish between the various parts of a person's name. In fact, as Java's Core APIs do not have a type for representing names, we ought to introduce another type for representing names. But to keep things simple we will not do this.

To represent a person's date of birth, we can use a field either of the class `java.util.Date` or of the class `Date` that was developed in the previous chapter.

By not having an import declaration for `java.util.Date`, the declaration of `PersonImpl` (given in Figure 12.7) chooses the latter.

In order to represent a person's phone number, we could look at representing the various parts of a phone number, e.g. the country code, the area code, the person's number and their extension (if there is one). However, once again, we will cheat and ignore this detail by representing a phone number by a `String`.

Finally, a person's height is represented by a `double`.

So this class declaration has four private fields: one of these is of a primitive type (the type `double`), two fields are of the class `String` defined in the `java.lang` package, and the other one is of an interface/class that we have produced ourselves.

12.5.4 Choosing to share objects or clone objects

If a field of your class is of a reference type (e.g. the field `iDateOfBirth`), then, when creating an object of this class, your constructor will often be supplied with an object to be used to initialize the field. In the code of your constructor, you have to decide whether to assign to the field a pointer to this object or a pointer to a clone of this object.

For example, consider the following constructor of the `PersonImpl` class. When a client uses this constructor, it needs to supply a `Date` object as the second argument of the call of the constructor. Should the constructor contain code that **share**s the supplied `Date` object, as in:

```
public PersonImpl(final String pName, final Date pDateOfBirth,
                  final String pPhoneNumber, final double pHeight)
{
    iName = pName;
    iDateOfBirth = pDateOfBirth;
    iPhoneNumber = pPhoneNumber;
    iHeight = pHeight;
}
```

Or should the constructor contain code that **clone**s the object, as in:

```
public PersonImpl(final String pName, final Date pDateOfBirth,
                  final String pPhoneNumber, final double pHeight)
{
    iName = pName;
    iDateOfBirth = new DateImpl(pDateOfBirth);
    iPhoneNumber = pPhoneNumber;
    iHeight = pHeight;
}
```

If you use the sharing code, you need to require the client to provide a `Date` object which is not inadvertently changed later. For example, there is no problem with using the sharing constructor in the following context:

```
Date tDate = null;
while (true)
{
    ...
    final String tLine = tKeyboard.readLine();
    tDate = new DateImpl(tLine);
    final Person tPerson = new PersonImpl(..., tDate, ..., ...);
    ...
}
```

This results in each of the `PersonImpl` objects having an `iDateOfBirth` field that is pointing to a different `DateImpl` object.

However, suppose the client instead uses:

```
Date tDate = new DateImpl();
while (true)
{
    ...
    final int tYear = ... ;
    tDate.setYear(tYear);
    final int tMonth = ... ;
    tDate.setMonth(tMonth);
    final int tDay = ... ;
    tDate.setDay(tDay);
    final Person tPerson = new PersonImpl(..., tDate, ..., ...);
    ...
}
```

Now each of the `PersonImpl` objects has an `iDateOfBirth` field that is pointing to the same `DateImpl` object, i.e. the one that `tDate` is pointing to. So each `Person-Impl` object will have the date of birth that is the date of birth of the last person created by the while loop.

To be on the safe side, it is probably best not to use constructors that share objects: instead write your constructor so that it clones the object. However, this can lead to a lot of unnecessary cloning (which is time-consuming). So if you trust your client, for efficiency reasons you may want to write your constructor so that it shares objects with the client.

Whatever approach you decide to adopt, it should be used for this field throughout your class declaration. Besides being used in the constructors, it also needs to be used in any get and set methods that manipulate this field.

The code of `PersonImpl` given in Figure 12.7 adopts the clone approach for the `iDateOfBirth` field. This affects the code of the constructors, the code of `getDateOfBirth` and the code of `setDateOfBirth`.

Note that we only have to make a choice between the share approach and the clone approach for a field that is of a class type when an object of this class can be changed after it has been created. It is quite safe to use the share approach if the field is of a class that is *immutable*. This is why the clone approach is not used for the iName and iPhoneNumber fields. Both of these fields are of the class type java.lang.String, and as was explained in Section 3.4.7, this class type produces objects that are immutable.

So one advantage of producing an immutable class (which implies that the class has no set methods) is that it enables the more efficient share approach to be used for any subsequent class declarations that have a field of this class.

12.5.5 Implementing the operations of the type

Because the interface declaration gives headers for four get methods, four set methods, equals, hashCode and toString, the class declaration has to provide declarations for these methods.

The declaration of equals needs to return *true* if and only if the object that is the target of the call of equals represents the same person as that represented by the object passed as an argument. At first glance, you might produce:

```
public boolean equals(final Object pObject)
{
    if ( pObject==null || getClass()!=pObject.getClass() )
    {
        return false;
    }
    final PersonImpl tPersonImpl = (PersonImpl)pObject;
    return iName.equals(tPersonImpl.iName) &&
           iDateOfBirth.equals(tPersonImpl.iDateOfBirth) &&
           iPhoneNumber.equals(tPersonImpl.iPhoneNumber) &&
           iHeight==(tPersonImpl.iHeight);
}
```

Note this is:

- using the method equals of the class java.lang.String when comparing the iName field of the target with the iName field of the object passed as an argument;
- using the method equals of the class DateImpl when comparing the iDateOfBirth fields (assuming that the DateImpl class produced in Chapter 11 is being used);
- using the == operator to compare the iHeight fields as this field is of a primitive type.

A disadvantage of the above declaration of equals is that it is too strict. If the two objects being compared come from information obtained several years apart, the person may have changed their phone number or their height, or they may have lied about their date of birth! Hence, the class declaration for PersonImpl shown in Figure 12.7 says that two PersonImpl objects represent the same person if their names are the same.

For the reasons given in Section 11.11.2, the `PersonImpl` class provides the following `hashCode` function:

```
public int hashCode()
{
    return 0;
}
```

The `toString` method of the class `PersonImpl` outputs a textual representation of a `PersonImpl` object. The code of the method uses `Date`'s `toString` method (produced in the last chapter). So it will produce a string like:

```
Smith, Rebecca%1981-02-27%44-1987-654321%1.75
```

In the previous chapter, it was suggested that a class should have a constructor that can parse the string produced by `toString`. The constructor of `PersonImpl` that has a `String` parameter can do this.

12.5.6 Providing a `compareTo` method

Sometimes there is a **natural order** to the values of a type. For example, all the values of the type `int` can be ordered according to their numerical values. For this reason, it makes sense for the Java programming language to provide relational operators, such as <, which allows us to find out whether one `int` value is less than (i.e. comes before) another `int` value.

In a similar way, when we looked at the `String` type, we saw that it provides a method called `compareTo` which compares two strings returning a negative value, zero, or a positive value, depending on whether the target string comes before, is the same as, or comes after the string supplied as the argument to the method. Here the ordering being used is what is called *lexicographic ordering* which is an extension of *alphabetic ordering*.

Whenever we produce an interface and a class for a new type, if the values of the type have a natural ordering, clients will find it useful for us to provide a method like `compareTo`.

Are the values of the type `Person` ordered? Well, depending on the context in which values of the type are used, there may be an obvious ordering or no appropriate ordering. However, we will suppose that we want an ordering determined by the alphabetic order of the names of the people.

The package `java.lang` provides an interface called `Comparable`. If you look at the WWW page $API/java/lang/Comparable.html, you will see that this interface is very simple:

```
public interface Comparable
{
    public int compareTo(Object pObject);
}
```

There are some parts of the Collections API that work better if your class implements this interface. So not only will we provide a method called `compareTo` that has the header:

```
public int compareTo(Object pObject);
```

but we will ensure that the class implements the Comparable interface.

There are a number of ways of doing this. The best way is to indicate that the Person interface is a **subinterface** of the Comparable interface:

```
public interface Person extends Comparable
{
    ...
}
```

If you do this, then:

- any class that implements the Person interface must provide declarations not only for the methods of the Person interface but also for the methods of the Comparable interface;
- if a client declares a variable of the interface type Person, methods of both the Person interface and the Comparable interface may be applied to this variable.

If you look at the Person interface given in Figure 12.6, you will see that the header of the interface declaration for Person is:

```
public interface Person extends Comparable
```

Note that this interface declaration does not have a header for the compareTo method. It does not have to because the compareTo method is declared in the Comparable interface. So if you want to see what methods are available, you not only have to look at the text of the interface, but also at the text of any **superinterfaces** (in this case, Comparable).

The header of the class declaration for PersonImpl (in Figure 12.7) is:

```
public class PersonImpl implements Person
```

Here there is no mention of Comparable. However, because Person is a subinterface of Comparable, the PersonImpl class has to provide a declaration for compareTo, the method that is declared in Comparable.

The declaration of compareTo provided by this class declaration is:

```
public int compareTo(final Object pObject)
{
    final PersonImpl tPersonImpl = (PersonImpl)pObject;
    return iName.compareTo(tPersonImpl.iName);
}
```

Previously, it was said that we wanted an ordering for values of type Person that is determined by the alphabetic order of the names of the people. This is achieved by using String's compareTo method on the two iName fields.

The WWW page that documents Comparable refers to a class's compareTo method as its **natural comparison method**. And it strongly recommends that

'natural orderings be consistent with equals'. This will be the case provided
e1.compareTo(e2)==0 has the same boolean value as e1.equals(e2) where
e1 and e2 are any two values of the class. See Curio 12.7.

Earlier it was said that we ought to implement the Comparable interface whenever we produce an interface and a class for values that have a natural ordering. So
really the Date interface (given in the previous chapter) ought to be a subinterface
of Comparable. This omission is remedied by Exercise 12.7.

(12.6) Using the **Person** interface and the **PersonImpl** class

A simple program that uses the Person interface and the PersonImpl class is the
PersonImplProg program given in Figure 12.8.

Note that this program only uses the PersonImpl class when it wants to create
an object of that class: on all other occasions it uses the Person interface instead. A
similar comment applies to its use of the Date interface and the DateImpl class.

```
// A program that uses the Person interface and the PersonImpl class.
// Barry Cornelius, 19 June 2000
import java.io. BufferedReader;
import java.io. InputStreamReader;
import java.io. IOException;
public class PersonImplProg
{
    public static void main(final String[] pArgs) throws IOException
    {
        final BufferedReader tKeyboard =
                    new BufferedReader(new InputStreamReader(System.in));
        System.out.println("Type in a person using the format " +
                    "Name%DateOfBirth%PhoneNumber%Height");
        final String tLine = tKeyboard.readLine();
        final Person tPerson = new PersonImpl(tLine);
        System.out.println("The person is: " + tPerson);
        final String tName = tPerson.getName();
        System.out.println("Their name is: " + tName);
        final Date tDateOfBirth = tPerson.getDateOfBirth();
        System.out.println("Their date of birth is: " + tDateOfBirth);
        final String tPhoneNumber = tPerson.getPhoneNumber();
        System.out.println("Their phone number is: " + tPhoneNumber);
        final double tHeight = tPerson.getHeight();
        System.out.println("Their height is: " + tHeight);
        final Person tAnotherPerson =
                    new PersonImpl("Smith, Rebecca",
                                new DateImpl(1981, 2, 27),
                                "44-1987-654321", 1.6);
        System.out.println(tPerson.equals(tAnotherPerson));
    }
}
```

Figure 12.8 A program that uses the Person interface and the PersonImpl class.

When this program is executed, it first outputs a prompt:

```
Type in a person using the format Name%DateOfBirth%PhoneNumber%Height
```

If the user types in:

```
Smith, Rebecca%1981-2-27%44-1987-654321%1.75
```

the program then outputs:

```
The person is: Smith, Rebecca%1981-02-27%44-1987-654321%1.75
Their name is: Smith, Rebecca
Their date of birth is: 1981-02-27
Their phone number is: 44-1987-654321
Their height is: 1.75
true
```

12.7 Illustrating the dependencies by class diagrams

Each interface declaration or class declaration is put into a separate file: it forms a **unit** of compilation (or **compilation unit**). The term **dependency** (or **coupling**) is used to refer to the use of one unit by some other unit. In this book, a **class diagram** will be used to illustrate the dependencies of the units that constitute a program.

Figure 12.9 contains a class diagram for the `PersonImplProg` program. In a class diagram, each arrow indicates that a particular unit is dependent on some other unit.

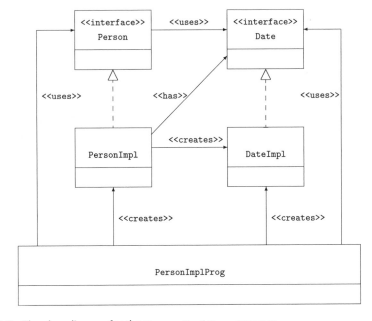

Figure 12.9 The class diagram for the `PersonImplProg` program.

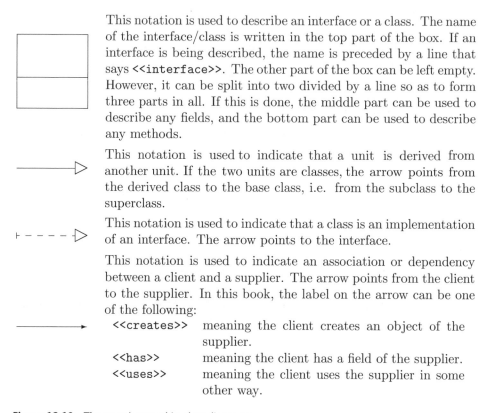

This notation is used to describe an interface or a class. The name of the interface/class is written in the top part of the box. If an interface is being described, the name is preceded by a line that says <<interface>>. The other part of the box can be left empty. However, it can be split into two divided by a line so as to form three parts in all. If this is done, the middle part can be used to describe any fields, and the bottom part can be used to describe any methods.

This notation is used to indicate that a unit is derived from another unit. If the two units are classes, the arrow points from the derived class to the base class, i.e. from the subclass to the superclass.

This notation is used to indicate that a class is an implementation of an interface. The arrow points to the interface.

This notation is used to indicate an association or dependency between a client and a supplier. The arrow points from the client to the supplier. In this book, the label on the arrow can be one of the following:

<<creates>>   meaning the client creates an object of the supplier.

<<has>>   meaning the client has a field of the supplier.

<<uses>>   meaning the client uses the supplier in some other way.

Figure 12.10   The notation used in class diagrams.

This notation is explained in Figure 12.10. It is a variant of the notation used for class diagrams by the **Unified Modeling Language** (UML).

In this book, we will concentrate on five kinds of dependencies. The ⟶▷ symbol will be used when a unit is *derived* from another unit: this symbol is not used until the next chapter. And the ⊢----▷ symbol is used when a class implements an interface. The other three kinds of dependencies will be indicated by a ⟶ symbol. When this symbol is used, it will be labelled with either <<creates>>, <<has>> or <<uses>>.

A <<creates>> arrow indicates that a class uses a constructor of another class. Note that it only makes sense to use a <<creates>> arrow between a client and a supplier when both of these are classes (i.e. neither of them can be interfaces). The <<has>> arrow will be used when a class declares a field (that is private or public) that is of some class type or interface type. Finally, the <<uses>> arrow will be used for all other dependencies. For example, it will be used when a method of a class calls a method of another interface/class or has a parameter that is of some interface/class type.

When drawing a class diagram, only the most important level of dependency will be indicated. The order of importance is given by the order in which the dependencies appear in Figure 12.10. For example, if a class A creates an object of class B, has a field of class B and uses some methods of class B, then there is no need to draw three arrows from A to B indicating <<creates>>, <<has>> and <<uses>> dependencies: instead just a <<creates>> arrow will be used (because this is more important than the other two).

A class diagram can be used to determine the **order** in which the interfaces and classes of the program need to be compiled. For the PersonImplProg program, the diagram in Figure 12.9 shows that there are two possible orders. One order is:

1. javac Date.java
2. javac DateImpl.java
3. javac Person.java
4. javac PersonImpl.java
5. javac PersonImplProg.java

The other order is obtained by interchanging steps 2 and 3.

12.8 Reducing the dependencies

If a program is still under development (and most programs are!), it is best if there are few dependencies as this means that there is less to re-compile (and re-test) when a change is made.

In this book, it has been suggested that an interface declaration is produced, and a class declaration that implements the interface is then produced. If you can foresee all the uses of a class, it may be possible to produce an interface that does not change. Usually, it is the code of the class declaration that will be changing: this will be because:

● the code does not do the right thing – it has a bug;
● the code can be made more efficient, e.g. takes up less space in memory or executes faster.

Because it is usually the code of a class rather than an interface that is changed, it is preferable for a client to be dependent on the interface rather than on the class (which implements that interface). If it is solely dependent on the interface, it need not be re-compiled if the class is changed.

Although, when coding the PersonImpl class (and the PersonImplProg program), we have chosen whenever possible to use Date rather than DateImpl and Person rather than PersonImpl, the class diagram points out that the code of the PersonImpl class is still dependent on the code of the DateImpl class. The problem lies in this area of the diagram:

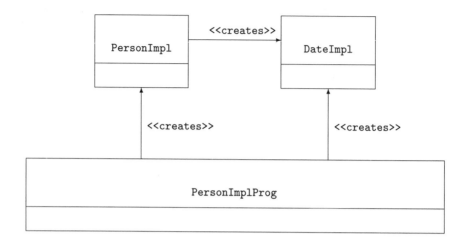

If we change `DateImpl`, we need to re-compile `PersonImpl` and `Person-ImplProg`. If we change `PersonImpl`, we need to re-compile `PersonImplProg`. Unless you take steps to avoid these sorts of dependencies, a change to one class can mean that you have to re-compile all the classes of a program.

However, the problem is not as easy as just re-compiling everything: we could make a change to `DateImpl` that affects the way in which it is used by `PersonImpl` and `PersonImplProg`. So whenever we re-compile a class, we ought also to re-test the class. For example, the `PersonImpl` class contains:

```
new DateImpl(tDateOfBirthString)
```

If we alter `DateImpl` so that the constructor that has a string as an argument now interprets it as *day-month-year* instead of *year-month-day*, then we will need to alter the code of `PersonImpl`.

So, if a client is dependent on a class (rather than on an interface), then any changes to the code of a class mean that we need to re-test the client, checking how the client uses the class and if necessary altering the client. Whether we make changes to the client or not, the client will need to be re-compiled.

So this is the reason why, when designing the code of a program, it is best to arrange the design so that classes are not dependent on each other. If there has to be a dependency, then it is better for an interface/class to be dependent on an interface rather than on a class.

We just have to look at the class diagram in order to see how well we have succeeded at this task. It is not a problem for a class to implement an interface, or for there to be `<<uses>>` or `<<has>>` arrows when the arrow points to an interface. However, if there are any other arrows between two classes, the two classes are said to be **tightly coupled**.

Obviously, we will have to create instances of classes somewhere. Creating them in the class that contains the `main` method is good because there is no code that is dependent on that class. In Section 21.5, we look at how the *factory pattern* can be used to reduce the tight coupling between the `PersonImpl` and the `DateImpl` classes.

12.9 Ensuring the same class is used for each `Date`

There is another problem with the `DateImpl`, `PersonImpl` and `PersonImplProg` classes. Each of these contains the use of constructors that commit to a particular implementation of an interface. For example, the `PersonImpl` class contains:

```
new DateImpl()
```

and

```
new DateImpl(tDateOfBirthString)
```

and the `PersonImplProg` program contains:

```
new DateImpl(1981, 2, 27)
```

On each occasion, we have chosen to use `DateImpl` rather than some other implementation such as `DateImplY`. So, luckily, on each occasion we have chosen the same class to represent a `Date`.

Suppose we now wish to switch to using some other class (e.g. `DateImplY`). Although this is manageable with this program, finding all the occurrences in a large program can be difficult. Problems will arise if we change most but not all of the occurrences. Depending on the actual circumstances, we may get a compilation error, an exception (such as a `NoClassDefFoundError` exception), or the program may not do what we want it to do.

One of the principles of software engineering is that the commitment to some decision should be made in one place and not all over the place. We have already seen an example of this. If a design decision is that we are going to use a tax rate of 17.5, then, instead of the value 17.5 appearing in the code on numerous occasions, the decision is documented using:

```
final double tTaxRate = 17.5;
```

and the constant `tTaxRate` is used in the code.

So, instead of our code containing numerous calls of the constructor of `DateImpl`, e.g.:

```
iDateOfBirth = new DateImpl(tDateOfBirthString);
```

we should call a method:

```
iDateOfBirth = pPopFactory.createDate(tDateOfBirthString);
```

where this method has a result type of `Date`. Thus most of our code does not contain any references to `DateImpl`. The code of the `createDate` method contains the only occurrence of a call of `DateImpl`'s constructor, i.e. the commitment to use `DateImpl` rather than `DateImplY` occurs in only one class.

This is an example of the use of the *factory pattern* (that was mentioned above); for more details, see Section 21.5.

Tips for programming and debugging

12.1   Section 12.5.6 introduced the `Comparable` interface that provides the `compareTo` method. Later, Curio 17.8 will briefly mention the `Comparator` interface that provides the `compare` method. So, watch out for a possible confusion between the names `Comparable`, `Comparator`, `compare` and `compareTo`.

12.2   In Section 12.7, five javac commands were given: these are the commands required to compile the interfaces and classes that make up the `PersonImplProg` program. When a Java program consists of several `.java` files, it is best to put the files into a new directory (also known as a folder). If you do this, then you can easily compile all of the `.java` files by typing:

```
javac *.java
```

In UNIX/MS-DOS, the notation `*.java` refers to all of the files in the current directory that have a `.java` extension.

When a `.java` file is changed, you need to re-compile the file that has been changed together with any files that depend on it. A class diagram (like the one in Figure 12.9) shows you the dependencies between the files, so it can be used to work out which of the javac commands need to be re-issued.

With earlier versions of javac, you could use a `-depend` or a `-Xdepend` option on the javac command line. If you did this, the javac compiler would automatically detect which `.class` files were out of date and would re-compile the associated `.java` files and their dependents. However, this facility is not available with the compiler of the Java 2 SDK v 1.3.0.

If you are using a system that has a `make` facility, you could use that. For UNIX, you could use a **Makefile** that has the following lines:

```
PersonImplProg.class: PersonImplProg.java \
                      Person.class PersonImpl.class \
                      Date.class DateImpl.class
        javac PersonImplProg.java
PersonImpl.class: PersonImpl.java \
                  Person.class \
                  Date.class DateImpl.class
        javac PersonImpl.java
Person.class: Person.java Date.class
        javac Person.java
DateImpl.class: DateImpl.java Date.class
        javac DateImpl.java
Date.class: Date.java
        javac Date.java
clean:
        rm PersonImplProg.class
        rm PersonImpl.class Person.class
        rm DateImpl.class Date.class
```

where each line that contains a UNIX command begins with a tab character.

Finally, if you become confused as to what needs to be re-compiled, one strategy is to re-compile everything. For this example, type:

```
erase *.class
javac *.java
```

in an MS-DOS environment, or:

```
rm *.class
javac *.java
```

in a UNIX environment.

Curios, controversies and cover-ups

12.1   In many ways, a declaration of a constant is similar to a declaration of a function. For example, the declaration of the constant:

```
public static final double tSpeedOfLight = 2.9979245858E8;
```

could be replaced by the function declaration:

```
public static double tSpeedOfLight()
{
    return 2.9979245858E8;
}
```

If you take this view, there is then no difference between the first and second categories of class declarations (given in Section 12.1).

12.2   Although it was suggested in Section 12.2 that a class declaration like `MathsConstants` has no constructors, this is not quite right. Because the class declaration does not declare a constructor, there is a *default no-arg constructor* (as was mentioned in Section 11.9.2). So it would be possible for a client to use this constructor, as in:

```
MathsConstants tMathsConstants = new MathsConstants();
```

Although the class `MathsConstants` provides some *class methods*, it does not have any *instance methods*. So, although a client can use this constructor to create a `MathsConstants` object and then make `tMathsConstants` point to it, there are no methods that the client can apply to it.

If you want to prevent a client from executing such code, you can add the following constructor to the class:

```
private MathsConstants()
{
}
```

Because this constructor has the modifier `private`, it cannot be used by a client. So a client is unable to create instances of the class.

12.3 If there is going to be only one instance of a class, is there any need for this instance to be created? That is, instead of the `KeyboardInput` class given in Figure 12.4 being coded in terms of instance methods that are applied to the only instance, why not use a class that has class methods that change class variables? So the class `KeyboardInput` is rewritten as follows:

```
public class NewKeyboardInput
{
    private static final BufferedReader iKeyboard =
                new BufferedReader(new InputStreamReader(System.in));
    private static StringTokenizer iTokens = null;
    private NewKeyboardInput()
    {
    }
    public static int nextInt()
    ...
    public static double nextDouble()
    ...
    private static String iGetToken() throws Exception
    ...
}
```

And instead of using:

```
final KeyboardInput tKeyboardInput = new KeyboardInput();
final int tAge = tKeyboardInput.nextInt();
```

we could then use:

```
final int tAge = NewKeyboardInput.nextInt();
```

If it were not for the presence of the private method `iGetToken`, it may look as if we have converted this class declaration from category 3 into a hybrid of categories 1 and 2, i.e. it now looks similar in style to the class `java.lang.Math`. However, the big difference is that one of the fields (`iTokens`) is not a constant.

Although this works, it is inelegant to use class variables and class methods in this way. If you really want to alter the value of a field from one call to another, it is more appropriate to have instance methods and to provide a constructor in order to create an object of the class.

12.4 It is sometimes necessary to guarantee that only one instance of a class can be created. You can do this by making the constructor private, by using a class variable to point to an instance of the class and by providing a method that returns a reference to this instance. If this were done to the class

KeyboardInput given in Figure 12.4, it would become:

```
public class KeyboardInput
{
    private static final KeyboardInput iKeyboardInput =
                                        new KeyboardInput();
    private final BufferedReader iKeyboard =
        new BufferedReader(new InputStreamReader(System.in));
    private StringTokenizer iTokens = null;
    private KeyboardInput()
    {
    }
    public static KeyboardInput getInstance()
    {
        return iKeyboardInput;
    }
    public int nextInt()
    ...
```

Because the constructor of this class is marked as `private`, it is not possible for a client to create an instance of this class. However, the class itself provides an instance:

```
private static final KeyboardInput iKeyboardInput =
                                        new KeyboardInput();
```

A client can get a pointer to this instance by using the method `getInstance` (which is a class method):

```
final KeyboardInput tKeyboardInput = KeyboardInput.getInstance();
```

It can then apply instance methods of the `KeyboardInput` class to this object in the usual way, e.g.:

```
final int tAge = tKeyboardInput.nextInt();
```

This way of hiding the constructor and making one instance of a class available to clients is sometimes employed in writing Java programs: it is called the **singleton pattern**.

More information about this pattern is given in the book *Design Patterns: Elements of Reusable Object-Oriented Software* ([17]). The examples in this book are given in C++ and Smalltalk. There is another book that covers similar material but which uses Java rather than C++ and Smalltalk. It is *Patterns in Java: Volume 1* by Mark Grand ([18]).

12.5   When designing an interface and class to represent a new type, it may be thought to be inappropriate to include `compareTo` because there is no obvious ordering to the values of the type. However, in some problems in which the type is going to be used, there is an ordering and you may have wished that the type had a compareTo method. It is possible using *inheritance* (introduced in Chapter 19) to produce a *subtype* (i.e. a new interface and class) that inherits all the facilities of the existing interface and class but which also implements Comparable. In some situations, it may be useful to produce several subtypes each of which implements Comparable in a different way.

12.6 A client may find that the compareTo method that is provided by a class is inappropriate. For example, it may be that it wants the objects that it is adding to a *collection* to be stored using some other ordering. In Curio 17.8, we will find out that the methods of the Collections API enable the client to do this so long as the client provides an object that implements the Comparator interface (from the java.util package).

12.7 In Section 12.5.6, it is suggested that a class's declaration of compareTo should be consistent with its equals. The WWW page (for the Comparable interface) says that this is 'because sorted sets (and sorted maps) without explicit comparators behave *strangely* when they are used with elements (or keys) whose natural ordering is inconsistent with equals'. Perhaps, it would be better if there were some way in which this consistency were adopted by default. It is possible to achieve this using a special kind of *superclass* called an *abstract class* (which will be mentioned in Section 19.3.5). The use of an abstract class to ensure that equals and compareTo are consistent is considered in Curio 19.9.

12.8 In some programming languages (such as C++ and Ada), it is possible to give new meanings to operators. In such languages, instead of a class declaring a method called compareTo, it could instead add new meanings for the relational operators when used with objects of the class. This is called **operator overloading**. The designers of Java chose not to add this feature to Java.

12.9 Often when producing a class Y you decide that it should have a field of some class X that already exists. This is called *composition* (or *aggregation*). Sometimes instead you choose to *derive* the class Y from the class X. This is called *inheritance*, and it is a topic that we will look at later. It is easy to see from a class diagram which of these is being used: the ———▷ symbol will be used for inheritance, and the ———• symbol with a <<has>> arrow will be used for composition.

(**Exercises**)————————————————————————————————

◊ **12.1** In Section 12.3, it was suggested that we could devise our own class declaration for some mathematical functions – say, a class called Math. If you have done Exercise 9.5 and Exercise 9.6, you will already have functions that calculate approximations to sin and sqrt. So, produce a class declaration containing these two functions. A skeleton of the required class is given in Figure 12.3.
    Write a program to test this class.

◇   **12.2**   Produce a new class called `Math2` that is similar to `Math` (produced in Exercise 12.1) except that:

● the code of the two functions should be written in terms of a variable called `iAccuracy`;

● this variable should be a private field of the class `Math2` and initialized to the value 0.00005;

● you should also provide a public method called `setAccuracy` which allows a client to set the accuracy to some other value – this method has a parameter which is the new value of the accuracy.

Write a program to test this class.

12.3   Produce a class called `ConvertConstants` that defines a number of constants that are useful in formulae to convert from one set of units to another. You will need to know that: 1 inch is 2.54 centimetres, 1 mile is about 1.6093 kilometres, 1 (imperial) gallon is about 4.5461 litres, 1 US gallon is about 3.7853 litres, 1 pound is about 0.4536 kilograms. The formula for converting between Fahrenheit and Celsius is given in Section 5.8.2.

Your class declaration should therefore contain appropriate constants for the values 2.54, 1.6093, 4.5461, 3.7853, 0.4536, 32.0, and 5.0/9.0.

Write a program to test this class.

12.4   Produce a class called `ConvertFunctions` that defines a number of functions each of which converts from one set of units to another. For example, you could include two functions (one in each direction) for each of the following: inches and centimetres, miles and kilometres, gallons and litres, pounds and kilograms, degrees Fahrenheit and degrees Celsius, etc. The class should use the constants of the class `ConvertConstants` – see Exercise 12.3.

Write a program to test this class.

12.5   Suppose that it is required to monitor the number of calls that a program makes of each of the following `java.lang.Math` functions: sin, cos, tan, exp, log and sqrt. Produce a class declaration for a class called `Math-Monitor` that includes method declarations for each of these functions. Each function of `MathMonitor` should do two things:

● it should increase a count of the number of calls by 1;

● it should return the value obtained from its appropriate counterpart in the `java.lang.Math` class.

Also provide a function that returns the current value of the count.

You could test this class by using it in the program you wrote to tabulate the values of sines and cosines – see Exercise 7.4.

12.6   A program is needed that produces a table of temperatures. Each line of the table should contain a temperature given in both degrees Fahrenheit and degrees Celsius. The table should have 190 lines covering temperatures from 30°F to 219°F (in steps of 1°F).

Suppose it is required for this output to be sent to a file, so that, later on, it can be output to a printer. Because there are a large number of lines of output, the file is to be divided up into chunks, so that, when the file is printed, each chunk gets output onto a separate page. One other requirement is that there should be a six-line *header* at the start of each chunk.

So, assuming the printer uses paper that has 66 lines to a page, a chunk of output to the file actually has the following format:

- the first three lines of the chunk are blank;
- the fourth line contains a number identifying which chunk it is;
- the next two lines are blank;
- the next 60 lines of the chunk contains the next 60 lines of output.

In order to implement this, you will have to keep track of how many lines have been output. So, instead of your program doing:

```
System.out.println();
```

at the end of each line of the table, get it to call a method called `println` provided by a class called `Pager`.

The `Pager` class should hide the count of the number of lines that have been output. Normally, its `println` method will just apply `println` to `System.out`; however, when `Pager`'s `println` has been called an appropriate number of times, it should output the header that starts a new chunk.

Produce the `Pager` class, and then write the program that uses the `Pager` class whilst producing a table of temperatures.

12.7   In Section 11.12, an interface and a class were produced for dates. Modify the interface declaration (which was given in Figure 11.14) so that it is a subinterface of `java.lang.Comparable`. Modify the class declaration (given in Figure 11.16) so that it declares an appropriate `compareTo` method.

Write a program to test the new versions of the interface and the class.

12.8   In Exercise 11.3, you produced an interface and a class for ISBNs. Modify the interface declaration so that it is a subinterface of `java.lang.Comparable`. Modify the class declaration so that it declares an appropriate `compareTo` method.

Write a program to test the new versions of the interface and the class.

12.9   Produce an interface called `Book` and a class called `BookImpl` that can be used to represent a book. Internally, the class should use a `String` to store the title of the book, a `String` to store the author of the book, an `int` to store the year of publication and an `ISBN` value to store the book's ISBN.

The interface should provide four get methods (to return these four values) and three methods called `equals`, `hashCode` and `toString` (that have their usual meanings). It should also be a subinterface of `java.lang.Comparable`.

Besides providing declarations for each of the methods of this interface (and a declaration of a `compareTo` method), the class should have a constructor that creates a `BookImpl` object from four parameters: a `String` giving the title, a `String` giving the author, an `int` giving the year of publication and an `ISBN` value giving the ISBN of the book. And it should also have a constructor that can be used to create a `BookImpl` object from a `Book` object that already exists.

You should use the ISBN interface and ISBNImpl class that were produced for Exercise 12.8.

Write a program to test Book and BookImpl.

12.10 In Exercise 11.5, an interface and a class were produced for representing a value that is a longitude or a latitude. Now produce an interface called Position and a class called PositionImpl that can be used to represent a position on the earth's surface. The class PositionImpl should declare two Angle(private) fields to represent the longitude and the latitude of the position.

The interface should provide:

- a get method that returns an Angle value that is the longitude;

- a get method that returns an Angle value that is the latitude;

- a set method with an Angle parameter that enables a client to set the longitude;

- a set method with an Angle parameter that enables a client to set the latitude;

- methods called equals, hashCode and toString (that have their usual meanings).

Besides declarations for each of these methods, the class should have a constructor that can create a PositionImpl object from two parameters that are a longitude and a latitude. It should also have a constructor that creates a PositionImpl object from a String. As mentioned in the text, the format of the string that is accepted by this constructor should be the same as that produced by the toString method of the class. And it should also have a constructor that can be used to create a PositionImpl object from a Position object that already exists.

Write a program called PositionImplProg that creates three objects representing the following three positions:

- 64° 50' W, 32° 14' N which is the location of Bermuda;

- 66° 30' W, 18° 15' N which is the location of Puerto Rico;

- 80° 5' W, 26° 0' N which is where Fort Lauderdale is located in Florida.

Anything that lies inside the triangle formed by these three positions is inside the so-called **Bermuda Triangle**.

So how do you find out whether a point is inside a triangle? On 29 December 1998, Horst Kraemer (horst.kraemer@snafu.de) posted an article on this topic to the sci.math newsgroup to answer a previous posting to this newsgroup.

Here is the code that results from reading Horst's article:

```
// The method iIsInside has four parameters of type Position.
// The first three are those for the vertices of the triangle.
// The last parameter is for the point.
// It returns true if and only if the point is inside the triangle.
private static boolean iIsInside(final Position pPosition1,
                                 final Position pPosition2,
```

```
                                    final Position pPosition3,
                                    final Position pPoint)
    {
        final double x1 = pPosition1.getLongitude().getDistance();
        final double y1 = pPosition1.getLatitude().getDistance();
        final double x2 = pPosition2.getLongitude().getDistance();
        final double y2 = pPosition2.getLatitude().getDistance();
        final double x3 = pPosition3.getLongitude().getDistance();
        final double y3 = pPosition3.getLatitude().getDistance();
        final double x0 =       pPoint.getLongitude().getDistance();
        final double y0 =       pPoint.getLatitude().getDistance();
        // thanks to Horst Kraemer for the clever stuff from here on
        final double  d = (x2-x1)*(y3-y1) -(y2-y1)*(x3-x1);
        final double  a = (x0-x1)*(y3-y1) -(y0-y1)*(x3-x1);
        final double  b = (x2-x1)*(y0-y1) -(y2-y1)*(x0-x1);
        if (d==0)
        {
            return true;
        }
        return 0<=a/d && 0<=b/d && a/d+b/d<=1;
    }
```

Arrange for the `PositionImplProg` program to output the following grid:

```
          West
North     85848382818079787776757473727170696867666564636261 60
    35: .  .  .  .  .  .  .  .  .  .  .  .  .  .  .  .  .  .  .  .  .  . . .
    34: .  .  .  .  .  .  .  .  .  .  .  .  .  .  .  .  .  .  .  .  .  . . .
    33: .  .  .  .  .  .  .  .  .  .  .  .  .  .  .  .  .  .  .  .  .  . . .
    32: .  .  .  .  .  .  .  .  .  .  .  .  .  .  .  .  .  . X  .  .  . . .
    31: .  .  .  .  .  .  .  .  .  .  .  .  .  .  . X X X  .  .  . . .
    30: .  .  .  .  .  .  .  .  .  .  .  . X X X X X  .  .  . . .
    29: .  .  .  .  .  .  .  .  .  . X X X X X X X  .  .  . . .
    28: .  .  .  .  .  .  . X X X X X X X X X X  .  .  . . .
    27: .  .  .  .  . X X X X X X X X X X X X X  .  .  . . .
    26: .  .  .  . X X X X X X X X X X X X X X X  .  .  . . .
    25: .  .  .  . X X X X X X X X X X X X X X  .  .  . . .
    24: .  .  .  .  . X X X X X X X X X X X X  .  .  . . .
    23: .  .  .  .  . X X X X X X X X X X  .  .  .  . . .
    22: .  .  .  .  .  . X X X X X X X  .  .  .  . . .
    21: .  .  .  .  .  .  . X X X X X  .  .  .  . . .
    20: .  .  .  .  .  .  . X X X  .  .  .  . . .
    19: .  .  .  .  .  .  . X  .  .  .  . . .
    18: .  .  .  .  .  .  .  .  .  .  .  .  .  .  .  .  .  .  .  .  .  . . .
    17: .  .  .  .  .  .  .  .  .  .  .  .  .  .  .  .  .  .  .  .  .  . . .
    16: .  .  .  .  .  .  .  .  .  .  .  .  .  .  .  .  .  .  .  .  .  . . .
    15: .  .  .  .  .  .  .  .  .  .  .  .  .  .  .  .  .  .  .  .  .  . . .
```

This grid shows values of longitude (in the range 85 to 60) running along the top, and values of latitude (in the range 35 to 15) running down the left. An X is used to indicate that a particular point is inside the Bermuda triangle.

Here are some points about this exercise:

- As has already been mentioned, the main method of Position-ImplProg should create three Position objects that represent the three vertices of the Bermuda Triangle.

- The main method should also include a for statement with a latitude degrees value stepping down from 35 to 15. Inside this loop, there should be another loop with a longitude degrees value stepping down from 85 to 60.

- Inside this inner loop, four things should happen:

    1. Form an appropriate string that can be passed as an argument to one of your Position constructors. The string should contain a longitude, a separator and a latitude.

    2. Construct a Position value from this string.

    3. Call iIsInside with this Position value as its fourth argument.

    4. If the result is true, output an X; otherwise output a dot.

Finally, draw a class diagram that shows the dependencies between the interfaces/classes of your program.

◇ **12.11** Produce an interface called Qe and a class called QeImpl that can be used to represent a quadratic equation.

The interface should provide:

- three get methods that return the coefficients of the quadratic equation;

- three set methods that set the coefficients of the quadratic equation;

- methods called equals, hashCode and toString (that have their usual meanings);

- a method called isReal that returns *true* if and only if the quadratic equation has real roots;

- a method called getRoot1 that returns one of the roots (provided isReal would return *true*);

- a method called getRoot2 that returns the other root (provided isReal would return *true*).

Besides declarations for each of these methods, the class should have a constructor that can create a QeImpl from three double parameters.

Here are some hints about one way to tackle the coding of the QeImpl class:

- provide three private fields of type double in which to store the three coefficients;

- provide two private fields of type double called iRoot1 and iRoot2 in which to store the roots of the quadratic equation;

- provide a private field of type `boolean` called `iRootsAreOutOfDate` which is initialized to *true* and is again set to *true* whenever any of the coefficients is changed;

- provide a private void method called `iSolve` which solves the quadratic equation and sets `iRootsAreOutOfDate` to *false*;

- the body of `getRoot1` can be coded in two steps: the first step is to call `iSolve` if `iRootsAreOutOfDate` is *true* and the second step is to return the value of `iRoot1`;

- `getRoot2` can be coded like `getRoot1`.

An example of the use of this interface and class is:

```
// read in a, b and c
...
// create the quadratic equation
final Qe tQe = new QeImpl(a, b, c);
// obtain the two roots of the quadratic equation if it has real roots
if (tQe.isReal())
{
    final double x1 = tQe.getRoot1();
    final double x2 = tQe.getRoot2();
    System.out.println("The quadratic equation is:");
    System.out.println(tQe);
    System.out.println("It has the following roots:");
    System.out.println(x1);
    System.out.println(x2);
}
```

Use the above code in a program that can find and output the roots of a quadratic equation. Test your program using the data given in Exercise 5.3.

[Hint: there is further information about quadratic equations in Section 6.8.]

Chapter 13

Providing a GUI: textfields and buttons

....

In this chapter, we look at how a program can create a new window and place GUI components such as textfields and buttons inside the window. We also look at how to produce a form from GUI components and at how to display a dialog box.

13.1) Using a graphical user interface

So far in this book, we have mainly obtained input from the user of a program by reading a value from the keyboard and the results of a program have been displayed by writing values to the terminal window being used to run the program.

This approach has been adopted because the amount of code you have to produce in order to read a value or display a value has been small.

Although these techniques for performing input and output were prevalent during the 1970s, during the 1980s and the 1990s the use of windowing systems has caused a change in the way in which input and output are often achieved. For example, these days, input is achieved through responding to dialog boxes, filling in forms, clicking on buttons, and so on. This technique for communicating values from and to the user of a program uses what is called a **graphical user interface** (or **GUI**).

Although the amount of code required to read a value or display a value will be larger than what we have been producing so far, the use of a GUI will make our programs more interesting to use.

13.2) AWT through the ages

One of the attractive features of Java is that there is an API for developing GUIs. The API is called the **Abstract Window Toolkit** (or **AWT**), and it is provided in the package java.awt. Although the AWT has been present from the start, the facilities that it provides for developing GUIs have changed with each major release of Java.

In JDK 1.0, a reasonably comprehensive set of features were provided. However, events such as mouse movements, button clicks and window closing had to be handled in a way which led to inefficient code, and code that was inappropriate in an object-oriented system.

In JDK 1.1, the event-handling mechanism was changed: instead, an object can register itself to handle any events on a particular component (such as a mouse, a button or a window).

The classes of the AWTs of JDK 1.0 and JDK 1.1 are implemented in terms of code written in the programming language C making use of existing libraries. This has the advantage that a Java program running on some platform (e.g. Windows 98) would look and feel like any other program written for that platform.

The disadvantage is that this scheme is inflexible: it is difficult for a programmer to add new components that have the correct *look and feel*. Late in 1996, Netscape Communications produced an API called the **Internet Foundation Classes** (or **IFC**) that was more flexible. Building on this, in April 1997, Sun, Netscape and IBM announced that they would produce an API called the **Java Foundation Classes** (or **JFC**) that would 'bring together the best of AWT with the best of IFC to create a unified set of APIs for developing robust, cross-platform Java applications'. Although beta versions of the JFC had been available for some time, the JFC first appeared as part of the development kit when the Java 2 Platform was announced in December 1998.

13.3 The Swing API

13.3.1 What is the Swing API?

The major part of the JFC is an API called the **Swing API**. The reason for calling it the *Swing API* is explained in Curio 13.1.

The Swing API is an API that provides components for producing GUIs. Unlike the AWT, it is completely written in Java. Because of this, it is easy for a programmer to add new GUI components that can be used alongside the Swing components. However, when writing programs that use the Swing API, it is still necessary to use some of the basic classes of the `java.awt` package.

The Swing API also has a **pluggable look-and-feel**. The *look* of a window in a Windows 95/98/NT environment is different from that in a Motif environment running on a UNIX workstation. With the Swing API, you can choose the look-and-feel to be that of a particular platform, to be a platform-independent look-and-feel, or to be a look-and-feel that depends on the platform on which the program is running.

13.3.2 What the Swing API includes and how it is organized

The Swing API is in the package `javax.swing`, and it contains many classes. It provides GUI components such as buttons, checkboxes, lists, menus, tables, text areas, and trees. It also includes GUI components that are containers (such as menu bars and windows), and higher-level components (such as dialog boxes, including dialog boxes for opening or saving files). And there are also classes for basic drawing operations, and for manipulating images, fonts and colours, and for handling events such as mouse clicks.

Many of these GUI components will have common features. For example, there is a method called `setBackground` that can be used to alter the background colour of a GUI component. Although it would be possible to include a method declaration called `setBackground` in each of the classes, this is not sensible. Instead, Java allows classes to be grouped into a **class hierarchy**: this means the Swing designers can declare the `setBackground` method in a class high up in the class hierarchy and it is automatically available in the classes that are lower down in the class hierarchy.

In this way, a class lower down in the class hierarchy can offer facilities that are actually declared higher up in the class hierarchy. This is one of the key aspects of *inheritance*.

13.3.3 A digression to introduce inheritance

So far, the classes we have used from the Core APIs, and the classes we have produced ourselves, have been for classes that are distinct from one another: a date is nothing like a person, and vice-versa. However, there will be occasions when a new class is in fact a more specialized form of another class.

For example, if we had to produce a program that manipulated data about students, we would need a class to represent a student. Such a class would have a lot in common with the class representing a person (produced in Section 12.5). For example, we would want a name field and a date of birth field; we would want methods called getName and getDateOfBirth; and so on.

Instead of producing a completely new class for a student, we can **derive** the class for a student from the class for a person. This is known as **inheritance**, and we will look at this topic in more detail in Chapter 19. Having derived a student class in this way, if a program creates a student object, it can apply not only the methods of the student class to the student object but also those of the person class. Suppose the StudentImpl class provides the methods getStudentNumber, getCourseName and toString. This is illustrated by the class hierarchy given in Figure 13.1.

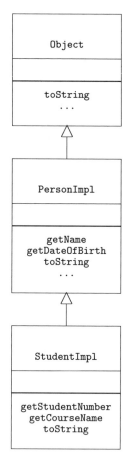

Figure 13.1 The class hierarchy of StudentImpl, PersonImpl and Object.

If we have an object of the class StudentImpl, the methods getStudentNumber, getCourseName, toString, getName and getDate-OfBirth can be applied to it.

Note that this is no different from the situation described in Section 11.7. There it was explained that if a client applies the toString method to an object of class Date when Date does not declare toString, the toString method of Object would be called.

Looking again at the class hierarchy in Figure 13.1, here is some more jargon:

- `StudentImpl` is a **subclass** of `PersonImpl`;
- `PersonImpl` and `Object` are the **superclasses** of `StudentImpl`;
- `PersonImpl` is the **direct superclass** of `StudentImpl`.

Sometimes the latter is abbreviated to *superclass*, i.e. `PersonImpl` is the *superclass* of `StudentImpl`.

13.3.4 Inheritance in the design of the Swing API

Inheritance is very useful when you have objects of different classes that have a large amount of similarity. As explained earlier, a class higher up in the class hierarchy can be used to represent the behaviour that is common. Sometimes the class used for this is not one that would be used for a real-world object: instead, a class is invented solely to represent the bits that are common.

This can be illustrated by looking at the way in which the Swing API represents buttons. It has many different kinds of buttons including:

- `JButton` which is the basic kind of button;
- `JToggleButton` which, when pushed, changes state until pushed again;
- `JCheckBox` which is like `JToggleButton` except it uses an icon to indicate whether it is on/off;
- `JRadioButton` which occurs in a group of which only one is selected at any point in time;
- `JMenuItem` which is a special kind of button that is used in conjunction with a `JMenu` object which we will look at in the chapter on creating menus (Chapter 18).

Because much of the functionality of a button is the same no matter what kind of button it is, the designers of the Swing API have chosen to put the common features into a class called `AbstractButton`. And because a `JCheckBox` and a `JRadioButton` are both special forms of a `JToggleButton`, these classes are derived from `JToggleButton`. These decisions (of the designers of the Swing API) are shown in the class hierarchy given in Figure 13.2.

So if you declare an object to be a `JRadioButton`, it may be that the methods you will want to apply to this object are declared in any of the following:

- the classes `JRadioButton`, `JToggleButton`, `AbstractButton` and `JComponent` from the `javax.swing` package;
- the classes `Container` and `Component` from the `java.awt` package;
- the class `Object` from the `java.lang` package.

Although inheritance is a design technique that is invaluable because it enables the reuse of methods and fields from other classes, it can at times be confusing as to where to find the documentation for a method. The WWW pages for the Core APIs are helpful in that, with each class, it also lists the methods and fields that are inherited from each of the superclasses of that class.

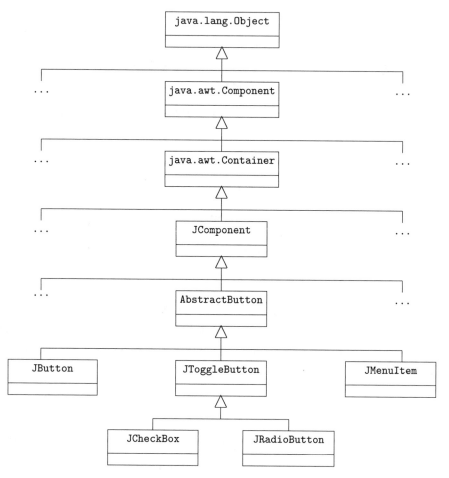

Figure 13.2 The class hierarchy of the buttons part of the Swing API.

13.4 Working within a window

When producing a GUI, we will need to create windows on the screen. The Swing API has a number of classes that enable a program to create a new window on the screen or to make use of an existing window.

The classes are:

- JWindow – which is for a window without a border or a menu bar;
- JFrame – which is for a window with a border and possibly a menu bar;
- JDialog – which is for a dialog box;
- JInternalFrame – which is for creating a frame inside an existing frame;
- JApplet – which is for the frame of a WWW page (for use by an *applet*).

All of these Swing classes (apart from JInternalFrame) inherit features from their counterparts of the java.awt package (as shown in Figure 13.3).

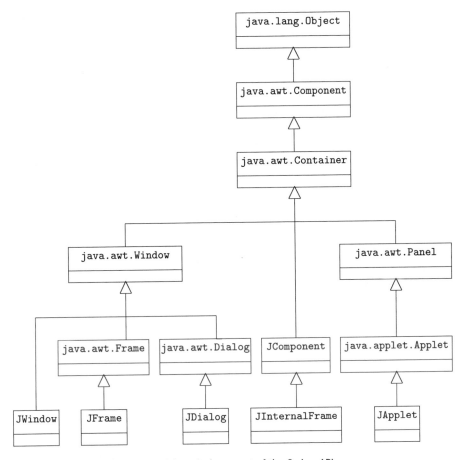

Figure 13.3 The class hierarchy of the windows part of the Swing API.

The JWindow class will not be considered in this book as the JFrame class is more useful. The JFrame and JDialog classes will be considered in this chapter; the JInternalFrame class will be considered in Section 18.5; and the JApplet class will be considered in Chapter 20.

Although each of these five classes fulfils different purposes, having created an object of one of these classes, you will want to do similar things to the object. The Swing designers have recognized this: so each class has a field to represent a pane called the **root pane**. So having created an object of one of the above classes, it is its JRootPane field on which operations will be performed.

The JRootPane field is used to represent four aspects of the window:

- a glass pane;
- a layered pane;

- a content pane;
- an optional menu bar.

The **content pane** is the main area of the window. It can be displayed with a **menu bar** but this is optional. The **layered pane** allows the possibility of having additional layers in front of the content pane, for placing tool boxes, dialog boxes, pop-up menus, etc. The **glass pane** sits in front of all of the other panes: it can be used to intercept mouse events such as those that occur when one internal window is dragged in front of another. To begin with, we will only be concerned with the content pane. We will look at menu bars in Chapter 18.

13.5) A simple example of a GUI

Suppose we want a Java program that creates a window that has a button and a textfield (an area for storing a line of text), and each time the button is clicked the textfield is updated to show the current date and time.

Rather than just present the program that accomplishes this task, the program will be developed in stages, each stage conquering some of the problems that occur.

13.6) Stage A: displaying the current date and time

The first step is to find out how to display the current date and time. It so happens that the class `java.util.Date` has a constructor that allows you to create an object with a value that represents the current date and time. A program that uses this class is given in Figure 13.4.

```
// Stage A: outputting the current date and time to the screen.
// Barry Cornelius, 19 June 2000
import java.util. Date;
public class GetDateProg
{
   public static void main(final String[] pArgs)
   {
      final Date tDate = new Date();
      System.out.println(tDate);
   }
}
```

Figure 13.4   Stage A: displaying the current date and time.

Because this program contains an import declaration for `java.util.Date`, the two occurrences of `Date` that appear in this program refer to the class `java.util.Date` (rather than any other class such as the class `Date` that was produced in Chapter 11).

The program produces output such as:

```
Mon Feb 19 12:36:43 GMT 2001
```

We will use the code of this program later.

13.7 Stage B: creating a window

The next step is to find out how we can get a Java program to display a new window on the screen. A simple program that does this is shown in Figure 13.5. It involves creating an object of the class JFrame. One of JFrame's constructors allows you to choose the string that is to be put into the title bar of the window:

```
final JFrame tJFrame = new JFrame("GetDateProg: Stage B");
```

The use of this class instance creation expression just creates the JFrame object: it does not display the window on the screen. This is done by a call of the method setVisible:

```
tJFrame.setVisible(true);
```

If you look at the WWW page documenting JFrame (at $API/javax/swing/ JFrame.html), you will find that the method setVisible is not declared in JFrame. So where is it declared? It must be declared in one of JFrame's superclasses. So the other possibilities are illustrated by the class hierarchy in Figure 13.3. This list of possibilities also appears at the top of JFrame's WWW page:

```
java.lang.Object
  |
  +--java.awt.Component
        |
        +--java.awt.Container
              |
              +--java.awt.Window
                    |
                    +--java.awt.Frame
                          |
                          +--javax.swing.JFrame
```

Besides listing the methods provided by JFrame, the WWW page also lists those

```
// Stage B: creating a window.
// Barry Cornelius, 19 June 2000
import javax.swing. JFrame;
public class GetDateProg
{
    public static void main(final String[] pArgs)
    {
        final JFrame tJFrame = new JFrame("GetDateProg: Stage B");
        tJFrame.setLocation(50, 100);
        tJFrame.setSize(300, 200);
        tJFrame.setVisible(true);
    }
}
```

Figure 13.5 Stage B: creating a window.

methods that JFrame inherits from its superclasses. If you look at the WWW page, you will see something like:

```
Methods inherited from class java.awt.Frame
    addNotify, finalize, getCursorType, getFrames, ..., setTitle
Methods inherited from class java.awt.Window
    addWindowListener, applyResourceBundle, dispose, ..., toFront
Methods inherited from class java.awt.Container
    add, addContainerListener, countComponents, ..., validateTree
Methods inherited from class java.awt.Component
    action, add, addComponentListener, ..., setVisible, ..., transferFocus
Methods inherited from class java.lang.Object
    clone, equals, getClass, hashCode, notify, notifyAll, wait
```

So, from all this information, we can see that setVisible is not declared in javax.swing.JFrame, nor in java.awt.Frame, nor in java.awt.Window, nor in java.awt.Container, but in the class java.awt.Component.

Unless you specify otherwise, when the window is displayed, it will be positioned in the top left-hand corner of the screen. The call:

```
tJFrame.setLocation(50, 100);
```

says that you want the top left-hand corner of the window to be positioned 50 pixels from the left-hand side of the screen and 100 pixels down from the top of the screen. And the call:

```
tJFrame.setSize(300, 200);
```

says that you want the window to be 300 pixels wide and 200 pixels high.

Because the program shown in Figure 13.5 uses the Swing API, it must be compiled with a compiler that understands the Java 2 Platform, e.g. the javac command of the Java 2 SDK. If you attempt to compile this program with a compiler from JDK 1.0 or JDK 1.1, you will get the compilation error:

```
GetDateProg.java:3: Class javax.swing.JFrame not found in import.
```

Having compiled the program, it can be executed by using the java command of the Java 2 SDK:

```
java GetDateProg
```

However, because this program displays a new window on the screen, you will need to be running some windowing system. This will not be a problem if you are using Windows 95/98/NT, but on a computer running UNIX you will need to be running a Motif-based windowing system.

The specific details of the appearance of the window will depend on this underlying windowing system. But, having written a Java program that creates a GUI, the program will execute in any Java environment: you do not have to write code that distinguishes between say Windows 98 and Motif.

When this program is executed, it just displays a blank window on the screen, as shown in Figure 13.6.

The program has no code to understand the removal of the window, so if you want to stop the execution of this program, you will need to press *Ctrl/C* in the window in

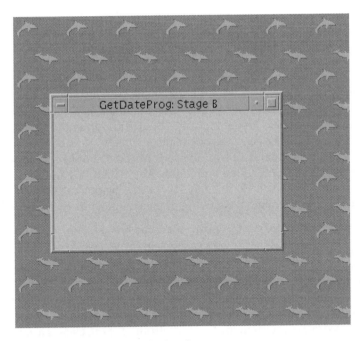

Figure 13.6 Stage B: a blank window is displayed.

which you typed the command:

```
java GetDateProg
```

We will look at how to overcome this problem in Section 13.11.

13.8 Stage C: adding GUI components to the window

Some GUI components will now be put into the window that is displayed by the program. As with the previous program, the first step is to create an object to represent that window:

```
final JFrame tJFrame = new JFrame("GetDateProg: Stage C");
```

In order to get our program to display a textfield and a button, the program needs to create these GUI components and add them to the content pane of the frame.

The Swing API contains classes that enable us to represent textfields and buttons:

```
final JTextField tJTextField = new JTextField("hello", 35);
final JButton tJButton = new JButton("Get Date");
```

There are a number of constructors for these classes (as shown at $API/javax/swing/JTextField.html and $API/javax/swing/JButton.html). The ones used above create a textfield containing 35 columns which is initialized to the string "hello", and a button containing a label with the characters "Get Date". Once again, this just creates two objects within an executing Java program that represent a textfield and a button. It does not do anything with them, such as make them visible.

These GUI components need to be added to the content pane of the JFrame window. We can get a reference to the JFrame's content pane by executing the method getContentPane:

```
final Container tContentPane = tJFrame.getContentPane();
```

The actual way in which GUI components are displayed within a container such as this content pane is controlled by a **layout manager**. The default layout manager for a content pane is a layout known as BorderLayout.

The BorderLayout layout manager allows you to use a method called add to place components in five divisions of the content page appropriately known as **North**, **West**, **Center**, **East** and **South**. These divisions are illustrated by the diagram in Figure 13.7. You do not have to put a component in each division: the layout manager will arrange the spacing of the components that you do provide:

```
tContentPane.add(tJTextField, BorderLayout.NORTH);
tContentPane.add(tJButton, BorderLayout.SOUTH);
```

The class java.awt.BorderLayout conveniently provides constants named NORTH, WEST, CENTER, EAST and SOUTH.

If you are unhappy with the layout, you can either use Container's setLayout method to choose another layout manager or you can use an object of class Box or JPanel to group items together. Both of these classes are in the javax.swing package: the Box class uses a layout called BoxLayout, and the JPanel class uses a layout called FlowLayout. We look at how to use the class Box in Section 13.16, and JPanel is mentioned in Curio 13.8.

When you have added all of the components to the content pane, you should apply the method pack (from the class java.awt.Window) to the frame. This arranges for the size of the frame to be just big enough to accommodate the components. So this time we have chosen not to call setSize: instead the call of pack determines an appropriate size for the window. A call of pack often appears just before a call of setVisible:

```
tJFrame.pack();
tJFrame.setVisible(true);
```

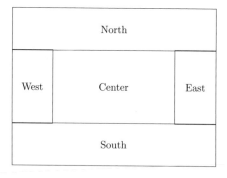

Figure 13.7 BorderLayout divides the content pane into five divisions.

Figure 13.8 shows the complete program, and Figure 13.9 shows what gets displayed when this program is executed. As there is no call of `setLocation`, the window will appear in the top left-hand corner of the screen.

```
// Stage C: adding GUI components to the window.
// Barry Cornelius, 19 June 2000
import java.awt.    BorderLayout;
import java.awt.    Container;
import javax.swing. JButton;
import javax.swing. JFrame;
import javax.swing. JTextField;
public class GetDateProg
{
    public static void main(final String[] pArgs)
    {
        final JFrame tJFrame = new JFrame("GetDateProg: Stage C");
        final JTextField tJTextField = new JTextField("hello", 35);
        final JButton tJButton = new JButton("Get Date");
        final Container tContentPane = tJFrame.getContentPane();
        tContentPane.add(tJTextField, BorderLayout.NORTH);
        tContentPane.add(tJButton,    BorderLayout.SOUTH);
        tJFrame.pack();
        tJFrame.setVisible(true);
    }
}
```

Figure 13.8   Stage C: adding GUI components to the window.

Figure 13.9   Stage C: a window containing a button and a textfield is displayed.

13.9 Stage D: responding to a click of the button

Having arranged for the textfield and the button to appear in the window, we need to be able to react to the user clicking the button. As was mentioned earlier, the handling of **events**, such as mouse clicks, mouse movements, key presses, window iconizing and window removal, is an area in which Java was improved between JDK 1.0 and JDK 1.1. Here we will look at how events are handled in versions of Java from JDK 1.1 onwards.

In order to handle the event of a user clicking on the JButton component, you need to do two things:

- create an object that has an actionPerformed method containing the code that you want to be executed (when the user clicks on the JButton component);
- indicate that this object is responsible for handling any events associated with the JButton component.

To put this a little more formally:

1. the program needs to create an object that is of a class that implements the ActionListener interface (which is declared in the package java.awt.event);

2. the program needs to use the addActionListener method to register this object as the **listener** for events on the JButton component.

If you look at the WWW page $API/java/awt/event/ActionListener.html, you will see that in order to implement the java.awt.event.ActionListener inter-face you just need to have a class that declares one method, a method called actionPerformed that has the header:

```
public void actionPerformed(ActionEvent pActionEvent)
```

So here is a class that does that:

```
import java.awt.event. ActionEvent;
import java.awt.event. ActionListener;
import java.util.       Date;
public class JButtonListener implements ActionListener
{
    public JButtonListener()
    {
    }
    public void actionPerformed(final ActionEvent pActionEvent)
    {
        final Date tDate = new Date();
        System.out.println(tDate);
    }
}
```

As with any class that implements an interface, it is important for the class not only to have a method called actionPerformed (with appropriate parameters and result type) but also to include the implements clause:

```
implements ActionListener
```

The GetDateProg program can create an object of this class in the usual way:

```
final JButtonListener tJButtonListener = new JButtonListener();
```

That satisfies the first requirement given above.

The program also needs to say that this object is going to be responsible for handling the clicks on the button. What we are effectively wanting to do is to say: 'please execute this object's `actionPerformed` method whenever there is a click on the `JButton` component'. In order to do this, we need to associate the object that has the `actionPerformed` method with the `JButton` object; or, in the jargon of Java, our `JButtonListener` object needs to be added as a *listener* for any events associated with the `JButton` object. This can be done using:

```
tJButton.addActionListener(tJButtonListener);
```

Because the `addActionListener` method has been applied to `tJButton`, the `actionPerformed` method of the object passed as an argument to

```
// Stage D: a class whose actionPerformed method writes to standard output.
// Barry Cornelius, 19 June 2000
import java.awt.event. ActionEvent;
import java.awt.event. ActionListener;
import java.util.      Date;
public class JButtonListener implements ActionListener
{
    public JButtonListener()
    {
    }
    public void actionPerformed(final ActionEvent pActionEvent)
    {
        final Date tDate = new Date();
        System.out.println(tDate);
    }
}
..................................................................
// Stage D: responding to a click of a button.
// Barry Cornelius, 19 June 2000
import java.awt.      BorderLayout;
import java.awt.      Container;
import javax.swing. JButton;
import javax.swing. JFrame;
import javax.swing. JTextField;
public class GetDateProg
{
    public static void main(final String[] pArgs)
    {
        final JFrame tJFrame = new JFrame("GetDateProg: Stage D");
        final JTextField tJTextField = new JTextField("hello", 35);
        final JButton tJButton = new JButton("Get Date");
        final JButtonListener tJButtonListener = new JButtonListener();
        tJButton.addActionListener(tJButtonListener);
        final Container tContentPane = tJFrame.getContentPane();
        tContentPane.add(tJTextField, BorderLayout.NORTH);
        tContentPane.add(tJButton, BorderLayout.SOUTH);
        tJFrame.pack();
        tJFrame.setVisible(true);
    }
}
```

Figure 13.10   Stage D: doing something when the user clicks on the button.

addActionListener (i.e. tJButtonListener) will be executed at each
click of this JButton component.

Figure 13.10 contains a listing of the JButtonListener class together with the
code of the GetDateProg program. The latter is the same as that given in Figure 13.8
apart from the inclusion of the two statements given above. These two classes need
to be stored in the files JButtonListener.java and GetDateProg.java. A diagram showing part of the class diagram for this program appears in Figure 13.11.
Although most of our programs rely on classes of the Core APIs, when producing
these class diagrams it is usually useful to leave out the dependences on classes of
the Core APIs.

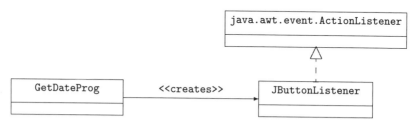

Figure 13.11   Stage D: part of the class diagram of the GetDateProg program.

Figure 13.12 gives an example of what happens when the JButton component is
clicked.

Figure 13.12   Stage D: whenever the button is clicked, the date and time are output.

Note that we do not have any precise control over when the `actionPerformed` method is called: this is at the whim of the person using the program. The act of registering code that will be executed later is sometimes referred to as creating a **callback**.

(13.10) Stage E: altering the `JTextField` component

Although the program of Stage D outputs the current date and time whenever the `JButton` component is clicked, the program sends this output to the *standard output*, i.e. to the terminal window that runs the program. What we really want to do is to copy the date and time into the `JTextField` component. And it is the variable `tJTextField` of the `main` method of `GetDateProg` that points to the `JTextField` object that we want to be updated each time the user clicks on the button.

How can we refer to this `JTextField` object within the `actionPerformed` method? We cannot just write `tJTextField` as this variable is local to the `main` method, and, anyway, the `main` method is in a different class from the `actionPerformed` method.

The easiest way is to alter the constructor for the listener object so that `tJTextField` is passed as an argument:

```
JButtonListener tJButtonListener = new JButtonListener(tJTextField);
```

In this way, when the `JButtonListener` object is being created, the constructor knows which `JTextField` object we want to be altered: it is the one pointed to by `tJTextField`.

What can the constructor do with this information? Well, it can make its own copy of the pointer:

```
public JButtonListener(final JTextField pJTextField)
{
    iJTextField = pJTextField;
}
```

where `iJTextField` is a private field of the `JButtonListener` object.

So when a `JButtonListener` object is created, its constructor stores a pointer to the `JTextField` object in a field of the `JButtonListener` object. Whenever the `actionPerformed` method is executed, it just has to alter the contents of the object pointed to by `iJTextField`.

Some of the methods that can be applied to a `JTextField` object are shown in Figure 13.13. Strictly speaking, some of these methods are methods of the class `javax.swing.JTextField` whereas the others are methods of the class `javax.swing.text.JTextComponent` which is the *direct superclass* of `javax.swing.JTextField`.

You can see from Figure 13.13 that, in order to change the value of a `JTextField` object, we need to apply the `setText` method to the object, passing the appropriate string as an argument, e.g. the statement:

```
iJTextField.setText("goodbye");
```

would put the characters of the string `"goodbye"` into the textfield. Since we actually

```
public JTextField(int pColumns);
```
   Initializes the new JTextField object to be an empty textfield that has pColumns columns.
```
public JTextField(String pString);
```
   Initializes the new JTextField object to be a textfield containing the string pString.
```
public JTextField(String pString, int pColumns);
```
   Initializes the new JTextField object to be a textfield that has pColumns columns and contains the string pString.
   ....
```
public String getText();
```
   Returns the text contained in the target textfield.
```
public void setEditable(boolean pEditable);
```
   Sets whether the text of the target textfield can be changed to the value of pEditable.
```
public void setFont(Font pFont);
```
   Sets the current font of the target textfield to be the font pFont.
```
public void setText(String pString);
```
   Sets the text of the target textfield to be the string pString.

Figure 13.13   Constructors and methods of the `javax.swing.JTextField` class.

want to set the textfield to a string describing the current date and time, we need to do:

```
Date tDate = new Date();
iJTextField.setText("" + tDate);
```

The complete text of this program is shown in Figure 13.15.

Figure 13.14 gives an example of what happens when the JButton component is clicked.

Figure 13.14   Stage E: whenever the button is clicked, the textfield is updated.

(13.11) Stage F: closing the window

Although this has achieved our goal of altering the JTextField component whenever the JButton component is clicked, there is one other thing that needs to be done. Up until now, the only way in which we have been able to terminate the execution of the program has been to press Ctrl/C. With this example, it may be useful to terminate the execution when the user closes the window.

```
// Stage E: a class which implements the ActionListener interface.
// Barry Cornelius, 19 June 2000
import java.awt.event. ActionEvent;
import java.awt.event. ActionListener;
import java.util.        Date;
import javax.swing.     JTextField;
public class JButtonListener implements ActionListener
{
   private JTextField iJTextField;
   public JButtonListener(final JTextField pJTextField)
   {
      iJTextField = pJTextField;
   }
   public void actionPerformed(final ActionEvent pActionEvent)
   {
      final Date tDate = new Date();
      iJTextField.setText("" + tDate);
   }
}
```
. . . .
```
// Stage E: achieving the goal of altering the JTextField component.
// Barry Cornelius, 19 June 2000
import java.awt.     BorderLayout;
import java.awt.     Container;
import javax.swing. JButton;
import javax.swing. JFrame;
import javax.swing. JTextField;
public class GetDateProg
{
   public static void main(final String[] pArgs)
   {
      final JFrame tJFrame = new JFrame("GetDateProg: Stage E");
      final JTextField tJTextField = new JTextField("hello", 35);
      final JButton tJButton = new JButton("Get Date");
      final JButtonListener tJButtonListener =
                              new JButtonListener(tJTextField);
      tJButton.addActionListener(tJButtonListener);
      final Container tContentPane = tJFrame.getContentPane();
      tContentPane.add(tJTextField, BorderLayout.NORTH);
      tContentPane.add(tJButton,    BorderLayout.SOUTH);
      tJFrame.pack();
      tJFrame.setVisible(true);
   }
}
```

Figure 13.15 Stage E: altering a JTextField whenever the user clicks the button.

In the same way that an ActionListener object is created to handle clicks on the JButton, we can establish an object which is responsible for handling events on a window. Unlike the ActionListener interface where we only had to provide one method, the WindowListener interface requires us to provide seven methods to provide for seven events concerning the manipulation of windows. The details are given on java.awt.event.WindowListener's WWW page which is at $API/java/awt/event/WindowListener.html.

A class (called ExitWindowListener) that implements the WindowListener interface is given in Figure 13.16. Note that this class has the implements clause implements WindowListener and has method declarations for each of the seven methods.

Because we only want to do something special when a window is about to close, some code has been provided for the windowClosing method whereas the other six method declarations have empty blocks.

When using the ActionListener interface, we had to:

- provide an object of a class that implements the ActionListener interface;
- register this object as a listener for clicks on the JButton component.

We have to do similar things when using the WindowListener interface.

The GetDateProg program in Figure 13.17 creates an ExitWindowListener object:

```
ExitWindowListener tExitWindowListener = new ExitWindowListener();
```

and registers this object as a listener for window events on the window associated with the tJFrame object:

```
tJFrame.addWindowListener(tExitWindowListener);
```

The following statement (from the GetDateProg program) ensures that, when the user clicks on the window's close button, the window is not removed from the screen:

```
tJFrame.setDefaultCloseOperation(JFrame.DO_NOTHING_ON_CLOSE);
```

The window is only removed when the program executes setVisible with an argument of *false*. See Curio 13.7.

Now when the user manipulates the window, one of the methods of the ExitWindowListener class will get executed. Most of these do not do anything. However, when the user clicks on the button to close the window, the code of the following method declaration gets executed:

```
public void windowClosing(final WindowEvent pWindowEvent)
{
    final Window tWindow = pWindowEvent.getWindow();
    tWindow.setVisible(false);
    tWindow.dispose();
    System.exit(0);
}
```

```
// Stage F: a class which implements the WindowListener interface.
// Barry Cornelius, 19 June 2000
import java.awt.        Window;
import java.awt.event. WindowEvent;
import java.awt.event. WindowListener;
public class ExitWindowListener implements WindowListener
{
    public void windowActivated(final WindowEvent pWindowEvent)
    {
    }

    public void windowClosed(final WindowEvent pWindowEvent)
    {
    }

    public void windowClosing(final WindowEvent pWindowEvent)
    {
        final Window tWindow = pWindowEvent.getWindow();
        tWindow.setVisible(false);
        tWindow.dispose();
        System.exit(0);
    }

    public void windowDeactivated(final WindowEvent pWindowEvent)
    {
    }

    public void windowDeiconified(final WindowEvent pWindowEvent)
    {
    }

    public void windowIconified(final WindowEvent pWindowEvent)
    {
    }

    public void windowOpened(final WindowEvent pWindowEvent)
    {
    }
}
```

Figure 13.16   Stage F: a class that implements the `WindowListener` interface.

You can see that when the `windowClosing` method is called, some object (that is of the class `WindowEvent`) is passed as an argument to `windowClosing`. This object contains details of what caused the window event to take place. The `WindowEvent` class has various methods that can be applied to this `WindowEvent` object: one of these is called `getWindow`. So, the first statement of the `windowClosing` method makes `tWindow` point to the `Window` object associated with the window being closed. For `GetDateProg`, this is the `JFrame` object that was created by its `main` method.

Back in Section 11.10, it was mentioned that a reference variable (that is of a class type) can point to an object of its class or any subclass. Here, `tWindow`, a reference variable of the class type `java.awt.Window` is pointing to an object of the class

```
// Stage F: using a WindowListener to handle a window-closing event.
// Barry Cornelius, 19 June 2000
import java.awt.    BorderLayout;
import java.awt.    Container;
import javax.swing. JButton;
import javax.swing. JFrame;
import javax.swing. JTextField;
public class GetDateProg
{
    public static void main(final String[] pArgs)
    {
        final JFrame tJFrame = new JFrame("GetDateProg: Stage F");
        final JTextField tJTextField = new JTextField("hello", 35);
        final JButton tJButton = new JButton("Get Date");
        final JButtonListener tJButtonListener =
                                    new JButtonListener(tJTextField);
        tJButton.addActionListener(tJButtonListener);
        final Container tContentPane = tJFrame.getContentPane();
        tContentPane.add(tJTextField, BorderLayout.NORTH);
        tContentPane.add(tJButton,    BorderLayout.SOUTH);
        final ExitWindowListener tExitWindowListener =
                                    new ExitWindowListener();
        tJFrame.addWindowListener(tExitWindowListener);
        tJFrame.setDefaultCloseOperation(JFrame.DO_NOTHING_ON_CLOSE);
        tJFrame.pack();
        tJFrame.setVisible(true);
    }
}
```

Figure 13.17   Stage F: using a `WindowListener` to handle a window-closing event.

`javax.swing.JFrame`, one of the subclasses of `java.awt.Window` (as shown in Figure 13.3).

The next statement of the `windowClosing` method calls the `setVisible` method. The call of `setVisible` with argument *false* ensures that the window is no longer displayed on the screen. When a `Window` object (such as a `JFrame` object) is created, some other objects are created. The call of `dispose` indicates that the space for these objects is no longer required. Although in general it is useful to execute these calls of `setVisible` and `dispose`, they are unnecessary in this program as they are followed by the call of `System.exit` that terminates the program.

13.12 Stage G: producing a class for a GUI component

We have effectively built a new GUI component, one that enables a user to display the current date and time. Instead of putting the code for doing this in the main method of a program, we could put the code in the constructor of a new class. Having done

```java
// Stage G: a class which implements the ActionListener interface.
// Barry Cornelius, 19 June 2000
import java.awt.event. ActionEvent;
import java.awt.event. ActionListener;
import java.util.        Date;
import javax.swing.      JTextField;
public class JButtonListener implements ActionListener
{
    private JTextField iJTextField;
    public JButtonListener(final JTextField pJTextField)
    {
        iJTextField = pJTextField;
    }
    public void actionPerformed(final ActionEvent pActionEvent)
    {
        final Date tDate = new Date();
        iJTextField.setText("" + tDate);
    }
}
```
....
```java
// Stage G: the class that implements the user interface.
// Barry Cornelius, 19 June 2000
import java.awt.        BorderLayout;
import java.awt.        Container;
import javax.swing. JButton;
import javax.swing. JFrame;
import javax.swing. JTextField;
public class GetDateJFrame
{
    public GetDateJFrame(final String pString, final int pX, final int pY)
    {
        final JFrame tJFrame =
                        new JFrame("GetDateJFrame: Stage G: " + pString);
        final JTextField tJTextField = new JTextField("hello", 35);
        final JButton tJButton = new JButton("Get Date");
        final JButtonListener tJButtonListener =
                                    new JButtonListener(tJTextField);
        tJButton.addActionListener(tJButtonListener);
        final Container tContentPane = tJFrame.getContentPane();
        tContentPane.add(tJTextField, BorderLayout.NORTH);
        tContentPane.add(tJButton,    BorderLayout.SOUTH);
        tJFrame.setLocation(pX, pY);
        tJFrame.pack();
        tJFrame.setVisible(true);
    }
}
```

Figure 13.18   Stage G: using a separate class for the user interface.

this, it means that if subsequently this capability is needed by a program all we have to do is to create an object of this class.

Figure 13.18 contains a class declaration called GetDateJFrame whose constructor does all the work that was done by the previous version of the GetDateProg program. Figure 13.19 shows a new version of the GetDateProg program which just creates two of these GetDateJFrame objects. Figure 13.20 shows a typical state during the execution of this program.

```
// Stage G: a program that creates two instances of the user interface.
// Barry Cornelius, 19 June 2000
public class GetDateProg
{
    public static void main(final String[] pArgs)
    {
        final int tFirstX = 100;
        final int tFirstY = 100;
        final int tSecondX = 100;
        final int tSecondY = 200;
        final GetDateJFrame tFirstGetDateJFrame =
                    new GetDateJFrame("First", tFirstX, tFirstY);
        final GetDateJFrame tSecondGetDateJFrame =
                    new GetDateJFrame("Second", tSecondX, tSecondY);
    }
}
```

Figure 13.19   Stage G: using GetDateJFrame (twice) in the GetDateProg program.

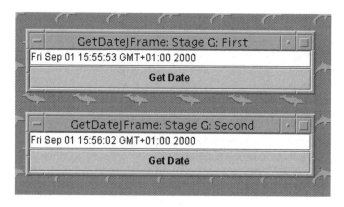

Figure 13.20   Stage G: two GetDateJFrame components are created.

(13.13) Stage H: getting a component to handle events

Having produced a class like JButtonListener, we usually have some code that creates an object of this class (e.g. tJButtonListener). This object handles the action events caused by an object of the GetDateJFrame class. So, usually, we are

```
// Stage H: a user interface that implements the ActionListener interface
// itself and creates a window listener (to handle window closing events).
// Barry Cornelius, 19 June 2000
import java.awt.event. ActionEvent;
import java.awt.event. ActionListener;
import java.awt.        BorderLayout;
import java.awt.        Container;
import java.util.       Date;
import javax.swing.     JButton;
import javax.swing.     JFrame;
import javax.swing.     JTextField;
public class GetDateJFrame implements ActionListener
{
    private JTextField iJTextField;
    public GetDateJFrame(final String pString, final int pX, final int pY)
    {
        final JFrame tJFrame =
                    new JFrame("GetDateJFrame: Stage H: " + pString);
        iJTextField = new JTextField("hello", 35);
        final JButton tJButton = new JButton("Get Date");
        tJButton.addActionListener(this);
        final Container tContentPane = tJFrame.getContentPane();
        tContentPane.add(iJTextField, BorderLayout.NORTH);
        tContentPane.add(tJButton,    BorderLayout.SOUTH);
        final ExitWindowListener tExitWindowListener =
                                        new ExitWindowListener();
        tJFrame.addWindowListener(tExitWindowListener);
        tJFrame.setDefaultCloseOperation(JFrame.DO_NOTHING_ON_CLOSE);
        tJFrame.setLocation(pX, pY);
        tJFrame.pack();
        tJFrame.setVisible(true);
    }
    public void actionPerformed(final ActionEvent pActionEvent)
    {
        final Date tDate = new Date();
        iJTextField.setText("" + tDate);
    }
}
```

Figure 13.21 Stage H: getting a component to handle its own events.

producing this class in order to create a single object of the class. Some people think that it is longwinded to have to do this in order to create just one object.

There are two alternative techniques that can be used. One of these techniques involves the use of an *anonymous class*, a topic which is not described in any detail in this book: for a brief introduction, see Curio 13.6. The other technique for avoiding the introduction of another class involves getting GetDateJFrame to handle its own events.

To do this, we need to achieve the following three tasks:

1. to say that GetDateJFrame implements the ActionListener interface;

2. to include a method called `actionPerformed` in the `GetDateJFrame` class;

3. to indicate that the object of the `GetDateJFrame` class is going to act as the listener for clicks on its button object.

In the listing of `GetDateJFrame` given in Figure 13.21, the first task is achieved by the following implements clause:

```
public class GetDateJFrame implements ActionListener
```

The second task is achieved because `GetDateJFrame` contains:

```
public void actionPerformed(final ActionEvent pActionEvent)
{
    final Date tDate = new Date();
    iJTextField.setText("" + tDate);
}
```

Note that the access to the `JTextField` field from the `actionPerformed` method is now a lot easier.

Finally, the third task can be achieved by `GetDateJFrame`'s constructor executing:

```
tJButton.addActionListener(this);
```

The `this` is a piece of magic. As explained in Curio 11.4, it is a way in which a class declaration can refer to the target. When it occurs in a constructor, it is a way of referring to the object that is being constructed. So the above statement arranges for the object being constructed to be responsible for listening for clicks on the `tJButton` component.

The new version of the `GetDateJFrame` class can be tested using the `GetDateProg` shown in Figure 13.19.

13.14 Using `ActionEvent` methods

Although the use of the `ActionListener` interface has been described for responding to a click on a `JButton` component, its use applies to any GUI component that generates an **action event**. For the Swing API, the other GUI components that generate action events are the other forms of buttons (that were mentioned in Section 13.3.4, i.e. `JToggleButton`, `JCheckBox`, `JRadioButton` and `JMenuItem`), `JComboBox`, `JFileChooser`, `JTextField` and `JPasswordField`.

If you look at the header for `actionPerformed`:

```
public void actionPerformed(ActionEvent pActionEvent);
```

you will see that, when it is called, some object (of the class `ActionEvent`) is passed as an argument to `actionPerformed`. This object contains details of what caused the action event to take place. The `actionPerformed` method can apply various methods to the `pActionEvent` object.

Two important methods are `getSource` and `getActionCommand`. The `getSource` function returns a pointer to the object that caused the action event, which might be a `JButton`, a `JTextField`, and so on.

So, suppose `GetDateJFrame`'s `actionPerformed` method (Figure 13.21) were altered to include:

```
Object tEventSource = pActionEvent.getSource();
JButton tEventButton = (JButton)tEventSource;
```

When the user clicks on the button, the value returned by `getSource` will be a pointer to the `JButton` object, i.e. `tEventButton` will point to the object that was pointed to by `tJButton` when `GetDateJFrame`'s constructor was being executed.

In a program where a listener object is a listener for only one GUI component, it is not necessary to include code that can be used to identify the source. However, if an object acts as a listener for several GUI components, `getSource` may be useful:

```
private JButton iFirstJButton;
private JButton iSecondJButton;
...
iFirstJButton = new JButton("first");
iFirstJButton.addActionListener(this);
iSecondJButton = new JButton("second");
iSecondJButton.addActionListener(this);
...
public void actionPerformed(final ActionEvent pActionEvent)
{
    final JButton tEventButton = (JButton)pActionEvent.getSource();
    if (tEventButton==iFirstJButton)
    ...
```

In order for this to work, the `actionPerformed` method needs to be able to refer to the reference variables that point to the buttons. When a component is acting as a listener for its own events (as shown above), this is easy to do: you can make the reference variables private fields of the class.

If this cannot easily be arranged, there are two alternative ways of identifying the source of an action event, both of which include the use of `getActionCommand` instead of `getSource`.

By default, for a button, `getActionCommand` will return (as a `String`) the label that is on the button. So, suppose we have set up two buttons using:

```
final JButton tFirstJButton = new JButton("first");
final JButton tSecondJButton = new JButton("second");
```

then the `actionPerformed` method can use:

```
public void actionPerformed(final ActionEvent pActionEvent)
{
    final String tCommand = pActionEvent.getActionCommand();
    if (tCommand.equals("first"))
    ...
```

If, for some reason, it is inappropriate to use the label, it is possible to use
setActionCommand to define your own string:

```
final JButton tAddJButton = new JButton("insert the person");
tAddJButton.setActionCommand("add");
tAddJButton.addActionListener(...);
final JButton tRemoveJButton = new JButton("delete the person");
tRemoveJButton.setActionCommand("remove");
tRemoveJButton.addActionListener(...);
```

Now the actionPerformed method can be coded using:

```
public void actionPerformed(final ActionEvent pActionEvent)
{
    final String tCommand = pActionEvent.getActionCommand();
    if (tCommand.equals("add"))
    ...
```

13.15 Providing a GUI for the I/O of a group of values

In the previous sections, we have seen how the JTextField, JButton and JFrame
components can be used to display information. Although these components can
also be used to provide a user interface for reading a single value into a program, for
anything more complicated than a single value, it will be useful to have something
more sophisticated.

We now look at how to provide a user interface for reading a value of the class
PersonImpl. We will need the user to supply a name, a date of birth, a phone
number and a height. For this, it will be best to provide a **form**. One possible form is
shown in Figure 13.22.

Figure 13.22 A form for use with the PersonImpl class.

To group things together in the shape of a form, it will be easiest to use the Box
class. There are more details about this class in the next section.

A button will be provided below the form: when the user clicks on the button, the
data in the various fields of the form will be combined to produce a value of the class
PersonImpl. To ensure that the user clicks on the button, it is best to use a window
that is a *dialog box*. This can be done using a JDialog object instead of a JFrame
object. We will look at this in more detail in later sections of this chapter.

Although a form can be used as part of a dialog box in order to provide a means
for inputting the details about a person, it could also be used on its own (i.e. not as

part of a dialog box) if we want to display the details about a person on the screen. We will use it for this purpose later.

(13.16) Stage A: introducing the `Box` and `JLabel` classes

The class Box (from the javax.swing package) allows a group of GUI components to be collected together, either as a horizontal row of components:

```
Box tBox = new Box(BoxLayout.X_AXIS);
```

or as a vertical column of components:

```
Box tBox = new Box(BoxLayout.Y_AXIS);
```

where the values X_AXIS and Y_AXIS are constants declared in the class BoxLayout (which is also in the javax.swing package). For more details about the possibilities of the Box and BoxLayout classes, look at $API/javax/swing/Box.html and at $API/javax/swing/BoxLayout.html.

Having created a Box object, GUI components can be added to the box one at a time:

```
tBox.add(tJTextField);
tBox.add(tJButton);
```

assuming that tJTextField and tJButton have already been assigned values.

We will usually want to **label** the textfields that appear in a form. This can be done using an object of the class JLabel. Suppose we want a textfield for inputting a person's name. A label for the textfield can be created by:

```
JLabel tNameJLabel = new JLabel("Name", SwingConstants.RIGHT);
```

where the value RIGHT ensures that the text of the label appears right-justified in the space that will be allocated for the label. The value RIGHT is a constant declared in the interface javax.swing.SwingConstants. There is more information about JLabel and SwingConstants at $API/javax/swing/JLabel.html and $API/javax/swing/SwingConstants.html.

So if we use:

```
JLabel tNameJLabel = new JLabel("Name", SwingConstants.RIGHT);
JTextField tNameJTextField = new JTextField(25);
Box tNameBox = new Box(BoxLayout.X_AXIS);
tNameBox.add(tNameJLabel);
tNameBox.add(tNameJTextField);
```

we have created a horizontal box containing two items: the first is a label with the string "Name" right-justified, and the second is a textfield that has 25 visible characters.

(13.17) Stage B: creating a form for a person's details

We now look at how the Box class can be used to produce a form for grouping together values that record the details about a person.

The form shown in Figure 13.22 has three rows of information. The full code to construct these rows is given in the constructor of the `PersonForm` class (given in Figure 13.23).

In the first row, there is a label and a textfield. These can be grouped together by using a horizontal `Box`. The statements given above that manipulate `tNameBox` can be used to create this row.

The second row is used for the date of birth: it also contains a label and a textfield. So a variable (called `tDateOfBirthBox`) can be manipulated in a similar way to `tNameBox`.

Just to be different, in the third row, there are two data items, a phone number and a height. So we can use a horizontal `Box` containing a label, a textfield, another label and another textfield. A variable called `tThirdRowBox` can be made to point to this `Box`.

To ensure that the labels (for the textfields) appear under one another, each label is given the same size using `javax.swing.JComponent`'s `setPreferredSize` method, e.g.:

```
tNameJLabel.setPreferredSize(tDimension);
```

```
// A class that can be used to create a form for a person
// Barry Cornelius, 19 June 2000
import javax.swing. Box;
import javax.swing. BoxLayout;
import java.awt.    Component;
import java.awt.    Dimension;
import javax.swing. JLabel;
import javax.swing. JTextField;
import javax.swing. SwingConstants;
public class PersonForm
{
    private JTextField iNameJTextField;
    private JTextField iDateOfBirthJTextField;
    private JTextField iPhoneNumberJTextField;
    private JTextField iHeightJTextField;
    private Box iBox;
    public PersonForm()
    {
        final Dimension tDimension = new Dimension(120, 20);
        // deal with the Name
        final JLabel tNameJLabel = new JLabel("Name", SwingConstants.RIGHT);
        tNameJLabel.setPreferredSize(tDimension);
        iNameJTextField = new JTextField(25);
        // deal with the NameBox
        final Box tNameBox = new Box(BoxLayout.X_AXIS);
        tNameBox.add(tNameJLabel);
        tNameBox.add(iNameJTextField);
```

Figure 13.23 *Continues on the next page.*

```
        // deal with the DateOfBirth
        final JLabel tDateOfBirthJLabel =
                        new JLabel("DateOfBirth", SwingConstants.RIGHT);
        tDateOfBirthJLabel.setPreferredSize(tDimension);
        iDateOfBirthJTextField = new JTextField(15);
        // deal with the DateOfBirthBox
        final Box tDateOfBirthBox = new Box(BoxLayout.X_AXIS);
        tDateOfBirthBox.add(tDateOfBirthJLabel);
        tDateOfBirthBox.add(iDateOfBirthJTextField);
        // deal with the PhoneNumber
        final JLabel tPhoneNumberJLabel =
                        new JLabel("PhoneNumber", SwingConstants.RIGHT);
        tPhoneNumberJLabel.setPreferredSize(tDimension);
        iPhoneNumberJTextField = new JTextField(10);
        // deal with the Height
        final JLabel tHeightJLabel = new JLabel("Height", SwingConstants.RIGHT);
        tHeightJLabel.setPreferredSize(tDimension);
        iHeightJTextField = new JTextField(5);
        // deal with the ThirdRowBox
        final Box tThirdRowBox = new Box(BoxLayout.X_AXIS);
        tThirdRowBox.add(tPhoneNumberJLabel);
        tThirdRowBox.add(iPhoneNumberJTextField);
        tThirdRowBox.add(tHeightJLabel);
        tThirdRowBox.add(iHeightJTextField);
        // now create the form
        iBox = new Box(BoxLayout.Y_AXIS);
        iBox.add(tNameBox);
        iBox.add(tDateOfBirthBox);
        iBox.add(tThirdRowBox);
    }
    public Component getGUI()
    {
        return iBox;
    }
    public Person getPerson()
    {
        return new PersonImpl(iNameJTextField.getText() +
                        "%" + iDateOfBirthJTextField.getText() +
                        "%" + iPhoneNumberJTextField.getText() +
                        "%" + iHeightJTextField.getText());
    }
    public void setPerson(final Person pPerson)
    {
        iNameJTextField.setText(pPerson.getName());
        iDateOfBirthJTextField.setText(pPerson.getDateOfBirth().toString());
        iPhoneNumberJTextField.setText(pPerson.getPhoneNumber());
        iHeightJTextField.setText("" + pPerson.getHeight());
    }
}
```

Figure 13.23   A class that can be used to create a form for a person.

The parameter of this method is a reference to an object of the class `java.awt.Dimension`. The code of `PersonForm`'s constructor sets up `tDimension` using:

```
Dimension tDimension = new Dimension(120, 20);
```

This refers to an area that is 120 pixels wide and 20 pixels high.

In order to construct the form, the three `Box`es representing the three rows can be put into a vertical `Box`. In the following code, `iBox` is a `Box` variable:

```
iBox = new Box(BoxLayout.Y_AXIS);
iBox.add(tNameBox);
iBox.add(tDateOfBirthBox);
iBox.add(tThirdRowBox);
```

In Section 13.12, the `GetDateJFrame`'s constructor not only builds a `JFrame` but also uses `setVisible` in order to display the GUI component. However, we want to use a `PersonForm` object in a number of different ways, e.g. as part of a dialog box for inputting a person, or on its own for displaying the details about a person.

So we will just get `PersonForm`'s constructor to build a `Box` but not display it. In fact, it makes a private variable called `iBox` point to this `Box`. In order for this to be accessible to a client that wants to use this form, a `getGUI` method is provided.

The obvious result type of the `getGUI` method is the type `Box`. However, instead, `Component` (from the `java.awt` package) has been used.

It is possible to use a `Box` value in the return statement (when the result type is `Component`) because a `Box` value is assignment compatible with `Component` (because `Box` is a subclass of `Component`).

So, why choose `Component` rather than `Box`? The use of the `Box` class for representing the form is an internal design decision of the `PersonForm` class. If we use a result type of `Component`, then, even though the value that is returned is actually a `Box` object, the client can only use it as if it were a `Component` object. By doing this, the designer of the `PersonForm` class can instead, in the future, use some other representation (e.g. a `JPanel`) and the code of the client would not need to be altered. See Curio 13.9.

So, after a client has executed:

```
PersonForm tPersonForm = new PersonForm();
```

it can get a pointer to the form that the constructor creates by executing:

```
Component tPersonFormGUI = tPersonForm.getGUI();
```

There are two main uses of `tPersonForm` and `tPersonFormGUI`:

1. to display the details about a person in a window on the screen;

2. to be used as part of a dialog box that allows a user to input the details of a person.

We will look at these two possibilities in the remaining sections of this chapter.

13.18 Stage C: using `PersonForm` to display a person

The previous section describes how we can produce a GUI component that is a form containing a person's details:

```
PersonForm tPersonForm = new PersonForm();
Component tPersonFormGUI = tPersonForm.getGUI();
```

The `PersonForm`'s `setPerson` can be used to put the details of a particular person into the form:

```
tPersonForm.setPerson(tPerson);
```

And the GUI component, i.e. `tPersonFormGUI`, can be used like any other GUI component (such as an object that is a `JButton` or a `JTextField`), e.g.:

```
tContentPane.add(tPersonFormGUI, BorderLayout.CENTER);
```

where `tContentPane` has been set up to point to the content pane of some window.

A simple program that demonstrates the use of `PersonForm` to display a person's details is given in Figure 13.24. Figure 13.25 shows what happens: after the user has typed in the details of a person in the terminal screen, these details are output in the form.

13.19 Stage D: using `PersonForm` as part of a dialog box

Earlier, we saw that the Swing API provides many classes for representing a window and we chose to create a `JFrame` object to represent a window. If you want to represent a dialog box, then it is best to use `JDialog` (or one of its subclasses). In order to use `JDialog`, you must already have created a window and, when the dialog box is made visible, it will appear in front of that window.

Sometimes dialog boxes appear that force a response from the user: he/she is unable to do anything else until the response is given. Such a dialog box is called a **modal dialog box**. You can construct a modal dialog box by passing the value *true* as the third argument of a `JDialog` constructor:

```
final JFrame tJFrame = new JFrame("master window");
final JDialog tJDialog = new JDialog(tJFrame, "dialog box window", true);
```

The `JDialog` class instance creation expression creates a `JDialog` object that represents a dialog box which:

- is a child window of the window represented by `tJFrame`;
- has the title `"dialog box window"` in its title bar;
- is modal.

```
// A program that uses a PersonForm to display the details about a person.
// Barry Cornelius, 19 June 2000
import java.awt.    BorderLayout;
import java.io.     BufferedReader;
import java.awt.    Component;
import java.awt.    Container;
import java.io.     InputStreamReader;
import java.io.     IOException;
import javax.swing. JFrame;
public class PersonOutputProg
{
    public static void main(final String[] pArgs) throws IOException
    {
        final PersonForm tPersonForm = new PersonForm();
        final Component tPersonFormGUI = tPersonForm.getGUI();
        final JFrame tJFrame = new JFrame("PersonOutputProg");
        final Container tContentPane = tJFrame.getContentPane();
        tContentPane.add(tPersonFormGUI, BorderLayout.CENTER);
        final ExitWindowListener tExitWindowListener = new ExitWindowListener();
        tJFrame.addWindowListener(tExitWindowListener);
        tJFrame.pack();
        tJFrame.setVisible(true);
        final BufferedReader tKeyboard =
                    new BufferedReader(new InputStreamReader(System.in));
        System.out.println("Type in a person using the format " +
                        "Name%DateOfBirth%PhoneNumber%Height");
        final String tLine = tKeyboard.readLine();
        final Person tPerson = new PersonImpl(tLine);
        System.out.println("The person is: " + tPerson);
        tPersonForm.setPerson(tPerson);
    }
}
```

Figure 13.24 Using a `PersonForm` to display the details about a person.

We will now produce a class called `PersonInputDialog` that can be used to display a dialog box for inputting the details about a person. The complete code of the class is given in Figure 13.26.

One GUI component of the dialog box is the form:

```
iPersonForm = new PersonForm();
final Component tPersonFormGUI = iPersonForm.getGUI();
```

The other component is a button:

```
final JButton tJButton = new JButton("OK");
```

and we make the `PersonInputDialog` object being constructed by this constructor a listener for clicks on this button by:

```
tJButton.addActionListener(this);
```

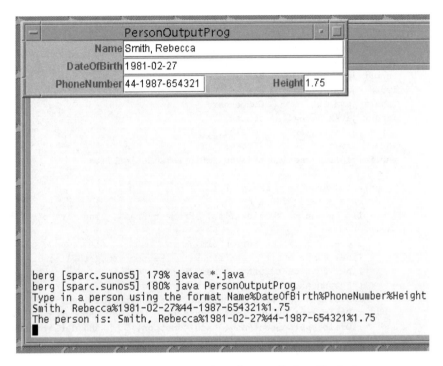

Figure 13.25   The details typed in the terminal window are displayed in the form.

Having created two Java objects to represent a form and a button, the constructor moves on to use these when creating a dialog box. First, it executes:

```
iJDialog = new JDialog(pJFrame, "PersonInputDialog", true);
```

where pJFrame, a pointer to the parent window, is a value passed as an argument to the constructor.

It then adds the form and the button to the dialog box. It could use:

```
final Container tContentPane = iJDialog.getContentPane();
tContentPane.add(tPersonFormGUI, BorderLayout.CENTER);
tContentPane.add(tJButton,       BorderLayout.SOUTH);
```

but instead it abbreviates this to:

```
iJDialog.getContentPane().add(tPersonFormGUI, BorderLayout.CENTER);
iJDialog.getContentPane().add(tJButton,       BorderLayout.SOUTH);
```

The dialog box is then displayed on the screen using:

```
iJDialog.setLocation(pX, pY);
iJDialog.pack();
iJDialog.setVisible(true);
```

where pX and pY are values passed as arguments to the constructor.

```
// A class that presents a dialog box for inputting values about a person.
// Barry Cornelius, 19 June 2000
import java.awt.event. ActionEvent;
import java.awt.event. ActionListener;
import java.awt.        BorderLayout;
import javax.swing.     Box;
import java.awt.        Component;
import javax.swing.     JButton;
import javax.swing.     JDialog;
import javax.swing.     JFrame;
public class PersonInputDialog implements ActionListener
{
    private PersonForm iPersonForm;
    private JDialog iJDialog;
    public PersonInputDialog(final JFrame pJFrame, final int pX, final int pY)
    {
        iPersonForm = new PersonForm();
        final Component tPersonFormGUI = iPersonForm.getGUI();
        final JButton tJButton = new JButton("OK");
        tJButton.addActionListener(this);
        iJDialog = new JDialog(pJFrame, "PersonInputDialog", true);
        iJDialog.getContentPane().add(tPersonFormGUI, BorderLayout.CENTER);
        iJDialog.getContentPane().add(tJButton,        BorderLayout.SOUTH);
        iJDialog.setLocation(pX, pY);
        iJDialog.pack();
        iJDialog.setVisible(true);
    }
    public void actionPerformed(final ActionEvent pActionEvent)
    {
        iJDialog.setVisible(false);
        iJDialog.dispose();
    }
    public Person getPerson()
    {
        return iPersonForm.getPerson();
    }
}
```

Figure 13.26   A class that presents a dialog box for inputting values about a person.

All of this code is executed when a client uses `PersonInputDialog`'s constructor. An example of a call of this constructor is:

```
PersonInputDialog tPersonInputDialog =
    new PersonInputDialog(tJFrame, 100, 200);
```

Because the constructor displays a modal dialog box, the program's execution will
then pause. The user completes the form and clicks on the button. As the object being
constructed has been registered as a listener for this button, its `actionPerformed`
method will get executed when the button gets clicked. The `actionPerformed`
method removes the dialog box from the screen, and then disposes of the resources
that `iJDialog` has acquired.

A program that uses the `PersonInputDialog` constructor is shown in Figure 13.27. First, the program creates a `JFrame` object (that is pointed to by `tJFrame`) and makes that visible. Then it uses `PersonInputDialog`'s constructor to display a dialog box:

```
PersonInputDialog tPersonInputDialog =
      new PersonInputDialog(tJFrame, tJDialogX, tJDialogY);
```

Note that `tJFrame` and two `int` constants (`tJDialogX` and `tJDialogY`) are passed as arguments to this constructor.

```
// A program that uses PersonInputDialog twice and compares the two people.
// Barry Cornelius, 19 June 2000
import java.awt.       BorderLayout;
import javax.swing. JFrame;
import javax.swing. JTextArea;
public class PersonInputDialogProg
{
   public static void main(final String[] pArgs)
   {
      final int tJFrameX = 100;
      final int tJFrameY = 100;
      final int tJDialogX = 100;
      final int tJDialogY = 200;
      final JFrame tJFrame = new JFrame("PersonInputDialogProg");
      final JTextArea tJTextArea = new JTextArea(3, 40);
      tJFrame.getContentPane().add(tJTextArea, BorderLayout.CENTER);
      final ExitWindowListener tExitWindowListener =
                                    new ExitWindowListener();
      tJFrame.addWindowListener(tExitWindowListener);
      tJFrame.setDefaultCloseOperation(JFrame.DO_NOTHING_ON_CLOSE);
      tJFrame.setLocation(tJFrameX, tJFrameY);
      tJFrame.pack();
      tJFrame.setVisible(true);
      PersonInputDialog tPersonInputDialog =
             new PersonInputDialog(tJFrame, tJDialogX, tJDialogY);
      final Person tFirstPerson = tPersonInputDialog.getPerson();
      tJTextArea.append("" + tFirstPerson);
      tPersonInputDialog =
             new PersonInputDialog(tJFrame, tJDialogX, tJDialogY);
      final Person tSecondPerson = tPersonInputDialog.getPerson();
      tJTextArea.append("\n" + tSecondPerson);
      tJTextArea.append("\n" + "same person is " +
                       tFirstPerson.equals(tSecondPerson));
   }
}
```

Figure 13.27   Using `PersonInputDialog` twice and comparing the two people.

When the user clicks on the button, the dialog box automatically disappears and the program proceeds to create a `PersonImpl` object for the first person by the call:

```
final Person tFirstPerson = tPersonInputDialog.getPerson();
```

The program then displays another dialog box, containing another form and button, in order to get the details about a second person. These details are stored in the `PersonImpl` object that is pointed to by `tSecondPerson`.

The program also adds a `JTextArea` to its `JFrame` object. A `JTextArea` is similar to a `JTextField` except that a `JTextArea` allows several lines of output to be displayed. The class is documented at **$API/javax/swing/JTextArea.html**. The `JTextArea` constructor that is used in the `PersonInputDialogProg` is:

```
final JTextArea tJTextArea = new JTextArea(3, 40);
```

This permits three lines of up to 40 characters. On these three lines, the program outputs the values of `tFirstPerson`, `tSecondPerson` and either the value *true* or the value *false* depending on whether the two people are the same person. Remember, the `equals` method for the `PersonImpl` class only compares the names of the two people.

Figure 13.28 shows what gets displayed when the user has already filled in the form for the first person and is now part way through filling in the form for the second person.

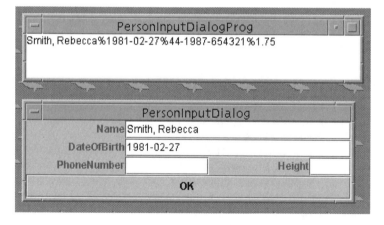

Figure 13.28   The screen when the user has filled in part of the second form.

Tips for programming and debugging

13.1   If a variable (e.g. `iBox`) is a field of a class, and you want to assign a value to it from a constructor or a method, do not fall into the trap of declaring it again in the constructor or method.

For example, consider the `PersonForm` class shown in Figure 13.23. The first draft of this class contained:

```
...
private Box iBox;
public PersonForm()
{
    ...
    Box iBox = new Box(BoxLayout.Y_AXIS);
    ...
}
...
public Component getGUI()
{
    return iBox;
}
...
```

Although this is syntactically valid, it will not do what is intended. When the program later calls `getGUI`, it will crash with a `NullPointerException` exception when it tries to access the object being pointed to by the field `iBox` (because `iBox` still has the value `null`, its default initial value). The error is caused by the redeclaration of `iBox` within `PersonForm`'s constructor. The code should have been:

```
...
private Box iBox;
public PersonForm()
{
    ...
    iBox = new Box(BoxLayout.Y_AXIS);
    ...
```

13.2 In the text of this chapter, a call like:

```
tContentPane.add(tJButton, BorderLayout.CENTER);
```

is used to add a component to a `BorderLayout` component. You can also do this by using:

```
tContentPane.add("Center", tJButton);
```

or by using:

```
tContentPane.add(tJButton, "Center");
```

However, both of these calls will not work if you misspell the string indicating the position. For the above example, you might accidentally spell `"Center"` as `"center"`, or a person from the UK (and elsewhere?) might spell `"Center"` as `"Centre"` (which is the British spelling of the word). If you do not get the string exactly right, your code will not do what you want it to do but it fails quietly, i.e. no error message is given. For these reasons, it is better to use:

```
tContentPane.add(tJButton, BorderLayout.CENTER);
```

Since CENTER is the name of a constant from the class java.awt.BorderLayout, if you misspell CENTER or spell it with lower-case letters, your program will not compile.

Curios, controversies and cover-ups

13.1 In their book *Programming with JFC* [54], Scott Weiner and Stephen Asbury say:

> A group of JavaSoft engineers came up with the name **Swing** while they were developing a demo to show off the features of their new UI component set at the 1997 JavaOne conference. The demo showed the graphical capabilities of the library and made extensive use of music, featuring the sound capabilities for this UI library. They thought that relating their Java library with the type of music played by Duke Ellington, Swing, was a great tie-in with the Java mascot, **Duke**. The name stuck.

13.2 Unfortunately, during the various beta releases of the JFC, the position of the Swing API has moved. This has been inconvenient for those developing code (or books) that use this API. Although it has previously resided at com.sun.java.swing and later at java.awt.swing, in the Java 2 Platform the Swing API is in the javax.swing package.

13.3 Even though the javax packages usually contain **extensions**, i.e. packages that are not part of the Core APIs, Sun say that the javax.swing package is part of the Core APIs.

13.4 If you have a JFrame object, you can use methods called getToolkit and getScreenSize in order to get some information about the size of the screen being used by your computer. So, if you want a window to be centred on the screen, but indented from the sides of the screen by 100 pixels on all four sides of the window, you could use the following code. It uses the Dimension and Toolkit classes from the java.awt package.

```
final JFrame tJFrame = new JFrame("some title");
tJFrame.setLocation(100, 100);
final Toolkit tToolkit = tJFrame.getToolkit();
final Dimension tDimension = tToolkit.getScreenSize();
tJFrame.setSize(tDimension.width - 200, tDimension.height - 200);
```

13.5 When a JTextField appears on a screen, by default its contents can be altered by the user of the program. This causes an action event to occur, and you can register an action listener on the JTextField if you want to know when this happens. Alternatively, a program can indicate that the contents of a JTextField are not to be changed. It can be do this using the setEditable method (that was mentioned in Figure 13.13):

```
tJTextField.setEditable(false);
```

13.6   If you only ever want to create a single instance of a class and want to pass it as an argument to some method, it may be possible to use an **anonymous class**. For example, the program shown in Figure 13.15 consists of the program class (GetDateProg) and the class JButtonListener, and the program class just creates one instance of JButtonListener:

```
final JButton tJButton = new JButton("Get Date");
final JButtonListener tJButtonListener =
                new JButtonListener(tJTextField);
tJButton.addActionListener(tJButtonListener);
```

Instead of producing the class JButtonListener, you can use an anonymous class:

```
final JButton tJButton = new JButton("Get Date");
tJButton.addActionListener(
    new ActionListener()
    {
        public void actionPerformed(final ActionEvent pActionEvent)
        {
            final Date tDate = new Date();
            tJTextField.setText("" + tDate);
        }
    }
);
```

If you use javac to compile this version of the GetDateProg program, it will create two .class files: as usual, the file GetDateProg.class contains the bytecodes of the program class whereas the file GetDateProg$1.class contains the bytecodes of the anonymous class.

13.7   It is common for a program to want to terminate when the user of the program closes any of the windows that have been created by the program. This is the reason why the GetDateProg program of Section 13.11 has an ExitWindowListener object:

```
final ExitWindowListener tExitWindowListener =
                                new ExitWindowListener();
tJFrame.addWindowListener(tExitWindowListener);
tJFrame.setDefaultCloseOperation(JFrame.DO_NOTHING_ON_CLOSE);
```

In versions of Java from the Java 2 Platform v 1.3 onwards, the class JFrame has a constant called EXIT_ON_CLOSE. So there is then no need for an ExitWindowListener class, and the above three statements can be replaced by:

```
tJFrame.setDefaultCloseOperation(JFrame.EXIT_ON_CLOSE);
```

13.8   Although the class `JPanel` from the `javax.swing` package (and `Panel` from `java.awt`) can be used to group GUI components together, if you want to have more control over how they appear on the screen, it is easier to use one or more `Box`es (as was explained in Section 13.17). And, although the classes `GridLayout` and `GridBagLayout` (from `java.awt`) can also be used to form a grid of GUI components, it is often easier to use `Box` objects.

13.9   In Section 13.17, it was claimed that, by returning a value of type `Component`, 'the client can only use it as if it were a `Component` object'. This is untrue. If the person developing the client is aware that the value being returned is actually of type `Box`, he/she can use a cast to convert the object into a `Box` object, as in:

```
Box tBox = (Box)(tPersonForm.getGUI());
```

Exercises

13.1   Draw a class diagram for the `GetDateProg` program shown in Figure 13.19 and Figure 13.18.

13.2   Write a Java program called `BasicCalculator` that can be used for a primitive calculator. The program should display three textfields and one button. The button should have the label *add*. The user of the program should enter integers in the first two textfields and, when he/she clicks the button, the program should put the sum of the two integers in the third textfield.

Here are some points about this exericse:

● You can obtain the text that is in a textfield by applying the `getText` method to the textfield, i.e. the call:

```
iJTextField.getText()
```

(where `iJTextField` is a `JTextField`) returns a `String`.

● You will also have to use `parseInt` to convert the `String` that contains digits into a value of type `int`.

● You can convert an `int` into a `String` by using a class method of `java.lang.Integer` called `toString`. So if `tValue` is an `int`, the following call produces a `String`:

```
Integer.toString(tValue)
```

Alternatively, you can use:

```
"" + tValue
```

● Do not bother to handle window events: just use Ctrl/C to abort the execution of your program.

13.3   When you have got the `BasicCalculator` program of Exercise 13.2 working, modify it so that there are now two buttons, one for addition and the other for subtraction.

Note that `BorderLayout` divides a pane into five areas which is convenient because you now have three textfields and two buttons. If you use the getActionCommand method mentioned in Section 13.14, you will only need one listener object. However, you will need to register this object as a listener for both buttons.

13.4 From the program produced as a solution for Exercise 13.3, move on to produce a program called Calculator that is more sophisticated.

It should provide 15 JButtons for the 15 keys of the calculator that have labels 0, 1, ... 9, +, -, *, / and =. It should also provide a JTextField which is set to the result of the calculation whenever the = button is clicked. The program should terminate when the window of the GUI is closed.

13.5 In Exercise 11.5, you produced an interface called Angle and a class called AngleImpl. Now produce a class called AngleForm that can be used to create a form for an angle.

The constructor for the class should be responsible for creating the form. It should use a horizontal box containing four JTextFields, one each for the degrees, minutes, seconds and direction values. The class should also provide methods called getGUI, getAngle and setAngle. The getGUI method returns a pointer to this box; the getAngle method returns the Angle value represented by the contents of the four textfields; and the setAngle method is used to set these textfields to the values that are appropriate for the Angle value passed as an argument to setAngle.

Write a program called AngleFormProg to test this class.

13.6 In Exercise 12.10, you produced an interface called Position and a class called PositionImpl. Now produce a class called PositionForm that can be used to create a form for a position.

The PositionForm class should include the declaration of two private fields of type AngleForm, one to represent the form for the longitude and the other to represent a form for the latitude.

PositionForm's constructor should use two AngleForm constructors to assign values to these two fields. It should then use a vertical Box to create a form. In one component of this Box, it should put the longitude's Box and in the other the latitude's Box. Hint: an AngleForm object has a getGUI method that can be used to get at its Box.

The PositionForm class should also provide methods called getGUI, getPosition and setPosition. The getGUI method returns a pointer to this box; the getPosition method returns the Position value represented by the two angles; and the setPosition method is used to set these angles to the values that are appropriate for the Position value passed as an argument to setPosition.

Write a program called PositionFormProg to test this class.

13.7 Produce a class called PositionInputDialog that can be used to present a dialog box for inputting a value that is a Position value.

The constructor for the class should be responsible for creating the dialog box. The pane of the dialog box should contain a PositionForm and a JButton. The class should also provide methods called actionPerformed and getPosition. The actionPerformed method is used to listen for clicks on the JButton object; and the getPosition method returns the Position value represented by the PositionForm object.

Modify your solution to Exercise 12.10 so that each of the three vertices of the triangle is read in by presenting a dialog box for each one in turn. Also get the program to add a JTextArea to its JFrame and arrange for the output of the grid to be sent to this textarea (instead of to System.out).

13.8   In Exercise 11.3 and Exercise 12.9, you produced interfaces and classes called ISBN, ISBNImpl, Book and BookImpl. Now produce a class called BookForm that can be used to create a form for a book.

The constructor for the class should be responsible for creating the form. It should use a vertical box containing four JTextFields, one each for the title, author, year and ISBN. The class should also provide methods called getGUI, getBook and setBook. The getGUI method returns a pointer to this box; the getBook method returns the Book value represented by the contents of the four textfields; and the setBook method is used to set these textfields to the values that are appropriate for the Book value passed as an argument to setBook.

Also, produce a class called BookInputDialog that can be used to present a dialog box for inputting a value that is a Book value.

The constructor for the class should be responsible for creating the dialog box. The pane of the dialog box should contain a BookForm and a JButton. The class should also provide methods called actionPerformed and getBook. The actionPerformed method is used to listen for clicks on the JButton object; and the getBook method returns the Book value represented by the BookForm object.

Write a program called BookInputDialogProg to test this class.

13.9   The JComponent class (from the package javax.swing) has the method:

```
public void setToolTipText(String pString);
```

This method registers the string to be used as a **tool tip**. This is the text that is displayed if a user leaves the mouse over a component.

The JComponent class also has the methods:

```
public void setBackground(Color pColor);
public void setForeground(Color pColor);
```

that change the background and the foreground colours of a component to the colour that is passed as an argument. The possible values for the Color argument are defined at $API/java/awt/Color.html.

Modify one of the programs that you have written to use these methods.

13.10   The JPasswordField class is like the JTextField class except that it can be used to hide the characters that are typed. The class has the method:

```
public void setEchoChar(char pChar);
```

This method is used to set the character that is echoed each time the user types a character.

Write a program that uses this class.

Chapter 14

Manipulating collections: lists, queues and stacks

Besides having an API for GUIs, another attraction of Java is that it has a comprehensive API for representing collections of values. This API, which was new with the Java 2 Platform, is known as the Collections API. It allows the representation of real-world objects that are *lists*, *sets* or *maps*. This chapter starts by briefly distinguishing between each of these, and indicates when you might use each of them. Full details about sets and maps are given in Chapter 17. The remainder of this chapter looks at lists.

We will see that a *list* should be used when we wish to retain full control over the order of the elements of a collection, or when we want the collection to be able to store duplicates as separate elements. An example of a collection where a list could be used is the collection of messages in a mailbox.

The chapter looks at the Collections API's `List` interface and at the two classes (provided by the API) that implement this interface: they are `ArrayList` and `LinkedList`. The chapter discusses how to choose between these two implementations.

Often we will use a list in a restrained fashion: we will perform the transactions only at the ends of the list. So the chapter also looks at two specific kinds of list called *queue*s and *stacks*.

14.1 Representing a collection of values

Although we have an interface–class to represent a person, the programs that we have written that use this interface–class are not very interesting: they just have one or two variables each of which is made to refer to a person. Although handling up to five people would be possible, the code would get horrendous if it were necessary to represent lots of people. So, how are we to represent a large group of people in a Java program, or, to put it more generally, how do we represent a collection of values?

We will find that we often want to write a program that manipulates a collection of values. Examples are:

- a collection of CDs;
- a queue of people;
- the list of messages in a mailbox;
- the entries of a phone directory.

In other programming languages, two constructs are provided in the language to represent a collection of values: an array and a pointer. Although Java has constructs which are equivalent to these, we will not look at them just yet for two reasons:

- it is very easy to get things wrong when you use an array or when you use pointers;
- we will want to represent more abstract ideas, like queues, lists and sets, and we will have to do a lot of work to represent these ideas if we use arrays/pointers.

At this point, in a book/course that teaches programming, many of the books/courses get heavily involved in looking at how collections like queues, lists and sets can be realized using arrays and/or pointers. Effectively, each book/course produces its own set of methods for handling the various kind of collections. All this duplication of effort ought to be unnecessary.

When we looked at producing a graphical user interface, we did not look at the problems of:

- how to draw the rectangle that forms the outline of a window;
- how to write the text of a label in the middle of a button;
- how to work out when someone has clicked a button;

and so on. We found that some clever guys had already done the hard work, and that they had provided an API for us to use.

So, although with earlier programming languages, programmers had to *roll their own* set of methods to handle the likes of queues, lists and sets, more recently, language designers have realized the benefits of providing these. At the point when the programming language C++ was being standardized, a set of classes called the **Standard Template Library** (**STL**) was added to C++. And, with the release of the Java 2 Platform, Java now has an API called the **Collections API**.

In an article entitled 'Get started with the Java Collections Framework' ([5]), Dan Becker writes:

> ...the Collections framework is worth your effort and will benefit your programming in many ways. Three big benefits come immediately to mind:
>
> - It dramatically increases the readability of your collections by providing a standard set of interfaces to be used by many programmers in many applications.
> - It makes your code more flexible by allowing you to pass and return interfaces instead of concrete classes, generalizing your code rather than locking it down.
> - It offers many specific implementations of the interfaces, allowing you to choose the collection that is most fitting and offers the highest performance for your needs.
>
> And that's just for starters.

Before looking at the details of any specific interfaces and classes, we will first look at the overall design of the Collections API.

14.2 An introduction to the Collections API

The designers of the Collections API have decided that there are three main ways in which we will want to represent a collection of values:

- as a **list** – a sequence of values that are ordered: there may be duplicates;
- as a **set** – each value appears only once: there are no duplicates;
- as a **map** – there is a mapping from keys to values: the keys are unique.

They have provided interfaces called `List`, `Set` and `Map` that define the methods that can be applied to objects that are lists, sets and maps. See Figure 14.1.

One of the benefits of using a `List` is that it allows duplicates, i.e. it allows the same value to appear more than once in the collection. This may be important. For example, if you are representing a collection of CDs, it may be that you have the same CD more than once. Or it may be that you are some kind of collector; perhaps you collect beermats (also known as dripmats). In this case, you will often have duplicates because these allow you the possibility of swopping one of your duplicates with another collector.

The other benefit of using a `List` is that it allows values to be ordered in any way you like. For example, suppose you want to represent a mailbox as a collection of messages. The user might want to add a message to this mailbox at some particular position in the mailbox, or they might want to delete a particular message from the mailbox. Or, if you have a queue of people, you will want insertions to be made at the tail of the queue whereas deletions are to be made at the head of the queue. For both of these examples, a `List` could be used.

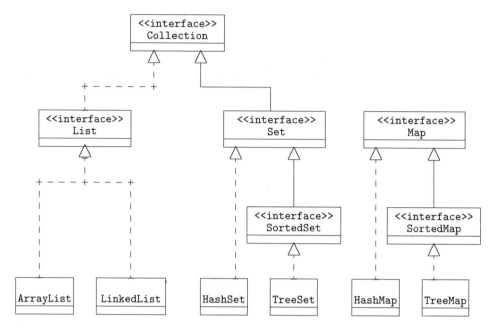

Figure 14.1   Part of the class hierarchy of the Collections API.

For the List interface, the API provides two classes that implement the interface. They are called ArrayList and LinkedList. The class ArrayList should be used if you want to make random accesses to the values of a collection, e.g. for a collection of messages in a mailbox, you will want to access each individual message: you might want to access the fifth message, then the second, then the seventh, and so on. This is a typical situation in which an ArrayList would be used.

The other class that implements the List interface is called LinkedList. This should be considered if you want to make frequent insertions and deletions at the beginning of a list. If these sort of insertions/deletions dominate the activities that are performed on a List, then a LinkedList should be considered (instead of an ArrayList). For more details about how to make the decision between using an ArrayList and a LinkedList, see Section 14.3.6.

However, if your collection has no duplicates or you do not want such flexibility about ordering, you may want to consider representing the collection using a Set. For the Set interface, a class called HashSet is provided. This gives a fast implementation of:

- adding new elements to a set;

- removing elements from a set;

- seeing whether a set contains a particular value.

Unlike the List, it makes no sense to want to control the order in which values are stored in a Set. However, it may be that the values being added to a Set are naturally ordered in some way. This is not an ordering that is as flexible as that for a List but is an ordering that is based on comparing the values of the collection.

For example, for a set of strings, the collection may be ordered in alphabetical order; for a set of people, the collection may be ordered by alphabetical order of the name field of each person; and so on.

For this kind of collection, the designers of the Collections API have provided a *subinterface* of Set called `SortedSet`, and a class called `TreeSet` that implements the `SortedSet` interface. For an object that is of the `TreeSet` class, it is possible:

- to find the first element;
- to iterate through the elements which gives each of the values in turn;

where the order depends on the sorting that has been chosen.

Finally, for some collections, a particular part of each value in the collection in some way identifies the value: it is called the *key*. The distinguishing feature of the `Map` interface is that it permits us to represent a mapping from keys to values. It could be used to represent a dictionary, a mapping from words to meanings. Or a database that, given a person's name, delivers the personal details of that person.

With the database, it may not be important for the values to be ordered: we may have no requirement to go through the thousands of people in the database in some order. Instead, we just want the values of the collection to be stored as efficiently as possible. For such a collection, the Collections API provides a class called `HashMap` (that implements the `Map` interface).

However, in the case of the dictionary, we may want the values of the collection to be sorted by the order of the words, as this will allow us easily to output the dictionary. There is a subinterface of the `Map` interface called `SortedMap`, and a class called `TreeMap` that implements this interface.

The preceding paragraphs summarize the overall design of a large part of the Collections API, and also briefly indicates the situations in which you might use the various interfaces and classes. `Set`s and `Map`s will be covered in Chapter 17: in this chapter, we will be looking at `List`s.

14.3 Representing lists

14.3.1 `List`, `ArrayList` and `LinkedList`

A **list** is an ordered collection of **element**s, where each element is a pointer to some object. You can visualize a list with four elements like this:

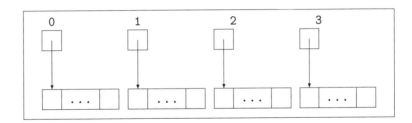

Some of the methods that can be applied to a `List` are shown in Figure 14.2. A full list of the methods is given at $API/java/util/List.html.

The elements of a list that has n elements are numbered from 0 to $n-1$. The unchecked exception called `IndexOutOfBoundsException` will occur if the value of `pIndex` is:

- outside this range when using the `get`, `remove` and `set` methods;
- outside the range 0 to n when using the `add` method.

....

```
public void add(Object pValue);
public void add(int pIndex, Object pValue);
```

Adds a new element to the target list. The element is assigned the value `pValue`, a pointer to some object. If `pIndex` is given, the element is inserted at position `pIndex`; otherwise, it is inserted after the last element of the target list. See Curio 14.1.

```
public boolean contains(Object pValue);
```

Returns the value *true* if and only if the target list contains an object having a value which `equals` that of the object pointed to by `pValue`.

```
public boolean equals(Object pList);
```

Returns the value *true* if and only if the objects of the target list and the list `pList` contain the same values in the same order.

```
public Object get(int pIndex);
```

Returns a pointer to the object that is at position `pIndex` of the target list.

```
public int indexOf(Object pValue);
```

Returns the position of the first object of the target list having a value which `equals` that of the object pointed to by `pValue`. If there is no such an object, -1 is returned; otherwise, for a list that has n elements, a value in the range 0 to $n-1$ is returned.

```
public boolean isEmpty();
```

Returns the value *true* if and only if the target list does not have any elements.

```
public Iterator iterator();
```

Returns an iterator over the elements of the target list that retains their ordering.

```
public int lastIndexOf(Object pValue);
```

Returns the position of the last object of the target list having a value which `equals` that of the object pointed to by `pValue`. If there is no such an object, -1 is returned; otherwise, for a list that has n elements, a value in the range 0 to $n-1$ is returned.

```
public boolean remove(Object pValue);
```

Removes from the target list the first object having a value which `equals` that of `pValue` (if such an object exists). Returns the value *true* if and only if it exists.

```
public Object remove(int pIndex);
```

Removes the element at position `pIndex` from the target list. Returns a pointer to the object of the element that was removed.

```
public Object set(int pIndex, Object pValue);
```

Changes the element at position `pIndex` of the target list so that it now points to the object pointed to by `pValue`. Returns a pointer to the object that was at this position before this call.

```
public int size();
```

Returns the number of elements in the target list.

Figure 14.2 Methods of the `java.util.List` interface.

To begin with, we will just consider the following methods of the List interface:

- add – which adds a new element to a list;
- remove – which removes an element from a list;
- get – which returns a pointer to the object that is at a particular position in the list;
- set – which changes the element (at some position in the list) so that it points to a different object;
- size – which returns how many elements there are in the list.

We will now look at an example that shows how these methods can be used.
   Suppose we have three people:

```
Person tTom   = new PersonImpl("Tom%1981-12-25%44-1987-654321%1.6");
Person tDick  = new PersonImpl("Dick%1980-3-18%44-1987-654322%1.7");
Person tHarry = new PersonImpl("Harry%1979-8-4%44-1987-654323%1.8");
```

Suppose we want to create a list containing these three people.
   List is an interface, and (as was mentioned earlier) the Collections API provides two classes that implement this interface: they are ArrayList and LinkedList. So a list can be created using either:

```
List tList = new ArrayList();
```

or:

```
List tList = new LinkedList();
```

We will look at how to make this choice in Section 14.3.6. Both of these statements create an **empty list**.
   Suppose we use an ArrayList. We can visualize the ArrayList's empty list as follows:

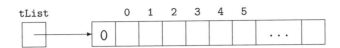

Having created the empty list, the statements:

```
int tSize = tList.size();
boolean tIsEmpty = tList.isEmpty();
```

assign 0 to the variable tSize and the value *true* to tIsEmpty.
   The variable tTom points to a PersonImpl object. We can add the tTom object to the list using:

```
tList.add(tTom);
```

The result can be visualized as:

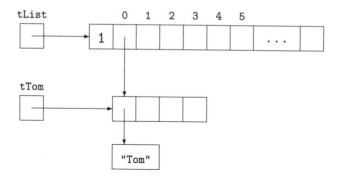

where only the first field of the `PersonImpl` object has been shown in detail.

Section 12.5.4 distinguished between using the *share approach* and the *clone approach*. The designers of the Collections API have chosen to use the share approach. This means that the `add` method does not make its own copy of the object pointed to by `tTom`. So, any elements of the list that point to the `tTom` object will be affected if we later choose to change the value of the object pointed to by `tTom`.

If we now do:

```
tList.add(tHarry);     // TH
```

the list will contain two elements, the first one describing Tom, the second one describing Harry. The comment after the call of `add`, i.e. `// TH`, gives a cryptic indication of the state of the list after the method call has been executed.

So we now have the following situation:

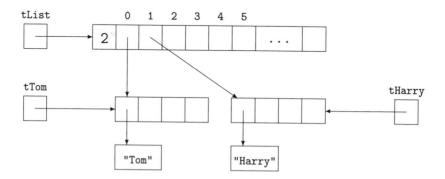

Figure 14.2 indicates that the `add` method has a parameter that is of the class `Object`. Because the class `Object` is at the top of Java's class hierarchy, it means that this method can be used with an object of any class. Suppose the argument points to an object of the class `PersonImpl`. Then, when the `add` method is called, its parameter, `pValue`, is made to point to the `PersonImpl` object. Because this parameter is of a

type (`Object`) that is higher in the class hierarchy than `PersonImpl`, this is called an **upcast**.

Each time we call the `add` method, we have to supply an argument. However, these arguments do not have to point to objects that are of the same class. We will look at the possibility of building lists where the objects of the list are of several classes in Section 14.3.7.

When we use `ArrayList`'s constructor, we get an `ArrayList` with some **capacity** that has been decided by the implementors of the `ArrayList` class. In the above diagrams, this has been left vague by using the . . . notation. Although an `ArrayList` has some **initial capacity**, it will automatically increase in capacity whenever the number of adds that our program performs exceeds its current capacity. We will look at how to control the initial capacity in Section 15.2.

The `get` method can be used to obtain a pointer to any object of a list. This method has one parameter: it indicates the position of the element in the list. The numbering starts from 0 (rather than from 1). So, to get a pointer to the object at the first element of the list, use:

```
Person tFirstPerson = (Person)tList.get(0);
```

Because a `List` can be used to store objects of any class, the result type of `get` is `Object`. So `tList.get(0)` returns a value of class `Object` and we have to cast this in order to treat the object as a `Person` object. As mentioned in Section 11.10, this cast is called a **downcast**. The above statement results in a situation that can be visualized as:

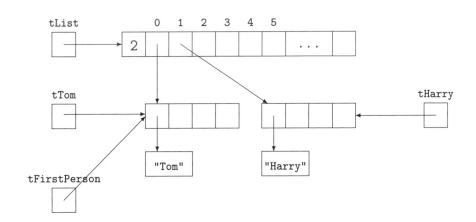

Note again that, because the Collections API adopts the *share approach*, `tFirst-Person` points to the same object as that of one of the elements of the list.

If we also execute the statements:

```
System.out.println(tFirstPerson);
System.out.println((Person)tList.get(1));
System.out.println(tList.size());
```

then the following would be output:

```
Tom%1981-12-25%44-1987-654321%1.6
Harry%1979-08-04%44-1987-654323%1.8
2
```

When add is used with one argument as in the calls given earlier, the new element is added at the end of the list. Instead, we can use add with an additional argument that indicates a position:

```
tList.add(1, tDick);      // TDH
```

This means that tDick is to be inserted at position 1 and the element previously at position 1 is now at position 2.

Here are some other examples of calls of methods from the List interface:

```
tList.add(3, tHarry);     // TDHH
tList.add(0, tDick);      // DTDHH
tList.remove(tHarry);     // DTDH
tList.remove(1);          // DDH
tList.set(0, tTom);       // TDH
```

where the comments give a cryptic description of the state of the list after each statement has been executed.

14.3.2 Using the Iterator interface

We often want to do some task to each element of a list. This is known as *iterating* through the elements of the list. With a List, it is possible to do this using the following code:

```
for (int tPersonNumber = 0; tPersonNumber<tList.size(); tPersonNumber++)
{
    final Person tPerson = (Person)tList.get(tPersonNumber);
    iProcessPerson(tPerson);
}
```

where iProcessPerson is a method that contains the code that we want to execute on each element of the list. Although this would be reasonably efficient for a list that is implemented as an ArrayList, for a LinkedList it is very inefficient. This is because a LinkedList is implemented as a **doubly-linked list**. This is a list where each element not only has a pointer to the value of the element but also has pointers to the elements that come before and after. You can visualize a LinkedList that has three elements as follows:

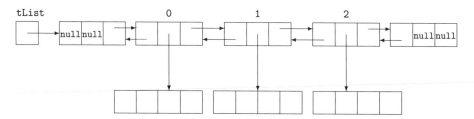

This diagram shows two fictitious elements, one at the start of the list and one at the end. An implementor of ArrayList often includes these elements in order to make it easier for him/her to write the code of the ArrayList class.

Consider what happens when get is called (when tList is pointing to a LinkedList object). Suppose we are executing the call tList.get(2). The get method needs to follow the pointers from tList down to element number 2. Given the above structure, in order to do this it needs to look at the values of four pointers, i.e. it needs to step over three elements, in order to get to element number 2. Of course, if the list contained 10 000 elements and we executed tList.get(4567), it would have to look at the values of 4569 pointers. For this reason, executing get on a LinkedList can be time-consuming.

Now consider what happens when the above for statement is used when tList points to a LinkedList object. When get is called, the code of get has to work its way down the list starting from the first element, and this has to be done on each of the calls of get.

So, we will avoid calling get in a loop. A different approach uses the iterator method that is defined in the List interface:

```
Iterator tIterator = tList.iterator();
```

No matter whether tList is pointing to an ArrayList object or a LinkedList object, the call of iterator will create information that enables the list to be iterated efficiently. Assuming tList is pointing to a LinkedList object, then, after the above statement has been executed, some sort of structure like the following will have been set up:

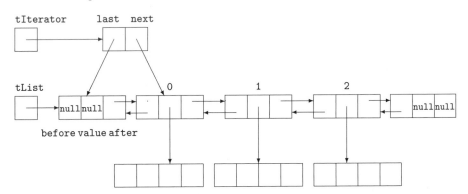

The call of iterator returns a pointer to an object which supports the Iterator interface. This interface contains the methods shown in Figure 14.3: they are officially documented at $API/java/util/Iterator.html. The methods iterator, hasNext and next can be used as follows:

```
final Iterator tIterator = tList.iterator();
while (tIterator.hasNext())
{
    final Person tPerson = (Person)tIterator.next();
    iProcessPerson(tPerson);
}
```

```
public boolean hasNext();
```
    Returns the value *true* if and only if the target iterator has another element.
```
public Object next();
```
    If there is another element, returns a pointer to the object that is at this element; otherwise throws a `NoSuchElementException` exception.
```
public void remove();
```
    Removes from the underlying list the element whose object was returned by the last call of `next`. Throws an `IllegalStateException` exception if `next` has not been called or the element has already been removed by a previous call of `remove`.

Figure 14.3   Methods of the `java.util.Iterator` interface.

The methods `hasNext` and `next` can be efficiently implemented: a call of `hasNext` just has to detect whether `tIterator.next` is pointing to the fictitious element at the end of the list, and a call of `next` just returns the value of `tIterator.next.value` and also moves the `last` and `next` pointers on by one element. More details are given in Curio 14.7.

    For a `LinkedList`, this code will execute a lot faster than the loop with `gets` given earlier.

14.3.3 The `contains` method

Given the method called `iterator`, it is very easy to find out whether a collection contains a particular value. Suppose we have a `List` which contains a collection of values all of which are `PersonImpl` objects. Suppose we now want to write a method called `iIsInList` that returns *true* if and only if the `List` object `pList` has an element which points to an object representing a person with the name `pName`:

```
private static boolean iIsInList(final List pList, final String pName)
{
    final Iterator tIterator = pList.iterator();
    while (tIterator.hasNext())
    {
        final Person tPerson = (Person)tIterator.next();
        if (pName.equals(tPerson.getName()))
        {
            return true;
        }
    }
    return false;
}
```

Here is an example of a call of this method:

```
final boolean tFound = iIsInList(tList, "Dick");
```

However, it is a waste of time declaring this method as the `List` interface has a method called `contains` that does this job for us:

```
public boolean contains(Object pValue);
```

So, instead of the call of `iIsInList`, we can use:

```
final Person tTargetPerson = new PersonImpl();
tTargetPerson.setName("Dick");
final boolean tFound = tList.contains(tTargetPerson);
```

The call of `contains` requires the target list (`tList`) to be searched from the head of the list to find an object of the list that has the same value as the object pointed to by `pValue` (which is the `tTargetPerson` object in the above call).

The WWW page that documents this interface (**$API/java/util/List.html**) states that the `contains` method looks for an element e such that `pValue.equals(e)`. So the following code describes what happens when the `contains` method is called:

```
public boolean contains(final Object pValue)
{
   final Iterator tIterator = iterator();
   while (tIterator.hasNext())
   {
      final Object tObject = tIterator.next();
      if (pValue.equals(tObject))
      {
         return true;
      }
   }
   return false;
}
```

Because the parameter of the call of `equals` is `tObject` which is of the type `Object`, the `equals` method being used here is one that has the header:

```
public boolean equals(Object pObject);
```

The actual `equals` method that is used depends on the class of the target object of the call of `equals`. In the above code, `pValue` is pointing to a `PersonImpl` object, and because the class declaration for `PersonImpl` declares a method with the above header then that method will be used.

So, to summarize, when executing:

```
final Person tTargetPerson = new PersonImpl();
tTargetPerson.setName("Dick");
final boolean tFound = tList.contains(tTargetPerson);
```

the `contains` method searches to see if it can find an object which `equals` that of `tTargetPerson`. It will use the method called `equals` declared in the class `PersonImpl`. This method says that two `PersonImpl` objects are equal if and only if the names are the same.

14.3.4 The methods `indexOf`, `lastIndexof` and `remove`

Each of the methods:

```
public boolean     contains(Object pValue);
public int            indexOf(Object pValue);
public int       lastIndexOf(Object pValue);
public boolean      remove(Object pValue);
```

(of the `List` interface) is similar in that each of them requires the target list to be searched from the head (or the tail for `lastIndexOf`) to find an object having the same value as the object pointed to by `pValue`. In order to do this, each of these methods uses the method:

```
public boolean equals(Object pObject);
```

applied to the object pointed to by `pValue`.

The method `contains` is not particularly useful if you want to do something to an element of the collection. Instead, it is better to use `indexOf` which will return the position of the element. Here is an example:

```
final Person tTargetPerson = new PersonImpl();
tTargetPerson.setName("Dick");
final int tPosition = tList.indexOf(tTargetPerson);
if (tPosition>=0)
{
    final Person tPerson = (Person)tList.get(tPosition);
    tPerson.setName("Richard");
    ...
}
```

Because the Collections API uses the *share approach*, `tPerson` is pointing to the same object that an element of `tList` is pointing to. So, the statement:

```
tPerson.setName("Richard");
```

also changes one of the objects of `tList` (which may or may not be what you want). If you prefer not to alter an object of the list, the result of the call of `get` should be cloned:

```
final Person tPerson = new PersonImpl((Person)tList.get(tPosition));
tPerson.setName("Richard");
...
```

It is also possible to use `indexOf` when you want to remove an element from a list: first find the appropriate position in the list and then remove the element at that position:

```
final Person tTargetPerson = new PersonImpl();
tTargetPerson.setName("Dick");
final int tPosition = tList.indexOf(tTargetPerson);
if (tPosition>=0)
{
    tList.remove(tPosition);
}
```

However, the `List` interface has another `remove` method which is more suitable (as it eliminates the need to call `indexOf`). So, the above is better coded as:

```
final Person tTargetPerson = new PersonImpl();
tTargetPerson.setName("Dick");
tList.remove(tTargetPerson);
```

14.3.5 An example of a complete program that manipulates a list

Figure 14.4 contains a complete program that manipulates a list. The program begins by obtaining the name of a file from the command line. It then reads lines from this file, each line containing the details about one person. As it reads each line, it creates a `PersonImpl` object and adds this object to a list. Having read the file, the program uses an `Iterator` to output the contents of the list. Finally, the program keeps reading lines from the keyboard (each line containing the details of a person) and finding out whether the person is in the list. It keeps doing this until the user of the program types in an empty line.

```
// Read a list of people from a file, output the list, and then examine it.
// Barry Cornelius, 19 June 2000
import java.util. ArrayList;
import java.io.   BufferedReader;
import java.io.   FileReader;
import java.io.   InputStreamReader;
import java.io.   IOException;
import java.util. Iterator;
import java.util. List;
public class ExamineList
{
   public static void main(final String[] pArgs) throws IOException
   {
      if (pArgs.length!=1)
      {
         System.out.println("Usage: java ExamineList datafile");
         System.exit(1);
      }
      final List tList = new ArrayList();
      // read a list of people from a file
      final BufferedReader tInputHandle =
                  new BufferedReader(new FileReader(pArgs[0]));
      while (true)
      {
         final String tFileLine = tInputHandle.readLine();
         if (tFileLine==null)
         {
            break;
         }
         final Person tFilePerson = new PersonImpl(tFileLine);
         tList.add(tFilePerson);
      }
```

Figure 14.4 *Continues on the next page.*

```
// output the list that has been read in
final Iterator tIterator = tList.iterator();
while (tIterator.hasNext())
{
    final Person tIteratePerson = (Person)tIterator.next();
    System.out.println(tIteratePerson);
}
// ask the user to examine the list
final BufferedReader tKeyboard =
            new BufferedReader(new InputStreamReader(System.in));
while (true)
{
    System.out.print("Person? ");
    System.out.flush();
    final String tKeyboardLine = tKeyboard.readLine();
    if (tKeyboardLine.equals(""))
    {
        break;
    }
    final Person tTargetPerson = new PersonImpl(tKeyboardLine);
    final int tPosition = tList.indexOf(tTargetPerson);
    System.out.print(tTargetPerson);
    if (tPosition>=0)
    {
        System.out.println(" is at position " + tPosition);
    }
    else
    {
        System.out.println(" is absent");
    }
}
}
}
```

Figure 14.4 Reading a file containing a list and asking the user to examine it.

14.3.6 Choosing between an `ArrayList` and a `LinkedList`

Although, in the previous sections, we have mainly used an `ArrayList`, all of
the method calls that were given can be executed no matter whether `tList` is an
`ArrayList` or a `LinkedList`. As explained earlier, these two classes implement a
list in two different ways. The `ArrayList` allocates a sequence of locations:

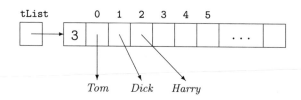

whereas a LinkedList uses a *doubly-linked list*:

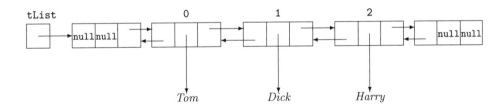

Earlier it was recommended that an ArrayList 'should be used if you want to make random accesses to the elements of a collection' and a LinkedList 'should be considered if you want to make frequent insertions and deletions at the beginning of a list'. Looking at the above diagrams, it should now be clearer as to why these recommendations were made. For example, if you want to use get to access a particular element, then it is immediately available if you use an ArrayList, whereas with a LinkedList the implementation of get has to work its way down from the first element. And if you want to use add to add a new value at the beginning of a list, then it looks as if this should be quicker with a LinkedList than with an ArrayList.

Some comments about this choice are given on one of the WWW pages of Sun's tutorial on Java ([30]). The page says:

> Most of the time, you'll probably use ArrayList. It offers constant time positional access, and it's just plain fast, because it does not have to allocate a node object for each element in the List, and it can take advantage of the native method System.arraycopy when it has to move multiple elements at once ...

> If you frequently add elements to the beginning of the List, or iterate over the List deleting elements from its interior, you might want to consider LinkedList. These operations are constant time in a LinkedList but linear time in an ArrayList. But you pay a big price! Positional access is linear time in a LinkedList and constant time in an ArrayList. Furthermore, the constant factor for LinkedList is much worse. If you think that you want to use a LinkedList, measure the performance with both LinkedList and ArrayList. You may be surprised.

Consider the ListTimes program shown in Figure 14.5. It uses the EggTimer class shown in Figure 14.6. Depending on a command line argument, this program creates an ArrayList or a LinkedList. So if you want to use an ArrayList type the command:

```
java ListTimes A
```

or if you want to use a LinkedList type the command:

```
java ListTimes L
```

```
// A program that measures the time taken to perform operations on a List.
// Barry Cornelius, 23 July 2000
import java.util. ArrayList;
import java.util. Iterator;
import java.util. LinkedList;
import java.util. List;
public class ListTimes
{
    public static void main(final String[] pArgs)
    {
        final EggTimer tEggTimer = new EggTimer();
        final int tNumberOfNews = 10000;
              int tNumberOfGets = 20000;
        final int tGetIndex      = 4567;
        final int tNumberOfAdds = 10000;
        List tList = null;
        switch (pArgs[0].charAt(0))
        {
            case 'A':
            {
                tNumberOfGets *= 1000;
                tList = new ArrayList();
            }
            break;
            case 'L':
            {
                tList = new LinkedList();
            }
            break;
            default:
            {
                System.out.println("Usage: java ListTimes [A|L]");
                System.exit(1);
            }
        }
        tEggTimer.reset();                                    // create list
        for (int tNewNumber = 1; tNewNumber<=tNumberOfNews; tNewNumber++)
        {
            tList.add(new PersonImpl("" + tNewNumber + "%1999-2-7%1234%1.7"));
        }
        double tAddEndTime = tEggTimer.get()/(double)tNumberOfNews;
        System.out.println(tAddEndTime);
        tEggTimer.reset();                            // get a particular element
        for (int tGetNumber = 1; tGetNumber<=tNumberOfGets; tGetNumber++)
        {
            Object tObject = tList.get(tGetIndex);
        }
```

Figure 14.5 *Continues on the next page.*

```
        double tGetTime = tEggTimer.get()/(double)tNumberOfGets;
        System.out.println(tGetTime);
        tEggTimer.reset();                        // get each element in turn
        for (int tWalkNumber = 0; tWalkNumber<tList.size(); tWalkNumber++)
        {
            Person tPerson = (Person)tList.get(tWalkNumber);
        }
        double tWalkTime = tEggTimer.get()/(double)tList.size();
        System.out.println(tWalkTime);
        tEggTimer.reset();                        // use Iterator to get each one
        final Iterator tIterator = tList.iterator();
        while (tIterator.hasNext())
        {
            Person tPerson = (Person)tIterator.next();
        }
        double tIteratorTime = tEggTimer.get()/(double)tList.size();
        System.out.println(tIteratorTime);
        tEggTimer.reset();                        // use add at start of list
        for (int tAddNumber = 1; tAddNumber<=tNumberOfAdds; tAddNumber++)
        {
            tList.add(0, new PersonImpl("Bloggs, Fred%1999-2-7%1234%1.7"));
        }
        double tAddStartTime = tEggTimer.get()/(double)tNumberOfAdds;
        System.out.println(tAddStartTime);
    }
}
```

Figure 14.5 A program to measure the performance of operations on lists.

The program measures:

- the amount of time it takes to add an element to the end of the list;
- the amount of time it takes using get to obtain a particular element of the list;
- the average amount of time it takes to get each element of the list in turn;
- the average amount of time it takes to get each element of the list in turn using Iterator;
- the amount of time it takes to add an element to the start of the list.

The following values were obtained using Java 2 SDK v 1.3.0 on a Windows 95 computer. These values are in milliseconds:

operation	ArrayList	LinkedList
time to add to the end of the list	0.072	0.072
time to get the 4567th element	0.000099	0.305
time to get element using get	0.0	0.16
time to get element using Iterator	0.005	0.0
time to add to the start of the list	0.264	0.049

These figures demonstrate that a get from a LinkedList is inefficient and a sequence of gets is better done using an Iterator. They also demonstrate that an ArrayList usually performs better than a LinkedList.

```
// A class that can be used to measure the time taken to perform operations.
// Barry Cornelius, 23 July 2000
public class EggTimer
{
    private long iStartTime;
    public EggTimer()
    {
        iStartTime = 0;
    }
    public void reset()
    {
        iStartTime = System.currentTimeMillis();
    }
    public double get()
    {
        if (iStartTime==0)
        {
            throw new IllegalArgumentException();
        }
        final long tFinishTime = System.currentTimeMillis();
        final long tPeriod = tFinishTime - iStartTime;
        iStartTime = 0;
        return (double)tPeriod;
    }
}
```

Figure 14.6   A class for measuring the time taken to perform operations.

14.3.7 Heterogeneous lists

So far, we have built lists where the objects of the list have all been objects of the same class. Such lists are called **homogeneous lists**. However, as was mentioned in Section 14.3.1, the methods of the Collections API are written in terms of the class Object. This means that the objects of a collection need not all be of the same class. A list whose objects are not objects of the same class is called a **heterogeneous list**.

The add method that is used to add a new element to a list has a parameter of the type Object. This means that we can pass a pointer to any object as an argument, i.e. a value of any reference type (but not a value of a primitive type). And it does not need to be the same type for each call of add.

So, for the first call we might use add with a PersonImpl object; for the next call of add we might use it with a DateImpl object; and so on:

```
tList.add(new PersonImpl("Tom%1981-12-25%44-1987-654321%1.6"));
tList.add(new DateImpl("1948-11-23"));
```

Whether it makes any sense to do this depends on what we are using the list for.

When we get objects from the list, we will usually want to perform a *downcast*, i.e. to cast each object into its appropriate class. This may not be easy to do if we have been adding objects belonging to various classes. If we get an object and cast it into an inappropriate class, our program will crash with a ClassCastException.

However, it may be that there is some commonality to the classes of the objects that have been added to the list: it may be that all of the classes implement some interface. In which case, we can apply any of the methods of the interface to any object no matter what its class is:

```
SomeInterface tSomeInterface = (SomeInterface)tList.get(tPosition);
tSomeInterface.someMethod(...);
```

where someMethod is a method that is included in the SomeInterface interface. When this code is executed, the actual someMethod method that gets executed will depend on the class of the object.

With the interfaces and classes that have been introduced so far, it is difficult to give a realistic example of this. When the Date interface was introduced, two classes (DateImpl and DateImplY) were given that implement this interface. Suppose, for some reason, our program randomly adds DateImpl and DateImplY objects to a list:

```
List tList = new ArrayList();
tList.add(new DateImpl(2000, 2, 5));
tList.add(new DateImplY(2000, 12, 25));
tList.add(new DateImplY(1948, 11, 23));
tList.add(new DateImpl(2000, 12, 25));
tList.add(new DateImplY(1752, 9, 2));
```

If we now want to iterate through the values of the list, some elements contain objects of the class DateImpl, whereas others contain of the class DateImplY. So we cannot easily cast to each object's class type. However, all the objects satisfy the Date interface. So, we can cast to the Date interface, as in:

```
Date tDate = (Date)tList.get(tPosition);
```

Or, we can use an iterator to iterate through this list:

```
final Iterator tIterator = tList.iterator();
while (tIterator.hasNext())
{
    final Date tDate = (Date)tIterator.next();
    iProcessDate(tDate);
}
```

Alternatively, there may be some regularity to the order of the classes of the objects. If so, we could use that. For example, a call that adds a PersonImpl object might always be followed by a call that adds a DateImpl object. In which case, we could use:

```
Person tPerson = (Person)tList.get(tPosition);
tPosition++;
Date tDate = (Date)tList.get(tPosition);
iProcessPersonDatePair(tPerson, tDate);
```

But if a `DateImpl` object has such a close association with a `PersonImpl` object, we should instead produce a new class that has a `PersonImpl` field and a `DateImpl` field, and add objects of that class to the list.

If, instead, the objects of the elements of the list belong to an almost random mix of classes, we could resort to code like the following:

```
Object tObject = tList.get(tPosition);
if (tObject instanceof Person)
{
    Person tPerson = (Person)tObject;
    iProcessPerson(tPerson);
}
else if (tObject instanceof Date)
{
    Date tDate = (Date)tObject;
    iProcessDate(tDate);
}
else
{
    ...
}
```

Not only is this inelegant, but the `instanceof` operators are also time-consuming to execute. Any use of this technique should be avoided. It indicates that some aspect of the design of the program is wrong.

14.3.8 Special forms of list

Sometimes a list is used in a particular way. We now look at two special uses of a list: first, we look at *queue*s where the transactions on the list take place at the ends of the list, and then we look at *stack*s where the transactions take place at one of the ends.

14.4 Representing queues

14.4.1 What is a queue?

In the UK, people form a *queue* when waiting to buy *cinema* tickets; in the USA, those waiting to buy *movie* tickets stand in a *line*. Since human beings are involved, there is often a lot of pushing in: if this happens, they are not in a queue! This is because we define a **queue** as an ordered list in which the activity of adding an element takes place at one of the ends, and the removal of an element takes place at the other end. The removal end is called the **head** (or **front**) of the queue; whereas the insertion end is called the **tail** (or **rear**) of the queue. A queue is sometimes known as a **first-in-first-out list** (or **FIFO**).

14.4.2 Representing a queue using `ArrayList`/`LinkedList`

Suppose we want to represent a queue in a program. For example, it may be that our problem requires us to represent a queue of people, or maybe it is a queue of files waiting to be printed on a printer.

For this, the program could use an object of class `ArrayList` or `LinkedList` using the `add` and `remove` methods to manipulate the queue. So the `add` method would be used to add an object to the end of the list, and the `remove` method would be used to remove the first element of the list. However, there would be nothing to stop us from using the `ArrayList`/`LinkedList` object in a way that subverts the fact that it is representing a queue. For example, we could write code that always puts us at the front of the queue!

14.4.3 Providing an interface and a class for a queue

If we want to ensure that a program abides by the rules of a queue, we could provide an interface for a queue called `Queue` together with a class that implements that interface. An obvious name for the class is either `ArrayQueue` or `LinkedQueue` depending on how we implement it.

We could provide the interface and class so that they are specific to the kind of element that we want to store in the queue, e.g. an interface and a class that manipulates a queue of people, and so they are written in terms of `Person` and `PersonImpl`. However, it could be argued that it is better to write these with elements of the class `Object`. In this way, the code can be used today for our program involving a queue of people, and reused later when we want to represent a queue of something else, e.g. a queue of files waiting to be printed.

14.4.4 The operations that are required for the `Queue` interface

So what operations do we need to provide in the `Queue` interface? One obvious one is:

 - `add` – which adds an element to the target queue.

This method will be called `add` to fit in with the naming conventions of the Collections API.

Sometimes when working with queues, programmers provide a method that just returns the object at the first element of the queue (without removing it) and another method which removes the first element of the queue. Other programmers provide just one method which returns a pointer to the first object and removes it from the queue.

Following the design of the Collections API, a hybrid of these two approaches will be adopted for the `Queue` interface. We will provide:

 - `getFirst` – which just returns a pointer to the object that is at the first element (without removing the element);
 - `remove` – which returns the value of the first element and removes the element.

We will also provide:

- `size` – which returns the number of elements in the target queue;
- `equals` – which returns the value *true* if and only if the objects of the target queue and the queue passed as an argument contain the same values in the same order;
- `hashCode` – which returns a hashcode value for the target queue;
- `toString` – which returns a textual representation of the target queue.

An interface for `Queue` is given in Figure 14.7.

```
// An interface for a queue.
// Barry Cornelius, 19 June 2000
public interface Queue
{
    // adds a new element (to the target queue) that is
    // assigned the value pObject, a pointer to some object
    public void add(Object pObject);

    // returns a pointer to the object that is at the first element
    // of the target queue (without removing the element)
    public Object getFirst();

    // returns a pointer to the object that is at the first element
    // of the target queue and removes that element from the queue
    public Object remove();

    // returns the number of elements in the target queue
    public int size();

    // returns the value true if and only if the objects of the
    // target queue and the queue passed as an argument have
    // the same values in the same order
    public boolean equals(Object pObject);

    // returns a hashcode value for the target queue
    public int hashCode();

    // returns a textual representation of the target queue
    public String toString();
}
```

Figure 14.7 The `Queue` interface.

14.4.5 Providing a `LinkedQueue` class that implements the `Queue` interface

A class called `LinkedQueue` that implements the `Queue` interface appears in Figure 14.8.

```
// A class that uses an object of the LinkedList class to implement Queue.
// Barry Cornelius, 19 June 2000
import java.util. LinkedList;
import java.util. Iterator;
import java.util. List;
public class LinkedQueue implements Queue
{
   private List iList;
   public LinkedQueue()
   {
      iList = new LinkedList();
   }
   public void add(final Object pObject)
   {
      iList.add(pObject);
   }
   public Object getFirst()
   {
      if (iList.isEmpty())
      {
         return null;
      }
      return iList.get(0);
   }
   public Object remove()
   {
      if (iList.isEmpty())
      {
         return null;
      }
      return iList.remove(0);
   }
   public int size()
   {
      return iList.size();
   }
   public boolean equals(final Object pObject)
   {
      if ( pObject==null || getClass()!=pObject.getClass() )
      {
         return false;
      }
      return iList.equals(((LinkedQueue)pObject).iList);
   }
   public int hashCode()
   {
      return 0;
   }
}
```

Figure 14.8 *Continues on the next page.*

```
public String toString()
{
    if (iList.isEmpty())
    {
        return new String("");
    }
    final StringBuffer tStringBuffer = new StringBuffer();
    final Iterator tIterator = iList.iterator();
    while (tIterator.hasNext())
    {
        final Object tObject = tIterator.next();
        tStringBuffer.append("@" + tObject);
    }
    tStringBuffer.deleteCharAt(0);
    return tStringBuffer.toString();
}
}
```

Figure 14.8 The `LinkedQueue` class.

The constructor of this class creates a `LinkedList` object and makes `iList` point to this `LinkedList` object. Although it is possible to provide a constructor that handles the `String` generated by `LinkedQueue`'s `toString` method, and a constructor that clones a queue, we will be lazy and not provide them.

The only thing that most of the methods of the `LinkedQueue` class do is to call the corresponding method of the class `LinkedList`. Providing an interface and a class that allows indirect access to an object of another class is an example of a design pattern known as the **adapter pattern**. In his book *Patterns in Java* ([18]), Mark Grand says that an Adapter class is used to provide 'an object that acts as an intermediary for method calls between client objects and *one other object* not known to the client objects'.

In the body of the `toString` method, it is possible to use the following code:

```
String tString = new String("");
final Iterator tIterator = iList.iterator();
while (tIterator.hasNext())
{
    final Object tObject = tIterator.next();
    tString += "@" + tObject.toString();
}
return tString.substring(1);
```

Each time round the loop, `tString` is made to point to a new string formed by appending to its previous value an @ followed by the result of applying `toString` to `tObject`. The actual `toString` that will get executed depends on what kind of object `tObject` is pointing to. Because we will be storing `PersonImpl` objects in the queue, the variable `tObject` will be pointing to a `PersonImpl` object, and so it will be `PersonImpl`'s `toString` that will get executed. The use of `substring` is to throw away the unwanted @ character that appears at the start of the string that has been built.

However, this code is not very efficient; each time round the loop, the use of the += operator results in the string currently pointed to by tString being thrown away after the new string has been created. As mentioned in Section 3.5, it is better to use StringBuffer in situations where you wish to build up a String gradually by performing a lot of string manipulation. The StringBuffer class is used by the code of the toString method given in Figure 14.8.

14.4.6 Using the Queue interface and the LinkedQueue class

The PersonLinkedQueueProg program (given in Figure 14.9) can be used to test the Queue interface and the LinkedQueue class. The user of this program is repeatedly asked for single-letter commands that allow him/her to manipulate a queue of people. The program provides a command to add a person to the queue, a command to remove a person from the queue, and so on.

The program naturally divides into two activities: one of these is to keep getting commands from the user and the other is to process each command. The main method handles the first of these whereas the second is handled by a subsidiary method called iProcessCommand. Although the code of the program could have been written so that the code of iProcessCommand appears **inline**, i.e. the code appears in place of the call of iProcessCommand, this would have led to a program which is less easy to understand. By placing the code to process a command in a method, the code of the main method is a lot easier to understand – it is only 17 lines long.

Having decided to use one or more subsidiary methods, it is likely to be the case that some variables will need to be accessed from both the main method and from subsidiary methods. This was discussed in Section 8.12. The choice is whether to pass the value of a variable as an argument of a subsidiary method or to make the variable a field of the program class. For the PersonLinkedQueueProg program, it is:

- appropriate for the iPersonQueue variable to be declared as a field of the program class;
- convenient for the iKeyboard variable to be declared as a field;
- debatable as to whether the tCommand variable should be declared as a field (and the PersonLinkedQueueProg program chooses not to do this).

A class diagram for the interfaces and classes forming the PersonLinkedQueue-Prog program is given in Figure 14.10. Because, earlier, it was decided to code the Queue interface and the LinkedQueue class in terms of the class Object instead of Person and PersonImpl, then Queue and LinkedQueue are not dependent on Person or PersonImpl. For this reason, we can make changes to Person or PersonImpl without having to re-compile and re-test Queue and LinkedQueue.

```
// A program that performs operations on a queue of people.
// Barry Cornelius, 19 June 2000
import java.io. BufferedReader;
import java.io. InputStreamReader;
import java.io. IOException;
public class PersonLinkedQueueProg
{
    private static Queue iPersonQueue;
    private static BufferedReader iKeyboard;
    public static void main(final String[] pArgs) throws IOException
    {
        iPersonQueue = new LinkedQueue();
        iKeyboard = new BufferedReader(new InputStreamReader(System.in));
        while (true)
        {
            System.out.print("Command? ");
            System.out.flush();
            final char tCommand = iKeyboard.readLine().toLowerCase().charAt(0);
            if (tCommand=='q')
            {
                break;
            }
            iProcessCommand(tCommand);
            System.out.println();
        }
    }
    private static void iProcessCommand(final char pCommand)
                                                        throws IOException
    {
        switch (pCommand)
        {
            case 'a':
            {
                System.out.print("Person? ");
                System.out.flush();
                final Person tPerson = new PersonImpl(iKeyboard.readLine());
                iPersonQueue.add(tPerson);
            }
            break;
            case 'd':
            {
                iPersonQueue = new LinkedQueue();
            }
            break;
```

Figure 14.9 *Continues on the next page.*

```
case 'e':
{
    System.out.print("The queue is ");
    if (iPersonQueue.size()!=0 )
    {
        System.out.print("not ");
    }
    System.out.println("empty");
}
break;
case 'g':
{
    if (iPersonQueue.size()==0)
    {
        System.out.println("The queue is empty");
    }
    else
    {
        final Person tPerson = (Person)iPersonQueue.getFirst();
        System.out.println("The first person is: " + tPerson);
    }
}
break;
case 'r':
{
    if (iPersonQueue.size()==0)
    {
        System.out.println("The queue is empty");
    }
    else
    {
        final Person tPerson = (Person)iPersonQueue.remove();
        System.out.println(tPerson + " has been removed");
    }
}
break;
default:
{
    System.out.println(pCommand + " is not a valid command letter");
}
break;
        }
    }
}
```

Figure 14.9 A program that tests the `Queue` interface and the `LinkedQueue` class.

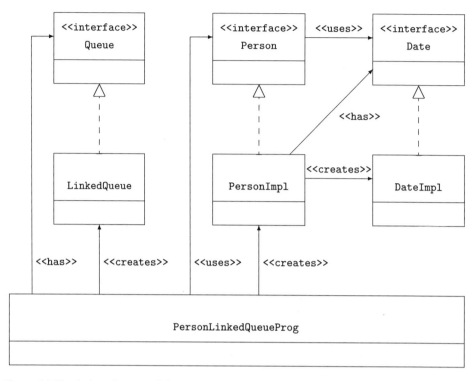

Figure 14.10   A class diagram of the `PersonLinkedQueueProg` program.

14.5 Representing stacks

14.5.1 What is a stack?

A list where the insertions and deletions take place at one of the ends of the list is called a **stack**. In the real world, there are many examples of stacks, and structures similar to stacks:

- small coin containers such as those carried by bus conductors;
- a pile of plates or trays in a restaurant;
- rifles in which cartridges are loaded by forcing down a spring which later feeds the bullets into the breech in reverse order of loading;
- a railway line that does a *reverse* (e.g. Battersby between Middlesbrough and Whitby in North Yorkshire) – here the last carriage in comes out of the station first.

We will be able to use the ideas of this section if our program has to model any of these stacks.

Stacks also occur frequently in computing. For example, the acquiring and releasing of storage for local variables when methods are called can best be modelled using a stack.

We now look at some jargon associated with stacks. The end of the stack where values are added and removed is called the **top** of the stack. The **bottom** of the stack is the least accessible element – it cannot be removed until all the other elements have been removed from the stack. Sometimes people say that they **push** down a value onto a stack and **pop** up the stack in order to remove a value. This terminology comes from imagining the stack as a spring-loaded pile of plates. A stack which contains no elements is referred to as an **empty stack**; and the term **underflow** is used to refer to an attempt to remove a value from an empty stack. Sometimes, there is a fixed amount of storage allocated for a stack; and the term **overflow** is used to refer to an attempt to add a value to a **full stack**. A stack is also known as a **last-in-first-out list**, a **LIFO**, a **push-down list** or a **nesting store**.

14.5.2 Using a stack to convert an expression into reverse Polish

Suppose a Java program contains the expression:

```
(-b + Math.sqrt(b*b - 4.0*a*c))/(2.0*a)
```

and suppose we pass this program to a Java compiler. Remember that the compiler has the task of converting our program into a binary form known as bytecodes. This process is a reasonably complicated task. And one area of difficulty is the generation of bytecodes from the notation that Java uses for arithmetic expressions.

Suppose we number the operations in the order in which they might be performed when the expression is being evaluated. This is the order in which they are likely to appear in the bytecodes being generated by the compiler:

```
(-b + Math.sqrt(b*b - 4.0*a*c))/(2.0*a)
 1  7          6   2 5    3 4  9    8
```

If the compiler works directly on this expression when compiling the program, it must engage in a great deal of back-and-forth scanning of the expression to find the next operation to be performed.

One method of eliminating this difficulty is for the compiler to make a preliminary translation of the arithmetic expression into a notation known as **reverse Polish** – named (?) after the Polish mathematician Jan Lukasiewicz who originated a similar notation. An alternative name for reverse Polish is **postfix notation**; the traditional way of writing an expression is often referred to as **infix notation**.

Although the operands of an expression appear in the same order in both notations, an operator appears between its two operands in infix notation, whereas in postfix notation it is written after its two operands. So the infix expression w+x would be written as wx+ in postfix notation. In this example of postfix notation, the two symbols immediately preceding the operator are operands. This is not always the case. Consider wxy*+. Here the two symbols preceding the + are y and *. Where one or both symbols are operators, the operands of these operators need to be found first. This can be done by proceeding through the postfix expression from left to right, finding in turn the operands for each of the operators. For example, in the postfix expression wxy*+, the operands of the * are x and y, and the operands of the + are w and the result of the operation xy*. If the postfix expression is wxy*+z-, the operands of the operators are as shown in the table:

operator	left operand	right operand
*	x	y
+	w	the result of xy*
−	the result of wxy*+	z

Here are some examples of arithmetic expressions written in both infix and postfix notations:

infix notation	postfix notation
w+x	wx+
w+x*y	wxy*+
(w+x)*y	wx+y*
w+x*y+z	wxy*+z+
(w+x)*(y+z)	wx+yz+*

In the postfix notation, the operators appear in the order in which they are needed in order to evaluate the expression. Note that, whereas parentheses are used in infix notation to override the priority of the operators, they are not needed in postfix notation since an operator is always applied to the previous two values.

We will now look at the translation of an infix expression into postfix in more detail. However, we will simplify the description by not discussing infix expressions containing parentheses and identifiers with more than one character – these are covered in Exercise 14.5 and Exercise 14.6. We will also not discuss more complex operands such as function calls.

Consider the expression shown in Figure 14.11. Although the operands occur in the same order in the two expressions, the order of the operators is quite different. If we are to generate the postfix from the infix, we need to know where to put the operators. How do we know, for example, where the + of this expression should appear in its postfix form?

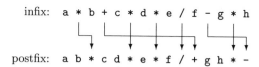

infix: a * b + c * d * e / f - g * h

postfix: a b * c d * e * f / + g h * -

Figure 14.11   Transforming an expression into reverse Polish.

The answer lies in the following observation. In infix notation, each operator lies between the two subexpressions on which it acts:

left-hand subexpression in infix notation	operator	right-hand subexpression in infix notation

In the translation to postfix notation, this operator will occur immediately to the right of the translation of the right-hand subexpression into postfix notation:

> *left-hand*   *right-hand*
> *subexpression*   *subexpression*
> *in postfix*   *in postfix*   *operator*
> *notation*   *notation*

For example, for the expression:

```
a*b+c*d*e/f-g*h
```

the left and right subexpressions operated on by the + are a*b and c*d*e/f. But how do we know where the end of the right-hand subexpression is? In this example, what is so special about the operand f? Why do we finish the right-hand subexpression when we get to f? This is because of the symbol following the f, namely, the symbol -. The reason that the - is not included in the right-hand subexpression is that it is an operator whose priority is not higher than that of the +.

This principle can be implemented by using a stack: the + needs to be stacked until we find an operator of the same or lower priority. The + is then moved from the stack to the next position in the postfix expression being generated. So, for each character of the infix expression, we need to do one of two things:

- *when the character being analysed is an operand*, it is immediately placed at the right-hand end of the postfix expression being created;

- *when the character being analysed is an operator*, the operator which is currently at the top of the stack is inspected. It is unstacked and transferred to the right-hand end of the postfix expression if its priority is equal to or higher than that of the new operator. The next operator in the stack is likewise inspected and the process is repeated until the stack is empty or an operator on the stack has a lower priority than that of the new operator. The new operator is then stacked.

After the last character of the expression has been processed, each operator on the stack needs to be unstacked and placed at the right-hand end of the postfix expression. Figure 14.12 shows a character-by-character use of this algorithm for the expression given in Figure 14.11.

14.5.3 A program to generate reverse Polish

Suppose we want a program to read in an expression and use the above algorithm to output the expression in reverse Polish. We will first provide an interface and a class that represents a stack.

14.5.4 The operations that are required for the Stack interface

The following operations will be provided in the Stack interface:

- add – which adds an element to (the top of) the target stack;

- getFirst – which just returns a pointer to the object that is the top element (without removing it);

character being analysed	bottom of stack is here top of stack is at this end stack becomes	postfix expression becomes
a		a
*	*	a
b	*	ab
+	+	ab*
c	+	ab*c
*	+*	ab*c
d	+*	ab*cd
*	+*	ab*cd*
e	+*	ab*cd*e
/	+/	ab*cd*e*
f	+/	ab*cd*e*f
−	−	ab*cd*e*f/+
g	−	ab*cd*e*f/+g
*	−*	ab*cd*e*f/+g
h	−*	ab*cd*e*f/+gh
		ab*cd*e*f/+gh*−

Figure 14.12 Using the algorithm to convert from infix to postfix notation.

```
// An interface for a stack.
// Barry Cornelius, 19 June 2000
public interface Stack
{
    // adds a new element (to the top of the target stack) that is
    // assigned the value pObject, a pointer to some object
    public void add(Object pObject);

    // returns a pointer to the object that is at the top element
    // of the target stack (without removing the element)
    public Object getFirst();

    // returns a pointer to the object that is at the top element
    // of the target stack and removes that element from the stack
    public Object remove();

    // returns the number of elements in the target stack
    public int size();

    // returns the value true if and only if the objects of the
    // target stack and the stack passed as an argument have
    // the same values in the same order
    public boolean equals(Object pObject);

    // returns a hashcode value for the target stack
    public int hashCode();

    // returns a textual representation of the target stack
    public String toString();
}
```

Figure 14.13 The Stack interface.

- remove – which returns a pointer to the object that is the top element and removes it;
- size – which returns the number of elements in the target stack;
- equals – which returns the value *true* if and only if the objects of the target stack and the stack passed as an argument contain the same values in the same order;
- hashCode – which returns a hashcode value for the target stack;
- toString – which returns a textual representation of the target stack.

The interface is given in Figure 14.13.

14.5.5 Implementing the Stack interface

Once again, it is easy to produce a class that implements the Stack interface: we can just produce a class whose methods are written in terms of calls of methods applied to either an ArrayList object or a LinkedList object. So this is another occurrence of the *adapter pattern*. A class called LinkedStack that uses a LinkedList object appears in Figure 14.14.

```java
// A class that uses an object of the LinkedList class to implement Stack.
// Barry Cornelius, 19 June 2000
import java.util. LinkedList;
import java.util. Iterator;
import java.util. List;
public class LinkedStack implements Stack
{
    private List iList;
    public LinkedStack()
    {
        iList = new LinkedList();
    }
    public void add(final Object pObject)
    {
        iList.add(0, pObject);
    }
    public Object getFirst()
    {
        if (iList.isEmpty())
        {
            return null;
        }
        return iList.get(0);
    }
    public Object remove()
    {
        if (iList.isEmpty())
```

Figure 14.14 *Continues on the next page.*

```
                {
                    return null;
                }
                return iList.remove(0);
            }
            public int size()
            {
                return iList.size();
            }
            public boolean equals(final Object pObject)
            {
                if ( pObject==null || getClass()!=pObject.getClass() )
                {
                    return false;
                }
                return iList.equals(((LinkedStack)pObject).iList);
            }
            public int hashCode()
            {
                return 0;
            }
            public String toString()
            {
                if (iList.isEmpty())
                {
                    return new String("");
                }
                final StringBuffer tStringBuffer = new StringBuffer();
                final Iterator tIterator = iList.iterator();
                while (tIterator.hasNext())
                {
                    final Object tObject = tIterator.next();
                    tStringBuffer.append("@" + tObject);
                }
                tStringBuffer.deleteCharAt(0);
                return tStringBuffer.toString();
            }
        }
```

Figure 14.14 The LinkedStack class.

The code given for the Stack interface and the LinkedStack class is similar to that for the Queue interface and the LinkedQueue class. This should be expected, as the only difference between a stack and a queue is that with a queue an element is added at the opposite end to the end where elements are removed whereas with a stack the two operations are performed at the same end.

14.5.6 A class which facilitates conversion to reverse Polish

The class called Infix given in Figure 14.15 has the task of implementing the algorithm (given in Section 14.5.2). It has a constructor that constructs an Infix

```java
// A class that represents an infix expression.
// Barry Cornelius, 19 June 2000
public class Infix
{
   private String iInfixString;
   private StringBuffer iPostfixStringBuffer;
   private Stack iOpStack;
   public Infix(final String pInfixString)
   {
      iInfixString = pInfixString;
      iOpStack = new LinkedStack();
   }
   public String toReversePolish()
   {
      iPostfixStringBuffer = new StringBuffer();
      for (int tCharNumber = 0; tCharNumber<iInfixString.length();
                            tCharNumber++)
      {
         iProcessChar(iInfixString.charAt(tCharNumber));
      }
      iProcessEndOfExpression();
      return iPostfixStringBuffer.toString();
   }
   private void iProcessChar(final char pChar)
   {
      switch (pChar)
      {
         case '+':
         case '-':
         case '*':
         case '/':
         {
            iProcessOp(pChar);
         }
         break;
         case ' ':
         {
            // do nothing
         }
         break;
         default:
         {
            iPostfixStringBuffer.append(pChar);
         }
         break;
      }
   }
```

Figure 14.15 *Continues on the next page.*

```
private void iProcessOp(final char pOp)
{
   while ( iOpStack.size()!=0 && iPriority(iTopChar())>=iPriority(pOp) )
   {
      iPostfixStringBuffer.append(iTopChar());
      iOpStack.remove();
   }
   // iOpStack.size()==0 !! iPriority(iTopChar())<iPriority(pOp)
   iOpStack.add(new Character(pOp));
}
private void iProcessEndOfExpression()
{
   while ( iOpStack.size()!=0 )
   {
      iPostfixStringBuffer.append(iTopChar());
      iOpStack.remove();
   }
   // iOpStack.size()==0
}
private char iTopChar()
{
   final Character tTopCharacter = (Character)iOpStack.getFirst();
   return tTopCharacter.charValue();
}
private int iPriority(final char pOp)
{
   int tPriority = 0;
   switch (pOp)
   {
      case '*':
      case '/':
      {
         tPriority = 20;
      }
      break;
      case '+':
      case '-':
      {
         tPriority = 10;
      }
      break;
   }
   return tPriority;
}
}
```

Figure 14.15 The Infix class represents an infix expression.

object from a string (containing the characters of the infix expression), and a method called `toReversePolish` that returns a string that is the reverse Polish form of the expression.

The algorithm requires us to put operators on to a stack. This is done by `Infix`'s `iProcessOp` method, and it has a `char` parameter that contains the operator to be stacked. Because the parameter of `Stack`'s `add` method is of the type `Object`, a `char` cannot be used as an argument. The code of the `iProcessOp` method uses the *wrapper class* `Character` to produce an object that can be added to the stack. This wrapper class is also used in `Infix`'s `iTopChar` method when the operator is removed from the stack.

14.5.7 A program to convert an expression to reverse Polish

Finally, a program which uses the `Infix` class is given in Figure 14.16. It reads in an infix expression from the keyboard and outputs the reverse Polish form of the expression to the screen.

```java
// A program that reads an infix expression and outputs reverse Polish.
// Barry Cornelius, 19 June 2000
import java.io. BufferedReader;
import java.io. InputStreamReader;
import java.io. IOException;
public class ToReversePolishProg
{
    public static void main(final String[] pArgs) throws IOException
    {
        final BufferedReader tKeyboard =
                        new BufferedReader(new InputStreamReader(System.in));
        System.out.print("Type in an expression (using infix notation): ");
        System.out.flush();
        String tInfixString = tKeyboard.readLine();
        Infix tInfix = new Infix(tInfixString);
        System.out.println("The equivalent reverse Polish is: " +
                        tInfix.toReversePolish());
    }
}
```

Figure 14.16 `ToReversePolish` reads infix and outputs reverse Polish.

Tips for programming and debugging

14.1 As mentioned earlier, the values that we can `add` to a `List` have to be objects. So you will need to use a *wrapper class* if you want to add a value that is of a primitive type. For more details, look at how `Character` is used in Section 14.5.6.

14.2 When you `get` an object from a `List`, you will often need to cast the object from the class `Object` into the real class of the object. If you cast it into an inappropriate class, a `ClassCastException` will be produced.

Curios, controversies and cover-ups

14.1 The table of List's methods (given in Figure 14.2) lists the two add methods as:

```
public void add(Object pValue);
public void add(int pIndex, Object pValue);
```

and we have used both of these methods as void methods. However, the first of these two add methods is really a function:

```
public boolean add(Object pValue);
```

This function always returns the value true. For more details, see the WWW pages at $API/java/util/List.html.

14.2 Besides implementing the List interface, the classes ArrayList and LinkedList also provide other public methods (that do not belong to the interface). For more details, see the WWW pages at $API/java/util/ArrayList.html and $API/java/util/LinkedList.html.

14.3 The ExamineList program (given in Figure 14.4) includes the statements:

```
final Person tIteratePerson = (Person)tIterator.next();
System.out.println(tIteratePerson);
```

Here there is no need for a *downcast*. The statements could instead be:

```
final Object tIterateObject = tIterator.next();
System.out.println(tIterateObject);
```

Here the call of println will arrange for the toString method to be applied to the object pointed to by tIterateObject. Because this variable is pointing to a PersonImpl object, it is PersonImpl's toString that will get executed.

We can only avoid a downcast if the method we wish to apply to the object is one that overrides a method of the class Object. In practice, this is likely to occur only for the toString method.

14.4 Although the Collections API was not present in JDK 1.0 and JDK 1.1, these earlier versions of the JDK did have a class called Vector. This class provides similar functionality to the ArrayList class. For compatibility reasons, it is also present in the Java 2 Platform. However, in this book, the ArrayList class is used instead.

14.5 The unmodifiableList method from the java.util.Collections class allows you to convert a list into an unmodifiable list. Any attempt to alter the contents of the list results in an unchecked exception called UnsupportedOperationException.

14.6 In Section 21.2, we will look at programs that have more than one *thread*. If a List object is accessed from more than one thread, it may be useful for the program to use the synchronizedList method from the java.util.Collections class. This method converts a list into a synchronized (i.e. a thread-safe) list.

14.7   A class that implements the Iterator interface needs to provide code for hasNext, next and remove. Assuming that a LinkedList implementation creates the structures illustrated in Section 14.3.2, the body of the hasNext method can be:

```
return next.after!=null;
```

The body of the next method can be:

```
if (next.after==null)
{
    throw NoSuchElementException;
}
last = next;
next = next.after;
return last.value;
```

The body of the remove method can be:

```
if (last==null || last.before==null)
{
    throw IllegalStateException;
}
last.before.after = last.after;
next.before = last.before;
last = null;
```

Note that the last pointer is just used to implement Iterator's remove method.

14.8   Although JDK 1.0 and JDK 1.1 have an interface called Enumeration (in the java.util package), these earlier versions of the JDK do not include the Iterator interface. According to one of Sun's WWW pages ([31]), Sun 'view the method names for Enumeration as unfortunate. They're very long, and very frequently used. Given that we were adding a method and creating a whole new framework, we felt that it would be foolish not to take advantange of the opportunity to improve the names.' For compatibility reasons, the Java 2 Platform includes Enumeration. However, although you may see code using Enumeration, it is preferable to write new code in terms of Iterator.

14.9   The List interface also contains a method called listIterator which returns a value of the ListIterator interface type. This interface is more sophisticated than the Iterator interface in that it allows a client to traverse the list in either direction, to move up and down the list at will, or to change the list while traversing it. For more details, look at $API/java/util/ListIterator.html.

14.10 Although this chapter provides a class called `Stack`, there is a class called `Stack` in the Core APIs. It is in the package `java.util`, and so it is documented at $API/java/util/Stack.html.

14.11 The interface `List` (and its supporting classes `ArrayList` and `LinkedList`) can be used to manipulate lists of objects of any classes. We can have lists of dates, lists of people, lists of points, and so on. This is possible because the interface and the classes are written in terms of the class `Object`.

However, as mentioned in Section 14.3.7, it is possible to add objects of any class to a list. If we do not intend to do this (i.e. our intention is to build a *homogeneous list*), then this error will not be detected at compilation time as what we have written is allowed. Unless we detect it when testing the program, the bug will surface as a `ClassCastException` when someone uses the program (as was mentioned in Tip 14.2).

Although the definition of the Java language has not changed much recently, in April 1999 Sun Microsystems made a suggestion that Java should be altered to include **generic types**. This proposal is being considered under Sun's **Java Community Process**. More details are on the WWW at [32].

Philip Wadler has written an article about generic types and what might happen to Java. The article is on the WWW at [51].

If this change were to be accepted, it would mean that you would need to use the type `Object` less often. In particular, the Collections API would be altered to allow you to specify that each object in a list belongs to some class/interface type. So, when adding a value to a collection, it must be an object of this type; and, when an element is retrieved from a collection, it would automatically be of this class/interface type, and you would not need to use a downcast.

Although a draft of the proposed change has not yet been produced, it would mean that instead of writing:

```
List tList = new ArrayList();
Person tPersonToAdd = new PersonImpl("Joe%2000-12-25%1234%0.3");
tList.add(tPersonToAdd);
Person tPersonGot = (Person)tList.get(0);
```

we could write something like the following:

```
List<Person> tList = new ArrayList<PersonImpl>();
Person tPersonToAdd = new PersonImpl("Joe%2000-12-25%1234%0.3");
tList.add(tPersonToAdd);
Person tPersonGot = tList.get(0);
```

As mentioned above, one of the drawbacks of using the type `Object` for collections is that some errors in programming are not detected until a program crashes at runtime. Unless a program is exhaustively tested, it may be that such an error is not in fact detected at testing, and embarrassingly materializes a lot later. The benefit of accepting generic types is that most of these sorts of errors could be detected when a program is compiled.

It is a pity that this did not form part of the original definition of the Java programming language, and that Sun Microsystems have taken so long to bite this bullet.

Exercises

14.1   In this chapter, classes called `LinkedQueue` and `LinkedStack` were presented that implement interfaces called `Queue` and `Stack`. Both of these classes are written in terms of the class `LinkedList` from the `java.util` package. What changes have to be made to the classes `LinkedQueue` and `LinkedStack` to use `ArrayList` instead?

If these changes were made to the classes, what changes (if any) are needed to the interfaces `Queue` and `Stack`? What changes (if any) need to be made to clients that use these interfaces and classes?

14.2   Modify the `PersonLinkedQueueProg` program (given in Figure 14.9) so that it calls `toString` on the `iPersonQueue` variable if the user types in the letter `'t'` as a command.

14.3   Suppose that there is a fictitious operator, say, $, that has a priority of 0. If such an operator were placed at the bottom of the stack prior to any calls of `iProcessOp`, there would be no need to check for an empty stack in the while statement of `iProcessOp` (see Figure 14.15). We can replace the while statement by:

```
while (iPriority(iTopChar())>=iPriority(pOp))
{
    iPostfixStringBuffer.append(iTopChar());
    iOpStack.remove();
}
// iPriority(iTopChar())<iPriority(pOp)
```

Make these changes. Note that you only have to alter the code of the `Infix` class – do not make changes anywhere else. Re-compile this class and the `ToReversePolishProg` class, and then run the program again.

14.4   Modify the interface `Stack` (given in Figure 14.13) and the class `Linked-Stack` (given in Figure 14.14) so that they support the following methods:

- a function called `isEmpty` that returns the value *true* if and only if the stack has no elements;

- a void method called `interchangeTopTwo` that reverses the order of the top two elements of the stack;

- a void method called `duplicateTop` that adds to the stack a new element which points to an object that has the same value as that of the element which was the top element of the stack.

Write a program to test the new version.

14.5 The algorithm for converting an expression to postfix notation can be changed to handle parentheses by including the following two new cases:

- *when the character being analysed is a* ' (', *a fictitious operator,* ' (', should be added to the stack. This operator should be given the priority 2;

- *when the character being analysed is a* ') ', each operator on the stack up to (but not including) the first ' (' operator should be unstacked. As each operator is unstacked, it should be placed at the right-hand end of the postfix expression. The ' (' operator should then be unstacked (but it should not be output).

Modify the `Infix` class so that it contains code to implement these changes. (This is the only file that needs to be altered.) Re-compile `Infix` and `ToReversePolishProg`, and test the new version.

14.6 Modify the program for converting an expression to postfix notation so that it can handle operands that are identifiers with more than one character.

14.7 A string of characters can be reversed by putting each character of the string on to a stack and then popping the stack until it is empty. Write a method that reverses the string value passed as an argument to the method. It should return a `String` that is the reversed string. Your method should perform its task using the interface `Stack` and the class `LinkedStack`. Write a program that tests this method.

14.8 The flight plan for the flight of a plane consists of a sequence of points. For example, the flight from London Heathrow to Seattle might go via Manchester, Prestwick, Reykjavik, Greenland, Hudson Bay and Yellowstone. The aim of this exercise is to write a program that reads a sequence of points and manipulates them as a `List`.

Create a file containing the positions of Heathrow, Manchester, Prestwick, Reykjavik, Greenland, Hudson Bay, Yellowstone and Seattle. These points have the following positions:

```
000-20-00-W:51-20-00-N
002-20-00-W:53-25-00-N
004-30-00-W:55-35-00-N
021-30-00-W:64-00-00-N
044-00-00-W:60-00-00-N
083-00-00-W:55-00-00-N
111-00-00-W:44-00-00-N
122-30-00-W:48-00-00-N
```

In your program, you will be representing the sequence of points by an `ArrayList` where each object of the list is of the type `Position` (which was given in Exercise 12.10).

Like the `PersonLinkedQueueProg` program (given in Figure 14.9), your program should read commands from the user. The following commands should be accepted:

- r   Read the details of a flight. When the program receives the r command, it should read a filename from the keyboard, open that file, read the lines of that file (assuming that there is a textual representation of a `PositionImpl` value on each of the lines), and add each `PositionImpl` value to the `List`.

- t   Output the result of running `toString` on the `ArrayList` variable.

- f   Output the position of the starting point of the flight. Within the program, set a `iPointNumber` variable to 0, `get` that particular element of the list and output it.

- n   Output the position of the next point of the flight. Increase the `iPointNumber` variable by 1, `get` that particular element of the list and output it.

- m   Change the position of the current point to a new value. Read the textual representation of a `Position` value from the keyboard and `set` the current element to that value.

- q   To exit from the program.

When you run your program, use f followed by a number of n commands in order to get to the seventh point. Then use the m command to change it from Yellowstone to Lake Winnipeg which is at 99-00-00-W:53-00-00-N. Then use the q command.

14.9   Create a file called `FigureProg.java` that contains the following values of data where each value is on a separate line: 1, 0.5, 2, 3.0, 5.0, 1, 1.0, 2, 1.0 and 1.0. This file contains descriptions about geometrical figures. The value 1 means that the next line contains the radius of a circle, whereas the value 2 means that the next two lines contain the width and height of a rectangle. So the above file describes:

- a circle of radius 0.5;

- a rectangle with width of 3.0 and height of 5.0;

- a circle of radius 1.0;

- a rectangle with width of 1.0 and height of 1.0.

Create a file called `Figure.java` containing the following interface:

```
public interface Figure
{
    public double area();
    public double perimeter();
    public String toString();
}
```

Provide a class called `Circle` that implements this interface. The class should have one constructor that has one parameter (of type `double`) that is the radius of a circle. Also provide suitable methods called `area`, `perimeter` and `toString` that return appropriate values. Do not provide any other constructors and do not provide methods called `equals`, `hashCode` or `compareTo`. Hints: if pi is the value of `Math.PI` and r is the radius of a circle, the area of the circle is pi*r*r and the perimeter of the circle is 2*pi*r.

Provide a class called `Rectangle` that also implements the `Figure` interface. The class should have one constructor that has two parameters (of type `double`) that are the width and height of a rectangle. Also provide suitable methods called `area`, `perimeter` and `toString`. Hints: if a rectangle has a width of w and a height of h, the area of the rectangle is w*h and the perimeter of the rectangle is (h+w)*2.

Write a program (called `FigureProg`) that reads in a data file like the one given above. The program should also create an `ArrayList` object and make a `List` variable, e.g. one called `tList`, point to it. For each of the figures described in the file that is read by the program, the program should either create an appropriate value of class `Circle` and add it to `tList` or it should create an appropriate value of class `Rectangle` and add that to `tList`.

After the program has read the file, the program should then output the details about each element of the list. Do this by using the `iterator` method on `tList` to produce an `Iterator` object, and then use a while statement containing calls of the `hasNext` and `next` methods applied to the `Iterator` object. The `next` method returns a value of type `Object`. Cast this result to the type `Figure` and make a `Figure` variable called `tFigure` point to the result of this downcast. Also (inside the while loop), output the result of applying `toString`, `area` and `perimeter` to this `Figure` variable.

You should get output like:

```
Circle(0.5) 0.7853981633974483 3.141592653589793
Rectangle(3.0,5.0) 15.0 16.0
Circle(1.0) 3.141592653589793 6.283185307179586
Rectangle(1.0,1.0) 1.0 4.0
```

Note that the string at the start of each line depends on what coding you have for `toString`.

Chapter 15

Using an array to represent a collection of values

The `List` interface and the `ArrayList` and `LinkedList` classes make it easy to store a collection of values. One of the advantages of using them is that they provide a possibility of storing a collection whose size we are unable to predict beforehand.

An alternative to using this interface and these classes is to use the *array* construct. In this chapter, we will see that the array is more suitable when the number of values to be stored is known. And storing values that are of a primitive type is a lot easier with an array than it is with a `List`. So a typical example where it would be more appropriate to use an array is when you want to store 12 rainfall figures, one for each month of a year.

The final example of this chapter looks at how we can use an array in a class that implements the `List` interface. Effectively, we will produce a class that rivals `java.util`'s `ArrayList`.

15.1 The need for arrays

Suppose that the manufacturer of a coffee vending machine wants to determine the popularity of the various drink combinations that the vending machine dispenses. The machine has four buttons marked 1, 2, 3 and 4 together with a notice explaining which button to use:

1   Black coffee, without sugar
2   Black coffee, with sugar
3   White coffee, without sugar
4   White coffee, with sugar

Suppose that we have some data containing the selections that have been made by the customers; that each line of data contains a selection, a value in the range 1 to 4; and that an empty line is used to indicate the end of the data.

Here is some pseudo-code for a solution to the problem:

1. Initialize all the frequency counts to zero.

Process the   } loop until   { **1.** Read in a selection.
2. selections of } an empty line   { **2.** If it is in range,
the customers } is read   {   then Increase the appropriate
                                        frequency count by one.

3. Output the frequency counts.

To store the counts of the frequency of selection of each drink, we could use four int variables. They could be called tBlackWithout, tBlackWith, tWhite-Without and tWhiteWith. And having read in the selection of a customer we need to increase an appropriate variable by one. If the selection is 1, we need to increase tBlackWithout by 1; if it is 2, we increase tBlackWith by 1; and so on. Of course, this can be handled easily by a switch statement. The complete code for this problem is given in Figure 15.1 and Figure 15.2.

Although this is a reasonable solution to this particular problem, note that a large amount of the code of the VendingMachine class would have to be altered if we had, say, three or perhaps five drink combinations. We would have to alter the declarations, the initializations, the switch statement, and the output section. So the program is not very versatile.

However, there is really a much more significant problem. If the number of drink combinations is increased a little, the code we need gets horrendous. Consider the code which would be produced if we had 20 drink combinations. We would need 20 declarations, 20 initializations, a switch statement with 20 arms, and 20 parts to the output section. We need a less clumsy way than having 20 copies of each of these pieces of code.

```java
// This class uses simple variables to represent the frequency counts.
// Barry Cornelius, 19 June 2000
import java.io. BufferedReader;
import java.io. IOException;
public class VendingMachine
{
   private BufferedReader iKeyboard;
   private int iBlackWithout;
   private int iBlackWith;
   private int iWhiteWithout;
   private int iWhiteWith;
   public VendingMachine(final BufferedReader pKeyboard)
   {
      iKeyboard = pKeyboard;
   }
   public void setFrequencyCountsToZero()
   {
      iBlackWithout = 0;
      iBlackWith = 0;
      iWhiteWithout = 0;
      iWhiteWith = 0;
   }
   public void readInSelectionsAndUpdateFrequencyCounts()
                                                throws IOException

   {
      while (true)
      {
         final String tLine = iKeyboard.readLine();
         if (tLine.equals(""))
         {
            break;
         }
         final int tDrinkSelection = Integer.parseInt(tLine);
         switch (tDrinkSelection)
         {
            case 1:
            {
               iBlackWithout += 1;
            }
            break;
            case 2:
            {
               iBlackWith += 1;
            }
            break;
            case 3:
            {
               iWhiteWithout += 1;
            }
            break;
```

Figure 15.1 *Continues on the next page.*

```
                    case 4:
                    {
                        iWhiteWith += 1;
                    }
                    break;
                    default:
                    {
                        System.out.println("The value is out of range");
                        System.exit(1);
                    }
                }
            }
        }
    public void outputFrequencyCounts()
    {
        System.out.println("Black (no sugar): " + iBlackWithout);
        System.out.println("Black with sugar: " + iBlackWith);
        System.out.println("White (no sugar): " + iWhiteWithout);
        System.out.println("White with sugar: " + iWhiteWith);
    }
}
```

Figure 15.1 A class that uses simple variables for the frequency counts.

```
// This program determines the popularity of the various
// combinations of drinks offered by a vending machine.
// Barry Cornelius, 19 June 2000
import java.io. BufferedReader;
import java.io. InputStreamReader;
import java.io. IOException;
public class VendingMachineProg
{
    public static void main(final String[] pArgs) throws IOException
    {
        final BufferedReader tKeyboard =
                new BufferedReader(new InputStreamReader(System.in));
        final VendingMachine tVendingMachine = new VendingMachine(tKeyboard);
        tVendingMachine.setFrequencyCountsToZero();
        tVendingMachine.readInSelectionsAndUpdateFrequencyCounts();
        tVendingMachine.outputFrequencyCounts();
    }
}
```

Figure 15.2 A program that processes the transactions of a vending machine.

15.2 Using a `List` for the vending machine problem

In Chapter 14, we used a `List` to represent a collection of values. So perhaps we can set up an `ArrayList` to contain the counts of the frequencies of the selections of each drink.

So, suppose (after receiving many complaints!) the manufacturer decides to offer tea as well as coffee. The machine is modified so that it now has eight buttons, and the frequency analysis program needs to be altered so that it can handle the following codes in the data:

1   Black coffee, without sugar
2   Black coffee, with sugar
3   White coffee, without sugar
4   White coffee, with sugar
5   Black tea, without sugar
6   Black tea, with sugar
7   White tea, without sugar
8   White tea, with sugar

It will need eight variables to count the number of selections of each drink combination.

We can create an `ArrayList` object in which to store these values as follows:

```
ArrayList iFrequencyCounts = new ArrayList();
```

As mentioned in Section 14.3.1, the initial capacity of any `ArrayList` object has some value that has been chosen by the designers of the Collections API:

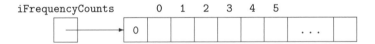

But we know that our program only needs space for eight values. We can indicate this by using a different constructor of the `ArrayList` class, one that indicates how many elements are needed:

```
ArrayList iFrequencyCounts = new ArrayList(8);
```

The execution of this declaration leads to the following situation:

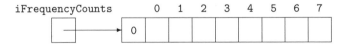

One of the subproblems given in the pseudo-code in the previous section is *Read in a selection*. In the `VendingMachine` class (given in Figure 15.1), this was coded using:

```
final String tLine = iKeyboard.readLine();
final int tDrinkSelection = Integer.parseInt(tLine);
```

The next subproblem is *Increase the appropriate frequency count by one*. When providing code for this subproblem, the version of the `VendingMachine` class shown in Figure 15.1 used a switch statement. If we use an `ArrayList`, we can use get to retrieve the current value of one of the eight elements and use set to change its value. Each of the frequency counts is an int. However, as was pointed out in Section 14.5.6, we cannot store a value of a primitive type in an element of this list: we will need to use the *wrapper class* Integer to create an object containing the int value. And, because, the value of tDrinkSelection is in the range 1 to 8 and the elements are numbered from 0 to 7, we will need code like:

```
final int tElementNumber = tDrinkSelection - 1;
final Integer tOldInteger =
                   (Integer)iFrequencyCounts.get(tElementNumber);
final Integer tNewInteger = new Integer(tOldInteger.intValue() + 1);
iFrequencyCounts.set(tElementNumber, tNewInteger);
```

Although it is possible to write statements like these in which you subtract one each time you want to move from a value in the range 1 to 8 to one in the range 0 to 7, it is easy to forget to do this. This would be another occurrence of a *one-off error*. An alternative approach is to allocate one extra element:

```
ArrayList iFrequencyCounts = new ArrayList(9);
```

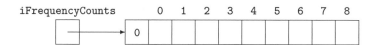

and to ignore the first element (the one with an index of zero). If you do this, the calls of get and set in the above code for updating the frequency counts by one can be written in terms of tDrinkSelection instead of tElementNumber.

The complete code of this new version of the VendingMachine class is given in Figure 15.3.

```
// This class uses an ArrayList to represent the frequency counts.
// Barry Cornelius, 19 June 2000
import java.util. ArrayList;
import java.io.   BufferedReader;
import java.io.   IOException;
public class VendingMachine
{
    private BufferedReader iKeyboard;
    private int iNumberOfDrinks;
    private ArrayList iFrequencyCounts;
    public VendingMachine(final BufferedReader pKeyboard,
                          final int pNumberOfDrinks)
    {
        iKeyboard = pKeyboard;
        iNumberOfDrinks = pNumberOfDrinks;
    }
```

Figure 15.3 *Continues on the next page.*

```
public void setFrequencyCountsToZero()
{
   iFrequencyCounts = new ArrayList(iNumberOfDrinks + 1);
   final Integer tZeroInteger = new Integer(0);
   for (int tDrinkNumber = 0; tDrinkNumber<=iNumberOfDrinks;
                             tDrinkNumber++)
   {
      iFrequencyCounts.add(tZeroInteger);
   }
}
public void readInSelectionsAndUpdateFrequencyCounts()
                                        throws IOException
{
   while (true)
   {
      final String tLine = iKeyboard.readLine();
      if (tLine.equals(""))
      {
         break;
      }
      final int tDrinkSelection = Integer.parseInt(tLine);
      if (tDrinkSelection<1 || tDrinkSelection>iNumberOfDrinks)
      {
         System.out.println("The value is out of range");
         System.exit(1);
      }
      // tDrinkSelection>=1 && tDrinkSelection<=iNumberOfDrinks
      final Integer tOldInteger =
                      (Integer)iFrequencyCounts.get(tDrinkSelection);
      final Integer tNewInteger = new Integer(tOldInteger.intValue() + 1);
      iFrequencyCounts.set(tDrinkSelection, tNewInteger);
   }
}
public void outputFrequencyCounts()
{
   for (int tDrinkNumber = 1; tDrinkNumber<=iNumberOfDrinks;
                             tDrinkNumber++)
   {
      final Integer tFrequencyCount =
                      (Integer)iFrequencyCounts.get(tDrinkNumber);
      System.out.println(tDrinkNumber + " " + tFrequencyCount.intValue());
   }
}
}
```

Figure 15.3 A class that uses an `ArrayList` for the frequency counts.

Here is a diagram that shows a typical state in the execution of the program:

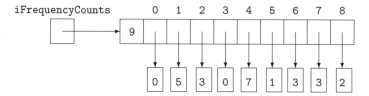

Instead of using:

```
iFrequencyCounts = new ArrayList(9);
```

the code of this class uses:

```
iFrequencyCounts = new ArrayList(iNumberOfDrinks + 1);
```

where iNumberOfDrinks is a private field of the class. This field gets its value from a value that is passed as an argument to the constructor when an object of the class is being created. By doing this, it is possible for the decision on the number of drink combinations to be made by the client. In the new version of the VendingMachine-Prog program (shown in Figure 15.4), the value 8 is used.

```
// This program determines the popularity of the various
// combinations of drinks offered by a vending machine.
// Barry Cornelius, 19 June 2000
import java.io. BufferedReader;
import java.io. InputStreamReader;
import java.io. IOException;
public class VendingMachineProg
{
    public static void main(final String[] pArgs) throws IOException
    {
        final BufferedReader tKeyboard =
                new BufferedReader(new InputStreamReader(System.in));
        final int tNumberOfDrinks = 8;
        final VendingMachine tVendingMachine =
                new VendingMachine(tKeyboard, tNumberOfDrinks);
        tVendingMachine.setFrequencyCountsToZero();
        tVendingMachine.readInSelectionsAndUpdateFrequencyCounts();
        tVendingMachine.outputFrequencyCounts();
    }
}
```

Figure 15.4   The new client determines the size of the vending machine.

15.3 Using an array for the vending machine problem

This new version of the VendingMachineProg program is better than the previous one because little work has to be done to the program if you want to change the number of drink combinations. However, it is not really appropriate to use an `ArrayList` for this kind of problem. Because the collection contains a predictable number of values, e.g. eight values, it is better to use Java's *array* construct. We will also find that the array construct makes it easier to handle collections of values that are of a primitive type: we will not have to use a wrapper class.

As will be shown in the next section, we can provide a statement that creates an **array object**. This object can be used instead of eight simple variables. In our program, we will declare a variable, called an **array variable**, that can point to this object. Suppose we have an array variable called `iFrequencyCounts`. Then, instead of referring to the variables:

        tBlackCoffeeWithout, tBlackCoffeeWith, ... , tWhiteTeaWith

we can use:

        iFrequencyCounts[0], iFrequencyCounts[1], ... , iFrequencyCounts[7]

You can visualize an array object as a group of boxes:

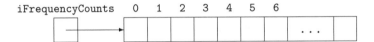

To refer to a particular box, we use the identifier of the array variable followed by an **index** within square brackets. So, in `iFrequencyCounts[4]`, the 4 is the index. This is similar to the subscripts used in mathematics, e.g. x_1 and x_2. A particular box is called an **element** or a **component** of the array. For the technical distinction between an *element* and a *component*, see Curio 15.2.

Not much would be achieved if we could only use a literal as an index. In the same way as a mathematician uses x_i and x_{i+1}, we can represent the subproblem *Increase the appropriate frequency count by one* (from the pseudo-code given earlier) by:

        add 1 to iFrequencyCounts[tDrinkSelection]

i.e. by:

```
iFrequencyCounts[tDrinkSelection] = iFrequencyCounts[tDrinkSelection] + 1;
```

or by:

```
iFrequencyCounts[tDrinkSelection] += 1;
```

Here we are referring to the variable `tDrinkSelection`; and so the particular element of the array object that gets increased by one depends on the value of `tDrinkSelection`.

In general, the index can be any expression whose type is `int` (or `char` or `byte` or `short` but not `long`).

The complete code for the subproblem *Process the selections of the customers* is given in the `readInSelectionsAndUpdateFrequencyCounts` method of the `VendingMachine` class that is shown in Figure 15.5. Once again, note that, unlike

```java
// This class uses an array to represent the frequency counts.
// Barry Cornelius, 19 June 2000
import java.io.BufferedReader;
import java.io.IOException;
public class VendingMachine
{
   private BufferedReader iKeyboard;
   private int iNumberOfDrinks;
   private int[] iFrequencyCounts;
   public VendingMachine(final BufferedReader pKeyboard,
                         final int pNumberOfDrinks)
   {
      iKeyboard = pKeyboard;
      iNumberOfDrinks = pNumberOfDrinks;
   }
   public void setFrequencyCountsToZero()
   {
      iFrequencyCounts = new int[iNumberOfDrinks + 1];
      for (int tDrinkNumber = 1; tDrinkNumber<=iNumberOfDrinks;
                                 tDrinkNumber++)
      {
         iFrequencyCounts[tDrinkNumber] = 0;
      }
   }
   public void readInSelectionsAndUpdateFrequencyCounts()
                                              throws IOException
   {
      while (true)
      {
         final String tLine = iKeyboard.readLine();
         if (tLine.equals(""))
         {
            break;
         }
         final int tDrinkSelection = Integer.parseInt(tLine);
         if (tDrinkSelection<1 || tDrinkSelection>iNumberOfDrinks)
         {
            System.out.println("The value is out of range");
            System.exit(1);
         }
         // tDrinkSelection>=1 && tDrinkSelection<=iNumberOfDrinks
         iFrequencyCounts[tDrinkSelection] += 1;
      }
   }
   public void outputFrequencyCounts()
   {
      for (int tDrinkNumber = 1; tDrinkNumber<=iNumberOfDrinks;
                                 tDrinkNumber++)
      {
         System.out.println(tDrinkNumber + " " +
                            iFrequencyCounts[tDrinkNumber]);
      }
   }
}
```

Figure 15.5 A class that uses an array for the frequency counts.

the switch statement given in the first version of `VendingMachine` class, this code does not have to be altered if the number of drink combinations is changed.

15.4 The declaration of array variables

In a Java program, we need to indicate that `iFrequencyCounts` is an *array variable*. This can be done by the declaration:

```
int[] iFrequencyCounts;
```

However, this just declares a *reference variable*, i.e. a variable that has the ability to point to an array object.

We can create an array object and make `iFrequencyCounts` point to it as follows:

```
iFrequencyCounts = new int[8];
```

This is an assignment statement where the right-hand side is an **array creation expression**.

As usual, the above declaration and assignment statement can be combined:

```
int[] iFrequencyCounts = new int[8];
```

Using the square brackets, the `int`s and the 8 indicates that we want to create:

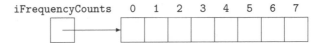

where each element of the array object contains an `int`. In Java, the elements of an array object all have the same type. The element type may be one of the primitive types (such as the type `int`) or a reference type (as will be shown in Section 15.10).

For the reasons explained when using an `ArrayList`, with the vending machine problem we will find it easier to use an array object that is one element bigger, i.e. to use:

```
int[] iFrequencyCounts = new int[9];
```

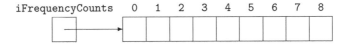

We can ignore element 0 and just use elements 1 to 8 for storing the eight frequency counts. Here is a diagram that shows a typical state in the execution of the program:

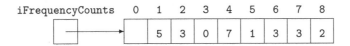

15.5 Completion of the vending machine program

There are two other subproblems of the pseudo-code that we have yet to reconsider. These are the subproblems *Initialize all the frequency counts to zero* and *Output the frequency counts*.

We will look at the second of these subproblems first. The program has gradually been updating eight elements of the array object pointed to by iFrequencyCounts, and the objective of this final subproblem is to output the final values of these elements. So we need to output the values of iFrequencyCounts[1], iFrequency-Counts[2],..., iFrequencyCounts[8]. This can be done by executing the statement:

```
System.out.println(iFrequencyCounts[tDrinkNumber]);
```

repeatedly with tDrinkNumber getting all of the values in the range 1 to 8, i.e. we need:

```
for (int tDrinkNumber = 1; tDrinkNumber<=iNumberOfDrinks;
                           tDrinkNumber++)
{
   System.out.println(iFrequencyCounts[tDrinkNumber]);
}
```

(where tNumberOfDrinks has the value 8). This will produce eight lines of output with each frequency count appearing on a separate line.

The subproblem of initializing all the elements of the array iFrequencyCounts to zero can also be done by a for statement:

```
for (int tDrinkNumber = 1; tDrinkNumber<=iNumberOfDrinks;
                           tDrinkNumber++)
{
   iFrequencyCounts[tDrinkNumber] = 0;
}
```

The complete code of the version of the VendingMachine class that uses an array is shown in Figure 15.5. It has a slightly more detailed output section than that described above. However, the output is still not very meaningful – see Exercise 15.1.

This class can be used with the same program class that was used with the previous version of the class (see Figure 15.4).

15.6 Avoiding **ArrayIndexOutOfBoundsException**

We have seen that the actual element of iFrequencyCounts that is accessed depends on the value of the index that is used. It is most important that this value is in range. If the index has a value that is less than 0 or is greater than tNumberOf-Drinks, the program will be attempting to refer to an element of the array that does not exist. Such an attempt will produce an unchecked exception known as an ArrayIndexOutOfBoundsException exception.

In this latest version of the VendingMachine class, there are four references to an element of the array object pointed to by iFrequencyCounts. We need not worry about the references in:

```
iFrequencyCounts[tDrinkNumber] = 0;
```

and:

```
System.out.println(tDrinkNumber + " " +
                   iFrequencyCounts[tDrinkNumber]);
```

since it is obvious that the surrounding for statement is giving tDrinkNumber appropriate values.

However, the same is not true for the assignment statement:

```
iFrequencyCounts[tDrinkSelection] += 1;
```

and so we ought to examine it more closely. Note that the variable tDrinkSelection is of type int, and that its value is obtained from the user typing in a value at the keyboard. So the variable can have any of the values of the type int. However, because of the if statement that occurs immediately before this assignment statement, this statement will not be executed when tDrinkSelection has a value that is outside the range from 1 to the value of tNumberOfDrinks.

15.7 Other tasks that are often performed on arrays

So far, we have seen two situations in which it has been useful to step through the elements of an array one at a time: these occur in the statements to initialize the array object and in those to output the contents of the array object. There are two other tasks that are often performed on the elements of an array object:

- finding the element with the smallest/largest value;
- finding the sum of the elements of the array object.

We will look at both of these in the context of the vending machine program.

To find the element of the iFrequencyCounts array that has the largest value, we need to introduce a new variable, tMostPopularDrinkNumber. We will start by assuming that the first drink is the most popular. Hence the code of the program can assign 1 to tMostPopularDrinkNumber. The code can then visit each element of the array object in turn, and if it finds a value that is greater than the value indicated by tMostPopularDrinkNumber, it changes the value of the variable tMostPopularDrinkNumber so that it contains the index of this new element. The code to do this task appears in the outputTheMostPopularDrink method of the VendingMachine class that is given in Figure 15.6. A program that uses this method is shown in Figure 15.7.

Besides outputting which is the most popular drink, the output method of this new version of the class also outputs a percentage value for each drink – it is the number of selections of the drink as a percentage of the total number of selections. In order

```java
// The output method outputs percentages as well as frequency counts.
// The class also has a method that finds the most popular drink.
// Barry Cornelius, 19 June 2000
import java.io. BufferedReader;
import java.io. IOException;
public class VendingMachine
{
   private BufferedReader iKeyboard;
   private int iNumberOfDrinks;
   private int[] iFrequencyCounts;
   public VendingMachine(final BufferedReader pKeyboard,
                         final int pNumberOfDrinks)
   {
      iKeyboard = pKeyboard;
      iNumberOfDrinks = pNumberOfDrinks;
   }
   public void setFrequencyCountsToZero()
   {
   ... same as in Figure 15.5
   }
   public void readInSelectionsAndUpdateFrequencyCounts()
                                                throws IOException
   {
   ... same as in Figure 15.5
   }
   public void outputFrequencyCountsAndPercentages()
   {
      int tNumberOfSelections = 0;
      for (int tDrinkNumber = 1; tDrinkNumber<=iNumberOfDrinks;
                                 tDrinkNumber++)
      {
         tNumberOfSelections += iFrequencyCounts[tDrinkNumber];
      }
      for (int tDrinkNumber = 1; tDrinkNumber<=iNumberOfDrinks;
                                 tDrinkNumber++)
      {
         final int tFrequencyCount = iFrequencyCounts[tDrinkNumber];
         final int tPercentage = 100*tFrequencyCount/tNumberOfSelections;
         System.out.println(tDrinkNumber + " " +
                            tFrequencyCount + " " + tPercentage);
      }
   }
}
```

Figure 15.6 *Continues on the next page.*

```java
public void outputTheMostPopularDrink()
{
    int tMostPopularDrinkNumber = 1;
    for (int tDrinkNumber = 2; tDrinkNumber<=iNumberOfDrinks;
                               tDrinkNumber++)
    {
        if (iFrequencyCounts[tDrinkNumber] >
                            iFrequencyCounts[tMostPopularDrinkNumber])
        {
            tMostPopularDrinkNumber = tDrinkNumber;
        }
    }
    System.out.println("The most popular drink is drink number " +
                        tMostPopularDrinkNumber);
}
}
```

Figure 15.6   A class providing additional operations on the frequency counts.

```java
// This program determines the popularity of the various
// combinations of drinks offered by a vending machine.
// It uses a class that has an output method that outputs percentages as well
// as frequency counts and has a method to output the most popular drink.
// Barry Cornelius, 19 June 2000
import java.io. BufferedReader;
import java.io. InputStreamReader;
import java.io. IOException;
public class VendingMachineProg
{
    public static void main(final String[] pArgs) throws IOException
    {
        final BufferedReader tKeyboard =
                new BufferedReader(new InputStreamReader(System.in));
        final int tNumberOfDrinks = 8;
        final VendingMachine tVendingMachine =
                new VendingMachine(tKeyboard, tNumberOfDrinks);
        tVendingMachine.setFrequencyCountsToZero();
        tVendingMachine.readInSelectionsAndUpdateFrequencyCounts();
        tVendingMachine.outputFrequencyCountsAndPercentages();
        tVendingMachine.outputTheMostPopularDrink();
    }
}
```

Figure 15.7   A program that uses the new methods.

to do this, the method needs code for the two subproblems:

1. Find the sum of the elements of the array.

2. Output each element as a percentage of the sum.

The code to do this is shown in the `outputFrequencyCountsAndPercentages` method that is given in Figure 15.6.

This version of the VendingMachine class has been written using four methods. You should note that:

● The code that finds the total number of selections that have been made could be combined with the code that reads in the selections.

● The loop to find the most popular drink number could be combined with the loop that outputs the frequency counts and percentages.

However, such code would be more complicated to understand as it is not so cleanly cut into subproblems.

15.8 Searching an array

Searching an array looking for a value is another frequently performed task – we will look at it in a fairly simple context.

Suppose a program uses elements 1 to 12 of the array:

```
double[] tRainfall = new double[13];
```

to represent the number of inches of rainfall for each of the months of a year.

The program is to find the first month of the year which had less than 2.4 inches of rainfall. So, if the rainfall figures are:

January	3.54
February	2.72
March	2.36
April	2.32
May	2.48
June	2.32
July	2.40
August	2.87
September	3.43
October	3.35
November	3.86
December	3.70

the program has to work out that the third figure is the first one that has a value less then 2.4, and so it should set a variable, say, tFirstDryMonthNumber to the value 3.

The code of the program has to work its way along the array looking for the first value which is less than 2.4. Thus, it can start with tMonthNumber equal to 1 and keep increasing tMonthNumber by 1 so long as tRainfall[tMonthNumber]>=2.4. Here is the code:

```
tMonthNumber = 1;
while (tRainfall[tMonthNumber]>=2.4)
{
    tMonthNumber++;
}
// tRainfall[tMonthNumber]<2.4
tFirstDryMonthNumber = tMonthNumber;
```

However, what happens when the year is a very wet year and there are no months with under 2.4 inches of rainfall? The values of tRainfall[tMonthNumber] will be greater than or equal to 2.4 for all values of tMonthNumber. The above code will produce an ArrayIndexOutOfBoundsException exception at the evaluation of tRainfall[tMonthNumber]>=2.4 when tMonthNumber has the value 13.

This error can be avoided once we recognize that the program needs to quit the loop in two ways:

- when it finds a value which is less than 2.4,
- when it reaches the end of the array.

One possible way of coding this is:

```
tMonthNumber = 1;
while (tRainfall[tMonthNumber]>=2.4 && tMonthNumber!=12)
{
    tMonthNumber++;
}
// tRainfall[tMonthNumber]<2.4 || tMonthNumber==12
if (tRainfall[tMonthNumber]<2.4)
{
    tDryMonthFound = true;
    tFirstDryMonthNumber = tMonthNumber;
}
else
{
    tDryMonthFound = false;
}
```

If this code finds a month that had under 2.4 inches of rainfall, it sets the variable tDryMonthFound to the value *true* and assigns an appropriate value to tFirstDryMonthNumber; otherwise, it sets tDryMonthFound to the value *false*.

15.9 Other points about arrays

Here are some other points about arrays:

1. This particular form of array is called a **one-dimensional array**. A **two-dimensional array** (or **matrix**) can be constructed by assigning array objects to each element of an array.

2. The following code creates an array object and assigns initial values to each of the elements:

```
double[] tRainfall = new double[13];
tRainfall[ 0] = 0.0;
tRainfall[ 1] = 3.54;
tRainfall[ 2] = 2.72;
...
tRainfall[12] = 3.70;
```

An **array initializer** can be used to abbreviate the above declaration and 13 assignment statements:

```
double[] tRainfall = { 0.0, 3.54, 2.72, 2.36, 2.32, 2.48, 2.32,
                       2.40, 2.87, 3.43, 3.35, 3.86, 3.70 };
```

Note that, when you use an array initializer, you do not have to give the size of the array as this is automatically deduced from the list of initial values.

3. You can find out the size of an array using the array's `length` variable. For example, the statement:

```
int tSize = tRainfall.length;
```

will assign the value 13 to `tSize`.

If an array is used as a parameter of a method, then, within the method, you can use `length` to find out the size of the array that has been passed as an argument. An example of this appears in Section 10.11 where `length` is applied to `pArgs`. For a possible confusion about the name `length`, see Tip 10.1.

4. Each array object has a method called `clone` that overrides `Object`'s `clone` method. It can be used to produce a copy of an array object:

```
double[] tRainfall = { 0.0, 3.54, 2.72, 2.36, 2.32, 2.48, 2.32,
                       2.40, 2.87, 3.43, 3.35, 3.86, 3.70 };
double[] tAnotherRainfall = (double[])tRainfall.clone();
```

5. The class `java.util.Arrays` provides a number of methods for manipulating arrays, including many overloadings of methods called `equals`, `fill`, `sort` and `binarySearch`.

The various `equals` methods can be used to compare two arrays that have the same type of elements. It is a *class method*; the two arrays are passed as parameters; and it returns the value *true* if and only if the two arrays have the same size and corresponding elements of the two arrays have the same value:

```
if ( Arrays.equals(tRainfall, tAnotherRainfall) )
...
```

The various `fill` methods can be used to fill an array with some value:

```
Arrays.fill(tRainfall, 1.0);
```

would assign the value 1.0 to all elements of the array `tRainfall`.

The various `sort` methods can be used to sort an array into numerical order, and the various `binarySearch` methods can be used to search a sorted array for a particular value. There is an example that uses these two methods in Section 15.10.

Note: `java.util.Arrays` was not present in JDK 1.0 and JDK 1.1.

6. The class `java.lang.System` provides a class method called `arraycopy` that can be used to copy part of an array into another array (or into the same array). There is an example of the use of this method in Section 15.11.5.

15.10 Using an array of objects

In the examples of arrays that have been given so far, the elements have been of some primitive type. As explained earlier, the elements of an array object all have the same type which may be one of the primitive types or may be a reference type. We now look at an example where the elements are of a reference type.

Suppose we want to represent the seating of people in a plane or a theatre. We have a fixed number of seats, and each seat is either empty or contains a person. In order to represent a person, we could use the type `String`, and so the array of seats could be represented by:

```
String[] iSeats = new String[iNumberOfSeats];
```

We could then execute assignment statements such as:

```
iSeats[0] = new String("Joe");
iSeats[1] = new String("Sue");
...
```

and this would result in the following:

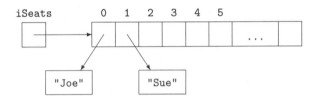

However, instead we will reuse the type `Person` and so represent the collection of seats by:

```
Person[] iSeats = new Person[iNumberOfSeats];
```

As the type of each element of this array object is the interface type `Person`, each element can be assigned any value that can be assigned to a `Person` variable. For example, we could execute:

```
iSeats[0] = new PersonImpl("Joe%2000-12-25%2468%1.85");
```

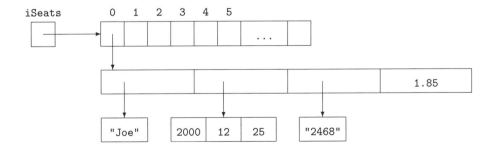

A class that uses an array to implement a collection of seats is shown in Figure 15.8. The class provides a method called checkIn that can be used to fill the seats with passengers; a method called outputSeats that can be used to output details of who is sitting in the seats; a method called sortTheEntries that can be used to sort the elements of the array; and a method called querySeats that keeps on reading the

```java
// This class uses an array to implement a collection of seats.
// Barry Cornelius, 19 June 2000
import java.util. Arrays;
import java.io.   BufferedReader;
import java.io.   IOException;
public class Seats
{
    private BufferedReader iKeyboard;
    private int iNumberOfSeats;
    private Person[] iSeats;
    public Seats(final BufferedReader pKeyboard, final int pNumberOfSeats)
    {
        iKeyboard = pKeyboard;
        iNumberOfSeats = pNumberOfSeats;
        iSeats = new Person[iNumberOfSeats + 1];
        final Person tEmptyPerson = new PersonImpl();
        for (int tSeatNumber = 1; tSeatNumber<=iNumberOfSeats; tSeatNumber++)
        {
            iSeats[tSeatNumber] = tEmptyPerson;
        }
    }
    public void checkIn() throws IOException
    {
        int tSeatNumber = 0;
        while (true)
        {
            final String tLine = iKeyboard.readLine();
            if (tLine.equals(""))
            {
                break;
            }
            tSeatNumber++;
            if (tSeatNumber>iNumberOfSeats)
            {
                System.out.println("More than " +
                                    iNumberOfSeats + " passengers");
                System.exit(1);
            }
            iSeats[tSeatNumber] = new PersonImpl(tLine);
        }
    }
}
```

Figure 15.8 *Continues on the next page.*

```java
public void outputSeats()
{
    for (int tSeatNumber = 1; tSeatNumber<=iNumberOfSeats; tSeatNumber++)
    {
        System.out.println(tSeatNumber + " " + iSeats[tSeatNumber]);
    }
}
public void sortTheEntries()
{
    Arrays.sort(iSeats, 1, iNumberOfSeats + 1);
}
public void querySeats() throws IOException
{
    while (true)
    {
        final String tName = iKeyboard.readLine();
        if (tName.equals(""))
        {
            break;
        }
        final Person tTargetPerson = new PersonImpl();
        tTargetPerson.setName(tName);
        final int tTargetPosition =
                        Arrays.binarySearch(iSeats, tTargetPerson);
        if (tTargetPosition>=0)
        {
            System.out.println("Position " + tTargetPosition + " contains " +
                                iSeats[tTargetPosition]);
        }
        else
        {
            System.out.println(tName + " was not found");
        }
    }
}
}
```

Figure 15.8   This class uses an array to implement a collection of seats.

details of a person from the keyboard and outputting the number of the seat that is occupied by that person. A program that declares and uses an object of this class is shown in Figure 15.9.

The `sortTheEntries` method of the `Seats` class uses the `sort` method (provided by the class `java.util.Arrays`) in order to sort the elements of the array.

The `querySeats` method of the `Seats` class uses the `binarySearch` method (provided by the class `java.util.Arrays`) in order to search the array for a particular element.

```
// This program creates an object of the Seats class
// and processes it.
// Barry Cornelius, 19 June 2000
import java.io. BufferedReader;
import java.io. InputStreamReader;
import java.io. IOException;
public class SeatsProg
{
    public static void main(final String[] pArgs) throws IOException
    {
        final BufferedReader tKeyboard =
                new BufferedReader(new InputStreamReader(System.in));
        final int tNumberOfSeats = 8;
        final Seats tSeats = new Seats(tKeyboard, tNumberOfSeats);
        tSeats.checkIn();
        tSeats.outputSeats();
        tSeats.sortTheEntries();
        tSeats.outputSeats();
        tSeats.querySeats();
    }
}
```

Figure 15.9   Using an object of the Seats class.

(15.11) Implementing the List interface using an array

15.11.1 Introduction

Chapter 14 introduced the List interface and two classes, called ArrayList and LinkedList, that implement that interface. Now that we know about arrays, we are in a position to write our own class that uses an array to implement the List interface. As this will be a rival to the ArrayList class, we will call the class MyArrayList.

When producing the code for MyArrayList, we could cheat, and just look at the file containing the source code of the java.util.ArrayList class. However, this has not been done.

So, why would we want to provide our own class? Mainly to give another example of how the array construct is used, and also to see whether we can produce anything that comes close to the performance of ArrayList. However, this is not a serious attempt to replace ArrayList, as its code has been subjected to close scrutiny since 1998 and so it should perform very well and, unlike our code, it should not have any bugs.

15.11.2 What methods need to be provided?

Some of the methods of the List interface are given in Figure 14.2. However, the WWW page at $API/java/util/List.html shows that the List interface provides a total of 25 methods. So our class declaration needs to implement all of these methods. However, to save space, we will not provide real implementations for some of the less commonly-used methods. So we will cheat for the method declarations for containsAll, removeAll, retainAll and subList, and two overloaded method declarations for each of addAll, listIterator and toArray. So, for each of these ten method declarations, the MyArrayList class provides a body for the method declaration that does not do anything useful.

For example, for the subList method, we could provide:

```
public List subList(final int pFromIndex, final int pToIndex)
{
    System.out.println("MyArrayList does not implement subList");
    System.exit(1);
}
```

However, java.lang provides an unchecked exception called UnsupportedOperationException, and it seems more appropriate to arrange for one of these to be generated. As mentioned in Section 11.9.1, we can arrange for an exception to occur by creating an object of the appropriate class, and using that object in a *throw statement*. So the MyArrayList class given in Figure 15.10 provides the following subList method:

```
public List subList(final int pFromIndex, final int pToIndex)
{
    throw new UnsupportedOperationException();
}
```

The UnsupportedOperationException exception is not available in JDK 1.0.2 and JDK 1.1.

```
// Using an array to implement the List interface.
// Barry Cornelius, 19 June 2000
import java.util. Collection;
import java.util. Iterator;
import java.util. List;
import java.util. ListIterator;
public class MyArrayList implements List
{
    // iCapacity indicates the current capacity of the iElements array, and so
    // iElements[0], iElements[1], ..., iElements[iCapacity-1] are available.
    // iSize indicates how many of these elements are being used, and so
    // iElements[0], iElements[1], ..., iElements[iSize-1] are being used.
    private int iCapacity;
    private Object[] iElements;
    private int iSize;
    public MyArrayList()
    {
        this(10);
    }
    public MyArrayList(final int pCapacity)
    {
        iCapacity = pCapacity;
        // the call of clear initializes the fields iElements and iSize
        clear();
    }
```

Figure 15.10 *Continues on the next page.*

```
private static void iCheckIndex(final int pIndex, final int pMaxIndex)
{
   if (pIndex<0 || pIndex>pMaxIndex)
   {
      throw new IndexOutOfBoundsException();
   }
   // pIndex>=0 && pIndex<=pMaxIndex
}
public void add(final int pIndex, final Object pValue)
{
   iCheckIndex(pIndex, iSize);
   if (iSize==iCapacity)
   {
      final int tNewCapacity = iCapacity*2;
      final Object[] tNewElements = new Object[tNewCapacity];
      System.arraycopy(iElements, 0, tNewElements, 0,
                       pIndex);
      System.arraycopy(iElements, pIndex, tNewElements, pIndex + 1,
                       iSize - pIndex);
      iCapacity = tNewCapacity;
      iElements = tNewElements;
   }
   else
   {
      System.arraycopy(iElements, pIndex, iElements, pIndex + 1,
                       iSize - pIndex);
   }
   iElements[pIndex] = pValue;
   iSize++;
}
public boolean add(final Object pValue)
{
   add(iSize, pValue);
   return true;
}
public boolean addAll(final int pIndex, final Collection pCollection)
{
   throw new UnsupportedOperationException();
}
public boolean addAll(final Collection pCollection)
{
   throw new UnsupportedOperationException();
}
```

Figure 15.10   *Continues on the next page.*

```java
public void clear()
{
   iElements = new Object[iCapacity];
   iSize = 0;
}
public boolean contains(final Object pValue)
{
   return indexOf(pValue)>=0;
}
public boolean containsAll(final Collection pCollection)
{
   throw new UnsupportedOperationException();
}
public boolean equals(final Object pObject)
{
   if (pObject==null || getClass()!=pObject.getClass())
   {
      return false;
   }
   final MyArrayList tMyArrayList = (MyArrayList)pObject;
   if (this.iSize!=tMyArrayList.iSize)
   {
      return false;
   }
   for (int tElementNumber = 0;
            tElementNumber<this.iSize; tElementNumber++)
   {
      final Object tThisObject = this.iElements[tElementNumber];
      final Object tParaObject = tMyArrayList.iElements[tElementNumber];
      if (! tThisObject.equals(tParaObject))
      {
         return false;
      }
   }
   return true;
}
public Object get(final int pIndex)
{
   iCheckIndex(pIndex, iSize - 1);
   return iElements[pIndex];
}
public int hashCode()
{
   return 0;
}
```

Figure 15.10 *Continues on the next page.*

```
public int indexOf(final Object pValue)
{
   int iPosition = 0;
   while (true)
   {
      if (iPosition==iSize)
      {
         return -1;
      }
      if (iElements[iPosition].equals(pValue))
      {
         return iPosition;
      }
      iPosition++;
   }
}
public boolean isEmpty()
{
   return iSize==0;
}
public Iterator iterator()
{
   return new MyArrayListIterator(iElements, iSize);
}
public int lastIndexOf(final Object pValue)
{
   int iPosition = iSize;
   while (true)
   {
      if (iPosition==0)
      {
         return -1;
      }
      iPosition--;
      if (iElements[iPosition].equals(pValue))
      {
         return iPosition;
      }
   }
}
public ListIterator listIterator()
{
   throw new UnsupportedOperationException();
}
public ListIterator listIterator(final int pIndex)
{
   throw new UnsupportedOperationException();
}
```

Figure 15.10 *Continues on the next page.*

```java
public Object remove(final int pIndex)
{
    iCheckIndex(pIndex, iSize - 1);
    final Object tObject = iElements[pIndex];
    System.arraycopy(iElements, pIndex + 1, iElements, pIndex,
                     iSize - pIndex - 1);
    iSize--;
    return tObject;
}
public boolean remove(final Object pValue)
{
    final int tPosition = indexOf(pValue);
    if (tPosition==-1)
    {
        return false;
    }
    final Object tObject = remove(tPosition);
    return true;
}
public boolean removeAll(final Collection pCollection)
{
    throw new UnsupportedOperationException();
}
public boolean retainAll(final Collection pCollection)
{
    throw new UnsupportedOperationException();
}
public Object set(final int pIndex, final Object pValue)
{
    iCheckIndex(pIndex, iSize - 1);
    final Object tObject = iElements[pIndex];
    iElements[pIndex] = pValue;
    return tObject;
}
public int size()
{
    return iSize;
}
public List subList(final int pFromIndex, final int pToIndex)
{
    throw new UnsupportedOperationException();
}
public Object[] toArray()
{
    throw new UnsupportedOperationException();
}
public Object[] toArray(final Object[] pObjects)
{
    throw new UnsupportedOperationException();
}
}
```

Figure 15.10 Using an array to implement the List interface.

15.11.3 Using an array to store the elements of the `List`

If `MyArrayList` is going to implement the `List` interface using an array, the class must declare an array variable. Suppose the variable is called `iElements`. Of course, we will not know what objects will be stored in the `List`, and so the array will be declared to have elements of the type `Object`:

```
private Object[] iElements;
```

Because the type of each element is `Object`, each element of the array can be made to point to an object of any class.

MyArrayList can provide a constructor that creates an array object of some arbitrarily-chosen capacity and a constructor that creates one of a capacity chosen by the client. `MyArrayList` can provide a field that records how big the array is:

```
private int iCapacity;
```

Only some of these elements will be in use at any point in time, and `MyArrayList` needs to record how many are in use:

```
private int iSize;
```

Given these fields, here is the code that could be used for the two constructors:

```
public MyArrayList()
{
    this(10);
}
public MyArrayList(final int pCapacity)
{
    iCapacity = pCapacity;
    iElements = new Object[iCapacity];
    iSize = 0;
}
```

The `MyArrayList` class that is given in Figure 15.10 provides constructors that are similar to these.

15.11.4 Writing some of the methods in terms of other methods

If you look at the code of the `MyArrayList` class that is given in Figure 15.10, you will see that the code of three methods are written in terms of other methods of the class:

- the method to add to the end of the list can be written in terms of the other add method;
- the `contains` method can be written in terms of `indexOf`;
- the method to remove the first element of the list having a given value can be written in terms of `indexOf` and the other remove method.

15.11.5 Implementing the add method

The code for the method that adds a new value at some position in the list is a little tricky. Unless we are adding the new value to the end of the list, we will have to move some of the current elements along in order to make room for the new value.

Suppose the list currently has elements numbered from 0 to $s - 1$, and that we want to insert the new value at position i. The add method will have to arrange for elements i to $s - 1$ to be moved along by one element so that they are now at positions $i + 1$ to s.

Although we could write our own code for moving the elements along:

```
for (tElementNumber = iSize; tElementNumber>tIndex; tElementNumber--)
{
    iElements[tElementNumber] = iElements[tElementNumber - 1];
}
```

the class java.lang.System provides a method called arraycopy. This method was mentioned earlier in Section 15.9. You need to pass the source array, the position in the source array, the destination array, the position in the destination array and the number of elements to be copied:

```
System.arraycopy(iElements, tIndex, iElements, tIndex + 1, iSize - tIndex);
```

We should use this instead of a for statement because the code of arraycopy executes faster.

There is one other issue we need to consider when writing the code of the add method: the first thing the method must do is to check whether there is any room in the array for the new value. If iSize is equal to iCapacity, the array is full. What can we do? One possibility is to create a new array object that has more elements and to copy the old elements into the new array object and to use that one instead. In more detail, we can execute the following steps:

1. Create an array called tNewElements that has twice as many elements.

2. Copy elements 0 to $i - 1$ from iElements to tNewElements.

3. Copy elements i to $s - 1$ of iElements to elements $i + 1$ to s of tNewElements.

4. Now make iElements point to this new array object.

If the array is not full, we just have to do the following step instead:

1. Move elements i to $s - 1$ of iElements to elements $i + 1$ to s of iElements.

No matter whether the four steps or the single step are executed, the ith element of the array object iElements is now available to be overwritten:

```
iElements[pIndex] = pValue;
iSize++;
```

The complete code of the add method is shown in Figure 15.10.

15.11.6 Implementing List's iterator method

List's iterator method has to return an object that can be used to help a client iterate through the elements of a List. One thing this object has to provide is a means by which a client can easily get to the next element of the list. For a List that is implemented by an array, all it need do is to keep track of the index of the next element.

The iterator method of the MyArrayList class (shown in Figure 15.10) just returns a pointer to a MyArrayListIterator object. The MyArrayListIterator class is shown in Figure 15.11. Note that it states that it implements the Iterator interface (of the package java.util). When an object of this class is created, the constructor stores a position of 0. It also stores a pointer to the array object and the

```java
// A class implementing the Iterator interface for MyArrayList.
// Barry Cornelius, 19 June 2000
import java.util. Iterator;
import java.util. NoSuchElementException;
public class MyArrayListIterator implements Iterator
{
    private Object[] iElements;
    private int iSize;
    private int iPosition;
    public MyArrayListIterator(final Object[] pElements, final int pSize)
    {
        iElements = pElements;
        iSize = pSize;
        iPosition = 0;
    }
    public boolean hasNext()
    {
        return iPosition<iSize;
    }
    public Object next()
    {
        if (iPosition==iSize)
        {
            throw new NoSuchElementException();
        }
        final Object tObject = iElements[iPosition];
        iPosition++;
        return tObject;
    }
    public void remove()
    {
        throw new UnsupportedOperationException();
    }
}
```

Figure 15.11 A class implementing the Iterator interface for MyArrayList.

size of the array object:

```
iElements = pElements;
iSize = pSize;
iPosition = 0;
```

Whenever the client applies the next method to this MyArrayListIterator object, the method just returns the value of the element with index iPosition and also increases iPosition by one:

```
final Object tObject = iElements[iPosition];
iPosition++;
return tObject;
```

The code of the next method that is given in Figure 15.11 also has code that checks whether iPosition is too big:

```
if (iPosition==iSize)
{
    throw new NoSuchElementException();
}
```

The code needed for the hasNext method is simple: all it has to do is to find out whether iPosition has a value that refers to an element of the array that is in use:

```
return iPosition<iSize;
```

15.11.7 Implementing the other methods of the MyArrayList class

Having looked at the add and iterator methods of MyArrayList in great detail, the remaining methods are a lot easier. They are clear, equals, get, hashCode, indexOf, isEmpty, lastIndexOf, remove, set and size. The code for each of these methods appears in Figure 15.10.

15.11.8 Comparing the performance of MyArrayList with ArrayList

In Section 14.3.6, a program called ListTimes was used to compare the performance of the ArrayList and the LinkedList classes.

The following table includes the times (in milliseconds) that were obtained when MyArrayList was used instead of ArrayList (using Java 2 SDK v 1.3.0 on a Windows 95 computer):

operation	ArrayList	LinkedList	MyArrayList
time to add to the end of the list	0.072	0.072	0.071
time to get the 4567th element	0.000099	0.305	0.000105
time to get element using get	0.0	0.16	0.0
time to get element using Iterator	0.005	0.0	0.0
time to add to the start of the list	0.264	0.049	0.258

These figures demonstrate that, in these tests, a MyArrayList object performs as well as an ArrayList object.

Tip for programming and debugging

15.1 Note that `System`'s `arraycopy`'s method is called `arraycopy` rather than `arrayCopy` (which would be more consistent with other capitalizations).

Curios, controversies and cover-ups

15.1 Because C and C++ allow:

```
int iFrequencyCounts[];
```

in Java the declaration:

```
int[] iFrequencyCounts;
```

may alternatively be written as:

```
int iFrequencyCounts[];
```

However, this is not recommended. The book *The Java Programming Language* (3rd edition) ([4]) by Ken Arnold, James Gosling and David Holmes says 'the first style is preferable because it places the type declaration entirely in one place'.

15.2 The JLS says that 'all the components of an array have the same type, called the **component type** of the array. ... The component type of an array may itself be an array type. ... eventually one must reach a component type that is not an array type: this is called the **element type** of the original array, and the components at this level of the data structure are called the **element**s of the original array'. So, for a *one-dimensional array*, the words *component* and *element* are interchangeable.

15.3 Consider the statements:

```
double[] tRainfall = new double[13];
System.out.println(tRainfall[7]);
```

When an array creation expression is executed, each element of the array object is assigned a value. The value that is assigned is the *default initial value* that is appropriate for the element type. These values are listed in Figure 11.2. So the `tRainfall` elements will all have the value 0, and the above `println` statement will output the value 0.

For this reason, the `setFrequencyCountsToZero` method of Figure 15.5 can be shortened. After the execution of the statement:

```
iFrequencyCounts = new int[iNumberOfDrinks + 1];
```

all of the elements of the array will automatically have the value 0. So the for statement that follows:

```
for (int tDrinkNumber = 1; tDrinkNumber<=iNumberOfDrinks;
                           tDrinkNumber++)
{
    iFrequencyCounts[tDrinkNumber] = 0;
}
```

may be omitted. However, it is the view of this book that it is better to retain the statements that initialize the elements of the array, as this clarifies that the programmer intended the elements to get these values. A more efficient way of initializing this array is to use:

```
Arrays.fill(iFrequencyCounts, 0);
```

where `fill` is a class method from the `java.util.Arrays` class – see Section 15.9.

15.4 Although the elements of an array all have the same type, it is easy to create an array with elements that are objects of different classes. If the type of the elements is the type `Object`, a value of any class may be assigned to the elements:

```
final Object[] tSillyArray = new Object[3];
tSillyArray[0] = new DateImpl(2000, 8, 28);
tSillyArray[1] = new PersonImpl("Joe%2000-12-25%1234%1.85");
tSillyArray[2] = new Integer(42);
```

This creates a **heterogeneous array**.

15.5 Consider the statements:

```
final String tLine = tKeyboard.readLine();
final int tNumberOfDrinks = Integer.parseInt(tLine);
final int[] tFrequencyCounts = new int[tNumberOfDrinks];
System.out.println(tFrequencyCounts.length);
```

If `tNumberOfDrinks` has the value 0, an array object with no elements will be assigned to `tFrequencyCounts`. So, it is not an error as far as the Java programming language is concerned to have an array that has no elements.

15.6 Section 15.9 points out that a *two-dimensional array* or *matrix* is formed if array objects are assigned to each element of an array. If these array objects are of different sizes, the result is a **jagged matrix**. However, if the array objects are all of the same size, the result is a **rectangular matrix**.

Exercises

15.1 Modify the class given in Figure 15.5 so that, having read a selection, it outputs a message like `Black coffee with no sugar`. You should use a method to do this task. Also alter the `outputFrequencyCounts` method so that, as well as outputting each drink number together with its frequency, it calls the above method to output a description of the drink. Test the new version of this class with the program given in Figure 15.4.

15.2 Modify the class given in Figure 15.5 so that it outputs the amount of money that has to be paid when a selection is made. Choose a different price for each choice of drink. Test the new version of this class with the program given in Figure 15.4.

15.3 In the class given in Figure 15.6, the code that determines the most popular drink does not properly handle the situation where there are two or more drinks that are equally the most popular, i.e. when there is a *draw*. Modify the class so that it outputs all the drink numbers that are the most popular. Test the new version of this class with the program given in Figure 15.7.

15.4 What happens to the execution of the program given in Figure 15.7 if the data indicates that no drinks have been selected, i.e. the first line of the data is an empty line? Modify the class given in Figure 15.6 to cater for this possibility.

15.5 The following code is proposed as an alternative to that given at the end of Section 15.8:

```
tMonthNumber = 1;
while (tMonthNumber<=12 && tRainfall[tMonthNumber]>=2.4)
{
    tMonthNumber++;
}
// (tMonthNumber>12) || (tRainfall[tMonthNumber]<2.4)
if (tMonthNumber>12)
{
    tDryMonthFound = false;
}
else
{
    tDryMonthFound = true;
    tFirstDryMonthNumber = tMonthNumber;
}
```

Does this code produce the desired effect? Does the order of the two subconditions of the while statement's boolean expression matter?

15.6 Write a program that reads in 12 monthly rainfall figures and then outputs each figure together with each figure's difference from the average monthly rainfall. Why do you need an array to solve this problem?

15.7 The railway line between Newcastle and Hexham has seven intermediate stations. The distances in miles between successive stations are:

```
2.25    3.25    4.5    2.0    2.5    2.5    2.25    3.0
```

Write a program that reads in the above data (putting one value on each line) and then outputs a triangular table that gives the distance between any pair of stations. Label the columns and rows of the table by placing station numbers above each column and before each row:

	1	2	3	4	...	9
1	0.00E+0					
2	2.25E+0	0.00E+0				
3	5.50E+0	3.25E+0	0.00E+0			
4	1.00E+1	7.75E+0	4.50E+0	0.00E+0		
...						
9	2.23E+1	2.00E+1	1.68E+1	1.23E+1	...	0.00E+0

◇ **15.8** The table:

x	3.0	3.3	3.6	4.0	4.5
y	14.9	18.2	22.3	27.2	33.3

gives the value of y for certain values of x. It is to be used for estimating the values of y for other values of x given as data. Write a program that reads in the above table of values, then reads in other values of x, and, for each value of x, outputs an approximation to the corresponding value of y.

An approximation to the value of y can be obtained by the method of **linear interpolation**. With this method, a straight line is fitted between the two points that lie either side of the desired point (x,y). If the points before and after (x,y) are (x_b,y_b) and (x_a,y_a), the value of y is given by:

$$y = y_b + \frac{y_a - y_b}{x_a - x_b} \times (x - x_b)$$

For example, suppose we want to find y when the value of x is 3.5. So, the point (x_b,y_b) is (3.3,18.2); and the point (x_a,y_a) is (3.6,22.3).

Use your program to find approximations to the value of y for $x = 3.5$ and $x = 3.1$. It should produce the values 20.9333 and 16.0000. What have you asked your program to do if the value of x lies outside the table, i.e. it has a value which is less than 3.0 or greater than 4.5?

Your program can assume that the table of values given in the data has its values of x in increasing numerical order. Your program should be written so that it can handle any table of values that has not more than 50 entries.

15.9 A **snakes and ladders** board which has n squares can be represented within a program by an array. Each component of the array represents one square of the board, tSquare[1] being the first square and tSquare[n] being the final square. The contents of each component of this array is:

m	if this square has a ladder leading to square m	$(1 \leq m \leq n)$,
$-m$	if this square has a snake leading to square m	$(1 \leq m \leq n)$,
0	if this square has neither a ladder nor a snake.	

The rules of the game are that, at each move, you throw one dice and move the number of squares shown on the dice. However:

 ◦ you need to throw a six to start (and hence the first square on which you land is always tSquare[6]);

 ◦ if you land on a square containing a ladder, you go up the ladder to the square at the other end;

 ◦ if you land on a square containing a snake, you have to go down to the square at the other end of the snake;

 ◦ you finish when you land on the final square.

Write a program that first reads in the details of a snakes and ladders board from a file, storing appropriate information about the board in the array tSquare. The program should then read in (from the keyboard) the throws of a dice by a player, outputting (to the screen), for each throw, the square reached by the player. The program should stop if the value 0 is given as a throw or if the player has reached the final square.

Produce a file containing the following values:

```
49   0   0   0    0    0    0  32
     0   0   0   37    0    0    0  29    0    0    0    0  -4    0
     0   0   0   -1    0    0    0    0  42    0    0    0 -21   47
     0   0   0  -33    0   45    0    0    0    0 -27    0 -36    0
```

Rather than adopting the layout shown here, put each value on a separate line of the file. The first value indicates that the board contains 49 squares – there are then 49 values, one for each square of the board. Execute your program with this data file and with the following values typed at the keyboard:

```
5  6  1  2  1  1  6  3  2  3  6  5  2  0
```

Each value should be typed on a separate line. These are the values obtained at each throw of a dice.

The above representation of a snakes and ladders board uses the sign of the value in the square in order to distinguish between a square containing a ladder and a square containing a snake. This makes it easier for a person to understand the file of data. Is there any other reason why this is done?

In what other ways can a snakes and ladders board be represented?

Chapter 16

Decoupling the model from the user interface

In Chapter 13, we looked at how several objects could be registered as listeners for some event such as a click on a button. More generally, what we might want to do is to set up several objects that get notified whenever the value of some other object gets changed, i.e. to create objects that are *observers* of changes to an object that is *observable*.

It is very easy to do this in Java, as the Core APIs provide an interface called Observer and a class called Observable.

In this chapter, we first look at how these can be used with a simple example, and then we look to see how the queue class (LinkedQueue) of Chapter 14 can be modified so that an instance of the class LinkedQueue can have more than one observer.

16.1 Using MVC to disentangle views from a model

In Chapter 14, we developed a program that represented a queue, and allowed the user of the program to manipulate it. When we make a change to the queue, who needs to know that this has happened? It may be that we would like to write the details of the change to a file, or e-mail the changes to someone, or update a display on the screen that indicates the size of the queue, and so on. Or we may want a program that includes all of these *views* of the data.

The actual pieces of code that make a change to a queue occur in the methods `add` and `remove` of the `LinkedQueue` class. If we want to be able to update each of the views, do we put all the code to update the views into the methods `add` and `remove`? Obviously, this would lead to:

- horrendous code in these methods;
- a lot of tight coupling between the `LinkedQueue` class and the classes that implement the views;
- the `LinkedQueue` class needing to be changed whenever a new view is required.

More importantly, it would be an inappropriate use of `LinkedQueue` as it is written in terms of `Object` and so it is currently independent of the objects being stored in the queue.

What we need is a way of disentangling the views of a real-world object from the model of the real-world object. A design technique known as **Model-View-Controller** (**MVC**) can be used to achieve this.

16.2 Applying MVC to a simple example

16.2.1 The need for an `Observable` class

Suppose we want to set up several observers of an object. In the MVC jargon, this object is called the **model** as it is usually modelling some object in the real world. And each **observer** (also known as a **viewer**) is presenting a different **view** of the model. Elsewhere there is another object which causes the model to change: this object is a **controller**.

To represent some data, we are likely to be using an interface and a class. In practice, we may be using something as complicated as a queue (e.g. `Queue` and `LinkedQueue`) or as simple as a date (e.g. `Date` and `DateImpl`). However, to begin with, while exploring the ideas of MVC, we will keep things even simpler: we will just use a class rather than an interface and a class. We will see later how to employ MVC with an interface as well as a class.

Suppose that the purpose of a class called `Model` is to provide a means by which we can hide a value of type `int` and provide a method (called `get`) to obtain its current value, a method (called `set`) to change its value to some other value, and a method (called `inc`) that increases the hidden `int`'s value by 1.

Suppose we also have a class (called ViewOne) that we want to use for an object that is some sort of viewer: it may want to display the latest value of the model on the screen, or write it to a file whenever the model changes, or something else.

What we want is a way in which a view can indicate that it wishes to be informed whenever the model changes. One way of achieving this is similar to the way in which objects can be registered as listeners for clicks on a button.

In more detail, we can arrange for the model to have a public method called addObserver. This method can be used whenever a client wants to register an object as a viewer for changes on the model:

```
Model tModel = new Model();
ViewOne tViewOne = new ViewOne(tModel);
tModel.addObserver(tViewOne);
```

The addObserver method can be called many times registering different objects as viewers on the object tModel.

In order to be able to inform each of the viewer objects whenever the model changes, it is necessary for the addObserver method of Model to keep a note of these objects. One way that it can do this is to store the objects in a collection such as a Set (which we will be looking at in detail in the next chapter). In this case, Model's addObserver method is simply:

```
public void addObserver(final Object pObject)
{
    iViewerSet.add(pObject);
}
```

where iViewerSet is a Set that is declared as a private field of the Model class.

So the Model needs a private field that is of the Set interface together with the above method declaration. If you do this, then, in the course of time, you could find yourself developing many classes containing a private field of type Set and a public method called addObserver. When we looked at the classes of the Swing API, we found that when a group of related classes had commonality, such as common fields and common methods, the designers of the Swing API found it convenient to put the common code into a superclass rather than including the code in each of the classes of the group.

So we could put the Set field and the addObserver method into a superclass – we could call it ViewableModel – and derive Model from ViewableModel. However, there is no need to produce a class called ViewableModel as it already exists: it is called Observable.

16.2.2 Using java.util's Observable class

As shown in Figure 16.1 (and at $API/java/util/Observable.html), the class java.util.Observable provides a method called addObserver. And each time this method is called it stores the object passed as an argument in a collection of objects wanting to be observers.

```
public void addObserver(Observer pObserver);
```
>   Adds the object **pObserver** to the set of observers for the target object. The
>   object **pObserver** must be of a class that implements the **Observer** interface.
```
protected void clearChanged();
```
>   Indicates that the target object has not been changed.
```
public int countObservers();
```
>   Returns the number of observers of the target object.
```
public void deleteObserver(Observer pObserver);
```
>   Deletes the object **pObserver** from the set of observers for the target object.
```
public void deleteObservers();
```
>   Empties the set of observers for the target object.
```
public boolean hasChanged();
```
>   Returns the value *true* if and only if the **setChanged** method has been applied
>   to the target object more recently than the **clearChanged** method.
```
public void notifyObservers();
public void notifyObservers(Object pObject);
```
>   If **hasChanged** applied to the target object returns the value *true*, call the **update**
>   method of each of the model's observers and then apply the **clearChanged**
>   method to the target object. The **update** method is called with two arguments:
>   the target object and the argument passed to **notifyObservers** if there is one,
>   or **null** if there is not.
```
protected void setChanged();
```
>   Indicates that the target object has been changed.

Figure 16.1   The methods of the `java.util.Observable` class.

The class declaration of `Model` in Figure 16.2 shows how we can indicate that we want the class `Model` to acquire all the facilities of the `Observable` class. Consider the header of `Model`'s declaration:

```
public class Model extends Observable
```

This header says that the class `Model extends Observable`, i.e. it is derived from `Observable`. The intention is that the common aspects of observable classes have been provided in this superclass, and so we do not have to declare them in a class like `Model`. This is *inheritance*, which will be explained in more detail in Chapter 19.

If a client creates an object of class `Model`, it can apply the methods declared in `Observable` to the object (because `Model` is derived from `Observable`). For example, in the `MVCProg` program (shown in Figure 16.3), `Observable`'s `addObserver` method is applied to `tModel`:

```
Model tModel = new Model();
ViewOne tViewOne = new ViewOne();
tModel.addObserver(tViewOne);
```

16.2.3 Notifying a viewer that the model has changed

When a method of the model makes a change to the data of the model, the model needs to inform each object that has been registered as a viewer. Looking at the

```
// A Model class that extends the Observable class.
// Barry Cornelius, 19 February 2000
import java.util. Observable;
public class Model extends Observable
{
    private int iValue;
    public Model()
    {
        iValue = 0;
    }
    public synchronized int get()
    {
        return iValue;
    }
    public synchronized void set(final int pValue)
    {
        iValue = pValue;
        setChanged();
        notifyObservers();
    }
    public synchronized void inc()
    {
        iValue++;
        setChanged();
        notifyObservers();
    }
}
```

Figure 16.2 A Model class that extends the Observable class.

button-clicking analogy again, what happens there is that, when there is a click of the button, the `actionPerformed` method of each listener object is executed. So, whenever there is a change to the model, we could arrange for the model to apply a particular method to each of the objects that has been registered as a viewer.

The model can achieve this by using Observable's notifyObservers method. This will call a method called update on each object that has been registered (using addObserver).

So any method of Model that changes the data of the model should call notifyObservers:

```
public synchronized void set(final int pValue)
{
    iValue = pValue;
    setChanged();
    notifyObservers();
}
```

```
// MVCProg uses addObserver to register tViewOne as a viewer of tModel.
// Barry Cornelius, 19 June 2000
import java.io. BufferedReader;
import java.io. InputStreamReader;
import java.io. IOException;
public class MVCProg
{
    public static void main(final String[] pArgs) throws IOException
    {
        final Model tModel = new Model();
        final ViewOne tViewOne = new ViewOne();
        tModel.addObserver(tViewOne);
        final BufferedReader tKeyboard =
                    new BufferedReader(new InputStreamReader(System.in));
        while (true)
        {
            System.out.print("Type in an int: ");
            System.out.flush();
            final String tLine = tKeyboard.readLine();
            if (tLine.equals(""))
            {
                break;
            }
            final int tNewValue = Integer.parseInt(tLine);
            tModel.set(tNewValue);
        }
    }
}
```

Figure 16.3 Using `addObserver` to register `tViewOne` as a viewer of `tModel`.

Rather than just calling `notifyObservers`, the `set` method actually calls two methods (of the `Observable` class):

- `setChanged`: A call of `setChanged` is used to record the fact that the model has changed: an observer is not notified at this stage.

- `notifyObservers`: If there has been an execution of `setChanged` since `notifyObservers` was last called, a call of `notifyObservers` will execute the `update` method of each observer.

It can sometimes be useful that the API has split this into two methods. Rather than informing the viewers as soon as a change in the model has been detected, it may be better just to record this (using `setChanged`), and to notify viewers (using `notifyObservers`) later. If the viewers were notified straightaway, there may be a lot of unnecessary notifications taking place. For more details about this, see Curio 16.4.

Note that, because `Model` is derived from `Observable`, methods of the `Observable` class can be called as if they had been declared in the class `Model`.

```
// A viewer implements the Observer interface.
// Barry Cornelius, 19 June 2000
import java.util. Observable;
import java.util. Observer;
public class ViewOne implements Observer
{
   public ViewOne()
   {
   }
   public void update(final Observable pObservable, final Object pObject)
   {
      final Model tModel = (Model)pObservable;
      System.out.println("Now got " + tModel.get());
   }
}
```

Figure 16.4 A viewer implements the `Observer` interface.

The above method declaration (and all of the other method declarations of the `Model` class) includes the `synchronized` keyword in its header. The role of `synchronized` will be considered in Section 16.4.

16.2.4 Providing the code of a viewer

Whenever an `Observable` object calls `notifyObservers`, the `update` method of the objects that have been registered as viewers will be called. The class `ViewOne` (shown in Figure 16.4) gives an example of a viewer.

Previously we have seen that any object wanting to be a listener for clicks on a button needs to implement the `ActionListener` interface. In a similar way, an object that wants to be notified by an `Observable` object has to implement the `Observer` interface. This interface consists of one method called `update`, as shown in Figure 16.5 (and at $API/java/util/Observer.html).

```
public void update(Observable pObservable, Object pObject);
```
   If an object implementing the `Observer` interface has registered itself as an observer for a model object, this method will be called by the `notifyObservers` method of the model object. The code of the `update` method can access the model object by casting `pObservable` to an appropriate type, and it can access the argument of the call of `notifyObservers` (if there is one) by casting `pObject` to an appropriate type.

Figure 16.5 The `java.util.Observer` interface.

The `ViewOne` class indicates that it implements the `Observer` interface (from `java.util`) by the implements clause:

```
implements Observer
```

and in order to satisfy this requirement it has a declaration for a method called `update`.

Whenever an Observable object calls notifyObservers, the update method of the registered objects will be called. The update method has two parameters. The first parameter (pObservable) will be set by notifyObservers to point to the Observable object, and the second parameter (pObject) will point to the object passed as a parameter to notifyObservers. If there is no such parameter, pObject will have the value null.

In the Model class (given in Figure 16.2), there are two calls of the notifyObservers method. Because both calls do not supply an argument, at the call of the update method pObject will have the value null.

So, if the viewer wants to access the model, it has to take the pObservable object and cast it to the type Model. The update method of ViewOne does this and then executes the get method of Model. This will return the new value of the hidden int. The update method then uses println to display this value.

16.2.5 Putting it all together

So the MVC program is now complete. The MVCProg program (shown in Figure 16.3) continually reads an integer from the keyboard, calling tModel.set to set the hidden value to this integer. In the MVC jargon, this program is acting as a *controller*. Each time the set method of the *model* object tModel is called, tModel's notify-Observers will be called. This method will call the update method of the *view* object (tViewOne). So each time set is called, the call of update will get println to display the new value.

```
// Another class (called ViewTwo) that implements the Observer interface.
// Barry Cornelius, 19 June 2000
import javax.swing. JLabel;
import java.util.    Observable;
import java.util.    Observer;
public class ViewTwo implements Observer
{
    private JLabel iJLabel;
    public ViewTwo()
    {
        iJLabel = new JLabel("unset");
    }
    public JLabel getGUI()
    {
        return iJLabel;
    }
    public void update(final Observable pObservable, final Object pObject)
    {
        final Model tModel = (Model)pObservable;
        iJLabel.setText("" + tModel.get());
    }
}
```

Figure 16.6 Another class (ViewTwo) that implements the Observer interface.

16.3 Other views and controllers

16.3.1 Adding a new view

The whole purpose of using Observable/Observer to implement MVC is to enable several observers to show different views of a model. Another class that implements the Observer interface is ViewTwo (shown in Figure 16.6). When the

```java
// A program which registers tViewOne and tViewTwo as viewers of tModel.
// Barry Cornelius, 19 June 2000
import java.awt.    BorderLayout;
import java.io.     BufferedReader;
import java.awt.    Container;
import java.io.     InputStreamReader;
import java.io.     IOException;
import javax.swing. JLabel;
import javax.swing. JFrame;
public class MVCProg
{
    public static void main(final String[] pArgs) throws IOException
    {
        final Model tModel = new Model();
        final ViewOne tViewOne = new ViewOne();
        tModel.addObserver(tViewOne);
        final ViewTwo tViewTwo = new ViewTwo();
        tModel.addObserver(tViewTwo);
        final JLabel tJLabel = tViewTwo.getGUI();
        final JFrame tJFrame = new JFrame("MVCProg");
        final Container tContentPane = tJFrame.getContentPane();
        tContentPane.add(tJLabel, BorderLayout.NORTH);
        tJFrame.pack();
        tJFrame.setVisible(true);
        final BufferedReader tKeyboard =
                    new BufferedReader(new InputStreamReader(System.in));
        while (true)
        {
            System.out.print("Type in an int: ");
            System.out.flush();
            final String tLine = tKeyboard.readLine();
            if (tLine.equals(""))
            {
                break;
            }
            final int tNewValue = Integer.parseInt(tLine);
            tModel.set(tNewValue);
        }
        System.exit(0);
    }
}
```

Figure 16.7 MVCProg registers tViewOne and tViewTwo as viewers of tModel.

update method of this class is called, a JLabel is updated with the latest value of the hidden int.

As shown in Figure 16.7, we can get the MVCProg program to use an object of this class by adding the following code to its main method:

```
final ViewTwo tViewTwo = new ViewTwo();
final JLabel tJLabel = tViewTwo.getGUI();
final JFrame tJFrame = new JFrame("MVCProg");
final Container tContentPane = tJFrame.getContentPane();
tContentPane.add(tJLabel, BorderLayout.NORTH);
tJFrame.pack();
tJFrame.setVisible(true);
```

This creates a ViewTwo object and adds its GUI component to the content pane of a JFrame object. We can register this ViewTwo object as an observer of changes to tModel by including the following statement in the MVCProg program:

```
tModel.addObserver(tViewTwo);
```

Now, whenever set is called, the call of notifyObservers will notify both of the observers. Both of their update methods will be called. So the new value of the hidden int will be displayed both using println and in the label of the JFrame window.

16.3.2 Adding another controller and yet another view

Earlier, it was pointed out that the call of set in the MVCProg program acts as the trigger for changes to the model: the MVCProg object acts as the *controller*.

Rather than being in separate classes, a controller and a view are often presented in the same class. This derivative of Model-View-Controller is sometimes called **Model-UserInterface** or the **Separable Model Architecture**.

An example is the VCThree class given in Figure 16.8. An object of this class has a JButton and a JLabel. The class provides a method called getGUI which returns a Box object that includes these two GUI components. The constructor registers the object being constructed as a listener for any clicks on the button. So when a click occurs, the object's actionPerformed method is executed. The action-Performed method applies inc to the Model object that was passed as an argument to the constructor of this class.

Because this call of inc leads to a call of notifyObservers, the update method of this class (and the other Observer classes) will be executed. The update method of this class obtains the new value of the hidden int and displays its value in the JLabel.

This class is providing both actionPerformed and update, i.e. it is implementing both the ActionListener interface and the Observer interface. For this reason, its implements clause mentions both of these interfaces:

```
public class VCThree implements ActionListener, Observer
```

```
// A class (called VCThree) that acts as a controller as well as a viewer.
// Barry Cornelius, 19 June 2000
import java.awt.event. ActionEvent;
import java.awt.event. ActionListener;
import javax.swing.     Box;
import javax.swing.     BoxLayout;
import javax.swing.     JButton;
import javax.swing.     JLabel;
import java.util.       Observable;
import java.util.       Observer;
public class VCThree implements ActionListener, Observer
{
   private Model iModel;
   private JButton iJButton;
   private JLabel iJLabel;
   public VCThree(final Model pModel)
   {
      iModel = pModel;
      iJButton = new JButton("increment");
      iJLabel = new JLabel("unset");
      iJButton.addActionListener(this);
   }
   public Box getGUI()
   {
      final Box tBox = new Box(BoxLayout.Y_AXIS);
      tBox.add(iJButton);
      tBox.add(iJLabel);
      return tBox;
   }
   public void actionPerformed(final ActionEvent pActionEvent)
   {
      iModel.inc();
   }
   public void update(final Observable pObservable, final Object pObject)
   {
      iJLabel.setText("" + iModel.get());
   }
}
```

Figure 16.8 A class (called VCThree) that acts as a controller as well as a viewer.

An object of the VCThree class could be incorporated into the MVCProg program by including the following statements in its main method:

```
final VCThree tVCThree = new VCThree(tModel);
tModel.addObserver(tVCThree);
final Box tBox = tVCThree.getGUI();
tContentPane.add(tBox, Borderlayout.SOUTH);
```

16.4 The need to synchronize the methods

Although, at a first glance, it may appear that when a Java program is being executed it simply works through the code of your program, it is not as simple as that. A program's execution actually involves many **threads** of code being executed.

For example, in addition to your code being executed, at the same time the *garbage collector* will be executing. This is the thread of code that collects up unwanted areas of storage. Here is another example: when you set up a listener for a click on a button, a separate thread of code is executed that mainly sits there waiting for a click of the button.

Although this book has not wanted to get involved in these details, there are occasions when they do have an impact. And, guess what, we now have one!

If we use the MVC technique, a viewer might want to inspect the value of a field of the model at the same time as a controller is updating it, or two controllers might both want to update the model at the same time. We have two threads trying to access the same variable simultaneously. To avoid these problems, you need some way of indicating that access to a variable is restricted to only one thread at a time. In Java, this can be done in two ways:

1. A block of code can indicate that it wants exclusive access to a variable as follows:

```
Obj tObj = new Obj();

...

synchronized(tObj)
{

    ...

}
```

2. Or you can say that you would like a method (of a class) to have exclusive access to the fields of the target, i.e. to the fields of the object to which the method is being applied. This is done by adding the synchronized keyword to the header of the method.

When we are using MVC, the second technique can be used to ensure that only one thread is accessing the model at any time. We simply add the synchronized keyword to each of the methods (of the model's class) that accesses any fields of the class.

For example, the class Model (shown in Figure 16.2) has a field called iValue and this is accessed by the get, set and inc methods. So, the headers of these methods have been declared as:

```
public synchronized int get()
public synchronized void set(final int pValue)
public synchronized void inc()
```

Curio 16.1 discusses why it is inappropriate for a constructor to have synchronized in its header.

If the class for the model implements an interface, the method headers that appear in the interface declaration may not include the synchronized keyword: only the headers of the method declarations appearing in the class declaration can include synchronized. The JLS ([19]) says the synchronized keyword is not allowed because it is describing 'implementation properties rather than interface properties'. Whether the use of the methods is synchronized is a design decision of the person who writes the class.

One of the paragraphs given earlier uses the strange wording 'you can say that you *would like* a method (of a class) to have exclusive access'. You will only get exclusive access to a variable/field if and only if every statement that accesses the variable/field appears in a synchronized block or a synchronized method.

16.5 The complete version of the MVCProg program

Note that the MVCProg program now has:

- one model: the tModel object;
- three views:

  1. the display caused by the println of the update method of the tViewOne object;

  2. the label of the tViewTwo object;

  3. the label of the tVCThree object;

- two controllers:

  1. the reading of a new int by MVCProg's main method;

  2. the clicking of the button in the VCThree object.

16.6 Revisiting the queue example

16.6.1 Making LinkedQueue into an Observable class

We now return to the interface and the class that implement a queue. This is the interface Queue and the class LinkedQueue of Section 14.4.4 and Section 14.4.5. The aim now is to enable any changes to a queue to be observable by any object that has registered to be an observer.

In order to do this, the following four changes need to be made:

1. Alter the Queue interface so that it includes the method:

```
public void addObserver(Observer pObserver);
```

The new form of this interface is given in Figure 16.9.

2. Alter the LinkedQueue class so that it indicates that it is derived from java.util.Observable. We can do this by altering its header to:

```
public class LinkedQueue extends Observable implements Queue
```

The new version of the LinkedQueue class is shown in Figure 16.10.

```
// An interface for an Observable queue.
// Barry Cornelius, 19 June 2000
import java.util. Observer;
public interface Queue
{
    // adds a new element (to the target queue) that is
    // assigned the value pObject, a pointer to some object
    public void add(Object pObject);

    // returns a pointer to the object that is at the first element
    // of the target queue (without removing the element)
    public Object getFirst();

    // returns a pointer to the object that is at the first element
    // of the target queue and removes that element from the queue
    public Object remove();

    // returns the number of elements in the target queue
    public int size();

    // returns the value true if and only if the objects of the
    // target queue and the queue passed as an argument have
    // the same values in the same order
    public boolean equals(Object pObject);

    // returns a hashcode value for the target queue
    public int hashCode();

    // returns a textual representation of the target queue
    public String toString();

    // adds the object pObserver to the set of observers for the target queue
    public void addObserver(Observer pObserver);
}
```

Figure 16.9   An interface for an Observable queue.

```
// An Observable version of the LinkedQueue class.
// Barry Cornelius, 19 June 2000
import java.util. LinkedList;
import java.util. Iterator;
import java.util. List;
import java.util. Observable;
import java.util. Observer;
public class LinkedQueue extends Observable implements Queue
{
    private List iList;
    public LinkedQueue()
    {
        iList = new LinkedList();
    }
    public synchronized void add(final Object pObject)
    {
        iList.add(pObject);
```

Figure 16.10   *Continues on the next page.*

```
         setChanged();
         notifyObservers("add");
      }
      public synchronized Object getFirst()
      {
         if (iList.isEmpty())
         {
            return null;
         }
         return iList.get(0);
      }
      public synchronized Object remove()
      {
         if (iList.isEmpty())
         {
            return null;
         }
         final Object tObject = iList.remove(0);
         setChanged();
         notifyObservers("remove");
         return tObject;
      }
      public synchronized int size()
      {
         return iList.size();
      }
      public synchronized boolean equals(final Object pObject)
      {
         if ( pObject==null || getClass()!=pObject.getClass() )
         {
            return false;
         }
         return iList.equals(((LinkedQueue)pObject).iList);
      }
      public synchronized int hashCode()
      {
         return 0;
      }
      public synchronized String toString()
      {
         if (iList.isEmpty())
         {
            return new String("");
         }
         final StringBuffer tStringBuffer = new StringBuffer();
         final Iterator tIterator = iList.iterator();
         while (tIterator.hasNext())
         {
            final Object tObject = tIterator.next();
            tStringBuffer.append("@" + tObject);
         }
         tStringBuffer.deleteCharAt(0);
         return tStringBuffer.toString();
      }
   }
}
```

Figure 16.10 An Observable version of the LinkedQueue class.

3. Add the synchronized keyword to the header of those method declarations of LinkedQueue that need to access the iList field.

4. Alter the bodies of LinkedQueue's add and remove methods to include calls of setChanged and notifyObservers, e.g. the body of add is changed to:

```
iList.add(pObject);
setChanged();
notifyObservers("add");
```

Previously, we have called notifyObservers with no arguments; here notifyObservers is called with an argument. This will automatically be used as the second argument when the update method of an observer is called. In this way, the model can pass an object to the viewer. In this example, notifyObservers is called with a String argument that describes whether the object was added or removed; thus each viewer can now easily find this out. For some discussion about whether information should be passed from the model to the viewer in this way, see Curio 16.3.

16.6.2 Changing PersonLinkedQueueProg into an MVC program

In the previous section, we modified Queue and LinkedQueue so that any objects of this class are Observable. The PersonLinkedQueueProg program (given in Figure 14.9) creates a LinkedQueue object, acts as a controller for this object (by means of the a, d and r commands) and also provides views of the LinkedQueue object (using the e and g commands).

Suppose we now want to change this program into one that has a GUI. One possibility is shown by the PersonLinkedQueueDriver program given in Figure 16.11. This program creates an LinkedQueue object; a PersonQueueController object that is going to be used to trigger changes to the queue; a QueueCounter

```
// A version of the PersonLinkedQueueProg program rewritten to use MVC.
// Barry Cornelius, 19 June 2000
public class PersonLinkedQueueDriver
{
    public static void main(final String[] pArgs)
    {
        final Queue iPersonQueue = new LinkedQueue();
        final PersonQueueController tPersonQueueController =
                        new PersonQueueController(iPersonQueue, 100, 100);
        final QueueCounter tQueueCounter = new QueueCounter(100, 300);
        iPersonQueue.addObserver(tQueueCounter);
        final QueueLister tQueueLister = new QueueLister(100, 500);
        iPersonQueue.addObserver(tQueueLister);
    }
}
```

Figure 16.11 The PersonLinkedQueueProg program rewritten to use MVC.

```java
// A class providing a controller for the PersonQueue.
// Barry Cornelius, 19 June 2000
import java.awt.event. ActionEvent;
import java.awt.event. ActionListener;
import java.awt.          BorderLayout;
import java.awt.          Container;
import javax.swing.    JButton;
import javax.swing.    JFrame;
public class PersonQueueController implements ActionListener
{
    private Queue iPersonQueue;
    private JFrame iJFrame;
    private int iJFrameX;
    private int iJFrameY;
    public PersonQueueController(final Queue pPersonQueue,
                              final int pJFrameX, final int pJFrameY)
    {
        iPersonQueue = pPersonQueue;
        iJFrameX = pJFrameX;
        iJFrameY = pJFrameY;
        iJFrame = new JFrame("PersonQueueController");
        final JButton tAddJButton = new JButton("Add");
        final JButton tRemoveJButton = new JButton("Remove");
        tAddJButton.addActionListener(this);
        tRemoveJButton.addActionListener(this);
        final Container tContentPane = iJFrame.getContentPane();
        tContentPane.add(tAddJButton,    BorderLayout.NORTH);
        tContentPane.add(tRemoveJButton, BorderLayout.SOUTH);
        final ExitWindowListener tExitWindowListener =
                                        new ExitWindowListener();
        iJFrame.addWindowListener(tExitWindowListener);
        iJFrame.setDefaultCloseOperation(JFrame.DO_NOTHING_ON_CLOSE);
        iJFrame.setLocation(iJFrameX, iJFrameY);
        iJFrame.setSize(300,100);
        iJFrame.setVisible(true);
    }
    public void actionPerformed(final ActionEvent pActionEvent)
    {
        final String tJButtonString = pActionEvent.getActionCommand();
        if (tJButtonString.equals("Add"))
        {
            final PersonInputDialog tPersonInputDialog =
                    new PersonInputDialog(iJFrame, iJFrameX + 20, iJFrameY + 20);
            final Person tPerson = tPersonInputDialog.getPerson();
            iPersonQueue.add(tPerson);
        }
        else
        {
            final Object tObject = iPersonQueue.remove();
        }
    }
}
```

Figure 16.12 A class providing a controller for the PersonQueue.

object, a viewer that displays in a JLabel the number of elements in the queue; and a QueueLister object, a viewer that displays a list of the elements of the queue in a JTextArea.

The QueueLister class passes its JTextArea as the argument of a JScrollPane constructor. The resulting GUI component is a JTextArea that has a **scroll bar**. It is very useful to do this, i.e. whenever you provide a JTextArea transform it into a scrollable JTextArea by using the result of passing it to JScrollPane's constructor.

Note that the classes PersonQueueController, QueueCounter and QueueLister (shown in Figures 16.12, 16.13 and 16.14) are written in terms of the interface Queue rather than in terms of LinkedQueue. This means that if the client (i.e. PersonLinkedQueueDriver) chooses to use a class other than LinkedQueue to implement the Queue interface, there is no need to change these classes as they only refer to Queue and not to LinkedQueue. It also means that if some changes are made to the code of LinkedQueue (which means that it has to be re-compiled), these classes do not have to be re-compiled and re-tested.

```
// A class providing a Queue viewer that outputs the size of the queue.
// Barry Cornelius, 12 February 2000
import java.awt.     BorderLayout;
import javax.swing. JFrame;
import javax.swing. JLabel;
import java.util.    Observable;
import java.util.    Observer;
public class QueueCounter implements Observer
{
    private JLabel iJLabel;
    public QueueCounter(final int pJFrameX, final int pJFrameY)
    {
        final JFrame tJFrame = new JFrame("QueueCounter");
        iJLabel = new JLabel("unused");
        tJFrame.getContentPane().add(iJLabel, BorderLayout.CENTER);
        tJFrame.setLocation(pJFrameX, pJFrameY);
        tJFrame.setSize(300,100);
        tJFrame.setVisible(true);
    }

    public void update(final Observable pObservable, final Object pObject)
    {
        final Queue tQueue = (Queue)pObservable;
        final String tOperationString = (String)pObject;
        iJLabel.setText("After " + tOperationString + ":" + tQueue.size());
    }
}
```

Figure 16.13 A class providing a Queue viewer that outputs the size of the queue.

```
// A class providing a Queue viewer that lists the items of the queue.
// Barry Cornelius, 12 February 2000
import java.awt.      BorderLayout;
import javax.swing.  JFrame;
import javax.swing.  JScrollPane;
import javax.swing.  JTextArea;
import java.util.     Observable;
import java.util.     Observer;
public class QueueLister implements Observer
{
    private JTextArea iJTextArea;
    public QueueLister(final int pJFrameX, final int pJFrameY)
    {
        final JFrame tJFrame = new JFrame("QueueLister");
        iJTextArea = new JTextArea("unused");
        final JScrollPane tJScrollPane = new JScrollPane(iJTextArea);
        tJFrame.getContentPane().add(tJScrollPane, BorderLayout.CENTER);
        tJFrame.setLocation(pJFrameX, pJFrameY);
        tJFrame.setSize(300,100);
        tJFrame.setVisible(true);
    }
    public void update(final Observable pObservable, final Object pObject)
    {
        final Queue tQueue = (Queue)pObservable;
        iJTextArea.setText(tQueue.toString().replace('@', '\n'));
    }
}
```

Figure 16.14 A class providing a Queue viewer that lists the items of the queue.

The classes QueueCounter and QueueLister are also independent of the type of the elements being stored in the queue.

All of this is shown by the class diagram (given in Figure 16.15). In this diagram, the following notation is used:

I	Implements	Q	Queue
C	Creates	P	Person
H	Has	D	Date
U	Uses	QC	QueueCounter
		QL	QueueLister
		LQ	LinkedQueue
		EWL	ExitWindowListener
		PQC	PersonQueueController
		PID	PersonInputDialog
		PF	PersonForm
		PI	PersonImpl
		DI	DateImpl

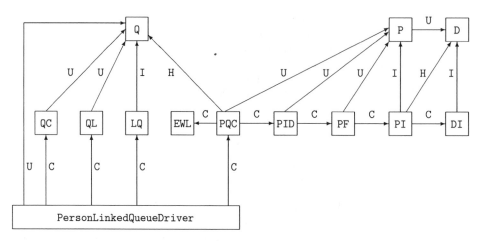

Figure 16.15   A class diagram for the `PersonLinkedQueueDriver` program.

16.7 Being an observer of more than one model

In this chapter, we have seen how to create an observer that reacts whenever there is some change to an object known as the model. However, more generally, it may be the case that an observer is actually a viewer of several objects, i.e. it may be presenting a view that is based on changes to several objects.

For example, it may be a viewer of several queues, i.e. several objects of the class `LinkedQueue`. Another example is illustrated by the code:

```
final Model tModelOne = new Model();
final Model tModelTwo = new Model();
final Model tModelThree = new Model();
final Monitor tMonitor = new Monitor();
tModelOne.addObserver(tMonitor);
tModelTwo.addObserver(tMonitor);
tModelThree.addObserver(tMonitor);
```

Here `tMonitor` is a viewer of several objects of the same class. However, it could be that a viewer is set up to observe changes to objects of different classes.

If an observer is only observing one object, the constructor of the observer can be passed an argument that is the model. This is the approach that was taken by the VCThree class of Figure 16.8. If we do this, there is no need for the observer's `update` method to interrogate the parameter `pObservable`. However, when an observer is observing several models, its `update` method can be called by any of them. In this situation, the `pObservable` parameter provides a means of determining which model has been updated.

Tips for programming and debugging

16.1 When a class declaration contains both an *extends clause* and an *implements clause*:

```
public class LinkedQueue extends Observable implements Queue
```

the extends clause must come before the implements clause (as is shown in Figure 11.4).

16.2 Section 16.4 points out that 'you will only get exclusive access to a variable/field if and only if every statement that accesses the variable/field appears in a `synchronized` block or a `synchronized` method'. Having to ensure that we add `synchronized` to each method of a class that accesses a `private` field is something that is prone to error. Forgetting to include a `synchronized` might cause weird unpredictable behaviour at runtime which would be difficult to debug.

Curios, controversies and cover-ups

16.1 Because no method can access the fields of an object until the constructor of the object has completed its execution, it is not appropriate (and not allowed) to add the `synchronized` keyword to the header of a constructor.

16.2 The class `Model` (given in Figure 16.2) contains a `set` method that can be used to change the value of the `iValue` field. The value of this variable is also changed by the `inc` method and the constructor of this class. It could be argued that the details of what to do when the field is updated appears three times. To avoid this, the three statements in the body of the constructor could be changed to:

```
set(0);
```

And the three statements of the body of `inc` could be changed to:

```
set(iValue + 1);
```

16.3 When `notifyObservers` was first introduced (in Section 16.2.3), it was called without any arguments; whereas, in Section 16.6.1, it was called with an argument. There it was shown that this argument can be used to pass information from the model to the viewer. Page 298 of the book *Design Patterns* ([17]) by Gamma *et al.* discusses how information should be passed between the model (which it calls the *subject*) and the observer. It says:

> At one extreme, which we call the **push model**, the subject sends observers detailed information about the change, whether they want it or not. At the other extreme is the **pull model**; the subject sends nothing, but the most minimal notification, and observers ask for details

explicitly thereafter. The pull model emphasizes the subject's igno-
rance of its observers, whereas the push model assumes subjects know
something about their observer's needs. The push model might make
observers less reusable, because Subject classes make assumptions
about Observer classes that might not always be true. On the other
hand, the pull model may be inefficient, because Observer classes
must ascertain what changed without help from the Subject.

16.4   There is some discussion on who triggers the update method, and how often
it should be called, on page 297 of *Design Patterns* ([17]) by Gamma *et al.* They
point out that calling the update method(s) for each operation that changes
the state of the model may mean that 'several consecutive operations will
cause several consecutive updates, which may be inefficient'. Another option
is to 'wait to trigger the update until after a series of state changes has been
made, thereby avoiding needless intermediate updates'. In Java, the provision
of two methods (setChanged and notifyObservers) rather than one
makes this easier to do. However, Gamma *et al.* say that, with this option,
errors are more likely since a call of notifyObservers may be forgotten.

Exercise

16.1   Add another view to the PersonLinkedQueueDriver program (described
in Section 16.6.2). This view should overwrite the file QueueDump.txt with
a textual representation of the contents of the queue whenever the queue is
changed. The class for this view can be written so that it is independent of the
class of the elements being stored in the queue.

Chapter 17

Using enumerations, sets and maps

Sometimes a type has a small number of values. For example, there will only be seven values in a type that is used for the days of a week. With such types, it is easy to enumerate (i.e. list) the values belonging to the type: so these types are sometimes called *enumerations*. Although it is possible to represent such a type in a Java program by an int, problems often arise if you do this: an alternative method is presented in this chapter.

Collections were introduced in Chapter 14, and in that chapter only lists were considered. The remainder of this chapter deals with the other two kinds of collections: *sets* and *maps*.

Besides providing interfaces called Set and Map, the java.util package also provides classes that implement these interfaces: it provides classes called HashSet, TreeSet, HashMap and TreeMap. This chapter looks at each of these.

Behind the scenes, the HashSet and HashMap classes use the hashCode method of the objects that have been stored in the collection. So, in this chapter, we also look at how we can write a hashCode method that gives a better performance for some of the operations that are performed on a HashSet/HashMap object.

17.1 Enumerations

17.1.1 What are enumerations?

Some objects of the real world that we may need to represent within a program are associated with a small set of possible values. There are usually names attached to each of the possible values that the object takes. For example, if we are writing a program for some game involving a pack of playing cards, each card belongs to one of the four suits called *clubs*, *diamonds*, *hearts* and *spades*.

Here are some examples of types where there are only a small number of values:

type	*values*
Suit	clubs, diamonds, hearts, spades
Gender	female, male
Day	Monday, Tuesday, Wednesday, Thursday, Friday, Saturday, Sunday
Month	January, February, March, April, May, June, July, ..., December
Figure	circle, rectangle, square, triangle
Voice	soprano, alto, tenor, bass
Beer	Adnams, Bass, Camerons, Fullers, Theakstons
Fish	anchovy, bass, cod, halibut, salmon, turbot

In some cases (such as *Suit*, *Day* and *Month*), there is an established number of values, whereas in other cases (such as *Figure*, *Beer* and *Fish*), we may wish to restrict our program to a certain set of values even though others may be possible.

And, for some **enumeration**s, there is an order associated with the values. For example, the values of the enumerations *Suit*, *Day*, *Month* and *Voice* have a recognized ordering. With other enumerations, there is no obvious ordering for the values.

Some programming languages (e.g. Pascal, Modula-2, Ada and C++) provide a means for declaring types that represent a small number of values. They are called **enumeration type**s. However, this is not the case for Java.

So we will have to find some other way of representing enumerations. We now consider three methods: the last one will be preferred.

17.1.2 Method One: using an `int` and literals of type `int`

Suppose we want to represent the current day of the week. We could declare a variable called `tDay` that is of the type `int`, and then a literal of the type `int` could be used to represent a particular day. For example, we could assign the value 2 to `tDay`. This might mean that `tDay` now has a value representing *Tuesday*.

The problem with this approach is that it is error-prone because the programmer/reader of the program has to remember the chosen mapping between the `int` values and the days. In particular, he/she has to remember whether the numbering starts from 0 or 1, and whether *Sunday* or *Monday* is the first day of the week.

17.1.3 Method Two: using an `int` and constants of type `int`

An improvement would be to introduce some constants for these `int` values. A class could be used to declare the constants. On some occasions, we will want to display an appropriate string (e.g. "Tuesday") instead of a numeric value. So the class could also provide methods to convert from a numeric value to a string and vice-versa. Such a class is provided for the type Day in Figure 17.1. Note the class breaks the conventions for the layout of switch statements that were recommended in Section 9.13.

```java
// A class that provides seven constants to represent the days of the week.
// Barry Cornelius, 19 June 2000
public class Day
{
    public static final int monday    = 1;
    public static final int tuesday   = 2;
    public static final int wednesday = 3;
    public static final int thursday  = 4;
    public static final int friday    = 5;
    public static final int saturday  = 6;
    public static final int sunday    = 7;
    public static int getInstance(final String pString)
    {
        int tDayNumber = -1;
        if (pString.length()>1)
        {
            final String tLowerCaseString = pString.toLowerCase();
            switch (tLowerCaseString.charAt(0))
            {
                case 'm': { tDayNumber = monday;    } break;
                case 'w': { tDayNumber = wednesday; } break;
                case 'f': { tDayNumber = friday;    } break;
                case 't':
                {
                    switch (tLowerCaseString.charAt(1))
                    {
                        case 'u': { tDayNumber = tuesday;  } break;
                        case 'h': { tDayNumber = thursday; } break;
                    }
                }
                break;
                case 's':
                {
                    switch (tLowerCaseString.charAt(1))
                    {
                        case 'a': { tDayNumber = saturday; } break;
                        case 'u': { tDayNumber = sunday;   } break;
                    }
                }
                break;
            }
        }
        return tDayNumber;
    }
}
```

Figure 17.1 *Continues on the next page.*

```
public static String getString(final int pInt)
{
  switch (pInt)
  {
    case    monday:  { return "Monday";    }
    case   tuesday:  { return "Tuesday";   }
    case wednesday:  { return "Wednesday"; }
    case  thursday:  { return "Thursday";  }
    case    friday:  { return "Friday";    }
    case  saturday:  { return "Saturday";  }
    case    sunday:  { return "Sunday";    }
         default:    { return "Unknown";   }
  }
}
}
```

Figure 17.1   A class that provides seven `int` constants for the days of a week.

```
// A program that tests the class Day.
// Barry Cornelius, 19 June 2000
public class DayProg
{
  public static void main(final String[] pArgs)
  {
    for (int tDayNumber = Day.monday; tDayNumber<=Day.sunday; tDayNumber++)
    {
      final String tDayString = Day.getString(tDayNumber);
      final int tDayNumberAgain = Day.getInstance(tDayString);
      System.out.println(tDayNumber + " " + Day.getString(tDayNumber) +
                                      " " + tDayNumberAgain);
    }
  }
}
```

Figure 17.2   A program that tests the use of the class `Day`.

A program (called `DayProg`) that tests this class is shown in Figure 17.2. It produces the output:

```
1 Monday 1
2 Tuesday 2
3 Wednesday 3
4 Thursday 4
5 Friday 5
6 Saturday 6
7 Sunday 7
```

17.1.4 The three problems with Method Two

There are three problems with Method Two:

1. The client needs to use the fact that the type is being represented by an `int`. For example, the `DayProg` program contains:

```
int tDayNumber = Day.monday;
```

The client could use a value which does not represent a value of the type:

```
tDayNumber = 42;
```

Or the client could use the numerical properties of the type `int`. For example, it could add *Tuesday* and *Wednesday* to produce *Friday* !

```
int tFirstDayNumber = Day.getInstance("Tuesday");
int tSecondDayNumber = Day.getInstance("Wednesday");
int tDayNumber = tFirstDayNumber + tSecondDayNumber;
System.out.println(Day.getString(tDayNumber));
```

2. The class has three places where the names associated with the values of the type appear. For example, *Monday* appears on the following three lines of the class Day:

```
public static final int monday    = 1;
case 'm': { tDayNumber = monday;    } break;
case    monday:  { return "Monday";    }
```

If we have to change this type, say to include an additional value, we must remember to alter all three places. With the Day class, this problem is unlikely to arise (as no-one is arguing for an extra day in the week!): however, in other cases this may be a problem.

3. Method Two shows how `int`s can be used to represent an enumeration. However, if a method has several parameters of type `int`, it will be easy to be confused about the order in which these should occur. For example, the class `java.awt.Font` contains a constructor described at $API/java/awt/Font.html as:

```
public Font(String name, int style, int size);
```

The intention is that the constructor gets called like:

```
final Font tFont = new Font("SansSerif", Font.PLAIN, 12);
```

where `Font.PLAIN` is an `int` constant of the class `java.awt.Font`. However, several people have moaned on the WWW that they have spent much time debugging a program because they inadvertently wrote something like:

```
final Font tFont = new Font("SansSerif", 12, Font.PLAIN);
```

For more details, see Curio 17.3.

17.1.5 Method Three: using a class with a private constructor

Using the classification of Chapter 12, the class Day that is given in Figure 17.1 is a hybrid of categories 1 and 2. Instead, we could provide a proper class (i.e. a class of category 4), and create instances of this class, one for each day of the week. We do not want clients to be able to create their own instances of the class, and so the class will not have any public constructors. However, we do want to create seven instances, and make these available. This can be done by making the constructor private; getting the class to construct the seven instances; and declaring public constants to point to these values. If this were all that is required, it could be satisfied by the class

```
// A class that declares seven constants and provides toString.
// Barry Cornelius, 19 June 2000
public class Day
{
    private String iString;
    private Day(final String pString)
    {
        iString = pString;
    }
    public String toString()
    {
        return iString;
    }
    public static final Day monday    = new Day("Monday");
    public static final Day tuesday   = new Day("Tuesday");
    public static final Day wednesday = new Day("Wednesday");
    public static final Day thursday  = new Day("Thursday");
    public static final Day friday    = new Day("Friday");
    public static final Day saturday  = new Day("Saturday");
    public static final Day sunday    = new Day("Sunday");
}
```

Figure 17.3   Using a class with seven constants and toString.

shown in Figure 17.3. A program that tests some aspects of this class is shown in Figure 17.4.

```
// A program that tests the intermediate version of the class Day.
// Barry Cornelius, 19 June 2000
public class DayProg
{
    public static void main(final String[] pArgs)
    {
        final Day tDay = Day.friday;
        System.out.println(tDay);
    }
}
```

Figure 17.4   A program that uses the intermediate version of the class Day.

However, we will also want to provide the ability to examine a string to see whether it is associated with one of the seven values. For this, the class can provide a method called getInstance having a parameter of type String and returning one of the seven values or the value null if the string is inappropriate.

For enumerations that have a natural ordering, a client may want to be able to iterate through the values of the type from the first one to the last one. This can be done if the class provides a method called iterator that returns a value that satisfies the java.util.Iterator interface. It will also be useful to provide a compareTo method to allow two values to be compared to see if one comes before the other.

One way in which a class can easily satisfy these new requirements is to use an array to store the seven values. Such a class is provided for the type Day in

Figure 17.5. As before, this class has seven constants, but each class instance creation expression has been replaced by a call of the class method iCreateDay, e.g. new Day("Monday") has been replaced by iCreateDay("Monday"). This method not only creates a new value of the class Day but it also assigns this value to the next unused element of the array iDays. The variable iNumberOf-Days records the number of elements of this array that have been used. Both iDays and iNumberOfDays are class variables.

When a new value of the class Day is created, Day's constructor not only stores the string (e.g. "Monday") in the iString field but it also stores the position of the string in the enumeration (e.g. 0) in the iPosition field. The reason for doing this is to make the code of methods like equals and compareTo more efficient.

We will defer consideration of the hashCode function until Section 17.4.

The getInstance method has to work its way through the elements of the array to find the element that has an appropriate iString value. In order to be more user-friendly to the client, it uses equalsIgnoreCase rather than equals in order to compare the strings. So the client can use any case in the spelling of the name of a day:

```
Day tMonday = Day.getInstance("MONDAY");
```

The easiest way of providing an iterator method is to use a class method called asList from java.util.Arrays. The asList method returns a List view of

```java
// Using a proper class with a private constructor to represent a day.
// Barry Cornelius, 19 June 2000
import java.util. Arrays;
import java.util. Iterator;
import java.util. List;
public class Day implements Comparable
{
   private String iString;
   private int iPosition;
   private Day(final String pString)
   {
      iString = pString;
      iPosition = iNumberOfDays;
   }
   public boolean equals(final Object pObject)
   {
      if ( pObject==null || getClass()!=pObject.getClass() )
      {
         return false;
      }
      return iPosition==((Day)pObject).iPosition;
   }
   public int hashCode()
   {
      return iPosition;
   }
```

Figure 17.5 *Continues on the next page.*

```
public int compareTo(final Object pObject)
{
    final Day tDay = (Day)pObject;
    return iPosition - tDay.iPosition;
}
public String toString()
{
    return iString;
}

private static Day iCreateDay(final String pString)
{
    final Day tDay = new Day(pString);
    iDays[iNumberOfDays] = tDay;
    iNumberOfDays++;
    return tDay;
}
private static int iNumberOfDays = 0;
private static final Day[] iDays = new Day[7];
public static final Day monday    = iCreateDay("Monday");
public static final Day tuesday   = iCreateDay("Tuesday");
public static final Day wednesday = iCreateDay("Wednesday");
public static final Day thursday  = iCreateDay("Thursday");
public static final Day friday    = iCreateDay("Friday");
public static final Day saturday  = iCreateDay("Saturday");
public static final Day sunday    = iCreateDay("Sunday");
public static Day getInstance(final String pString)
{
    for (int tDayNumber = 0; tDayNumber<iNumberOfDays; tDayNumber++)
    {
        final Day tArrayDay = iDays[tDayNumber];
        final String tArrayDayString = tArrayDay.iString;
        if (tArrayDayString.equalsIgnoreCase(pString))
        {
            return tArrayDay;
        }
    }
    return null;
}
public static Iterator iterator()
{
    final List tList = Arrays.asList(iDays);
    return tList.iterator();
}
}
```

Figure 17.5   Using a proper class with a private constructor to represent a day.

the elements of the array passed as an argument. Note that it does not generate a new `List` where the elements are copies of the elements of the array. Instead the `List` that is returned shares the elements of the array. `Day`'s `iterator` method can then be provided by applying the `iterator` method to this `List`.

A program that tests this class is shown in Figure 17.6.

```
// A program that tests the class Day.
// Barry Cornelius, 19 June 2000
import java.util. Iterator;
public class DayProg
{
   public static void main(final String[] pArgs)
   {
      final Day tWednesday = Day.getInstance("weDneSdaY");
      final Iterator tDayIterator = Day.iterator();
      while (tDayIterator.hasNext())
      {
         final Day tDay = (Day)tDayIterator.next();
         final String tDayString = tDay.toString();
         final Day tDayAgain = Day.getInstance(tDayString);
         System.out.println(tDay + " " + tDayString + " " + tDayAgain +
                                  " " + tDay.compareTo(tWednesday));
      }
   }
}
```

Figure 17.6 A program that tests the use of the new version of the class `Day`.

The program produces the output:

```
Monday Monday Monday -2
Tuesday Tuesday Tuesday -1
Wednesday Wednesday Wednesday 0
Thursday Thursday Thursday 1
Friday Friday Friday 2
Saturday Saturday Saturday 3
Sunday Sunday Sunday 4
```

Although, for this example, there is an obvious order for the values of the type, where there is no obvious order it is suggested that the values are ordered by the alphabetical order of the names that are associated with the values.

One advantage of using values of type `int` to represent a type that is an enumeration is that it is easy to use a switch statement to decide which value a variable (of this type) has. This is not possible if a class like that shown in Figure 17.5 is used for the enumeration.

17.1.6 The enumeration pattern

The ideas presented in Section 17.1.5 enable you to produce a class for any type that has a small number of values. The code given in Figure 17.5 can be used as a *pattern* for types that have a small number of values: we will call it the **enumeration pattern**. The classes that are produced in this way avoid the three problems mentioned in Section 17.1.4.

Some papers dealing with enumerations in Java are mentioned in Curio 17.2 and Curio 17.3.

17.2 Sets

17.2.1 What is a set?

If a program uses a variable of some type in order to represent a real-world object, the variable can be used to record a single value that represents some particular state of the object. Sometimes real-world objects possess a combination of values rather than just one, and it is often appropriate to refer to the *set* of values possessed by an object. In Java, such a real-world object can be represented by an object that is a Set, an interface provided in the Collections API of the Java 2 Platform.

17.2.2 The interface Set

Some of the methods of the Set interface are shown in Figure 17.7. The full set of methods is given at $API/java/util/Set.html.

```
public boolean add(Object pValue);
```
    Adds a new element to the target set. The element is assigned the value pValue, a pointer to some object. However, the element is only added if the target set does not contain an object having a value which equals that of pValue. Returns the value *true* if and only if the value pValue was not already in the set.
```
public boolean contains(Object pValue);
```
    Returns the value *true* if and only if the target set contains an object having a value which equals that of pValue.
```
public boolean equals(Object pSet);
```
    Returns the value *true* if and only if the target set and the set pSet contain the same objects.
```
public int hashCode();
```
    Returns the hashcode value of the target set.
```
public boolean isEmpty();
```
    Returns the value *true* if and only if the target set does not have any elements.
```
public Iterator iterator();
```
    Returns an iterator over the elements of the target set.
```
public boolean remove(Object pValue);
```
    Removes from the target set the object having a value which equals that of pValue (if such an object exists). Returns the value *true* if and only if it exists.
```
public int size();
```
    Returns the number of elements in the target set.

Figure 17.7 Methods of the `java.util.Set` interface.

In particular, the interface includes methods called:

- add – which adds a value to a set;
- remove – which removes a value from a set;
- contains – which indicates whether a particular value is in a set;
- size – which returns how many elements there are in the set.

Note that using add to add a value to a Set does not change the Set if the Set already contains the value. So, unlike a List, a Set cannot be used to store duplicates.

We now look at an example that shows how these methods can be used.

17.3 Using a Set in a program that creates a pizza

The menus of pizzerias usually offer a large number of different kinds of pizzas each with a different set of toppings. Suppose that we wish to record the set of toppings that each pizza contains. First, we need a type that represents the possible toppings. The class given in Figure 17.8 assumes that a pizzeria provides the following toppings: anchovies, cheese, egg, ham, mushrooms, onions, peppers, salami, tomatoes. This class is similar to the Day class (given in Section 17.1.5). However, because there is no natural ordering to the values of the enumeration, there is no need for the compareTo and iterator methods, and so these have not been provided.

We want to record the specific values of this type that are appropriate for a particular pizza. A Set can be used for this.

```
// A class that represents a topping.
// Barry Cornelius, 19 June 2000
public class Topping
{
   private String iString;
   private int iPosition;
   private Topping(final String pString)
   {
      iString = pString;
      iPosition = iNumberOfToppings;
   }
   public boolean equals(final Object pObject)
   {
      if ( pObject==null || getClass()!=pObject.getClass() )
      {
         return false;
      }
      return iPosition==((Topping)pObject).iPosition;
   }
}
```

Figure 17.8 *Continues on the next page.*

```
public int hashCode()
{
   return iPosition;
}
public String toString()
{
   return iString;
}

private static Topping iCreateTopping(final String pString)
{
   final Topping tTopping = new Topping(pString);
   iToppings[iNumberOfToppings] = tTopping;
   iNumberOfToppings++;
   return tTopping;
}
private static int iNumberOfToppings = 0;
private static final Topping[] iToppings = new Topping[9];
public static final Topping anchovies = iCreateTopping("anchovies");
public static final Topping cheese    = iCreateTopping("cheese");
public static final Topping egg       = iCreateTopping("egg");
public static final Topping ham       = iCreateTopping("ham");
public static final Topping mushrooms = iCreateTopping("mushrooms");
public static final Topping onions    = iCreateTopping("onions");
public static final Topping peppers   = iCreateTopping("peppers");
public static final Topping salami    = iCreateTopping("salami");
public static final Topping tomatoes  = iCreateTopping("tomatoes");
public static Topping getInstance(final String pString)
{
   for (int tToppingNumber = 0; tToppingNumber<iNumberOfToppings;
                                tToppingNumber++)
   {
      final Topping tArrayTopping = iToppings[tToppingNumber];
      final String tArrayToppingString = tArrayTopping.iString;
      if (tArrayToppingString.equalsIgnoreCase(pString))
      {
         return tArrayTopping;
      }
   }
   return null;
}
}
```

Figure 17.8 A class that represents a topping.

The Collections API provides two classes that implement the Set interface. They are called HashSet and TreeSet. The TreeSet class should be used when we would like TreeSet's iterator to produce the elements of the set in an order determined by the values of the elements. TreeSet implements the SortedSet interface, a subinterface of Set. In order to use TreeSet, the type of the values of the set must implement the Comparable interface (from java.lang) and/or the set must be created using a constructor that has an argument of a class that implements the Comparator interface (of the java.util package). For more details, see Curio 17.8. The HashSet class should be used when we are not bothered with order.

The class Pizza given in Figure 17.9 uses a HashSet.

```java
// A class that represents a pizza.
// Barry Cornelius, 19 June 2000
import java.util. HashSet;
import java.util. Iterator;
import java.util. Set;
import java.util. StringTokenizer;
public class Pizza
{
    private Set iSet;
    public Pizza()
    {
        iSet = new HashSet();
    }
    public Pizza(final String pString)
    {
        this();
        final StringTokenizer tTokens = new StringTokenizer(pString, "-");
        while (tTokens.hasMoreTokens())
        {
            final String tToppingString = tTokens.nextToken();
            add(tToppingString);
        }
    }
    public void add(final String pString)
    {
        final Topping tTopping = Topping.getInstance(pString);
        if (tTopping!=null)
        {
            iSet.add(tTopping);
        }
    }
    public boolean equals(final Object pObject)
    {
        if ( pObject==null || getClass()!=pObject.getClass() )
        {
            return false;
        }
        return iSet.equals(((Pizza)pObject).iSet);
    }
    public int hashCode()
    {
        return iSet.hashCode();
    }
```

Figure 17.9 *Continues on the next page.*

```
public String toString()
{
   if (iSet.isEmpty())
   {
      return new String("");
   }
   else
   {
      final StringBuffer tStringBuffer = new StringBuffer();
      final Iterator tIterator = iSet.iterator();
      while (tIterator.hasNext())
      {
         final Topping tTopping = (Topping)tIterator.next();
         tStringBuffer.append("-" + tTopping);
      }
      tStringBuffer.deleteCharAt(0);
      return tStringBuffer.toString();
   }
}
}
```

Figure 17.9   A class that represents a pizza.

A simple program that tests the `Pizza` class is given in Figure 17.10.

Consideration of the `hashCode` functions of the `Topping` and `Pizza` classes will be deferred until Section 17.4.

17.4 Providing better versions of `hashCode`

17.4.1 Why do we wish to provide a better version of `hashCode`?

As we have just seen, the `java.util` package provides two classes (`HashSet` and `TreeSet`) that implement the `Set` interface. This interface provides methods like `contains`, `add` and `remove` that need to check whether a collection contains a particular object. If you are using `HashSet`, you can speed up the execution of these methods by providing a good implementation of `hashCode`.

When we first looked at `hashCode` back in Section 11.11.2, it was suggested that for the time being you should provide:

```
public int hashCode()
{
   return 0;
}
```

In Section 11.11.2, it was said that, although this may not give good performance with collections, at least it will work in all situations whereas producing a better version of `hashCode` might produce one for which this is not the case. We now look at the difficulties of producing a better version of `hashCode`.

```
// A program that tests the use of the class Pizza.
// Barry Cornelius, 19 June 2000
import java.io. BufferedReader;
import java.io. InputStreamReader;
import java.io. IOException;
public class PizzaProg
{
    public static void main(final String[] pArgs) throws IOException
    {
        final Pizza tPizza = new Pizza();
        final BufferedReader tKeyboard =
                    new BufferedReader(new InputStreamReader(System.in));
        System.out.print("How many toppings do you want? ");
        System.out.flush();
        final String tNumberOfToppingsString = tKeyboard.readLine();
        final int tNumberOfToppings =
                        Integer.parseInt(tNumberOfToppingsString);
        for (int tToppingNumber = 1; tToppingNumber<=tNumberOfToppings;
                                tToppingNumber++)
        {
            System.out.print("Type in the name of a topping: ");
            System.out.flush();
            final String tToppingString = tKeyboard.readLine();
            tPizza.add(tToppingString);
        }
        System.out.println("Toppings are " + tPizza);
    }
}
```

Figure 17.10 A program that tests the use of the class Pizza.

17.4.2 Providing other code for the hashCode function

Returning to the Date–DateImpl example, another possibility for the hashCode function is:

```
public int hashCode()
{
    return iMonth;
}
```

If we use this hashCode function, an integer in the range 1 to 12 is associated with each of the values of the class DateImpl. For example:

```
final Date tNoelDate = new DateImpl(2000, 12, 25);
final int tValue = tNoelDate.hashCode();
```

will assign the value 12 to tValue.

So, if we were to store values of the type Date in a collection (such as a HashSet), the designer of the collection class could arrange for the values of the collection to be stored in 12 **buckets**: all the values of the collection that have a hashcode of 1 would be stored in the first bucket; all those with a hashcode of 2 would be stored in the second bucket; and so on. When we later call the contains method to check whether a particular Date value is in the collection, the code of the contains method can find the hashcode of the Date value and then it need only look at the values in the appropriate bucket.

For example, suppose we want to set up a HashSet containing the dates when various composers died:

Bach	1750-08-28
Beethoven	1827-03-26
Cage	1992-08-12
Chopin	1849-10-17
Copland	1990-12-02
Elgar	1934-02-23
Handel	1759-04-14
Mendelssohn	1847-11-04
Purcell	1695-11-21
Sibelius	1957-09-20
Stanford	1924-03-29
Tallis	1585-11-23
Tchaikovsky	1893-11-06
Vaughan-Williams	1958-08-26
Walton	1983-03-08

Suppose we add each of these dates to a HashSet, e.g. for Bach:

```
final Date tDeathOfBach = new DateImpl(1750, 8, 28);
tHashSet.add(tDeathOfBach);
```

The add method could use Date's hashCode function to store the values in 12 buckets:

1.

2. 1934-02-23

3. 1924-03-29, 1827-03-26, 1983-03-08

4. 1759-04-14

5.

6.

7.

8. 1750-08-28, 1992-08-12, 1958-08-26

9. 1957-09-20

10. 1849-10-17

11. 1847-11-04, 1695-11-21, 1893-11-06, 1585-11-23

12. 1990-12-02

Then, when later we ask the collection class whether it has the value 1893-11-06 (the date when Tchaikovsky died), the contains method can call hashCode on this value and, because this produces the value 11, the contains method need only check the four values that are in the 11th bucket. The code of the contains method uses equals on each of these values in turn returning the value *true* if and only if it finds the value (in this case, the value 1893-11-06).

Besides the above coding of the hashCode function, there are many other possibilities we could choose instead. Here is another example:

```
public int hashCode()
{
    return iYear+10000 + iMonth*100 + iDay;
}
```

17.4.3 The reason for using a zero-returning hashCode

However, there is one problem which we have not yet considered. If a client chooses to change a value after it has been put in a collection, the value will no longer be in the right bucket. So it will not be found if we later search for it.

For example, contrary to what it says above, Bach actually died on 28 July 1750 rather than on 28 August 1750. So we might want to change this date:

```
tDeathOfBach.setMonth(7);
```

and this would change this value in the collection. So it becomes:

1.
2. 1934-02-23
3. 1924-03-29, 1827-03-26, 1983-03-08
4. 1759-04-14
5.
6.
7.
8. 1750-07-28, 1992-08-12, 1958-08-26
9. 1957-09-20
10. 1849-10-17
11. 1847-11-04, 1695-11-21, 1893-11-06, 1585-11-23
12. 1990-12-02

Suppose we now use contains to search for the value 1750-07-28. Because when hashCode is applied to this value it produces the value 7, the contains method will look in the 7th bucket which is empty. So the method will not find the value as the appropriate value is in the wrong bucket.

Rule 1: Here is an important rule: a hashCode function should not be written in terms of fields that can be altered.

Since the class DateImpl provides setYear, setMonth and setDay, we ought not to provide a hashCode function that is written in terms of the iYear, iMonth and/or iDay fields. So this is the reason why the DateImpl class (of Figure 11.16) uses:

```
public int hashCode()
{
    return 0;
}
```

If we use this hashCode function, a collection class will use one bucket for all the objects we put into the collection. Although this means that a method like contains will execute more slowly as all the values of the collection are in one bucket, it does mean that we need not worry about values being changed after they have been added to a collection.

17.4.4 It is not a problem for immutable classes

Of course, this problem will not occur if you are providing an *immutable class*. With such classes, once an object has been created, there are no fields that can be altered. In such circumstances, you will be able to choose a hashCode function that helps to speed up searching.

17.4.5 Revisiting examples of earlier chapters

So if we removed setYear, setMonth and setDay from Date–DateImpl, its objects would now be immutable. We could then use either of the two hashCode functions that were given above in Section 17.4.2. This would speed up the searching for dates when they have been stored in a HashSet.

For the above reason, a zero-returning hashCode function has been provided for all of the classes developed in previous chapters of this book.

For example, consider the PersonImpl class again: it is given in Section 12.7. This class provides set methods for all of its fields. However, suppose we do not provide a setName method. We would then be in a position to provide a hashCode method that is based on the value of the iName field. For example, we could return the length of the name:

```
public int hashCode()
{
    return iName.length();
}
```

However, normally with Strings, you return the hashcode of the string:

```
public int hashCode()
{
    return iName.hashCode();
}
```

Rule 2: Here is another important rule: the same hashcode values must be produced for any two objects that are equal (according to the `equals` method).

In practice, this means that a `hashCode` function must always return the same value (e.g. the value 0) or it is just dependent on some or all of the fields used in the definition of `equals`.

17.4.6 Looking at the examples of this chapter

So far in this chapter, three classes have had `hashCode` functions. Each of these classes results in objects that are immutable.

Figure 17.5 contains a class for a `Day`. Each object of this class contains an `int` value (called `iPosition`) which is its position (in the enumeration) and the `equals` function is written in terms of this field. We can therefore provide:

```
public int hashCode()
{
    return iPosition;
}
```

Like `Day`, the class `Topping` in Figure 17.8 is a type representing an enumeration. So it has a similar `hashCode` function.

Figure 17.9 provides a class for representing a pizza. As has already been noted, this is an immutable class. And its `equals` method is written in terms of `iSet` which is of the `Set` interface type. As this type provides a `hashCode` method, we can use this in `Pizza`'s `hashCode` method:

```
public int hashCode()
{
    return iSet.hashCode();
}
```

17.4.7 What is the effect on performance?

The `HashCodeTimes` program shown in Figure 17.11 can be used to measure how long it takes to execute the `contains` method on a `HashSet` object. The program creates a `HashSet` that contains 10 000 elements that are objects of the `DateImpl` class. The program times the execution of 10 000 calls of `contains`. The following results were obtained for different codings of the `hashCode` method of the `DateImpl` class:

the code of the `hashCode` *method*	*time taken*
`return 0;`	14826
`return iMonth;`	1235
`return iYear*10000 + iMonth*100 + iDay;`	36

The times are given in milliseconds. These results demonstrate how a carefully chosen `hashCode` method can affect the performance of some programs.

```java
// A program for comparing the performance of DateImpl's hashCode method.
// Barry Cornelius, 19 June 2000
import java.util. HashSet;
import java.util. Iterator;
import java.util. Random;
import java.util. Set;
public class HashCodeTimes
{
    public static void main(final String[] pArgs)
    {
        final Random tRandom = new Random();
        final Set tSet = new HashSet();
        for (int tCount = 1; tCount<=10000; tCount++)
        {
            final int tYear = 1990 + tRandom.nextInt(10);
            final int tMonth = 1 + tRandom.nextInt(12);
            final int tDay = 1 + tRandom.nextInt(28);
            final Date tAddDate = new DateImpl(tYear, tMonth, tDay);
            boolean tResult = tSet.add(tAddDate);
        }
        final Iterator tIterator = tSet.iterator();
        final long tStartTime = System.currentTimeMillis();
        while (tIterator.hasNext())
        {
            final Date tNextDate = (Date) tIterator.next();
            final boolean tResult = tSet.contains(tNextDate);
        }
        final long tFinishTime = System.currentTimeMillis();
        System.out.println(tFinishTime - tStartTime);
    }
}
```

Figure 17.11   A program for comparing the performance of DateImpl's hashCode.

17.5) Maps

17.5.1 What is a map?

Although we will often want to represent a collection of items using a list or a set, it may be that one part of each item of data is important: it acts as a **key** to the other part(s) of the item.

Here are two examples:

- For a phone directory, the key is the name of the person. The other part of the item is the person's phone number.

- For a dictionary, the key is the spelling of the word. The other parts of the item are the meaning of the word; how the word is derived (i.e. the etymology); when the word was first used; and so on.

These are examples of a **map**. Given a key, e.g. "Joe Bloggs", the phone directory defines a value, e.g. "01987-654321". Each map contains a collection of **entries** (or **associations**), each entry **associating** a *key* with a *value*. With some maps (e.g. the dictionary given above), each value is actually several pieces of data, whereas with other maps (e.g. the phone directory) the value is just one piece of data.

17.5.2 The interface `Map` and the classes `HashMap` and `TreeMap`

In Java, a map can be represented using the `Map` interface of the Collections API. Some of the methods of this interface are shown in Figure 17.12. The full set of methods is given at $API/java/util/Map.html. In particular, the interface includes methods called:

- `put` – which associates a given key with a given value;
- `remove` – which removes the entry for a given key;

```
public boolean containsKey(Object pKey);
```
Returns the value *true* if and only if the target map contains an entry whose key part has a value which `equals` the value of `pKey`.
```
public boolean containsValue(Object pValue);
```
Returns the value *true* if and only if the target map contains at least one entry whose value part has a value which `equals` the value of `pValue`.
```
public Set entrySet();
```
Returns a `Set` view of all the key-value entries of the target map.
```
public boolean equals(Object pMap);
```
Returns the value *true* if and only if the target map and the map `pMap` contain the same entries.
```
public Object get(Object pKey);
```
Returns a pointer to the object associated with the key `pKey` in the target map or `null` if there is no such entry.
```
public int hashCode();
```
Returns the hashcode value of the target map.
```
public boolean isEmpty();
```
Returns the value *true* if and only if the target map does not have any entries.
```
public Set keySet();
```
Returns a `Set` view of all the keys of the target map.
```
public Object put(Object pKey, Object pValue);
```
Associates, in the target map, the key `pKey` with the value `pValue`, a pointer to some object. Returns a pointer to the object which was previously associated with the key `pKey` or `null` if this is a new entry.
```
public Object remove(Object pKey);
```
Removes the entry with the key `pKey` from the target map if such an entry exists. Returns the value which was associated with the key `pKey` or `null` if there was no such entry.
```
public int size();
```
Returns the number of entries in the target map.
```
public Collection values();
```
Returns a `Collection` view of all the values of the target map.

Figure 17.12 Methods of the `java.util.Map` interface.

- `get` – which returns the value associated with a given key;
- `containsKey` – which indicates whether the map contains an entry for a given key;
- `size` – which returns how many entries there are in the map.

The Collections API provides two classes that implement this interface: they are called `HashMap` and `TreeMap`. The `TreeMap` class should be used when we would like the entries of the map to be in the order determined by the values of the keys. `TreeMap` implements the `SortedMap` interface, a subinterface of `Map`. When you want to use `TreeMap`, the type of the keys of the map must implement the `Comparable` interface and/or the map must be created using a constructor that has an argument of a class that implements the `Comparator` interface. For more details, see Curio 17.8. The `HashMap` class should be used when we are not bothered with order.

17.5.3 A simple example that uses the `Map` interface

Suppose we want to create an object that represents a phone directory. Since names are to be associated with phone numbers, we will use a map. It can be created using the declaration:

```
final Map tPhoneDirectory = new HashMap();
```

Currently, the map is empty, as can be shown by:

```
System.out.println(tPhoneDirectory.size());
```

This statement outputs the value 0. A new entry can be added by:

```
tPhoneDirectory.put("University of Durham", "2000-374-0191");
```

Another one can be added by:

```
tPhoneDirectory.put("Joe Bloggs", "01987-654321");
```

An entry can be updated by:

```
tPhoneDirectory.put("University of Durham", "0191-374-2000");
```

We can examine the map using code like:

```
if (tPhoneDirectory.isEmpty())
{
    System.out.println("map is empty");
}
else
{
    System.out.println("size of map is " + tPhoneDirectory.size());
}
final String tPersonName = "University of Durham";
if (tPhoneDirectory.containsKey(tPersonName))
```

```
{
    final String tPhoneNumber = (String)tPhoneDirectory.get(tPersonName);
    System.out.println(tPersonName + "'s phone number is " + tPhoneNumber);
}
```

Given the previous calls, the above statements should output:

```
2
University of Durham's phone number is 0191-374-2000
```

17.5.4 Iterating through the entries of a map

The Map interface provides three methods which allow the entries of a map to be viewed in three different ways. One method (keySet) allows you to view all the keys; another (called values) views a collection of all the values; and the third method (entrySet) views a set of key-value entries.

When using HashMap and TreeMap, it is important to know that the implementations of these classes are such that none of these three methods creates a new collection of objects. What they do is to provide a different view of an existing collection.

keySet is the method that produces a view of all the keys. Since all the keys of a map have different values, the method returns a Set. If the map is a SortedMap, the keySet method returns a SortedSet.

So the call of keySet in:

```
final Set tKeySet = tPhoneDirectory.keySet();
```

returns a set containing the values "University of Durham" and "Joe Bloggs". This can be shown using the code:

```
final Iterator tKeySetIterator = tKeySet.iterator();
while (tKeySetIterator.hasNext())
{
    final String tPersonName = (String)tKeySetIterator.next();
    final String tPhoneNumber = (String)tPhoneDirectory.get(tPersonName);
    System.out.println(tPersonName + "'s phone number is " + tPhoneNumber);
}
```

Since tPhoneDirectory is a HashMap object, the order in which the entries appear is unpredictable. If tPhoneDirectory were created as a TreeMap object, then the entries would appear sorted by the keys. Since the keys of tPhoneDirectory are Strings, then by default the order of the keys would be the alphabetical order of these strings, i.e. the above code would output the line for "Joe Bloggs" before that for "University of Durham". If some other order is required, this is possible by passing an object that is of a class that implements the Comparator interface as an argument to the constructor used to create the TreeMap. For more details, see Curio 17.8.

The method that returns a view of the values of a map is called values. Unlike the keys, the values of a map may not have distinct values. (In our example, two people may have the same phone number.) Thus it would be inappropriate for the result type of the `values` method to be a `Set`: instead, it is a `Collection`. As was shown in Figure 14.1, the `Collection` interface is the interface for which `List` and `Set` are subinterfaces. This interface includes the operations `add`, `contains`, `iterator` and `size`.

So the call of `values` in:

```
final Collection tValuesCollection = tPhoneDirectory.values();
```

returns an object (supporting the `Collection` interface) that contains pointers to the objects of `tPhoneDirectory` containing the values `"0191-374-2000"` and `"01987-654321"`. So we can do:

```
final Iterator tValuesCollectionIterator = tValuesCollection.iterator();
while (tValuesCollectionIterator.hasNext())
{
    final String tPhoneNumber = (String)tValuesCollectionIterator.next();
    System.out.println(tPhoneNumber);
}
```

The third method (called `entrySet`) returns a view that is a `Set` containing all the key-value entries:

```
final Set tEntrySet = tPhoneDirectory.entrySet();
```

Each element of this set supports the `java.util.Map.Entry` interface. Some of the methods of this interface are shown in Figure 17.13. For more details, see $API/java/util/Map.Entry.html.

```
public boolean equals(Object pEntry);
```
Returns the value *true* if and only if the target entry and the entry `pEntry` represent the same entry.
```
public Object getKey();
```
Returns a pointer to the object that is the key part of the target entry.
```
public Object getValue();
```
Returns a pointer to the object that is the value part of the target entry.
```
public int hashCode();
```
Returns the hashcode value of the target entry.
```
public Object setValue(Object pValue);
```
Changes the value part of the target entry to the value `pValue`, a pointer to some object. Returns the previous value of the value part.

Figure 17.13 Methods of the `java.util.Map.Entry` interface.

You can iterate through the elements of this set using the code:

```
final Iterator tEntrySetIterator = tEntrySet.iterator();
while (tEntrySetIterator.hasNext())
{
    final Entry tEntry = (Entry)tEntrySetIterator.next();
    final String tPersonName = (String)tEntry.getKey();
    final String tPhoneNumber = (String)tEntry.getValue();
    System.out.println(tPersonName + "'s phone number is " + tPhoneNumber);
}
```

17.6) Using a Map to manipulate a population

17.6.1 Representing a population by a TreeMap

In Section 12.5, an interface called Person and a class called PersonImpl were introduced as a means of describing details about a person. Suppose we want to store information about a number of people, i.e. to store details about a **population**.

Although earlier (in Section 14.4.4 to Section 14.4.6) we did something similar – we represented a queue of people – this time we do not need the entries to be ordered according to when they were added to the collection.

We could instead use a Set, perhaps a SortedSet, where the elements are sorted according to the names of the people. However, because we are primarily interested in retrieving information from the population based on the person's name, it is better to use a Map.

We will want to iterate through the Map in the alphabetical order of the names, and so it would be useful to use a TreeMap (because it implements the SortedMap interface). However, if this were not important, a HashMap could be used instead.

So TreeMap will be used to implement the population. However, how the population is represented is something which we may wish to reconsider later. So a class will be used for the population: in this way, we will be able to hide the implementation details.

17.6.2 Using an interface called Pop

We can provide this class with an interface (as shown in Figure 17.14). This Pop interface includes the following methods (as well as some other methods that are not listed here):

- To add a new person to the population:

```
public boolean add(Person pPerson);
```

The method returns the value *true* if and only if the person was not already in the population.

- To remove the person with a given name from the population:

```
public boolean remove(String pName);
```

The method returns the value *true* if and only if the person was in the population.

- To get the details about the person with a given name from the population:

```
public Person get(String pName);
```

The method returns a pointer to the object representing the person or the value null if the person is not in the population.

- To get the details about the first person in the population:

```
public Person getFirst();
```

The method returns a pointer to the object representing the person or the value null if the population is empty.

```
// An interface for a population.
// Barry Cornelius, 19 June 2000
import java.util. Observer;
public interface Pop
{
    // returns true if and only if pPerson is not already in the population
    public boolean add(Person pPerson);

    // returns true if and only if a person with the name pName is
    // in the population
    public boolean remove(String pName);

    // returns null if and only if there is not a person with the name pName
    public Person get(String pName);

    // returns null if and only if there is no first person
    public Person getFirst();

    // returns null if and only if there is no next person
    public Person next();

    // returns the size of the target population
    public int size();

    // return the value true if and only if the target population
    // represents the same population as pObject
    public boolean equals(Object pObject);

    // returns a hashcode for the target population
    public int hashCode();

    // returns a textual representation of the target population
    public String toString();

    // registers pObserver as an observer of the target population
    public void addObserver(Observer pObserver);
}
```

Figure 17.14   An interface for a population.

To get the details about the next person in the population:

```
public Person next();
```

The method returns a pointer to the object representing the person or the value
`null` if there is no other person.

To register some given object as an observer of changes to the population:

```
public void addObserver(Observer pObserver);
```

The object must be of a class that implements the `Observer` interface.

17.6.3 A class called PopImpl that implements the Pop interface

Whenever you use the Map interface, you will need a type for the key and a type for the value. Having decided to use a Map for the population, we need a type for the person's name and a type for the personal details about the person.

For the person's name, we could use a type that properly represents the name of a person. For example, it could represent a person's family name, and their first name, and so on. Of course, like when designing the class PersonImpl, we could cheat and just use one String for a person's name. Even if you do this, it would still be useful to introduce an interface called Name, and a class called NameImpl that hides this design decision. One of the advantages of using Name rather than String means that it is obvious as to which parts of the code are dependent on this decision. However, we will not even do this: we will just use the type String for a person's name.

We also need a type for the personal details about a person. We already have a type called Person, and for this we are recording a person's name, their date of birth, their phone number and their height. As we are mapping from a person's name to their personal details, it is really inappropriate to use the type Person for the personal details, as then the person's name would appear on both sides of the map.

However, as we have already done all the work for producing the interface Person and its implementation PersonImpl, we will use these and ignore the fact that they are inappropriate. Using them means that we have the usual problems caused by duplication:

- if we change one occurrence of the name, we will need to remember to change the other;
- the data will take up more space.

In Java, the amount of additional space required is small as the two variables can both be reference variables that refer to the same String.

The code for PopImpl is given in Figure 17.15.

PopImpl's constructor needs to create a TreeMap and make some variable point to it. The variable is called iPop.

In the interface, add is declared as:

```
public boolean add(Person pPerson);
```

In the class PopImpl, the code of add just has to associate a person's name, i.e. pPerson.getName() with their personal details, i.e. pPerson. So the code of this method contains the call:

```
iPop.put(pPerson.getName(), pPerson)
```

The Map interface says that the put method returns null if and only if the map did not already contain this key (i.e. this person's name). So the code of add checks the result produced by this call of put. Although this could be coded as:

```
final Person tPreviousPerson = (Person)iPop.put(pPerson.getName(), pPerson);
return tPreviousPerson==null;
```

it instead uses:

```
final Object tObject = iPop.put(pPerson.getName(), pPerson);
return tObject==null;
```

```
// A class that implements the Pop interface.
// Barry Cornelius, 19 June 2000
import java.util. Iterator;
import java.util. Map;
import java.util. Observable;
import java.util. Observer;
import java.util. TreeMap;
public class PopImpl extends Observable implements Pop
{
   private Map iPop;
   private Iterator iIterator;
   public PopImpl()
   {
      iPop = new TreeMap();
      iIterator = null;
   }
   public synchronized boolean add(final Person pPerson)
   {
      final Object tObject = iPop.put(pPerson.getName(), pPerson);
      setChanged();
      notifyObservers();
      return tObject==null;
   }
   public synchronized boolean remove(final String pName)
   {
      final Object tObject = iPop.remove(pName);
      setChanged();
      notifyObservers();
      return tObject!=null;
   }
   public synchronized Person get(final String pName)
   {
      return (Person)iPop.get(pName);
   }
   public synchronized Person getFirst()
   {
      iIterator = iPop.values().iterator();
      return next();
   }
   public synchronized Person next()
   {
      if (iIterator.hasNext())
      {
         return (Person)iIterator.next();
      }
      else
      {
         return null;
      }
   }
}
```

Figure 17.15 *Continues on the next page.*

```
public synchronized int size()
{
    return iPop.size();
}
public synchronized boolean equals(final Object pObject)
{
    if ( pObject==null || getClass()!=pObject.getClass() )
    {
        return false;
    }
    return iPop.equals(((PopImpl)pObject).iPop);
}
public synchronized int hashCode()
{
    return iPop.hashCode();
}
public synchronized String toString()
{
    return iPop.toString();
}
}
```

Figure 17.15   A class that implements the Pop interface.

The population is providing an addObserver method in order to allow observers. So, there are calls of setChanged and notifyObservers in the body of add.

The code of remove needs to remove from the map the entry that it has for pName if there is one. This can be done by applying the remove method to iPop. The result of this call is an indication of whether the map had an entry for pName. This value is used when producing the result of remove. The remove method also has calls of setChanged and notifyObservers.

In order to code get, we can use the get method on the map iPop.This will return the value with which pName is associated (if there is an entry). Because get returns a value of type Object, the get method needs to cast this value to the type Person. If there is no entry, then get will return null and this is the value which is returned by get.

In order to implement getFirst and next, an iterator will be used. This iterator will have to be accessible from both methods: this can be accomplished by making it a private field of the class:

```
private Iterator iIterator;
```

The iterator can be created by the getFirst method. It can do this using:

```
final Collection tCollection = iPop.values();
iIterator = tCollection.iterator();
```

This can be abbreviated to:

```
iIterator = iPop.values().iterator();
```

The getFirst method then needs to deliver the first object of the iterator. In order to do this, it first has to use hasNext on tIterator to check whether one exists and if one does it has to use next on tIterator to get hold of its value. However, this is exactly the same task that has to be performed by the PopImpl's next method and so getFirst just returns the result of calling PopImpl's next.

As you can see, all the methods of PopImpl apply methods to iPop in order to update the map that has been created. Once again, this is a use of the *adapter pattern*.

17.6.4 Using Pop and PopImpl to manipulate a population

The PopImplProg program (given in Figure 17.16) can be used to test the Pop interface and the PopImpl class. Like the PersonLinkedQueueProg program (given in Section 14.4.6) the user of this program is repeatedly asked for single-letter commands that allow him/her to manipulate a population. The program provides a command to add a person to the population, a command to remove a person from the population, and so on.

As with the PersonLinkedQueueProg program, the program naturally divides into two activities: one of these is to keep getting commands from the user and the other is to process each command. The main method handles the first of these whereas the second is handled by a subsidiary method called iProcessCommand.

```
// A program that tests the Pop interface and the PopImpl class.
// Barry Cornelius, 19 June 2000
import java.io. BufferedReader;
import java.io. InputStreamReader;
import java.io. IOException;
public class PopImplProg
{
    private static Pop iPop;
    private static BufferedReader iKeyboard;
    public static void main(final String[] pArgs) throws IOException
    {
        iPop = new PopImpl();
        iKeyboard = new BufferedReader(new InputStreamReader(System.in));
        while (true)
        {
            System.out.print("Command? ");
            System.out.flush();
            final char tCommand = iKeyboard.readLine().toLowerCase().charAt(0);
            if (tCommand=='q')
            {
                break;
            }
            iProcessCommand(tCommand);
            System.out.println();
        }
    }
```

Figure 17.16 *Continues on the next page.*

```java
private static void iProcessCommand(final char pCommand)
                                                throws IOException
{
    switch (pCommand)
    {
        case 'a':
        {
            System.out.print("Person? ");
            System.out.flush();
            final Person tPerson = new PersonImpl(iKeyboard.readLine());
            if ( ! iPop.add(tPerson) )
            {
                System.out.println("The person is already in the population");
            }
        }
        break;
        case 'd':
        {
            iPop = new PopImpl();
        }
        break;
        case 'g':
        {
            System.out.print("Name? ");
            System.out.flush();
            final String tName = iKeyboard.readLine();
            final Person tPerson = iPop.get(tName);
            if (tPerson==null)
            {
                System.out.println("No such person in the population");
            }
            else
            {
                System.out.println(tPerson);
            }
        }
        break;
        case 'r':
        {
            System.out.print("Name? ");
            System.out.flush();
            final String tName = iKeyboard.readLine();
            if ( ! iPop.remove(tName) )
            {
                System.out.println("The person is not in the population");
            }
        }
        break;
        default:
        {
            System.out.println(pCommand + " is not a valid command letter");
        }
        break;
    }
}
}
```

Figure 17.16 A program that tests the `Pop` interface and the `PopImpl` class.

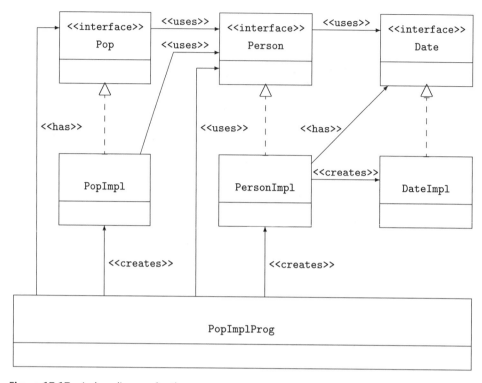

Figure 17.17 A class diagram for the PopImplProg program.

A class diagram for the interfaces and classes forming the PopImplProg program is given in Figure 17.17. Note that because the Pop interface and the PopImpl class are written in terms of Person rather than PersonImpl, Pop and PopImpl are independent of PersonImpl. So if we make some changes to the code of Person-Impl, there will be no need to recompile Pop and PopImpl.

Tips for programming and debugging

17.1 In Figure 17.5, the declaration:

```
public static final Day monday = iCreateDay("Monday");
```

assigns to the class variable monday the result of executing the class method iCreateDay. This method looks at the value of iNumberOfDays, assigns a value to an element of the iDays array, and then increases the value of iNumberOfDays by 1. So it is important that the variables iNumberOfDays and iDays have been assigned values before iCreateDay is called. For this reason, the declarations:

```
private static int iNumberOfDays = 0;
private static final Day[] iDays = new Day[7];
```

precede the first call of iCreateDay. A NullPointerException exception would be produced (at runtime) if the declaration of iDays appears after the declaration containing the first call of iCreateDay.

17.2 When working with a collection class, methods of a class such as hashCode or equals are often called behind the scenes by methods such as contains, add or remove. However, it is sometimes unclear as to whether hashCode/equals is actually being called. You can easily find out whether this is happening by temporarily including a println statement in the body of the method. If you get output, you know that the method is being called.

17.3 Suppose you create a TreeSet or a TreeMap (using the constructor that has no arguments). If the class of the objects of the Set, or the class of the keys of the Map, do not implement the Comparable interface, then those operations that require a comparison to be made with an object of the collection will lead to a ClassCastException. For more details, see Curio 17.8.

Curios, controversies and cover-ups

17.1 This chapter introduces the idea of an *enumeration*.There is no connection between an *enumeration* and the interface Enumeration of the java.util package. See Curio 14.8 for a few more details about the Enumeration interface.

17.2 The WWW contains several articles on how to provide enumerations in Java programs. So, for alternatives to the enumeration pattern presented in Section 17.1.5, look at 'Type safe constants in C++ and Java' ([6]) by Philip Bishop, 'Create enumerated constants in Java' ([3]) by Eric Armstrong, 'The Type-Safe Enumeration Idiom' ([52]) by Rodney Waldhoff and the 'Replace Enums with Classes' section of Joshua Bloch's article entitled 'Substitutes for Missing C Constructs' ([7]).

17.3 The WWW page [22] has an article entitled 'Overloading int considered harmful' written by Elliotte Rusty Harold. He says that some parts of the Core APIs misuse int. When two parameters of a method are both of type int, it is easy to get the order of them wrong, and such programs are difficult to debug. He argues that, instead of using an int, it would be better to introduce a new class providing some objects that can be used as constants. This is exactly the approach we took for Day in Section 17.1.5.

17.4 The enumeration pattern presented in Section 17.1.6 is in many ways similar to the singleton pattern that was mentioned in Curio 12.4.

17.5 The package java.util has a class called BitSet that can be used to represent a set of binary digits. For more details, see $API/java/util/BitSet.html.

17.6 If all of the set methods were removed from Person–PersonImpl, it would then be possible to provide a hashCode method that is dependent on the values of iName, iDateOfBirth, iPhoneNumber and iHeight. Here is one possibility:

```
public int hashCode()
{
    return iName.hashCode() + iDateOfBirth.hashCode() +
            iPhoneNumber.hashCode() + (int)iHeight;
}
```

Note that:

- this function uses the hashCode method of java.lang.String (twice) and the hashCode method declared for DateImpl (that was given in Figure 11.16);

- although DateImpl's hashCode currently returns the value zero, it is still appropriate for DateImpl's hashCode method to be called as this decision may be changed in the future;

- the evaluation of the expression may produce a value that overflows (perhaps several times) but this does not matter (as the result of an overflow is a predictable integer value).

17.7   As the Collections API was not part of JDK 1.0 and JDK 1.1, it was not so easy to represent sets and maps in these earlier versions of the JDK. However, these versions did have a class called Hashtable and an abstract class called Dictionary. For compatibility reasons, these classes are also present in the Java 2 Platform. However, in this book, the HashMap class and the Map interface are used instead.

17.8   In order to use TreeSet, the type of the values of the set must implement the Comparable interface (from java.lang) and/or the set must be created using a constructor that has an argument of a class that implements the Comparator interface (of the java.util package). Similarly, when you want to use TreeMap, the type of the keys of the map must implement the Comparable interface and/or the map must be created using a constructor that has an argument of a class that implements the Comparator interface.

As pointed out at $API/java/util/Comparator.html, a class that wishes to implement the Comparator interface must provide two methods:

```
int compare(Object pFirstObject, Object pSecondObject);
```

and:

```
boolean equals(Object pObject);
```

The compare method is required to return a negative integer, zero, or a positive integer depending on whether the value of pFirstObject is less than, equal to, or greater than that of pSecondObject. The contract of Comparator's equals is similar to that normally imposed on equals, but in addition the two objects being compared for equality must have comparators that impose the same ordering.

17.1 Modify the Day class (given in Figure 17.5) so that is is easy to cycle through the values of the type.

Provide three methods:

```
public static Object getFirst();
public Object getNext();
public boolean isLast();
```

The getFirst method is a class method that returns a pointer to the first value of the class. The getNext method is applied to a value of the class, and it returns a pointer to the next value of the class. When applied to the last value of the type, it will cycle round to deliver a pointer to the first value of the type. And isLast applied to a value of the class returns *true* if and only if it is the last value of the class.

Write a suitable program to test this version of the class.

17.2 Add a method called getKind to the Pizza class. This method should attempt to identify the pizza and return an appropriate String. The following values should be returned:

toppings	String
no toppings	"Not A Pizza"
cheese, tomatoes	"Boring"
mushrooms, tomatoes, cheese, onions	"Margherita"
mushrooms, ham, tomatoes, cheese, onions	"Calzone"
mushrooms, ham, tomatoes, cheese, peppers	"Capricciosa"
mushrooms, onions, ham, tomatoes, cheese, anchovies, peppers	"Quatro Stagioni"
anchovies, egg, peppers, salami, mushrooms, ham, tomatoes, cheese, onions	"Awful"
none of the above	"Unknown"

Modify the PizzaProg program to call this method.

17.3 Provide a class declaration (called SetUtils) that has the following methods:

```
public static Set union(Set pFirstSet, Set pSecondSet);
public static Set intersection(Set pFirstSet, Set pSecondSet);
public static Set difference(Set pFirstSet, Set pSecondSet);
public static boolean subset(Set pFirstSet, Set pSecondSet);
public static boolean superset(Set pFirstSet, Set pSecondSet);
```

where:

- the union method returns a set of elements whose values are in either pFirstSet or pSecondSet or both sets;

- the intersection method returns a set of elements whose values are in both pFirstSet and pSecondSet;

- the `difference` method returns a set of elements whose values are in `pFirstSet` but are not in `pSecondSet`;

- the `subset` method returns the value *true* if and only if the elements of `pFirstSet` are a subset of those of `pSecondSet`;

- the `superset` method returns the value *true* if and only if the elements of `pFirstSet` are a superset of those of `pSecondSet`.

17.4   Modify the `PopImplProg` program so that it uses the letters f and n to trigger calls of the `getFirst` and `next` methods of `PopImpl`.

17.5   In Section 14.4.6, the `PersonLinkedQueueProg` program was presented. And in the previous chapter, this program was altered to be a program (called `PersonLinkedQueueDriver`) that uses a GUI. Modify the `PopImplProg` program so that it uses a GUI.

17.6   Produce a class called `BookingSystem` that models a system to be used for booking seats on flights. The details should be stored in a `Map` mapping flight numbers (e.g. KL5941) to planes. Use a `String` to represent a flight number and introduce a new class called `Plane` to represent the plane.

The `Plane` class should have two private fields: an `int` representing the capacity of the plane (i.e. the total number of seats), and a `Pop` field to represent the passengers that have bookings for the flight.

The `BookingSystem` class should have methods to perform the following operations:

- add a flight (with a given flight number and a given number of seats) to the system;

- remove a flight from the system;

- find out how many empty seats there are on a given flight;

- output details about each person that is booked on a given flight;

- add a person to a given flight;

- remove a person from a given flight.

Provide a program that tests this class.

17.7   Produce a program (called `CrossReference`) that generates a **cross-reference** listing of a text file. This means that your program should read a file containing some lines of text, and display a list of all the words used in the file. This output should be in alphabetical order and, alongside each word, there should be a list of the line numbers of the line(s) on which the word is used.

You can use `StringTokenizer` to break a line up into words. Of course, the text is likely to contain punctuation characters but, to begin with, ignore this problem.

There are many possibilities for storing the cross-reference information. One possibility would be to use a map mapping words to sets, where each set contains elements that are line numbers.

17.8   Suppose a file called `Points.data` contains a *database* of the positions of places:

```
Greenland         44-00-00-W:60-00-00-N
Reykjavik         21-30-00-W:64-00-00-N
Hudson Bay        83-00-00-W:55-00-00-N
Lake Winnipeg     99-00-00-W:53-00-00-N
New York          74-00-00-W:40-40-00-N
Yellowstone       111-00-00-W:44-00-00-N
Seattle           122-30-00-W:48-00-00-N
Vancouver         123-00-00-W:49-50-00-N
Heathrow          0-20-00-W:51-20-00-N
Manchester        2-20-00-W:53-25-00-N
Newcastle         1-35-00-W:55-00-00-N
Prestwick         4-30-00-W:55-35-00-N
Amsterdam         4-50-00-E:52-20-00-N
Frankfurt         8-40-00-E:50-10-00-N
Paris             2-20-00-E:48-50-00-N
```

Suppose another file called `Flight.data` contains details of a flight plan (given as a list of places):

```
Heathrow
Manchester
Prestwick
Reykjavik
Greenland
Hudson Bay
Lake Winnipeg
Seattle
```

Write a program (called `TranslateFlight`) that first reads in the file `Points.data`, and stores the details of each line as an entry of a `Map` mapping a place-name to a position. As some of the place-names include spaces, use `lastIndexOf(" ")` to divide a line into two parts, and use `trim` on the left-hand part to remove the trailing spaces.

Then get the program to read the file `Flight.data` and for each place-name the program should look the place-name up in the `Map` so as to be able to output the place-name and its position.

So given the above data, the program should output:

```
Heathrow              0-20-00-W:51-20-00-N
Manchester            2-20-00-W:53-25-00-N
Prestwick             4-30-00-W:55-35-00-N
Reykjavik             21-30-00-W:64-00-00-N
Greenland             44-00-00-W:60-00-00-N
Hudson Bay            83-00-00-W:55-00-00-N
Lake Winnipeg         99-00-00-W:53-00-00-N
Seattle               122-30-00-W:48-00-00-N
```

The program should have the name of the first file (i.e. `Points.data`) embedded in the program. For an example of how to do this, see the `SumFixed` program given in Figure 10.4. Your program should obtain the name of the second file from the command line used to execute the program, e.g.:

```
java TranslateFlight Flight.data
```

The details of how to do this are given in Section 10.11.

17.9 In this exercise, you are going to represent the comings and goings of cars at a car park. The exercise uses the Model-View-Controller technique.

For the Model, we need a class that can store details of what cars are in the car park. To do this properly you ought to have one class called `Car` and another called `CarPark`. However, do not provide a `Car` class: to represent a car just use a `String` for the car's number plate. For the `CarPark`, use a `Set` to represent the collection of cars that the car park contains.

You can create a `Set` using:

```
iSet = new HashSet();
```

assuming you already have:

```
private Set iSet;
```

The rest of the `CarPark` class can be similar to the `LinkedQueue` class given in Figure 14.8. However, do not bother to produce an interface as well as a class for the car park. Just provide one constructor with no arguments and two methods that a client can use to record the arrival/departure of cars. Instead of calling them `add` and `remove`, call these methods `arrive` and `depart`. In the bodies of `arrive` and `depart` you need to add/remove an object from the `iSet` set; there are methods called `add` and `remove` that can be used to add/remove elements from a set (as explained in Figure 17.7).

Also provide methods called `equals` and `hashCode` and `toString`. For `toString`, you can just use `toString` on the `iSet` variable or you can produce code like the `toString` method of the `LinkedQueue` class (given in Figure 14.8). This would require you to use the `iterator` method on the `iSet` variable.

There are two entrances to this car park: one from the west, and the other from the east. They both have a car park attendant who is responsible for noticing when a car arrives and when it leaves.

So produce a `CarParkController` class. This will be used to model a car park entrance. Later (see below), you will create two objects of this class, one for the West entrance, and the other for the East entrance.

The constructor of the `CarParkController` class can create a `JFrame` and make it visible. The `JFrame` has a `JTextField` and two `JButtons` marked *Add* and *Remove*. The idea is that the attendant types the number plate of a car in the text field and then clicks the appropriate button. This leads to a call of either the `arrive` or the `depart` method. The code of this class can be similar to that of the `PersonQueueController` class given in Figure 16.12.

And so to the viewer. Produce a class called CarParkLister that has an update method which outputs the latest state of the car park whenever the CarPark object changes. Just use println for this output. You can use the toString method on the CarPark object in order to do this. In places, your code can be similar to that of the QueueLister class in Figure 16.14 but it will be a lot simpler because this exercise uses println rather than a GUI output.

Finally, produce a program class (called CarParkProg) that can be used to create objects of the above classes. You need one CarPark object, two CarParkController objects (one for the West entrance and the other for the East entrance), and one CarParkLister object. This class can be similar to the PersonLinkedQueueDriver class given in Figure 16.11.

17.10 Produce a class called Library that models a system to be used for loaning books from a library. The details of the loans should be stored in a Map mapping books to people. Use Book (from Exercise 12.9) to represent a book, and use Person (from Section 12.5) to represent a person.

The Library class should declare appropriate methods including methods to perform the following operations:

- add a new book to the library;
- loan a book to a person;
- return a book to the library;
- enquire whether a book is in the library;
- find out who has borrowed a particular book.

Provide a program that tests this class.

Chapter 18

Providing a GUI: menus and internal frames

Chapter 13 introduced some classes that can be used to produce graphical user interfaces. In particular, we looked at how to create windows on the screen, how to display GUI components (such as buttons and textfields) within a window, and how to react to some kinds of events (such as clicks on buttons and window events).

This chapter takes another look at GUIs: we first find out how to produce a GUI that has a *menu system*. So we will look at how to create *menu bars*, *menus* and *menu items*. Often we will add a *menu item* to a menu; however, if instead we add a menu to a menu, then we are building a menu that has a *submenu*.

The chapter also provides details about how to create *popup menus*.

So far, programs that have displayed many windows have produced them as separate windows. Instead, it is possible to create windows within a parent window. So, in this chapter, we will also look at how to create a window that has *internal frames*.

18.1 Adding a menu system

18.1.1 A menu system has three components

In Java, it is reasonably easy to add a **menu system** to a GUI: you can use the JMenuBar, JMenu and JMenuItem classes that form part of the Swing API (and so are in the javax.swing package). These classes are used to represent the three parts of a menu system that are shown in Figure 18.1.

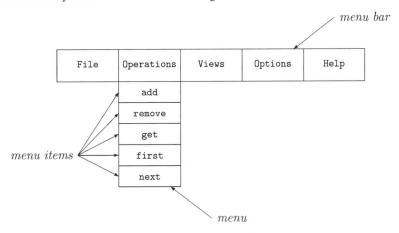

Figure 18.1   The three parts of a menu system.

18.1.2 Adding a menu bar

The key component of a menu system is its **menu bar**. In Java, a menu system's menu bar can be created using an object of the class JMenuBar:

```
final JMenuBar tJMenuBar = new JMenuBar();
```

Having created this JMenuBar object, it can be used just like any other GUI component (e.g. a JButton object). For example, it could be added to the SOUTH part of a JFrame's content pane. However, having said that, JMenuBar objects are not usually used in this way.

So what should we do instead? Well, as pointed out in Section 13.4, each object of the classes JFrame, JDialog, JInternalFrame and JApplet has a *root pane*, and one aspect of this root pane is an optional menu bar. And you can set what gets used as the menu bar for one of these objects by applying a method called setJMenuBar to the object, as in:

```
tJFrame.setJMenuBar(tJMenuBar);
```

A comment about the setJMenuBar method is given in Curio 18.1.

18.1.3 Adding menus to the menu bar

The purpose of a menu bar is to provide a number of **menus**. In the diagram in Figure 18.1, the menu bar has five menus labelled *File, Operations, Views, Options* and *Help*. In Java, we can create a menu and give it a label using an object of the class JMenu:

```
final JMenu tFileJMenu = new JMenu("File");
```

It can be added to a menu bar by using a call of add:

```
tJMenuBar.add(tFileJMenu);
```

Another menu can be added using:

```
final JMenu tOperationsJMenu = new JMenu("Operations");
tJMenuBar.add(tOperationsJMenu);
```

When the menu system is displayed, the various menus will appear on the menu bar in the order that the calls of add were executed.

18.1.4 Adding menu items to each menu

Each menu provides a number of **menu item**s. In the diagram, the *Operations* menu is being displayed. It has five menu items labelled *add*, *remove*, *get*, *first* and *next*. In Java, a menu item can be created and given a label using an object of the class JMenuItem:

```
JMenuItem tJMenuItem = new JMenuItem("add");
```

It can be added to a menu by using a call of add:

```
tOperationsJMenu.add(tJMenuItem);
```

Often a menu provides **keyboard short-cut**s to the menu items. So, instead of clicking on a menu item, the user can press a key on the keyboard. We can get this effect by using a call of setMnemonic to associate a key with a menu item:

```
tJMenuItem.setMnemonic('A');
```

If we do this, pressing the Alt key at the same time as the A key has the same effect as clicking on the menu item labelled add. Because the positions of the keys of a keyboard can be configured to suit the practice of a particular country, it is better to use constants from the class KeyEvent (which forms part of the java.awt.event package):

```
tJMenuItem.setMnemonic(KeyEvent.VK_A);
```

The WWW page at $API/java/awt/event/KeyEvent.html says: 'Virtual key codes do not identify a physical key, they depend on the platform and keyboard layout. For example, the key that on a Windows U.S. keyboard layout generates VK_Q, generates VK_A on a Windows French keyboard layout.'

A JMenuItem component behaves very much like a button: for this reason, it is a subclass of AbstractButton (as was mentioned in Section 13.3.4). When the user clicks on a menu item (or uses a keyboard short-cut), an *action event* is generated. We will want some code executed when this happens. We can arrange for this code to be executed by putting it in the actionPerformed method of a class (which implements the ActionListener interface), and by using addActionListener to register an object of this class as a listener for action events on the menu item.

So for the tOperationsJMenu, we could use:

```
JMenuItem tJMenuItem = new JMenuItem("add");
tOperationsJMenu.add(tJMenuItem);
tJMenuItem.setMnemonic(KeyEvent.VK_A);
tJMenuItem.addActionListener(this);

tJMenuItem = new JMenuItem("remove");
tOperationsJMenu.add(tJMenuItem);
tJMenuItem.setMnemonic(KeyEvent.VK_R);
tJMenuItem.addActionListener(this);
```

In this code, the variable tJMenuItem is made to point to a new JMenuItem object; a pointer to this object is then added to the operations menu; a keyboard short-cut is then established for the menu item; and then the current object is made a listener for action events on the JMenuItem object. All of this needs to be performed for each of the menu items. Note that the various menu items will appear on a menu in the order that the calls of add are executed.

Because, in the above code, the current object is acting as a listener for clicks on any of the menu items, its actionPerformed method will get executed when a click occurs. This method can find out which menu item has been clicked by using the getActionCommand method (which was mentioned in Section 13.14):

```
public void actionPerformed(final ActionEvent pActionEvent)
{
    final String tCommand = pActionEvent.getActionCommand();
    if (tCommand.equals("add"))
    ...
```

18.2 Adding a menu system to the population program

18.2.1 Replacing PopImplProg by PopMenuProg

The population program (PopImplProg) given in Section 17.16 is old-fashioned because it gets its input from the keyboard. We can make it more exciting to use by adding a menu system to the program. The new version of this program (PopMenuProg) is given in Figure 18.2.

This program creates a PopImpl object and makes tPop point to it. Later, it creates a PopMenu object. As we find out in the next section, the constructor of this class creates a JMenuBar object. The PopMenuProg program can set up a pointer (tJMenuBar) to this JMenuBar object by using PopMenu's getJMenuBar method. The program also sets up a JFrame object (tJFrame) and uses setJMenuBar in order to establish this JMenuBar object as the menu bar for the JFrame object.

The program creates a JTextField object (tResultsJTextField) that will be used to display the results of performing operations on the population. It also creates a JTextArea object (tLogJTextArea) that will be used to record the transactions that are performed on the population. Following the advice given in Section 16.6.2,

```
// A population-manipulation program that uses a menu.
// Barry Cornelius, 20 June 2000
import java.awt.    BorderLayout;
import java.awt.    Container;
import javax.swing. JFrame;
import javax.swing. JMenuBar;
import javax.swing. JScrollPane;
import javax.swing. JTextArea;
import javax.swing. JTextField;
public class PopMenuProg
{
    public static void main(final String[] pArgs)
    {
        final int tJFrameX = 100;
        final int tJFrameY = 100;
        final int tJDialogX = 100;
        final int tJDialogY = 200;
        final Pop tPop = new PopImpl();
        final JFrame tJFrame = new JFrame("PopMenuProg");
        final ExitWindowListener tExitWindowListener =
                                          new ExitWindowListener();
        tJFrame.addWindowListener(tExitWindowListener);
        final JTextField tResultsJTextField = new JTextField();
        final JTextArea tLogJTextArea = new JTextArea(5, 30);
        final Container tContentPane = tJFrame.getContentPane();
        tContentPane.add(tResultsJTextField,          BorderLayout.CENTER);
        tContentPane.add(new JScrollPane(tLogJTextArea), BorderLayout.SOUTH);
        final PopMenu tPopMenu =
                new PopMenu(tJFrame, tPop, tJDialogX, tJDialogY,
                          tResultsJTextField, tLogJTextArea);
        final JMenuBar tJMenuBar = tPopMenu.getJMenuBar();
        tJFrame.setJMenuBar(tJMenuBar);
        tJFrame.setLocation(tJFrameX, tJFrameY);
        tJFrame.pack();
        tJFrame.setVisible(true);
    }
}
```

Figure 18.2   A population-manipulation program that uses a menu.

this `JTextArea` object is given a scroll bar by passing it to `JScrollPane`'s constructor. The program adds the `JTextField` and the `JScrollPane` objects to the `JFrame`'s content pane.

18.2.2 The `PopMenu` class handles the menu

The code of the `PopMenu` class is given in Figure 18.3. The main task of this class's constructor is to construct a menu system (`iJMenuBar`). The menu bar has just two menus: one is labelled *File* and the other is labelled *Operations*.

```
// A class presenting a menu for the manipulation of a population.
// Barry Cornelius, 20 June 2000
import java.awt.event. ActionEvent;
import java.awt.event. ActionListener;
import javax.swing.    JFrame;
import javax.swing.    JMenu;
import javax.swing.    JMenuBar;
import javax.swing.    JMenuItem;
import javax.swing.    JTextArea;
import javax.swing.    JTextField;
import java.awt.event. KeyEvent;
public class PopMenu implements ActionListener
{
    private JMenuBar iJMenuBar;
    private JFrame iJFrame;
    private Pop iPop;
    private int iX;
    private int iY;
    private JTextField iResultsJTextField;
    private JTextArea iLogJTextArea;

    private void iAddJMenuItem(final JMenu pJMenu, final int pKeyEvent,
                              final String pString)
    {
        final JMenuItem tJMenuItem = new JMenuItem(pString);
        pJMenu.add(tJMenuItem);
        tJMenuItem.setMnemonic(pKeyEvent);
        tJMenuItem.addActionListener(this);
    }

    private void iCreateFileJMenu(final JMenuBar pJMenuBar)
    {
        final JMenu tFileJMenu = new JMenu("File");
        pJMenuBar.add(tFileJMenu);
        iAddJMenuItem(tFileJMenu, KeyEvent.VK_Q, "quit");
    }

    private void iCreateOperationsJMenu(final JMenuBar pJMenuBar)
    {
        final JMenu tOperationsJMenu = new JMenu("Operations");
        pJMenuBar.add(tOperationsJMenu);
        iAddJMenuItem(tOperationsJMenu, KeyEvent.VK_A, "add");
        iAddJMenuItem(tOperationsJMenu, KeyEvent.VK_R, "remove");
        iAddJMenuItem(tOperationsJMenu, KeyEvent.VK_G, "get");
        iAddJMenuItem(tOperationsJMenu, KeyEvent.VK_F, "first");
        iAddJMenuItem(tOperationsJMenu, KeyEvent.VK_N, "next");
    }
```

Figure 18.3 *Continues on the next page.*

```
public PopMenu(final JFrame pJFrame, final Pop pPop,
               final int pX, final int pY,
               final JTextField pResultsJTextField,
               final JTextArea pLogJTextArea)
{
   iJFrame = pJFrame;
   iPop = pPop;
   iX = pX;
   iY = pY;
   iResultsJTextField = pResultsJTextField;
   iLogJTextArea = pLogJTextArea;
   iJMenuBar = new JMenuBar();
   iCreateFileJMenu(iJMenuBar);
   iCreateOperationsJMenu(iJMenuBar);
}

private void iDisplayPersonOutputDialog(final Person pPerson)
{
   if (pPerson==null)
   {
      iResultsJTextField.setText("No person has been found");
   }
   else
   {
      iResultsJTextField.setText("                          ");
      final PersonOutputDialog tPersonOutputDialog =
                    new PersonOutputDialog(iJFrame, pPerson, iX, iY);
   }
}

public void actionPerformed(final ActionEvent pActionEvent)
{
   switch (pActionEvent.getActionCommand().charAt(0))
   {
      case 'a':
      {
         final PersonInputDialog tPersonInputDialog =
                           new PersonInputDialog(iJFrame, iX, iY);
         final Person tPerson = tPersonInputDialog.getPerson();
         final boolean tResult = iPop.add(tPerson);
         iResultsJTextField.setText("Person:" + tPerson + " OK:" +
                                                          tResult);
         iLogJTextArea.append("add\n");
      }
      break;
```

Figure 18.3 *Continues on the next page.*

```
        case 'r':
        {
            final NameInputDialog tNameInputDialog =
                                    new NameInputDialog(iJFrame, iX, iY);
            final String tName = tNameInputDialog.getName();
            final boolean tResult = iPop.remove(tName);
            iResultsJTextField.setText("Name:" + tName + " OK:" + tResult);
            iLogJTextArea.append("remove\n");
        }
        break;
        case 'g':
        {
            final NameInputDialog tNameInputDialog =
                                    new NameInputDialog(iJFrame, iX, iY);
            iDisplayPersonOutputDialog(iPop.get(tNameInputDialog.getName()));
            iLogJTextArea.append("get\n");
        }
        break;
        case 'f':
        {
            iDisplayPersonOutputDialog(iPop.getFirst());
            iLogJTextArea.append("first\n");
        }
        break;
        case 'n':
        {
            iDisplayPersonOutputDialog(iPop.next());
            iLogJTextArea.append("next\n");
        }
        break;
        case 'q':
        {
            System.exit(0);
        }
        break;
      }
   }

   public JMenuBar getJMenuBar()
   {
      return iJMenuBar;
   }
}
```

Figure 18.3 A class presenting a menu for the manipulation of a population.

Most of the code that is executed by PopMenu's constructor arises from the calls of subsidiary methods called iCreateFileJMenu and iCreateOperationsJMenu. These two methods do all the laborious work of creating the two menus. To do this, they use another subsidiary method called iAddJMenuItem.

Figure 18.4 shows the result of selecting the *Operations* menu from the menubar. Shown behind the menu are the GUI components resulting from tResultsJTextField and tLogJTextArea.

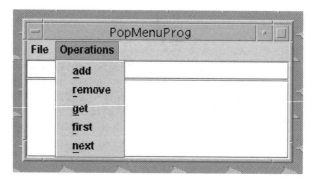

Figure 18.4   Selecting the *Operations* menu presented by the PopMenuProg program.

When the user selects a menu item (or presses the appropriate keyboard shortcut), it is PopMenu's actionPerformed method that gets executed. This method uses getActionCommand to determine which menu item was selected by the user. Because the labels that have been put on the menu items of both menus start with unique letters, the actionPerformed method just looks at the first character of the String produced by getActionCommand.

18.2.3 The *add* operation uses PersonInputDialog

If the user has chosen the *add* operation, a PersonInputDialog object is created. This class was produced back in Section 13.19: its constructor displays a form and a button (as shown in Figure 18.5), and the user is expected to fill in the form and click the button. The information on the form is used to create a PersonImpl object, and the code of actionPerformed adds that person to the population. Whether this operation was successful is reported to PopMenuProg's JTextField object and the fact that an add operation has taken place is recorded in PopMenuProg's JTextArea object.

18.2.4 The *first* operation uses PersonOutputDialog

When the user chooses the *first* operation, actionPerformed first applies the getFirst method to iPop, and then it passes the result to a subsidiary method called iDisplayPersonOutputDialog. Unless the population is empty, this method arranges for details about the person to be output to the screen. To do this, it uses an object of the class PersonOutputDialog. The code of this class is given in Figure 18.6.

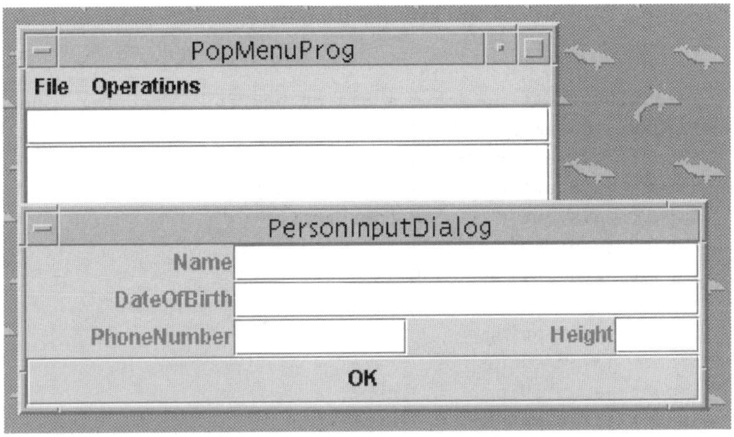

Figure 18.5 Selecting the *Add* menu item presents a `PersonInputDialog` box.

```java
// A class that presents a dialog box for outputting values about a person.
// Barry Cornelius, 20 June 2000
import java.awt.event. ActionEvent;
import java.awt.event. ActionListener;
import java.awt.        BorderLayout;
import java.awt.        Component;
import javax.swing.     JButton;
import javax.swing.     JDialog;
import javax.swing.     JFrame;
public class PersonOutputDialog implements ActionListener
{
    private JDialog iJDialog;
    public PersonOutputDialog(final JFrame pJFrame, final Person pPerson,
                              final int pX, final int pY)
    {
        final PersonForm tPersonForm = new PersonForm();
        tPersonForm.setPerson(pPerson);
        final Component tPersonFormGUI = tPersonForm.getGUI();
        final JButton tJButton = new JButton("OK");
        tJButton.addActionListener(this);
        iJDialog = new JDialog(pJFrame, "PersonOutputDialog", true);
        iJDialog.getContentPane().add(tPersonFormGUI, BorderLayout.CENTER);
        iJDialog.getContentPane().add(tJButton,        BorderLayout.SOUTH);
        iJDialog.setLocation(pX, pY);
        iJDialog.pack();
        iJDialog.setVisible(true);
    }
    public void actionPerformed(final ActionEvent pActionEvent)
    {
        iJDialog.setVisible(false);
        iJDialog.dispose();
    }
}
```

Figure 18.6 A class that presents a dialog box for outputting values about a person.

```
// A class that presents a dialog box for inputting a name.
// Barry Cornelius, 20 June 2000
import java.awt.event. ActionEvent;
import java.awt.event. ActionListener;
import java.awt.        BorderLayout;
import javax.swing.     Box;
import javax.swing.     BoxLayout;
import javax.swing.     JButton;
import javax.swing.     JDialog;
import javax.swing.     JFrame;
import javax.swing.     JLabel;
import javax.swing.     JTextField;
public class NameInputDialog implements ActionListener
{
    private JTextField iNameJTextField;
    private JDialog iJDialog;
    public NameInputDialog(final JFrame pJFrame,
                           final int pX, final int pY)
    {
        final Box tNameFormBox = new Box(BoxLayout.X_AXIS);
        final JLabel tNameJLabel = new JLabel("Name");
        tNameFormBox.add(tNameJLabel);
        iNameJTextField = new JTextField(40);
        tNameFormBox.add(iNameJTextField);
        final JButton tJButton = new JButton("OK");
        tJButton.addActionListener(this);
        iJDialog = new JDialog(pJFrame, "NameInputDialog", true);
        iJDialog.getContentPane().add(tNameFormBox, BorderLayout.CENTER);
        iJDialog.getContentPane().add(tJButton,     BorderLayout.SOUTH);
        iJDialog.setLocation(pX, pY);
        iJDialog.pack();
        iJDialog.setVisible(true);
    }
    public void actionPerformed(final ActionEvent pActionEvent)
    {
        iJDialog.setVisible(false);
        iJDialog.dispose();
    }
    public String getName()
    {
        return iNameJTextField.getText();
    }
}
```

Figure 18.7 A class that presents a dialog box for inputting a name.

18.2.5 The *get* operation uses `NameInputDialog`

If the user chooses the *get* operation, the `actionPerformed` method (that is shown in Figure 18.3) creates a `NameInputDialog` object:

```
final NameInputDialog tNameInputDialog =
                        new NameInputDialog(iJFrame, iX, iY);
```

The code of this class is given in Figure 18.7.

As with the `PersonInputDialog` mentioned above, the constructor of this class displays a form and a button, and the user is expected to fill in the form and click the button. The form is used to find out from the user the name of the person whose details he/she is interested in obtaining.

In the `actionPerfomed` method, this name is used as an argument for the call of `get` applied to `iPop`. As with the *first* operation, the `iDisplayPersonOutput-Dialog` method is then used to display the details of the person on the screen.

18.3 Providing a menu that has a submenu

So far, we have just added objects of class `JMenuItem` to a `JMenu`, and such objects behave like buttons. However, an item of a `JMenu` does not have to be a `JMenuItem` object: other objects can be added, including any object that is of the class `java.awt.Component` or of any subclass of that class.

For example, we could add a `JMenu` object to a `JMenu` object. If we do this, we create a **submenu**.

So, suppose we want to alter the `PopMenuProg` program so that the items of the *Operations* menu are split into two submenus: one for the operations that modify the population and the other one for operations that just view the population.

To do this, we first create the *Operations* menu and add it to the `JMenuBar`:

```
final JMenu tOperationsJMenu = new JMenu("Operations");
pJMenuBar.add(tOperationsJMenu);
```

This is as before. Then we can create two other `JMenu` objects for the two submenus:

```
final JMenu tModifyJMenu = new JMenu("Modify");
final JMenu tViewJMenu = new JMenu("View");
```

and add these to the *Operations* menu:

```
tOperationsJMenu.add(tModifyJMenu);
tOperationsJMenu.add(tViewJMenu);
```

Having done that, we can create `JMenuItem` objects for the *add, remove, get, first* and *next* operations, adding them to either `tModifyJMenu` or `tViewJMenu`.

So the only part of the `PopMenuProg` program that needs to be changed is the code of the `iCreateOperationsJMenu` method, the method that creates the *Operations* menu. The new code is given in Figure 18.8 (and this can be used instead of the code for this method that is given in Figure 18.3).

```
private void iCreateOperationsJMenu(final JMenuBar pJMenuBar)
{
    final JMenu tOperationsJMenu = new JMenu("Operations");
    pJMenuBar.add(tOperationsJMenu);
    final JMenu tModifyJMenu = new JMenu("Modify");
    tOperationsJMenu.add(tModifyJMenu);
    final JMenu tViewJMenu = new JMenu("View");
    tOperationsJMenu.add(tViewJMenu);
    iAddJMenuItem(tModifyJMenu, KeyEvent.VK_A, "add");
    iAddJMenuItem(tModifyJMenu, KeyEvent.VK_R, "remove");
    iAddJMenuItem(tViewJMenu,   KeyEvent.VK_G, "get");
    iAddJMenuItem(tViewJMenu,   KeyEvent.VK_F, "first");
    iAddJMenuItem(tViewJMenu,   KeyEvent.VK_N, "next");
}
```

Figure 18.8   Altering `iCreateOperationsJMenu` to use two submenus.

If this code is used, then, when the *Operations* menu is displayed, two items will be displayed: one is labelled `Modify` and the other is labelled `View`. Both menu items contain a symbol indicating that a submenu is available. When you click on one of these items, the submenu will be revealed (as shown in Figure 18.9).

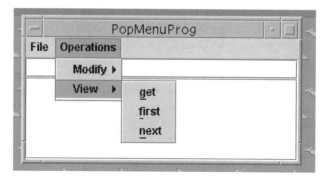

Figure 18.9   Clicking on a menu item of the *Operations* menu reveals a submenu.

18.4 Providing popup menus

The Swing API also includes a class called `JPopupMenu` that can be used to display a **popup menu**. So, you can arrange for a menu to be shown whenever an appropriate **mouse event** occurs.

Here are some brief details of how to do this:

- Create a `JPopupMenu` object and add menu items to this object in the same way as they are added to a `JMenu` object.

- Produce a class implementing the `MouseListener` interface (from the `java.awt.event` package). This interface requires you to implement five methods. Each one of these methods has a parameter of the MouseEvent class. Provide empty bodies for the methods mouseClicked, mouseEntered and mouseExited. For the mousePressed and mouseReleased methods, first apply the method isPopupTrigger to the MouseEvent parameter. If this returns the value *true*, apply JPopupMenu's show method to the JPopupMenu object. This method requires three arguments: a pointer to the GUI component in whose space the menu is to be displayed, together with the x and y offsets within this space at which the menu is to be displayed. For more details, see $API/javax/swing/JPopupMenu.html.

- Create an object of the class that implements the MouseListener interface.

- Use addMouseListener to register the MouseListener object as a listener for any mouse events on each of the GUI components, e.g.:

```
final Container tContentPane = tJFrame.getContentPane();
tContentPane.add(tResultsJTextField, BorderLayout.CENTER);
tContentPane.add(tJScrollPane,        BorderLayout.SOUTH);
final PopMenu tPopMenu = ... ;
tResultsJTextField.addMouseListener(tPopMenu);
tLogJTextArea.addMouseListener(tPopMenu);
```

(18.5) Creating a window with several internal frames

So far, when a program has to create several windows, these have been created as separate entities on the screen. Although there are some environments where this is a common thing to do, elsewhere a different approach is taken. Instead, one **parent window** is created, and all the other windows are created inside it. This technique is often used by applications running in Microsoft Windows. In that environment, the **child window**s are often displaying different documents, and so this technique is referred to as the **Multiple Document Interface (MDI)**.

If you wish to produce this effect, first create a JFrame that is going to be the parent window:

```
final JFrame tJFrame = new JFrame("title for the parent window");
```

If it is appropriate, you may want to add a menu bar to this window.

Then create a JDesktopPane, and add it to the JFrame:

```
final JDesktopPane tJDesktopPane = new JDesktopPane();
final Container tContentPane = tJFrame.getContentPane();
tContentPane.add(tJDesktopPane, BorderLayout.CENTER);
```

Having created the JDesktopPane object, you can create as many JInternal-Frame objects as you wish: you can make each of these appear as a separate window within the parent window. Here is the declaration of one of the JInternalFrame objects:

```
final JInternalFrame tFirstJInternalFrame =
   new JInternalFrame("title for the child window", true, true, true, true);
```

```
// Replacing the PopMenuProg program by a program that uses internal frames.
// Barry Cornelius, 20 June 2000
import java.awt.      BorderLayout;
import java.awt.      Container;
import java.awt.      Dimension;
import javax.swing.   JDesktopPane;
import javax.swing.   JFrame;
import javax.swing.   JInternalFrame;
import javax.swing.   JLabel;
import javax.swing.   JMenuBar;
import javax.swing.   JScrollPane;
import javax.swing.   JTextArea;
import javax.swing.   JTextField;
import java.awt.      Toolkit;
public class PopInternalProg
{
   public static void main(final String[] pArgs)
   {
      final Pop tPop = new PopImpl();

      // build a JInternalFrame containing the LogJTextArea
      final JTextArea tLogJTextArea = new JTextArea(5, 30);
      tLogJTextArea.setText("start\n");
      final JInternalFrame tLogJInternalFrame =
              new JInternalFrame("Internal frame", true, true, true, true);
      tLogJInternalFrame.getContentPane().add(new JScrollPane(tLogJTextArea),
                                       BorderLayout.CENTER);
      tLogJInternalFrame.setLocation(100, 300);
      tLogJInternalFrame.setSize(400, 100);
      tLogJInternalFrame.setVisible(true);

      // build another JInternalFrame containing the ResultsJTextField
      final JTextField tResultsJTextField = new JTextField();
      final JInternalFrame tResultsJInternalFrame =
              new JInternalFrame("Internal frame", true, true, true, true);
      tResultsJInternalFrame.getContentPane().add(tResultsJTextField,
                                       BorderLayout.CENTER);
      tResultsJInternalFrame.setLocation(100, 50);
      tResultsJInternalFrame.setSize(250, 50);
      tResultsJInternalFrame.setVisible(true);

      // build a JDeskTopPane and add the two JInternalFrames to it
      final JDeskTopPane tJDesktopPane = new JDesktopPane();
      tJDesktopPane.add(tLogJInternalFrame);
      tJDesktopPane.add(tResultsJInternalFrame);
```

Figure 18.10   *Continues on the next page.*

```
        // build a JFrame and add the JDesktopPane to it
        final JFrame tJFrame = new JFrame("PopInternalProg");
        final Container tContentPane = tJFrame.getContentPane();
        tContentPane.add(tJDesktopPane, BorderLayout.CENTER);
        final ExitWindowListener tExitWindowListener =
                                        new ExitWindowListener();
        tJFrame.addWindowListener(tExitWindowListener);
        tJFrame.setDefaultCloseOperation(JFrame.DO_NOTHING_ON_CLOSE);
        final PopMenu tPopMenu =
            new PopMenu(tJFrame, tPop, 400, 400,
                        tResultsJTextField, tLogJTextArea);
        final JMenuBar tJMenuBar = tPopMenu.getJMenuBar();
        tJFrame.setJMenuBar(tJMenuBar);
        tJFrame.setLocation(100, 100);
        // the code on these next 4 lines first finds out the screen size and
        // then sets the size of the JFrame appropriately
        final Toolkit tToolkit = tJFrame.getToolkit();
        final Dimension tDimension = tToolkit.getScreenSize();
        tDimension.height -= 200;
        tDimension.width -= 200;
        tJFrame.setSize(tDimension);
        tJFrame.setVisible(true);
    }
}
```

Figure 18.10   Replacing the `PopMenuProg` program by one that uses internal frames.

Having declared an internal frame object, it needs to be added to the `JDesktop-Pane`. You should also include a call of `setVisible` to make the `JInternalFrame` appear on the screen.

```
tJDesktopPane.add(tFirstJInternalFrame);
tFirstJInternalFrame.setVisible(true);
```

For more details about the need to use `setVisible`, see Tip 18.1. The five parameters of this constructor of the `JInternalFrame` class are used as follows:

1. a `String` that is to be displayed in the title bar of the internal frame;

2. a `boolean` that indicates whether the user can resize the internal frame;

3. a `boolean` that indicates whether the user can close the internal frame;

4. a `boolean` that indicates whether the user can maximize the internal frame;

5. a `boolean` that indicates whether the user can iconify the internal frame.

Providing the value *true* for each of the last four arguments means that the user is able to do whatever they want to the internal frame.

Having created the `JInternalFrame` and added it to the desktop, you can use it just like a `JFrame`. So, it has a root pane, and GUI components can be added to the content pane of the root pane. And, if it is appropriate, you may want to call `setJMenuBar` to add a menu bar to the `JInternalFrame`.

Figure 18.2 shows the text of the program class of the `PopMenuProg` program. The program displays a `JFrame` containing a `JTextField` and a `JTextArea` in the CENTER and SOUTH parts of the `JFrame`'s content pane. This program class uses the `PopMenu` class (Figure 18.3), the `PersonOutputDialog` class (Figure 18.6) and the `NameInputDialog` class (Figure 18.7) together with many classes (and interfaces) from earlier chapters.

In order to demonstrate internal frames, we will suppose that we want to alter this program class so that it uses separate windows for the `JTextField` and `JTextArea`. So we will create one `JInternalFrame` that has a `JTextField` GUI component and another `JInternalFrame` that has a `JTextArea` GUI component. Both of these `JInternalFrame`s need to be added to a `JDesktopPane`.

The program class (`PopInternalProg`) shown in Figure 18.10 can be used instead of using `PopMenuProg`'s program class. It can use unaltered versions of all of the supporting classes (`PopMenu`, `PersonOutputDialog`, `NameInputDialog` and so on).

Figure 18.11 shows a point in the execution of the `PopInternalProg` program.

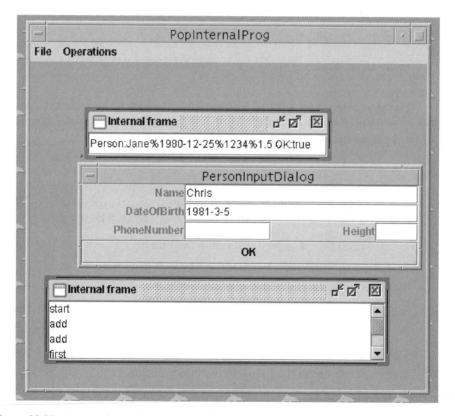

Figure 18.11 A point during the execution of the `PopInternalProg` program.

18.1   In versions of Java from the Java 2 Platform v 1.3 onwards, it is necessary to apply the `setVisible` method to a `JInternalFrame` object in order to make it appear on the screen. This was not the case with Java 2 Platform v 1.2. So, if you are using Java 2 Platform v 1.3 and you have acquired some Java source code that has been written for Java 2 Platform v 1.2, you may need to add calls of `setVisible` to the code in order to make its `JInternalFrame` objects appear on the screen.

Curios, controversies and cover-ups

18.1   It was pointed out in Section 18.1.2 that you can apply the `setJMenuBar` method to any objects of the classes `JFrame`, `JDialog`, `JInternalFrame` and `JApplet`. Normally, in Java's Core APIs, any method that is common to a set of classes is not declared in each of the classes but is instead declared once in a common superclass of the classes. However, these classes do not have a common superclass, and so all four classes provide their own `setJMenuBar` method.

18.2   The `iDisplayPersonOutputDialog` method shown in Figure 18.3 contains the statement:

```
PersonOutputDialog tPersonOutputDialog =
                new PersonOutputDialog(iJFrame, pPerson, iX,  iY);
```

The purpose of this statement is to display a dialog box containing the details about a person. Although `tPersonOutputDialog` is made to point to a `PersonOutputDialog` object, the method does not use this variable again. Because of this, and because Java allows a class instance creation expression to be used as a statement, the above statement can be abbreviated to the statement:

```
new PersonOutputDialog(iJFrame, pPerson, iX, iY);
```

However, this looks confusing, and so it is not recommended.

Exercises

18.1   Add a GUI interface (that uses menus) to the `BookingSystem` program produced as a solution to Exercise 17.6.

18.2   Add a GUI interface (that uses menus) to the `CarParkProg` program produced as a solution to Exercise 17.9.

18.3   Add a GUI interface (that uses menus) to the `Library` program produced as a solution to Exercise 17.10.

Chapter 19

Deriving a class
from another class

When producing a new class declaration, it makes sense to utilize classes that already exist. For example, when producing a class to represent people (the `PersonImpl` class) we used a field of type `Date` to represent the person's date of birth. A person has no special connection with a date; it is just useful to have a field of this type when constructing the `PersonImpl` class. This is a technique known as *composition*.

When a class is a more specialized form of an existing class, we will save a lot of time and effort by indicating that we wish to reuse the code of the existing class. If we use an *extends clause* in the declaration of the new class, the new class immediately has all the fields of the existing class and all of its methods. This is a technique known as *inheritance*.

In this chapter, we look at some examples that explore the ideas of inheritance.

The chapter also compares the techniques of composition and inheritance, pointing out the situations in which it is appropriate to use them.

The chapter ends by providing a better method for cloning an object.

19.1 Revisiting four key aspects of inheritance

Many of the key aspects of inheritance have already been explained. So, first, we will briefly review these.

In Java, all classes are arranged in a class hierarchy. In this chapter, we will find out how to add a new class to this class hierarchy: we will use an *extends clause* to make the new class a *subclass* of some other class. If a class declaration has no extends clause (as has been the case with most of the classes we have produced so far), the class is derived from the class Object:

1. So a class (other than the class Object) is always derived from some other class – this class is called its **direct superclass**.

Having grafted the new class onto the class hierarchy, it is possible to wander up the hierarchy: as has already been stated, the new class is derived from a class called its direct superclass; and that class will be derived from another class which is *its* direct superclass; and so on. The top of the hierarchy is reached when we reach the class Object:

2. So a class that is some way down the class hierarchy:

- has a class that is called its direct superclass;
- has a number of other classes that are also superclasses of the class;
- has Object as its *most indirect superclass*.

As has already been mentioned, the extends clause indicates where the new class is to be put into the class hierarchy. So how do you decide which class to make the direct superclass of a new class? The choice depends on whether there is an existing class that has *members* (i.e. fields and methods) that you would also like to be part of your new class. If this is the case, that class may be suitable as a direct superclass of the new class. This means that:

3. Having declared an object of the new class, any method of the direct superclass and of any other superclasses of this class can be applied to the object.

Arranging classes into a class hierarchy so that common members can be placed in a superclass is the main purpose of inheritance. This was pointed out (in Section 13.3.2) in the first chapter on GUIs:

> Many of these GUI components will have common features. For example, there is a method called setBackground that can be used to alter the background colour of a GUI component. Although it would be possible to include a method declaration called setBackground in each of the classes, this is not sensible. Instead, Java allows classes to be grouped into a **class hierarchy**: this means the Swing designers can declare the setBackground method in a class high up in the class hierarchy and it is automatically available in the classes that are lower down in the class hierarchy.

In this way, a class lower down in the class hierarchy can offer facilities that are actually declared higher up in the class hierarchy. This is one of the key aspects of *inheritance*.

In Section 11.7, it was also pointed out that, if a class does provide a method declaration called `toString` (that has the same *signature* as that of `Object`'s `toString` method), the `toString` method of the new class is used if `toString` is applied to an object of the new class. This is another important idea of inheritance:

4. A class can provide a method declaration with the same signature as that of a declaration in a superclass – this is known as *method overriding*.

Although many of the key aspects of inheritance have already been introduced, there are some others that have yet to be considered:

- how to use an *extends clause* to indicate the direct superclass of a class;
- the interaction between interfaces and inheritance;
- the use of an *abstract class* to signify that a class exists just to provide common features of subclasses;
- the use of *abstract methods*;
- the use of the *Hollywood principle*;
- the situations in which to use and not to use inheritance.

In this chapter, we look at some examples in order to explore these new ideas.

19.2 Deriving a new class by inheritance

19.2.1 Introducing a type to represent students

So far we have used interfaces and classes in order to represent objects that are distinct from one another: a date is nothing like a person, and vice-versa. However, there will be occasions when we will want to represent objects that are specialized forms of objects for which we have already produced a class.

For example, if we now have to produce a program that manipulates data about students, we will need an interface and a class to represent a student. What we need to represent has a lot in common with the interface and the class representing a person that was produced in Chapter 12. So a lot of the hard work has already been done.

For a person, we chose to represent the person's name, their date of birth, their phone number and their height. Suppose that for a student we need to represent their student registration number and the name of their course as well.

19.2.2 Coding the `Student` interface

The `Person` interface was given in Figure 12.6. It contains the declarations of 11 methods: there are four get methods, four set methods, and methods called `equals`, hashCode and toString. As it is a subinterface of the Comparable interface, it also provides a method called compareTo. For the Student interface, we need all of these together with four more declarations for methods called getStudentNumber, getCourseName, setStudentNumber and setCourseName.

An interface declaration called Student could be produced by copying the file Person.java to the file Student.java, and by adding the four new declarations; however, this is not the way to do it. If we ever wished to change the Person interface, we would probably want to change Student as well. It is always difficult to keep multiple copies (of what is meant to be the same code) up to date and in step.

In Section 12.5.6, we saw that an *extends clause* can be used to express the fact that an interface is a more specialized form of another interface: the new interface is said to be a *subinterface* of the existing interface. So the interface for Student can use an **extends clause** to declare that Student is a subinterface of Person:

```
public interface Student extends Person
{
    public int getStudentNumber();
    public String getCourseName();
    public void setStudentNumber(int pStudentNumber);
    public void setCourseName(String pCourseName);
}
```

If we use this interface declaration:

- the Student interface has all of the 11 method headers of the Person interface and the method header of the compareTo method (of the Comparable interface) as well as the four new method headers;

- any class implementing the Student interface has to provide declarations for all of these 16 methods;

- any client declaring a Student variable can apply any of these 16 methods to the variable.

The full declaration of the Student interface is given in Figure 19.1.

19.2.3 Coding the StudentImpl class

We have three choices when coding the StudentImpl class.

Choice 1: duplicating the code of the PersonImpl class

The code of the PersonImpl class is given in Figure 12.7. When producing the code of the StudentImpl class, we could copy the file PersonImpl.java to the file StudentImpl.java and then add the appropriate new declarations that are needed to handle students. As explained above, this is not a good way of implementing StudentImpl because it is difficult to maintain duplicate copies of the same code.

```
// A type to represent a student.
// Barry Cornelius, 20 June 2000
public interface Student extends Person
{
    // return the StudentNumber part of the target student
    public int getStudentNumber();

    // return the CourseName part of the target student
    public String getCourseName();

    // set the StudentNumber part of the target student to pStudentNumber
    public void setStudentNumber(int pStudentNumber);

    // set the CourseName part of the target student to pCourseName
    public void setCourseName(String pCourseName);
}
```

Figure 19.1   The Student interface.

Choice 2: including a Person field in the StudentImpl class

We could instead include a Person field as one of the fields of the StudentImpl class. Any of the methods that belong to the Person interface is then implemented by applying the method to the Person field:

```
public class StudentImpl implements Student
{
    ...
    private Person iPerson;
    public StudentImpl(final String pName, final Date pDateOfBirth,
                       final String pPhoneNumber, final double pHeight,
                       final int pStudentNumber, final String pCourseName)
    {
        iPerson = new PersonImpl(pName, pDateOfBirth, pPhoneNumber, pHeight);
        iStudentNumber = pStudentNumber;
        iCourseName = pCourseName;
    }
    ...
    public String getName()
    {
        return iPerson.getName();
    }
    ...
    public void setName(final String pName)
    {
        iPerson.setName(pName);
    }
    ...
}
```

Once again, it would also be necessary to add the appropriate new declarations that are needed to handle students.

This class uses the *adapter pattern* as, essentially, all it does is to present a new interface for an existing class.

It also uses a design technique known as *composition*: the class StudentImpl is *composed* of a field, or *has* a field, that is of the interface type Person. Although it is often better to use composition rather than inheritance, this is not the case with this example. We will look at the issues involved with choosing between composition and inheritance in Section 19.7.

Choice 3: using inheritance to form a subclass

In Java, we can use **inheritance** if a class wants to be the same as some other class but with additional functionality. If we declare StudentImpl using an **extends clause**:

```
public class StudentImpl extends PersonImpl
{
    ...
}
```

it means that the class StudentImpl has all the declarations of PersonImpl as well as the ones that textually appear in StudentImpl.

So, as soon as we include the above extends clause, any object of the class StudentImpl has:

- private fields called iName, iDateOfBirth, iPhoneNumber and iHeight;
- 12 method declarations: they are the four get methods, the four set methods, and the methods called equals, hashCode, compareTo and toString.

This is called **inheritance**. The class StudentImpl is said to **inherit** from the class PersonImpl; the class StudentImpl is said to be a *subclass* of PersonImpl; and the class PersonImpl is said to be a *superclass* of StudentImpl.

The full declaration of StudentImpl is given in Figure 19.2. Note that it has an extends clause:

```
extends PersonImpl
```

to say that it is derived from PersonImpl, and it has an implements clause:

```
implements Student
```

to say that it implements the Student interface. Other aspects about the coding of StudentImpl will now be considered.

19.2.4 Method overriding

As explained earlier, you can give a method of a subclass the same *signature* as a method of the superclass, and this is called **method overriding**. It is often used when more appropriate code can be devised for the method of the subclass.

```java
// A class that implements the Student interface.
// Barry Cornelius, 20 June 2000
import java.util. StringTokenizer;
public class StudentImpl extends PersonImpl implements Student
{
   private String iCourseName;
   private int iStudentNumber;
   public StudentImpl()
   {
      this("", new DateImpl(), "", 0.0, "", 0);
   }
   public StudentImpl(final String pName, final Date pDateOfBirth,
                      final String pPhoneNumber, final double pHeight,
                      final String pCourseName, final int pStudentNumber)
   {
      super(pName, pDateOfBirth, pPhoneNumber, pHeight);
      iCourseName = pCourseName;
      iStudentNumber = pStudentNumber;
   }
   public StudentImpl(final String pStudentString)
   {
      super(pStudentString.substring(0, pStudentString.indexOf("@")));
      try
      {
         final StringTokenizer tTokens =
                        new StringTokenizer(pStudentString, "@");
         final String tPersonString = tTokens.nextToken();
         iCourseName = tTokens.nextToken();
         String tStudentNumberString = tTokens.nextToken();
         if (tStudentNumberString.equals(""))
         {
            tStudentNumberString = "0";
         }
         iStudentNumber = Integer.parseInt(tStudentNumberString);
      }
      catch(final Exception pException)
      {
         iCourseName = "";
         iStudentNumber = -1;
         throw new IllegalArgumentException();
      }
   }
   public String getCourseName()
   {
      return iCourseName;
   }
```

Figure 19.2 *Continues on the next page.*

```
     public int getStudentNumber()
     {
        return iStudentNumber;
     }
     public void setCourseName(final String pCourseName)
     {
        iCourseName = pCourseName;
     }
     public void setStudentNumber(final int pStudentNumber)
     {
        iStudentNumber = pStudentNumber;
     }
     public String toString()
     {
        return super.toString() + "@" + iCourseName + "@" + iStudentNumber;
     }
}
```

Figure 19.2 A class that implements the Student interface.

Of the methods declared in the PersonImpl class, the methods equals, hashCode, compareTo and toString are the obvious candidates for method overriding, i.e. for each of these methods, there may be more appropriate code to be executed when the person is a student.

Because (in Chapter 12) we chose to say that two PersonImpl objects are the same if their iName fields are the same, it is useful to do the same with StudentImpl objects. So, equals does not need to be overridden: the one given in PersonImpl is good enough for StudentImpl objects. Because hashCode and compareTo are linked with equals, the same decision also applies to hashCode and compareTo.

However, because a StudentImpl object stores additional information, the code that is executed for the toString method could be different. So the class declaration for StudentImpl given in Figure 19.2 provides its own declaration of toString. As you would expect, when toString is applied to a Person object, PersonImpl's toString will be used; when it is applied to a Student object, StudentImpl's toString will be used.

19.2.5 Accessing fields and methods of the superclass

Since an object of the class StudentImpl has fields iName, iDateOfBirth, iPhoneNumber and iHeight, it is tempting to code StudentImpl's toString as:

```
public String toString()
{
    return iName + "%" + iDateOfBirth + "%" + iPhoneNumber + "%" + iHeight +
               "@" + iCourseName  + "@" + iStudentNumber;
}
```

However, iName, iDateOfBirth, iPhoneNumber and iHeight are all marked as private in the class PersonImpl and, even though a StudentImpl object has these fields, it is not possible to access them directly from within the code of StudentImpl. See Curio 19.2.

Instead, we can use PersonImpl's public methods: getName, getDateOf- Birth, getPhoneNumber and getHeight. When used within a method (e.g. toString) of a subclass of PersonImpl, they can be used without specifying a target in which case they are being applied to whatever target the method (e.g. toString) is being applied:

```
public String toString()
{
    return getName() + "%" + getDateOfBirth() +
                    "%" + getPhoneNumber() + "%" + getHeight() +
                    "@" + iCourseName      + "@" + iStudentNumber;
}
```

Because this code uses getName, getDateOfBirth, getPhoneNumber and getHeight, it introduces a *dependency* between the StudentImpl and Person- Impl classes. If we were to add another field to the PersonImpl class, we would probably need to alter toString of StudentImpl as well. So, although the above toString would work, it is not the ideal code for StudentImpl's toString.

As all of the work of outputting the details about the person part of a student is done by PersonImpl's toString, we should use that instead. However, a call of toString from within the body of StudentImpl would call StudentImpl's toString. In order to call PersonImpl's toString from within StudentImpl, we need to use super.toString() as in:

```
public String toString()
{
    return super.toString() + "@" + iCourseName + "@" + iStudentNumber;
}
```

This version of the declaration of toString is the one that appears in the StudentImpl class given in Figure 19.2.

19.2.6 Coding the constructor of a subclass

Whenever you use inheritance, the constructor of the subclass needs to be able to initialize the fields that are inherited from the superclass.

In the StudentImpl example, a StudentImpl object has a set of fields from the PersonImpl class as well as its own fields (iStudentNumber and iCourseName). Because of this, the constructor of StudentImpl has to initialize not only its own fields but also those of the superclass. Consider the StudentImpl constructor that has six parameters (shown in Figure 19.2). In the body of this constructor, a statement involving the super keyword is used to initialize the fields of the superclass:

```
super(pName, pDateOfBirth, pPhoneNumber, pHeight);
```

Here the super keyword is being used to form what is called an **explicit constructor invocation statement**.

When using inheritance, you will usually want to use this form of `super` in order to initialize fields of the superclass. There are a number of restrictions on this form of `super`. Firstly, the call of `super` must appear as the first statement of the constructor. Consider the constructor of `StudentImpl` that has a `String` parameter. This could be used as follows:

```
Student tStudent =
        new StudentImpl("Smith%1970-6-12%01987-654322%1.85@Computing@27");
```

An obvious coding for this constructor is:

```
public StudentImpl(final String pStudentString)
{
    try
    {
        final StringTokenizer tTokens =
                        new StringTokenizer(pStudentString, "@");
        final String tPersonString = tTokens.nextToken();
        super(tPersonString);
        iCourseName = tTokens.nextToken();
        String tStudentNumberString = tTokens.nextToken();
        if (tStudentNumberString.equals(""))
        {
            tStudentNumberString = "0";
        }
        iStudentNumber = Integer.parseInt(tStudentNumberString);
    }
    catch(final Exception pException)
    {
        iCourseName = "";
        iStudentNumber = -1;
        throw new IllegalArgumentException();
    }
}
```

The idea is that `pStudentString` is broken up into three substrings. The first substring is something like `"Smith%1970-6-12%01987-654322%1.85"`. Using this as an argument of `super` means that the `PersonImpl`'s constructor that has a `String` parameter will be called, and this will ensure that the `PersonImpl` fields will be initialized.

However, the above `StudentImpl` constructor is not allowed because this use of `super` does not appear in the first statement of the constructor. The code given in Figure 19.2 finds a way round this problem: it is not very elegant.

Curio 19.4 contains details of the other restrictions on the use of this form of `super`. For details of what happens if the superclass has fields and you fail to initialize them using this form of `super`, see Curio 19.5.

19.2.7 Not overriding `equals`

In Section 19.2.4, we chose not to provide a declaration of `equals` within the class `StudentImpl`. So, what happens when `equals` is applied to an object of class `StudentImpl`? Here is an example:

```
Student tFirstStudent =
        new StudentImpl("Smith", new DateImpl(1970, 6, 12),
                            "01987-654322", 1.85, "Computing", 27);
Student tSecondStudent =
        new StudentImpl("Smith", new DateImpl(1970, 6, 12),
                            "01987-654322", 1.85, "Computing", 27);
boolean tIsSameStudent = tFirstStudent.equals(tSecondStudent);
```

Because `StudentImpl` does not have a method called `equals`, and because `PersonImpl` is a superclass of `StudentImpl`, `PersonImpl`'s `equals` will be called. Here is the code of `PersonImpl`'s `equals` method (extracted from Figure 12.7):

```
public boolean equals(final Object pObject)
{
    if ( pObject==null || getClass()!=pObject.getClass() )
    {
        return false;
    }
    return iName.equals(((PersonImpl)pObject).iName);
}
```

It has a parameter of class `Object`, and so any object of any class can be passed as an argument. In the above call of `equals`, we are passing `tSecondStudent` as an argument, and the method is being applied to `tFirstStudent`. So, both the argument and the target are of the class `StudentImpl`. When the method is executed, `pObject` is assigned the value of `tSecondStudent`, and then the value of `pObject` is checked to see whether it has the value `null`. Because the boolean expression `if ( pObject==null || getClass()!=pObject.getClass() )` has the value *false*, the execution of the `equals` method moves to the next statement and returns the value of the expression `iName.equals(((PersonImpl)pObject).iName)`. Although `pObject` is pointing to a `StudentImpl` object, here the *cast* will treat the object as if it only had the parts associated with a `PersonImpl` object. So, this expression returns *true* if and only if the `iName` fields of the two objects have the same string of characters.

19.2.8 Using the `Student` interface and the `StudentImpl` class

The `PopImplProg` program given in Figure 17.16 manipulates a population. It uses an object of the `PopImpl` class in order to maintain the data about a collection of people. The program assumes the user of the program types the letter a when a person is to be added to the population; the program uses the following code to arrange for this to happen:

```
case 'a':
{
    System.out.print("Person? ");
    System.out.flush();
    final Person tPerson = new PersonImpl(iKeyboard.readLine());
    if ( ! iPop.add(tPerson) )
    {
        System.out.println("The person is already in the population");
    }
}
break;
```

Suppose that we now want to modify this program so that we can add students (to the population) as well as ordinary people. Assuming the letter s is going to be used for this, then one way of reading in a student and adding the student to the population is to use the following code:

```
case 's':
{
    System.out.print("Student? ");
    System.out.flush();
    final Student tStudent = new StudentImpl(iKeyboard.readLine());
    if ( ! iPop.add(tStudent) )
    {
        System.out.println("The student is already in the population");
    }
}
break;
```

So now the program is maintaining a collection of objects where some objects are of class PersonImpl and other objects are of class StudentImpl. This map is said to have **heterogeneous values**. There is some similarity to the heterogeneous lists that were mentioned in Section 14.3.7.

The user of the program types the letter g if they wish to find out the details about someone in the population. They then have to type in the person's name and the variable tName is made to point to this String. The program then executes:

```
final Person tPerson = iPop.get(tName);
System.out.println(tPerson);
```

When the println is executed, the variable tPerson is pointing to an object that is either of the class PersonImpl or of the class StudentImpl: the particular toString that gets executed (by println) depends on this. The program will output something like:

```
Smith%1970-06-12%01987-654322%1.85
```

if it is a `PersonImpl` object or something like:

```
Smith%1970-06-12%01987-654322%1.85@Computing@27
```

if it is a `StudentImpl` object.

19.3 A class hierarchy that uses an abstract class

We now look at another example where inheritance can be used. The main aim of introducing this additional example is to reinforce some of the new ideas (that were presented in the previous section).

19.3.1 The class `Shape`

Suppose we need to represent some two-dimensional geometrical shapes in a program. We can use the class `Shape` given in Figure 19.3 for objects that are two-dimensional geometrical shapes. The class declaration includes a constructor to create an object representing a shape at some position in two-dimensional space. As well as the usual methods, it also includes a method called `translate` that moves a shape to a new position relative to its current position.

19.3.2 The class `Circle`

Suppose we now want a class `Circle` to represent circles. As a circle is a specialized form of a shape, we will produce this class using inheritance from the class `Shape`. See Figure 19.4.

Objects of this class have three fields: `iX` and `iY` (from `Shape`) and `iRadius` (from `Circle`). One of the constructors of this class uses an *explicit constructor invocation statement*:

```
super(pX, pY);
```

in order to initialize the `iX` and `iY` fields.

Circle's declaration also provides methods called `equals`, `hashCode` and `toString`. These method declarations override the declarations that have the same name that are given in the class `Shape`. Each of these three methods use the notation `super.`*methodname*`()` in order to execute `Shape`'s version of the method.

19.3.3 The class `Rectangle`

In a similar way, the class `Rectangle` (given in Figure 19.5) can be built from the class `Shape`.

19.3.4 Using the class `Shape` and its subclasses

The `ShapesCollection` class given in Figure 19.6 uses the class `Shape`, the class `Circle` and the class `Rectangle`. An object of the `ShapesCollection` class

```java
// A class that represents a two-dimensional geometrical figure.
// Barry Cornelius, 20 June 2000
public class Shape
{
    private int iX;
    private int iY;
    public Shape()
    {
        this(0, 0);
    }
    public Shape(final int pX, final int pY)
    {
        iX = pX;
        iY = pY;
    }
    public int getX()
    {
        return iX;
    }
    public int getY()
    {
        return iY;
    }
    public void translate(final int pX, final int pY)
    {
        iX += pX;
        iY += pY;
    }
    public boolean equals(final Object pObject)
    {
        if ( pObject==null || getClass()!=pObject.getClass() )
        {
            return false;
        }
        final Shape tShape = (Shape)pObject;
        return iX==tShape.iX && iY==tShape.iY;
    }
    public int hashCode()
    {
        return iX + iY;
    }
    public String toString()
    {
        return iX + ":" + iY;
    }
}
```

Figure 19.3   A class that represents a two-dimensional geometrical figure.

```
// A class that represents a circle.
// Barry Cornelius, 20 June 2000
public class Circle extends Shape
{
    private int iRadius;
    public Circle()
    {
        this(0, 0, 0);
    }
    public Circle(final int pRadius, final int pX, final int pY)
    {
        super(pX, pY);
        iRadius = pRadius;
    }
    public int getRadius()
    {
        return iRadius;
    }
    public boolean equals(final Object pObject)
    {
        if ( pObject==null || getClass()!=pObject.getClass() )
        {
            return false;
        }
        return super.equals(pObject) && iRadius==((Circle)pObject).iRadius;
    }
    public int hashCode()
    {
        return super.hashCode() + iRadius;
    }
    public String toString()
    {
        return super.toString() + ":" + iRadius;
    }
}
```

Figure 19.4 A class that represents a circle.

is created by the ShapesToScreen program that is given in Figure 19.7. This program first associates a BufferedReader object with a file called ShapesToScreen.data and then passes this object as an argument of ShapesCollection's constructor. In this way, ShapesCollection's constructor can read lines from this file.

ShapesCollection's constructor assumes that the file contains data describing some shapes. The file could contain the values: 1, 63, 82, 8, 2, 130, 40, 160, 60, 2, 235, 50, 40, 40, 2, 120, 72, 140, 4, 2, 228, 72, 59, 4, 1, 210, 82, 8, 1, 247, 82, 8 (where each value is on a separate line of the file). In this data, there is a sequence of values for each shape. The first value in each sequence is a key to the kind of shape: if the key

```java
// A class that represents a rectangle.
// Barry Cornelius, 20 June 2000
public class Rectangle extends Shape
{
    private int iWidth;
    private int iHeight;
    public Rectangle()
    {
        this(0, 0, 0, 0);
    }
    public Rectangle(final int pWidth, final int pHeight,
                     final int pX, final int pY)
    {
        super(pX, pY);
        iWidth = pWidth;
        iHeight = pHeight;
    }
    public int getWidth()
    {
        return iWidth;
    }
    public int getHeight()
    {
        return iHeight;
    }
    public boolean equals(final Object pObject)
    {
        if ( pObject==null || getClass()!=pObject.getClass() )
        {
            return false;
        }
        final Rectangle tRectangle = (Rectangle)pObject;
        return super.equals(pObject) &&
                iWidth==tRectangle.iWidth &&
                iHeight==tRectangle.iHeight;
    }
    public int hashCode()
    {
        return super.hashCode() + iWidth + iHeight;
    }
    public String toString()
    {
        return super.toString() + ":" + iWidth + ":" + iHeight;
    }
}
```

Figure 19.5   A class that represents a rectangle.

```
// A class that stores a collection of Shapes read from a BufferedReader.
// Barry Cornelius, 20 June 2000
import java.util. ArrayList;
import java.io.    BufferedReader;
import java.io.    IOException;
import java.util. List;
public class ShapesCollection
{
    private List iList;
    public ShapesCollection(final BufferedReader pInputHandle)
    {
        iList = new ArrayList();
        try
        {
            while (true)
            {
                String tLine = pInputHandle.readLine();
                if (tLine==null)
                {
                    break;
                }
                final int tKey = Integer.parseInt(tLine);
                tLine = pInputHandle.readLine();
                final int tX = Integer.parseInt(tLine);
                tLine = pInputHandle.readLine();
                final int tY = Integer.parseInt(tLine);
                switch (tKey)
                {
                    case 1:
                    {
                        tLine = pInputHandle.readLine();
                        final int tRadius = Integer.parseInt(tLine);
                        final Circle tCircle = new Circle(tRadius, tX, tY);
                        iList.add(tCircle);
                    }
                    break;
                    case 2:
                    {
                        tLine = pInputHandle.readLine();
                        final int tWidth = Integer.parseInt(tLine);
                        tLine = pInputHandle.readLine();
                        final int tHeight = Integer.parseInt(tLine);
                        final Rectangle tRectangle =
                                        new Rectangle(tWidth, tHeight, tX, tY);
                        iList.add(tRectangle);
                    }
                    break;
```

Figure 19.6 *Continues on the next page.*

```
                    default:
                    {
                        System.out.println("unknown value for the key: " + tKey);
                    }
                    break;
                }
            }
        }
        catch(final IOException pIOException)
        {
            System.out.println("ignoring an IOException");
        }
    }
    public int size()
    {
        return iList.size();
    }
    public Shape get(final int pShapeNumber)
    {
        return (Shape)iList.get(pShapeNumber);
    }
}
```

Figure 19.6 A class that stores a collection of Shapes read from a BufferedReader.

```
// A program to read some data about shapes and output this to the screen.
// Barry Cornelius, 20 June 2000
import java.io. BufferedReader;
import java.io. FileNotFoundException;
import java.io. FileReader;
public class ShapesToScreen
{
    public static void main(final String[] pArgs) throws FileNotFoundException
    {
        final BufferedReader tInputHandle =
                    new BufferedReader(new FileReader("ShapesToScreen.data"));
        final ShapesCollection tShapesCollection =
                    new ShapesCollection(tInputHandle);
        final int tNumberOfShapes = tShapesCollection.size();
        for (int tShapeNumber = 0;
                tShapeNumber<tNumberOfShapes; tShapeNumber++)
        {
            final Shape tShape = tShapesCollection.get(tShapeNumber);
            tShape.translate(1, 2);
            System.out.println(tShape);
        }
    }
}
```

Figure 19.7 Reading data about shapes and outputting this to the screen.

is a 1, the shape is a circle; or if it is a 2, the shape is a rectangle. So the above data is meant to be interpreted as follows: the first shape is a circle with an x-coordinate of 63, a y-coordinate of 82, and a radius of 8; the second shape is a rectangle with an x-coordinate of 130, a y-coordinate of 40, a width of 160, and a height of 60; and so on. You should find that the above data describes four rectangles and three circles.

The constructor stores the details about the shapes in a list called `iList`:

```
iList = new ArrayList();
```

It adds a value to the list either by executing:

```
final Circle tCircle = new Circle(tRadius, tX, tY);
iList.add(tCircle);
```

or by executing:

```
final Rectangle tRectangle = new Rectangle(tWidth, tHeight, tX, tY);
iList.add(tRectangle);
```

So the constructor does not store any references to objects of the class `Shape` in the list: instead, each element of the list is a reference either to a `Circle` object or to a `Rectangle` object.

The `ShapesCollection` class provides two methods: one returns the number of elements in the list, and the other returns the value of the element stored at a given position in the list.

At the end of the `ShapesToScreen` program, there is a for statement that outputs details about the shapes that have been stored. It repeatedly executes the following three statements:

```
final Shape tShape = tShapesCollection.get(tShapeNumber);
tShape.translate(1, 2);
System.out.println(tShape);
```

In the first of these, the `Shape` variable `tShape` is made to refer to either a `Circle` object or a `Rectangle` object. Then the `translate` method is applied to the object. Because neither `Circle` nor `Rectangle` declare a `translate` method, it will be the `translate` method of the superclass (`Shape`) that will be used. Finally, the call of `println` will use either `Circle`'s or `Rectangle`'s `toString` method in order to print the shape referred to by `tShape`.

When the program is executed with the above data, this for statement produces the output:

```
64:84:8
131:42:160:60
236:52:40:40
121:74:140:4
229:74:59:4
211:84:8
248:84:8
```

19.3.5 Turning Shape into an abstract class

Often a superclass is introduced merely as a useful place to store common fields and common methods. This is the case with the class AbstractButton which is the direct superclass of classes like JButton and JMenuItem. It is also the case with the class Shape. There is no intention to have any objects of the class Shape: it is really just a useful place to put the x and y coordinates of a shape's position and a useful place to provide methods (such as translate) which are applicable to all shapes.

In Java, you can use the abstract modifier if you wish to document in a class declaration that there is no intention to create any objects of the class. Such a class is called an **abstract class**:

```
abstract public class Shape
{
    . . .
}
```

Since this class is now an abstract class, it is not possible to create instances of the class. So, the class instance creation expression of:

```
Shape tShape = new Shape();
```

would cause a compilation error.

Even if a class is abstract, it will still be important for it to have constructors: such a constructor will be used when the constructor of a subclass wants to initialize fields of its superclass, e.g. by executing:

```
super(pX, pY);
```

19.4 Producing a subclass of JComponent

As we saw in Chapter 13, inheritance is also used in the design of the Swing API. For example, all of the GUI components (such as JButton, JLabel, ...) are derived from JComponent.

Whenever we declare an object that is of the class JComponent or is of one of its subclasses (JButton, JLabel, ...), then in order for it to be useful it has to be added to another GUI component that is a container (e.g. a JFrame or a JDialog). One of the things that happens when this container is displayed on the screen is that the paintComponent method of each of its GUI components is called. And any of these paintComponent methods will be re-executed whenever its GUI component gets *damaged*, e.g. a part of the window that it occupies needs to be repainted because some window that has been in front of it has been moved away.

The paintComponent method of the JComponent class does not do anything useful as it has an empty block:

```
public void paintComponent(Graphics pGraphics)
{
}
```

However, if we have declared a class to be a subclass of the JComponent class, we can override this paintComponent method, declaring one that does something. For example, the HelloJComponent class shown in Figure 19.8 (which is declared to be a subclass of JComponent) has a paintComponent method which paints the string "Hello world" at the position 50,30.

```
// A class for an object that outputs "Hello world" when it gets displayed.
// Barry Cornelius, 20 June 2000
import java.awt.    Dimension;
import java.awt.    Graphics;
import javax.swing. JComponent;
public class HelloJComponent extends JComponent
{
    public HelloJComponent()
    {
    }
    public void paintComponent(final Graphics pGraphics)
    {
        pGraphics.drawString("Hello world", 50, 30);
    }
    public Dimension getPreferredSize()
    {
        return new Dimension(220, 70);
    }
}
```

Figure 19.8 A class for an object that can display "Hello world".

A program that uses the HelloJComponent class is shown in Figure 19.9.

Note there is no call of paintComponent in the code that we have written. Instead, this method is called by some of the *supporting code*, the code of the classes that are used by our program. And it is called whenever there is a need to display/re-display the HelloJComponent component. This is sometimes referred to as the **Hollywood principle** – *don't call us: we'll call you.*

Note that whenever this supporting code calls the paintComponent method, it passes an object of the class java.awt.Graphics as an argument: this object is a **graphics context**, a means by which we can change the drawing surface.

The graphics context has an origin which is at the top left-hand corner of the drawing surface. It also has a background colour, a foreground colour, and a font that is used if text is painted onto the drawing surface. All of these aspects have default values that can be changed by calling an appropriate method.

In the call of drawString given in Figure 19.8, the text "Hello world" is painted at the position that is 50 pixels from the left of the drawing surface and 30 pixels down from its top, as shown in Figure 19.10.

When a client of HelloJComponent includes an object of this class as a GUI component of a container, the container will want to know how much space to allocate for the component: it does this by calling the object's getPreferredSize method. The JComponent class provides a getPreferredSize method that returns a value

```
// A program that displays a HelloJComponent object.
// Barry Cornelius, 20 June 2000
import java.awt.    BorderLayout;
import java.awt.    Container;
import javax.swing. JFrame;
import javax.swing. JLabel;
public class HelloJComponentProg
{
    public static void main(final String[] pArgs)
    {
        final HelloJComponent tHelloJComponent = new HelloJComponent();
        final JFrame tJFrame = new JFrame("HelloJComponentProg");
        final ExitWindowListener tExitWindowListener =
                                        new ExitWindowListener();
        tJFrame.addWindowListener(tExitWindowListener);
        final Container tContentPane = tJFrame.getContentPane();
        tContentPane.add(new JLabel("NORTH"), BorderLayout.NORTH);
        tContentPane.add(tHelloJComponent,    BorderLayout.CENTER);
        tContentPane.add(new JLabel("SOUTH"), BorderLayout.SOUTH);
        tJFrame.pack();
        tJFrame.setVisible(true);
    }
}
```

Figure 19.9 A program that displays a `HelloJComponent` object.

of the class `Dimension` (from the `java.awt` package) that represents a size of 1 pixel by 1 pixel. The `HelloJComponent` class given in Figure 19.8 overrides this method in order to provide a more appropriate value for the size of the drawing surface: it returns a `Dimension` representing 220 pixels by 70 pixels.

As well as `drawString` that can be used to paint text, there are numerous other methods that can be applied to a graphics context, i.e. to an object of the class `java.awt.Graphics`. A table of some of these methods is given in Figure 19.11.

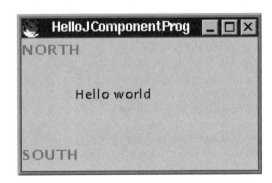

Figure 19.10 The output of the `HelloJComponentProg` program.

Where a description mentions a rectangle, the left-hand side of the rectangle is pX pixels in from the left of the drawing surface and the top side of the rectangle is pY pixels down from the top of the drawing surface. The rectangle has a width of pWidth pixels and a height of pHeight pixels.

```
public void clearRect(int pX, int pY, int pWidth, int pHeight);
```
Clears from the target the rectangle given by pX, pY, pWidth and pHeight by filling it with the background colour of the target.

```
public void drawArc(int pX, int pY, int pWidth, int pHeight,
                    int pStartAngle, int pArcAngle);
```
Draws on the target the outline of an elliptical arc defined by pStartAngle and pArcAngle covering the rectangle given by pX, pY, pWidth and pHeight.

```
public void drawLine(int pX1, int pY1, int pX2, int pY2);
```
Draws on the target a line between the point defined by pX1 and pY1 and the point defined by pX2 and pY2.

```
public void drawOval(int pX, int pY, int pWidth, int pHeight);
```
Draws on the target the outline of an oval covering the rectangle given by pX, pY, pWidth and pHeight.

```
public void drawPolygon(int[] pXPoints, int[] pYPoints, int pNumPoints);
```
Draws on the target the outline of a closed polygon defined by the arrays pXPoints and pYPoints which contain the x and y coordinates and the integer pNumPoints which gives the number of points.

```
public void drawPolyline(int[] pXPoints, int[] pYPoints, int pNumPoints);
```
Draws on the target a sequence of connected lines defined by the arrays pXPoints and pYPoints which contain the x and y coordinates and the integer pNumPoints which gives the number of points.

```
public void drawRect(int pX, int pY, int pWidth, int pHeight);
```
Draws on the target the outline of the rectangle given by pX, pY, pWidth and pHeight.

```
public void drawString(String pString, int pX, int pY);
```
Draws the string pString on the target at the position given by pX and pY.

```
public void fillArc(int pX, int pY, int pWidth, int pHeight,
                    int pStartAngle, int pArcAngle);
```
Fills on the target the elliptical arc defined by pStartAngle and pArcAngle covering the rectangle given by pX, pY, pWidth and pHeight.

```
public void fillOval(int pX, int pY, int pWidth, int pHeight);
```
Fills on the target the oval covering the rectangle given by pX, pY, pWidth and pHeight.

```
public void fillPolygon(int[] pXPoints, int[] pYPoints, int pNumPoints);
```
Fills on the target the closed polygon defined by the arrays pXPoints and pYPoints which contain the x and y coordinates and the integer pNumPoints which gives the number of points.

```
public void fillRect(int pX, int pY, int pWidth, int pHeight);
```
Fills on the target the rectangle given by pX, pY, pWidth and pHeight.

```
public void setColor(Color pColor);
```
Sets the target's foreground colour to pColor (which is a value of the type java.awt.Color).

```
public void setFont(Font pFont);
```
Sets the target's font to pFont (which is a value of the type java.awt.Font).

```
public String toString();
```
Returns a String representing the value of the target.

Figure 19.11 Methods of the java.awt.Graphics class.

19.5) Modifying `ShapesToScreen` to draw its shapes

19.5.1 Using a `paintComponent` that calls `draw` for each shape

The loop of the `ShapesToScreen` program (given in Figure 19.7) is used just to output details of some geometrical shapes:

```
final Shape tShape = tShapesCollection.get(tShapeNumber);
tShape.translate(1, 2);
System.out.println(tShape);
```

Instead of using `println` to output the object pointed to by `tShape`, we could instead use methods like `drawRect` and `fillOval` (from `java.awt.Graphics`) in order to display the shapes in a window on the screen (as shown in Figure 19.12).

It may be tempting to achieve this using an if statement that uses the `instanceof` operator to determine the class of the object pointed to by `tShape`:

```
public void paintComponent(final Graphics pGraphics)
{
    final int tNumberOfShapes = iShapesCollection.size();
    for (int tShapeNumber = 0; tShapeNumber<tNumberOfShapes; tShapeNumber++)
    {
        final Shape tShape = iShapesCollection.get(tShapeNumber);
        if (tShape instanceof Circle)
        {
            final Circle tCircle = (Circle)tShape;
            final int tRadius = tCircle.getRadius();
            final int tXTopLeft = tCircle.getX() - tRadius;
            final int tYTopLeft = tCircle.getY() - tRadius;
            pGraphics.fillOval(tXTopLeft, tYTopLeft, tRadius*2, tRadius*2);
        }
        else
        {
            final Rectangle tRectangle = (Rectangle)tShape;
            final int tWidth = tRectangle.getWidth();
            final int tHeight = tRectangle.getHeight();
            final int tXLeft = tRectangle.getX() - tWidth/2;
            final int tYTop = tRectangle.getY() - tHeight/2;
            pGraphics.drawRect(tXLeft, tYTop, tWidth, tHeight);
        }
    }
}
```

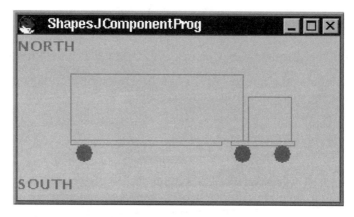

Figure 19.12   The output of the `ShapesJComponentProg` program.

However, this is not recommended because:

- it would be necessary to modify this code whenever some other geometrical shape (such as a triangle) were introduced;
- it introduces a dependency between this class and the class `Circle`, the class `Rectangle, ...` ;
- it is time-consuming to execute an `instanceof` operator.

Instead, it is better to include a method in each of the classes that represent geometrical shapes and to apply that method to `tShape`. If the method were called `draw`, `paintComponent` could be:

```
public void paintComponent(final Graphics pGraphics)
{
    final int tNumberOfShapes = iShapesCollection.size();
    for (int tShapeNumber = 0; tShapeNumber<tNumberOfShapes; tShapeNumber++)
    {
        final Shape tShape = iShapesCollection.get(tShapeNumber);
        tShape.draw(pGraphics);
    }
}
```

This `paintComponent` method could be included as one of the methods of a `ShapesJComponent` class, a class that is derived from `JComponent`. A program (`ShapesJComponentProg`) that creates an object of this class and incorporates it in a `JFrame` is given in Figure 19.13. The full code of the `ShapesJComponent` class is given in Figure 19.14. It uses the `ShapesCollection` class: this can be left unchanged from the code given in Figure 19.6.

The file of data (`ShapesJComponentProg.data`) used by the `ShapesJComponentProg` program is the same as that used by the `ShapesToScreen` program (given in Figure 19.7) except two lines containing the values 300 and 100 appear at the start of the file.

```
// A program that displays the shapes it finds in a file of data.
// Barry Cornelius, 20 June 2000
import java.awt.    BorderLayout;
import java.io.     BufferedReader;
import java.awt.    Container;
import java.io.     FileNotFoundException;
import java.io.     FileReader;
import javax.swing. JFrame;
import javax.swing. JLabel;
public class ShapesJComponentProg
{
    public static void main(final String[] pArgs) throws FileNotFoundException
    {
        final BufferedReader tInputHandle =
                new BufferedReader(new FileReader("ShapesJComponentProg.data"));
        final ShapesJComponent tShapesJComponent =
                new ShapesJComponent(tInputHandle);
        final JFrame tJFrame = new JFrame("ShapesJComponentProg");
        final ExitWindowListener tExitWindowListener =
                                                    new ExitWindowListener();
        tJFrame.addWindowListener(tExitWindowListener);
        final Container tContentPane = tJFrame.getContentPane();
        tContentPane.add(new JLabel("NORTH"), BorderLayout.NORTH);
        tContentPane.add(tShapesJComponent,   BorderLayout.CENTER);
        tContentPane.add(new JLabel("SOUTH"), BorderLayout.SOUTH);
        tJFrame.pack();
        tJFrame.setVisible(true);
    }
}
```

Figure 19.13   A program that displays the shapes it finds in a file of data.

19.5.2 Supplying draw for each class representing a shape

As mentioned above, if we want to apply the draw method to tShape, the Circle
and the Rectangle classes need to be altered to include a declaration of a draw
method.

The draw method of the Circle class can be:

```
public void draw(final Graphics pGraphics)
{
    final int tXTopLeft = getX() - iRadius;
    final int tYTopLeft = getY() - iRadius;
    pGraphics.setColor(Color.magenta);
    pGraphics.fillOval(tXTopLeft, tYTopLeft, iRadius*2, iRadius*2);
}
```

```java
// A class for a GUI component that displays a collection of shapes.
// Barry Cornelius, 20 June 2000
import java.io.      BufferedReader;
import java.awt.     Dimension;
import java.awt.     Graphics;
import java.io.      IOException;
import javax.swing.  JComponent;
public class ShapesJComponent extends JComponent
{
    private ShapesCollection iShapesCollection;
    private int iTotalWidth;
    private int iTotalHeight;
    public ShapesJComponent(final BufferedReader pInputHandle)
    {
        try
        {
            String tLine = pInputHandle.readLine();
            iTotalWidth = Integer.parseInt(tLine);
            tLine = pInputHandle.readLine();
            iTotalHeight = Integer.parseInt(tLine);
            iShapesCollection = new ShapesCollection(pInputHandle);
        }
        catch(final Exception pException)
        {
            iTotalWidth = 0;
            iTotalHeight = 0;
            iShapesCollection = null;
            throw new IllegalArgumentException();
        }
    }
    public void paintComponent(final Graphics pGraphics)
    {
        final int tNumberOfShapes = iShapesCollection.size();
        for (int tShapeNumber = 0;
                tShapeNumber<tNumberOfShapes; tShapeNumber++)
        {
            final Shape tShape = iShapesCollection.get(tShapeNumber);
            tShape.draw(pGraphics);
        }
    }
    public Dimension getPreferredSize()
    {
        return new Dimension(iTotalWidth, iTotalHeight);
    }
}
```

Figure 19.14 A class for a GUI component that displays a collection of shapes.

and the draw method of the Rectangle class can be:

```
public void draw(final Graphics pGraphics)
{
    final int tXLeft = getX() - iWidth/2;
    final int tYTop = getY() - iHeight/2;
    pGraphics.setColor(Color.green);
    pGraphics.drawRect(tXLeft, tYTop, iWidth, iHeight);
}
```

The revised versions of these classes are given in Figures 19.15 and 19.16.

```
// The Circle class is augmented with a draw method.
// Barry Cornelius, 20 June 2000
import java.awt. Color;
import java.awt. Graphics;
public class Circle extends Shape
{
    private int iRadius;
    ... same as in Figure 19.4
    public String toString()
    {
        return super.toString() + ":" + iRadius;
    }
    public void draw(final Graphics pGraphics)
    {
        final int tXTopLeft = getX() - iRadius;
        final int tYTopLeft = getY() - iRadius;
        pGraphics.setColor(Color.magenta);
        pGraphics.fillOval(tXTopLeft, tYTopLeft, iRadius*2, iRadius*2);
    }
}
```

Figure 19.15   The Circle class is augmented with a draw method.

19.5.3 Introducing an abstract method called draw

There is one other change that has to be made. The code of the paintComponent method of the ShapesJComponent class (in Figure 19.14) includes:

```
tShape.draw(pGraphics);
```

The variable tShape is a reference variable of the class type Shape. With the declaration of the Shape class given previously (in Figure 19.3), it is not possible to call draw with tShape as a target because the Shape class does not have a draw method (even though each subclass of Shape has a draw method).

We could get round this problem by adding the following declaration to Shape:

```
public void draw(final Graphics pGraphics)
{
}
```

```
// The Rectangle class is augmented with a draw method.
// Barry Cornelius, 20 June 2000
import java.awt. Color;
import java.awt. Graphics;
public class Rectangle extends Shape
{
    private int iWidth;
    private int iHeight;
    ... same as in Figure 19.5
    public String toString()
    {
        return super.toString() + ":" + iWidth + ":" + iHeight;
    }
    public void draw(final Graphics pGraphics)
    {
        final int tXLeft = getX() - iWidth/2;
        final int tYTop = getY() - iHeight/2;
        pGraphics.setColor(Color.green);
        pGraphics.drawRect(tXLeft, tYTop, iWidth, iHeight);
    }
}
```

Figure 19.16   The `Rectangle` class is augmented with a `draw` method.

However, it is better style to use the following declaration:

```
abstract public void draw(Graphics pGraphics);
```

This is the declaration of an **abstract method**. It looks weird as it does not have a method body. Its inclusion in the `Shape` class means that it is now possible to write:

```
tShape.draw(pGraphics);
```

If a class has an abstract method, the class must be an *abstract class* (see Section 19.3.5).

```
abstract public class Shape
{
    ...
}
```

The revised version of the `Shape` class is given in Figure 19.17. Consider `Shape`'s declaration of `draw` again:

- The use of `abstract` with `draw`'s declaration means that a subclass is required to give a full (i.e. a non-abstract) declaration of `draw` – however, the subclass can give an abstract declaration of `draw` if the subclass is also abstract.

- The use of the `abstract` modifier and the absence of a method body is better than an empty method body. This is because the use of an abstract method documents that, although it is sensible to apply `draw` to an object that is of a subclass of `Shape`, it is not sensible (and not permitted) to apply `draw` to an object that is of the `Shape` class itself.

```
// An abstract class for two-dimensional shapes that has a draw method.
// Barry Cornelius, 20 June 2000
import java.awt. Graphics;
abstract public class Shape
{
    private int iX;
    private int iY;
    ... same as in Figure 19.3
    public String toString()
    {
        return iX + ":" + iY;
    }
    abstract public void draw(Graphics pGraphics);
}
```

Figure 19.17   An abstract class for two-dimensional shapes that has a draw method.

19.5.4 Adding a new geometrical shape

In Section 19.5.1, the use of the instanceof operator was frowned on. If instanceof were used, it would be necessary to modify the code of paintComponent each time some other geometrical shape were introduced. Instead, a draw
method was added to each class that represents a shape. By this means, the only part
of the code that needs to be altered when a new shape is added is the code that reads
the data, i.e. the code of the ShapesCollection class. Because the rest of the code
of the program is written in terms of the abstract superclass Shape, new subclasses
can be added and immediately used without any impact on the code.

19.6 Upgrading by inheritance

Suppose you have produced a class (called X) and that this has been successfully used
by a number of programs for several years. Suppose that some new program requires
a class that is similar to X, but which has some new features.

For example, X might be the class PersonImpl if you are upgrading it to provide
details about a person's home address as well as their name, date of birth, phone
number and height.

If you modify the code of X, you would need to re-compile and re-test each program
that used the previous version of X. Instead, you could derive a new class (e.g. Y)
from X:

```
public class Y extends X
{
    ...
}
```

In this way, existing programs can continue to use X and new programs can be written in terms of Y (which has all the features of X and some additional features).

Of course, if later on some more features are required, you could then derive a class Z from Y:

```
public class Z extends Y
{

    ...

}
```

This class would offer not only the new features, but those declared in Y and X as well.

As you can see, this technique provides an easy way to reuse existing code. However, it should be used with caution. Nigel Warren and Philip Bishop say '... be very careful with inheritance for reuse; it is one of those techniques that is extremely appealing because it offers very powerful and simple ways to add features to your software at apparently little cost, but it also carries a number of downsides. If you are looking at some code and you find deep inheritance hierarchies, you may find that inheritance for reuse is the culprit that is making the code hard to understand, slow, and occupy far too much memory.' For more details about this, look at their book *Java in Practice* ([53]).

19.7 Choosing between composition and inheritance

19.7.1 Distinguishing between *is a* and *has a* relationships

Back in Section 12.5, we used Date and DateImpl when constructing the PersonImpl class. And in Section 19.2.3 we used PersonImpl when constructing the class StudentImpl. Two different techniques are being used to construct a new class from an existing class. We used *inheritance* to produce the class StudentImpl from the class PersonImpl, whereas the class PersonImpl contains a field (called iDateOfBirth) of type Date (and this is made to point to a DateImpl object). This is called **composition** (or **aggregation**): the class PersonImpl is *composed* of a field of type Date.

Earlier, we said we used inheritance because the new class 'is a more specialized form of another class'. It is best to use inheritance for what are sometimes called **is-a relationships** and to use composition for **has-a relationships**. So, one test for deciding whether to use inheritance or composition is to see whether it makes sense to use the word *every* with either the words *is a* or the words *has a*. For example, *every person is a date* is nonsense whereas *every person has a date* (for their date of birth) makes sense.

For a new class, it is sometimes difficult to decide whether to use inheritance or composition, i.e. to decide whether it should be derived from an existing class or whether it should have a field of that class.

When making a decision about this, we need to be very clear about the purpose of each class. Consider the class Circle which we derived from Shape. Both the phrases *every circle is a shape* and *every circle has a shape* make sense. So, this does not help. If, instead, we had used the name Figure instead of Shape, then *every circle is a figure* makes sense, whereas *every circle has a figure* does not. From this analysis, it was right to use inheritance, i.e. to derive Circle from Shape although it would probably be better to use the name Figure rather than Shape. However, if we had chosen the name Position instead of Shape, then, because *every circle has a position* makes sense whereas *every circle is a position* does not, we might have chosen composition rather than inheritance.

19.7.2 Sometimes it is obvious as to which to use

For some classes, the answer about whether to use inheritance or composition is clear-cut. For example, if we want to declare a paintComponent method then we will not get the desired effect unless we use inheritance, i.e. we have to subclass the JComponent class. However, if we want full control over what methods a client uses, then we had better use composition – this is a use of the *adapter pattern*. If, instead, we use inheritance a client is able to use any of the methods of the superclass.

19.7.3 Reworking previous classes to use inheritance

In this book, we take the view that programmers often use inheritance when it may be preferable to use composition. Many of the classes given in earlier chapters have been coded using composition whereas other programmers might have used inheritance.

The obvious sign is a class where the adapter pattern has been used, i.e. a class has a private field that is of some class type and it uses many of the methods of this other class. It is indicated by a <<has>> dependency in a class diagram.

Consider the class PersonForm given in Figure 13.23. This is being used to display a PersonForm like that shown in Figure 13.22. To achieve this, the PersonForm class has a private field called iBox that is a Box and PersonForm's constructor applies some of Box's methods to this object. So the class PersonForm uses composition: the class PersonForm is composed of an object of type Box.

Instead of PersonForm having a private field of type Box, it could be derived from Box. The new version of PersonForm is given in Figure 19.18. In the new code, the iBox field has been removed, and so all of the references to iBox have been changed.

As PersonForm is derived from Box, a PersonForm object is a Box object and so there is no longer a need for the getGUI method, hence this has also been removed. This has an effect on any clients of PersonForm: the new form of PersonInput-Dialog is given in Figure 19.19.

So should PersonForm be coded using inheritance or composition? i.e. should the code of Figure 19.18 and Figure 19.19 be preferred to that of Figure 13.23 and Figure 13.26?

```
// A class that can be used to create a form for a person
// Barry Cornelius, 20 June 2000
...  same as in Figure 13.23
public class PersonForm extends Box
{
    private JTextField iNameJTextField;
    private JTextField iDateOfBirthJTextField;
    private JTextField iPhoneNumberJTextField;
    private JTextField iHeightJTextField;
    public PersonForm()
    {
        super(BoxLayout.Y_AXIS);
        final Dimension tDimension = new Dimension(120, 20);
        ...  same as in Figure 13.23
        tThirdRowBox.add(iHeightJTextField);
        // now create the form
        add(tNameBox);
        add(tDateOfBirthBox);
        add(tThirdRowBox);
    }
    public Person getPerson()
    {
        ...  same as in Figure 13.23
    }
    public void setPerson(final Person pPerson)
    {
        ...  same as in Figure 13.23
    }
}
```

Figure 19.18 A class that can be used to create a form for a person.

Although it might be argued that a `PersonForm` object is a specialized form of a `Box` and that inheritance should be used, this book argues that this is incorrect:

- The `Box` object is just used for one aspect of the `PersonForm` object.
- There are many methods of the `Box` class that we do not wish a client to use. For example, it would make no sense for a client to apply `add` to a `PersonForm` object to add additional rows to the form because the other methods of `PersonForm` just know about the first three rows. If inheritance is used, it is very easy for the client to apply `add` to the `PersonForm` object. However, if composition is used, it is a little more difficult: the client would first have to cast the result of the call of `getGUI` to the `Box` class before the method can be called.

So, if we use composition rather than inheritance, we retain a little more control over the way in which this class is used.

```
// A class that presents a dialog box for inputting values about a person.
// Barry Cornelius, 20 June 2000
... same as in Figure 13.26
public class PersonInputDialog implements ActionListener
{
    private PersonForm iPersonForm;
    private JDialog iJDialog;
    public PersonInputDialog(final JFrame pJFrame, final int pX, final int pY)
    {
        iPersonForm = new PersonForm();
        final JButton tJButton = new JButton("OK");
        tJButton.addActionListener(this);
        iJDialog = new JDialog(pJFrame, "PersonInputDialog", true);
        iJDialog.getContentPane().add(iPersonForm, BorderLayout.CENTER);
        iJDialog.getContentPane().add(tJButton,    BorderLayout.SOUTH);
        iJDialog.setLocation(pX, pY);
        iJDialog.pack();
        iJDialog.setVisible(true);
    }
    public void actionPerformed(final ActionEvent pActionEvent)
    {
        ... same as in Figure 13.26
    }
    public Person getPerson()
    {
        ... same as in Figure 13.26
    }
}
```

Figure 19.19   A class that presents a dialog box for inputting values about a person.

19.8) Providing a better way of cloning

19.8.1 What is wrong with using a constructor for cloning

So far, when producing a new class, we have often added a constructor that enables us to clone an object of the class. For example, suppose that we have at some point created a `PersonImpl` object:

```
Person tPerson = new PersonImpl("Smith%1970-6-12%01987-654322%1.85");
```

we can at some later point create a clone of this object by:

```
Person tClonePerson = new PersonImpl(tPerson);
```

We can do this because `PersonImpl` provides a constructor that can be used for cloning.

This works fine provided `tPerson` is pointing to a `PersonImpl` object, but it may in fact instead be pointing to an object of some subclass. If we do:

```
Person tPerson =
        new StudentImpl("Smith%1970-6-12%01987-654322%1.85@Computing@27");
```

and later do:

```
Person tClonePerson = new PersonImpl(tPerson);
```

then we will not get `tClonePerson` pointing to a copy of the `StudentImpl` object. This would be a real problem if, for instance, we were trying to make a copy of a list where some of the elements are of class `PersonImpl` and some are of class `StudentImpl`.

Although we could provide:

```
Person tClonePerson = null;
if (tPerson instanceof StudentImpl)
{
    tClonePerson = new StudentImpl(tPerson);
}
else
{
    tClonePerson = new PersonImpl(tPerson);
}
```

this is not a good programming style.

Suppose that instead of using a constructor:

```
Person tClonePerson = new PersonImpl(tPerson);
```

we execute something like:

```
Person tClonePerson = tPerson.clone();
```

By providing both `PersonImpl` and `StudentImpl` with suitable `clone` methods, this will execute `PersonImpl`'s `clone` method if `tPerson` points to a `PersonImpl` object, and `StudentImpl`'s `clone` method if `tPerson` points to a `StudentImpl` object.

19.8.2 Overriding `Object`'s `clone` method

The class `java.lang.Object` provides a method called `clone`. The header of this method is:

```
public Object clone();
```

When it is used on an object, it returns a new instance of the existing object which contains a copy of all the fields of the existing object. If you want a class to support cloning, it is best to override this method.

So, suppose we want to modify the Date interface and the DateImpl class so that it supports a clone method. To say that our class now supports a clone method, we will add the following header to the Date interface:

```
public Object clone();
```

and add the following method to the DateImpl class:

```
public Object clone()
{
    try
    {
        return super.clone();
    }
    catch(final CloneNotSupportedException pCloneNotSupportedException)
    {
        throw new InternalError();
    }
}
```

This method might be used as follows:

```
Date tDate = new DateImpl(2000, 5, 1);
...
Date tCloneDate = (Date)tDate.clone();
```

The call tDate.clone() is an execution of DateImpl's clone method. When this happens, the following statement will get executed:

```
return super.clone();
```

So, the value that is returned is the value produced by the clone method of DateImpl's superclass which is the class Object. This just returns a copy of the object to which this method is being applied: in this example, the method is being applied to tDate. So we get:

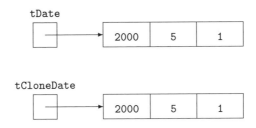

Figure 19.20 shows the new modified versions of the Date interface and the DateImpl class.

```
// A type for representing dates that provides a clone method.
// Barry Cornelius, 20 June 2000
public interface Date extends Cloneable
{
    public int getYear();
    ... same as in Figure 11.14
    public Object clone();
}
...........................................................................
// A class implementing the Date interface that has a clone method.
// Barry Cornelius, 20 June 2000
import java.util. StringTokenizer;
public class DateImpl implements Date
{
    private int iYear;
    private int iMonth;
    private int iDay;
    ... same as in Figure 11.16
    public Object clone()
    {
      try
      {
        return super.clone();
      }
      catch(final CloneNotSupportedException pCloneNotSupportedException)
      {
        throw new InternalError();
      }
    }
}
```

Figure 19.20   Modifying Date-DateImpl to implement clone.

Note that if the code of a method of a class wishes to call Object's clone method, then:

● The class must implement the Cloneable interface. Above we have done this by making Date a subinterface of Cloneable. This interface forms part of the java.lang package. As the Cloneable interface is empty:

```
public interface Cloneable
{
}
```

you do not have to supply any method declarations in order to implement it.

● The code must catch the CloneNotSupportedException exception even though this exception cannot actually happen.

For some details about why this is the case, see Curio 19.8.

19.8.3 Providing a deep copy rather than a shallow copy

When writing the code of `clone`, we need to consider whether we want to adopt the *share approach* or the *clone approach* when a class has one or more fields that are of a reference type. This is illustrated by the code shown in Figure 19.21 which contains modified versions of the `Person` interface and the `PersonImpl` class.

```
// A type for representing people that provides a clone method.
// Barry Cornelius, 20 June 2000
public interface Person extends Cloneable, Comparable
{
    public String getName();
    ... same as in Figure 12.6
    public Object clone();
}
.............................................................................
// A class implementing the Person interface that has a clone method.
// Barry Cornelius, 20 June 2000
import java.util. StringTokenizer;
public class PersonImpl implements Person
{
    private String iName;
    private Date iDateOfBirth;
    private String iPhoneNumber;
    private double iHeight;
    ... same as in Figure 12.7
    public Object clone()
    {
        try
        {
            final PersonImpl tPersonImpl = (PersonImpl)super.clone();
            if (iDateOfBirth!=null)
            {
                tPersonImpl.iDateOfBirth = (Date)iDateOfBirth.clone();
            }
            return tPersonImpl;
        }
        catch(final CloneNotSupportedException pCloneNotSupportedException)
        {
            throw new InternalError();
        }
    }
}
```

Figure 19.21 Modifying `Person-PersonImpl` to implement `clone`.

Suppose a client contains:

```
Person tPerson = new PersonImpl("Smith%1970-6-12%2468%1.85");
...
Person tClonePerson = tPerson.clone();
```

When this call of `clone` is executed, the following statement from `PersonImpl`'s `clone` method:

```
final PersonImpl tPersonImpl = (PersonImpl)super.clone();
```

uses `Object`'s `clone` method to produce a copy of the object to which `clone` is being applied, in this case, `tPerson`.

The result is illustrated by this diagram:

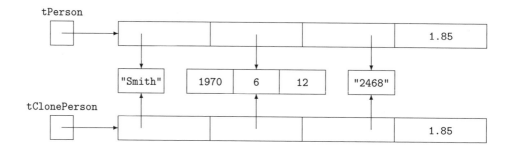

Because all the objects are shared, this is known as a **shallow copy**.

Although there is no problem with the sharing of the fields that are `Strings` (because `Strings` are immutable), the code of `PersonImpl`'s `clone` method moves on to ensure that the `iDateOfBirth` fields are not shared. It executes:

```
tPersonImpl.iDateOfBirth = (Date)iDateOfBirth.clone();
```

This alters the `iDateOfBirth` field of `tPersonImpl` to be a clone of `tPerson`'s `iDateOfBirth` field. This code uses the new versions of `Date` and `DateImpl` that were given in Figure 19.20.

This extra code ensures that the mutable field is not shared: it ensures that a **deep copy** is produced.

The value of `tPersonImpl` then gets returned by the `clone` method, and this is the value that is assigned to `tClonePerson`:

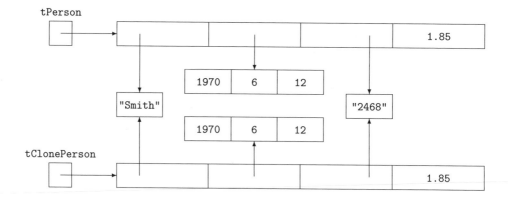

19.8.4 Using a `clone` method in preference to a constructor

At the moment, `Date-DateImpl` (and `Person-PersonImpl`) provide both a constructor and a method for cloning. For example, `Date-DateImpl` provides the constructor:

```
public DateImpl(final Date pDate)
{
    this(pDate.getYear(), pDate.getMonth(), pDate.getDay());
}
```

as well as the method:

```
public Object clone()
{
    ...
}
```

Given that we are providing a `clone` method, there is now no need for this class to provide the constructor, as any uses of the constructor can be replaced by calls of the `clone` method.

For example, the code of the `PersonImpl` class currently contains:

```
public Date getDateOfBirth()
{
    return new DateImpl(iDateOfBirth);
}
...
public void setDateOfBirth(final Date pDateOfBirth)
{
    iDateOfBirth = new DateImpl(pDateOfBirth);
}
```

This code can be replaced by:

```
public Date getDateOfBirth()
{
    return (Date)iDateOfBirth.clone();
}
...
public void setDateOfBirth(final Date pDateOfBirth)
{
    iDateOfBirth = (Date)pDateOfBirth.clone();
}
```

19.8.5 Providing a `clone` method for a subclass

Suppose we now move on to provide `clone` for the `Student-StudentImpl` type. When `clone` is applied to a `StudentImpl` object, `StudentImpl`'s `clone` method needs to execute two steps:

1. Execute PersonImpl's clone method. This will do two things:

    (a) Execute Object's clone method which will create a new instance of the StudentImpl object.

    (b) Make the iDateOfBirth field point to a clone of the DateImpl object rather than to the original DateImpl object.

2. Do a *deep copy* of any fields declared in StudentImpl that are of a reference type which has mutable objects.

As the only fields of StudentImpl are a String and an int, there is nothing to do for the second step. And the first step can be performed simply by doing:

```
return super.clone():
```

The changes for Student and StudentImpl are shown in Figure 19.22.

```
// A type for representing students that provides a clone method.
// Barry Cornelius, 20 June 2000
public interface Student extends Person
{
    public int getStudentNumber();
    ... same as in Figure 19.1
    public Object clone();
}
..........................................................................
// A class implementing the Student interface that has a clone method.
// Barry Cornelius, 20 June 2000
import java.util. StringTokenizer;
public class StudentImpl extends PersonImpl implements Student
{
    private String iCourseName;
    private int iStudentNumber;
    ... same as in Figure 19.2
    public Object clone()
    {
        return super.clone();
    }
}
```

Figure 19.22   Modifying Student-StudentImpl to implement clone.

Note that, unlike the new code for Date-DateImpl and Person-PersonImpl, the new code for Student-StudentImpl does not say that it implements the Cloneable interface and the code of StudentImpl's clone method does not catch the CloneNotSupportedException exception. The need to do these two things occurs only when you are providing clone for a class that is a direct subclass of Object.

For more details about cloning, see Curio 19.7.

19.1 If you want a class to have a `paintComponent` method (that overrides the `paintComponent` method of `JComponent`), it is necessary to derive the class from the `JComponent` class.

19.2 If you produce a new class as a subclass of `JComponent`, and you override `paintComponent`, you should also override `getPreferredSize` as was mentioned in Section 19.4. If you fail to do this, your subclass of `JComponent` will be allocated a size of 1 pixel by 1 pixel, and so whatever you are painting will not immediately be visible. You could make it visible by resizing the `JFrame`'s window (using the window manager of the environment in which you are running the Java program).

19.3 If a class is a direct subclass of `Object` and it wishes to provide a `clone` method that overrides `Object`'s `clone` method, then:

● the class must implement the `Cloneable` interface;

● the `clone` method must either handle the `CloneNotSupportedExcep-tion` exception or the header of the `clone` method must include the throws clause:

```
throws CloneNotSupportedException
```

19.4 Although a class that wishes to implement `clone` must provide a method with the header:

```
public Object clone();
```

do not confuse this with the `Cloneable` interface. The `clone` method is not in this interface: instead, the `Cloneable` interface is empty:

```
public interface Cloneable
{
}
```

19.5 The WWW pages for `Object`'s `clone` method says that any method that overrides `Object`'s `clone` method should not call a constructor.

19.1 In Curio 4.2, it was mentioned that when calling a class method it is possible for the name appearing on the left-hand side of the dot to be either the name of a class or the name of a reference variable (of the appropriate class). In Curio 4.2, it was suggested that it is a lot less confusing and a lot more helpful to use the name of a class. An example is:

```
double tFirst = Double.parseDouble(tLine);
```

Suppose the classes `PersonImpl` and `StudentImpl` both provide a class method called `someMethod`, and suppose we have the following call of the method someMethod:

```
Person tPerson = ... ;
double tSomeValue = tPerson.someMethod(tSomeArguments);
```

Here the class method is being called with the name of a reference variable on the left of the dot. By using the name of a variable rather than the name of a class, the particular someMethod method that gets called depends on what kind of object tPerson is pointing to when the statement gets executed.

19.2 So far, a *member* of a class has had either a public or a private modifier. If a member of a class has no modifier at all, it can be accessed by the code of any class within the same *package*. As mentioned in Curio 11.12, this sort of access is sometimes called *package access*. The topic of packages is considered in more detail in Section 21.4. If, instead, a member of a class has a protected modifier, it can be accessed by the code of any class within the same package or by the code of any subclass (whether or not it is in the same package).

So, the code of any method of a subclass may access any public and protected members of a superclass.

Consider the class Shape again. It is given in Figure 19.3. If we want some members of the class Shape to be accessible in Shape and in any subclass of Shape but generally to be inaccessible, those members should be made protected members of the class Shape. However, if we want a member of the class Shape to be inaccessible in the code of a subclass, it needs to be a private member of the class Shape.

The class declaration for Shape has iX and iY as private fields. So the code of a method of the class Circle is unable to access these fields directly, and uses Shape's getX and getY to access their values. Instead, Shape could declare iX and iY to be protected in which case they would not only be accessible from the code of Shape but they could also be accessed from the code of Circle (and any other subclasses of Shape).

Some people argue that it is inappropriate for a subclass to be able to access fields of its superclass: they would argue that, like the Shape given in Figure 19.3, it is better for these fields to be private and for the superclass to provide public methods to access them.

19.3 Although an interface can extend more than one interface, it is not possible for a class to extend more than one class. So, unlike C++, in Java you cannot derive a class from more than one class, i.e. Java does not have **multiple inheritance**.

19.4 In Section 19.2.6, it was pointed out that, if a constructor uses an *explicit constructor invocation statement* to initialize the fields of its superclass, that statement must appear as the first statement of the constructor. There are other restrictions: an explicit constructor invocation statement cannot refer to any instance variables or instance methods declared in the class or in any superclass.

19.5   If the first statement of the constructor of a subclass is not an *explicit constructor invocation statement*, the fields of the superclass are initialized by executing the constructor of the superclass that has no parameters. In this situation, a compilation error will occur if the superclass provides at least one constructor but does not provide one with no parameters.

19.6   Several examples of inheritance have been provided in this chapter. For example, in Section 19.2.3, StudentImpl was derived from PersonImpl and, in Section 19.3.2 and Section 19.3.3, Circle and Rectangle were derived from Shape.

When producing StudentImpl we chose (in Section 19.2.4) not to provide an equals method, and so the equals of PersonImpl will be used if equals is applied to a StudentImpl object: so two people/students are the same person/student if their names are the same.

However, when producing Circle (and Rectangle) from Shape, we chose (in Section 19.3.2) to provide Circle with an equals method (that overrides Shape's equals method): this is because we need to say that two circles are the same if and only if they have the same radius (as well as the same x and y values).

Since Chapter 11, we have been using the same skeleton for the code of equals:

```
public boolean equals(final Object pObject)
{
    if ( pObject==null || getClass()!=pObject.getClass() )
    {
        return false;
    }
    return ... ;
}
```

This code involves two calls of getClass. Another coding for equals that is often used is illustrated by the following skeleton:

```
public boolean equals(final Object pObject)
{
    if ( ! (pObject instanceof X) )
    {
        return false;
    }
    return ... ;
}
```

where X is the name of the class. Although this code using the instanceof operator looks easier to understand, it is not really appropriate to use this code when you use inheritance and you want a subclass to override the version of equals provided by the superclass.

So, although there would be no problem with using the instanceof code in the equals method provided by PersonImpl (and used by StudentImpl), there would be a problem with using it in the equals method provided by Shape which is overridden by Circle (and Rectangle). The problem is that the version of equals provided by Shape would then not satisfy one of the rules of the contract of equals mentioned at $API/java/lang/Object.html. This rule says that the equals method 'is **symmetric**: for any reference values x and y, x.equals(y) should return true if and only if y.equals(x) returns true'.

Suppose we were to provide Shape with the following version of equals:

```
public boolean equals(final Object pObject)
{
    if ( ! (pObject instanceof Shape) )
    {
        return false;
    }
    final Shape tShape = (Shape)pObject;
    return iX==tShape.iX && iY==tShape.iY;
}
```

and provided Circle with the following version of equals:

```
public boolean equals(final Object pObject)
{
    if ( ! (pObject instanceof Circle) )
    {
        return false;
    }
    return super.equals(pObject) && iRadius==((Circle)pObject).iRadius;
}
```

Then, we would have a problem when we use equals with two objects, one of which is of class Shape and the other is of one of the subclasses of Shape, e.g. Circle. This can be illustrated by executing the code:

```
Shape tShape = new Shape(1, 2);
Circle tCircle = new Circle(5, 1, 2);
System.out.println(tShape.equals(tCircle));
System.out.println(tCircle.equals(tShape));
```

The first call of equals is being applied to a Shape object and so we will use Shape's equals method. The call will lead to pObject pointing to an object of class Circle. So what happens with the test pObject instanceof Shape? Is this going to deliver *true* or *false* when pObject is pointing to a Circle object? Well, for a condition that has the form:

RelationalExpression instanceof *ReferenceType*

the JLS says: 'At run time, the result of the instanceof operator is true if the value of the *RelationalExpression* is not null and the reference could be cast to the *ReferenceType* without raising a ClassCastException'. Since the cast (Shape)pObject is allowed when pObject is pointing to a Circle object, then pObject instanceof Shape is allowed and has the value *true*. So the code moves on and produces the value *true* or *false* depending on whether the x and y values of the two objects are the same. In the above example, they are the same, and so the value *true* will be produced.

The second call of equals will always produce the value *false*: this is because tShape does not satisfy the test that checks whether the parameter is an instanceof Circle.

So, when an equals method is written using instanceof, it does not always satisfy the symmetric rule. For more information about this, see:

- pages 44 to 59 of the book *Practical Java* ([21]) by Peter Haggar;

- at [29], there is a WWW page containing an article by Mark Roulo entitled 'How to avoid traps and correctly override methods from java.lang.Object'.

In his article, Mark Roulo uses equals to compare the results of the two calls of getClass, i.e. instead of:

```
if (pObject==null || getClass()!=pObject.getClass())
```

he has code like:

```
if (pObject==null || !(getClass().equals(pObject.getClass())))
```

However, this book argues that it is unnecessary to use equals as there is no problem with using ==. This view is supported by the code given by Peter Haggar.

Both authors point out that instanceof (rather than getClass) is used in the code of the equals methods of some of the classes of Java's Core APIs. And so you will run into the non-symmetric problem if you want to produce a subclass of one of these classes. In his book, Peter Haggar says: 'A quick glance through the source code of the Java libraries shows the use of instanceof in equals method implementations is common. You also find the use of getClass. The Java libraries are not consistent in how they implement the equals methods of their classes, thereby making consistent equality comparisons difficult'.

19.7 Section 19.8 gave details of how to provide a clone method. For more details about cloning, see:

- the article by Mark Roulo mentioned in Curio 19.6;

- at [48], you will find an article by Bill Venners entitled 'The canonical object idiom'.

19.8 If a method of a class calls `Object`'s `clone` method, the class must implement `Cloneable` and the method must handle the `CloneNotSupported Exception` exception. This is because the code of `Object`'s `clone` method looks like this:

```
public Object clone() throws CloneNotSupportedException
{
    if (this instanceof Cloneable)
    {
        return ...   // return a clone of this;
    }
    throw new CloneNotSupportedException();
}
```

19.9 Since the `equals` method and the `compareTo` method are related, you may wish to ensure each class establishes the correct relationship between these two methods. One way of doing this would be to define an abstract class that provides an implementation of `equals` in terms of `compareTo` declaring `compareTo` to be an abstract method. Such a class appears in Figure 19.23.

```
// An abstract class providing equals implemented in terms of compareTo.
// Barry Cornelius, 20 June 2000
abstract public class Equality implements Comparable
{
    final public boolean equals(final Object pObject)
    {
        if (pObject==null || getClass()!=pObject.getClass())
        {
            return false;
        }
        return this.compareTo(pObject)==0;
    }
    abstract public int compareTo(Object pObject);
}
```

Figure 19.23   An abstract class that implements `equals` in terms of `compareTo`.

Having produced this abstract class, we can derive subclasses of `Equality` that automatically have an appropriate `equals` method.

This code shows a new use of the `final` modifier. Its use with the declaration of the `equals` method means that no subclass of `Equality` may override this declaration of `equals`.

19.10 Figure 8.4 and Figure 11.4 present simplified views of the syntax of method declarations and class declarations as they incorrectly do not allow for the possibility of abstract methods and abstract classes.

19.11 If you ever want to get a drawing surface repainted, do not call the `paintComponent` method (or the `paint` method): your program should call `JComponent`'s `repaint` method instead.

19.12 Before the Java 2 Platform and the Swing API appeared, the painting facilities of the class `java.awt.Graphics` were used with a class called `Canvas` that is in the `java.awt` package. When using the Java 2 Platform, it is better to use the Swing API's `JComponent` class rather than `java.awt`'s `Canvas` class.

19.13 Before the Java 2 Platform and the Swing API appeared, painting was done by overriding a method called `paint`. The `JComponent` class also has a method called `paint`, and it is possible to override that method instead of `paintComponent`. However, this is not recommended. At [14], you will find an article by Amy Fowler entitled 'Painting in AWT and Swing'. In it, she says:

> [Swing] ... factors the `paint()` call into three separate methods, which are invoked in the following order:
>
> ```
> protected void paintComponent(Graphics g)
> protected void paintBorder(Graphics g)
> protected void paintChildren(Graphics g)
> ```
>
> Swing programs should override `paintComponent()` *instead of* overriding `paint()`. Although the API allows it, there is generally no reason to override `paintBorder()` or `paintChildren()` (and if you do, make sure you know what you're doing!).

If you want to give a drawing surface a border then, rather than overriding `paintBorder()`, you should instead call `JComponent`'s `setBorder` method. The argument that is passed to this method must be an object of a class that implements the `javax.swing.border.Border` interface (such as an object of any of the classes listed in the 'Direct known subclasses' section of the WWW page at $API/javax/swing/border/AbstractBorder.html). If you have used `setBorder`, you must override `paintComponent` rather than `paint` because the border only gets painted when `paintBorder` is called. It is `JComponent`'s `paint` method that calls the `paintBorder` method, and so, if you override `paint`, `JComponent`'s `paintBorder` will not get called.

19.14 In Section 13.11, an `ExitWindowListener` class was produced by implementing the interface `java.awt.event.WindowListener` – it appears in Figure 13.16. Although we only wanted to provide code for one of the methods, we had to provide empty blocks for the other six methods. Instead of providing a `WindowListener` class by implementing this interface, the class can instead be provided by extending `java.awt.event.WindowAdapter`. Such a class is shown in Figure 19.24.

    An `ExitWindowAdapter` object is used in the same way as an `ExitWindowListener` object:

```
final ExitWindowAdapter tExitWindowAdapter = new ExitWindowAdapter();
tJFrame.addWindowListener(tExitWindowAdapter);
```

```
// A class that extends WindowAdapter and exits when its window is closed.
// Barry Cornelius, 20 June 2000
import java.awt.         Window;
import java.awt.event. WindowAdapter;
import java.awt.event. WindowEvent;
public class ExitWindowAdapter extends WindowAdapter
{
    public void windowClosing(final WindowEvent pWindowEvent)
    {
        final Window tWindow = pWindowEvent.getWindow();
        tWindow.setVisible(false);
        tWindow.dispose();
        System.exit(0);
    }
}
```

Figure 19.24   A class extending `WindowAdapter` that exits on closing the window.

19.15   Although this chapter has developed its own classes called `Circle` and
`Rectangle`, in practice these would not be used: there are more suitable
classes in the `java.awt` and `java.awt.geom` packages. In particular, the
subclasses of `java.awt.geom.RectangularShape` are useful. A list of
these subclasses is given in the 'Direct known subclasses' section of the WWW
page at $API/java/awt/geom/RectangularShape.html.

Exercises

19.1   Modify the `PopImplProg` program (that was given in Figure 17.16) in the
way suggested by Section 19.2.8.

19.2   Produce an interface called `Employee` and a class `EmployeeImpl`. The
`Employee` interface should be a subinterface of `Person` and the class
`EmployeeImpl` should be derived from `PersonImpl` (and implement
`Employee`). Employees should be represented by their name, their date of
birth, their phone number, their height, their employee number and their
jobtitle.
   Modify the program produced as a solution to Exercise 19.1 so that it
can handle employees as well. Use the letter `e` to add an employee to the
population.

19.3   Modify the `ShapesJComponentProg` program (described in Section 19.5)
so that it can handle the following lines of data:

```
0
60
50
Eddie Stobart
```

So a 0 in the data signifies this new kind of geometrical shape. When drawn, it should output the string at the given x and y coordinates using bold characters in a sans serif font. You will need to use `Graphics`'s `setFont` method in order to do this. This method has a parameter that is of the type `java.awt.Font`. For more details about this class, see the WWW page at $API/java/awt/Font.html.

19.4 Modify the declarations of the `Circle` and `Rectangle` classes (given in Figure 19.15 and Figure 19.16) so that they both declare a method with the following heading:

```
public void drawAreaValue(final Graphics pGraphics,
                          final int pX, final int pY);
```

This method should calculate the area of the circle/rectangle and use `Graphic`'s `drawString` method to output the value of the area to the drawing surface at the position given by `pX` and `pY`. Hint: if you need the formulae for the area of a circle/rectangle, look at the details given in Exercise 14.9.

Modify the `Shape` class (given in Figure 19.17) so that it has the declaration of an abstract method called `drawAreaValue`.

Modify the `ShapesJComponent` class (given in Figure 19.14) so that its `paintComponent` method calls `drawAreaValue` as well as `draw`. Use appropriate values for the second and third arguments of the call of `drawAreaValue` to ensure that the output appears nicely on the screen.

Test the new versions of these classes with the `ShapesJComponentProg` program (given in Figure 19.13).

Chapter 20

Producing applets (for use with the WWW)

One of the main reasons why Java is so well known is that it is possible for Java code to be run when you visit a WWW page. Such pieces of code are called *applets*.

In this chapter, we look at how to write Java source code so that it can be run as an applet from a WWW page. This will be done by overriding methods such as `init`, `start` and `paint`. We also need to be aware of the restrictions that are placed on code that is executed as an applet.

We will find that the Java interpreters embedded in most WWW browsers are not able to run applets that use the new facilities of the Java 2 Platform. We will look at how the *Java Plug-in* can be used to circumvent this problem.

This chapter also looks at *Java Archives*, a way in which we can bundle together a collection of files. In particular, we will see that a Java Archive speeds up the downloading from the WWW of an applet's `.class` files.

20.1 Using HTML to code WWW pages

When you use a WWW browser (such as Netscape's Navigator or Microsoft's Internet Explorer) to display a WWW page, you will see a combination of paragraphs of text, bulleted lists of information, tables of information, images, links to other pages, and so on. The people that have prepared WWW pages have coded them (or have arranged for them to be coded) using the **HyperText Markup Language** (**HTML**).

An example of some HTML is given in Figure 20.1 – we will suppose that this text has been stored in a file called `Simple.html`. The HTML language involves the use of **tags** which usually occur in pairs. An example is `<P>` and `</P>` which are used to indicate that the embedded text should be displayed by the WWW browser as a paragraph.

```
<HTML>
<HEAD>
<TITLE>A Simple Example</TITLE>
</HEAD>
<BODY>
<P>
This is the first sentence of the first paragraph.   And here is the
second.
Here is a third sentence.   And
here is the last one of the first paragraph.
</P>
<P>
Here is a second paragraph.
It has a list of items:
<OL>
<LI>first point;</LI>
<LI>second point;</LI>
<LI>third point;</LI>
</OL>
</P>
</BODY>
</HTML>
```

Figure 20.1 An example of instructions in HTML (HyperText Markup Language).

When someone (perhaps on the other side of the world) uses a browser to visit this WWW page, the HTML instructions are transferred across the Internet to the browser; the browser interprets these instructions and then displays something within the browser's window. The HTML given in Figure 20.1 would cause a browser to display something like that given in Figure 20.2.

20.2 Executing Java when visiting a WWW page

Since the inception of the WWW in the early 1990s, people have been finding different ways of making a WWW page more appealing to the visitor to the page. When Sun

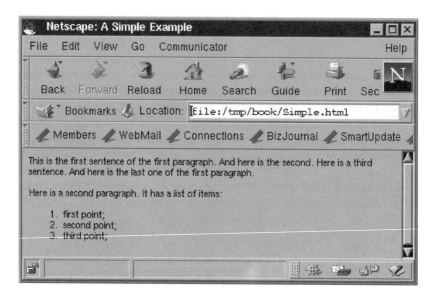

Figure 20.2 The output produced by the WWW page given in `Simple.html`.

produced Java in 1995, they thought it would be useful if Java code could be executed as part of browsing a WWW page. The Java code could do some processing and display its output within the pane of the WWW browser. They showed that this was possible by producing a WWW browser that had this capability – it was first called **WebRunner** and later called **HotJava**. They then persuaded Netscape whose browser (Navigator) was the most popular at that time to include a Java interpreter as part of the code of Navigator. Support for Java within Microsoft's Internet Explorer came later.

In order that the author of a WWW page could indicate which Java `.class` file was to be executed when the WWW page was loaded, HTML was altered to include an APPLET tag. An example of some HTML that includes an APPLET tag is given in Figure 20.3.

WWW browsers ignore tags that they do not understand. So if a WWW browser is given this HTML and it does not understand the APPLET tag, it will display the message `Java does not seem to be supported by your WWW browser`. However, if a WWW browser is capable of running Java, then, when the HTML interpreter of the browser sees this APPLET tag, it will start to obtain the bytecodes from the file mentioned in the CODE attribute of the APPLET tag (and ignore the text that appears between the APPLET and the /APPLET tag). So, with the HTML given in Figure 20.3, it would download the bytecodes that are in the file `HelloApplet.class`. Unless you also include a CODEBASE attribute, the browser will assume that this file is in the same directory from which it is obtaining the file containing the HTML instructions. There are details about using CODEBASE in Curio 20.1.

```
<HTML>
<HEAD>
<TITLE>The HelloApplet Example</TITLE>
</HEAD>
<BODY>
<P>
Start.
</P>
<APPLET CODE="HelloApplet.class" WIDTH="150" HEIGHT="25">
<P>Java does not seem to be supported by your WWW browser</P>
</APPLET>
<P>
Finish.
</P>
</BODY>
</HTML>
```

Figure 20.3 HTML having an `APPLET` tag referring to the `HelloApplet` class.

These bytecodes will be transferred from the `.class` file into a storage area known to the Java interpreter of the WWW browser. Often the bytecodes of a `.class` file will take some time to be transferred and so the rest of the WWW page is likely to be displayed before the bytecodes arrive. When the bytecodes have finally arrived, the browser's Java interpreter will execute them.

So, although the author of the WWW page compiled the Java source code on his/her computer, the `.class` file(s) that were produced by the compiler will be executed by the Java interpreter which forms part of the code of the WWW browser (that is running on the computer of the person visiting the WWW page).

20.3 Deriving from `Applet` instead of declaring `main`

The Java source code that we have produced in previous chapters has been for programs that we have run on our own computer. Such programs are called **Java applications**. We are now about to produce Java source code that is to be run by the Java interpreter of a WWW browser. This kind of source code is called a **Java applet**.

The source code for an applet is different from that for an application. For an application, we have been providing a class that has a method called `main`, and this is the method that is executed first when we run the `java` command, the command that executes a Java interpreter. For an applet, we do not provide a `main` method: instead, we derive a class from `java.applet.Applet` and override methods like `paint`, `init`, `start`, `stop` and `destroy`. We do this because this is what the Java interpreter contained in the WWW browser expects.

```
// The code of the HelloApplet applet paints a string.
// Barry Cornelius, 20 June 2000
import java.applet. Applet;
import java.awt.    Graphics;
public class HelloApplet extends Applet
{
   public void paint(Graphics pGraphics)
   {
      pGraphics.drawString("Hello world", 50, 25);
   }
}
```

Figure 20.4   The code of the HelloApplet applet paints a string.

An example of some Java source code that is a Java applet is given in Figure 20.4. This can be compiled in the usual way:

```
javac HelloApplet.java
```

in order to produce the file HelloApplet.class.

If we tell a WWW browser to read the WWW page given in Figure 20.3, then, when it reaches the APPLET tag, it knows it has to obtain the bytecodes contained in the file HelloApplet.class. When these bytecodes have arrived, the Java interpreter contained in the WWW browser will create an object of the HelloApplet class. And, because we have overridden the paint method, the code of this method will be executed. The result is displayed within the window of the browser (as shown in Figure 20.5).

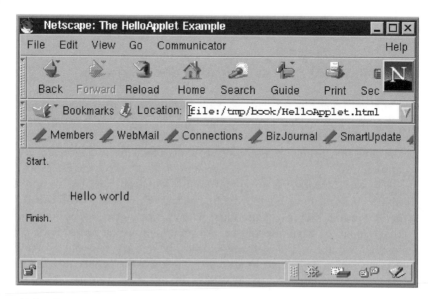

Figure 20.5   The output produced by the WWW page given in HelloApplet.html.

The code of `HelloApplet` is simple, and so the only classes that it depends on are classes from Java's Core APIs. However, normally the code for an applet will be dependent on other classes that the author has written. If this is the case, then, as the Java interpreter executes the bytecodes, it will detect that the bytecodes of other classes need to be downloaded, and so it will return to the author's WWW site to download the bytecodes from the appropriate `.class` files.

20.4 Dealing with the different versions of Java

Early versions of WWW browsers contain a Java interpreter that understands JDK 1.0.2, the version of Java that was prevalent at the time they were released. Each time a new version of a WWW browser is released, the latest version of the Java interpreter can be included in the browser. So the Java interpreter of some WWW browsers understand JDK 1.1.x (although, unfortunately, with many versions of WWW browsers, some parts of JDK 1.1.x are missing).

During the years 1996–1998, this led to a chaotic state of affairs: some browsers would only execute applets coded with JDK 1.0.2, and other browsers only understood parts of JDK 1.1. It also seemed unlikely that any browsers would provide a Java interpreter for the Java 2 Platform. The best advice during this time was to write the Java source code for Java applets in terms of the language and the APIs of JDK 1.0.2, and to compile the source code with the JDK 1.0.2 compiler. Even today, JDK 1.0.2 is still available from Sun at [33].

Of course, such an approach does not mean that you can reap the benefits of later versions of the Java Platform. For example, the way of handling events (such as the event of a user clicking a button) was improved between JDK 1.0 and JDK 1.1. And the Java 2 Platform brought the introduction of the Swing and Collection APIs.

The Java 2 Platform version of the `HelloApplet` applet (of Figure 20.4) is the `NewHelloApplet` applet that is given in Figure 20.6. This applet is derived from `JApplet`, a class that is in the `javax.swing` package. And, as shown in Figure 13.3, `JApplet` is itself derived from `java.applet.Applet`.

But, because `NewHelloApplet` uses the Java 2 Platform, what WWW browser can we use to run this applet?

```
// A version of the HelloApplet applet that uses the Swing API from Java 2.
// Barry Cornelius, 20 June 2000
import java.awt.    Graphics;
import javax.swing. JApplet;
public class NewHelloApplet extends JApplet
{
    public void paint(final Graphics pGraphics)
    {
        pGraphics.drawString("Hello world", 50, 25);
    }
}
```

Figure 20.6 A version of `HelloApplet` that uses the Swing API from Java 2.

Recognizing that browsers supporting different versions of Java interpreters was a major problem, Sun looked at how this problem might be overcome. They now suggest that developers of WWW pages that use Java applets code their HTML in such a way that the visitor to the WWW page is asked to download a plug-in to their computer if the plug-in appropriate to the version of Java required by the applet is not present on the computer. The applet is then executed using the Java interpreter contained in this plug-in. Any Java interpreter contained in the WWW browser will be ignored.

This plug-in is known as the **Java Plug-in**: it was previously called the **Java Activator**.

In this way, the author of a Java applet can ensure that the right version of the Java Platform is used with his/her applet and that the version being used is complete. However, there are a few snags with this approach:

1. The way in which the HTML is written in order for this to happen depends on which browser is being used. For example, the HTML that is required for Netscape's Navigator is different from that which is needed for Microsoft's Internet Explorer. Although you could provide HTML that only works for one of these browsers, it is better for your HTML to allow any browser. So the reasonably simple APPLET tag of the file HelloApplet.html (given in Figure 20.3) needs to be replaced by the HTML of the file NewHelloApplet.html which is shown in Figure 20.7.

   This file contains a large number of difficult lines of HTML in order for it to work with both Navigator and Internet Explorer. Essentially, the lines immediately following the OBJECT tag are used by Internet Explorer, whereas those immediately following the EMBED tag are used by Navigator. The WWW page at [34] contains some details about what all this means. On that WWW page, Sun give an even more complicated version that can deal with situations not catered for by the HTML given in Figure 20.7.

   Even though it is complicated, once you have got it right there are only a few things that have to be changed when you need to produce a HTML file for a different applet: you just have to change the two sets of references to the name of the .class file (NewHelloApplet.class), the width (150) and the height (25).

2. As mentioned above, the HTML is coded so that the appropriate Java Plug-in is downloaded if it is not present in the visitor's computer. The HTML given in Figure 20.7 illustrates this, as it refers to some WWW pages at http://java.sun.com/products/plugin/1.2/. Depending on your connectivity to the Internet, a plug-in may take some time to download.

3. Sun only produce versions of the Java Plug-in for their Solaris operating system, for Linux and for the various Microsoft Windows platforms. And, although there is support for Netscape's Navigator and Microsoft's Internet Explorer, the position of other WWW browsing software (such as **Opera** and **StarOffice**) is currently unclear.

Sun provide different versions of the Java Plug-in for the different versions of the Java 2 Platform. For example, there is a version that supports v 1.2 and another

```
<HTML>
<HEAD>
<TITLE>The NewHelloApplet Example</TITLE>
</HEAD>
<BODY>
<P>
Start.
</P>
<OBJECT classid="clsid:8AD9C840-044E-11D1-B3E9-00805F499D93"
  width="150" height="25"
  codebase=
"http://java.sun.com/products/plugin/1.2/jinstall-12-win32.cab#Version=1,2,0,0"
>
  <PARAM NAME="code" VALUE="NewHelloApplet.class">
  <PARAM NAME="type" VALUE="application/x-java-applet;version=1.2">
  <COMMENT>
  <EMBED type="application/x-java-applet;version=1.2"
    width="150" height="25"
    code="NewHelloApplet.class"
    pluginspage="http://java.sun.com/products/plugin/1.2/plugin-install.html">
    <NOEMBED>
      </COMMENT>
        Java 2 Platform v 1.2 is needed to run this applet
    </NOEMBED>
  </EMBED>
</OBJECT>
<P>
Finish.
</P>
</BODY>
</HTML>
```

Figure 20.7 Getting an applet to use the Java Plug-in.

version that also supports v 1.3. Unless the code of your Java applet requires a feature that was introduced with v 1.3, it is best to write the HTML so that it indicates that it requires v 1.2. This is why there are lot of occurrences of *1.2* in the HTML given in Figure 20.7. By doing this, your applet can run without any downloading being required provided the computer has the Java Plug-in for v 1.2 (or for some later version).

20.5 Using appletviewer when developing Java applets

When developing a Java applet, the `.class` file will often be changed before the final version is produced. One problem that authors of Java applets often face is the difficulty in persuading a WWW browser to load a new version of a `.class` file if the `.class` file has changed on the author's WWW site. With some releases of some WWW browsers on some platforms, pressing the *Shift* key at the same time as clicking the browser's *Reload/Refresh* button may cause it to reload everything. If this does not work, the only sure way to get round this problem is to exit from the WWW browser and to start it up again.

If you are developing a WWW applet, it will be very tedious if you have to restart the WWW browser frequently.

However, the Java 2 SDK comes with a tool called **appletviewer** that can be used to view the output of an applet whose `.class` file is mentioned in a WWW page. So, having compiled some Java source code, e.g.:

```
javac NewHelloApplet.java
```

the `NewHelloApplet.class` file can be executed and its output can be displayed by running the following UNIX/MS-DOS command:

```
appletviewer NewHelloApplet.html
```

You can keep this appletviewer program running. If you subsequently make a change to the `NewHelloApplet.java` file and then recompile it, you can get appletviewer to load the new version of the `NewHelloApplet.class` file by clicking on the *Reload* option of the appletviewer's menu. So this appletviewer program provides a useful tool for testing Java applets.

(20.6) The life cycle of a Java applet

The `NewHelloApplet` applet just overrides the `paint` method. Most applets do something more involved than just `painting`. In order to write any code for an applet you need to be aware of the **life cycle** of an applet, i.e. the various stages that an applet goes through from birth to death.

When the bytecodes of an applet are loaded (or reloaded), the `init` method of the applet is executed. Then the applet's `start` method is executed. The `start` method is also re-executed when the user comes back to the WWW page associated with the applet after having visited another page. Whenever the user leaves this page, the `stop` method is executed. Finally, the `destroy` method is executed if the WWW browser has to unload the applet.

The `paint` method will first get executed after the `init` and `start` methods have been executed. It will automatically get re-executed whenever the window has to be redrawn.

The class `java.applet.Applet` declares methods for `init`, `start`, `stop`, `destroy` and `paint` that do nothing, i.e. they have empty blocks. These methods are inherited by `javax.swing.JApplet`, and by any classes that you derive from `javax.swing.JApplet`. So, if you want to define some actions to take place at the various points in the life cycle of an applet, you just need to override the appropriate methods.

Although overriding the `start` and `stop` methods is important for applets which start a new **thread**, the topic of multithreading is only briefly mentioned by this book: see Section 21.2.

We now look at an example of an applet that overrides the `init` method. Other examples that do this appear in later sections of this chapter.

20.7 `JLabelApplet` overrides the `init` method

Back in Section 13.4, we discovered that all of the classes that create a window on the screen (i.e. `JWindow`, `JFrame`, `JDialog`, `JInternalFrame` and `JApplet`) have a *content pane*. This is the main area of the window, and, in Section 13.8, we saw that a program can access the content pane of an object of one of these classes by executing its `getContentPane` method.

So, instead of overriding the `paint` method to output the string `"Hello world"` as is done by the `NewHelloApplet` applet, we could instead add a `JLabel` containing this string to the applet's content pane. As we only want to execute the code to add the `JLabel` object to the content pane once, it is appropriate to put the call of `add` in an `init` method of an applet. An applet that does this is the `JLabelApplet` applet shown in Figure 20.8.

```
// An applet that adds a JLabel to its content pane.
// Barry Cornelius, 20 June 2000
import java.awt.     BorderLayout;
import java.awt.     Container;
import javax.swing.  JApplet;
import javax.swing.  JLabel;
public class JLabelApplet extends JApplet
{
   public void init()
   {
      final JLabel tJLabel = new JLabel("Hello world");
      final Container tContentPane = getContentPane();
      tContentPane.add(tJLabel, BorderLayout.CENTER);
   }
}
```

Figure 20.8 An applet that adds a `JLabel` to its content pane.

As mentioned in Section 20.6, whenever a browser starts to execute the bytecodes of an applet, it will first execute the applet's `init` method. So this is the reason why we have put the statements in `JLabelApplet` init's method.

The result of running this applet is shown in Figure 20.9.

20.8 Restrictions imposed on Java applets

So far, programs have been able to read from files, to write to files, and to call methods (such as `System.exit`) that behind the scenes make system calls, i.e. calls to routines of the underlying operating system. Using some of the APIs that have not

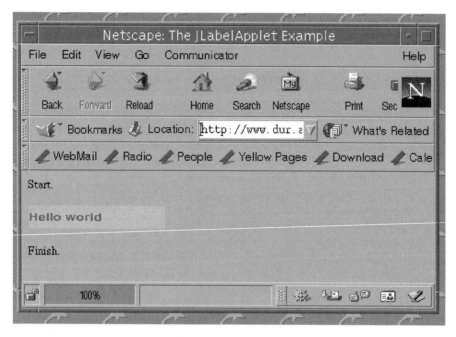

Figure 20.9   The output produced by the `JLabelApplet` applet.

been considered, it is also possible to write Java source code that communicates with other computers. Although it is reasonable for these sort of activities to be performed by Java source code that is a program, i.e. a *Java application*, is it appropriate for these activities to be performed by *Java applets*?

To be more specific: if you visit a WWW page, and the author of that WWW page causes your WWW browser to execute some bytecodes produced by the author, are you happy for these bytecodes to be able to write to files on your computer, or to read any of your files?

The designers of Java took the view that it is not always appropriate for these activities to be performed by Java applets that have been downloaded from the Internet. Instead, the environment of an applet is controlled by the user of the WWW browser. For example, there is no access to local files from Netscape's Navigator, whereas HotJava users can configure HotJava as to which files can be read from and which can be written to. More details are given at [36].

This approach is often called the **Sandbox** approach. This was Sun's first attempt at controlling what an applet can do. With later revisions of the Java Platform, Sun have been providing ways in which an applet can be allowed to perform these activities. It is now possible for the author of an applet to add to the applet a **digital signature** authorized by a **certificate** obtained from a **certificate authority**. If a visitor downloads this **signed applet** and allows their WWW browser to accept its certificate, the applet is said to be a **trusted applet**. There are more details about signed applets at [37].

Sun's main WWW page on security restrictions is at [38].

Converting PopMenuProg

Many of the programs that have appeared in previous chapters can easily be rewritten as Java applets. Often this can be done by putting the code of the main method into an applet's init method. For example, we could take the statements of the main method of the PopMenuProg program (given in Figure 18.2) and put them into an init method of a PopMenuApplet class. The resulting code is shown in Figure 20.10.

```
// An applet produced by copying most of the code of the PopMenuProg program.
// Barry Cornelius, 20 June 2000
import java.awt.    BorderLayout;
import java.awt.    Container;
import javax.swing. JApplet;
import javax.swing. JFrame;
import javax.swing. JMenuBar;
import javax.swing. JScrollPane;
import javax.swing. JTextArea;
import javax.swing. JTextField;
public class PopMenuApplet extends JApplet
{
    public void init()
    {
        final int tJFrameX = 100;
        final int tJFrameY = 100;
        final int tJDialogX = 100;
        final int tJDialogY = 200;
        final Pop tPop = new PopImpl();
        final JFrame tJFrame = new JFrame("PopMenuApplet");
        final JTextField tResultsJTextField = new JTextField();
        final JTextArea tLogJTextArea = new JTextArea(5, 30);
        final Container tContentPane = tJFrame.getContentPane();
        tContentPane.add(tResultsJTextField,                BorderLayout.CENTER);
        tContentPane.add(new JScrollPane(tLogJTextArea), BorderLayout.SOUTH);
        final PopMenu tPopMenu =
                new PopMenu(tJFrame, tPop, tJDialogX, tJDialogY,
                            tResultsJTextField, tLogJTextArea);
        final JMenuBar tJMenuBar = tPopMenu.getJMenuBar();
        tJFrame.setJMenuBar(tJMenuBar);
        tJFrame.setLocation(tJFrameX, tJFrameY);
        tJFrame.pack();
        tJFrame.setVisible(true);
    }
}
```

Figure 20.10 An applet produced by copying most of the code of PopMenuProg.

In producing this class, the two statements of PopMenuProg that establish a window listener:

```
final ExitWindowListener tExitWindowListener = new ExitWindowListener();
tJFrame.addWindowListener(tExitWindowListener);
```

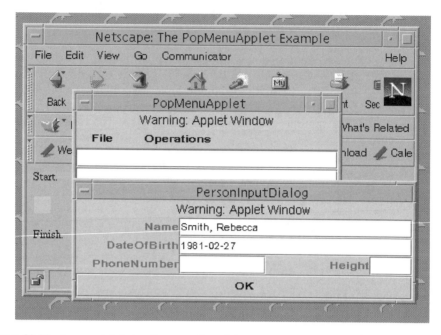

Figure 20.11   Some point during the execution of the `PopMenuApplet` applet.

have been omitted. This is because the `ExitWindowListener` class has a `windowClosing` method that calls `System.exit`. For the reasons explained in Section 20.8, it is not appropriate for the `PopMenuApplet` class to have this code.

When an applet is executed, any windows that it creates will have a **yellow warning banner** displaying the text `Warning: Applet Window`. This text warns the user of the WWW browser that the window being displayed has not been produced by a *trusted applet*. The WWW page at [35] says that the 'yellow warning banner is an important security feature. It cannot be disabled by untrusted applets. If you use a signed applet, where the signing key is trusted by the end user, then the warning banner will not be shown.' Some point during the execution of this applet is shown in Figure 20.11.

Curio 20.4 describes what you can do if the warning banner coincides with the GUI components being displayed by your applet.

(20.10) Converting `ShapesJComponentProg`

Suppose we want to be able to use the `ShapesJComponentProg` shown in Figure 19.13 as an applet.

A problem with the `main` method of this class is that it reads its data from a file (from a file called `ShapesJComponentProg.data`). As explained in Section 20.8, it is not usually possible for an applet (which is downloaded from the Internet) to read from a file stored on the computer of the person visiting the WWW page. However, the restrictions on applets do allow an applet to read a data file that is provided on the applet author's WWW site.

For example, in order to read a data file that is stored in the same directory as the .html file, the applet first needs to determine the URL of the directory containing this .html file. It can do this by using the method getDocumentBase from the class java.applet.Applet. This method returns an object of the class java.net.URL. The applet can then associate another object of the class URL with the file ShapesJComponentProg.data by using:

```
final URL tURL = new URL(getDocumentBase(), "ShapesJComponentProg.data");
```

An input stream can then be established with ShapesJComponentProg.data by the statement:

```
final BufferedReader tInputHandle =
             new BufferedReader(new InputStreamReader(tURL.openStream()));
```

This statement uses URL's openStream method. See the WWW page at $API/java/net/URL.html for more details about java.net's URL class. Lines can now be read from the WWW, i.e. from the file ShapesJComponentProg.data. This can be done in the usual way, i.e. by using readLine on tInputHandle.

The above statements appear in the code of the ShapesJComponentApplet applet that is shown in Figure 20.12. The result of running this applet is shown in Figure 20.13.

20.11 Reading data from an applet's WWW page

It is possible to get the code of an applet to read strings that have been created in the HTML of the WWW page that is used to run the applet. To demonstrate this, the NewHelloApplet applet will be modified so that it obtains from the HTML the information about what string to output and where to output it.

The HTML given in Figure 20.7 needs to have the following lines added to the OBJECT section:

```
<PARAM NAME="greeting" VALUE="Hello Java!">
<PARAM NAME="x"        VALUE="50">
<PARAM NAME="y"        VALUE="25">
```

and the following lines added to the EMBED section:

```
greeting="Hello Java!"
x="50"
y="25"
```

The new code of the HTML file is shown in Figure 20.14.

The applet can use a method called getParameter in order to get the value associated with a parameter. It is demonstrated by the code shown in Figure 20.15.

Note that this applet overrides both the init method and the paint method.

```
// An applet that reads a data file from the applet's WWW site.
// Barry Cornelius, 20 June 2000
import java.awt.    BorderLayout;
import java.io.     BufferedReader;
import java.awt.    Container;
import java.io.     InputStreamReader;
import java.io.     IOException;
import javax.swing. JApplet;
import javax.swing. JLabel;
import java.net.    URL;
public class ShapesJComponentApplet extends JApplet
{
    public void init()
    {
      try
      {
        final URL tURL =
            new URL(getDocumentBase(), "ShapesJComponentProg.data");
        final BufferedReader tInputHandle =
            new BufferedReader(new InputStreamReader(tURL.openStream()));
        final ShapesJComponent tShapesJComponent =
            new ShapesJComponent(tInputHandle);
        final Container tContentPane = getContentPane();
        tContentPane.add(new JLabel("NORTH"), BorderLayout.NORTH);
        tContentPane.add(tShapesJComponent,   BorderLayout.CENTER);
        tContentPane.add(new JLabel("SOUTH"), BorderLayout.SOUTH);
      }
      catch(final IOException pIOException)
      {
        throw new IllegalArgumentException();
      }
    }
}
```

Figure 20.12   An applet that reads a data file from the applet's WWW site.

(20.12) Producing code for an application and an applet

If you want to use some Java source code sometimes as an application and sometimes as an applet, it would be better not to have duplicate copies of the code as is
the case with the main method of the PopMenuProg class (given in Figure 18.2)
and the init method of the PopMenuApplet class (shown in Figure 20.10). It is
usually easy to rewrite the code of the program and applet classes so as to avoid the
duplication.

   In this example, the code of the PopMenuApplet class can be reworked so that
it can be used by the PopMenuProg class. The new code for PopMenuApplet is
shown in Figure 20.16. The main difference between the PopMenuApplet classes of
Figure 20.10 and Figure 20.16 is that the JFrame object is now pointed to by a private

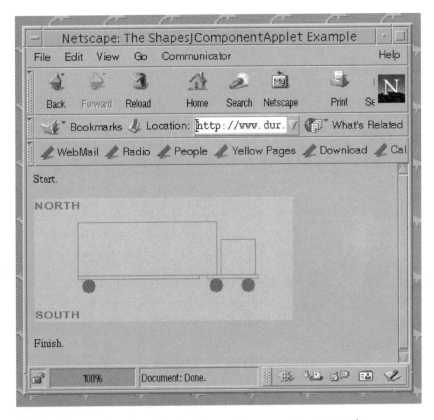

Figure 20.13   The output produced by the `ShapesJComponentApplet` applet.

field of the class and the class has a `getJFrame` method that returns a pointer to this `JFrame` object.

The `PopMenuProg` program can now be written in terms of this class as is shown in Figure 20.17.

(20.13) Using a Java Archive file produced by `jar`

As was mentioned earlier, the `CODE` attribute in the HTML that is used to run an applet identifies the name of the file containing the bytecodes of the applet's class. However, normally, the author of an applet will provide a number of supporting classes as well as the class of the applet. It was pointed out in Section 20.3 that the bytecodes of each of the `.class` files will be downloaded from the author's WWW site as the Java interpreter being used by the WWW browser detects that it requires them.

For example, suppose a directory contains the files for the `PopMenuApplet` applet. The following files would have to be downloaded in order to execute all of the

```
<HTML>
<HEAD>
<TITLE>The ParamApplet Example</TITLE>
</HEAD>
<BODY>
<P>
Start.
</P>
<OBJECT classid="clsid:8AD9C840-044E-11D1-B3E9-00805F499D93"
   width="150" height="25"
   codebase=
"http://java.sun.com/products/plugin/1.2/jinstall-12-win32.cab#Version=1,2,0,0"
>
  <PARAM NAME="code" VALUE="ParamApplet.class">
  <PARAM NAME="greeting" VALUE="Hello Java!">
  <PARAM NAME="x"        VALUE="50">
  <PARAM NAME="y"        VALUE="25">
  <PARAM NAME="type" VALUE="application/x-java-applet;version=1.2">
  <COMMENT>
  <EMBED type="application/x-java-applet;version=1.2"
    width="150" height="25"
    code="ParamApplet.class"
    greeting="Hello Java!"
    x="50"
    y="25"
    pluginspage="http://java.sun.com/products/plugin/1.2/plugin-install.html">
    <NOEMBED>
      </COMMENT>
        Java 2 Platform v 1.2 is needed to run this applet
    </NOEMBED>
  </EMBED>
</OBJECT>
<P>
Finish.
</P>
</BODY>
</HTML>
```

Figure 20.14   Passing information from an HTML file to a Java applet.

code of this applet:

```
Date.class  DateImpl.class   Person.class     PersonImpl.class
NameInputDialog.class        PersonForm.class
PersonInputDialog.class      PersonOutputDialog.class
Pop.class   PopImpl.class    PopMenu.class  PopMenuApplet.class
```

The Java 2 SDK contains a tool that enables the author of an applet to combine a number of files into a single file. The resulting file is called a **Java Archive**. The tool is called jar, and, like the other commands of the Java 2 SDK, it can be run from a UNIX/MS-DOS command line. The documentation for the jar command

```
// Reading information from the HTML file used to run an applet.
// Barry Cornelius, 20 June 2000
import java.awt.    Graphics;
import javax.swing. JApplet;
public class ParamApplet extends JApplet
{
    private String iGreeting;
    private int iX;
    private int iY;
    public void init()
    {
        iGreeting = getParameter("greeting");
        final String tXString  = getParameter("x");
        iX = Integer.parseInt(tXString);
        final String tYString  = getParameter("y");
        iY = Integer.parseInt(tYString);
    }
    public void paint(final Graphics pGraphics)
    {
        pGraphics.drawString(iGreeting, iX, iY);
    }
}
```

Figure 20.15 Using `getParameter` to get information from an applet's HTML file.

says 'When the components of an applet or application (`.class` files, images and sounds) are combined into a single archive, they may be downloaded by a java agent (like a browser) in a single HTTP transaction, rather than requiring a new connection for each piece. This dramatically improves download times. `jar` also compresses files and so further improves download time.'

Assuming that the directory containing the files for the `PopMenuApplet` applet only contains `.class` files that are associated with this applet, then a Java Archive can be produced from these `.class` files by the UNIX/MS-DOS command line:

```
jar cvf PopMenuApplet.jar *.class
```

The first argument to the `jar` command, which in this example is `cvf`, indicates the options that you want to be passed to the `jar` command. There are three main ways in which the `jar` command is used. If the options contain a c, then this means that you want to create an archive; if they contain a t, you want the `jar` command just to list the contents of an archive (that already exists); and if they contain an x, you want the command to extract some files from an archive.

If the options include the letter v, then the `jar` command will produce some output to tell you what it is doing – v means *verbose*. Finally, the f means that the name of an archive is given as the next argument. When a c option is present, the remaining arguments give the names of the `.class` files that you want to be put into

```
// The code of PopMenuApplet reworked so that it can be used by PopMenuProg.
// Barry Cornelius, 20 June 2000
import java.awt.     BorderLayout;
import java.awt.     Container;
import javax.swing. JApplet;
import javax.swing. JFrame;
import javax.swing. JMenuBar;
import javax.swing. JScrollPane;
import javax.swing. JTextArea;
import javax.swing. JTextField;
public class PopMenuApplet extends JApplet
{
    private JFrame iJFrame;
    public void init()
    {
        final int iJFrameX = 100;
        final int iJFrameY = 100;
        final int tJDialogX = 100;
        final int tJDialogY = 200;
        final Pop tPop = new PopImpl();
        iJFrame = new JFrame("PopMenuApplet");
        final JTextField tResultsJTextField = new JTextField();
        final JTextArea tLogJTextArea = new JTextArea(5, 30);
        final Container tContentPane = iJFrame.getContentPane();
        tContentPane.add(tResultsJTextField,           BorderLayout.CENTER);
        tContentPane.add(new JScrollPane(tLogJTextArea), BorderLayout.SOUTH);
        final PopMenu tPopMenu =
                new PopMenu(iJFrame, tPop, tJDialogX, tJDialogY,
                            tResultsJTextField, tLogJTextArea);
        final JMenuBar tJMenuBar = tPopMenu.getJMenuBar();
        iJFrame.setJMenuBar(tJMenuBar);
        iJFrame.setLocation(iJFrameX, iJFrameY);
        iJFrame.pack();
        iJFrame.setVisible(true);
    }
    public JFrame getJFrame()
    {
        return iJFrame;
    }
}
```

Figure 20.16 PopMenuApplet reworked so that it can be used by PopMenuProg.

the archive. In UNIX/MS-DOS, the notation * . class refers to all of the files in the current directory that have a . class extension.

So the above jar command produces a file called PopMenuApplet.jar that contains a compressed archive of all of the .class files that constitute the PopMenuApplet applet.

```
// PopMenuProg rewritten so that it uses the revised PopMenuApplet class.
// Barry Cornelius, 20 June 2000
import javax.swing. JFrame;
public class PopMenuProg
{
   public static void main(final String[] pArgs)
   {
      final PopMenuApplet tPopMenuApplet = new PopMenuApplet();
      tPopMenuApplet.init();
      final JFrame tJFrame = tPopMenuApplet.getJFrame();
      final ExitWindowListener tExitWindowListener =
                                        new ExitWindowListener();
      tJFrame.addWindowListener(tExitWindowListener);
   }
}
```

Figure 20.17 PopMenuProg rewritten to use the revised PopMenuApplet class.

Suppose a WWW page contains a CODE attribute to say that the bytecodes of an applet's class are stored in the file PopMenuApplet.class. If you want the WWW browser to download the bytecodes in the Java Archive PopMenuApplet.jar instead of downloading each .class file, you will need to include an ARCHIVE attribute as well as the CODE attribute.

If your HTML uses an APPLET tag or an EMBED tag, the syntax of the ARCHIVE attribute is:

```
archive="PopMenuApplet.jar"
```

and, if your HTML uses an OBJECT tag, you need to include:

```
<PARAM NAME="archive" VALUE="PopMenuApplet.jar">
```

Note you need a CODE attribute as well as the ARCHIVE attribute: the latter gives the name of the file containing the Java Archive (in which all the .class files are stored) and the CODE attribute gives the name of the particular class file that contains the applet class, i.e. effectively it identifies the bytecodes that are executed first.

As mentioned earlier, there are two advantages in using a Java Archive:

● One HTTP connection from the computer running the WWW browser to the computer of the author's WWW site is made to obtain the bytecodes in the Java Archive instead of making lots of HTTP connections, one for each of the .class files.

● Because the information in the Java Archive is stored in a compressed format, there is less bytes to be downloaded. For example, the .class files of the PopMenuApplet applet occupy a total of 18 212 bytes, whereas the size of the PopMenuApplet.jar file is 11 415 bytes.

Tip for programming and debugging ────────────────────────────────

20.1 One problem that authors of Java applets often face is the difficulty in persuading a WWW browser to load a new version of a `.class` file if the `.class`
file has changed on the author's WWW site. One solution is to test applets
using the `appletviewer` program. For more details about this problem, and
for details of the `appletviewer` program, see Section 20.5.

Curios, controversies and cover-ups ──────────────────────────────

20.1 If the `.class` files that form your applet are not stored in the same directory
as the `.html` file, this can be indicated by using a CODEBASE attribute in the
HTML. So, suppose you have stored the `.class` files in a subdirectory of the
directory containing the `.html` file, and suppose the subdirectory is called
`classes`. If your HTML uses an APPLET tag or an EMBED tag, the syntax of
the CODEBASE attribute is:

```
codebase="classes"
```

and, if your HTML uses an OBJECT tag, you need to include:

```
<PARAM NAME="codebase" VALUE="classes">
```

In Section 20.10, it was mentioned that an applet can call the
`getDocumentBase` method in order to find out the URL of the directory
containing the `.html` file. There is also a method called `getCodeBase` that
can be used by an applet to find out the URL of the directory containing the
`.class` files. If this method is called when the CODEBASE attribute has not
been set, it will return the same URL as the `getDocumentBase` method.

20.2 In this book, we normally use a `final` keyword with each parameter of a
method if we do not intend to alter the value of the parameter within the body
of the method. Support for this use of the `final` keyword was introduced with
JDK 1.1. The `final` keyword has not been used in the code for the `paint`
method of the `HelloApplet` applet (given in Figure 20.4). By making this
decision, it means that this code can be compiled by a JDK 1.0.2 compiler. In
this way, we can be sure that the code of the applet can be downloaded by
any WWW browser that only has support for JDK 1.0.2.

20.3 Many of the applets given in this chapter override the `paint` method.
Although the previous chapter suggested that it is better to override
`paintComponent` rather than `paint`, this is only true for subclasses of the
`JComponent` class. The classes `JApplet` and `Applet` are not subclasses of
`JComponent`.

20.4 The WWW page at [35] contains an FAQ page for the Java Plug-in. One of the
questions is concerned with preventing the *yellow warning banner* covering
the area occupied by an applet's GUI components. The answer is:

You should use the getInsets method to find the size of your frame's decorative border. This includes the warning banner. For example, if you create a Frame with size 100 × 100, you might find it has insets [top=42, left=5, bottom=5, right=6] giving you a drawable area of 89 × 53. You need to position your work within the drawable area. If you need to create a drawable area of a particular size, first create and show the Frame, then use getInsets to find the insets' sizes, then figure out the desired frame size by adding your desired size to the insets, then use frame.setsize() to set your frame to that size.

20.5 The command line used to run the jar tool is similar to that of UNIX's tar command.

Exercises

20.1 Produce an applet from the calculator program produced as a solution to Exercise 13.2, Exercise 13.3 or Exercise 13.4.

20.2 Produce an applet from the BookingSystem program produced as a solution to Exercise 18.1.

20.3 Produce an applet from the CarParkProg program produced as a solution to Exercise 18.2.

20.4 Produce an applet from the Library program produced as a solution to Exercise 18.3.

Chapter 21

Looking briefly at other topics

· ·

Previous chapters have provided incomplete coverage or passing references to topics such as exceptions, threads, the Swing API, packages and the factory pattern. These and other topics are briefly considered in this chapter. Pointers to other sources of information about these topics are also given.

The chapter ends with some pointers to useful books and WWW pages about Java.

21.1 Exception handling

21.1.1 Dealing with unexpected situations

A method often detects situations which it knows it cannot handle. It may be that the arguments for the method were inappropriate; it may be that a series of calculations has led to a situation that should not occur; it may be that its attempt to allocate space using new has failed; and so on. What should the programmer of this method do when such unexpected situations (**exceptions**) arise?

The method could output an error message and then terminate the execution of the program. However, the user of the method might be extremely unhappy if this happens: he/she might want to do some *cleanup* code before the program terminates.

Instead, the programmer of the method could return some value that signifies that an error has occurred. Examples of this technique are given for the methods of the Pop interface and the PopImpl class (shown in Figure 17.14 and Figure 17.15). However, returning an error value may be inconvenient to the user of the method as the point of the call of the method may not be the best place to handle the error. In such situations, his/her code may be littered with error-handling code.

Since Java has a construct for handling exceptions, the method could instead signify that an exception has occurred, and the caller of the method could then handle that exception at a point that is convenient. For example, it could be handled by a try statement at the point where the method is called, or, instead, the header of the method whose body contains the point of the call could have a throws clause to signify that it is not dealing with the exception.

21.1.2 Throwing an exception

In Java, you can indicate that some exception has occurred by executing a **throw statement**. Syntactically, a throw statement looks like a return statement: it consists of the throw keyword followed by an expression. This expression must be of the type Throwable. Rather than using an expression of this type, it is usual to subclass the class Exception (which is itself a subclass of Throwable) to produce your own Exception class.

Suppose we want to modify the add method of Pop–PopImpl so that it generates an exception if the person is already in the population. So instead of the method having the header:

```
// returns true if and only if pPerson is not already in the population
public boolean add(Person pPerson);
```

it now has the header:

```
// throws PopPresentException if pPerson is already in the population
public void add(Person pPerson) throws PopPresentException;
```

Previously, a client could find out whether a person was already in the population by looking at the value that was returned by add. With the new version of add, the method does not return a value: instead, an exception will be thrown if an attempt is made to add a person who is already in the population.

So the code of the add method is changed from:

```
public synchronized boolean add(final Person pPerson)
{
    final Object tObject = iPop.put(pPerson.getName(), pPerson);
    setChanged();
    notifyObservers();
    return tObject==null;
}
```

to:

```
public synchronized void add(final Person pPerson) throws PopPresentException
{
    final Object tObject = iPop.put(pPerson.getName(), pPerson);
    if (tObject!=null)
    {
        throw new PopPresentException();
    }
    setChanged();
    notifyObservers();
}
```

If the throw statement is executed, an object of the class PopPresentException is created, and this is then passed as the argument to the catch clause of the exception handler that can handle this exception.

The above code assumes that there is a class called PopPresentException. Here is some code that can be used for this class:

```
public class PopPresentException extends Exception
{
    public PopPresentException()
    {
        super();
    }
}
```

Because of the defaults that Java has, this can be abbreviated to:

```
public class PopPresentException extends Exception
{
}
```

The caller of add can decide where it handles this exception. One possibility would be to handle the exception at the point where add is called, i.e. to replace:

```
final Person tPerson = new PersonImpl(iKeyboard.readLine());
if ( ! iPop.add(tPerson) )
{
    System.out.println("The person is already in the population");
}
```

by:

```
final Person tPerson = new PersonImpl(iKeyboard.readLine());
try
{
    iPop.add(tPerson);
}
catch(final PopPresentException pPopPresentException)
{
    System.out.println("The person is already in the population");
}
```

When you produce a class that subclasses Exception, it is sometimes useful to pass information from the point where the exception occurred to the point where it is to be handled. For example, we could modify the throw statement in the add method to be:

```
throw new PopPresentException(tObject);
```

Here we are passing as an argument a pointer to the object describing the person that was found in the population.

We also need to modify the PopPresentException class:

```
public class PopPresentException extends Exception
{
    private Person iPerson;
    public PopPresentException()
    {
        iPerson = null;
    }
    public PopPresentException(final Object tObject)
    {
        iPerson = (Person)pObject;
    }
    public Person getPerson()
    {
        return iPerson;
    }
}
```

A catch clause can now use:

```
catch(final PopPresentException pPopPresentException)
{
    final Person tPerson = pPopPresentException.getPerson();
    System.out.println("The person is already in the population: " + tPerson);
}
```

If you are going to change the add method, it makes sense to do something similar with the remove method, i.e. to change it to a method that has the following header:

```
// throws PopAbsentException if there is no person with name pName
public synchronized void remove(String pName) throws PopAbsentException;
```

21.1.3 When should exceptions be used?

Although exceptions look as if they could be very useful, many people hold the view that they should only be used for situations that should not happen rather than situations which are expected. The book *Fault Tolerance: Principles and Practice* ([2]) by Tom Anderson and Peter Lee uses the term **fault tolerance** to refer to the fact 'that an implemented system will not be perfect, and that measures are therefore required to enable the operational system to cope with the faults that remain or develop'. The book also says:

> ... exceptions can be used for both normal and fault tolerance activities within a program. Indeed, [in 'Exception Handling: Issues and a Proposed Notation', *Communications of the ACM*, **18**(12), 683–696] Goodenough proposes exception handling for use as a normal programming construct to handle unusual but valid situations [such as adding a person to a population when they are already in the population]. However, it does not seem appropriate to indiscriminately use an exception mechanism for both abnormal activities and normal processing – a clear separation of these activities is necessary to ensure a coherent approach to fault tolerance. Thus, this book ... will assume that exceptions and their handlers are used solely for the implementation of fault tolerance.

Given this point of view, altering Pop–PopImpl so that its methods generate exceptions (as we did in Section 21.1.2) is an inappropriate use of exceptions.

If you want to learn more about this topic, a good article on the topic is 'Designing with exceptions' by Bill Venners. You will find it at [47].

21.2 Starting another thread

21.2.1 The class java.lang.Thread

Often the user of a program does something that causes the program to do some task that is time-consuming. In this situation, you may prefer the user to have the ability to get on with something else at the same time as the time-consuming task. In Java, you can put the time-consuming task into a separate **thread** of execution.

It is easy to start another thread: you just need to create an object of the class Thread (from the package java.lang), and execute its start method. So, suppose a method, e.g. the main method of a program, contains:

```
final Thread tThread = new Thread();
...
tThread.start();
```

then the call of start does two things:

- it starts the execution of tThread.run() in a separate thread;
- it then immediately returns to the statement following the call of tThread.start().

So we now have two threads of activity that are running concurrently: the main method and the tThread.run method.

This is not so exciting as it sounds because java.lang.Thread's run method does nothing because it has an empty block, and so it stops executing straightaway. We are just left with the thread of execution that is executing the main method.

21.2.2 Deriving the class ClockStdout from java.lang.Thread

Because Java has inheritance, we can derive a class from java.lang.Thread and provide a run method that does something useful.

In the code given in Figure 21.1, a class called ClockStdout is derived from java.lang.Thread, and ClockStdout's declaration of run overrides Thread's run method. The code of ClockStdout's run method is an infinite loop inside which we first get the current date and time, then output that to the *standard output*, and then use sleep to wait for two seconds.

```
// Overriding Thread's run method.
// Barry Cornelius, 21 June 2000
import java.util. Date;
public class ClockStdout extends Thread
{
    public void run()
    {
        while (true)
        {
            final Date tDate = new Date();
            System.out.println(tDate);
            try
            {
                Thread.sleep(2000);
            }
            catch(final InterruptedException pInterruptedException)
            {
            }
        }
    }
}
```

Figure 21.1 Overriding Thread's run method.

```
// Using ClockStdout to start a new thread.
// Barry Cornelius, 21 June 2000
public class ClockStdoutProg
{
    public static void main(final String[ ] pArgs)
    {
        System.out.println("ClockStdoutProg program");
        final ClockStdout tClockStdout = new ClockStdout();
        tClockStdout.start();
        for (int tCount = 0; tCount<8; tCount++)
        {
            System.out.println("tCount is: " + tCount);
            try
            {
                Thread.sleep(1000);
            }
            catch(final InterruptedException pInterruptedException)
            {
            }
        }
        System.out.println("ClockStdoutProg program");
    }
}
```

Figure 21.2   Using `ClockStdout` to start a new thread.

21.2.3 Using `ClockStdout` in the `ClockStdoutProg` program

The main method of the `ClockStdoutProg` program (given in Figure 21.2) creates an object (`tClockStdout`) of the class `ClockStdout`, and then calls `tClock-Stdout`'s `start` method. However, the class `ClockStdout` does not itself declare a `start` method, and so it is `java.lang.Thread`'s `start` method that gets called. As explained earlier, this does two things:

- it causes `tClockStdout`'s `run` method (i.e. the infinite loop) to start executing in a separate thread;

- it immediately returns to execute the rest of the `main` method.

So we now have two threads of activity that are running concurrently: the `main` method and `tClockStdout`'s `run` method. Having started the `tClockStdout` thread, the `main` method then goes on to output the digits from 0 to 7 stopping for one second after it has output each digit.

Here is the sort of output that the `ClockStdoutProg` program produces:

```
ClockStdoutProg program
tCount is: 0
Wed Jun 21 19:49:15 GMT+01:00 2000
tCount is: 1
tCount is: 2
```

```
Wed Jun 21 19:49:17 GMT+01:00 2000
tCount is: 3
tCount is: 4
Wed Jun 21 19:49:19 GMT+01:00 2000
tCount is: 5
tCount is: 6
Wed Jun 21 19:49:21 GMT+01:00 2000
tCount is: 7
ClockStdoutProg program
Wed Jun 21 19:49:23 GMT+01:00 2000
Wed Jun 21 19:49:25 GMT+01:00 2000
Wed Jun 21 19:49:27 GMT+01:00 2000
Wed Jun 21 19:49:29 GMT+01:00 2000
...
```

You can see that the output is from both threads, and that the program will not finish because the `tClockStdout` thread is an infinite loop. Ctrl/C can be used to stop this program's execution.

One way of getting the program to terminate properly is for its `main` method to call:

```
System.exit(0);
```

21.2.4 Using `synchronized` for accessing a variable

If you wish to access the same variable from more than one thread, you will need to use the `synchronized` keyword to ensure that accesses to the variable are performed correctly. For more details, see Section 16.4.

21.2.5 Using another thread in a GUI

The `ClockStdoutProg` program (given in Figure 21.2) keeps on outputting the current date and time every two seconds. It writes its output to the standard output. Suppose that we now want this output displayed in a textfield of a window that we have created.

In our new program, we can use the `Clock` class (given in Figure 21.3). This class is similar to the `ClockStdout` class that was used by the `ClockStdoutProg` program. The new program is the `ClockProg` program shown in Figure 21.4. Note that this program passes a reference to a textfield and the value of an interval of time as arguments to `Clock`'s constructor.

Instead of `Clock`'s `run` method having an infinite loop, the loop now depends on the value of the variable `iContinueExecution`. This is initialized by `Clock`'s constructor to *true*: its value can be changed to *false* by executing the method called `finish`, a public method that is provided by the class.

When a field of an object is accessed by more than one thread, Java allows each thread to keep its own working copy of the field. By doing this, access to the field can be faster. Only at certain points does it reconcile its copy with the master copy.

```
// Providing a thread class that repeatedly updates a textfield.
// Barry Cornelius, 21 June 2000
import java.util.    Date;
import javax.swing. JTextField;
public class Clock extends Thread
{
    private JTextField iJTextField;
    private int iSleepTime;
    private volatile boolean iContinueExecution;
    public Clock(final JTextField pJTextField, final int pSleepTime)
    {
        iJTextField = pJTextField;
        iSleepTime = pSleepTime;
        iContinueExecution = true;
    }
    public void finish()
    {
        iContinueExecution = false;
    }
    public void run()
    {
        while (iContinueExecution)
        {
            final Date tDate = new Date();
            iJTextField.setText(tDate.toString());
            try
            {
                Thread.sleep(iSleepTime);
            }
            catch(final InterruptedException pInterruptedException)
            {
            }
        }
    }
}
```

Figure 21.3 Providing a thread class that repeatedly updates a textfield.

As mentioned in Section 16.4, the synchronized keyword can be used to ensure that a method has exclusive access to a variable. An alternative method is to use the volatile keyword: if you declare a field as volatile, a thread must, at every access to the field, reconcile its working copy of the field with the master copy.

In the Clock class (shown in Figure 21.3), the variable iContinueExecution is declared to be volatile. As explained above, if some thread calls Clock's finish method, this variable is set to *false*. The use of volatile ensures that the thread executing the run method always has an up-to-date copy of the value of the iContinueExecution field whenever the thread accesses the field.

The ClockProg program (given in Figure 21.4) creates a frame and a textfield, and adds the textfield to the frame. It passes this textfield and the value 2000 (meaning

```
// Using the Clock thread in the ClockProg program.
// Barry Cornelius, 21 June 2000
import java.awt.    BorderLayout;
import java.awt.    Container;
import javax.swing. JFrame;
import javax.swing. JTextField;
public class ClockProg
{
    public static void main(final String[] pArgs)
    {
        System.out.println("ClockProg program");
        final JFrame tJFrame = new JFrame("ClockProg program");
        final JTextField tJTextField = new JTextField(35);
        final Container tContentPane = tJFrame.getContentPane();
        tContentPane.add(tJTextField, BorderLayout.CENTER);
        tJFrame.pack();
        tJFrame.setVisible(true);
        final Clock tClock = new Clock(tJTextField, 2000);
        tClock.start();
        for (int tCount = 0; tCount<8 ; tCount++)
        {
            System.out.println("tCount is: " + tCount);
            try
            {
                Thread.sleep(1000);
            }
            catch(final InterruptedException pInterruptedException)
            {
            }
        }
        System.out.println("ClockProg program");
    }
}
```

Figure 21.4 Using the `Clock` thread in the `ClockProg` program.

2 seconds) as arguments to a `Clock` constructor, and then calls `Clock`'s `start` method.

21.2.6 `ClockApplet` overrides `init`, `start` and `stop`

So the `ClockProg` program updates a textfield with the current date and time every two seconds. Suppose that we want to do this in an applet.

In Java, this example is an ideal situation in which to start a new thread. One thread of activity is the life cycle of the applet: the other thread is the loop that is periodically updating the textfield. So, we need an applet whose `start` method starts off the thread with the loop and whose `stop` method stops the thread with the loop. Recall from Section 20.6 that, when we leave the WWW page associated with an applet, the applet's stop method is executed and when we revisit the page the applet's start method is executed.

So, the applet's start method could create a new Clock object and then call Clock's start method. This will in turn start the execution of Clock's run method. The applet's stop method needs to stop the execution of the thread with the loop. It can do this by calling Clock's finish method.

The code of the ClockApplet applet is shown in Figure 21.5. It uses the Clock class shown in Figure 21.3. The ClockApplet applet can be run in the usual way, i.e. by having a WWW page that refers to the file ClockApplet.class.

```java
// Using the Clock thread in the ClockApplet program.
// Barry Cornelius, 21 June 2000
import java.awt.    BorderLayout;
import java.awt.    Container;
import javax.swing. JApplet;
import javax.swing. JTextField;
public class ClockApplet extends JApplet
{
    private JTextField iJTextField;
    private Clock iClock;
    public ClockApplet()
    {
        iJTextField = new JTextField(50);
        iClock = null;
    }
    public void init()
    {
        final Container tContentPane = getContentPane();
        tContentPane.add(iJTextField, BorderLayout.CENTER);
    }
    public void start()
    {
        if (iClock==null)
        {
            iClock = new Clock(iJTextField, 2000);
            iClock.start();
        }
    }
    public void stop()
    {
        if (iClock != null && iClock.isAlive())
        {
            iClock.finish();
        }
        iClock = null;
    }
}
```

Figure 21.5   Using the Clock thread in the ClockApplet program.

```
// Using the Runnable interface.
// Barry Cornelius, 21 June 2000
import java.awt.    BorderLayout;
import java.awt.    Container;
import java.util.   Date;
import javax.swing. JApplet;
import javax.swing. JTextField;
public class ContinuousClockApplet extends JApplet implements Runnable
{
   private JTextField iJTextField;
   private Thread iThread;
   private volatile boolean iContinueExecution;
   public ContinuousClockApplet()
   {
      iJTextField = new JTextField(50);
      iThread = null;
      iContinueExecution = true;
   }
   public void init()
   {
      final Container tContentPane = getContentPane();
      tContentPane.add(iJTextField, BorderLayout.CENTER);
   }
   public void start()
   {
      if (iThread == null)
      {
         iThread = new Thread(this);
         iThread.start();
      }
   }
   public void stop()
   {
      if (iThread != null && iThread.isAlive())
      {
         iContinueExecution = false;
      }
      iThread = null;
   }
   public void run()
   {
      while (iContinueExecution)
      {
         final Date tDate = new Date();
         iJTextField.setText(tDate.toString());
         try
         {
            Thread.sleep(2000);
         }
         catch(final InterruptedException pInterruptedException)
         {
         }
      }
   }
}
```

Figure 21.6 Using the `Runnable` interface.

So, in this applet, the class `ClockApplet` requires the overriding of `java.applet.Applet`'s init, start and stop methods.

Starting a new thread in which to run the infinite loop is the easiest way of managing this problem. If, instead, we put the infinite loop in either the `init` or the `start` methods of the applet, the method would never end. Indeed, the method would continue to run even if we moved away from the WWW page associated with the applet: it would continue to run until we left the browser.

21.2.7 Using the `Runnable` interface

So far, we have achieved the possibility of running more than one thread by deriving a class (e.g. `Clock`) from the class `java.lang.Thread`. There is a bit of difficulty here: it may be that a class is already a subclass of some other class, and we would now also like to make it a subclass of `java.lang.Thread`. As mentioned in Curio 19.3, producing a class that is derived from more than one superclass (*multiple inheritance*) is not possible in Java. However, we are in luck because the class `java.lang.Thread` also provides an interface called `Runnable`.

The use of the `Runnable` interface is demonstrated by the reworking of the `ClockApplet` applet to produce the `ContinuousClockApplet` applet (shown in Figure 21.6).

This applet's `start` method uses the statement:

```
iThread = new Thread(this);
```

Here we are using `this` to pass the target of the applet's `start` method as an argument to a constructor of `java.lang.Thread`. Having done that, we can start off this thread by calling `iThread.start`. Because of the constructor we used to create the `Thread` object, the `start` method of the `Thread` class calls a method called `run` of the object passed as the argument to the constructor. So our applet has to put the actions that we want performed in the new thread into a method called `run`.

21.2.8 Further information about threads

Sun's *Tutorial* on Java includes many pages about threads. These start at [39] and at [40]. A comprehensive book on threads is *Java Threads* (2nd edition) by Scott Oaks and Henry Wong ([26]). There is also a useful article entitled 'Why are `Thread.stop`, `Thread.suspend`, `Thread.resume` and `Runtime.runFinalizersOnExit` Deprecated' at [41].

(21.3) The Swing API

Chapter 13 and Chapter 18 introduce some of the important aspects of the Swing API. However, there is a lot more to it. In particular, the classes `JTable` and `JTree` are useful.

One helpful book on the Swing API is *Programming with JFC* by Scott Weiner and Stephen Asbury ([54]). Sun's *Tutorial* on Java includes many pages about the Swing API: these pages start at [42]. Another book on the Swing API is *Java Swing* by

Robert Eckstein, Marc Loy and Dave Wood ([13]). Sun have released a set of WWW pages that are connected with developing GUIs using the Swing API. These are at [43].

Declaring your own packages

21.4.1 Package declarations

By default, an interface/class declaration belongs to the *default package*. And .class files of the default package are stored in the current directory.

It is useful to be able to group related interfaces/classes together. And for this, Java has the concept of a **package**.

You can use a **package declaration** to indicate that an interface/class belongs to a particular package. For example, suppose you have a file containing the text of a class called Date and that you want it to belong to a package called dateutils. You just need to insert a package declaration at the start of the file:

```
package dateutils;
```

Any interface/class declaration that contains this line belongs to this package. The .class files associated with these files of source code must appear in a directory called dateutils. And any client that wishes to use this class could use an import declaration, such as:

```
import dateutils.Date;
```

If instead some interface/class declarations each have a package declaration that takes the form:

```
package utils.dateutils;
```

then the .class files should be in a subdirectory called dateutils that is itself in a directory called utils. Any client that wishes to use the class called Date belonging to this package could use the import declaration:

```
import utils.dateutils.Date;
```

21.4.2 Setting the CLASSPATH

When the Java compiler/interpreter is executed, it looks for any packages in the directories that are mentioned in the **CLASSPATH**. By default, the CLASSPATH is empty, and if this is the case it will instead look for packages in the current directory.

So, if you have put some interface/class declarations into a package called utils.dateutils, the utils directory must be a subdirectory of the current directory.

Although the use of a subdirectory of the current directory is a useful place to hide the files of a package, this mechanism can be too restrictive. For example, if you build a number of useful classes and store them in one or more packages, it would be useful to put these in a standard place, e.g. a directory called classes or a directory called `public_html`. However, if you want the Java compiler/interpreter to look for packages in other directories, you will have to set the CLASSPATH.

The way in which this is done depends on whether you are using a UNIX or an MS-DOS command line. When using UNIX, then for csh/tcsh an example would be:

```
setenv CLASSPATH .:/users/dcl0bjc/classes:/users/dxy3abc/public_html
```

or, if you are using sh, ksh or bash, this would be:

```
CLASSPATH=.:/users/dcl0bjc/classes:/users/dxy3abc/public_html
export CLASSPATH
```

At an MS-DOS prompt, you could type something like:

```
set CLASSPATH=.;C:\project\classes;D:\myjava
```

Note that for UNIX, items in the list of directories are separated by a colon, whereas semicolons are used when typing the command in MS-DOS.

If you also want the compiler/interpreter to look in the current directory, then it must be included in the CLASSPATH. A dot can be used in the CLASSPATH in order to refer to the current directory (as shown in the examples given above).

The Java compiler/interpreter knows how to find the packages that are a part of the Java 2 SDK, and so there is no need to include anything in the CLASSPATH to help the compiler/interpreter find these packages. Note: this was not the case with some earlier versions of the JDK.

21.4.3 It's a small world: how can unique names be generated?

Java specifies a convention for generating globally unique names for interfaces and classes. The convention is that a package name starts with the components of the author's Internet address (in reverse order). Examples are:

organization	domain name	an example of an interface/class name
Sun Microsystems	sun.com	com.sun.xxx.yyyyy
IBM	ibm.com	com.ibm.wwww.vvv.uuuuu
University of Durham	dur.ac.uk	uk.ac.dur.aaaaa.bbb.ccc.dddd

If the University of Durham wanted to establish a convention for the uniqueness of the names of interfaces/classes, it could utilize a person's username. So, because my username is dcl0bjc, I might prefer to put the `Date` class mentioned earlier into the package indicated by:

```
package uk.ac.dur.dcl0bjc.utils.dateutils;
```

And if I wanted this package to be accessible from the WWW (see below), then it is often sensible to put the files of this package into the directory:

```
/users/dcl0bjc/public_html/uk/ac/dur/dcl0bjc/utils/dateutils
```

Having done this, if you needed to use this package in a Java application, you would need something like:

```
import uk.ac.dur.dcl0bjc.utils.dateutils.Date;
```

and you would need to set the CLASSPATH:

```
setenv CLASSPATH .:/users/dcl0bjc/public_html
```

in order for the Java compiler/interpreter to find the `.class` files.

Many WWW servers are configured so that the files that are in or below a user's `public_html` directory are accessible to any WWW browser running anywhere in the world. So the reason for putting these `.class` files in a directory that is below a user's `public_html` directory is that they can then be accessed by a Java applet running on any WWW browser. As mentioned in Curio 20.1, you can use the CODEBASE attribute of an APPLET/OBJECT/EMBED tag if you want to indicate that an applet's `.class` files are all stored in a particular place; e.g.:

```
codebase="http://www.dur.ac.uk/~dcl0bjc/"
```

could be used for the `dateutils` example (when using an APPLET tag or an EMBED tag).

21.4.4 Compiling from a directory to one visible from the WWW

Although it may be useful to put your `.class` files into a publicly accessible place, you may want to hide the source files. If the current directory contains some Java source code and the current directory is inaccessible from the WWW, you can easily arrange for the Java compiler to put the `.class` files into a different directory (a directory that is accessible from the WWW) by using the d option of the `javac` command, e.g.:

```
setenv CLASSPATH .:/users/dcl0bjc/public_html
javac -d /users/dcl0bjc/public_html Date.java
```

If the file `Date.java` contains the line:

```
package uk.ac.dur.dcl0bjc.utils.dateutils;
```

then the directory:

```
/users/dcl0bjc/public_html/uk/ac/dur/dcl0bjc/utils/dateutils
```

will be used by the compiler to store the `Date.class` file. If need be, it will automatically create any directories that do not exist.

21.5 The factory pattern

In this book, two approaches have been taken when constructing a new class:

- just produce a class declaration;

● produce an interface declaration and a class declaration that implements that interface.

On many occasions, the book has been lazy, and has not bothered with an interface declaration. However, as was explained in Section 11.13:

Introducing an interface is preferable because:

● an interface declaration provides a clearer statement than a class declaration as to the contract (between the client and the supplier);

● writing the client in terms of an interface means that there is less work involved if you want to switch to a different implementation of a class.

Section 12.8 and Section 12.9 point out two problems. First, even though we have written most of the code of a client in terms of an interface type (e.g. Date) instead of a class type (e.g. DateImpl), the client will still need to create an instance of the class.

For example, the class PersonImpl contains:

```
iDateOfBirth = new DateImpl(tDateOfBirthString);
```

where iDateOfBirth is of the interface type Date. How can we remove this last set of dependencies between PersonImpl and DateImpl?

Section 12.9 mentions a second problem. We will get into difficulty if, at different places within the same program, we inadvertently use constructors of different classes (that implement the same interface). How can we avoid this problem?

Section 12.9 then moves on to give brief details of a solution to both of these problems. The solution is to introduce a class (PopFactoryImpl) that is responsible for creating objects. So it might have a method called createDate whose body includes:

```
return new DateImpl(...);
```

So if we ever want to change the actual class that is used to implement the Date interface, PopFactoryImpl is the only class that needs to be changed.

To ensure that we can make such a change without having to recompile all the clients of createDate, we will also introduce an interface called PopFactory, and we will arrange for the class PopFactoryImpl to be an implementation of this interface.

These methods can all belong to PopFactory–PopFactoryImpl. When a set of interfaces/classes are related, it is sensible to put them into a package (as was explained in Section 21.4). For example, we could put Date–DateImpl, Person–PersonImpl and Pop–PopImpl into a package called pop. At various points, we will need to create instances of DateImpl, PersonImpl and PopImpl. Instead of these class instance creation expressions appearing in the code, it would be better to introduce calls of methods called createDate, createPerson and createPop. These methods can all belong to PopFactory–PopFactoryImpl which should also be included in the pop package.

```
// The interface for the factory PopFactory.
// Barry Cornelius, 21 June 2000
package uk.ac.dur.dclObjc.pop;
public interface PopFactory
{
    public Date createDate();
    public Date createDate(Date pDate);
    public Date createDate(int pYear, int pMonth, int pDay);
    public Date createDate(String pString);
    public Person createPerson();
    public Person createPerson(Person pPerson);
    public Person createPerson(String pName, Date pDateOfBirth,
                               String pPhoneNumber, double pHeight);
    public Person createPerson(String pPersonString);
    public Pop createPop();
}
```

Figure 21.7 The interface for the factory `PopFactory`.

The codes of the `PopFactory` interface and the `PopFactoryImpl` class are shown in Figures 21.7 and 21.8. All the other classes that form this program need to be altered in two ways. First, they need to indicate that they also belong to the `uk.ac.dur.dclObjc.pop` package. Secondly, any class instance creation expressions need to be replaced by a call of an appropriate `createXXX` method. For example, the statement:

```
iDateOfBirth = new DateImpl(tDateOfBirthString);
```

is replaced by:

```
iDateOfBirth = iPopFactory.createDate(tDateOfBirthString);
```

There is now no reason why the constructors of `DateImpl`, `PersonImpl` and `PopImpl` should be `public`. The only calls of these constructors should be in the `PopFactoryImpl` class. If we leave out the `public`, i.e. using:

```
DateImpl(final int pYear, final int pMonth, final int pDay)
{
    ...
}
```

instead of:

```
public DateImpl(final int pYear, final int pMonth, final int pDay)
{
    ...
}
```

```
// The class that implements the factory PopFactory.
// Barry Cornelius, 21 June 2000
package uk.ac.dur.dclObjc.pop;
public class PopFactoryImpl implements PopFactory
{
    public Date createDate()
    {
        return new DateImpl();
    }
    public Date createDate(final Date pDate)
    {
        return new DateImpl(pDate);
    }
    public Date createDate(final int pYear, final int pMonth, final int pDay)
    {
        return new DateImpl(pYear, pMonth, pDay);
    }
    public Date createDate(final String pString)
    {
        return new DateImpl(pString);
    }
    public Person createPerson()
    {
        return new PersonImpl(this);
    }
    public Person createPerson(final Person pPerson)
    {
        return new PersonImpl(this, pPerson);
    }
    public Person createPerson(final String pName, final Date pDateOfBirth,
                               final String pPhoneNumber,
                               final double pHeight)
    {
        return new PersonImpl(this,
                        pName, pDateOfBirth, pPhoneNumber, pHeight);
    }
    public Person createPerson(final String pPersonString)
    {
        return new PersonImpl(this, pPersonString);
    }
    public Pop createPop()
    {
        return new PopImpl();
    }
}
```

Figure 21.8   The class that implements the factory `PopFactory`.

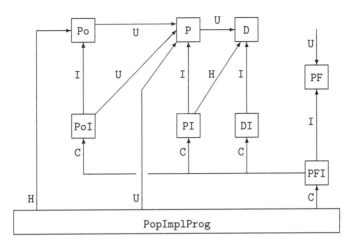

Figure 21.9 A class diagram for the version of `PopImplProg` that uses `PopFactory`.

then the constructor will not be accessible by a client: it will only be accessible by code that appears in the same package as the constructor. For more details about this, see Curio 19.2.

The class diagram that results from these changes is shown in Figure 21.9. In this diagram, the following notation is used:

I	Implements	Po	Pop
C	Creates	P	Person
H	Has	D	Date
U	Uses	PF	PopFactory
		PoI	PopImpl
		PI	PersonImpl
		DI	DateImpl
		PFI	PopFactoryImpl

In order to make the diagram less confusing, some of the <<uses>> lines have been omitted. This diagram should be compared with the one shown in Figure 17.17. By making these changes, both of the problems mentioned earlier are removed.

This idea of arranging the code of a program so that all objects are created by one class is called the *factory pattern*. There is more information about this pattern in the book *Design Patterns: Elements of Reusable Object-Oriented Software* by Erich Gamma, Richard Helm, Ralph Johnson and John Vlissides ([17]). The examples in this book are given in C++ and Smalltalk. There is another book that covers similar material but which uses Java rather than C++ and Smalltalk. It is *Patterns in Java: Volume 1* by Mark Grand ([18]). The factory pattern is also advocated by Mark Fussell in his excellent document 'ChiMu OO and Java Development' ([16]). Mark's document has a lot of useful ideas.

21.6 The JDBC API

21.6.1 What is JDBC?

The **Structured Query Language (SQL)** is a language for inspecting and updating tables in relational databases. One of the most used SQL statements is the `SELECT` statement: it is used to inspect one of the tables of information that has been stored in a database. For example, the statement:

```
SELECT last, first FROM ages WHERE age >= 21
```

would look at a table called `ages` and produce a new table containing the surnames and first names of the people having an age of at least 21 years.

Although SQL has been evolving since the early 1980s, it was in 1990 that the SQL Access Group defined the **Call Level Interface (CLI)** as a standard for accessing databases. To implement it, you need a **driver** that can translate a CLI call into the language used to access a particular database. Microsoft's **Open Database Connectivity (ODBC)**, an API for Microsoft Windows that implements an extended version of the CLI, was first released in 1992. Most database vendors (including CA/Ingres, IBM, Informix, Oracle and Sybase as well as Microsoft) support the ODBC API.

ODBC is an API that was written for the programming language C and although the **Java Native Interface (JNI)** allows a Java program to call a C function, there are many disadvantages with this approach:

- a Java program calling C code is one which is not so secure, robust and portable;

- calling C code is not usually possible from a Java applet because of security restrictions.

So, instead Java has its own API for submitting SQL statements to a database server: it is an API called **JDBC** (sometimes called the **Java DataBase Connectivity**).

The JDBC API is in the `java.sql` package. It is implemented via a driver manager that can support multiple drivers connecting to different databases. A JDBC **driver** can either be written entirely in Java so that it can be downloaded as part of an applet or it can be implemented using native methods to bridge to existing database access libraries.

At [44], Sun gives details of the drivers that are available from a number of vendors. You will find JDBC support for most of the popular database servers.

21.6.2 An example

Here is an outline of the sort of code that you need for connecting to a database server running on the computer `machine.company.com`, performing a query, and then disconnecting:

```
Connection tConnection = null;
Class.forName("com.somewhere.productname.sqldriver");
final String tURLString =
            "jdbc:sql://machine.company.com:portnumber/databasename";
```

```
final String tUsername = "guest";
final String tPassword = "tseug";
tConnection = DriverManager.getConnection(tURLString, tUsername, tPassword);
final Statement tStatement = tConnection.createStatement();
final String tSQLString = "SELECT last, first FROM ages WHERE age >= 21";
final ResultSet tResultSet = tStatement.executeQuery(tSQLString);
final ResultSetMetaData tResultSetMetaData = tResultSet.getMetaData();
final int tNumCols = tResultSetMetaData.getColumnCount();
boolean tMoreRows = tResultSet.next();
while (tMoreRows)
{
    for (int tColNum=1; tColNum<=tNumCols; tColNum++)
    {
        System.out.print(" " + tResultSet.getString(tColNum));
    }
    System.out.println();
    tMoreRows = tResultSet.next();
}
tResultSet.close();
tStatement.close();
tConnection.close();
```

21.6.3 More information about JDBC

Sun's main page about JDBC is at [45]. Sun's *Tutorial* on Java includes some pages about JDBC: they start at [46]. My own document on 'Developing Distributed Systems' includes a section on JDBC: it is on the WWW at [11].

21.7 Client-server computing

21.7.1 What is client-server computing?

In the past, many distributed systems have been built that are **two-tier**. This is a system that has a client program communicating with a server program. Often mailer programs are examples of two-tier systems. Typically, the user interface is in the client and the server is there to process data, e.g. to access a mailbox, or to manipulate a database. The complicated application logic (or business logic) is often put in the client.

21.7.2 Implementing client-server computing

Client-server computing has traditionally been implemented using **socket**s. A socket is a point of connection within a program to the Internet, and a program can start to communicate when it arranges for the socket to bind to a port of the computer that is running the program.

The Java classes java.net.DatagramSocket, java.net.ServerSocket and java.net.Socket provide easy-to-use ways of writing programs that use sockets. However, in Java, client-server computing can be performed without having to work at the level of sockets. This is because Java has several application programming interfaces (APIs) that offer higher levels of abstraction for client-server computing.

21.7.3 JDBC, RMI and CORBA

In this area, there are three APIs: Remote Method Invocation (**RMI**), Common Object Request Broker Architecture (**CORBA**) and Java DataBase Connectivity (**JDBC**). As seen earlier in this chapter, the latter is a way in which a Java program can use SQL to access a database server: the other two APIs allow us to rise up above the socket-level details of client-server computing when we want to access objects distributed across different computers.

With RMI, both the client and the server have to be Java applications/applets (running in some Java environment). However, with CORBA, the client and server programs may be in different languages. You need to provide an interface in a language called the Interface Definition Language (**IDL**). Each program can run on any operating system written in any language so long as you have a compiler to translate the interface from IDL into that language on that operating system.

Although Java applications can use these APIs to attempt to communicate with any computer on the Internet, Java applets are normally restricted to talking to the site from which the applet was downloaded. This hinders the use of applets in client-server computing. An applet has to be a *trusted applet* if it wishes to overcome these security restrictions.

21.7.4 Three-tier systems

In the past, client-server computing has usually involved just two computers talking to one another. Often a lot of the processing is going on in the client, which often means that the client is a big program. More recently, **three-tier** systems have come into favour. This is where an additional tier is interposed: it is there to handle the application logic (or business logic) leaving the client just to handle the user interface.

There are a number of advantages to this approach. For example, the code running on the client is small. And it is possible to write the code running on the middle tier so that it handles requests from more than one client. In this way, requests can be more efficiently handled.

21.7.5 Further information about client-server computing

One good book is *Client/Server Programming with Java and CORBA* (2nd edition) by Robert Orfali and Dan Harkey ([27]). It contains extensive sections on both CORBA and JDBC, and the use of CORBA and JDBC to build multi-tier systems. They also compare CORBA with other methods: sockets, HTTP/CGI and RMI. Another good book on this topic is *Java Programming with CORBA* (2nd edition) by Andreas Vogel and Keith Duddy ([50]).

RMI, CORBA, JDBC and three-tier systems are also explored in my document 'Developing Distributed Systems' which is stored at [11].

21.8 Finding other information about Java

21.8.1 Primary resources

Here is a list of URLs for the main WWW pages about Java:

- The most important URL for information about Java is: http://java.sun.com/.
- In particular, Sun's Java documentation is at http://developer.java.sun.com/developer/infodocs/index.shtml.
- A definition of the language is at http://java.sun.com/docs/books/jls/html/.
- A definition of the 1.0.2 API is at http://java.sun.com/products/jdk/1.0.2/api/.
- A definition of the 1.1 API is at http://java.sun.com/products/jdk/1.1/docs/api/packages.html.
- A definition of the 1.2 API is at http://java.sun.com/products/jdk/1.2/docs/api/.
- A definition of the 1.3 API is at http://java.sun.com/j2se/1.3/docs/api/.
- Sun's Java tutorial is at http://java.sun.com/docs/books/tutorial/.
- Sun has produced a list of Java FAQs at http://java.sun.com/docs/faqindex.html.

21.8.2 Important secondary resources

Cafe au Lait contains news about Java. It is updated daily. See http://www.ibiblio.org/javafaq/. It is a valuable source of information. Probably the best weekly/monthly magazine about Java is available at http://www.javaworld.com/. And a list of reports in the press concerning Java is maintained at http://www.javaworld.com/javaworld/netnews/netnews.index.html.

21.8.3 Books

Both Addison-Wesley and O'Reilly have an excellent series of books on Java. For more details, see http://www.awl.com/cseng/javaseries/index.shtml and http://java.oreilly.com/. A good book to read after you have read this book is *Beginning Java 2* by Ivor Horton ([24]).

For material on how to write good Java programs, look at the following books:

- *Java in Practice* by Nigel Warren and Philip Bishop ([53]);
- *Practical Java* by Peter Haggar ([21]);
- *The Elements of Java Style* by Al Vermeulen *et al.* ([49]);
- *Thinking in Java* by Bruce Eckel ([12]).

21.1   In this chapter, it is implied that the CLASSPATH is a list of entries each of which must be a directory. This is too restrictive: each entry must either be a directory or the full name of a *Java Archive* (for which see Section 20.13). An example is:

```
setenv CLASSPATH .:/users/dcl0bjc/public_html:/users/dcl0bjc/fred.jar
```

For historical reasons, an entry may also be a `.zip` file containing `.class` files – these days, Java Archive files are used instead of `.zip` files.

Appendix A

Obtaining the Java 2 SDK and an appropriate text editor

A.1 Obtaining the Java 2 SDK

In order to obtain a copy of the Java 2 SDK, you need to go to Sun Microsystem's main WWW site for Java:

http://java.sun.com/

There is a link on this page to *Products and APIs*. So click on this link. You are now looking for a link to the *Java 2 Platform Standard Edition (J2SE)*. At the time of writing, this takes you to:

http://java.sun.com/j2se/

and the current release is version 1.3 which is at:

http://java.sun.com/j2se/1.3/

On this page, you will need to choose between Solaris, Linux and Microsoft Windows. You will then get to an appropriate download page, e.g. for Microsoft Windows you will get to a page like:

http://java.sun.com/j2se/1.3/download-windows.html

You will then need to find the section of this page that invites you to download the Java 2 SDK. The page warns you that the download is quite large (about 30Mb). Click on the *continue* button. You will then be invited to read the *Terms and conditions*. If you are happy with them, click on the *ACCEPT* button. Then click on *FTP download*. If you are downloading the version of the Java 2 SDK for Microsoft Windows, you will eventually get a file with a name like j2sdk1_3_0-win.exe. This is a self-extracting archive: you can get the Java 2 SDK extracted by double-clicking on the icon for this file within Windows Explorer.

As well as downloading the Java 2 SDK, it is very useful to download a copy of the documentation. In particular, this documentation includes a copy of the WWW pages that document Java's Core APIs. To download the documentation, first return to the appropriate download page, e.g.:

http://java.sun.com/j2se/1.3/download-windows.html

You will then need to find the section of this page that invites you to *Download Java 2 SDK Docs – HTML Format*. Again, this is a large file (about 23Mb). Click on the *continue* button. Then click on *FTP download*. If you are downloading the version of the Java 2 SDK for Microsoft Windows, you will eventually get a file with a name like j2sdk1_3_0-doc.zip. This is a ZIP file, and to get at its contents you will need to run an unzip program on it. If you do not have WinZip or PKUNZIP or InfoZip, you might want to go to the following site where you will find a free version of InfoZip's UnZip program:

http://ftp.software.com/pub/infozip/UnZip.html

A.2) Obtaining an editor for editing Java programs

The process of typing in a Java program and correcting any typing mistakes you make needs to be done with a **text editor**. If you are using a UNIX system (such as Solaris or Linux), your UNIX system will come with various text editors such as vi, pico and emacs. You can choose one of these.

If, instead, you are using Microsoft Windows, you could use notepad. Some advice about how to edit Java programs with notepad appears in Appendix B. Although it is possible to use notepad, it is better to use a more powerful editor such as textpad or ntemacs. One of the main reasons why both of these are better for editing a Java program is that they present the various parts of the text of the program in different colours. When you make a syntactical error, this is more obvious as the colours are wrong.

If you are using Microsoft Windows, and you wish to obtain a copy of textpad, go to:

http://www.textpad.com/

```
(setq default-directory (getenv "HOME"))

(set-background-color "white")

(defconst my-c-style
  '((c-basic-offset . 3)
    (c-comment-only-line-offset . 0)
    (c-hanging-braces-alist     . ((substatement-open before after)))
    (c-offsets-alist . ((topmost-intro          . 0)
                        (topmost-intro-cont    . 0)
                        (substatement          . +)
                        (substatement-open     . 0)
                        (case-label            . +)
                        (access-label          . -)
                        (inclass               . +)
                        (inline-open           . 0)
                        ))
    )
  "My C Programming Style")

;; Customizations for all of c-mode, c++-mode, and objc-mode
(defun my-c-mode-common-hook ()
  ;; add my personal style and set it for the current buffer
  (c-add-style "PERSONAL" my-c-style t)
  ;; offset customizations not in my-c-style
  (c-set-offset 'member-init-intro '++)
  ;; other customizations
  (setq tab-width 8
        ;; this will make sure spaces are used instead of tabs
        indent-tabs-mode nil)
  ;; we like auto-newline and hungry-delete
  (c-toggle-auto-hungry-state 1)
  ;; keybindings for all supported languages.  We can put these in
  ;; c-mode-base-map because c-mode-map, c++-mode-map, objc-mode-map,
  ;; java-mode-map, and idl-mode-map inherit from it.
  (define-key c-mode-base-map "\C-m" 'newline-and-indent)
  )

(add-hook 'c-mode-common-hook 'my-c-mode-common-hook)
(global-font-lock-mode t)
```

Figure A.1 A .emacs file for use when editing Java programs.

Although an evaluation copy is free, this software is shareware, and so a small charge is made if you want to retain the software.

If you are using Microsoft Windows, and you wish to obtain a copy of ntemacs, go to:

http://www.gnu.org/software/emacs/windows/ntemacs.html

On this WWW page, you need to look under the heading *How do I get an Emacs distribution?* and at the subheadings *Where do I get precompiled versions?* and *How do I unpack the distributions?*. You will probably find it useful to read the material under the headings *How do I install Emacs?*, *How do I run Emacs?* and *Where do I put my* `.emacs` *(or* `_emacs`*) file?*.

A.3   A `.emacs` file for use with emacs or ntemacs

Figure A.1 contains the listing of a file that can be used with emacs or ntemacs. On a UNIX system, the file is best stored in a file called `.emacs`, whereas when using ntemacs on a computer running Microsoft Windows the file is best stored in a file called `_emacs`. For more details on how to use this file with ntemacs, see the section of the WWW page:

http://www.gnu.org/software/emacs/windows/ntemacs.html

that is entitled *Where do I put my* `.emacs` *(or* `_emacs`*) file?*.

Appendix B

Compiling and executing programs using the Java 2 SDK

• •

B.1 Creating a window in which you can type commands

If you are going to use the Java 2 SDK, then, in order to compile and execute Java programs, it is necessary to create a **terminal window**. If you are using a UNIX system (such as Solaris or Linux) running some variant of the X Window System, you will probably already be familiar with how to create a terminal window. When using Microsoft Windows, you can create a terminal window by clicking on *Start*, then *Programs*, and then either *MS-DOS Prompt* or *Command Prompt*. If you do this, a new window should appear on your screen.

B.2 Creating a directory for Java programs

Whenever you wish to use the Java 2 SDK, you should store the files containing Java programs in some separate directory. (A **directory** is also known as a **folder** in

Microsoft Windows.) Later, when you create your own classes, a program will consist of many files. At that stage, it will be useful to create a separate directory for each program. To begin with, however, each program will just consist of one file. In this appendix, it will be assumed that you will want to store your Java programs in a directory called `programs`.

You can create a directory called `programs` by using the command `mkdir` in the terminal window:

```
mkdir programs
```

Whenever you want to access your Java programs, switch to this directory by typing the following command in a terminal window:

```
cd programs
```

B.3 Choosing an editor

If you are using a UNIX system (such as Solaris or Linux), your UNIX system will come with various text editors such as `vi`, `pico` and `emacs`. The rest of this appendix assumes that you are already familiar with one of these.

If, instead, you are using Microsoft Windows, you could use `notepad`. However, there are some text editors that are better than notepad. Details about how to obtain `textpad` and `ntemacs` are given in Appendix A. The rest of this appendix assumes that you are using notepad.

B.4 Creating a Java program

So use the appropriate command to get into your text editor in order to create a file called `SimpleSum.java`. If you are using notepad, you can do this by typing the following command in the terminal window:

```
notepad SimpleSum.java
```

When notepad produces a dialog box warning you that the file does not exist, click on *Yes*.

Now type in the text of the `SimpleSum` program. It is given in Figure 1.1. However, when typing in the program, replace the author's name and the date the program was created by your name and today's date. And instead of typing in the line:

```
System.out.print(tSum);
```

type the following line:

```
System.out.print(tSump)
```

[There are two differences.]

Note: it is important that you type the rest of the text of the program exactly as it is in Figure 1.1. In particular, be careful that you include the punctuation symbols and that you use small and capital letters as shown.

Having typed in this program, use the command of your text editor that will store this text in the file SimpleSum.java. For example, with notepad, you need to go to the *File* menu and click on *Save*.

Return to the terminal window and type the command ls if you are using UNIX or dir if you are using Microsoft Windows. The output from this command should indicate that you now have a file called SimpleSum.java.

B.5 Compiling the SimpleSum program

As explained in Section 2.11, the process of getting a Java program to execute is a two-stage process: you first have to *compile* the program and then you can *execute* it. The process of compilation is performed by you using a Java compiler. The Java 2 SDK includes a Java compiler, and, if it has been installed properly (!), the compiler can be executed using a command called **javac**.

So, having typed in the code of a Java program, and stored it in a file called SimpleSum.java, you can get the compiler to compile the program by typing the following command in the terminal window:

```
javac SimpleSum.java
```

If you get an error message saying that this command could not be found, there is a problem with how the Java 2 SDK system was installed. Otherwise, the Java compiler will now start to compile your program. The rest of this appendix assumes that you have typed in the program correctly except for the changes suggested above. It may be that you have accidentally introduced other changes and in this case you will have other things to sort out.

However, if you have typed in the text as suggested, the javac command should output some compilation error messages. Unfortunately, the actual error messages that you will get depends on the version of the Java 2 SDK you are using. If you are using an early version of the Java 2 SDK, you will get the messages:

```
SimpleSum.java:12: Invalid type expression.
        System.out.print(tSump)
SimpleSum.java:13: Invalid declaration.
        System.out.println();
2 errors
```

However, the compiler of Java 2 SDK v 1.3.0 produces the following error messages:

```
SimpleSum.java:12: ';' expected
        System.out.print(tSump)
                              ^
SimpleSum.java:12: cannot resolve symbol
symbol  : variable tSump
location: class SimpleSum
        System.out.print(tSump)
2 errors
```

If you have only these two errors, then you typed in the program as was suggested.

Often the error messages you get will be a bit cryptic, and understanding them comes with time. However, the compiler has indicated which lines have problems on them. Sometimes the compiler will not know that an error has occurred until it is processing the line following the line that is really wrong.

One of the problems with the program you have typed is that the tSump should really be tSum. This is reported by the compiler of Java 2 SDK v 1.3.0 as a *symbol* that it cannot *resolve*. The other problem is that there should be a semicolon after:

```
System.out.print(tSum)
```

So go back to your text editor and make these two changes to this line of the file SimpleSum.java. Then, re-save the text in the file SimpleSum.java. Then re-issue the following command in the terminal window:

```
javac SimpleSum.java
```

This is the process of correcting the errors that have been detected by the compiler. If you have compilation errors which are different to the ones described above, try to understand what the error messages mean – this takes some practice! And then correct the text of the program.

This process needs to be repeated until you get no compilation errors.

B.6 Executing the SimpleSum program

Having produced a Java program that compiles without any errors, you can now move on to the second stage. This is where you execute the program.

The compiler will have created a file of bytecodes from your Java program. You can confirm this by returning to the terminal window and typing ls if you are using UNIX or dir if you are using Microsoft Windows. You should now have a file called SimpleSum.class.

You can get the Java interpreter (of the Java 2 SDK) to execute the bytecodes of this file by typing the following command in the terminal window:

```
java SimpleSum
```

The program should output the line:

```
The sum of the two numbers is: 6.9
```

Appendix C

Producing javadoc documentation

....

C.1 Using the javadoc tool

Whenever we have been wanting to find out the details about a class of one of Java's Core APIs, we have looked at the WWW pages that document the class. The same kind of documentation can be generated for our own interfaces and classes by using the **javadoc** tool that comes with the Java 2 SDK.

In order for javadoc to produce useful documentation, we need to augment the Java source code with **documentation comments**. For example, if you want to produce documentation for the Date interface (given in Figure 11.14), the file Date.java needs to be changed to something like that given in Figure C.1.

The javadoc tool ignores any comments unless they are documentation comments. These are comments that begin with /** and end with */. There should be a one-sentence documentation comment immediately before the interface/class declaration to explain the purpose of the interface/class that is declared in the file. If the file contains import declarations, this documentation comment should be positioned after the import declarations. And then each field/constructor/method of the interface/class should be preceded by a documentation comment describing the purpose of the field/constructor/method.

Within these documentation comments, you can use **tag**s to help javadoc. The example in Figure C.1 uses the following tags:

tag	purpose
@author	indicates the author of the code
@version	indicates the version of the code
@return	indicates the purpose of the value that is returned
@param	indicates the purpose of a parameter

```
/**
   * A type to represent a date.
   * @author Barry Cornelius
   * @version 1st September 2000
   */
public interface Date
{
    /** @return the year part of the target date */
    public int getYear();

    /** @return the month part of the target date */
    public int getMonth();

    /** @return the day part of the target date */
    public int getDay();

    /** @param pYear the value to set the year part of the target date */
    public void setYear(int pYear);

    /** @param pMonth the value to set the month part of the target date */
    public void setMonth(int pMonth);

    /** @param pDay the value to set the day part of the target date */
    public void setDay(int pDay);

    /** @param pObject the value with which to compare the target date
       * @return true if and only if the target represents the same date
       *            as pObject */
    public boolean equals(Object pObject);

    /** @return the hashcode for the value of the target */
    public int hashCode();

    /** @return a textual representation of the target date */
    public String toString();
}
```

Figure C.1   The Date interface with documentation comments.

The first word following a @param tag should be the identifier of the parameter.
There can be more than one occurrence of the @author and @param tags.

One of the simplest ways of running the javadoc tool is to pass as arguments to
javadoc the names of the .java files that you want it to examine. An example is:

```
javadoc Date.java
```

Another example is:

```
javadoc Date.java DateImpl.java
```

If you wish to apply javadoc to all of the .java files in the current directory, use:

```
javadoc *.java
```

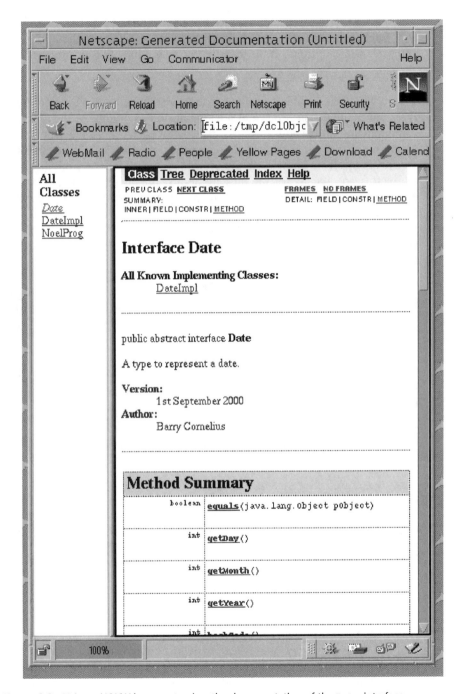

Figure C.2   Using a WWW browser to view the documentation of the Date interface.

However, there are two problems. First, javadoc does not process any @author and @version tags unless instructed to do so by means of the optional -author and -version options on the javadoc command line. For example, you could use:

```
javadoc -author -version *.java
```

And the second problem occurs because, when javadoc runs, it creates a lot of files. It examines the declarations and documentation comments of the files passed on its command line, and produces one .html file for each .java file. But it also produces a large number of supporting files. To save the directory containing the source of your Java programs from being cluttered up with all these files, it is probably best to create a directory specifically for the files created by the javadoc tool. Having created the directory, you can instruct javadoc to put its files into this directory by using a d option on the javadoc command line.

So, suppose you have created a directory called public_html. Suppose the current directory just contains the following .java files: Date.java, DateImpl.java and NoelProg.java. You could use:

```
javadoc -d public_html -author -version *.java
```

It would produce the files Date.html, DateImpl.html, NoelProg.html, allclasses-frame.html, deprecated-list.html, help-doc.html, index-all.html, index.html, overview-tree.html, package-list, packages.html, serialized-form.html and stylesheet.css. All of these files would be put into the public_html directory. If you use a WWW browser to look at the file index.html, you should get output like that shown in Figure C.2.

The javadoc tool has many more facilities besides the ones described above. For more details about the javadoc tool, look at the WWW pages that form the documentation of the Java 2 SDK. The javadoc page is at $API/../tooldocs/tools.html.

Tips for programming and debugging

C.1   With UNIX, if you need to create a directory and a set of intermediate directories, this is easy to do using the p option of the mkdir command. For example:

```
mkdir -p /users/dcl0bjc/public_html/uk/ac/dur/dcl0bjc/utils/dateutils
```

Curios, controversies and cover-ups

C.1   Although it is not obvious from the example given in Figure C.1, javadoc's documentation comments should be written in HTML. This means, for example, that you can embolden text by enclosing the text within <b> and </b> tags. However, it also means that you need to use <, > or &, if you want to put the characters <, > or & in a documentation comment.

References

[1] Addison-Wesley. 'The Addison-Wesley Java Series Page'.
http://www.awl.com/cseng/javaseries/index.shtml

[2] Tom Anderson and Peter Lee (1981). *Fault Tolerance: Principles and Practice.* Prentice-Hall. ISBN 0-13-308254-7.

[3] Eric Armstrong. 'Create enumerated constants in Java'.
http://www.javaworld.com/jw-07-1997/jw-07-enumerated.html

[4] Ken Arnold, James Gosling and David Holmes (2000). *The Java Programming Language* (3rd edn). Addison-Wesley. ISBN 0-201-70433-1.

[5] Dan Becker. 'Get started with the Java Collections Framework'.
http://www.javaworld.com/javaworld/jw-11-1998/jw-11-collections.html

[6] Philip Bishop. 'Type safe constants in C++ and Java'.
http://www.javaworld.com/javaworld/javatips/jw-javatip27.html

[7] Joshua Bloch. 'Substitutes for Missing C Constructs'.
http://developer.java.sun.com/developer/Books/shiftintojava/page1.html

[8] Patrick Chan, Rosanna Lee and Douglas Kramer (1998). *The Java Class Libraries* (2nd edn), Volume 1. Addison-Wesley. ISBN 0-201-31002-3.

[9] Patrick Chan and Rosanna Lee (1998). *The Java Class Libraries* (2nd edn), Volume 2. Addison-Wesley. ISBN 0-201-31003-1.

[10] Patrick Chan, Rosanna Lee and Douglas Kramer (1999). *The Java Class Libraries* (2nd edn), Volume 1: *Supplement for the Java 2 Platform, Standard Edition v 1.2.* Addison-Wesley. ISBN 0-201-48552-4.

[11] Barry Cornelius. 'Developing Distributed Systems with Java'.
http://www.dur.ac.uk/barry.cornelius/java/distributed/

[12] Bruce Eckel (2000). *Thinking in Java* (2nd edn). Prentice Hall. ISBN 0-13-027363-5.

[13] Robert Eckstein, Marc Loy and Dave Wood (1998). *Java Swing.* O'Reilly. ISBN 1-56592-455-X.

[14] Amy Fowler. 'Painting in AWT and Swing'.
http://jsp2.java.sun.com/products/jfc/tsc/articles/painting/

[15] Martin Fowler (with Kendall Scott) (1997). *UML Distilled*. Addison-Wesley. ISBN 0-201-32563-2.

[16] Mark Fussell. 'ChiMu OO and Java Development: Guidelines and Resources'.
http://www.chimu.com/publications/javaStandards/

[17] Erich Gamma, Richard Helm, Ralph Johnson and John Vlissides (1995). *Design Patterns: Elements of Reusable Object-Oriented Software*. Addison-Wesley. ISBN 0-201-63361-2.

[18] Mark Grand (1998). *Patterns in Java*, Volume 1. John Wiley. ISBN 0-471-25839-3.

[19] James Gosling, Bill Joy, Guy Steele and Gilad Bracha (2000). *The Java Language Specification* (2nd edn). Addison-Wesley. ISBN 0-201-31008-2.

[20] James Gosling, Bill Joy, Guy Steele and Gilad Bracha. *The Java Language Specification (2nd edn)*. http://java.sun.com/docs/books/jls/

[21] Peter Haggar (2000). *Practical Java*. Addison-Wesley. ISBN 0-201-61646-7.

[22] Elliotte Rusty Harold. 'Overloading Int Considered Harmful'.
http://www1.fatbrain.com/whatshot/sigs/javasig/guestcolumn1199.asp

[23] Allen Holub. 'Building user interfaces for object-oriented systems, Part 1'.
http://www.javaworld.com/javaworld/jw-07-1999/jw-07-toolbox.html

[24] Ivor Horton (1999). *Beginning Java 2*. Wrox Press. ISBN 1-861002-23-8.

[25] International Standardization Organization (1992). ISO 2108: *Information and documentation – International Standard Book Numbering (ISBN)*.

[26] Scott Oaks and Henry Wong (1999). *Java Threads* (2nd edn). O'Reilly. ISBN 1-56592-418-5.

[27] Robert Orfali and Dan Harkey (1998). *Client/Server Programming with Java and CORBA* (2nd edn). John Wiley. ISBN 0-471-24578-X.

[28] Arthur Riel (1996). *Object-Oriented Design Heuristics*. Addison-Wesley. ISBN 0-201-63385-X.

[29] Mark Roulo. 'How to avoid traps and correctly override methods from `java.lang.Object`'.
http://www.javaworld.com/javaworld/jw-01-1999/jw-01-object.html

[30] Sun Microsystems. 'Collections: General Purpose Implementations'.
http://java.sun.com/docs/books/tutorial/collections/implementations/general.html

[31] Sun Microsystems. 'Java Collections API Design FAQ'.
http://java.sun.com/j2se/1.3/docs/guide/collections/designfaq.html

[32] Sun Microsystems. 'Add Generic Types to the Java Programming Language'.
http://java.sun.com/aboutJava/communityprocess/jsr/jsr_014_gener.html

[33] Sun Microsystems. 'The Java Developers Kit 1.0.2'.
http://java.sun.com/products/jdk/1.0.2/

[34] Sun Microsystems. 'Java Plug-in HTML Specification'.
http://java.sun.com/products/plugin/1.2/docs/tags.html and
http://java.sun.com/products/plugin/1.3/docs/tags.html

[35] Sun Microsystems. 'Java Plug-in FAQ'.
http://java.sun.com/products/plugin/1.2/plugin.faq.html and
http://java.sun.com/products/plugin/1.3/plugin.faq.html

[36] Sun Microsystems. 'Frequently Asked Questions – Applet Security'.
http://java.sun.com/sfaq/

[37] Sun Microsystems. 'JDK 1.2 – Signed Applet Example'.
http://java.sun.com/security/signExample12/

[38] Sun Microsystems. 'Java Security API'.
http://java.sun.com/security/

[39] Sun MicroSystems. 'Lesson: Doing Two or More Tasks At Once: Threads'.
http://java.sun.com/docs/books/tutorial/essential/threads/

[40] Sun MicroSystems. 'How to Use Threads'.
http://java.sun.com/docs/books/tutorial/uiswing/misc/threads.html/

[41] Sun Microsystems. 'Why are `Thread.stop`, `Thread.suspend`,
`Thread.resume` and `Runtime.runFinalizersOnExit` Deprecated'.
http://java.sun.com/j2se/1.3/docs/guide/misc/
threadPrimitiveDeprecation.html

[42] Sun Microsystems. 'Trail: Creating a GUI with JFC/Swing'.
http://java.sun.com/docs/books/tutorial/uiswing/

[43] Sun Microsystems. 'Java Look and Feel Design Guidelines'.
http://java.sun.com/products/jlf/guidelines.html

[44] Sun Microsystems. 'JDBC Technology – Drivers'.
http://industry.java.sun.com/products/jdbc/drivers

[45] Sun Microsystems. 'JDBC Technology'. http://java.sun.com/products/jdbc/

[46] Sun Microsystems. 'Trail: JDBC Database Access'.
http://java.sun.com/docs/books/tutorial/jdbc/

[47] Bill Venners. 'Designing with exceptions'.
http://www.javaworld.com/javaworld/jw-07-1998/jw-07-techniques.html

[48] Bill Venners. 'The canonical object idiom'.
http://www.javaworld.com/javaworld/jw-10-1998/jw-10-techniques.html

[49] Al Vermeulen, Scott W. Ambler, Greg Bumgardner, Eldon Metz, Trevor
Misfeldt, Jim Shur and Patrick Thompson (2000). *The Elements of Java Style*.
Cambridge University Press. ISBN 0-521-77768-2.

[50] Andreas Vogel and Keith Duddy (1998). *Java Programming with CORBA*
(2nd edn). John Wiley. ISBN 0-471-24765-0.

[51] Philip Wadler. 'GJ: A Generic Java'.
http://www.ddj.com/articles/2000/0002/0002a/0002a.htm

[52] Rodney Waldhoff. 'The Type-Safe Enumeration Idiom'.
http://members.tripod.com/rwald/java/articles/TypeSafeEnumeration.html

[53] Nigel Warren and Philip Bishop (2000). *Java in Practice*. Addison-Wesley.
ISBN 0-201-36065-9.

[54] Scott Weiner and Stephen Asbury (1998). *Programming with JFC*. John Wiley.
ISBN 0-471-24731-6.

Index to the classes defined in the book

....

Index to the syntax diagrams

....

Index to the classes defined in the APIs

....

Main index